CRIMINAL PROCEDURE

second edition

John L. Worrall

University of Texas at Dallas

PEARSON

Boston   Columbus   Indianapolis   New York   San Francisco   Hoboken
Amsterdam   Cape Town   Dubai   London   Madrid   Milan   Munich   Paris   Montréal   Toronto
Delhi   Mexico City   São Paulo   Sydney   Hong Kong   Seoul   Singapore   Taipei   Tokyo

Editorial Director: Andrew Gilfillan
Senior Acquisitions Editor: Gary Bauer
Program Manager: Tara Horton
Editorial Assistant: Lynda Cramer
Director of Marketing: David Gesell
Marketing Manager: Mary Salzman
Senior Marketing Coordinator: Alicia Wozniak
Marketing Assistant: Les Roberts
Senior Managing Editor: JoEllen Gohr
Project Manager: Susan Hannahs
Creative Director: Andrea Nix
Art Director: Diane Ernsberger
Cover Designer: Cenveo
Cover Image: 145/Hisham Ibrahim/Ocean/Corbis
Full-Service Project Management: Bev Kraus/S4Carlisle Publishing Services
Composition: S4Carlisle Publishing Services
Printer/Binder: R. R. Donnelley/Owensville
Cover Printer: Lehigh/Phoenix Color Hagerstown
Text Font: Minion Pro-Regular 10/12

Library of Congress Cataloging-in-Publication Data
Worrall, John L., author.
  Criminal procedure / John L. Worrall.—Second edition.
    pages cm
  Includes bibliographical references and index.
  ISBN 978-0-13-358759-3 (alk. paper)—ISBN 0-13-358759-2 (alk. paper)
  1. Criminal procedure—United States.   I. Title.
  KF9619.W65 2015
  345.73'05—dc23
                                                    2014035223

Dedication

For Dylan, Jordyn, and Sabrina

10 9 8 7 6 5 4 3 2 1

Paper bound ISBN 10:   0-13-358759-2
ISBN 13: 978-0-13-358759-3
Loose leaf ISBN 10:   0-13-410579-6
ISBN 13: 978-0-13-410579-6

Brief Contents

Contents

PART 2   Search and Seizure

PART 3   Interrogations, Confessions, and Identification Procedures

Preface

Introducing the Justice Series

When best-selling authors and instructional designers come together, focused on one goal—improve student performance across the criminal justice (CJ) curriculum—you come away with a groundbreaking new series of print and digital content: the Justice Series.

Several years ago we embarked on a journey to create affordable texts that engage students without sacrificing academic rigor. We tested this new format with Fagin's *CJ 2010* and Schmalleger's *Criminology* and received overwhelming support from students and instructors.

The Justice Series expands this format and philosophy to more core CJ and criminology courses, providing affordable, engaging instructor and student resources across the curriculum. As you flip through the pages, you'll notice this book doesn't rely on distracting, overly used photos to add visual appeal. Every piece of art serves a purpose—to help students learn. Our authors and instructional designers worked tirelessly to build engaging info-graphics, flow charts, pull-out statistics, and other visuals that flow with the body of the text, provide context and engagement, and promote recall and understanding.

We organized our content around key learning objectives for each chapter and tied everything together in a new objective-driven end-of-chapter layout. Not only is the content engaging to the student, it's easy to follow and focuses the student on the key learning objectives.

Although brief, affordable, and visually engaging, the Justice Series is no quick, cheap way to appeal to the lowest common denominator. It's a series of texts and support tools that are instructionally sound and student approved.

Additional Highlights to the Author's Approach

- A comprehensive introduction to criminal procedure takes students from the point where individuals first come into contact with the police all the way through to appeal.

- Half of the book is devoted to "traditional" criminal procedure topics, notably search and seizure as well as interrogation and identification procedures. The remainder of the book moves beyond these topics and discusses the pretrial process; the roles of defense attorneys, prosecutors, and grand juries; plea bargaining and guilty pleas; rights of criminal defendants at trial; and appeals and *habeas corpus*.

- Many leading Supreme Court decisions are discussed; however, lengthy excerpts from the actual decisions are left out of the text in order to avoid distracting from the many important concepts introduced.

- For a "real-world" focus, the book incorporates several actual legal documents and excerpts from official policy manuals of police departments and other criminal justice agencies around the United States.

- The author avoids unnecessary legalese and takes special steps to thoroughly introduce basic legal concepts and issues, all the while adopting a conversational tone.

- "Think About It" exercises are intended to encourage classroom discussion and reflection. These exercises place readers in the position of a judge who must decide how the issue/scenario should be resolved. Some are based on actual court cases, but several are hypothetical.

- Chapter-opening vignettes and end-of-chapter case studies discuss current events in criminal procedure, including some of the most recent and controversial Supreme Court decisions and their effects on the criminal justice system.

New to This Edition

In addition to being updated with the latest U.S. Supreme Court decisions, the following chapter-by-chapter changes have been made:

Chapter 1: A new chapter-opening story features the constitutionality of police drones. A new section on the differences between the real world of law enforcement and the "theory" world of the courts is included, and the chapter wraps up with a new case on GPS tracking.

Chapter 2: An expanded section on history of the exclusionary rule is included. The qualified immunity section is updated with three recent Supreme Court decisions.

Chapter 3: A new "Think About It" exercise touches on the scope of private search. A new section on Fourth Amendment terminology has been added, as has a section on tracking devices that features the Supreme Court's decision in *U.S. v. Jones.* An expanded section on the role of informants in probable cause determination is included, and the new end-of-chapter case story features *U.S. v. Harris.*

Chapter 4: A new chapter-opening story features *Messerschmidt v. Millender* (2011), a Supreme Court case focusing on Fourth Amendment particularity. The chapter also includes a new section on flaws in and challenges to search warrants. Finally, the electronic surveillance section is updated and expanded.

When best-selling authors and instructional designers come together focused on one goal—to improving student performance across the CJ curriculum—they come away with a groundbreaking new series of print and digital content: the *Justice Series.*

Chapter 5: The chapter includes a new section on other actions sanctioned during a traffic stop. It is also updated with the most recent warrantless search/seizure cases.

Chapter 6: A new chapter-opening story features the NYPD stop-and-frisk class-action suit. The chapter also now includes an expanded treatment of *Terry v. Ohio.*

Chapter 7: The treatment of business and residential inspections is revised and expanded.

Chapter 8: A new chapter-opening story discusses the public safety exception as applied after the Boston Marathon bombing. The chapter also includes expanded coverage of *Miranda*, with addition of the most recent cases. A new *Miranda* timeline is also included.

Chapter 9: The chapter includes a new end-of-chapter identification case.

Chapter 10: The section on the prosecution's duty to disclose exculpatory evidence is expanded. A revised *Brady* timeline is included, as is a new end-of-chapter case featuring a *Brady* claim.

Chapter 11: Expanded grand jury composition coverage is provided. Case timelines are revised and include the latest U.S. Supreme Court cases governing effective assistance of counsel.

Chapter 12: The most recent U.S. Supreme Court cases pertaining to chapter content are now included.

Chapter 13: The chapter starts with a new opening story featuring the so-called *Allen* charge. A new end-of-chapter case discusses the goals of sentencing. The chapter includes expanded confrontation coverage and an updated sentencing timeline.

▶ Instructor Supplements

Instructor's Manual with Test Bank

This supplement includes content outlines for classroom discussion, teaching suggestions, and answers to "Think About It" exercises from the text. It also contains a Word document version of the test bank.

TestGen

This computerized test generation system gives you maximum flexibility in creating and administering tests on paper, electronically, or online. It provides state-of-the-art features for viewing and editing test bank questions, dragging a selected question into a test you are creating, and printing sleek, formatted tests in a variety of layouts. Select test items from test banks included with TestGen for quick test creation, or write your own questions from scratch. TestGen's random generator provides the option to display different text or calculated number values each time questions are used.

PowerPoint Presentations

Our presentations offer clear, straightforward outlines and notes to use for class lectures or study materials. Photos, illustrations, charts, and tables from the book are included in the presentations when applicable.

To access supplementary materials online, instructors need to request an instructor access code. Go to www.pearsonhighered .com/irc, where you can register for an instructor access code.

Within 48 hours after registering, you will receive a confirming email, including an instructor access code. Once you have received your code, go to the site and log on for full instructions on downloading the materials you wish to use.

Pearson Online Course Solutions

Criminal Procedure is supported by online course solutions that include interactive learning modules, a variety of assessment tools, videos, simulations, and current event features. Go to www.pearsonhighered.com or contact your local representative for the latest information.

Alternate Versions

eBooks

This text is also available in multiple eBook formats, including Adobe Reader and CourseSmart. *CourseSmart* is an exciting new choice for students looking to save money. As an alternative to purchasing the printed textbook, students can purchase an electronic version of the same content. With a *CourseSmart* eTextbook, students can search the text, make notes online, print out reading assignments that incorporate lecture notes, and bookmark important passages for later review. For more information, or to purchase access to the *CourseSmart* eTextbook, visit www.coursesmart.com.

▶ Acknowledgments

Several people contributed to this book, a few of whose names are almost certainly escaping me. First, my former department chair, Larry Gaines, deserves credit for introducing me to book writing. Thank you to the following reviewers for their insightful suggestions: Jason Waller, Tyler Junior College; Kevin Daugherty, Central New Mexico Community College; and Mohamad Khatibloo, National University. I would also like to thank the people at Pearson; they include: Gary Bauer, Tara Horton, and Susan Hannahs. I also want to thank my project manager, Bev Kraus, at S4Carlisle.

John L. Worrall is professor of criminology and program head at the University of Texas at Dallas (UTD). A Seattle native, both his M.A. (criminal justice) and Ph.D. (political science) are from Washington State University, where he graduated in 1999. From 1999 to 2006, he was a member of the criminal justice faculty at California State University, San Bernardino. He joined UTD in the fall of 2006. Dr. Worrall has published articles and book chapters on topics ranging from legal issues in policing to crime measurement. He is also the author or coauthor of numerous textbooks, including *Introduction to Criminal Justice* (with Larry J. Siegel, 15th ed., Cengage, 2016) and *Criminal Procedure: From First Contact to Appeal* (5th ed., Pearson, 2015); coeditor of *The Changing Role of the American Prosecutor* (SUNY, 2009); and editor of the journal *Police Quarterly*.

"Criminal procedure arms the police, judges, prosecutors, and defense attorneys with the knowledge necessary to preserve the rights of individuals accused of criminal activity."

Introduction to Criminal Procedure

1 Identify two key themes running throughout criminal procedure.

2 Summarize the constitutional basis for criminal procedure.

3 Explain the importance of precedent.

4 Describe the public order (crime-control) and individual rights (due process) perspectives of criminal justice and how criminal procedure balances the two.

5 Outline the structure of the court system, including the responsibilities and jurisdictions of each level.

6 Understand the parts of a court case.

7 Summarize the criminal process.

Drones became important assets in the wars in Iraq and Afghanistan. They have also been used for years now to assist with patrolling the U.S.–Mexico border. More recently, they are creeping into domestic law enforcement use, such as for search-and-rescue operations or performing reconnaissance ahead of raids. Ordinary citizens can readily access drones, too, albeit cheaper and less sophisticated versions of what government officials typically use. Drones have become so popular that privacy advocates have sounded the call for tight regulations.

The Federal Aviation Administration has enacted a number of rules restricting the activities of what it calls "unmanned aircraft,"[1] but states have truly led the charge with new laws and legislative proposals intended to place limits on drone use. Most such efforts have been designed to curtail unrestricted law enforcement use, such as by requiring police to secure a warrant based on probable cause before flying drones over private property. Other proposals have called for warrant requirements *any time* a drone is used. Some jurisdictions have faced so much backlash from concerned citizens that they have returned their new equipment to the manufacturers![2]

High courts have yet to answer questions about the constitutionality of drone use, but that will likely change in the not-too-distant future. But even if legislatures and courts place strict limitations on drone use in domestic

© Montgomery Martin/Alamy

law enforcement, civilian use remains an issue. Citizens are not bound by the same constitutional restrictions the government is. That coupled with the increased accessibility to the technology (many drones are homemade) means it is not difficult to imagine a situation in which drones armed with high-definition cameras fly across neighborhoods engaging in all manner of surveillance.

DISCUSS **What limits should be placed on law enforcement and civilian drone activities?**

▶ What Is Criminal Procedure?

Identify two key themes running throughout criminal procedure.

American **criminal procedure** consists of a vast set of rules and guidelines that describe how suspected and accused criminals are to be handled and processed by the justice system. Criminal procedure begins when the police first contact a person and ends well after his or her conviction. It continues on through charging, trial, and to the appellate stage. Along the way, the constitutional rights of the accused must be honored and preserved.

Two important themes run throughout criminal procedure. First, there is a concern with the constitutional rights of accused persons, as interpreted by the courts. People enjoy a number of important rights in the United States, but the bulk of criminal procedure consists of *constitutional procedure* or what the U.S. Constitution says—usually through the interpretation of the U.S. Supreme Court (that is, the Court)—with regard to the treatment of criminal suspects.

Second, criminal procedure contains an important historical dimension, one that defers regularly to how sensitive legal issues have been approached in the past. The role of *precedent*,

or past decisions by the courts, cannot be overemphasized. At the same time, though, the world continues to evolve, and it is sometimes necessary to part ways with the past and decide novel legal issues.

▶ The Constitutional Basis for Criminal Procedure

The Preamble to the U.S. Constitution states,

> We the People of the United States, in Order to form a more perfect Union, establish Justice, insure domestic Tranquility, provide for the common defence, promote the general Welfare, and secure the Blessings of Liberty to ourselves and our Posterity, do ordain and establish this Constitution for the United States of America.

Of particular relevance to criminal procedure are the terms *justice* and *liberty.* The Constitution helps ensure justice and liberty through both setting forth the various roles of government and protecting the rights of people within

The Constitution helps ensure justice and liberty through both setting forth the various roles of government and protecting the rights of people within the nation's borders.

the nation's borders. Throughout the years, the courts have devoted a great amount of energy to interpreting the Constitution and to specifying what rights are important and when they apply.

However, the Constitution is not the only source of rights; there are others worthy of consideration. In addition, some rights are more important than others, at least as far as criminal procedure is concerned. Finally, the two-tiered system of government in the United States creates a unique relationship between the federal and state levels. Criminal procedure cannot be understood without attention to the interplay between federal and states' rights.

Sources of Rights

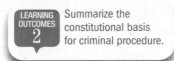

In addition to the Constitution, important sources of rights include court decisions, statutes, and state constitutions. Most of the court decisions discussed in this section and throughout the text are U.S. Supreme Court decisions.

Whenever the Supreme Court interprets the Constitution, it effectively makes an announcement concerning people's rights. For example, the Fourth Amendment states that unreasonable searches and seizures are impermissible. The term *unreasonable* is not self-explanatory, however, so the Court has taken steps to define it. One definition of *unreasonable* appears in the recent decision of *Wilson v. Layne* (526 U.S. 603 [1999]), in which the Court held that it is unreasonable for the police to bring reporters along when serving a warrant unless the reporters are there to serve a legitimate law enforcement objective.

Although the Constitution and the court decisions stemming from it reign supreme in criminal procedure, statutes also play an important role. Obviously, the Constitution and the courts cannot be expected to protect all of the interests that people represent. Statutes attempt to compensate for that shortcoming by establishing that certain rights exist. An example is Title VII of the 1964 Civil Rights Act. Among other things, it prohibits discrimination in employment. Another statute of relevance in criminal procedure is 42 U.S.C. Section 1983. As discussed further in the next chapter, it allows private citizens to sue local law enforcement officials for violations of federally protected rights.

In addition, each state has its own constitution, which can be considered an important source of rights. The supremacy clause of Article VI to the U.S. Constitution makes *it* the supreme law of the land and binds all states and the federal government to it. However, nothing in the U.S. Constitution precludes individual states from adopting stricter interpretations of the federal provisions. In general, if a state constitution gives *less* protection than

the federal Constitution, such a limitation is unconstitutional. But a stricter interpretation of the federal Constitution is perfectly reasonable. For example, the Supreme Court has interpreted the Fifth Amendment in such a way that it requires police to advise a suspect of his or her so-called *Miranda* rights when the suspect is subjected to custodial interrogation—an action that does not necessarily rise to the level of an arrest. A *state*, however, could require that *Miranda* rights be read whenever a person is arrested, regardless of whether he or she is interrogated.

Finally, although they are not a source of rights per se, the **Federal Rules of Criminal Procedure** are worth considering.[3] Excerpts from the Federal Rules are reprinted throughout this book because they sometimes clarify important rulings handed down by the U.S. Supreme Court. Additionally, the Federal Rules set forth the criminal procedure guidelines by which federal criminal justice practitioners are required to abide.

Rights of Relevance in Criminal Procedure

Of the many rights specified in the U.S. Constitution, the rights stemming from five amendments are of special importance in criminal procedure. They are the Fourth, Fifth, Sixth, Eighth, and Fourteenth Amendments (see Figure 1–1 for details). The first four of these are found in the Bill of Rights. The Bill of Rights consists of the first ten amendments. Beyond the Bill of Rights, the Fourteenth Amendment is of special relevance in criminal procedure. Sometimes the First Amendment, which protects assembly and speech, and the Second Amendment, which protects the right to bear arms, are relevant in criminal procedure, but only rarely.

- The **Fourth Amendment** is perhaps the most well-known source of rights in criminal procedure. In fact, it is considered so important that several books on criminal procedure devote the overwhelming majority of their chapters to it. Several rights can be distinguished by reading the text of the Fourth Amendment. It refers to the right of people to be free from unreasonable searches and seizures, and it provides that specific requirements are to guide the warrant process. That is, a warrant must be issued by a magistrate or judge, supported by probable cause, and sufficiently specific as to what is to be searched and/or seized. Because of the complexity of the Fourth Amendment, this book devotes an entire section to its interpretation (see Part II).

- The second constitutional amendment of special relevance to criminal procedure is the **Fifth Amendment**. This book also examines the Fifth Amendment in detail, focusing in particular on the role of the grand jury, the statement that no person shall be "twice put in jeopardy of life or limb" (known as the *double-jeopardy* clause), the statement that no one can be compelled "to be a witness against himself" (also known as the *self-incrimination* clause), and—perhaps most important of all—the requirement that an individual cannot be deprived of life, liberty, or property without due process of law.

- The **Sixth Amendment** is also of great importance in criminal procedure. Of relevance to criminal procedure is the Sixth Amendment's language concerning speedy

Fourth Amendment	The right of the people to be secure in their persons, houses, papers, and effects, against unreasonable searches and seizures, shall not be violated, and no Warrants shall issue, but upon probable cause, supported by Oath or affirmation and particularly describing the place to be searched, and the persons or things to be seized.
Fifth Amendment	No person shall be held to answer for a capital, or otherwise infamous crime, unless on a presentment or indictment of a Grand Jury, except in cases arising in the land or naval forces, or in the Militia, when in actual service in time of War or public danger; nor shall any person be subject for the same offense to be twice put in jeopardy of life or limb; nor shall be compelled in any criminal case to be a witness against himself, nor be deprived of life, liberty, or property, without due process of law; nor shall private property be taken for public use, without just compensation.
Sixth Amendment	In all criminal prosecutions, the accused shall enjoy the right to a speedy and public trial, by an impartial jury of the State and district wherein the crime shall have been committed, which district shall have been previously ascertained by law, and to be informed of the nature and cause of the accusation; to be confronted with the witnesses against him; to have compulsory process for obtaining witnesses in his favor, and to have the Assistance of Counsel for his defence.
Eighth Amendment	Excessive bail shall not be required, nor excessive fines imposed, nor cruel and unusual punishments inflicted.
Fourteenth Amendment (relevant portions)	All persons born or naturalized in the United States, and subject to the jurisdiction thereof, are citizens of the United States and of the State wherein they reside. No State shall make or enforce any law which shall abridge the privileges or immunities of citizens of the United States, nor shall any State deprive any person of life, liberty, or property, without due process of law; nor deny to any person within its jurisdiction the equal protection of the laws.

FIGURE 1–1 Constitutional Amendments of Relevance in Criminal Procedure.

and public trials, impartial juries, confrontation, and compulsory process. The Sixth Amendment also suggests that in addition to being public, trials should be open, not closed, proceedings. The Supreme Court has interpreted the Sixth Amendment as providing the right of the accused to be present at his or her trial and to be able to put on a defense.

- The **Eighth Amendment** is relevant in criminal procedure but to a limited extent. The Eighth Amendment's language on bail and the nature of cruel and unusual punishment are relevant in criminal procedure.

- The **Fourteenth Amendment** has an important home in criminal procedure. It is a fairly long amendment, however, and only a small portion is relevant to the handling and treatment of criminal suspects. The due process language of the Fourteenth Amendment mirrors that of the Fifth. Nonetheless, because the Fifth Amendment is part of the Bill of Rights, it is only binding on the federal government. The Fourteenth Amendment, by contrast, has been used by the Supreme Court to *incorporate*, or make applicable to the states, several of the rights provided for in the Bill of Rights. (The following subsection introduces the so-called incorporation controversy.) The Fourteenth Amendment's due process clause has been interpreted to consist of two types of due process: (1) **substantive due process** and (2) **procedural due process**. The essence of substantive due process is protection from arbitrary and unreasonable action on the part of state officials. By contrast, a procedural due process violation is one in which a violation of a significant life, liberty, or property interest occurs (for example, *Geddes* v. *Northwest Missouri State College*, 49 F.3d 426 [8th Cir. 1995]). Procedural due process is akin to procedural fairness.

Incorporation

The Bill of Rights, consisting of the first ten amendments to the U.S. Constitution, places limitations on the powers of the federal government. It does *not* limit the power of the states, however. In other words, the first ten amendments place no limitations on state and local governments and their agencies. Government power at the state and local levels is clearly limited by state constitutions.

Even though the Bill of Rights does not limit state and local governments, the Supreme Court has found a way to do so

The first ten amendments place no limitations on state and local governments and their agencies.

through the Fourteenth Amendment. In particular, the Court has used the Fourteenth Amendment's due process clause, which holds that no state shall "deprive any person of life, liberty, or property, without due process of law," to make certain protections specified in the Bill of Rights applicable to the states. This is known as **incorporation**.

The extent to which the Fourteenth Amendment should regulate state and local government power has been the subject of some disagreement—hence, the incorporation controversy. The basic question posed over the years has been "To what degree should the Fourteenth Amendment's due process clause incorporate the various provisions of the Bill of Rights so as to restrict state and local law enforcement in the same way federal law enforcement is restricted by the Bill of Rights?" In response to this question, there are several leading views on incorporation. They are depicted in Figure 1–2.

The incorporation debate is significant because of three concerns. First, because most contact between citizens and the police occurs at the state and local levels, it is critical to determine the role of the federal Constitution at the state level. Comparatively few people have contact with federal law enforcement, so the Bill of Rights actually regulates a limited number of police/citizen contacts. Second, incorporation, according to some, threatens *federalism*. Under the doctrine of federalism, states have the authority to develop their own rules and laws of criminal procedure, but if the Fourteenth Amendment incorporates the Bill of Rights, this authority can be compromised. Third, the incorporation debate raises important concerns about the separation of powers. Namely, the Supreme Court has decided which rights should be incorporated—a decision that may better be reserved for Congress.

Total Incorporation	The *total incorporation* perspective holds that the Fourteenth Amendment's due process clause incorporates the entire Bill of Rights. In other words, all protections specified in the Bill of Rights should be binding on the states. The primary proponent of this view was Supreme Court Justice Hugo Black (for example, *Adamson* v. *California*, 332 U.S. 46 [1947]; *Rochin* v. *California*, 342 U.S. 165 [1952]).
Selective Incorporation	The second leading view on incorporation is that of *selective incorporation*, or the *fundamental rights* perspective. It favors incorporation of certain protections enumerated in the Bill of Rights, not all of them. Further, this perspective deems certain rights as being more critical, or fundamental, than others. The Supreme Court's decision in *Snyder* v. *Massachusetts* (291 U.S. 97 [1934]) advocates this perspective, arguing that the due process clause prohibits state encroachment on those "principle[s] of justice so rooted in the traditions and consciences of our people as to be ranked as fundamental."
Total Incorporation Plus	The third view on incorporation can be termed *total incorporation plus*. This view holds that the Fourteenth Amendment's due process clause incorporates the whole Bill of Rights as well as additional rights *not* specified in the Constitution, such as the "right to privacy." This view can be found in such Supreme Court cases as *Adamson* v. *California* and *Poe* v. *Ullman* (367 U.S. 497 [1961]).
	Finally, some people believe that the topic of incorporation deserves case-by-case consideration. That is, no rights should be incorporated across the board. Rather, the facts and circumstances of each individual case should be weighed in order to determine if any protections listed in the Bill of Rights should apply at the state or local level.

FIGURE 1–2 Leading Views on Incorporation.

Right	Deciding Case	
First Amendment freedom of religion, speech, and assembly and the right to petition for redress of grievances	Fiske v. Kansas, 274 U.S. 380 (1927)	
Fourth Amendment prohibition of unreasonable searches and seizures	Wolf v. Colorado, 338 U.S. 25 (1949)	
Fifth Amendment protection against compelled self-incrimination	Malloy v. Hogan, 378 U.S. 1 (1964) ·	
Fifth Amendment protection from double jeopardy	Benton v. Maryland, 395 U.S. 784 (1969)	
Sixth Amendment right to counsel	Gideon v. Wainwright, 372 U.S. 335 (1963)	
Sixth Amendment right to a speedy trial	Klopfer v. North Carolina, 386 U.S. 213 (1967)	
Sixth Amendment right to a public trial	In re Oliver, 333 U.S. 257 (1948)	
Sixth Amendment right to confrontation	Pointer v. Texas, 380 U.S. 400 (1965)	
Sixth Amendment right to an impartial jury	Duncan v. Louisiana, 391 U.S. 145 (1968)	
Sixth Amendment right to compulsory process	Washington v. Texas, 388 U.S. 14 (1967)	
Eighth Amendment prohibition of cruel and unusual punishment	Robinson v. California, 370 U.S. 660 (1962)	

FIGURE 1–3 Rights Incorporated to the States.

Where does incorporation stand today? The Supreme Court has consistently held that some protections listed in the Bill of Rights are more applicable to the states than others. The Fourth Amendment, in its view, lists several *fundamental rights*. By contrast, the Fifth Amendment's grand jury clause has not been deemed fundamental and is not binding on the states (*Hurtado v. California*, 110 U.S. 516 [1884]).

Figure 1–3 lists the rights that have been deemed fundamental by the Supreme Court and, as a result, incorporated to the states.[4] The Supreme Court cases responsible for these incorporation decisions are listed as well.

Although not all of the Bill of Rights is binding on the states, it bears mentioning that the Supreme Court has repeatedly emphasized that Americans have a fundamental right to privacy, even though the Constitution makes no mention of privacy. It is commonly said that people do not enjoy an *expectation of privacy* in public places. It would seem, then, that certain rights not listed in the Constitution have also been identified as well as incorporated.

▶ *Precedent and Its Importance*

To many students of criminal procedure, legal research is a less-than-desirable pursuit. Even so, it is essential in everyday practice because of the importance of precedent. A **precedent** is a rule of case law (that is, a decision by a court) that is binding on all lower courts and the court that issued it. A past decision may not be available in each case, but when one is, the courts will defer to it. This is the doctrine of *stare decisis*.

Stare Decisis

Stare decisis is a Latin term that means to abide by or to adhere to decided cases. Most courts adhere to the principle of *stare decisis*. That is, when a court has handed down a decision on a specific set of facts or legal questions, future court decisions that involve similar facts or questions will defer to the previous decision. In short, *stare decisis* is simply the practice of adhering to a previous decision or precedent.

Why does *stare decisis* occupy such an important position in the U.S. court system? The answer is that it promotes consistency. It is well known that accused criminals enjoy the right to counsel (*Gideon v. Wainwright*, 372 U.S. 335 [1963]), but what if from one year to the next the Supreme Court vacillated on whether this right were constitutionally guaranteed? The criminal process, not to mention the rights of the accused, would be unpredictable and vary from one point to the next.

When a court has handed down a decision on a specific set of facts or legal questions, future court decisions that involve similar facts or questions will defer to the previous decision.

It is important to note that the practice of deferring to precedent is not always possible or desirable. First, *stare decisis* is usually only practiced by courts in a single jurisdiction. Suppose, for example, that a federal circuit appeals court handed down a decision. All the district courts within that circuit would then abide by the appeals court decision. Courts outside that circuit would *not* be bound to adhere to the decision (although some courts often do as a matter of professional courtesy). Perhaps more important, if a case coming before a court is unique and does not resemble one decided in the past, the court may *distinguish* it.

Distinguishing Cases

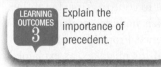

LEARNING OUTCOMES 3 Explain the importance of precedent.

When a previous decision does not apply to the current facts, a court will **distinguish** the case, saying, in effect, that this case is different and cannot be decided by looking to past rulings. Another way of understanding what it means to distinguish a case is to think of the present set of facts as unique and never before considered by an appellate court.

Because only a handful of cases make it to the appellate level, and even fewer still arrive at the Supreme Court, there is an untold number of cases waiting to be distinguished. This is a critical point. The case law in place currently addresses only a minute quantity of possible constitutional questions. Countless contacts occur between the police and citizens, and several of them may give rise to important constitutional questions. Yet they may never see the inside of a courtroom. So, although this book may appear heavy on case law, a thorough understanding of criminal procedure would require a review of the nearly infinite possible factual circumstances that could arise in the criminal process.

An example of a case that was distinguished is *Terry* v. *Ohio* (392 U.S. 1 [1968]). In that case, the Supreme Court held that police officers can stop and frisk suspects with reasonable suspicion, not probable cause (the latter standard appearing in the text of the Fourth Amendment). The Court felt that a stop-and-frisk is different from a search or a seizure and, as such, should be governed by a different set of standards. Had the Supreme Court *not* decided *Terry*, or any case like it, stop-and-frisk encounters would probably still be considered seizures and therefore subject to the Fourth Amendment's requirement for probable cause. *Terry* will be considered in more detail later, as will many other distinguished cases.

In nearly every class on criminal procedure, students ask, "What if . . . ?" The "what if" question reflects a concern over possible factual circumstances not already addressed in published court decisions. In order for a "what if" question to be answered, a court decision must result. Otherwise, the best approach to answering such a question is to look to the past and find a decision that closely resembles the hypothetical scenario posed by the question. In this vein, every case discussed

The case law in place currently addresses only a minute quantity of possible constitutional questions.

throughout this text should be thought of as a distinguished case. Every decision was based on a different set of factual circumstances and was deemed by the reviewing court as worthy of being distinguished. Were it not for distinguished cases, criminal procedure case law could be adequately covered in a matter of minutes, even seconds.

Theory Versus Reality

Criminal procedure consists mostly of rules and guidelines that have been handed down by the courts to dictate how the criminal process should play out. In some circumstances, however, court decisions may not have a great deal of influence. That is, some court decisions are made in the theoretical world, which is somewhat disconnected from the day-to-day operations of law enforcement within the real world. Understandably, there can be differences, even tensions, between the worlds of theory and reality.

Americans are taught that the courts—and the Supreme Court, in particular—are charged with interpreting the Constitution and the laws of the United States. They are further taught that law enforcement should accept such interpretations uncritically and without much reflection. Although these understandings are mostly true, theory and reality can still differ. Some Supreme Court decisions have little influence in the real world, and in some cases may even be flatly ignored. There are four reasons for this:

- First, the Supreme Court sometimes makes decisions on excruciatingly detailed matters that have almost no applicability to most law enforcement officers, most of the time. A good example is the Supreme Court's decision in *Atwater* v. *City of Lago Vista* (533 U.S. 924 [2001]). The Court decided that the Fourth Amendment does not prohibit the police from arresting people for seatbelt violations. To the parties involved in the actual case, this decision may have been significant. But in most jurisdictions, how many police officers are going to arrest people for seatbelt violations? The case probably has little relevance to most police officers because they usually have more important matters to address.

- Second, the Supreme Court frequently hands down decisions that would seem to have dramatic effects on the nature of law enforcement, but actually involve issues that are already being addressed by many police agencies. For example, the Supreme Court's decision in *Tennessee* v. *Garner* (471 U.S. 1 [1985]) made it a violation of the Fourth Amendment for the police to use deadly force to apprehend an unarmed and nondangerous fleeing felon. However, prior to *Garner*, many police agencies had already adopted restrictive deadly force policies—policies that, in many instances, were more restrictive than the ruling handed down in *Garner*. Police agency policy, therefore, can differ from, and even be more restrictive than, decisions reached by the Supreme Court.

- The third reason for the gap between theory and reality is that the courts sometimes hand down decisions that can be effectively circumvented or ignored by the police. Clearly, it is not in the best interest of law enforcement to ignore the courts, and probably quite rare that the police do so, but it does occur.

For example, in *Kyllo* v. *United States* (533 U.S. 27 [2001]), the Supreme Court held that a search occurs when the police scan a private residence with an infrared thermal imager without first obtaining a warrant. The consequence of conducting such a scan without a warrant is that any evidence subsequently obtained will not be admissible in court. However, in reality, what is to prevent the police from scanning someone's house if there is no intent to obtain evidence?

- Finally, what the courts say and the police do can differ simply as a consequence of some aspects of the U.S. legal system. It is well known, for example, that a police officer cannot stop a motorist without some level of justification. On how many occasions, though, are motorists stopped without justification? That is, how many people are pulled over every day simply because a police officer is suspicious of them? This cannot be established for certain, but it does happen. It *can* happen because the legal system cannot do much to prevent it. Someone who is wrongfully stopped can file a complaint, but research shows that many such complaints are resolved in favor of the police. A lawsuit can be filed, but such suits are rarely successful. And if nothing is discovered that leads to arresting the motorist, then it is doubtful that the illegal stop will draw attention in court.

▶ Competing Concerns in Criminal Procedure

Criminal procedure is an exciting topic because of the inherent tension it creates between two competing sets of priorities. On the one hand, there is a serious interest in the United States in controlling crime, with some Americans advocating doing whatever it takes to keep criminals off the streets. On the other hand, because of their country's democratic system of government, Americans value people's rights and become angry when those rights are compromised or threatened. These two competing sets of values have been described by Herbert Packer as the *crime-control* and *due process* perspectives.[5]

The values each opposing perspective subscribes to are probably familiar to many readers because the due process/crime-control debate invariably pops up all throughout criminal justice. Almost without exception, whenever there is disagreement as to how best to approach the crime problem—be it through court decisions or legislative measures—the due process/crime-control distinction rears its head. A delicate balance has to be achieved between the two perspectives.

The due process perspective closely resembles a liberal political orientation. Liberals often favor protection of people's rights and liberties to a higher degree than their conservative counterparts. By contrast, the crime-control perspective is the one most frequently subscribed to by conservative law-and-order types.

Of course, in reality, there can be a great deal of overlap between the two orientations. Liberals occasionally favor conservative crime-control policies, and conservatives can be concerned with protecting the rights of American citizens. That

is to say, although the two groups frequently stand in stark contrast to each other, they do sometimes meet in the middle. Regardless, the values espoused by each group—be it an interest in crime control, an interest in civil rights, or an interest in both—are here to stay. Given that, it is useful to consider each perspective in more detail, focusing special attention on the implications for criminal procedure.

Due Process

Packer's **due process perspective** is, first and foremost, concerned with people's rights and liberties. It also gives significant weight to human freedom. Due process advocates believe that the government's primary job is not to control crime but rather to maximize human freedom, which includes protecting citizens from undue government influence. Proponents of due process favor minimizing the potential for mistakes, as explained by Packer:

> People are notoriously poor observers of disturbing events. . . . [C]onfessions and admissions by persons in police custody may be induced by physical or psychological coercion so that the police end up hearing what the suspect thinks they want to hear rather than the truth; witnesses may be animated by a bias or interest that no one would trouble to discover except one specially charged with protecting the interests of the accused (as the police are not).[6]

Due process advocates also believe that each suspect is innocent until proven guilty, just as Americans are taught. In addition, they place greater emphasis on *legal guilt* (whether a person is guilty according to the law) rather than *factual guilt* (whether a person actually committed the crime with which he or she is charged).

Underlying the due process/crime-control perspectives are four ideals: (1) The criminal process looks, or should look, something like an obstacle course, (2) quality is better than quantity, (3) formality is preferred over informality, and (4) a great deal of faith is put in the courts.

The Obstacle Course

The "obstacle course" idea is rooted in a metaphor, of course. A criminal process that resembles an obstacle course is one that is complex and needs to be navigated by skilled legal professionals. Further, it is one that is somewhat difficult to operate in a predictable fashion. It is not a process that prides itself on speed and efficiency—values of great importance in the crime-control perspective. In fact, the opposite could be said. The obstacle-course metaphor also stresses that each case must pass through several complicated twists and turns before a verdict can be rendered.

Quality over Quantity

Another way to distinguish between due process and crime control is in terms of quantity and quality. The due process view favors quality—that is, reaching a fair and accurate decision at every stage of the criminal process. It stresses that each case should be handled on an individual basis and that special attention should be paid to the facts and circumstances surrounding

© Marmaduke St. John/Alamy

the event. In addition, the concern with quality is one that minimizes the potential for error. For example, due process advocates are in favor of allowing several death penalty appeals because the possibility of executing the wrong person should be avoided at all costs.

Insistence on Formality

Due process advocates do not favor informal processes. Because of the potential for human error and bias, they favor a full-blown adversarial criminal process. They also believe that early intervention by judges and other presumptively objective parties (besides, say, the police) is in the best interest of people accused of breaking the law.

Faith in the Courts

Another value inherent in the due process perspective is intense faith in the courts as opposed to law enforcement. Due process advocates correctly point out that the job of a judge is to interpret the U.S. Constitution. This, they argue, helps provide protection to people charged with crimes. Faith in the courts also corresponds with the previously mentioned insistence on formality. When guilt or innocence is determined in court, an air of fairness and objectivity must be maintained.

- -

Crime Control

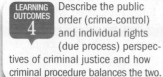

LEARNING OUTCOMES 4 Describe the public order (crime-control) and individual rights (due process) perspectives of criminal justice and how criminal procedure balances the two.

In contrast to the due process perspective, the **crime-control perspective** emphasizes the importance of controlling crime, perhaps to the detriment of civil liberties. From a cost/benefit perspective, crime-control advocates believe that the benefit of controlling crime to society at large outweighs the cost of infringing on some individuals' due process protections. Another way to distinguish between the due process and crime-control perspectives is to consider the distinction between *means* and *ends*: Crime control is more

concerned with the *ends*—with wiping out crime, or at a minimum, with mitigating its harmful effects. By contrast, due process is concerned with the *means*—with the methods by which people are treated by criminal justice officials. The result—either crime or the absence of it—is not of great concern to due process advocates.

The Assembly Line

The metaphor of an "assembly line" suggests that the criminal process should be automatic, predictable, and uniform. In other words, every criminal should be treated the same, with minimal variations in terms of charges and sentences. The assembly-line metaphor further suggests that the criminal process should be quick and efficient. The goal of the crime-control perspective is to move criminals through the justice process as swiftly as possible. A full-blown adversarial criminal process, replete with hearings and other pauses in the interest of the accused, is anathema to the crime-control view.

Quantity over Quality

As just mentioned, the due process model stresses quality over quantity. The crime-control model, by contrast, favors quantity over quality, a view that is consistent with the assembly-line metaphor. The goal is to move as many offenders as possible through the criminal justice system with as little delay as possible. If mistakes are made along the way and someone is wrongfully charged or convicted, so be it. That is, the *overall* goal of ensuring that as many criminals are dealt with as possible is superior to protecting any individual's constitutional rights.

Insistence on Informality

Whereas the due process perspective favors the formality of the criminal process, with particular emphasis on the courts, the crime-control perspective favors informality. The courts are to be avoided; instead, justice should be meted out beyond the walls of a courtroom. Plea bargaining, for instance, is favored because of its swift, behind-the-scenes nature (not to mention that it eliminates the need to go to trial). An insistence on

informality suggests further that the law enforcement establishment should be more involved in making determinations of guilt, not the courts.

Faith in the Police

Finally, whereas the due process perspective places a great deal of faith in the courts, the crime-control perspective puts a high degree of trust in the police. All Americans are taught that each suspect is innocent until proven guilty in a court of law. Clearly, the courts are charged with making this determination. However, crime-control advocates favor so-called street justice, giving the police vast discretion in deciding how to deal with people suspected of being involved in criminal activity. A fitting

quote describing the crime-control perspective is, therefore, "All criminals are guilty until proven innocent." In other words, all suspects should be considered guilty; if the courts determine otherwise, then so be it.

▶ Structure of the U.S. Court System

Criminal procedure can be complex, not only because of the many factual questions that arise in day-to-day police/citizen encounters (as well as throughout the rest of the justice process), but also because of the two-tiered structure of the U.S. court system. This two-tiered structure reflects the idea of *dual sovereignty*: The federal and state governments are considered separate, or *sovereign*, in their own right. Each state, as well as the federal government, has its own court structure.

There is no way to succinctly describe all the variations in state court structures, but, generally, they resemble one another. Typically, the lowest-level courts in a given state are **courts of limited jurisdiction**, which have jurisdiction over relatively minor offenses and infractions. A traffic court fits in this category. Next are the trial courts, also called **courts of general jurisdiction**, which try several types of cases. Courts of general jurisdiction are often county-level courts and are frequently called **superior courts**. At the next highest level are the **intermediate appellate courts**; verdicts from courts of general jurisdiction are appealed to these courts. Finally, each state has its own **state supreme court**, the highest court in the state. Figure 1–4 shows a typical state court structure—from the state of Washington. Importantly, state courts try cases involving state laws (and, depending on the level of the court, some county, city, and other local ordinances).

The *federal* court structure can be described succinctly because, for the purposes of criminal procedure, it consists of three specific types of courts. Federal courts try cases involving federal law. The lowest courts at the federal level are the so-called **district courts**. There are 94 federal district courts in the United States (as of this writing), including 89 district courts in the 50 states and 1 each in Puerto Rico, the Virgin Islands, the District of Columbia, Guam, and the Northern Mariana Islands. At the next level are the **U.S. courts of appeals**. There are 13 of these so-called circuit courts of appeals: 12 regional courts and 1 for the federal circuit. Each is charged with hearing appeals from several of the district courts that fall within its circuit. Finally, the **U.S. Supreme Court** is the highest court in the federal system. As will be discussed, however, the Supreme Court does not hear only federal appeals.[7] Figure 1–5 shows the structure of the federal court system; the courts of relevance in criminal procedure are highlighted. Figure 1–6 presents a map of the geographic boundaries of the U.S. courts of appeals and the U.S. district courts.

The federal government as well as each of the 50 states is considered a sovereign entity. That is why each has a court

LEARNING OUTCOMES **5** Outline the structure of the court system, including the responsibilities and jurisdictions of each level.

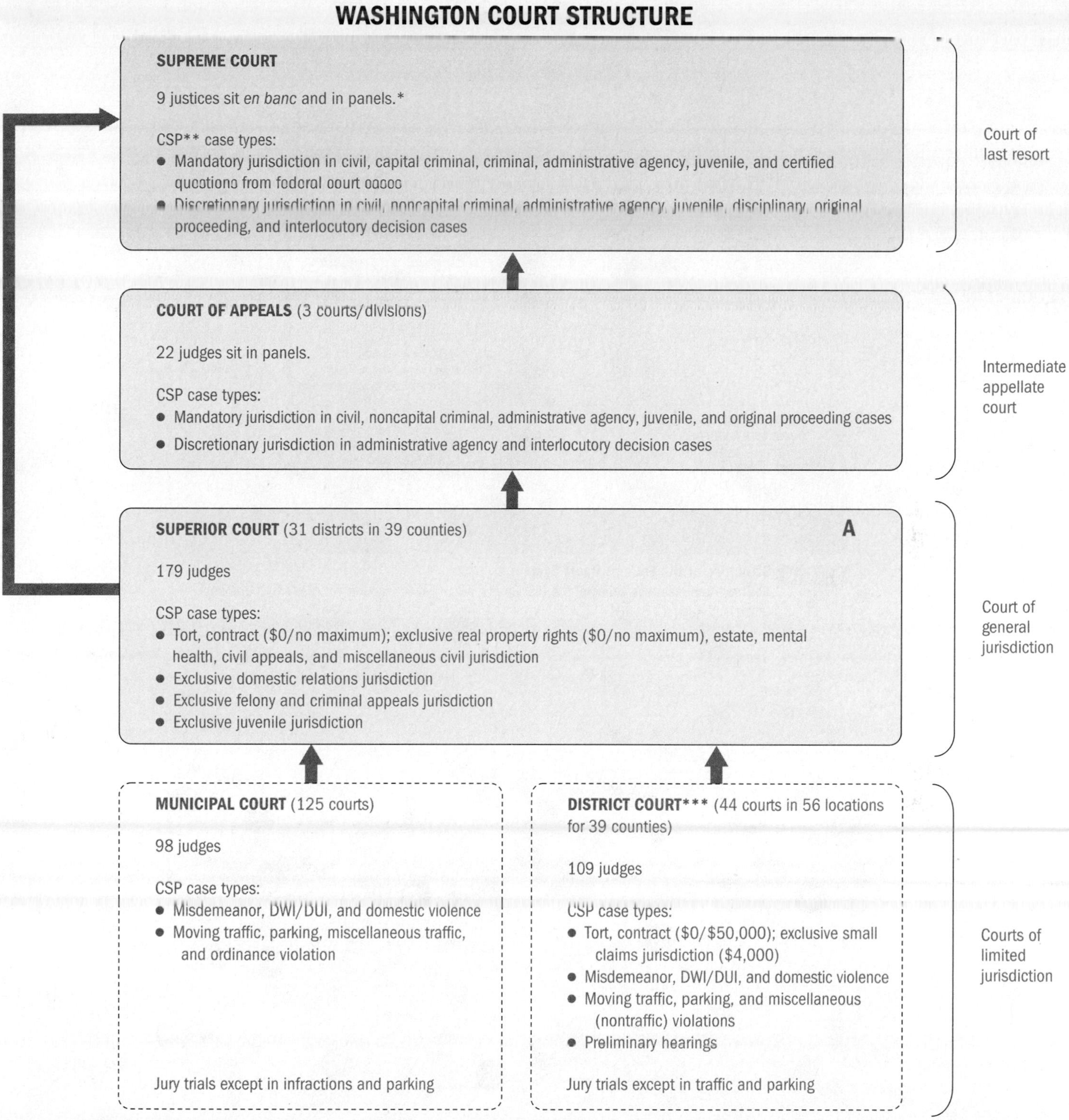

WASHINGTON COURT STRUCTURE

SUPREME COURT

9 justices sit *en banc* and in panels.*

CSP** case types:
- Mandatory jurisdiction in civil, capital criminal, criminal, administrative agency, juvenile, and certified questions from federal court cases
- Discretionary jurisdiction in civil, noncapital criminal, administrative agency, juvenile, disciplinary, original proceeding, and interlocutory decision cases

Court of last resort

COURT OF APPEALS (3 courts/divisions)

22 judges sit in panels.

CSP case types:
- Mandatory jurisdiction in civil, noncapital criminal, administrative agency, juvenile, and original proceeding cases
- Discretionary jurisdiction in administrative agency and interlocutory decision cases

Intermediate appellate court

SUPERIOR COURT (31 districts in 39 counties)   **A**

179 judges

CSP case types:
- Tort, contract ($0/no maximum); exclusive real property rights ($0/no maximum), estate, mental health, civil appeals, and miscellaneous civil jurisdiction
- Exclusive domestic relations jurisdiction
- Exclusive felony and criminal appeals jurisdiction
- Exclusive juvenile jurisdiction

Court of general jurisdiction

MUNICIPAL COURT (125 courts)

98 judges

CSP case types:
- Misdemeanor, DWI/DUI, and domestic violence
- Moving traffic, parking, miscellaneous traffic, and ordinance violation

Jury trials except in infractions and parking

DISTRICT COURT*** (44 courts in 56 locations for 39 counties)

109 judges

CSP case types:
- Tort, contract ($0/$50,000); exclusive small claims jurisdiction ($4,000)
- Misdemeanor, DWI/DUI, and domestic violence
- Moving traffic, parking, and miscellaneous (nontraffic) violations
- Preliminary hearings

Jury trials except in traffic and parking

Courts of limited jurisdiction

* *en banc* means all justices/judges hear the case at once. "In panels" means only some of the justices/judges hear the case.
** Court Statistics Project
*** District court provides services to municipalities that do not have a municipal court.

FIGURE 1–4 **Structure of a State Court System (Washington).**
Source: www.bjs.gov/content/pub/pdf/scou4.pdf (accessed November 6, 2013).

system of its own. There is another set of sovereigns, however: the Native American tribal courts. These tribal courts will receive no further attention in this book because, in general, they do not have to follow the same constitutional requirements as state and federal courts. Rather, they fall under the Indian Civil Rights Act of 1968. The U.S. military also has its own structure, in which the rules of criminal procedure differ markedly from those covered here. Because of the complexity of the Uniform Code of Military Justice, military courts and criminal procedure will not be covered in this book, either.

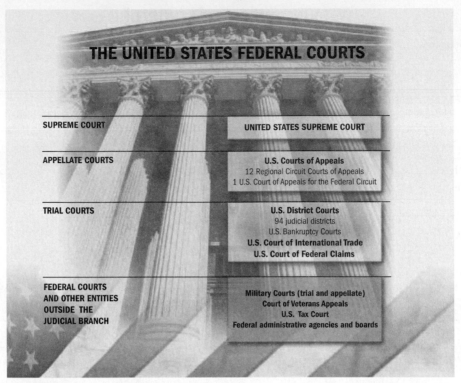

FIGURE 1-5 Structure of the Federal Court System.
Source: Administrative Office of the U.S. Courts, http://www.uscourts.gov/FederalCourts.aspx (accessed August 19, 2014).

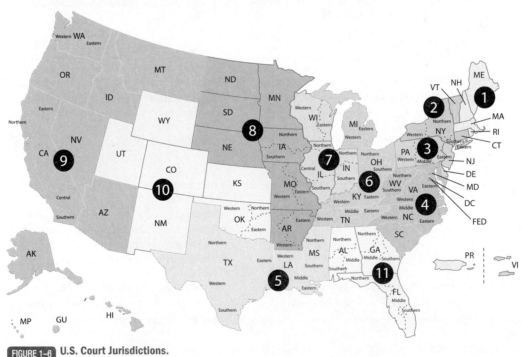

FIGURE 1-6 U.S. Court Jurisdictions.
Source: Administrative Office of the U.S. Courts, www.uscourts.gov/Court_Locator.aspx UnderstandingtheFederalCourts/FederalCourtsStructure.aspx (accessed November 6, 2013).

That said, what influences where a case will be decided? Generally, if the case involves federal law, it will be tried in federal court. If, by contrast, it involves state law, it will be heard in state court. Certain crimes—such as kidnapping, transportation of illegal narcotics across state lines, and robbing a federally insured bank—can be tried in both federal and state courts, if the prosecutors agree. As will be discussed later, such a dual prosecution does not violate the Fifth Amendment's double-jeopardy clause.

As indicated near the outset of this chapter, criminal procedure textbooks—this one included—focus almost exclusively on U.S. Supreme Court decisions. Why focus on *federal* Supreme Court decisions rather than *state* supreme court decisions? The answer is that many important cases move from the state supreme courts to the U.S. Supreme Court, which is the court of last resort. Decisions of the U.S. Supreme Court are therefore important because they represent the last word on what conduct is constitutional and what is not.

To understand the relationship between the federal and state courts, it is necessary to understand first where to find criminal cases and then how to trace the progress of criminal cases as they move from the trial to the appellate level. Following discussion of these topics, attention will turn to what types of cases are decided by the U.S. Supreme Court and how state-level court decisions arrive at the nation's highest court.

▶ Understanding Court Cases

Being able to find court cases requires that readers be familiar with legal citations as well as the publications in which cases can be found. Legal citations are somewhat cryptic but can be deciphered with relative ease (see Figure 1–7). After becoming familiar with case citations, it is necessary to learn where the cases can actually be found. First, most university libraries have one or several of the so-called reporters listed in Figure 1–8. They can be found in bound form on the library shelves. Online research is also an option. Cases can be found at such websites

Miranda v. *Arizona*, (384 U.S. 436 [1966])

Miranda and Arizona: the parties to the case. The party listed first is the one initiating the action. In this case, *Miranda* appealed his conviction, which is why he is listed first.

384: the volume of the publication in which the case is located

U.S.: the abbreviation of the publication in which the case can be found. "U.S." refers to the official U.S. Supreme Court reports.

436: the page on which the case starts

1966: the year the decision was published

FIGURE 1–7 Understanding Case Citations.

Abbreviation	Description
U.S.	*United States Reports*: This is the official publication for U.S. Supreme Court decisions.
S.Ct.	*Supreme Court Reporter*: This West Law publication reports U.S. Supreme Court decisions.
CrL	*Criminal Law Reporter*: This Bureau of National Affairs publication reports U.S. Supreme Court decisions.
L.W.	*United States Law Week*: This Bureau of National Affairs publication reports U.S. Supreme Court decisions.
F.2d	*Federal Reports, Second Series*: This West Law publication reports decisions of the Federal Courts of Appeals.
P.2d	*Pacific Reporter, Second Series*: This West Law publication reports decisions from the Pacific states.
A.2d	*Atlantic Reporter, Second Series*: This West Law publication reports decisions from the Atlantic states.
N.E.2d	*North Eastern Reporter, Second Series*: This West Law publication reports decisions from the northeastern states.
N.W.2d	*North Western Reporter, Second Series*: This West Law publication reports decisions from the northwestern states.
S.E.2d	*South Eastern Reporter, Second Series*: This West Law publication reports decisions from the southeastern states.
S.W.2d	*South Western Reporter, Second Series*: This West Law publication reports decisions from the southwestern states.
S.2d	*Southern Reporter, Second Series*: This West Law publication reports decisions from the southern states.

FIGURE 1–8 Publications Containing Court Cases.

as www.findlaw.com. U.S. Supreme Court cases can be found at www.supremecourtus.gov. Another website, maintained by Cornell University, is helpful for finding Supreme Court cases: www.law.cornell.edu/supct/.

Many university libraries also have access to subscription databases, such as LexisNexis, which contain cases from nearly all courts across the country. LexisNexis has a search feature known as *Shepard's Citations*, which allows researchers to enter a case citation and retrieve every other case that has cited it. Doing a Shepard's search is useful for tracing the history and current status of an important decision. Westlaw offers a similar service known as KeyCite.

For those who do not enjoy reading actual court decisions, other sources of legal information may be useful. For example, legal dictionaries and encyclopedias offer clarification of important legal concepts. Legal digests identify and consolidate legal issues, provide commentary on and interpret cases, and otherwise "digest" complex material. Finally, law reviews are useful places to find discussions of various aspects of the law as well as opinions on and interpretations of court cases. Databases such as LexisNexis contain full-text articles from nearly all law reviews.

Defendant	Person charged with the crime in question
Prosecutor	The official governmental representative tasked with bringing charges against the accused
Appellant	The party that appeals
Appellee	The party appealed against
Petitioner	Similar to an appellant, but one who files for *habeas corpus* review

FIGURE 1-9 The Parties to a Case.

Affirm The appellate court agrees with the lower court's decision.	**Remand** The case is sent back to the lower court for further action.
Reverse The lower court's decision is nullified or set aside.	**Vacate** The lower court's decision is cancelled or set aside (similar to a reversal).

FIGURE 1-10 Common Appellate Court Dispositions.

Tracing the Progress of a Criminal Case

LEARNING OUTCOMES 6 Understand the parts of a court case.

One of the more frustrating aspects of criminal procedure, especially for those who have little familiarity with the law or legal jargon, is the sometimes laborious task of tracing the progress of a criminal case. If final decisions were reached in a single court, then criminal procedure would be vastly simplified. In reality, though, a single case can bounce back and forth between trial and appellate courts, sometimes for years. Indeed, many U.S. Supreme Court decisions concern matters that occurred a decade or more ago. Thus, it is of particular importance for students of criminal procedure to learn how to trace a criminal case.

There are several essential steps to tracing the progress of a criminal case. First, it is necessary to have a basic understanding of the nation's court structure. This requires knowing where the criminal trial in question took place. If it took place in a federal circuit court, then tracing the progress of the case will be fairly easy. There are only three possible courts—district court, circuit appellate court, and the Supreme Court—that may have handed down decisions on the matter. If the case originated in state court, however, it can be decidedly more difficult to trace the case over time. Familiarity with the state court structure is needed, as well as an understanding of how cases can jump back and forth between the state and federal courts, which will be discussed later in this section.

Second, to adequately follow the progress of a criminal case, it is also necessary to understand the legal jargon, beginning with the parties to the case (see Figure 1–9). Next, to follow a

A single case can bounce back and forth between trial and appellate courts, sometimes for years.

criminal case, it is essential to have an understanding of how cases are decided and what possible decisions can be reached (see Figure 1–10). At the trial level, two decisions can result: guilty and not guilty. At the appellate level, however, the picture becomes more complex. Assume, for example, that a defendant is found guilty in a federal district court and appeals to one of the circuit courts of appeals. Assuming that the court agrees to hear the case, it can hand down one of several decisions. The most common decisions are to affirm or to reverse a lower court's decision.

If there were only one appellate court, tracing the progress of a case would be fairly simple. Unfortunately, multiple appellate courts exist, which means the decisions from court to court can change. This is a very important point. Assume, for example, that a defendant is found guilty in a state trial court. He or she could appeal to the state's intermediate appellate court, which could reverse the defendant's conviction. The case could then go to the state's supreme court, which could reverse the appellate court's decision and basically uphold the defendant's conviction. Finally, the case could go to the U.S. Supreme Court, which could again reverse the defendant's conviction. Believe it or not, this is a fairly simple progression. Nothing prevents a single case from going from the trial court to the appellate court, back to the trial court, up to the appellate court again, up to the state supreme court, back to the intermediate appellate court, and so on.

It is essential to understand what has happened with a criminal case before making any claims as to its importance or influence. In other words, doing incomplete legal research can be a recipe for disaster. If, for instance, a researcher finds a state supreme court decision that supports a point he or she wants to make, but that decision was later reversed, say, by the U.S. Supreme Court, whatever argument he or she makes in reliance on that state supreme court case will be inaccurate. Thus, in tracing the progress of a criminal case, it is necessary to understand whether the issue in question has been resolved or may currently be on the docket of an appellate court, which could render an altogether different decision.

In tracing a criminal case, especially when interpreting one decided at the appellate level, it is important to understand the components of a published decision (see Figure 1–11). An appellate court often consists of a panel of judges who may not always agree with one another, even though the court reaches a single decision. For example, a 5-to-4 decision by the U.S. Supreme Court is one in which the Court reached a single decision because of a majority, but four of the justices disagreed.

There is much more to tracing the progress of a criminal case than understanding the terminology encountered along the way. How is it that certain cases are appealed and others are not? Under what circumstances may the defendant, but not the prosecution, appeal, and vice versa? Why do some defendants file several appeals and others do not? Answers to these questions are presented in the last chapter of this text, where special attention is given to the appellate process and other methods for challenging the verdicts of trial courts throughout the United States.

Most criminal cases originate at the state level. This should be obvious because there are 50 state court structures and only 1 federal court system. Also, the number of state laws

Opinion	Voice of the majority of the court—the majority opinion
Concurring Opinion	An agreement with the majority decision, but using different reasoning
Dissenting Opinion	A disagreement (supported by reasoning) with the majority decision

FIGURE 1–11 Parts of a Supreme Court Decision.

criminalizing certain types of conduct vastly exceeds the number of federal laws with the same objective. But just because most cases are heard in state courts does not mean they cannot be heard at the federal level. State-level cases can arrive at the U.S. Supreme Court.

Stated simply, a state-level case can arrive at the U.S. Supreme Court if it raises a federal question, which is usually a question concerning the U.S. Constitution. First, however, such a case must proceed through several steps. It must move all the way to the state supreme court. That is, a case cannot jump from a state-level intermediate appellate court to the U.S. Supreme Court.

Next, like many appellate courts, the U.S. Supreme Court must decide whether it wants to hear the case. The party seeking

A state-level case can arrive at the U.S. Supreme Court if it raises a federal question, which is usually a question concerning the U.S. Constitution.

Think About It...

Brandon Bourdages/Shutterstock

Interpreting a Supreme Court Holding Assume that John Smith was subjected to a search that was not supported by probable cause. Assume further that he was convicted in a federal district court based on evidence obtained from the search. He appealed his conviction to the U.S. court of appeals, which remanded his case back to the district court to determine if the search to which Smith was subjected required probable cause. The district court concluded that the search did not require probable cause. The case was then appealed again to the U.S. court of appeals, which reversed the district court's decision. The U.S. Supreme Court then granted *certiorari* and reversed the U.S. court of appeals decision. In plain English, what happened here? In other words, what is the practical effect of this convoluted case progression?

Think About It...

ene/Shutterstock

Would the Supreme Court Hear This Case? Assume that a state supreme court heard an appeal from one of the state's intermediate appellate courts. In the appeal, the defendant argued that her conviction should be overturned, as the judge failed to declare that certain testimony provided by the government's lead witness should have been deemed inadmissible according to the state's rules of evidence. In making its decision, the appellate court sided with the government, upholding the defendant's conviction. Would the U.S. Supreme Court likely hear this case? What if instead the defendant argued that the original judge mistakenly permitted the prosecutor to comment to the jury concerning the defendant's refusal to take the stand and testify? Would that issue likely get a hearing from the Court?

a decision must file documents with the Court, asking to be heard. If the Supreme Court agrees the case is worth deciding, it issues what is known as a ***writ of certiorari***. This is an order by the court requiring the lower court to send the case and a record of its proceedings to the U.S. Supreme Court for review. Four of the nine U.S. Supreme Court justices must agree to hear a case before a *writ of certiorari* will be issued. This is known as the **rule of four**.

If four justices do not agree to hear the case, that is the end of the road in terms of legal options. When tracing the progress of a case, encountering a statement such as "cert. denied" will indicate this result: The case was denied a hearing by the Supreme Court. Figure 1–12 summarizes how cases arrive at the Supreme Court.

It cannot be overemphasized that only a handful of cases will ever reach the U.S. Supreme Court. It is not uncommon for the Supreme Court to review thousands of petitions yet grant fewer than 100 *writs of certiorari*. Most cases that are appealed stop short of reaching the Supreme Court, so it is necessary to find out at what level the final decision was reached. Not tracing a case to its final decision can be fatal to a legal argument. In other words, if a researcher wants to argue a specific point with reference to a previously decided case, he or she must be sure that the decision is, if only for the time being, a final one.

At the risk of simplification, there are two types of Supreme Court decisions: (1) **bright-line decisions** and (2) decisions requiring **case-by-case adjudication**. A bright-line decision is one in which the Court hands down a *specific rule*, one subject to very little interpretation. It is like the metaphorical "line drawn in the sand"; in other words, the Court emphatically communicates to the criminal justice community what it can and cannot do. An example of a bright-line decision is *Wilson* v. *Layne*, mentioned earlier. In it, the Supreme Court said that the police cannot bring the media along on the service of warrants unless media presence serves a legitimate law enforcement objective. It is easy to see that this is a clear, bright-line rule. Exactly what constitutes a "law enforcement objective" may be somewhat vague, but otherwise, this rule is quite clear. The advantage of a bright-line rule is that it promotes clarity and consistency. Also, it is easily understood by criminal justice officials.

A decision requiring case-by-case adjudication is quite different. In many cases, the Supreme Court refers to the concept of **totality of circumstances**. For example, in the case of ***Manson* v. *Braithwaite* (432 U.S. 98 [1977])**, the Supreme Court held that the totality of circumstances determines whether an identification procedure is unreliable. This means that all the facts and circumstances surrounding the case must be examined in order to determine whether a constitutional rights violation has taken place. Deciding whether the totality of circumstances supports the action in question requires looking at each case *individually*. There is no existing recipe specifying what authorities should or should not do. A case-by-case decision is preferable in some instances because it is rarely possible to know in advance all the possible twists and turns in a criminal case. That is, case-by-case decisions promote flexibility, leaving it up to the lower courts (usually, the trial court) to decide if the action in question conforms to constitutional guidelines. However, this approach can also create uncertainty for law enforcement officials.

► The Criminal Process

There is no easy or concise way to describe the criminal process. Figure 1–13 presents one variation. Importantly, however, there are many different variations. For example, cases are handled differently between the federal and state levels. Many differences exist between states, as well. Further, depending on the seriousness of a case, the criminal process may assume different forms.

Almost all criminal procedure texts present an overview of the criminal process, like the one that follows. But because of the variation from one jurisdiction to the next, readers should take steps to familiarize themselves with the criminal processes in the areas in which they reside. That said, think of the rest of this section as an overview of the criminal process. The rest of this book will detail the criminal process in this order.

Pretrial

The wheels of the criminal process are set in motion once an arrest occurs. This is the **pretrial** stage of the criminal process. An arrest may occur because an officer observed a crime in progress. Alternatively, an arrest may be made because an arrest warrant was out on the individual targeted. The officer may also have been serving a search warrant and discovered contraband, thus justifying an arrest. Finally, the officer may have been engaged in a proper warrantless search, found contraband, and made the arrest.

FIGURE 1–12 How Cases Arrive at the Supreme Court.

There is no easy or concise way to describe the criminal process.

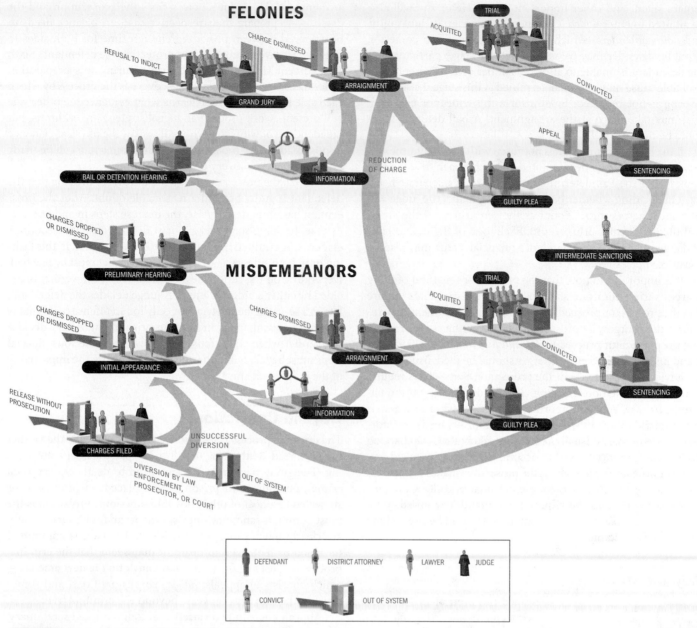

FELONIES

TRIAL

REFUSAL TO INDICT — CHARGE DISMISSED — ACQUITTED

GRAND JURY — ARRAIGNMENT — CONVICTED

BAIL OR DETENTION HEARING — INFORMATION — REDUCTION OF CHARGE — APPEAL — SENTENCING

GUILTY PLEA

CHARGES DROPPED OR DISMISSED — PRELIMINARY HEARING

INTERMEDIATE SANCTIONS

MISDEMEANORS

CHARGES DROPPED OR DISMISSED — INITIAL APPEARANCE — CHARGES DISMISSED — TRIAL — ACQUITTED

ARRAIGNMENT — CONVICTED

RELEASE WITHOUT PROSECUTION — INFORMATION — SENTENCING

CHARGES FILED — UNSUCCESSFUL DIVERSION — GUILTY PLEA

DIVERSION BY LAW ENFORCEMENT, PROSECUTOR, OR COURT — OUT OF SYSTEM

DEFENDANT   DISTRICT ATTORNEY   LAWYER   JUDGE

CONVICT   OUT OF SYSTEM

FIGURE 1–13 Sequence of Events in the Criminal Justice System.

In any case, once someone is arrested, he or she will be searched. This is done to protect the police and also to discover contraband that may be in the suspect's possession. Then the suspect will be transported to the police station and booked. *Booking* is the process in which the suspect is fingerprinted, processed, photographed, and probably placed in a holding cell. The suspect may also be required to submit to testing (such as a Breathalyzer) and possibly to participate in a lineup for identification by a witness to the crime.

After this, the police will present their case to the prosecutor, and, assuming the prosecutor believes the evidence is persuasive enough, he or she will bring charges against the suspect, subject to certain restrictions identified by the U.S. Supreme Court. The suspect will now be considered the *defendant*. If the charges are minor, the police may release the suspect, in which case he or she will be required to appear in court at some later date.

Suspects who are booked, placed in detention, and charged with a crime face a number of different court hearings, depending on the seriousness of the crime. Misdemeanors, because of their not-so-serious nature, tend to be fast-tracked through the courts. A misdemeanor defendant may appear at only one court hearing, in which the judge will decide guilt or innocence. Felony defendants, by contrast, face a longer legal road. If, as described already, the suspect is arrested without a warrant, he or she will be granted a probable cause hearing, in which the judge will decide whether the arresting officer had appropriate justification to make the arrest. (This hearing may, in fact, be merged with other hearings, but this book will treat it as a separate event.)

The next step in the criminal process is the *arraignment*. At the arraignment, the suspect comes before a judge and is, at a minimum, informed of the charges against him or her. The defendant will also be notified of the right to counsel, the right to remain silent, and other important rights. He or she will also be allowed to enter a *plea*. Common pleas are guilty, not guilty, and *nolo contendere* (which is akin to a plea of "no contest"). A public defender may be assigned at this stage, particularly if the defendant is unable to afford his or her own representation. Probable cause may also be determined at this stage if a separate hearing is not required. Finally, for a misdemeanor charge, a trial may take place at the arraignment. A bail determination could be made as well.

If the bail determination is not fused with the arraignment, a separate hearing may be warranted. (The approach taken in this book is that the bail determination is made in a separate hearing.) In deciding whether bail should be granted, the judge will take such factors into account as the seriousness of the crime and the defendant's prior record, likelihood of flight, and level of dangerousness. The defendant's financial status may also be considered.

It is important to note that the prosecutor's method of filing charges varies from one state to the next. Some states require that the prosecutor proceed by *information*, a document that describes the charges the prosecutor is filing. Other states require that the prosecutor proceed by a *grand jury indictment*. That is, a grand jury decides whether charges should be filed, usually with the advice and assistance of the prosecutor. Some states require or allow both methods of filing charges, depending on the nature of the case. What is important in this discussion, however, is that in jurisdictions in which the prosecutor proceeds by information, he or she is usually required to show that the charging decision is appropriate. This is accomplished in a so-called *preliminary hearing*, during which the prosecutor makes out what is known as a *prima facie case* of the defendant's guilt. A preliminary hearing can also be required in a grand jury jurisdiction, requiring the prosecutor to present his or her case before seeking a grand jury indictment.

Adjudication

Once the pretrial process has concluded and the charges have stood, **adjudication** occurs. This takes place following either a guilty plea or a trial. If, at arraignment, the defendant pleads guilty, then a trial is not necessary. In such an instance, special steps must be taken to ensure that the defendant's guilty plea is valid. The defendant may also agree to a *plea bargain* agreement, in which in exchange for leniency from the prosecutor and/or the court, he or she pleads guilty to the crime with which he or she is charged. Plea bargaining of this nature can occur at any stage of the criminal process, however. That is, a suspect can reach a plea agreement with the prosecutor as early as the pretrial stage, during the trial, and—in fact—well into jury deliberations. In any case, the plea bargain, if there is one, must be accepted by the court. The judge makes this determination.

If the defendant pleads not guilty, the case is set for trial. The trial is usually scheduled for some date well after the arraignment. This allows both sides—the prosecution and the defense—to prepare their respective cases. A balance needs to be achieved between providing enough time for both sides to present effective arguments and protecting the defendant's Sixth Amendment right to a speedy trial. During this preparation process, *discovery* takes place. Discovery is the process by which each side to a criminal case learns what evidence the other side will present. Work product and legal strategy are off limits, but the identities of witnesses who will testify, the physical evidence in possession of both parties, and other items must all be made available in the discovery process.

At trial, the prosecutor bears the burden of proving that the defendant is guilty beyond a reasonable doubt. After the prosecution has presented its case, the defense steps in and presents its case. In doing so, it seeks to cast doubt on the prosecution's evidence. A criminal trial may move back and forth in this fashion until both sides rest. At this point, a verdict must be reached. Depending on the seriousness of the offense, the verdict is decided by either a judge or a jury. A judge decides the defendant's fate in a so-called bench trial but only for an offense that is likely to result in less than six months' imprisonment. A jury decides the verdict when the offense at issue is more serious. Special steps must be taken in either instance to ensure the impartiality of the judge or the jury.

Beyond Conviction

The criminal process does not necessarily end once the verdict has been read. **Sentencing** usually takes place at a separate hearing. The guilty party may be sentenced to death (for a capital crime), committed to prison, fined, placed on probation, or subjected to a host of other possible sanctions. Probation is the most common sanction; imprisonment, and, of course, death, are clearly much more serious. When a person is committed to prison or sentenced to death, it may seem that the criminal process has just begun, as the **post-conviction review process**—which consists of appeals, *habeas corpus* petitions, and sometimes both—can drag on years beyond the criminal trial.

Appeals come in two varieties: automatic and discretionary. Most convicted criminals are entitled to at least one *automatic appeal* (also known as an *appeal of right*). An automatic appeal must be heard by an appellate court. With a discretionary appeal, however, it is up to the appellate court to decide whether the appeal will be heard. The right of a convicted criminal to file excessive discretionary appeals is deplored by supporters of the death penalty and other serious sanctions.

Making an appeal is not the only method of challenging a guilty verdict. The right of *habeas corpus*—a method of what is commonly called *collateral attack*—is guaranteed in the Constitution, providing every convicted criminal the right to petition a court to decide on the constitutionality of his or her confinement. All that is granted, however, is the right to *file* a petition, or to *request* to be heard. The decision about whether to grant a prisoner's *habeas* petition is up to the reviewing court. If a prisoner exhausts all available appellate mechanisms and is denied *habeas* review, he or she will remain in prison for the full term of his or her sentence.

GPS Tracking

Read the following facts from an October 22, 2013 decision by the U.S. Court of Appeals for the Third Circuit (which includes Delaware, New Jersey, and Pennsylvania):

> A spectre was haunting Delaware, Maryland, and New Jersey in 2009 and 2010—the three states had been hit by a wave of pharmacy burglaries, many of which affected Rite Aid pharmacies. The method used in the various crimes was largely consistent: In many cases, the alarm systems for the pharmacies would be disabled by cutting the external phone lines. The local police approached the Federal Bureau of Investigation (FBI) for help (collectively, "the police"), and the hunt was on.
>
> By mid-May 2010, a suspect emerged: a local electrician named Harry Katzin. Not only had he recently been caught burglarizing a Rite Aid pharmacy, but he and his brothers—Mark and Michael—had criminal histories that included arrests for burglary and theft. Over the course of the following months, the joint state and federal investigation began receiving reports of seeing Harry Katzin around Rite Aid pharmacies throughout the three states. For example, in late October 2010, local police in Pennsylvania encountered Harry Katzin crouching beside some bushes outside of a Rite Aid after responding to reports of suspicious activity. As the pieces began falling into place, the police proceeded with their next step: electronic tracking. The police knew that Harry Katzin regularly parked his van on a particular street in Philadelphia. Thus, in the early hours of a mid-December morning, after consulting with the United States Attorney's office, but without obtaining a warrant, the FBI affixed a "slap on" GPS tracker to the exterior of Harry Katzin's van.
>
> Although the police do not appear to have set a time limit for using the GPS tracker, the device yielded the results they were after within several days. According to the tracker, Harry Katzin's van had left Philadelphia on the evening of December 15, 2010, and had traveled to the immediate vicinity of a Rite Aid in a neighboring town. Through use of the device, the police could see that the van had been driven around the town for several minutes before parking at a specific location for over two hours. When the FBI noticed that the van was once again on the move, the call came in: the van was to be taken.
>
> While state troopers stopped Harry Katzin's van on a Pennsylvania highway, a squad of local police officers investigated the Rite Aid closest to where Harry Katzin's van had been parked; they found that it had been burglarized and relayed this information to the troopers. Inside the van, troopers found Harry at the wheel, with Mark and Michael as passengers. From outside of the van, the troopers could see merchandise and equipment from the burglarized Rite Aid, including pill bottles and Rite Aid storage bins. The police impounded the van and arrested the Katzin brothers. (*United States* v. *Katzin*, No. 12-2548 [Third Cir. 2013])

GPS tracking raises several interesting questions for criminal procedure:

1. A warrant was not used in this case. Do you think a warrant should have been used? Revisit this question later after reading Chapters 3–7 to see if your answer has changed.
2. Should it matter that the FBI actually affixed the GPS tracking device rather than the local police?
3. GPS tracking and other high-tech devices are very helpful for law enforcement. Drones, as featured in this chapter's opening story, fit the bill. At what point can technological advances go "too far" in terms of compromising people's privacy rights?

Identify two key themes running throughout criminal procedure.

Criminal procedure is concerned with the constitutional rights of accused persons and contains a strong historical dimension.

1. Why is criminal procedure synonymous with *constitutional* procedure?

2. What themes run throughout criminal procedure?

criminal procedure A vast set of rules and guidelines that describe how suspected and accused criminals are to be handled and processed by the justice system.

Summarize the constitutional basis for criminal procedure.

Criminal procedure is mostly about constitutional rights, primarily as they are interpreted by the U.S. Supreme Court.

1. What are the main sources of rights?

2. What constitutional amendments are relevant in criminal procedure?

3. What is incorporation, and why should we be concerned with it?

Federal Rules of Criminal Procedure The rules that govern the conduct of all criminal proceedings brought in federal courts.

Fourth Amendment Part of the U.S. Constitution, which states, "The right of the people to be secure in their persons, houses, papers, and effects, against unreasonable searches and seizures, shall not be violated, and no Warrants shall issue, but upon probable cause, supported by Oath or affirmation and particularly describing the place to be searched, and the persons or things to be seized."

Fifth Amendment Part of the U.S. Constitution, which states, "No person shall be held to answer for a capital, or otherwise infamous crime, unless on a presentment or indictment of a Grand Jury, except in cases arising in the land or naval forces, or in the Militia, when in actual service in time of War or public danger; nor shall any person be subject for the same offense to be twice put in jeopardy of life or limb; nor shall be compelled in any criminal case to be a witness against himself, nor be deprived of life, liberty, or property, without due process of law; nor shall private property be taken for public use, without just compensation."

Sixth Amendment Part of the U.S. Constitution, which states, "In all criminal prosecutions, the accused shall enjoy the right to a speedy and public trial, by an impartial jury of the State and district wherein the crime shall have been committed, which district shall have been previously ascertained by law, and to be informed of the nature and cause of the accusation; to be confronted with the witnesses against him; to have compulsory process for obtaining witnesses in his favor, and to have the Assistance of Counsel for his defence."

Eighth Amendment Part of the U.S. Constitution, which states, "Excessive bail shall not be required, nor excessive fines imposed, nor cruel and unusual punishments inflicted."

Fourteenth Amendment Part of the U.S. Constitution, which states, "All persons born or naturalized in the United States, and subject to the jurisdiction thereof, are citizens of the United States and of the State wherein they reside. No State shall make or enforce any law which shall abridge the privileges or immunities of citizens of the United States, nor shall any State deprive any person of life, liberty, or property, without due process of law; nor deny to any person within its jurisdiction the equal protection of the laws."

substantive due process Protection from arbitrary and unreasonable action on the part of state officials.

procedural due process Protection of significant life, liberty, or property interests, sometimes described as "procedural fairness."

incorporation The Supreme Court's practice of using the Fourteenth Amendment's due process clause, which holds that no state shall "deprive any person of life, liberty, or property, without due process of law," to make certain protections specified in the Bill of Rights applicable to the states.

Explain the importance of precedent.

Before making decisions, courts almost always look to the past for the purpose of determining whether a case with similar facts has already been decided. If one has not, the court will distinguish the present case and hand down a decision that may be relied on by some other court at some other date.

1. What is the relationship between precedent and *stare decisis*?

2. What does it mean when a court decides to "distinguish" a case?

precedent A rule of case law (that is, a decision by a court) that is binding on all lower courts and the court that issued it.

stare decisis A Latin term that means to abide by or to adhere to decided cases. Most courts adhere to the principle of *stare decisis*.

distinguish An appellate court's decision to treat a case before it as sufficiently distinct that it cannot be decided by looking to past rulings. In other words, the set of facts is unique and never before considered by an appellate court.

Describe the public order (crime-control) and individual rights (due process) perspectives of criminal justice and how criminal procedure balances the two.

Throughout criminal procedure—indeed, throughout all of criminal justice—two competing concerns can almost always be heard. The crime-control perspective favors controlling crime at whatever cost, and the due process perspective is concerned with protecting people's rights. Every court decision, every crime-control policy, and even every reaction by the criminal justice system to the threat of crime must balance both of these concerns. Some decisions and policies lean too far in the direction of crime control and, for that reason, become quite controversial.

The same holds true for decisions and policies that cater to due process. For the justice process to flow smoothly, a balance needs to be achieved.

1. Compare and contrast the due process and crime-control perspectives.

2. Which perspective, due process or crime control, do you prefer and why?

due process perspective A general concern with people's rights and liberties. The due process perspective is closely aligned with a liberal political orientation.

crime-control perspective A perspective that emphasizes the importance of controlling crime, perhaps to the detriment of civil liberties.

Outline the structure of the court system, including the responsibilities and jurisdictions of each level.

At the federal level, three types of courts are relevant: district courts, circuit courts of appeals, and the U.S. Supreme Court. State court structures vary from one state to the next but generally consist of courts of limited jurisdiction, trial courts of general jurisdiction, intermediate appellate courts, and supreme courts.

1. Summarize the typical state court structure.

2. Explain the difference between the three main federal courts.

courts of limited jurisdiction Courts that have jurisdiction over relatively minor offenses and infractions. An example of a limited jurisdiction court is a traffic court.

courts of general jurisdiction The main trial courts at the state level. They are usually located at the county level and are often called "superior courts."

superior courts The most common name for state-level courts of general jurisdiction.

intermediate appellate courts At the state level, courts to which verdicts from courts of general jurisdiction are appealed.

state supreme courts The highest courts at the state level.

district court Federal trial courts. There are 94 federal district courts in the United States, including 89 district courts in the 50 states and 1 each in Puerto Rico, the Virgin Islands, the District of Columbia, Guam, and the Northern Mariana Islands.

U.S. courts of appeals At the federal level, courts to which verdicts from the district courts are appealed.

U.S. Supreme Court The highest court in the federal court system.

Understand the parts of a court case.

To accurately trace a court case, it is necessary to understand the court structure, legal terminology, and outcomes of a decision.

Key Case

Manson v. Braithwaite

1. What are the essential steps needed to trace the progression of a criminal case through the courts?

2. Explain the process by which court cases arrive at the U.S. Supreme Court.

3. It is often said that Supreme Court cases represent the "tip of the iceberg." Why?

writ of certiorari An order by the court requiring the lower court to send the case and a record of its proceedings to the U.S. Supreme Court for review.

rule of four The requirement that four U.S. Supreme Court justices must agree to hear a case before it goes before the full Court.

bright-line decisions A decision in which a court hands down a *specific rule*, one subject to very little interpretation.

case-by-case adjudication The reality that some cases cannot result in bright-line rules. Courts often look to the "totality of circumstances" when taking a case-by-case approach.

totality of circumstances All the facts and circumstances surrounding the case. In case-by-case adjudication, these must be examined in order to determine whether a constitutional rights violation has taken place.

Summarize the criminal process.

The criminal process begins with a police/ citizen encounter and then moves into arrest, booking, pretrial hearings, trial, and appeals.

1. Explain what occurs during the pretrial phase of the criminal process.

2. Explain what occurs at the adjudication phase of the criminal process.

3. Explain what occurs *following* adjudication.

pretrial The period between arrest and trial.

adjudication The process by which a court arrives at a decision in a case.

sentencing The process by which the guilty party may be sentenced to death (for a capital crime), committed to prison, fined, placed on probation, or subjected to a host of other possible sanctions.

post-conviction review process The process, which consists of appeals and *habeas corpus* petitions, that begins when a person is committed to prison or sentenced to death.

2

"By far, the most significant remedy in criminal procedure is the exclusionary rule."

The Exclusionary Rule and Other Remedies

1 Distinguish between legal and extralegal remedies.

2 Summarize the exclusionary rule and the exceptions to it.

3 Summarize the "fruit of the poisonous tree" doctrine and the exceptions to it.

4 Describe criminal prosecution and civil remedies for constitutional rights violations.

INTRO A RECORD-KEEPING MISTAKE

Deputy Mark Anderson learned that Bennie Dean Herring, a man who was no stranger to law enforcement, drove to the Coffee County (Alabama) Sheriff's Department to retrieve an item from his impounded truck. Anderson asked the warrant clerk to check for any outstanding arrest warrants against Herring. When she found none, Anderson asked her to check with her counterpart in neighboring Dale County. Indeed, there was an outstanding arrest warrant for Herring in Dale County. Anderson and another deputy then followed Herring as he left the impound lot, stopped him, and arrested him. A search of Herring revealed methamphetamine in his pocket. The deputies also found a pistol in the vehicle.

The arrest in this case seemed like a slam dunk. However, unknown to the officers, the Dale County arrest warrant had been recalled several months earlier. Apparently the computer database had not been updated. In other words, there really was no Dale County arrest warrant for Herring. With no arrest warrant, and assuming there was no other reason for the deputies to stop Herring, a question arose as to whether the contraband found during the arrest should have been admissible against Herring at trial. If the arrest was not justified, should the evidence have been excluded? A strict reading of the exclusionary rule, the main topic of this chapter, would suggest yes. Yet in Herring's case, which went all the way to the U.S. Supreme Court, the answer is no. The Court basically held that the deputies made an honest mistake and that the evidence against Herring should have been admissible in court.[1]

© David Cole/Alamy

 Do you agree with the Supreme Court's decision?

▶ Remedies for Constitutional Rights Violations

Criminal procedure cannot be fully appreciated without some discussion of remedies. A **remedy** provides a method of rectifying wrongdoing. That is, when a person believes he or she has been harmed in some way, he or she may seek to ease the pain, make the person who caused the harm "pay," or both. For example, if Sandy is unjustifiably assaulted by Jim, an on-duty police officer, she may opt to remedy the wrong inflicted on her. A remedy is the mechanism for enforcing violations of people's rights.

Remedies fall into two categories: (1) legal and (2) extralegal. **Extralegal remedies** are those conducted outside the legal process. For example, if one man is assaulted by another, the assaulted individual may seek revenge and opt to resolve the perceived injustice with his fists. This is an extralegal remedy. In contrast, **legal remedies** are those made available by the law, by a court decision, or by a police agency policy or procedure.

The most frequently discussed remedy in criminal procedure is the *exclusionary rule*. It is an example of a remedy made

available because of court decisions; that is, it has no statutory basis. But in order to place the exclusionary rule in context, it is also important to examine other types of remedies, such as those provided in law and agency practice. These remedies are important because the exclusionary rule applies only in limited contexts.

> **LEARNING OUTCOMES 1** Distinguish between legal and extralegal remedies.

The bulk of criminal procedure concerns *constitutional* procedure. It focuses on the various forms of government action permitted and not permitted by the U.S. Constitution. Accordingly, the focus here is primarily on remedies for constitutional rights violations—particularly the exclusionary rule and 42 U.S.C. Section 1983 (or, simply, Section 1983), a statute that provides people with an avenue for suing criminal justice officials. There are several situations in which neither the exclusionary rule nor 42 U.S.C. Section 1983 applies, however. This chapter thus wraps up with an examination of additional remedies that are available to people whose *constitutional* rights are not violated but whose rights are violated, nonetheless. These include disciplinary procedures, civilian review, mediation, and even the criminal law.

Criminal procedure cannot be fully appreciated without some discussion of remedies.

This chapter is organized into three primary sections. The first two sections introduce the exclusionary rule and the so-called "fruit of the poisonous tree" doctrine. The last section touches on other remedies besides the exclusionary rule—namely, the criminal law, civil litigation (lawsuits), and various "nonjudicial" remedies (those that operate outside the official court process).

▶ The Exclusionary Rule

By far, the most significant remedy in criminal procedure is the **exclusionary rule**. It is, simply, a rule of exclusion. The exclusionary rule requires that evidence obtained in violation of the Constitution cannot be used in a criminal trial to prove guilt. It is a rule, as opposed to a constitutional provision, because nowhere in the Constitution does it say that illegally obtained evidence must be excluded at trial. In other words, the Supreme Court created the exclusionary rule.

History of the Exclusionary Rule

Somewhat surprisingly, the U.S. Constitution contains no provisions for enforcing the protections enunciated in the Bill of Rights. For example, even though people enjoy the right to be free from unreasonable searches and seizures, the Constitution does not specify how this right is to be enforced.

For a time, then, the Bill of Rights was more or less a sham, especially when it came to criminal procedure. Without a means for remedying an unlawful search, improperly obtained confession, or similar violation, evidence obtained in flagrant violation of the Constitution could be admissible at trial.

Fortunately, as early as 1886, the U.S. Supreme Court began to suggest that improperly obtained evidence be excluded. In *Boyd* v. *United States* (116 U.S. 616 [1886]), the Court held that business records should have been excluded because

> a compulsory production of the private books and papers of the owner of goods … is compelling him to be a witness against himself, within the meaning of the Fifth Amendment to the Constitution, and is the equivalent of a search-and-seizure—and an unreasonable search-and-seizure—within the meaning of the Fourth Amendment. (p. 634)

Then, in **Weeks v. United States (232 U.S. 383 [1914])**, the Court relied solely on the Fourth Amendment as a basis for exclusion. Without a warrant, police entered the home of Fremont Weeks and seized documents that tied him to criminal activity. The Court held that the documents were seized in violation of the Fourth Amendment and should have been returned to Weeks, rather than used in a criminal trial against the petitioner.

In *Silverthorne Lumber Co.* v. *United States* (251 U.S. 385 [1920]), a similar set of circumstances was presented. Silverthorne allegedly avoided paying taxes. Without a warrant,

Nowhere in the Constitution does it say that illegally obtained evidence must be excluded at trial.

federal agents seized documents from him and made copies. The Court declared that authorizing such activities would encourage law enforcement to circumvent the Constitution. Justice Holmes stated that without an enforcement mechanism, "the Fourth Amendment [is reduced] to a form of words" and little else.

It is important to note that *Boyd*, *Weeks*, and *Silverthorne Lumber* were all *federal* cases. Following these decisions, the Supreme Court continued for several years to apply the exclusionary rule only in federal cases. Then, in 1949, the Court began to turn its attention to constitutional rights violations occurring at the *state* level. In *Wolf* v. *Colorado*, 338 U.S. 25 (1949), a man was convicted of conspiring to perform abortions, based in part on evidence that was obtained improperly and without a warrant. The Supreme Court decided that the Fourth Amendment is applicable to the states under the due process clause of the Fourteenth Amendment, but it stopped short of mandating exclusion:

> Granting that in practice the exclusion of evidence may be an effective way to deterring unreasonable searches, it is not for this Court to condemn as falling below the minimal standards assured by the Due Process Clause a State's reliance upon other methods which, if consistently enforced, would be equally effective…. We cannot brush aside the experience of the States which deem the incidence of such conduct by the police too slight to call for a deterrent remedy not by way of disciplinary measure but by overriding the relevant rules of evidence. (p. 31)

Even though the Court was hesitant to mandate exclusion of improperly obtained evidence in state courts, at the time of the *Wolf* decision, many states had already adopted their own versions of the exclusionary rule. By 1960, 26 states had adopted exclusionary rules.

In *Elkins* v. *United States* (364 U.S. 206 [1960]), the Court denounced the so-called **"silver platter" doctrine**, which permitted the use of evidence in *federal* court that had been obtained illegally by *state* officials. For example, federal officials could not expect illegally obtained evidence to be admissible if they seized it themselves (as decided in *Weeks*). But under the silver platter doctrine, if they asked state law enforcement officials to seize the evidence, even in violation of the Constitution, it would be admissible in federal court. The silver platter doctrine was thus a convenient means of circumventing the *Weeks* decision. The Supreme Court caught on to this practice and scrapped the doctrine.

A Turning Point: *Mapp* v. *Ohio*

The year 1961 marked a watershed in criminal procedure, as it was the year the Supreme Court decided the landmark case of **Mapp v. Ohio (367 U.S. 643 [1961])**. Arguably, this was, and continues to be, one of the most significant criminal procedure cases the Supreme Court has decided.

On May 23, 1957, three Cleveland police officers arrived at Dollree Mapp's residence to search for a suspect who they thought was hiding there. The officers demanded entrance, but they were not allowed in. Ms. Mapp called her attorney and was advised not to let the officers in. The officers once again sought entrance three hours later. Ultimately, they forced entry and confronted Ms. Mapp in the entryway, who demanded to see a warrant. A paper claimed to be a warrant was held up by one of the officers. Ms. Mapp took it and placed it in her bosom. A struggle ensued, and Ms. Mapp was handcuffed and taken upstairs to her bedroom where officers searched a dresser, a closet, and some suitcases. The search fanned out from there. The officers eventually found obscene materials, which formed the basis of the conviction and ultimately were at issue in the case.

In a 5-to-4 decision, the Supreme Court decided that the exclusionary rule applied to the states. It concluded that other remedies, such as reliance on the due process clause to enforce Fourth Amendment violations, had proven "worthless and futile." It also noted that ". . . the State, by admitting evidence unlawfully seized, serves to encourage disobedience to the Federal Constitution which it is bound to uphold." The 5-to-4 decision reflects the controversy over the exclusionary rule. People are sharply divided on the issue of whether it is bane or boon for law enforcement. Arguments for and against the rule are summarized in Figure 2–1.

In *Ker* v. *California*, 374 U.S. 23 (1963), the Court extended the ruling in *Mapp* to state cases that were in violation of *federal* standards of constitutional law, even if the *state* court had upheld the search or seizure. In *Ker*, the California Supreme Court ruled that a search conducted by the police was lawful, and evidence seized in that search was admissible. The U.S. Supreme Court overruled the California court, holding that the search was in violation of the Fourth Amendment, and the evidence obtained should be excluded. The Court noted that it had no "supervisory authority over state courts, … and, consequently, [*Mapp*] implied no *total* obliteration of state laws relating to arrests and searches in favor of federal law." In essence, the Court must defer to the states to decide what constitutes a reasonable search or seizure, but only to the extent such decisions are "consistent with federal constitutional guarantees." Thus, whenever determining the reasonableness of a questionable Fourth Amendment action, federal standards must be applied. However, if a state adopts procedures that are *more restrictive* than federal standards, doing so complies with the *Mapp* decision.

One final limitation of *Mapp* is that it only mandates exclusion of evidence obtained in violation of the federal Constitution. If, instead, evidence is obtained in violation of a rule or state law, but is not a constitutional violation, exclusion is not required under *Mapp* (*Cady* v. *Dombrowski*, 413 U.S. 433 [1973]). Such evidence may be excluded, however, on some other basis in case law.

See the accompanying exclusionary rule case timeline. It summarizes the Supreme Court decisions just discussed and puts them in chronological order.

Applicability of the Exclusionary Rule Beyond the Fourth Amendment

There is a measure of debate concerning the applicability of the exclusionary rule to violations of constitutional rights besides those stemming from the Fourth Amendment. People have asked if the exclusionary rule should be applied to the Fifth Amendment. What about the Sixth Amendment? The short answer to both questions is that it does. As a general rule, evidence obtained in violation of either the Fifth or Sixth Amendment will be excluded at a criminal trial. The long answer, unfortunately, leaves the issue somewhat unresolved.

On the one hand, some people believe that because the Fourth Amendment contains no specific reference to what should happen when an improper search or seizure takes place, the purpose of the exclusionary rule is to enforce the Fourth Amendment. They argue, furthermore, that because the exclusionary rule operates differently outside the Fourth Amendment context, it was not meant to apply to Fifth and Sixth Amendment violations. For example, just because a confession is improperly obtained does not mean that any subsequently obtained physical evidence will be excluded.

On the other hand, some observers argue that evidence can still be excluded because of Fifth, Sixth, and even Fourteenth Amendment violations. Improperly obtained confessions are not admissible—that is, they will be excluded from a criminal trial. Coercive confessions will be excluded under the Fourteenth Amendment's due process clause, identifications stemming from Sixth Amendment violations will not be admissible, and so on. These observers' point is that evidence can technically be excluded when any constitutional provision giving rise to such evidence is violated.

The perspective adopted in this book is that the exclusionary rule applies across the board. Any constitutional provision that governs law enforcement's efforts to secure evidence that could be used in a criminal prosecution falls under the purview of the exclusionary rule. That is, whenever law enforcement violates one or more of the Fourth, Fifth, Sixth, and Fourteenth Amendments—the most common amendments in criminal procedure—the evidence resulting from such a violation will not be admissible in a court of law. It is important to note, however, that the exclusionary rule and its close cousin— the "fruit of the poisonous tree" doctrine (discussed later in this chapter)—do not always operate in the same manner outside the Fourth Amendment context.

When the Exclusionary Rule Does Not Apply

As indicated already, the exclusionary rule applies in criminal trials. But what of other proceedings, both criminal and noncriminal? The answer is that it depends. More specifically, it depends on whether the rule's remedial objective in a given context is deterrence. In other words, if in a particular circumstance the exclusion of evidence would not in theory deter misconduct, the rule does not apply. With a handful of exceptions, the exclusionary rule does not apply in four situations: grand jury investigations, *habeas corpus* proceedings, parole revocation hearings, and civil proceedings. Also see Figure 2–2.

- First, the exclusionary rule does not apply in the context of grand jury investigations. In *United States* v. *Calandra* (414 U.S. 338 [1974]), a witness called before a grand jury refused to answer questions that were based on evidence obtained from him during an unlawful search. Worried that enforcement of the exclusionary rule would impede

The debate over the exclusionary rule centers on three important issues: (1) whether the rule deters police misconduct; (2) whether the rule imposes unnecessary costs on society; and (3) whether alternative remedies would be effective and should be pursued.

Deterrence

Critics

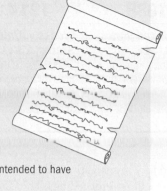

- The exclusionary rule does not deter police misconduct.
- Most constitutional rights violations are unintentional, making them undeterrable.
- Officers who act in bad faith will commit perjury to mask a constitutional rights violation.

Supporters

- The exclusionary rule is not intended to deter individual officers (i.e., specific deterrence) but is instead intended to have a broader, systemic deterrent effect (i.e., general deterrence).
- Many police departments have amended their policies in the wake of the *Mapp* v. *Ohio* decision and encouraged their officers to adhere to constitutional safeguards.

Social Costs

Critics

- The exclusionary rule requires throwing out some of the most reliable forms of evidence (e.g., confessions), letting suspected criminals go free.
- Innocent people have nothing to gain from the exclusionary rule because they have nothing to be seized by law enforcement officers who would infringe on constitutional protections.
- The exclusionary rule creates public cynicism because it allows some individuals to escape prosecution.
- The exclusionary rule is too extreme, in that a relatively trivial violation by a police officer may result in the exclusion of significant evidence.

Supporters

- The benefits of the exclusionary rule outweigh its costs.
- The exclusionary rule is rarely applied. Indeed, this is true; motions to exclude evidence because of alleged constitutional rights violations are relatively rare, and they succeed even more rarely.
- The rule is beneficial because it helps innocent people. That is, since *Mapp* and other significant decisions, innocent people have been subjected to fewer unconstitutional searches, not necessarily because the police fear the exclusion of evidence but because of the potential for civil liability, citizen complaints, and the like.
- Public cynicism, to the extent it exists, should be directed at wayward government officials, not the exclusionary rule.
- The exclusionary rule is not disproportionate in terms of its consequences but rather is intended to serve as a general deterrent.

Alternative Remedies

Critics

- Effective alternatives do exist and should be pursued, including civil litigation, criminal prosecution, and internal discipline.
- Overzealous law enforcement officers can be deterred from violating the Constitution by these enforcement mechanisms.

Supporters

- Juries are more likely to favor police officers in civil trials.
- Immunity is often extended to police officers in civil litigation cases.
- Internal police discipline is something of a sham (i.e., disciplinary decisions tend to favor the officer, not the citizen filing the complaint).

FIGURE 2–1 Arguments for and Against the Exclusionary Rule.

1886	**1914**	**1920**	**1949**
Boyd v. United States, 116 U.S. 616 Evidence obtained in violation of the Fourth and Fifth Amendment should be excluded.	**Weeks v. United States, 232 U.S. 383** Evidence obtained in violation of the Fourth Amendment should be excluded.	**Silverthorne Lumber Co. v. United States, 251 U.S. 385** The decision establishing the "fruit of the poisonous tree" doctrine, but it is important in exclusionary rule development because of Justice Holmes's observation that without an enforcement mechanism, the "Fourth Amendment [is reduced] to a form of words" (p. 392).	**Wolf v. Colorado, 338 U.S. 25** Evidence obtained in violation of the constitution *may* be excluded from state proceedings under the Fourteenth Amendment's due process clause, but it need not be.

grand jury investigations, the Court held that it did not apply in those proceedings. The Court noted that "[a]ny incremental deterrent effect which might be achieved by extending the rule to grand jury proceedings is uncertain at best" (p. 351). The reason for this is that grand juries serve investigative functions, and the evidence would still be excluded at trial.

- The rule also does not apply in *habeas corpus* proceedings. The topic of *habeas corpus* will be discussed later in this book (see Chapter 13), but it is worth defining the term here. Basically, every state or federal prisoner in the United States enjoys the constitutional right to challenge his or her conviction in federal court on the grounds that his or her constitutional rights were violated. *Habeas corpus* is not an appeal; it is known as a *collateral attack*.

  As far as the exclusionary rule goes, because a *habeas corpus* petition always *follows* a criminal trial, the Court removed Fourth Amendment issues from the list of violations that can be raised in such a petition, assuming the petitioner had a "full and fair" opportunity to challenge such violations at trial. In other words, the Court reasoned that because the exclusionary rule applies at trial, any deterrent effect is most likely served there. (Deterrence *after* the trial would essentially be pointless.) In the Court's words, "The view that the deterrence of Fourth Amendment violations would be furthered rests on the dubious assumption that law enforcement authorities would fear that federal habeas review might reveal flaws in a search or seizure that went undetected at trial and on appeal" (*Stone* v. *Powell*, 428 U.S. 465 [1976], p. 493).

- The third type of criminal proceeding in which the exclusionary rule does not apply is a parole revocation hearing. This was the decision reached in *Pennsylvania* v. *Scott* (524 U.S. 357 [1998]), in which the majority argued that

application of the exclusionary rule in a parole revocation hearing "would both hinder the function of state parole systems and alter the traditionally flexible administrative nature of parole revocation proceedings" (p. 364). The Court further noted that the relationship between a *parole officer* and a *parolee* (as opposed to the relationship between a *police officer* and a *suspect*) is supervisory rather than adversarial, so it would be "unfair to assume that the parole officer bears hostility against the parolee that destroys his neutrality" (p. 368). Although this view is clearly debatable, it is one of the main reasons the Court offered for its decision not to apply the exclusionary rule in parole revocation proceedings. Finally, in line with the Court's decision in *Scott*, several lower courts have decided that the exclusionary rule is inapplicable in sentencing hearings (for example, *United States* v. *Schipani*, 315 F. Supp. 253 [E.D.N.Y 1970]; *United States* v. *McCrory*, 930 F.2d 63 [D.C.Cir. 1991]).

- Moving into the realm of civil proceedings, the exclusionary rule does not apply in civil actions brought by the Internal Revenue Service (IRS) to collect taxes. This was the decision reached in *United States* v. *Janis* (428 U.S. 433 [1976]). Janis had successfully excluded evidence in his prior criminal trial, citing officer misconduct, and then moved to have the same evidence excluded in a civil action brought against him by the IRS. The Court held that the IRS case fell "outside the offending officer's zone of primary interest." Thus, excluding the evidence a second time would not deter the officer's misconduct that was remedied at the criminal trial in which the evidence was first excluded.

In another case, the Court held that the exclusionary rule does not apply in deportation hearings brought by the Immigration and Naturalization Service (INS), which are noncriminal. In *INS* v. *Lopez-Mendoza* (468 U.S. 1032 [1984]), the Court moved away from the "zone of interest" language expressed in *Janis* and adopted a balancing test similar to that espoused in *Calandra*. Specifically, the Court looked at the social benefits of applying the exclusionary rule versus the costs to society of excluding evidence. In support of its decision, the Court noted that because most illegal aliens do not defend themselves in deportation hearings and agree to leave voluntarily, it is doubtful that the exclusionary rule would deter

- Grand jury investigations (*United States* v. *Calandra*, 414 U.S. 338 [1974])
- *Habeas corpus* proceedings (e.g., *Stone* v. *Powell*, 428 U.S. 465 [1976], p. 493)
- Parole revocation (*Pennsylvania* v. *Scott*, 524 U.S. 357 [1998])
- Various civil actions (e.g., *United States* v. *Janis*, 428 U.S. 433 [1976])
- Deportation hearings (*INS* v. *Lopez-Mendoza*, 468 U.S. 1032 [1984])

FIGURE 2–2 **When the Exclusionary Rule Does Not Apply.**

1960	1961	1963	1973
***Elkins* v. *United States*, 364 U.S. 206** The Supreme Court denounced the "silver platter doctrine," the practice of using in federal court evidence unconstitutionally obtained by state officials.	***Mapp* v. *Ohio*, 367 U.S. 643** The exclusionary rule applies to the states through the due process clause of the Fourteenth Amendment.	***Ker* v. *California*, 374 U.S. 23** Federal standards must be applied when determining whether the exclusionary rule should apply. States can also apply more restrictive procedures for evaluating admissibility of evidence, but they cannot relax the *Mapp* standard.	***Cady* v. *Dombrowski*, 413 U.S. 433** Evidence obtained in violation of a state rule or law that is not of a constitutional dimension need not be excluded under *Mapp*. It may, however, be excluded under state law.

border agents from committing Fourth Amendment violations. On the other hand, the Court noted that releasing illegal aliens into the United States because of constitutional rights violations would frustrate the purpose of the INS.

There are some civil proceedings in which the exclusionary rule *does* apply. In particular, if the civil proceeding is the primary focus of the investigating law enforcement officer (for example, a civil forfeiture investigation in lieu of a criminal investigation), then the exclusionary rule may apply. The Supreme Court has not directly confronted this issue, but some lower courts have. For example, lower courts have applied the exclusionary rule in juvenile delinquency proceedings (for example, *State in Interest of T.L.O.*, 94 N.J. 331 [1983]; *New Jersey* v. *T.L.O.*, 469 U.S. 325 [1985]) and in some administrative proceedings (for example, *Donovan* v. *Sarasota Concrete Co.*, 693 F.2d 1061 [11th Cir. 1982]). The key in each situation was that the investigating law enforcement officer worked directly with the adjudicating body. Contrast this with, for example, *Janis*, in which the IRS's civil case was secondary to a criminal prosecution and the investigating officer was involved only with the criminal prosecution.

Exceptions to the Exclusionary Rule

 LEARNING OUTCOMES 2 Summarize the exclusionary rule and the exceptions to it.

Critics of the exclusionary rule routinely argue that it constitutes a loophole in the criminal justice process and is responsible for otherwise guilty criminals going free. On the whole, this argument is somewhat deceptive, in part because of the exceptions allowed to the exclusionary rule. Over the years, the Supreme Court has seen fit to *allow* evidence in light of honest mistakes as well as for other purposes. There are two exceptions to the exclusionary rule: (1) the "good faith" exception and (2) the impeachment exception.

Good Faith Exception

As a general rule, when an honest mistake is made during the course of a search or seizure, any subsequently obtained evidence will be considered admissible. Two cases decided together were responsible for this **"good faith" exception: *United States* v. *Leon* (468 U.S. 897 [1984])** and *Massachusetts* v. *Sheppard* (468 U.S. 981 [1984]).

In *Leon*, police relied on a search warrant that was later declared invalid because it was not supported by probable cause. The Court upheld the search because the officers acted in good faith.

In *Sheppard*, officers had a difficult time finding a warrant form because it was the weekend, so they settled on a form previously used in another search for controlled substances. They made some changes to the form and presented it to a judge at his residence. The judge signed off on the warrant after making some changes of his own. But the references to controlled substances remained in the warrant, even though that was not what the officers set out to search for. A trial judge declared the warrant invalid, but the Supreme Court disagreed.

In both *Leon* and *Sheppard*, the Supreme Court concluded that evidence obtained in reasonable (good faith) reliance on a defective warrant was admissible:

> [W]e cannot conclude that admitting evidence obtained pursuant to a warrant while at the same time declaring that the warrant was somehow defective will in any way reduce judicial officers' professional incentives to comply with the Fourth Amendment, encourage them to repeat their mistakes, or lead to the granting of all colorable warrant requests. (*United States* v. *Leon*, p. 917)

The good faith exception enunciated in *Leon* and *Sheppard* is not unqualified, however. If, for example, a warrant is "so lacking in indicia of probable cause as to render official belief in its existence entirely unreasonable, then evidence obtained following its service will not be admissible" (*United States* v. *Hove*, 848 F.2d 137 [9th Cir. 1988], p. 139). Similarly, if a warrant is "so facially deficient—i.e., in failing to particularize the place to be searched or things to be seized—that the executing officers cannot reasonably presume it to be valid, then the exception does not apply" (*United States* v. *Leary*, 846 F.2d 592 [10th Cir. 1988], p. 607). Furthermore, if the judge issuing the warrant is deliberately misled by information in the affidavit, as when a police officer acts in *bad* faith, then the good faith exception will not apply (*Lo-Ji Sales, Inc.* v. *New York*, 442 U.S. 319 [1979]). Also, if the judge issues a search warrant without sufficient consideration, then good faith cannot later be asserted.

The good faith exception is not held in the highest regard by some. Critics believe that it gives police officers an incentive to "forum shop" or to find judges who will be quick to sign off on a warrant. Justice Brennan argued in opposition to the exception as follows:

> Creation of this new exception for good faith reliance upon a warrant implicitly tells magistrates that they

need not take much care in reviewing warrant applications, since their mistakes will from now on have virtually no consequence: If their decision to issue a warrant is correct, the evidence will be admitted; if their decision was incorrect but [not "entirely unreasonable" and] the police rely in good faith on the warrant, the evidence will also be admitted. Inevitably, the care and attention devoted to such an inconsequential chore will dwindle. (*United States* v. *Leon*, p. 956)

The good faith exception has been extended to other situations besides searches and seizures based on defective warrants. For instance, if a police officer acts in reasonable reliance on a statute that is later found to be unconstitutional, then the good faith exception will apply (see *Michigan* v. *DeFillippo*, 443 U.S. 31 [1979]). In addition, if evidence is obtained following a search or seizure that is conducted in reasonable reliance on computer records that turn out to be inaccurate, then, again, the exception will apply. In *Arizona* v. *Evans* (514 U.S. 1 [1995]), for example, a defendant was arrested during a traffic stop because the officer's computer showed an outstanding warrant that, unknown to the officer, had been quashed 17 days earlier. Evidence obtained from a search of the vehicle was admissible because, according to the Court, "there is no basis for believing that application of the exclusionary rule in these circumstances will have a significant effect on court employees responsible for informing the police that a warrant has been quashed" (p. 15). As noted in the chapter-opening case, a similar decision was reached in the *Herring* case in which police arrested an individual and found contraband in a search incident to arrest, yet unbeknownst to the officers, the arrest warrant had been recalled months earlier (*Herring* v. *United States*, 555 U.S. 135 [2009]).

Impeachment Exception

The next leading exception to the exclusionary rule is the so-called **impeachment exception**. If one of the good faith exceptions does not apply, then the prosecution cannot use, as part of its case, evidence resulting from an illegal search or seizure. However, if the prosecution seeks to use such evidence for the purpose of impeaching (that is, attacking the credibility of) a witness, then it will be considered admissible for that purpose. In **Walder v. United States (347 U.S. 62 [1954])**, a narcotics case, the Supreme Court permitted the introduction of heroin that had been illegally seized from the defendant two years earlier (and excluded from the trial it was supposed to be used in) in order to attack his statement that he had never purchased, used, or sold drugs. An important restriction concerning the impeachment exception is that it applies only to criminal defendants, not other witnesses (*James* v. *Illinois*, 493 U.S. 307 [1990]).

Good faith and impeachment are, again, the only two recognized exceptions to the exclusionary rule. Three additional exclusionary rule–type exceptions (that is, inevitable discovery, independent source, and purged taint) are sometimes blended together with these two, but they should be kept separate. They are actually exceptions to the "fruit of poisonous tree" doctrine, to which the discussion turns now.

▶ The "Fruit of the Poisonous Tree" Doctrine

In **Silverthorne Lumber Co. v. United States (251 U.S. 385 [1920])**, the Supreme Court created the **"fruit of the poisonous tree" doctrine**.[2] In that case, Silverthorne Lumber Company was convicted on contempt charges for failing to produce documents that were learned of during the course of an illegal search. The Court reversed the conviction, stating that forcing the company to produce documents that were learned of strictly because of an illegal search violated the Fourth Amendment. The *Silverthorne* holding was reaffirmed in the case of *Nardone* v. *United States* (308 U.S. 338 [1939]). In it, the Court noted that it should be left to the discretion of "experienced trial judges" to determine whether "a substantial portion of the case against [the accused] was a fruit of the poisonous tree" (p. 341).

The metaphor of the "fruit of the poisonous tree" can be traced to the biblical story of the Garden of Eden. As the story goes, Adam and Eve ate the apple, the forbidden fruit, from the tree, bringing original sin into the world. The poisonous tree, then, is the initial unconstitutional search or seizure. Anything obtained from the tree is considered forbidden fruit.

In short, the exclusionary rule applies not only to evidence obtained as a direct result of a constitutional rights violation but also to evidence *indirectly* derived from a constitutional rights violation. In many ways, the fruit of the poisonous tree doctrine resembles a "but for" test, in which the courts have to ask, "But

> The exclusionary rule applies not only to evidence obtained as a direct result of a constitutional rights violation but also to evidence *indirectly* derived from a constitutional rights violation.

Think About It...

An Act of Good Faith? Police Officer Wesson stopped a car that met the description of one supposedly driven away by two suspects from the scene of a burglary. He arrested both occupants and searched the car, finding illegal weapons in the trunk. It turns out that the vehicle description was wrong and Wesson arrested the wrong men. Nevertheless, should Officer Wesson's arrest come under the good faith exception to the exclusionary rule?

Scott Richardson/Shutterstock

- A suspect is coerced to confess and alerts police to where evidence can be found. The evidence would be inadmissible because it is fruit of an unconstitutional confession.
- Police arrest a suspect without probable cause and he confesses. The confession would be inadmissible as fruit of the unconstitutional arrest.
- Police arrest a suspect without probable cause. The suspect rats out two co-conspirators whom the police then arrest. The second set of arrests would be considered fruit of the poisonous tree, assuming the police had no other basis for arresting the co-conspirators.

 **Fruit of the Poisonous Tree Examples.**

for the unconstitutional police conduct, would the evidence have been obtained regardless?" If the answer is no, then the evidence will be excluded. If the answer is yes, then the issue becomes more complicated. Several examples appear in Figure 2–3.

Exceptions to "Fruit of the Poisonous Tree"

There are three main exceptions to the fruit of the poisonous tree doctrine. They are purged taint, independent source, and inevitable discovery.

Purged Taint

The first exception to the fruit of the poisonous tree doctrine is known as the *attenuation*, or **"purged taint," exception**. In *Nardone*, Justice Frankfurter observed that in some cases, "sophisticated argument may prove a causal link obtained through [illegality] and the Government's proof. As a matter of good sense, however, such a connection may have become so attenuated as to dissipate the taint" (p. 341). This observation was somewhat prophetic in the sense that the Court did not actually admit evidence because of attenuation. Several years later, in the case of **Wong Sun v. United States (371 U.S. 471 [1963])**, however, the Court did admit evidence because of attenuation.

In making an attenuation analysis, the courts must decide whether the derivative evidence was obtained by exploitation of the initial unconstitutional act or instead by other means that are purged of the primary taint. In *Wong Sun*, the Court determined that statements provided by a defendant who was illegally arrested and released but later returned to the police stationhouse on his own initiative were admissible because the statements did not result from the illegal arrest. Instead, the defendant decided to come back *later*, following his release. The Court noted that his statement had become attenuated to the extent that it dissipated the taint of the initial unconstitutional act.

In *Brown v. Illinois* (422 U.S. 590 [1975]), the Supreme Court pointed to several factors that should be considered in determining whether the purged taint exception applies: (1) whether the *Miranda* warnings were given prior to a voluntary confession, (2) the "temporal proximity" of the illegal police conduct and verbal statements made by a suspect, (3) the presence of intervening events or circumstances, and (4) the "purpose and flagrancy of the official misconduct." Several later cases focused on these four factors to varying degrees.

For example, in *Dunaway v. New York* (442 U.S. 200 [1979]), the Court chose to decide whether a confession obtained following a questionable stationhouse detention was admissible. The *Miranda* warnings had been given, but the Court still held that stationhouse detention intruded "so severely on interests protected by the Fourth Amendment as necessarily to trigger the traditional safeguards against illegal arrest" (p. 216). The Court then held that despite the *Miranda* warnings, Dunaway's statements should not be admissible. To hold differently would allow "law enforcement officers to violate the Fourth Amendment with impunity, safe in the knowledge that they could wash their hands in the 'procedural safeguards' of the Fifth" (p. 219).

In another case, *Taylor v. Alabama* (457 U.S. 687 [1982]), the Court held that the purged taint exception should not apply even under these circumstances: (1) The defendant had been advised of his *Miranda* rights, (2) six hours had elapsed between the defendant's illegal arrest and confession, and (3) the defendant had been permitted to visit with friends before making his confession.

Think About It...

The Independent Source Suspecting that people were storing marijuana in a warehouse, several police officers entered the building without obtaining a warrant to do so. (Later, they argued that they had suspected that evidence would be destroyed or that the people would escape if they had waited to obtain a warrant.) In fact, the search revealed bales of marijuana but no people. The police then applied for a warrant to search the building, deliberately failing to mention their previous search. The warrant was granted, the search was conducted, and the police "discovered" the marijuana. Should the marijuana be considered admissible at trial?

Solid Web Designs LTD/Shutterstock

Contrast *Taylor* with *Rawlings* v. *Kentucky* (448 U.S. 98 [1980]), in which the Court held that statements made 45 minutes after an illegal arrest *were* admissible because the defendant (1) had been advised of his *Miranda* rights just before making an incriminating statement, (2) had been in a house instead of a police station, and (3) had made spontaneous statements that did not result from direct questioning. Furthermore, the Court noted that the illegal arrest was not flagrant and that the defendant never argued that his admission was an involuntary product of police questioning.

Independent Source

The second exception to the fruit of the poisonous tree doctrine is the so-called **independent source** exception. The first case to affirmatively establish this type of exception was **Segura v. United States (468 U.S. 796 [1984])**. There, the Court held that evidence found in an apartment pursuant to a valid search warrant was admissible, even though the police had entered the apartment illegally *prior* to serving the search warrant because the warrant was based on information totally disconnected with the initial illegal search. In other words, even though the police first entered the apartment illegally, the warrant they later served was based on information independent from that search.

Inevitable Discovery

The third exception to the fruit of the poisonous tree doctrine is known as the **inevitable discovery exception**. Stated simply, if evidence would be found regardless of unconstitutional police conduct, then it is admissible. This exception was first recognized by the Supreme Court in **Nix v. Williams (467 U.S. 431 [1984])**. In that case, the evidence was the body of a young girl, which was discovered after the police had illegally questioned the defendant concerning the body's whereabouts. Under ordinary circumstances, the body would not have been considered admissible, but the prosecution was able to prove that at the time of the illegal questioning, a search party looking for the girl's body had narrowed in on its target and would have "inevitably discovered" the body. The Iowa Supreme Court affirmed the lower court's decision to admit the body into evidence because "(1) the police did not act in bad faith for the purpose of hastening discovery of the evidence in question, and (2) . . . the evidence in question would have been discovered by lawful means" (*Iowa* v. *Williams*, 285 N.W.2d 248 [Iowa 1979], p. 260).

The inevitable discovery exception bears striking resemblance to the independent source exception. For all practical purposes, evidence that would be inevitably discovered comes from an independent source. The search that was under way in *Nix* v. *Williams*, for example, was totally disconnected from the questioning of the defendant. In light of the similarities between these two exceptions to the fruit of the poisonous tree doctrine, some courts have simply opted to call the inevitable discovery exception the *hypothetical independent source exception* (see *Nix*, p. 438).

The exceptions to the fruit of the poisonous tree doctrine are summarized in Figure 2–4.

Purged Taint
The Case: *Wong Sun* v. *United States*, 371 U.S. 471 (1963)
The Rule: If the taint of an unconstitutional search/seizure is sufficiently "purged" (such as with the passage of time), the evidence will be admissible. Example: Assume a police officer wrongfully arrests a suspect and releases him. If the suspect comes back to the police station months later on his own initiative and is arrested, the initial taint is purged.

Independent Source
The Case: *Segura* v. *United States*, 468 U.S. 796 (1984)
The Rule: Evidence brought forward by a source independent of an unconstitutional search or seizure will be admissible.
Example: If police wrongfully elicit a confession from a suspect as to the location of a murder weapon, the weapon won't be admissible; however, if a private person (one who is not acting in concert with police in any way) finds the weapon and turns it in, it will be admissible.

Inevitable Discovery
The Case: *Nix* v. *Williams*, 467 U.S. 431 (1984)
The Rule: Evidence that would have been discovered anyway will be admissible regardless of a wrongful search or seizure.
Example: The police wrongfully elicit a confession from a murder suspect as to the location of the victim's body. If the body would have been found anyway (e.g., a search for the victim was already under way), the body would be admissible as evidence.

FIGURE 2–4 Exceptions to Fruit of the Poisonous Tree Doctrine.

▶ Alternative Remedies

Various statutes at the federal and local levels provide criminal remedies for police misconduct, just like the exclusionary rule does. Some states make it criminal for police officers to trespass and/or to falsely arrest people. In fact, most criminal sanctions that apply to ordinary citizens also apply to police officers. Likewise, various statutes at the federal level make it not only improper but also criminal for police officers to engage in certain types of conduct.

Criminal Law

The most common federal statute for holding police officers criminally liable is **18 U.S.C. Section 242**. It states,

> Whoever, under color of any law, statute, ordinance, regulation, or custom, willfully subjects any inhabitant of any State, Territory, or District to the deprivation of any rights, privileges, or immunities secured or protected by the Constitution or laws of the United States, or to different punishments, pains, or penalties, on account of such inhabitant being an alien, or by reason of his color, or race, than are prescribed for the punishment of citizens, shall be fined not more than $1,000 or imprisoned not more than one year, or both; and if death results shall be subject to imprisonment for any term of years or for life.

Although it is a federal statute, Section 242 can be used to prosecute either a state or a federal law enforcement officer. In other words, a state police officer who violates Section 242 can be charged criminally in federal court.

To be held liable under Section 242, a law enforcement officer must act with specific intent to deprive a person of important constitutional (or other federal) rights (**Screws v. United States, 325 U.S. 91 [1945]**). Also, for criminal liability under Section 242, a constitutional right must be clearly established (*United States* v. *Lanier*, 520 U.S. 259 [1997]). Together, these restrictions have resulted in the filing of relatively few Section 242 cases. In fact, criminal liability under Section 242 is reserved for the most egregious forms of police misconduct. Some examples appear in Figure 2–5.

Additional federal statutes make it a criminal act to unlawfully search and seize individuals (18 U.S.C. Section 2236),

although applications of this statute are rare, as well. Section 2235 of 18 U.S.C. makes it criminal to maliciously procure a warrant, and Section 2234 makes it criminal to exceed the authority of a warrant. Regardless of which criminal statute applies, an important distinction needs to be made between the various criminal statutes and 42 U.S.C. Section 1983. An officer who is held *criminally* liable will receive a criminal conviction and can even go to prison. Section 1983, by contrast, is *civil*, meaning that it is used independently of the criminal process. A successful Section 1983 lawsuit will never result in imprisonment of the defendant.

The same *state* laws that apply to ordinary citizens also apply to police officers. For example, if a police officer knowingly and intentionally kills someone and is not legally justified in doing so (for example, to prevent injury to a third party), that officer can be held criminally liable for murder. Similarly, if a police officer trespasses on private property without appropriate justification, he or she can be held criminally liable. Criminal liability can extend to a police officer for virtually any conceivable offense.

Some crimes are committed by police officers more often than other crimes. Birzer places such offenses into three categories: (1) violent and sex crimes, (2) drug crimes, and (3) other crimes.[3] With respect to violent crimes, the so-called Miami River Cops were charged with murdering drug smugglers. As for sex crimes, a police officer in Fort Myers, Florida, was charged with sexual assault against a 19-year-old female. These examples are not offered to suggest that police officers frequently engage in criminal activity but only that it happens. No one is above the law, even police officers.

Clearly, police officers also engage in many actions that would be crimes if performed by ordinary citizens. Police officers, however, enjoy immunity from criminal liability for these actions if the actions are committed (justifiably) as part of their official duties. The so-called law enforcement or **public duty defense** to criminal liability is what shields police officers from criminal liability on most occasions. Assuming officers use deadly or nondeadly force properly, they will not be held criminally liable for their actions. The rules concerning deadly and nondeadly force appear in Figure 2–6.

Beyond the realms of deadly and nondeadly force, police officers do not have much in the way of defense against criminal liability. If a police officer who committed burglary for his or her own personal gain attempted to assert a public duty defense, he or she would almost certainly fail. Similarly, if a police officer shoots and kills a person not for the purpose of preventing a crime or effecting an arrest but, say, for vengeance, that officer will almost certainly be convicted of some degree of homicide and probably sentenced to prison.

Miller v. *United States* (404 F.2d 611 [5th Cir. 1968]): A police officer was held criminally liable for allowing his canine unit to bite a suspect.

Williams v. *United States* (341 U.S. 97 [1951]): A defendant had been beaten, threatened, and physically punished for several hours, so a police officer was held criminally liable.

Lynch v. *United States* (189 F.2d 476 [5th Cir. 1951]): Criminal charges were filed in the wake of the assault and battery of several criminal defendants.

FIGURE 2–5 Examples of 18 U.S.C. Section 242 Cases.

Civil Litigation

When a person's constitutional or other federal civil rights are violated, he or she can sue. Even if a person merely *believes* his or her rights have been violated, litigation is still an option.

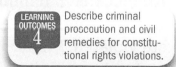

LEARNING OUTCOMES **4** Describe criminal prosecution and civil remedies for constitutional rights violations.

Deadly Force

<u>What it is</u>: Force that is likely to cause death or significant bodily injury

<u>Legal Standard</u>:

Preventing crime: A police officer can only use deadly force to prevent a felony if he or she reasonably believes that the other person is about to commit an "atrocious" or "forcible" felony (see *People v. Ceballos*, 526 P.2d 241 [Cal. 1974]).

Arrest: Deadly force can only be used to effect an arrest if (1) the force is necessary to prevent the suspect's flight; (2) the officer can attempt to warn the suspect of his or her intention to use deadly force (e.g., "Stop or I'll shoot!"); and (3) the officer has probable cause to believe that the suspect, if not immediately apprehended, poses a significant threat of death or serious bodily injury to the officer or others (*Tennessee v. Garner*, 471 U.S. 1 [1985]).

<u>Example</u>: Shooting a gun at a suspect

Nondeadly Force

<u>What it is</u>: Force that is unlikely to cause death or significant bodily harm.

<u>Legal Standard</u>: Nondeadly force can be used to apprehend a suspect so long as it is reasonable in terms of the Fourth Amendment (*Graham v. Connor*, 490 U.S. 386 [1989]). Three criteria are considered: (1) the severity of the crime, (2) whether the suspect posed a threat, and (3) whether the suspect was resisting or attempting to flee the scene.

<u>Example</u>: An officer uses her Taser to subdue a suspect.

FIGURE 2–6 Rules Governing Deadly and Nondeadly Force.

The worst (or best) that can happen is that the lawsuit will be dismissed. The civil liability process is summarized in Figure 2–7.

In this section, we look at one particular type of civil liability (casually referred to as "Section 1983"), but there are others, such as state tort liability, that are beyond the scope of this book. Before we continue, know that although civil liability may be an effective remedy for people whose rights are violated, litigation may come with a high price tag; it can be costly and time-consuming to sue.

What is the purpose of **civil litigation**? Aside from sometimes being the only remedy available, civil lawsuits are attractive because money can be awarded. A lawsuit in which one or more parties seek monetary compensation is called a **damage suit**. The *plaintiff*, or the person filing the lawsuit, seeks payment for injuries or perceived injuries suffered. In addition to damages, the plaintiff can also seek **injunctive relief**, which basically means he or she wants the court to bring the injurious or offensive action to a halt.

Although civil liability may be an effective remedy for people whose rights are violated, litigation may come with a high price tag; it can be costly and time-consuming to sue.

Think About It...

Color of Law Officer Webster regularly patronized a bar. One night, while off duty, he got into a fight, drew his gun, and shot and killed James Ramos. Ramos's heirs filed a Section 1983 lawsuit against the city for which Webster worked, alleging that it failed to adequately train him as to whether and how to react during off-duty altercations. Furthermore, Ramos's heirs alleged that this failure caused Webster, acting under color of law, to deprive Ramos of his constitutional rights. Will this lawsuit succeed?

Why should we care about civil remedies in a book about criminal procedure? One answer is that criminal remedies do not always apply. The exclusionary rule does not apply if there are no criminal charges. Likewise, criminal remedies made

1. *Citizen complaint*: The first step in filing a lawsuit normally involves a citizen complaint. In a citizen complaint, the aggrieved party can do one of two things: call attention to inappropriate police conduct *or* demand some form of remedial action (e.g., injunctive relief or monetary damages). This latter form of citizen complaint is considered a *demand*.

2. *Demand*: If the complaint filed with the police by a citizen (the *complainant*) requests some action on the part of the police, then the complainant will make a more or less informal demand of the police, who will then send a *response*. This may lead to informal discussions between the two sides. The complainant may retain the services of an attorney, but the procedure remains largely informal at this early juncture.

3. *Citizen complaint board*: In some jurisdictions (e.g., Spokane, WA), the complainant can further file a complaint with a local citizen complaint board if the police agency in question fails to take satisfactory action. Citizen complaint boards vary considerably in use, authority, and terminology, so they are only mentioned here in passing as one mechanism for dispute resolution. Other avenues of dispute resolution may well be in place.

4. *Lawyer's letter*: If the complainant and the police cannot work things out informally, the complainant usually brings in an attorney. The attorney will send a so-called lawyer's letter to the police agency, the officer(s) in question, and/or the city or county. While this letter may not have any legal significance, it usually gets a serious response.

5. *Prelitigation settlement discussion*: An informal prelitigation settlement discussion is often held, in which the police or their representatives and the complainant or his or her representatives work together to try to reach a settlement. If no settlement is reached, the complaint/demand will likely evolve into a full-blown lawsuit.

6. *Claim with city/county clerk*: Before being able to proceed with a lawsuit, the citizens in some states and counties are first required to file a claim with the city or county against which the complaint is made or to give the police agency a chance to respond to a formal complaint or a request for damages. This *claim* should be distinguished from a *citizen complaint*, discussed above. This claim is an explicit prerequisite that must be completed before a lawsuit can move forward; it is mandated by law. The purpose of such a claim is primarily to inform officials of what is about to transpire. Often, a lawsuit cannot be filed until the parties in question are given the opportunity to respond to a claim.

7. *Lawsuit*: A citizen complaint/demand evolves into a full-blown lawsuit when none of the informal proceedings discussed satisfy the complainant. To reach the stage of a lawsuit, two actions must occur: First, a *complaint* must be filed with the clerk of the court in which the lawsuit will be heard. (This complaint is a legal requirement and differs from the citizen complaint already filed.) Second, the court or an attorney must issue a *summons* to be *served* on the agencies or people named in the complaint. Sometimes, the summons is personally delivered; other times, it is sent by registered or certified mail. The parties named in the complaint (e.g., the police, their agencies, municipalities) are now known as the *defendants*, and the aggrieved party or parties filing the lawsuit are now known as the *plaintiffs*.

FIGURE 2–7 Stages of a Civil Lawsuit.

available by state and federal law generally apply in cases of the most egregious police misconduct. Another answer is that several important criminal procedure decisions (for example, *Tennessee v. Garner*) began as civil lawsuits.

42 U.S.C. Section 1983 provides a remedy in federal court for the "deprivation of any rights . . . secured by the Constitution and laws" of the United States. Section 1983 states,

> Every person who, under color of any statute, ordinance, regulation, custom, or usage, of any State or Territory, subjects, or causes to be subjected, any citizen of the United States or other persons within the jurisdiction thereof to the deprivation of any rights, privileges, or immunities secured by the Constitution and laws, shall be liable to the party injured in an action at law, suit in equity, or other proper proceeding for redress.

There are two key requirements for a Section 1983 lawsuit to succeed. First, the *defendant*, the person being sued, must have acted under "color of law." The Supreme Court has stated that

FIGURE 2–8 Situations in Which Officers Act Under Color of Law.

someone acts under **color of law** when he or she acts in an official capacity (*Lugar* v. *Edmondson Oil Co.*, 457 U.S. 922 [1982]). For example, a police officer who is on duty acts under color of law. By contrast, someone acting in a private capacity, such as an ordinary citizen, cannot be said to have acted under color of law. Several examples of the color of law appear in Figure 2–8.

Interestingly, plaintiffs *can* sue private parties under Section 1983 when private parties conspire with state officers. With regard to this point, the Supreme Court has held that "a state normally can be held responsible for a private decision only when it has exercised coercive power or has provided such significant encouragement, either overt or covert, that the choice must in law be deemed to be that of the state" (*Blum* v. *Yaretsky*, 457 U.S. 991 [1982], p. 1004).

The second requirement for a successful Section 1983 lawsuit is that a constitutional rights violation has taken place. In determining whether a constitutional rights violation has taken place, the plaintiff must establish that the defendant's conduct violated a specific constitutional provision, such as the Fourth Amendment. As noted in *Daniels* v. *Williams* (474 U.S. 327 [1986]), "[I]n any given Section 1983 suit, the plaintiff must still prove a violation of the underlying constitutional right" (p. 330).

Municipal/County Liability

Cities and counties can also be held liable under Section 1983, particularly if they adopt and implement policies or adopt customs that become responsible for constitutional rights violations (see *Monell* v. *Department of Social Services*, **436 U.S. 658 [1978]**). In general, a plaintiff will not succeed with a Section 1983 municipal/county liability claim if a common practice is engaged in by lower-ranking officials who have no authority to make policy in the traditional sense of the term. For example, if a group of police officers regularly use excessive force but do so on their own, with no authorization from the city or county, then the city or county cannot be held liable for these officers' actions.

In another city/county liability case, *City of Canton* v. *Harris* **(489 U.S. 378 [1989])**, the Supreme Court held that counties (and, by extension, cities) can be held liable for inadequately training their law enforcement officers. The facts of the case in *Canton* were that Harris was arrested and brought to the police station in a patrol wagon. On arrival, the officers found Harris lying on the floor of the wagon. She was asked if she needed medical attention, but she responded incoherently. After she was brought into the station, she slumped to the floor on two occasions. Eventually, she was left lying on the floor; no medical attention was summoned for her. Harris later sued, seeking to hold the city liable for a violation of her Fourteenth Amendment right, under the due process clause, to receive medical attention while in police custody. However, the Court held that "only where a municipality's failure to train its employees in a relevant respect evidences a 'deliberate indifference' to the rights of its inhabitants can such a shortcoming be properly thought of as a city 'policy or custom' that is actionable under [Section] 1983" (p. 389).

In *Board of Commissioners of Bryan County* v. *Brown* (520 U.S. 397 [1997]), the Supreme Court revisited the city/county liability issue. In particular, the question before the Court was whether a single hiring decision by a municipality's policymaker could give rise to an inadequate hiring claim under Section 1983. In that case, Brown's claim was fueled by the injuries she suffered at the hands of Bryan County Reserve Deputy Stacy Burns during a high-speed pursuit and by the fact that Burns had two previous misdemeanor convictions for assault and battery (both

Think About It...

Municipal Liability Danny Koller, 17 years old, stole a van from a car lot by driving it through the showroom window. Almost immediately, members of the local police department began to pursue him. After a dangerous and lengthy high-speed chase, the van was forced to stop. Danny emerged from the van unarmed. When the pursuing officers approached him, they hit him and pulled his hair. In the scuffle, the pistol of one of the officers discharged. The bullet struck Danny in the head and he died as a result of the wound. Danny's parents brought suit under 42 U.S.C. Section 1983, seeking damages from the city. They argued that the city maintained a formal policy of using excessive police force, and that this policy caused Danny's death. Assuming this tragedy is an isolated event, will the plaintiffs succeed with their lawsuit?

© Michael Matthews - Police Images/Alamy

of which were overlooked during the pre-employment screening process). Brown seemed to have a good case, but the Court felt otherwise, finding for Bryan County and setting a high standard for claims against a municipality for inadequate hiring. Specifically, the Court held that "[e]ven assuming without deciding that proof of a single instance of inadequate screening could ever trigger municipal liability, [the county commissioners'] failure to scrutinize Burns's record cannot constitute 'deliberate indifference' to [the] respondent's federally protected right to be free from the use of excessive force" (p. 412).

Defending Against Wrongful Litigation

Officials who are sued under Section 1983 can assert a **qualified immunity** defense. Qualified immunity is a judicially created defense, just like the exclusionary rule is a court creation. In some cases, qualified immunity is more than a defense; it may afford immunity from suit.

Qualified immunity was developed to accommodate two conflicting policy concerns: effective crime control vis-à-vis the protection of people's civil liberties. Although the Supreme Court has clearly intimated that Section 1983 should serve as a deterrent to official misconduct, the Court has also recognized that it is not fair to hold officials liable for lapses in judgment and honest mistakes. These issues were addressed in the seminal cases of *Harlow* v. *Fitzgerald* (457 U.S. 800 [1982]) and *Wood* v. *Strickland* (420 U.S. 308 [1975]).

Similar to the Fourth Amendment's test for reasonableness, an objective reasonableness standard has been applied in order to determine if qualified immunity should be extended to criminal justice officials who are defendants. For the purposes of qualified immunity, a defendant is said to have acted in an objectively reasonable fashion if he or she does not violate clearly established rights about which a reasonable person would have known (*Harlow* v. *Fitzgerald*). In some Section 1983 cases, defendants have benefited from qualified immunity even for violating clearly established constitutional rights, provided that the defendants' mistaken belief was objectively reasonable (e.g., *Malley* v. *Briggs*, 475 U.S. 335 [1988]).

Qualified immunity was strengthened in *Messerschmidt* v. *Millender*, 565 U.S. __ (2012). Police were seeking a sawed-off shotgun in connection with a gang shooting, but the search warrant authorized the officers to search for *all* firearms. The warrant was challenged as overbroad and not in compliance with the Fourth Amendment's particularity requirement. The Ninth Circuit Court of Appeals refused to grant the officers qualified immunity in the Section 1983 lawsuit that followed the search, but the Supreme Court sided with the officers, holding in part that the officers ". . . reasonably believed they had a fair probability of finding illegal firearms and other evidence relevant to the crime."

In some Section 1983 cases, defendants have benefited from qualified immunity even for violating clearly established constitutional rights, provided that the defendants' mistaken belief was objectively reasonable. *Ryburn* v. *Huff*, 565 U.S. __ (2012) illustrates this trend. Officers visited the home of a boy who had allegedly threatened to "shoot up" his school. The officers spoke to the boy and his mother after they opened the front door at the officers' request. When the officers asked if there were any guns in the house, the mother turned and retreated into the interior of the house. Fearing for their safety and others who may have been inside, the officers entered the house. The conversation continued and it was determined that the rumor implicating the boy was false. The officers were later sued under Section 1983 on the theory that they entered the home without a warrant. The Supreme Court decided they enjoyed qualified immunity for their actions because ". . . reasonable police officers in the petitioners' position could have come to the conclusion that the Fourth Amendment permitted them to enter the Huff residence if there was an objectively reasonable basis for fearing that violence was imminent," which there was.

Qualified immunity thus affords protection to defendant criminal justice officials not just for reasonably mistaken beliefs, but for any number of actions that are objectively reasonable under the circumstances—viewed from "the perspective of a reasonable officer at the scene, rather than with the 20/20 vision of hindsight" (*Ryburn*, 565 U.S. __ [2012]).

Figure 2–9 provides an overview of the Section 1983 process for lawsuits against individual police officers. Note that individual officers can enjoy qualified immunity if they act in an objectively reasonable fashion.

Nonjudicial Remedies

Nonjudicial remedies are available for situations in which neither the exclusionary rule nor civil liability are viable options. Consider the hypothetical case of a motorist who is stopped without proper justification. Assume the motorist is released. To be sure, he or she has suffered an inconvenience, but if no contraband was found and there was no egregious misconduct on the officer's part, what can this person do? About the only choice available is to file a written complaint. A complaint/commendation form from the Abilene, Texas, Police Department appears in Figure 2–10.

Think About It...

The Fourth Amendment and Qualified Immunity In a recent Supreme Court case, *Wilson* v. *Layne* (526 U.S. 603 [1999]), the Supreme Court considered (1) whether law enforcement officers violated the Fourth Amendment by allowing members of the media to accompany them on the service of warrants and (2) whether the officers were nonetheless entitled to qualified immunity if such activity violates the Fourth Amendment. The Court decided that "a media 'ride-along' in a home violates the Fourth Amendment, but because the state of the law was not clearly established at the time the entry in this case took place, respondent officers are entitled to qualified immunity" (p. 603). Do you see any problems with this decision?

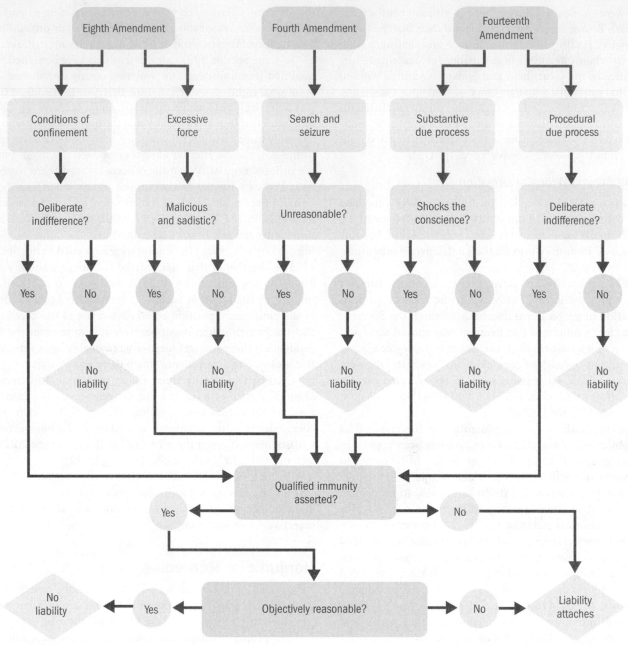

Individual Liability Under Section 1983.

Internal Review

Internal review is the process by which a police department (or other criminal justice agency if one of its employees was responsible for alleged misconduct) investigates a complaint against one of its employees. In its model police misconduct policy, the Police Executive Research Forum listed a number of means by which the police themselves can implement effective complaint procedures. They need to secure community support, monitor compliance, and maintain due process protections for officers and citizens alike.[4]

Figure 2–11 shows the District of Columbia Metropolitan Police Department's complaint review process, depicting one agency's approach to internal discipline.

Civilian Review

There has been a marked increase in the number of cities involving citizens at some stage of the police complaint process.[5] This has occurred because of the demand for some form of external input in the investigation process. It has also occurred

There has been a marked increase in the number of cities involving citizens at some stage of the police complaint process.

Abilene Police Department
Citizen Complaint/Commendation Form

File complaints or commendations about Police Department employees on this form. Return the completed form to the desk duty officer, 1st floor at the Police Department, 450 Pecan or hand deliver to the City Manager's Office, 555 Walnut, Room 203 or by mail to P.O. Box 60 Abilene, Texas 79604. Complaints will not be investigated until a Police Supervisor has contacted the Complaining Party.

Involved Officer/Employee(s) Information:			
Name:			
Name:			

Person Making the Complaint/Commendation:			
Name:		**Phone:**	
Address:		**Phone:**	

Information:
Please provide as much information about the reason you were contacted by the officer/employee. Specific information about the date, time and location will help in locating computer-based information if you do not know the officer/employee's name.

Date of Contact:		**Approximate Time:**		**AM/PM**
Location Contacted:				

Reason For The Complaint/Commendation: (attach additional pages if needed)

Witness Information:			
Name:		**Phone:**	
Address:		**Phone:**	
Name:		**Phone:**	
Address:		**Phone:**	

Submitted by _____ Date _____

FIGURE 2–10 Citizen Complaint Form.

MPD Complaint Investigation Process

A complaint may be submitted to either the MPD or Office of Police Complaints (OPC). The following flowcharts detail the complaint review processes.

Step 1

The complaint is filed with the MPD.

Step 2

The MPD official responsible for investigating the complaint contacts you to let you know he or she is investigating it. If necessary, the official will obtain additional information.

Step 3

The complaint is investigated–witnesses and the officer against whom the complaint is filed are interviewed. The officer is entitled to know the complainant's name, if it is known, and the nature of the complaint. However, the MPD will not reveal the complainant's name if the complainant requests to remain anonymous.

Step 4

- Investigation is completed and one of the following conclusions is made:
- Sustained – where the person's allegation is supported by sufficient evidence to determine that the incident occurred and the actions of the officer were improper.
- Insufficient Facts – where there are insufficient facts to decide whether the alleged misconduct occurred.
- Exonerated – where a preponderance of the evidence shows that the alleged conduct did occur but did not violate MPD policies, procedures, or training.
- Unfounded – where the investigation determined no facts to support that the incident complained of actually occurred.

Step 5

You are notified of the outcome of the investigation. If you do not agree with it, you may appeal the decision in writing by sending a letter to the Chief of Police at 300 Indiana Ave., NW, Rm. 5080, Washington, DC 20001.

 FIGURE 2–11 **Complaint Investigation Process.**
Source: District of Columbia Metropolitan Police Department, http://mpdc.dc.gov/page/mpd-complaint-investigation-process (accessed May 2, 2013).

due to some sentiments that citizens can investigate the police better than the police themselves can:

> Citizen involvement in the complaint process will produce (1) more objective and more thorough investigations; (2) a higher rate of sustained complaints and more disciplinary actions against guilty officers; (3) greater deterrence of police misconduct (through both general and specific deterrence); and (4) higher levels of satisfaction on the part of both individual complainants and the general public.[6]

West has identified three distinct forms of citizen review: (1) civilian review, (2) civilian input, and (3) civilian monitor.[7] Pure **civilian review** is the strongest form; a civilian panel investigates, adjudicates, and recommends punishment to the police chief. The second strongest form is **civilian input**; in this form, a civilian panel receives and investigates a complaint, leaving adjudication and discipline with the department itself. Finally, the **civilian monitor** form, the weakest of the three, leaves investigation, adjudication, and discipline inside the department; a civilian is allowed to review the adequacy and impartiality of the process. The research reported by West focused only on the first two forms: civilian review and civilian input. Both place investigative authority with an independent body and are arguably

more satisfactory to disgruntled citizens than the third form, civilian monitor.

Critics of civilian review argue that such procedures suffer from a number of drawbacks:

- They ignore existing legal resources at citizens' disposal.
- It is difficult for people disconnected from the police department to have an adequate understanding of the internal operations of a civilian review board.
- Citizen review damages morale.
- Civilian review invites abdication of authority by line supervisors.
- Such boards weaken the ability of top management to achieve conformity through discipline.
- They are tantamount to admitting that the police are incapable of policing themselves.[8]

Mediation

Some have argued that **mediation**, or relying on a neutral third party to render decisions, is a desirable approach to address the problem of police misconduct. In this technique, the decision of a neutral third party, or **ombudsman** (sometimes called a "mediator" or "arbitrator"), is sought.[9] As Whitebread and Slobogin observe,

> [Another] remedial system which, like the civilian review board, operates outside the judicial and internal police spheres, is the Scandinavian ombudsman system. The ombudsman is, most simply, an external critic of administration. His goal is improvement of administration rather than punishment of administrators or redress of individual grievances. Thus, instead of conducting formal hearings associated with adjudicating individual complaints, he relies primarily on his own investigations to gather information. On the basis of his findings, he may recommend corrective measure to the department, although he cannot compel an official to do anything.[10]

A key characteristic of the ombudsman system is that it is independent of the complainant and the person being complained against. The ombudsman should be a person to whom people may come with grievances connected to the government. The ombudsman stands between the citizen and the government, acting as something of an intermediary.

As another alternative, Chief Justice Burger suggested in *Bivens v. Six Unknown Named Agents* (403 U.S. 388 [1971]) that a quasi-judicial body be appointed for the purpose of recovering damages against the government. Under his plan, if damages are awarded, the record of what transpired will become part of the offending officer's permanent file. Neither of these systems has gained widespread acceptance, much less adoption.

Exclusionary Rule Objections

Critics of the exclusionary rule claim that it leads to otherwise guilty criminals going free. So does it? Ultimately, this is an empirical question, one several researchers have attempted to answer over the years. Here is a summary of some of the key studies:

1. Successful motions for the exclusion of evidence were made in only 1.3% of prosecuted cases (Government Accountability Office. [1979]. *Report of the Comptroller General of the United States, impact of the exclusionary rule on federal criminal prosecutions*. Washington, DC: Author).

2. Of the cases rejected for prosecution, 4.8% of them were rejected because of search-and-seizure problems. Approximately 50% of those released because of the exclusionary rule were re-arrested within two years of their release (National Institute of Justice. [1982]. *The effects of the exclusionary rule: A study in California*. Washington, DC: Author).

3. In a re-analysis of the previous study, one researcher found that prosecutors rejected only 0.8% of felony arrests because of Fourth Amendment concerns. He concluded further that "only about 2.35% of felony arrests are lost because of illegal searches" (Davies, T. Y. [1983]. A hard look at what we know (and still need to learn) about the "costs" of the exclusionary rule: The NIJ study and other studies of "lost" arrests. *American Bar Foundation Journal, 3*[8], 611).

4. A nine-county study of 7,500 felony court cases revealed that motions to suppress were filed in less than 5% of all cases. The success rate of such motions was reported to be 0.69%. The study's conclusion was that less than 0.6% of all cases were lost due to the exclusion of evidence (Nardulli, P. F. [1983]. The societal cost of the exclusionary rule: An empirical assessment. *American Bar Foundation Journal, 3*[8], 585).

5. Few cases were "lost" as a result of the exclusionary rule in seven jurisdictions when police used search warrants. "Twenty-one of 1,355 defendants (1.5%) were 'allowed to go free' as a result of a successful motion to suppress physical evidence" (Uchida, C. D., & Bynum, T. S. [1991]. Search warrants, motions to suppress, and "lost cases": The effects of the exclusionary rule in seven jurisdictions. *The Journal of Criminal Law and Criminology, 81*[4], 1034).

It has been several years since these studies were published, but their findings likely still ring true.

Research on the effects of the exclusionary rule raises a number of questions:

1. Is it possible that the picture has changed and that today more defendants than ever go free because of police mistakes? Why or why not?
2. Although the percentage of "lost cases" due to police mistakes is low, could it be lower? Should it be?
3. What other possible loopholes exist in the criminal justice system?

LEARNING OUTCOMES 1

Distinguish between legal and extralegal remedies.

Legal remedies are made available by law, court decisions, and agency policy/procedure. Examples include the exclusionary rule, criminal liability, civil litigation, and various alternative remedies. Extralegal remedies are those conducted outside the legal process.

1. Define the term *remedy*.
2. Distinguish between the two types of remedies.

remedy A method of rectifying wrongdoing.

extralegal remedies Remedies conducted outside the legal process, such as a personal vendetta.

legal remedies Remedies made available by the law, by a court decision, or by a police agency policy or procedure.

LEARNING OUTCOMES 2

Summarize the exclusionary rule and the exceptions to it.

The exclusionary rule requires that evidence obtained in violation of the Constitution be excluded from trial. Exceptions are good faith and impeachment.

Key Cases

> *Weeks* v. *United States*
> *Mapp* v. *Ohio*
> *United States* v. *Leon*
> *Walder* v. *United States*

1. What is the exclusionary rule?
2. Is the exclusionary rule applicable beyond the Fourth Amendment? Explain.
3. What are the two exceptions to the exclusionary rule?

exclusionary rule The Supreme Court–created rule requiring that evidence obtained in violation of the Constitution cannot be used in a criminal trial to prove guilt.

"silver platter" doctrine A practice prior to *Elkins* v. *United States* (364 U.S. 206 [1960]) that permitted the use of evidence in *federal* court that had been obtained illegally by *state* officials.

"good faith" exception An exception to the exclusionary rule providing that when an honest mistake is made during the course of a search or seizure, any subsequently obtained evidence will be considered admissible.

impeachment exception An exception to the exclusionary rule providing that evidence considered inadmissible at one trial can be used in a later trial to impeach (that is, cast doubt on the credibility of) the defendant.

LEARNING OUTCOMES 3

Summarize the "fruit of the poisonous tree" doctrine and the exceptions to it.

The exclusionary rule has been extended to require that derivative evidence obtained from a constitutional rights violation also be excluded. This is known as the "fruit of the poisonous tree" doctrine. Exceptions to this doctrine include inevitable discovery, independent source, and purged taint.

Key Cases

> *Silverthorne Lumber Co.* v. *United States*
> *Wong Sun* v. *United States*
> *Segura* v. *United States*
> *Nix* v. *Williams*

1. Define the "fruit of the poisonous tree" doctrine.
2. What are the three exceptions to the fruit of the poisonous tree doctrine?

"fruit of the poisonous tree" doctrine An extension of the exclusionary rule. The poisonous tree is the initial unconstitutional search or seizure. Anything obtained from the tree is considered forbidden fruit and is not admissible at trial.

"purged taint" exception An exception to the fruit of poisonous tree doctrine that permits the introduction of evidence if it has become attenuated to the extent that it dissipated the taint of the initial unconstitutional act.

independent source An exception to the fruit of the poisonous tree doctrine that permits the introduction of evidence if it has arrived via an independent source, such as a party disconnected from the case at hand.

inevitable discovery exception An exception to the fruit of the poisonous tree doctrine that permits the introduction of evidence if it would have been discovered anyway.

LEARNING OUTCOMES 4

Describe criminal prosecution and civil remedies for constitutional rights violations.

Police officers can be held criminally liable for misconduct. Civil lawsuits against government officials—the police, mainly—can be filed when neither the exclusionary rule nor other criminal remedies apply. Alternative remedies include internal review, civilian review, and mediation.

Key Cases

> *Screws v. United States*
>
> *Monell v. Department of Social Services*
>
> *City of Canton v. Harris*
>
> *Malley v. Briggs*

1. How does the criminal law operate as a remedy?
2. How does civil litigation act as a remedy?
3. What are the requirements of a successful Section 1983 lawsuit?
4. Compare and contrast three nonjudicial remedies.

18 U.S.C. Section 242 A federal statute used to hold police officers (and other government actors) criminally liable for actions that cause violations of people's constitutional or other federally protected rights.

public duty defense A defense that shields police officers from criminal liability when performing certain official functions, such as using deadly force.

civil litigation The same as a lawsuit.

damage suit A lawsuit in which one or more parties seek monetary compensation.

injunctive relief A court-ordered prohibition against a certain act or condition.

42 U.S.C. Section 1983 A federal statute that provides a remedy in federal court for the "deprivation of any rights . . . secured by the Constitution and laws" of the United States. Also called "Section 1983."

color of law One of two requirements for a successful Section 1983 lawsuit. An official acts under color of law when he or she acts in an official capacity.

qualified immunity Immunity from suit that applies some of the time and in certain situations. Sometimes qualified immunity serves as an "affirmative defense," meaning that it is raised at trial—if the case goes that far. If a criminal justice official acts on a reasonably mistaken belief, as gauged from the standpoint of a reasonable officer, then qualified immunity can be granted.

internal review A nonjudicial remedy in which the police investigate on their own complaints against officers.

civilian review The strongest method of citizen input in which a civilian panel investigates, adjudicates, and recommends punishment to the police chief.

civilian input A method of citizen input into the complaint review process in which a civilian panel receives and investigates a complaint, leaving adjudication and discipline with the department itself.

civilian monitor The weakest method of citizen input that leaves investigation, adjudication, and discipline inside the department. A civilian is allowed to review the adequacy and impartiality of the process.

mediation A method of alternative dispute resolution in which a neutral third party renders disciplinary decisions.

ombudsman A term used to describe the neutral third party who conducts mediation.

"By adopting the Fourth Amendment, the framers of the Constitution placed significant restrictions on searches conducted by government officials."

Introduction to the Fourth Amendment

1 Outline the history, purpose, and essential elements of the Fourth Amendment.

2 Define searches within the context of the Fourth Amendment.

3 Define seizures within the context of the Fourth Amendment.

4 Explain the concept of justification, including probable cause.

INTRO POLICE PURSUIT TECHNOLOGIES: CONSTITUTIONAL?

The so-called StarChase[1] system mounts a compressed air launcher behind the grille of a police cruiser. During a pursuit, a laser targets the fleeing vehicle and StarChase launches a small projectile containing a GPS module that attaches to it. The module then transmits the fleeing vehicle's coordinates back to dispatch, where a dispatcher can track it via a secure Internet connection. StarChase helps police avoid the risks associated with high-speed pursuits, but it also helps ensure that they "get their man." For the longest time, police were faced with a simple but difficult chase/don't chase decision. StarChase is designed to avoid pursuits altogether and ensure that the police can still locate criminals who refuse to stop.

StarChase is interesting from a criminal procedure standpoint. As soon as someone's movements are tracked, regardless of whether the person is a criminal suspect, Fourth Amendment questions are presented.

StarChase LLC

DISCUSS Does StarChase comply with Fourth Amendment requirements?

▶ Purpose and Elements of the Fourth Amendment

The Fourth Amendment to the U.S. Constitution reflects one of the primary grievances early American colonists had toward the Crown. The British Parliament, intent on rooting out smuggling activities taking place in the American colonies, issued writs of assistance, which permitted unlimited searches. Officials needed no justification to obtain writs of assistance, and there was no judicial supervision designed to limit the scope of the searches authorized by the writs. The practice was not well received in the American colonies. By adopting the Fourth Amendment, the framers of the Constitution placed significant restrictions on searches conducted by government officials.

The Fourth Amendment contains two basic clauses: The **reasonableness clause**, which proscribes unreasonable searches and seizures, is followed by the **warrant clause**, which says that "no Warrants shall issue, but upon probable cause, supported by Oath or affirmation, and particularly describing the place to be searched, and the persons or things to be seized." A fundamental question has been raised about these two clauses. They are joined in the text of the Fourth Amendment by the conjunction *and*, which has led to a great deal of debate over whether the two clauses are related or separate. Some people have argued that the warrant clause gives meaning to the reasonableness clause, in that it automatically renders unreasonable a search that is not conducted with a warrant. Others have argued that the search-and-seizure clause and the warrant clause should be read separately. Their position is that the reasonableness of a search should not depend on whether a warrant was obtained or on whether there was a good excuse for not obtaining a warrant.

The Supreme Court has staked out the middle ground. As it stated in *Mincey* v. *Arizona* (437 U.S. 385 [1978]), "The Fourth Amendment proscribes all unreasonable searches and seizures, and it is a cardinal principle that searches conducted outside the judicial process, without prior approval by judge or magistrate, are per se unreasonable under the Fourth Amendment, subject to a few specifically established and well delineated exceptions" (p. 390) (see also *Vale* v. *Louisiana*, 399 U.S. 30 [1970]).

Basically, the rule of thumb is that a search warrant (or an arrest warrant, in the case of a seizure of a person) should be procured whenever practical. If, however, there is an emergency or other such exception, such as a significant risk to public safety, a warrant may not be necessary. This third view is most common today.

Basic Terminology

The Fourth Amendment protects *persons*, *houses*, *papers*, and *effects* from unreasonable searches and seizures. Few court cases have turned on the meanings of these terms, but it is still important to define them.

LEARNING OUTCOMES 1 Outline the history, purpose, and essential elements of the Fourth Amendment.

The term *person* encompasses the individual as a whole, both internally and externally. An arrest, for example, is a seizure of a person. If a police officer pulls up the sleeves of a suspected drug user to look for needle tracks, this is a search of a *person* within the meaning of the Fourth Amendment.

In the early twentieth century, the Supreme Court ruled that the Fourth Amendment applied only to searches and seizures of tangible items (*Olmstead* v. *United States*, 277 U.S. 438 [1928]). Oral communications fell outside the scope of the Fourth Amendment, so surveillance of conversations, regardless of how it was pursued, did not enjoy constitutional protections. Today, however, in the wake of *Katz* v. *United States* (389 U.S. 347 [1967]), the Supreme Court has stated emphatically that oral communications trigger the protections of the Fourth Amendment. Thus, the definition of *person* for purposes of the Fourth Amendment not only includes the person's internal and external physical body but also (most) oral communications made by people.

House is a term that is broadly construed to mean any structure that a person uses as a residence (and frequently a business) on either a temporary or long-term basis. A hotel room or its equivalent is considered a "house," as it is a temporary residence that enjoys Fourth Amendment protection. Also, a garage or other structure not connected to a house can also fall within the meaning of a "house" under the Fourth Amendment. Whether a garage is actually a house, though, depends on a number of considerations, which we examine later in this chapter. An open field, by contrast, does not trigger the protection of the Fourth Amendment because it is not a house. (Open fields and curtilage are defined later on in this chapter.)

Papers and effects include nearly all personal items. Business records, letters, diaries, memos, and countless other forms of tangible evidence can be defined as *papers*. *Effects* is the catch-all category. Anything that is not a person, house, or paper is probably an effect. Effects can include cars, luggage, clothing, weapons, contraband, and the fruits of criminal activity. If the police activity in question does not involve a person, house, paper, or effect, no Fourth Amendment protections exist. In reality, though, almost any conceivable tangible item or form of communication falls within the protection of the Fourth Amendment. What becomes important, then, is determining precisely when the Fourth Amendment applies and when a search or seizure can be considered reasonable.

How to Analyze the Fourth Amendment

To fully grasp the Fourth Amendment, it is necessary to understand (1) which police activities trigger its protections and (2) what justification is required for the police to engage in certain types of activities (see Figure 3–1). In determining when the Fourth Amendment is triggered, it is important to draw a distinction between a **search** and a **seizure**. Each action triggers the protections of the Fourth Amendment, but each is distinctly different. In addition, the law that governs searches is not the same as the law that governs seizures.

The second stage in the Fourth Amendment analysis requires focusing on the **reasonableness** of the search or seizure. In other words, once the protections of the Fourth Amendment were triggered, did the police act in line with Fourth Amendment requirements? For example, if a person is arrested, did the police have adequate reason to believe that the person arrested

> To fully grasp the Fourth Amendment, it is necessary to understand (1) which police activities trigger its protections and (2) what justification is required for the police to engage in certain types of activities.

Step 1:
Identify activities that trigger the Fourth Amendment.

Step 2:
Identify the required justification.

FIGURE 3–1 Understanding the Fourth Amendment.

in fact committed the crime? When the courts focus on the reasonableness of a search or seizure, they speak in terms of *justification*. If the police (or other government actors) engage in a search or seizure without justification, they violate the Fourth Amendment.

The only justification mentioned in the Fourth Amendment is *probable cause*. The untrained observer may be inclined to think that any search or seizure based on a lesser degree of certainty than probable cause would violate the Fourth Amendment. For a time, this was the case. In recent decades, however, the Supreme Court has carved out exceptions to the Fourth Amendment's probable cause requirement. Basically, the Court has ruled that there are certain situations in which the police can seize people and/or look for evidence with a lesser degree of certainty than probable cause.

► When a Search Occurs

A search is, as the term suggests, an activity geared toward finding evidence to be used in a criminal prosecution. That said, not every act of looking for evidence can be considered a search *within the meaning of the Fourth Amendment*. To define when a search takes place, two important factors need to be considered: (1) whether the presumed search is a product of **government action** and (2) whether the intrusion violates a person's **reasonable expectation of privacy**. The following subsections look at these in some detail. Also see Figure 3–2.

> Not every act of looking for evidence can be considered a search *within the meaning of the Fourth Amendment.*

| government action | infringement on a person's reasonable oxpootation of privacy |

FIGURE 3–2 Elements of a Fourth Amendment Search.

Government Action

The Fourth Amendment's protection against unreasonable searches and seizures has been limited by the courts to conduct that is governmental in nature. Thus, when a private individual seizes evidence or otherwise conducts a search, the protections of the Fourth Amendment are not triggered. For example, if Angela knows that her neighbor Larry has a large supply of stolen stereo equipment in the garage behind his house, she could conceivably enter his garage, seize the evidence, and turn it over to the police. They, in turn, could use the evidence, and other information provided by Angela, to arrest Larry. Of course, Angela could be found guilty of criminal trespass, but as far as the Fourth Amendment is concerned, she committed no constitutional violations. Assuming that Angela acted independent of the police, she acted in a private capacity.

The inapplicability of the Fourth Amendment to searches or seizures carried out by private individuals was first recognized by the Supreme Court in **Burdeau v. McDowell (256 U.S. 465 [1921])**. In that case, some individuals illegally entered McDowell's business office and seized records. The records were later turned over to the attorney general of the United States, who planned to use them against McDowell in court. McDowell sought return of the records, and the district court granted his petition. However, the Supreme Court eventually stated that the Fourth Amendment's "origin and

history clearly show that it was intended as a restraint upon the activities of sovereign authority, and was not intended to be a limitation upon other than governmental agencies" (p. 475).

The Court's decision in *Burdeau* has survived through several subsequent landmark cases. For example, in *Coolidge* v. *New Hampshire* (403 U.S. 443 [1971]), the Court stated that if a private person "wholly on [his] own initiative" turns over evidence to authorities, "[t]here can be no doubt under existing law that the articles would later [be] admissible in evidence" (p. 487). Similarly, in *Walter* v. *United States* (447 U.S. 649 [1980]), the Court ruled that "a wrongful search and seizure conducted by a private party does not violate the Fourth Amendment and . . . does not deprive the government of the right to use evidence that it has acquired [from the third party] lawfully" (p. 656).

What Are Government Officials?

A uniformed police officer acting in his or her official capacity is a *government official* within the meaning of the Fourth Amendment. However, the police represent a comparatively small percentage of one branch of government: The executive branch. Numerous other officials are also responsible for enforcing the law.

Even those individuals whose actions will never result in a criminal prosecution are bound by Fourth Amendment restrictions. For example, in the case of *Camara* v. *Municipal Court* (387 U.S. 523 [1967]), the Court held that regulatory officials conducting health and safety inspections can be considered government actors for purposes of the Fourth Amendment. This ruling has been expanded, in fact, to apply to numerous other government officials, including fire inspectors (*Michigan* v. *Tyler*, 436 U.S. 499 [1978]); Occupational, Safety, and Health Administration (OSHA) inspectors (*Marshall* v. *Barlow's, Inc.*, 436 U.S. 307 [1978]); federal mine inspectors (*Donovan* v. *Dewey*, 452 U.S. 594 [1981]); and even public school teachers (*New Jersey* v. *T.L.O.*, 469 U.S. 325 [1985]).

The situation is decidedly less clear, however, for individuals who perform clear law enforcement functions but are not employed by the government per se. This includes store detectives (for example, *Gillett* v. *State*, 588 S.W.2d 361, Tex.

Think About It...

A "Moonlighting" Scenario Officer Clark is a sworn policeman by day and a private security guard by night. One night, while on duty in the parking lot outside a major retail store, Clark witnessed Lenore Rand, a patron whom he suspected of shoplifting, leaving the store. Clark confronted Rand, seized her bag, and discovered several items that she had not paid for. The incident was reported and the evidence was turned over to the police. May Rand mount a Fourth Amendment challenge to Clark's actions?

bikeriderlondon/Shutterstock

Government Actor		Not Totally Clear	Not a Government Actor
Uniformed police officer acting in his or her official capacity		Certain store detectives	Private person
Regulatory officials conducting health and safety inspections		Certain security guards	
Fire inspectors		Insurance inspectors	
Occupational, Safety, and Health Administration inspectors			
Federal mine inspectors			
Teachers			
Private person working at behest of a government actor			

FIGURE 3–3 Identifying Government Actors for Fourth Amendment Purposes (Some Examples).

Crim.App. [1979]), security guards (*Stanfield* v. *State*, 666 P.2d 1294 [Okl.Crim. 1983]), and insurance inspectors (*Lester* v. *State*, 145 Ga.App. 847 [1978]). At the risk of simplification, the rule is this: When a private source is used deliberately in place of the police, Fourth Amendment protections are triggered. That is, the officials are said to be acting in a government capacity. See Figure 3–3 for a summary of this discussion.

When Do Private Individuals Become Government Agents?

An otherwise private person can become a government official if he or she acts at the behest of a government official. In *Coolidge* v. *New Hampshire* (403 U.S. 443 [1971]), the Supreme Court stated that "[t]he test . . . is whether [the private person] in light of all the circumstances of the case, must be regarded as having acted as an 'instrument' or agent of the state" (p. 487). Simply put, when government officials join in on a private search or instruct a private individual to conduct a search, the private individual can be viewed as a government actor within the meaning of the Fourth Amendment.

A variation on this line of cases is one in which a government official does not actively participate in or order a search or seizure but instead merely provides information that leads to a private search or seizure. For example, in *People* v. *Boettner* (80 Misc.2d 3 [1974]), a court upheld a search conducted by private university officials based on information supplied to them by the police. In support of its decision, the court noted that the private search was carried out without the knowledge of the police, who, at the time, were proceeding with their own investigation of the incident.

When a Private Search Becomes Governmental

An otherwise private search may also be turned into a government search when the government recipient of the items seized by the private party subjects the evidence to a search that is *substantially more intrusive* than the private search. In **United States v. Jacobsen (466 U.S. 109 [1984])**, Federal Express employees (who are not government actors) opened a damaged package and found several packages containing a suspicious white powder. They closed the package and then summoned federal agents, who reopened the packages and conducted a field test on the substances. The Supreme Court held, "The agent's viewing of what a private party had freely made available for his inspection did not violate the Fourth Amendment" (p. 119), and the field test had nothing more than a "de minimus [minimal] impact on any protected property interest."

Think About It...

The Scope of a Private Search Glen Olson stands accused of poisoning dogs in his neighborhood by means of feeding them dog biscuits lined with a harmful chemical. Olson's girlfriend, in a desperate attempt to bring her boyfriend's cruelty to a halt, turned a bag of dog biscuits over to the police that presumably contained the chemical used to poison the helpless animals. Because the police were not sure what the substance in the biscuits was, they took the biscuits to a laboratory and subjected them to a chemical analysis. Laboratory technicians found that the substance was a chemical known to bring about violent illness. May Olson move to suppress the evidence on the grounds that the laboratory analysis triggered the protections of the Fourth Amendment?

Reasonable Expectation of Privacy

LEARNING OUTCOMES 2

Define searches within the context of the Fourth Amendment.

Government action alone is not enough to implicate the Fourth Amendment. Coupled with government action, the Fourth Amendment is triggered only when the law enforcement activity in question infringes on a person's reasonable expectation of privacy. In other words, there are times when police officers and other government officials look for evidence (as in an open field, for instance) but do not act intrusively enough so as to trigger the Fourth Amendment.

Prior to 1967, the definition of a *search* was closely tied to property interests. Police action would only be deemed a search if it physically infringed on an individual's property. The activity basically had to amount to common-law trespassing for it to be considered a search. Any police activity that was not trespassory in nature was not considered a search. This definition became outdated in the landmark decision of *Katz* v. *United States* (389 U.S. 347 [1967]).

In *Katz*, federal agents placed a listening device outside a phone booth in which Katz was having a conversation. Katz made incriminating statements during the course of his conversation, and the Federal Bureau of Investigation (FBI) sought to use the statements against him at trial. The lower court ruled that the FBI's activities did not amount to a search because there was no physical entry into the phone booth. The Supreme Court reversed that decision, holding that the Fourth Amendment "protects people, not places," and so its reach "cannot turn upon the presence or absence of a physical intrusion into any given enclosure" (p. 353). Instead, the Fourth Amendment definition of a *search* turns on the concept of privacy. In the Court's words, "The Government's activities in electronically listening to and recording words violated the privacy upon which [Katz] justifiably relied while using the telephone booth and thus constituted a 'search and seizure' within the meaning of the Fourth Amendment" (p. 353).

Despite the seemingly profound change in the search-and-seizure definition following *Katz*, several subsequent decisions have interpreted the *Katz* ruling rather narrowly. For instance, in *California* v. *Greenwood* (486 U.S. 35 [1988]), the Supreme Court ruled that a Fourth Amendment search or seizure occurs only when (1) the citizen has a manifested subjective expectation of privacy and (2) the expectation of privacy is one that society (through the eyes of a court) is willing to accept as objectively reasonable.

Undercover Agents and False Friends

What happens when a person privately conveys information to another individual who is, in fact, an undercover agent, or as

some people describe such a person, a "false friend"? In *Hoffa* v. *United States* (385 U.S. 293 [1966]), the Supreme Court sought to answer this question. The defendant, Hoffa, had a conversation with a union official who was in Hoffa's private suite by invitation but who was, in fact, a government informant. The informant reported what Hoffa said to government officials, and Hoffa sought to have the evidence excluded on the grounds that it was an illegal search. The Supreme Court disagreed with this decision, noting that the informant "was not a surreptitious eavesdropper" (p. 302) but a person who "was in the suite by invitation and every conversation which he heard was either directed to him or knowingly carried on in his presence" (p. 302).

A more difficult question arose in *United States* v. *On Lee* (343 U.S. 747 [1952]). *On Lee* addressed the issue of whether an undercover agent could wear a recording device during a conversation with a suspected criminal. The majority ruled that this activity did not constitute a search, again, because the informant was invited into the area where the conversation took place. Justice Burton dissented, however, noting that the recorder "amount[s] to [the agent] surreptitiously bringing [the police] with him" (p. 766). The majority countered by arguing that the listening device was simply designed to improve the accuracy of the evidence obtained by the informant. Other cases have been decided in a similar fashion (for example, *United States* v. *White*, 401 U.S. 745 [1971]; *Lopez* v. *United States*, 373 U.S. 427 [1963]).

At a glance, it may seem that *On Lee* and *Katz* are at odds with one another. After all, both involved surreptitious recordings. How do we draw a distinction? In *On Lee*, the information was conveyed voluntarily to a false friend. In *Katz*, the information was *not* voluntarily surrendered to the authorities who were listening in on the conversation. Also, in *On Lee* the recording was just that. It was not an intercepted communication, as was the case in *Katz*. Generally speaking, then, when people voluntarily convey information or provide material to third parties, they cannot have a reasonable expectation of privacy (even if those third parties are best friends) because the third parties could easily turn the information over to authorities.

Abandoned Property

What if an individual abandons his or her property, such as leaving it in a public place or discarding it in the trash? This question came up in the case of *California* v. *Greenwood*. In that case, the Court reached the following decision:

> [G]arbage bags left on or at the side of a public street are readily accessible to animals, children, scavengers, snoops, and other members of the public. Moreover, respondents placed their refuse at the curb for the express purpose of conveying it to a third party, the trash collector, who might himself have sorted through respondents' trash or permitted others, such as the police, to do so. Accordingly, having deposited their garbage in an area particularly suited for public inspection and, in a manner of speaking, public consumption, for the express purpose of having strangers take it, respondents could have no reasonable expectation of privacy in the inculpatory items they discarded. (p. 40)

Coupled with government action, the Fourth Amendment is triggered only when the law enforcement activity in question infringes on a person's reasonable expectation of privacy.

A "False Friend" Scenario John Quinn was put in jail after being arrested as a homicide suspect. The prosecutor did not think she had enough evidence to proceed to trial, so she asked a police officer to dress in street clothes, pose as a jail inmate, and strike up a conversation with Quinn. The officer was placed in the same cell with Quinn and began to make small talk with him. Eventually, Quinn mentioned that he was involved in the murder of Valerie Hutton but that he was not the "trigger man." Quinn's attorney moved to have the statements suppressed on the grounds that a Fourth Amendment violation took place, arguing that Quinn had a reasonable expectation of privacy that his conversation would not be shared with or repeated to other individuals. Does Quinn have a reasonable expectation of privacy in this regard?

Although *Greenwood* dealt exclusively with discarded trash, it extends to other types of abandonment. For example, if a murder suspect discarded a gun on public property, it would be considered abandoned. Why? A person cannot have a reasonable expectation of privacy in a public place or an "open field" (see the next section).

Open Fields and Curtilage

The physical setting in which police activity takes place is also important in determining whether the Fourth Amendment applies. Clearly, the inside of a residence is protected by the Fourth Amendment, but what about the outside? And if the outside is protected, how far beyond the residence can the strictures of the Fourth Amendment be expected to apply?

In providing answers to these questions, the courts refer to the term *curtilage*. According to the Supreme Court (***Oliver* v. *United States*, 466 U.S. 170 [1984]**), **curtilage** is the "area to which extends the intimate activity associated with the sanctity of a man's home and the privacies of life" (p. 225). This definition should be contrasted with the definition of an **open field**, which is any unoccupied or undeveloped real property falling outside the curtilage of a home (p. 170). Figure 3–4 distinguishes among a house, curtilage, and open field.

Open fields do not enjoy Fourth Amendment protection, but homes and curtilage do. Note, however, that open fields

Open field

Curtilage

House

FIGURE 3–4 Relationship between House, Curtilage, and Open Field.

need not be *open* or *fields* to fall beyond the reach of the Fourth Amendment. If a barn that is located 50 yards from a house is not used for "intimate activities," it *can* be considered an open field, even though it is located on private property (see *United States* v. *Dunn*, 480 U.S. 294 [1987]). This is because "[o]pen fields do not provide the setting for those intimate activities that the [Fourth] Amendment is intended to shelter from government interference or surveillance" (*Oliver* v. *United States*, p. 179). Likewise,

> [t]here is no societal interest in protecting the privacy of those activities, such as the cultivation of crops, that occur in open fields. Moreover, as a practical matter, these lands usually are accessible to the public and the police in ways that a home, office or commercial structure would not be. It is not generally true that fences or [No Trespassing] signs effectively bar the public from viewing open fields in rural areas. (p. 179)

What if police perform so-called flyovers (aerial surveillance from a fixed-wing aircraft and/or helicopter)? In *California* v. *Ciraolo* (476 U.S. 207 [1986]), the Supreme Court ruled that naked-eye observation of a fenced-in backyard from a height of 1,000 feet did not constitute a search. The logic offered by the Court was that in "an age where private and commercial flight in the public airways is routine, it is unreasonable for respondent to expect that his marijuana plants were constitutionally

Is a Public Street an Open Field? Officer Perez suspects that a local man is growing marijuana in his backyard but cannot tell for certain because of the large fence surrounding the house. To find out, Perez places a stepladder on a nearby public sidewalk, climbs up to the top, peers over the fence, and observes several dozen marijuana plants growing in the man's garden. Has a search occurred in this situation?

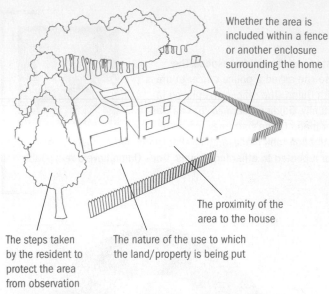

Whether the area is included within a fence or another enclosure surrounding the home

The proximity of the area to the house

The steps taken by the resident to protect the area from observation

The nature of the use to which the land/property is being put

FIGURE 3–5 Factors Courts Use to Distinguish Between Open Fields and Curtilage.

protected" from such observation (p. 215). Similarly, in *Florida* v. *Riley* (488 U.S. 445 [1989]), the Court held that the Fourth Amendment was not implicated when the police flew a helicopter at an altitude of 400 feet over the defendant's partially covered greenhouse, which was found to contain marijuana. Figure 3–5 summarizes factors courts will consider to distinguish between cartilage and open fields.

Tracking Devices

In **United States v. Knotts (460 U.S. 276 [1983])**, the Supreme Court decided on the constitutionality of federal agents' actions of placing a "beeper" (a tracking device) in a container and tracking the container to the defendant's cabin. The Court concluded that "[a] person travelling in an automobile on public thoroughfares has no reasonable expectation of privacy in his movements from one place to another" (p. 281) (see also *United States* v. *Karo*, 468 U.S. 705 [1984]).

In 2012, the Supreme Court was confronted with a similar scenario, this time involving global positioning system (GPS) monitoring. The government obtained a warrant to install a GPS tracking device on a woman's car. It authorized the device to be placed on the vehicle within 10 days, and within the District of Columbia. The device was actually placed on the vehicle on the 11th day, and in Maryland, in violation of the warrant. Thus, the device was put on the vehicle without a warrant. The government tracked the vehicle for 28 days and used information thereby obtained to bring a case against the woman's husband. The Supreme Court held that "[t]he Government's attachment of the GPS device to the vehicle, and its use of that device to monitor the vehicle's movements, constitutes a search under the Fourth Amendment" (**United States v. Jones, 565 U.S. ___ [2012]**).

Unanswered in *Jones* was the question of whether the police should have obtained a warrant before affixing the tracking device to Jones's vehicle.

The Third Circuit did answer this question, however, and the case was the subject of the case featured at the end of Chapter 1. It will be interesting to see whether the Supreme Court eventually tackles the issue.

Sensory Enhancement

The rules become significantly more complicated when law enforcement officials use so-called *enhancement devices* to look for evidence. Enhancement devices can include flashlights, drug dogs, satellite photography, thermal imagery, and so on. Whatever their form, the devices are designed to enhance or replace the ability of the police to identify and discern criminal evidence or crime itself.[2]

The availability of sophisticated technology is also determinative in deciding which sensory enhancement devices the police can use. In **Kyllo v. United States (533 U.S. 27 [2001])**, law enforcement officials were suspicious that marijuana was being grown in Kyllo's home. Agents scanned his home using a thermal imaging device (also known as FLIR, for Forward Looking Infrared). The scan revealed that Kyllo's garage roof and side wall were relatively hot compared to the rest of his home. Based in part on the results from the thermal imager, a federal magistrate issued a warrant to search Kyllo's home. However, the Supreme Court declared that

> [w]here . . . the Government uses a device that is not in general public use, to explore details of a private home that would previously have been unknowable without physical intrusion, the surveillance is a Fourth Amendment "search," and is presumptively unreasonable without a warrant. (p. 40)

The courts will also consider the extent to which a sensory enhancement device actually enhances the natural senses. In doing this, several courts have distinguished between devices that *enhance* the senses versus those that *replace* the senses (see Figure 3–6). Generally, an enhancement device that is used to assist the senses (as binoculars do, for instance) is less likely to implicate the Fourth Amendment than a device that replaces the senses (as some satellites do). The permissibility of the use of binoculars can be attributed to the argument that police officers sometimes wish to avoid detection during the course of observation. Flashlights are clearly devices that enhance the natural senses, and courts have ruled that, when used, they do not trigger the Fourth Amendment (*Texas* v. *Brown*, 460 U.S. 730 [1983]; *United States* v. *Dunn*).

- The nature of the place surveilled
- The nature of the activity surveilled
- The care taken to ensure privacy
- The lawfulness of the vantage point
- The availability of sophisticated technology
- The extent to which the technology used enhances or replaces the natural senses

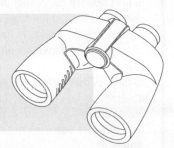

FIGURE 3–6 Factors Courts Use to Consider whether a Sensory Enhancement Device Is Appropriate.

A slightly more controversial device is a drug dog. Some courts have ruled that their use does not trigger the Fourth Amendment under certain circumstances (for example, **United States v. Place, 462 U.S. 696 [1983]**), but the issue is unresolved because one could argue that a drug dog's senses are used to *replace* an officer's senses. In fact, in *Commonwealth* v. *Johnston* (515 Pa. 454 [1987]), the court ruled that law enforcement officers' use of drug dogs violated the state constitution because "a free society will not remain free if police may use this, or any other crime detection device, at random and without reason" (p. 165). The courts also need to consider *where* drug-sniffing dogs are used.

In a 2013 case, *Florida* v. *Jardines*, 569 U.S. ___ (2013), the Supreme Court was confronted with the question of whether an officer's decision to let a narcotics-sniffing dog sniff around the front door of a man's house constituted a search. The Court decided it was, and based its reasoning on the concept of curtilage. Had the officer entered the house, a search would have undoubtedly occurred. In contrast, had the dog detected the narcotics from a public sidewalk, a search *would not* have occurred. But was the porch considered curtilage? Indeed it was. The Court applied this creative logic:

> To find a visitor knocking on the door is routine (even if sometimes unwelcome); to spot that same visitor exploring the front path with a metal detector, or marching his bloodhound into the garden before saying hello and asking permission, would inspire most of us to—well, call the police.

Figure 3–7 contains a summary of the discussion in this and the preceding few subsections. It calls attention to situations and places in which no expectation of privacy generally exists.

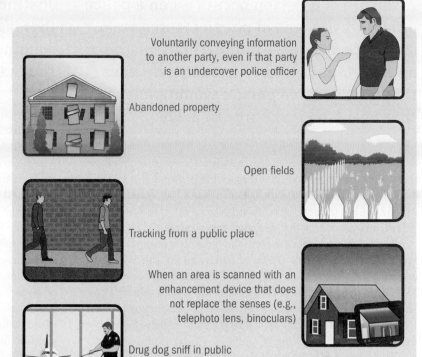

Voluntarily conveying information to another party, even if that party is an undercover police officer

Abandoned property

Open fields

Tracking from a public place

When an area is scanned with an enhancement device that does not replace the senses (e.g., telephoto lens, binoculars)

Drug dog sniff in public areas (e.g., airport)

FIGURE 3–7 Situations and Places in which No Expectation of Privacy Exists.

▶ When a Seizure Occurs

The definition of *seizure* has a very specific meaning in criminal procedure. It is not the case that something must be physically grasped for a seizure to take place. Indeed, the police can stop short of actually touching a person, but their actions can still constitute a seizure. At the other extreme, though, there are certain things the police can do to inconvenience people without triggering the Fourth Amendment. It is important to distinguish between two types of seizures: (1) seizures of property and (2) seizures of persons.

Seizures of Property

As the Supreme Court declared in *United States* v. *Jacobsen*, a **seizure of property** occurs "when there is some meaningful interference with an individual's possessory interest in that property."

In determining if a piece of property is seized, courts often refer to people's *actual* and *constructive* possessions. A piece of property is in a person's actual possession if he or she is physically holding or grasping the property. Constructive possession, by comparison, refers to possession of property without physical contact (for example, a bag that is next to a person on the ground but not in his or her hands). A piece of property is seized, therefore, if the police remove it from a person's actual or constructive possession, such as when they take a person's luggage at an airport and move it into another room to be searched (see *United States* v. *Place*).

Relatively few cases concerning seizures of property are encountered. Usually, property is seized *after* a search occurs. When a search is declared unlawful, the seizure of the property that follows is generally unconstitutional because of the exclusionary rule. However, there are certain cases in which seizure occurs apart from a search. For example, in **Soldal v. Cook County (506 U.S. 56 [1992])**, the question before the Supreme Court was whether the Fourth Amendment applied when a family's trailer was removed from a trailer park. The Court held that the Fourth Amendment applied, meaning a seizure occurred.

Seizures of Persons

A **seizure of a person** occurs when a police officer—by means of physical force or show of authority—intentionally restrains an individual's liberty 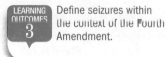 in such a manner that a reasonable person would believe that he or she is not free to leave (*Terry* v. *Ohio*, 392 U.S. 1 [1968]; *United States* v. *Mendenhall*, 446 U.S. 544 [1980]). Another way

LEARNING OUTCOMES 3 — Define seizures within the context of the Fourth Amendment.

> **A seizure of a person occurs when a police officer—by means of physical force or show of authority—intentionally restrains an individual's liberty in such a manner that a reasonable person would believe that he or she is not free to leave.**

of understanding what a Fourth Amendment seizure involves is to ask this question: Would a reasonable person believe that he or she is free to decline the officer's requests or otherwise terminate the encounter? (*Florida* v. *Bostick*, 501 U.S. 429 [1991]). A "no" answer means that a seizure has occurred.

The seizure of a person can take place in a number of ways. For example, a person is seized when he or she is arrested and taken to the police station for questioning (*Dunaway* v. *New York*, 442 U.S. 200 [1979]). A person is also seized if he or she is physically restrained on the street for the purpose of being frisked (for example, *Terry* v. *Ohio*) or if he or she is pulled over by the police while driving.

The seizure of a person does not have to be *physical* for the Fourth Amendment to be implicated. For example, a seizure can occur when a police officer simply questions a person. The Supreme Court stated in *Terry* v. *Ohio* that "not all personal intercourse between policemen and citizens involves 'seizures' of persons" (p. 20, n. 16). Even so, a seizure *does* occur when the officer's conduct in conjunction with the questioning would convince a reasonable person that he or she is not free to leave.

Another way a seizure can occur is by *pursuit*, even if the person sought by the police is never caught. However, it is not always clear whether a pursuit constitutes a seizure. This is important because if the pursuit of a suspect is *not* a seizure, then the police may lawfully chase people without justification. Moreover, if the person discards anything during the chase, the police may lawfully seize the item because the Fourth Amendment does not apply. In fact, as the Supreme Court noted in **California** v. **Hodari D. (499 U.S. 621 [1991])**, when an officer chases a suspect but does not lay hands on him or her, a seizure does not occur until the suspect submits to police authority.

In *Hodari D.*, a police officer chased a suspect on foot. The officer did not have justification to stop or arrest the suspect. The suspect discarded an item during the chase, which the officer stopped to pick up. The Supreme Court upheld the officer's action because the suspect was still in flight at the time the officer picked up the object. The Supreme Court did state in *Hodari D.*, however, that a seizure *does* occur the instant a police officer lays hands on a suspect during a chase, even if the suspect is able to break away from the officer's grasp.

▶ Justification

To this point, only the threshold question of whether the Fourth Amendment applies has been addressed—that is, has a search or seizure occurred? If the answer is no, then the issue will go

> **Justification needs to be in place *a priori*—that is, before a person or evidence is sought in an area protected by the Fourth Amendment.**

no further, and justification will not matter because a search or seizure did not occur. However, if the government's action constitutes a search or seizure, the next issue involves deciding whether the police acted within the limits of the Fourth Amendment. If they did not, then any evidence they obtained during the course of such an illegal search or seizure cannot be used in a criminal proceeding to determine guilt.

Once it has been determined *whether* the Fourth Amendment applies, it is then necessary to consider *what* the Fourth Amendment requires. The warrant requirement will be considered later, but the first and most fundamental inquiry in terms of Fourth Amendment requirements concerns the doctrine of justification. Put simply, the police need to have **justification**, or cause, before they can conduct a search or a seizure. Justification needs to be in place *a priori*—that is, before a person or evidence is sought in an area protected by the Fourth Amendment. The police cannot conduct an illegal search to obtain evidence and then argue *after the fact* that what they did was appropriate.

Justification can be viewed as something of a sliding scale that hinges on the type of intrusion the police make. Generally, the more intrusive the police action, the higher the level of justification required. Conversely, the lower the level of intrusion, the lower the justification needed.

Probable Cause

In principle, the definition of **probable cause** does not vary, regardless of the conduct in which the police engage. It was defined by the Supreme Court in **Beck v. Ohio (379 U.S. 89 [1964])** as more than bare suspicion; it exists when "the facts and circumstances within [the officers'] knowledge and of which they [have] reasonably trustworthy information [are] sufficient to warrant a prudent man in believing that the [suspect] had committed or was committing an offense" (p. 91). In **Brinegar v. United States (338 U.S. 160 [1949])**, the Court added, "The substance of all the definitions of probable cause is a reasonable ground for belief of guilt" (p. 175).

Unfortunately, these legal definitions are of little use to those on the front lines of law enforcement. A more practical definition of probable cause is *more than 50% certainty*. As such, it lies somewhere below absolute certainty and proof beyond a reasonable doubt (the latter of which is necessary to obtain a criminal conviction) and somewhere above a hunch or reasonable suspicion (the latter of which is required to conduct a stop-and-frisk).

The notion of a *prudent man* is akin to the idea of objective reasonableness already discussed. Basically, it means that courts consider what the average person on the street would believe, not what a person who has received special training in the identification and apprehension of lawbreakers (for example, police officer, judge, etc.) would believe. This is not to say, however, that the experience of a police officer is not relevant to a probable cause determination. On the contrary, in *United States* v. *Ortiz* (422 U.S. 891 [1975]), the Court ruled that "officers are entitled to draw reasonable inferences from these facts in light of their knowledge of the area and their prior experience with aliens and smugglers" (p. 897) and, by extension, other people suspected of criminal activity.

Figure 3–8 lists a number of the ingredients in the "recipe" for probable cause as well as examples of each ingredient. Each in isolation is rarely, if ever, enough. Rather, a combination of the factors listed in Figure 3–8 is necessary for probable cause to be established.

Probable cause is always required in the following scenarios:

- Arrests with warrants
- Arrests without warrants
- Searches and seizures of property with warrants
- Searches and seizures of property without warrants

One point needs to be underscored: Probable cause to search does not necessarily create probable cause to arrest, and, alternatively, probable cause to arrest does not necessarily create probable cause to search. With regard to the latter point, consider this hypothetical situation: Police officers pursue a drug suspect into her residence and, based on a hot-pursuit exigency, arrest her in her living room. Assuming probable cause was in place to pursue the suspect, the police do not possess unfettered latitude once in the house to search the place up and down. The courts have placed restrictions on what can be done in a situation such as this—that is, on how far the police can go with a search following (incident) to arrest.

Informants and Other Third Parties

The police routinely rely on information supplied to them by a sophisticated network of *informants*. Informants are not necessarily shady characters connected to the criminal lifestyle—they can also be victims of crime, witnesses of crime, and other police officers.

The courts have attempted to create tests to ensure that information supplied by informants is credible. In *Aguilar* v. *Texas* (378 U.S. 108 [1964]), the Supreme Court ruled that an affidavit based on a tip from an informant must show (1) sufficient information to demonstrate how the informant reached his or her conclusion and (2) sufficient information to establish the reliability of the informant. Stated differently, the first prong asks, "Why should the police believe this person?" and the second prong asks, "How does the informant know what he or she claims to know?"

Probable cause to search does not necessarily create probable cause to arrest, and, alternatively, probable cause to arrest does not necessarily create probable cause to search.

For both prongs of the *Aguilar* test to be satisfied, the police need to supply specific information in their affidavit. A statement to the effect that "this informant has provided reliable information in the past" is not enough. More appropriate is a statement such as "This informant has supplied information in the past that led to the conviction of John Doe" (see also *United States* v. *Freitas*, 716 F.2d 1216 [9th Cir. 1983]).

In *Spinelli* v. *United States* (393 U.S. 410 [1969]), the Supreme Court clarified the meaning of the first prong. It concluded that insufficient knowledge of the details of the reported criminal activity can be overcome if "the tip describe[s] the accused's criminal activity in sufficient detail that the magistrate knows that he is relying on something more substantial than a casual rumor . . . or an accusation based merely on a individual's general reputation" (p. 416). Similarly, in *Draper* v. *United States*, 358 U.S. 307 (1959), the Court ruled that the first prong—the credibility prong—may also be satisfied even though the informant implicates himself or herself in criminal activity, provided that such a statement is against self-interest. An example of a self-interested admission of criminal activity would be one in which the informant seeks to curry favor with the police and/or prosecutors in exchange for supplying information.

The *Aguilar* and *Spinelli* tests were heavily modified in **Illinois v. Gates (462 U.S. 213 [1983])**, when the Supreme Court basically abandoned the two-pronged probable cause analysis and replaced it with a *totality of circumstances* test. Thus, if "a particular informant is known for the unusual reliability of his predictions of certain types of criminal activities in a locality, his failure, in a particular case, to thoroughly set forth the basis of his knowledge surely should not serve as an absolute bar to a finding of probable cause based on his tip" (p. 233). In other words, a deficiency in one prong can be compensated for with an abundant supply of information in the other.

Aguilar, *Spinelli*, and *Gates* were all search cases, which would seem to limit their applicability in the arrest context, but the *Illinois* v. *Gates* totality of circumstances test is now used for determining probable cause based on information from informants in both the arrest and search/seizure contexts. The courts will give consideration to five factors in determining whether the totality of circumstances creates probable cause:

- when the informant describes how he or she found out about the criminal activity;
- when the informant gives a detailed description of that activity;
- when evidence for the informant's reliability exists;
- when the informant predicts criminal activity that is later corroborated by the police; and
- when the informant implicates himself or herself in criminal activity.

In cases where the informant is not implicated in some criminal activity, but is a victim or eyewitness, the Supreme Court has relaxed the *Aguilar/Spinelli/Gates* tests. For example, in *Jaben* v. *United States* (381 U.S. 214 [1965]), the Court held that "whereas some supporting information concerning the credibility of informants in narcotics cases or other common

1. Prior record
   Examples
   - Suspect has prior conviction for same activity.
   - Suspect is known to have committed similar offense in the past.
2. Flight from the scene
   Examples
   - Suspect sees police and runs away.
   - Suspect flees from an apartment known for drug dealing.
3. Suspicious conduct
   Examples
   - Suspect fails to make eye contact with officers.
   - Suspect demonstrates extreme inattention to police.
   - Suspect appears startled by police and turns quickly away.
   - Suspect is seen "casing" a jewelry store.
4. Admissions
   Examples
   - Suspect tells informant that he/she committed a crime.
   - Officer overhears two men talking about their involvement in a crime.
   - Officer hears one suspect tell another, "I told you not to do it."
5. Incriminating evidence
   Examples
   - Suspect found in possession of drug paraphernalia.
   - Burglary suspect found with pillowcase full of loot.
   - Sack of cash and ski mask found in robbery suspect's car.
6. Unusual hour
   Examples
   - At 2:30 AM, an officer saw a man depart a darkened property where valuables were kept.
   - At 3:30 AM, an officer observed two men walking in a business area who then fled at the sight of the officer.
7. Suspect resembles the perpetrator
   Examples
   - Suspect wears clothes similar to the perpetrator of a crime.
   - Suspect is an occupant of the same car thought to flee the scene of a robbery.
   - The number of suspects in the car is the same as the number of suspects reportedly involved in the crime.
8. Evasive and untruthful responses to questions
   Examples
   - Suspect caught in a lie about where she was coming from.
   - Suspect gives false name and/or identification.
   - Suspect uses an alias.
   - Suspect denies owning a car that is registered to him.
   - Suspect gives vague and confusing answers to an officer's questions.
9. Obvious attempt to hide something
   Examples
   - Officers hear a toilet flush when arriving to serve a search warrant.
   - Officer observes a suspect push something under the seat of his car.
   - Suspect is looking into the trunk of a vehicle but slams it quickly on seeing a police officer.
10. Presence in a high-crime area or near a crime scene
    Examples
    - Officer observes a vehicle leave the scene of a burglary at which no other people or vehicles were located.
    - The suspect is the only pedestrian near the scene of a burglary.
    - Officers observe an apparent drug transaction in an area known for narcotics activity.
11. Furtive gestures
    Examples
    - Officers observe the passenger in a vehicle duck from view.
    - Suspect makes a quick hand-to-mouth movement.
    - Suspect turns away from the officers when they announce their presence.
    - The driver of a vehicle reaches under the seat.
12. Knowing too much
    Example
    - Suspect volunteers information that only the perpetrator could possibly know.

FIGURE 3–8 Ingredients in the Probable Cause Recipe.

1959	1964	1969	1983
***Draper* v. *United States*, 358 U.S. 307** An informant's tip coupled with corroboration by officers may result in probable cause for arrest.	***Aguilar* v. *Texas*, 378 U.S. 108** An affidavit based on a tip from an informant must show (1) sufficient information to demonstrate how the informant reached his/her decision and (2) sufficient information to establish the reliability of the informant. These are known as the credibility and reliability prongs, respectively.	***Spinelli* v. *United States*, 393 U.S. 410** Insufficient knowledge about the details of the reported criminal activity can be overcome if "the tip describe[s] the accused's criminal activity in sufficient detail that the magistrate knows that he is relying on something more substantial than a casual rumor...or an accusation based merely on a individual's general reputation" (p. 416).	***Illinois* v. *Gates*, 462 U.S. 213** The *Aguilar/Spinelli* test is replaced with a "totality of circumstances" analysis. A weakness in one prong can be made up for with a stronger showing in the other. In other words, an informant who has proven quite reliable but not necessarily credible may provide enough information to support a probable cause determination.

garden varieties of crime may be required, such information is not so necessary in the context of the case before us." Similar rulings have been applied when the informants have been other police officers. For example, in *United States* v. *Ventresca* (380 U.S. 102 [1965], p. 111), the Supreme Court ruled that "[o]bservations of fellow officers of the Government engaged in a common investigation are plainly a reliable basis for a warrant applied for by one of their number." Of course, probable cause is still required. When probable cause is found lacking, the arrest will most likely be deemed unconstitutional.

Firsthand Knowledge

When is probable cause established by someone other than a third party—namely, the arresting officer? The courts usually do not worry about the truthfulness or accuracy of the arresting officer's observations but, instead, whether probable cause to arrest was in place. In particular, the courts have required that probable cause *to* arrest must be determined independently from the arrest itself, meaning that probable cause to arrest must be required *before* the arrest. In *Sibron* v. *New York* (392 U.S. 40 [1968]), the Supreme Court stated, "It is axiomatic that an incident search may not precede an arrest and serve as part of its justification" (p. 63). In simple terms, this means that police cannot search people and illegally seize evidence simply for the purpose of establishing probable cause to arrest. Stated differently, probable cause cannot be established in hindsight. It should be pointed out, though, that evidence encountered during law enforcement activity that does not constitute an arrest or a search (a pat down, for instance) can create or be used to establish probable cause to arrest or conduct a further search, depending on the circumstances. (Pat-down searches are discussed in a following section.)

In another case (*United States* v. *Di Re*, 332 U.S. 581 [1948]), the Supreme Court held that a suspect's proximity to criminal activity is not enough to establish probable cause to arrest. In that case, officers arrested Di Re from the front seat of a car on the grounds that there were two other men in the car passing counterfeit ration coupons between one another. The Court noted that had Di Re even seen the activity, "it would not follow that he knew they were ration coupons, and if he saw that they were ration coupons, it would not follow

that he would know them to be counterfeit" (p. 593). Simply put, then, proximity to criminal activity does not create probable cause to arrest (see also *Johnson* v. *United States*, 333 U.S. 10 [1948]).

In yet another case, one in which the police had a valid warrant authorizing them to search a tavern, the Court held that the search warrant did not give them permission to search the patrons of the bar, including the petitioner, because they were not named in the warrant (*Ybarra* v. *Illinois*, 444 U.S. 85 [1979]). If, however, the arresting officer were armed with additional information (from a third-party informant, for example), then probable cause would be easier to establish (see *Ker* v. *California*, 374 U.S. 23 [1963]). What is more, courts regularly defer to officers' judgments as to whether probable cause was in place (see *Maryland* v. *Pringle*, 540 U.S. 366 [2003]).

- -

Other Standards

To recap, the justification required to conduct a search or a seizure within the meaning of the Fourth Amendment is probable cause. However, much police activity does not reach the level of intrusion that occurs when a search or seizure is carried out. For example, the police routinely have to confront people on the street in order to question them and to pull over automobiles to enforce traffic laws. If probable cause were required under such circumstances, the police could do little in terms of investigating suspicious activity.

LEARNING OUTCOMES 4

Explain the concept of justification, including probable cause.

Reasonable Suspicion

Recognizing how essential certain *lesser intrusions* are to the police mission, the Supreme Court established in **Terry v. Ohio (392 U.S. 1 [1968])** a different level of justification for such activities, namely, **reasonable suspicion**. Reasonable suspicion is something below probable cause but above a hunch. *Terry* dealt with so-called stop-and-frisk activities, but reasonable suspicion as a standard of justification permeates other arenas of criminal procedure (for example, traffic stops).

In *Terry*, an officer's attention was drawn to two men on a street corner who appeared to the officer to be "casing" a store

Having Probable Cause to Arrest An observant police officer was on foot patrol and noticed a suspicious person standing at the counter in a convenience store. The person, who had one hand in his coat pocket, appeared to be carrying on a conversation with the clerk, who was reaching into the cash register and appeared to be very nervous. On a hunch that she was witnessing a robbery in progress, the officer quickly entered the store, surprised the person talking to the clerk, arrested him, and upon searching him incident to the arrest, found a handgun in his coat pocket. His attorney moved to suppress the handgun on the grounds that the police officer did not have probable cause to arrest. What should the courts decide?

for a robbery. The officer approached the men and asked them to identify themselves. The officer then proceeded to pat down the men and found a gun on each one. The men were placed under arrest. They tried to suppress the guns, but the Supreme Court eventually held the officer's actions valid in the interest of "effective crime prevention and detection" (p. 22). Balancing an intrusion that was arguably less serious than a search with the interests of society in apprehending lawbreakers, the Court held that a lower standard than probable cause was required because "street encounters between citizens and police officers are incredibly rich in diversity" (p. 13).

There is no clear definition of *reasonable suspicion*, just as there is no clear definition of *probable cause*. As stated in *United States* v. *Cortez* (449 U.S. 411 [1981]),

> Courts have used a variety of terms to capture the elusive concept of what cause is sufficient to authorize police to stop a person. Terms like "articulable reasons" and "founded suspicion" are not self-defining; they fall short of providing clear guidance dispositive of the myriad factual situations that arise. But the essence of all that has been written is that the totality of circumstances— the whole picture—must be taken into account. Based upon that whole picture the detaining officers must have a particularized and objective basis for suspecting the particular person stopped of criminal activity. (p. 417)

As a level of justification lying below probable cause, reasonable suspicion is "considerably less than proof of wrongdoing by a preponderance of evidence" (*United States* v. *Sokolow*, 490 U.S. 1 [1989], p. 7) but more than an unparticularized hunch. Figure 3–9 contains a list of specific factors that can contribute to reasonable suspicion—and some information that *cannot* give rise to reasonable suspicion. Like probable cause, reasonable suspicion can be based on a number of different sources, including informants, but because the reasonable suspicion standard falls below that for probable cause, less information is required.

In *Adams* v. *Williams* (407 U.S. 143 [1972]), for example, the Supreme Court held that reasonable suspicion may be based on an anonymous telephone tip, so long as the police can corroborate certain

details from the informant. In a similar case, **Alabama v. White (496 U.S. 325 [1990])**, the Supreme Court observed, "Reasonable suspicion is a less demanding standard than probable cause not only in the sense that reasonable suspicion can be established with information that is different but also in the sense that reasonable suspicion can arise from information that is less reliable than that required to show probable cause" (p. 330).

In *United States* v. *Hensley* (469 U.S. 221 [1985]), the Supreme Court unanimously held that the reasonable suspicion standard is satisfied when the police rely on "wanted" flyers, even those from other jurisdictions. A restriction on this ruling was that the flyer, regardless of its place of origin, must be based on articulable facts that connect the suspect to criminal activity. The key here is **articulable facts**. Articulable facts are events that are witnessed and can be explained. The opposite of articulable facts would be a gut reaction or a mere hunch.

The Court in *Hensley* also had to decide if a stop based on reasonable suspicion of *prior* criminal activity was permissible under the Fourth Amendment's reasonableness standard. All decisions up to that point had dealt with suspected criminal activity immediately before the officer's arrival or criminal activity likely to have occurred but for the officer's arrival. In *Hensley*, the police stopped a man 12 days after the commission of a robbery for which he was suspected. The Court upheld the police's action and stated that it "would not only hinder the investigation, but might also enable the suspect to flee in the interim and to remain at large" (p. 229) if the officers had not taken action.

To further illustrate the meaning of reasonable suspicion, consider the case of *Sibron* v. *New York*. In that case, the Court held that talking to known addicts and reaching into their

Factors That *May* Give Rise to Reasonable Suspicion	Factors That *Will Not* Give Rise to Reasonable Suspicion
Suspect in high–crime area at unusual hour.	Hunch
Suspect flees from officers.	Rumor
Suspect appears to receive cash in exchange for two small envelopes.	Intuition
Suspect puts television in the trunk of a car in an area where most businesses are closed.	Instinct
Suspect appears to be "casing" a convenience store.	Curiosity

FIGURE 3–9 **Factors that May and Do Not Give Rise to Reasonable Suspicion.**

pockets does not produce reasonable suspicion that criminal activity is afoot. In yet another case, *Brown* v. *Texas* (443 U.S. 47 [1979]), two police officers observed Brown and another man walking away from one another. One of the officers later testified that he thought the officers' arrival broke up some suspicious activity. Officer Venegas approached Brown and asked him to identify himself. Brown refused and was later convicted under a statute that made it illegal to refuse to give an officer one's name and address. According to the Court,

> There is no indication in the record that it was unusual for people to be in the alley. The fact that the appellant was in a neighborhood frequented by drug users, standing alone, is not a basis for concluding that the appellant himself was engaged in criminal conduct. In short, the appellant's activity was no different from the activity of other pedestrians in that neighborhood. (p. 52)

Contrast *Brown* v. *Texas* with the Supreme Court's decision in *Illinois* v. *Wardlow* (528 U.S. 119 [2000]). In that case, Chicago police officers were patrolling an area known for narcotics traffic. Upon seeing the officers, Wardlow ran and was chased down by the police. When he was patted down, the officers found a Colt .38 pistol and arrested him. Wardlow appealed his conviction, arguing that the stop-and-frisk was illegal because the officers did not have reasonable suspicion. The Court disagreed, noting that "a location's characteristics are relevant in determining whether the circumstances are sufficiently suspicious to warrant further investigation" (p. 119). In addition, the Court noted that it was Wardlow's unprovoked flight that aroused the officers' "suspicion" and that "nervous, evasive behavior is another pertinent factor in determining reasonable suspicion, and headlong flight is the consummate act of evasion" (p. 124). Thus, in the Court's view, the officers *did* have reasonable suspicion to stop and frisk Wardlow.

In *United States* v. *Arvizu* (534 U.S. 266 [2002]), the Supreme Court highlighted the importance of the totality of circumstances as well as officers' experience in making a determination of reasonable suspicion. In that case, a border patrol agent in a remote part of Arizona became suspicious of a van that slowed upon seeing him. Also, the driver failed to acknowledge the agent. The agent stopped the van, and the Supreme Court upheld this decision. The Court stated the agent was "entitled to make an assessment of the situation in light of his specialized training and familiarity with the customs of the area's inhabitants" (p. 276).

Because reasonable suspicion is of fundamental importance in criminal procedure, this text will devote an entire chapter to the role it plays in law enforcement activities. Chapter 6 will cover *Terry* stops in detail, focusing carefully on the definitions of *stop* and the scope of the *frisk*.

Administrative Justification

A third level of justification has arisen by virtue of the fact that government entities occasionally conduct searches in circumstances other than criminal investigations. As noted earlier, a search-and-seizure action aimed at obtaining evidence for use in a criminal proceeding cannot occur without appropriate justification. Noncriminal searches also occur, however, so the Supreme Court has created a different level of justification. Instead of being based on reasonableness, the **administrative justification** adopts a balancing approach, weighing the privacy interests of individuals with the interests of society in preserving public safety.

In *Colorado* v. *Bertine* (479 U.S. 367 [1987]), the Court stated that the "standard of probable cause is peculiarly related to criminal investigations, not routine, noncriminal procedures. . . . The probable-cause approach is unhelpful when analysis centers upon the reasonableness of routine administrative caretaking functions, particularly when no claim is made that the protective procedures are a subterfuge for criminal investigations" (p. 317). Accordingly, the courts have required that administrative searches be conducted according to objective, standardized procedures. Also important to note is that authorities cannot use an administrative search as a pretext for a full-blown search.

An informative example of the balancing approach taken in justifying administrative searches can be found in *Vernonia School District* v. *Acton* (115 S. Ct. 2386 [1995]). In that case, the Court decided the fate of a school policy that required athletes to submit to random urinalysis for drugs. The Court allowed the search because it was not geared toward any particular individual. Further, the Court reasoned that athletes in public schools enjoy a lesser expectation of privacy because they must participate in other examinations, they dress together in the locker room, and they participate in the sports *voluntarily*. The government interest cited by the Court was preventing "drug use by our Nation's school children" (p. 2395). This was a controversial decision, indeed, as it seemed to reduce the need for justification set forth explicitly in the Fourth Amendment.

The administrative search rationale has been applied in a number of related situations. For example, the courts have been rather liberal in terms of upholding questionable searches of highly regulated business establishments. In *New York* v. *Burger* (482 U.S. 691 [1987]), for instance, the Supreme Court authorized a warrantless search of an automobile junkyard. In *Donovan* v. *Dewey* (452 U.S. 594 [1981]), the Court upheld the warrantless inspection of mines. The same logic carried over to a case involving the inspection of a gun dealership (*United States* v. *Biswell*, 406 U.S. 311 [1972]). In support of its decisions, the Court argued that people who choose to conduct business in highly regulated environments enjoy a reduced expectation of privacy.

Other decisions have involved such varied enterprises as arson investigations (*Michigan* v. *Clifford*, 464 U.S. 286 [1984]; *Michigan* v. *Tyler*, 436 U.S. 499 [1978]), border checkpoints to stop vehicles in an effort to detect illegal aliens (*United States* v. *Martinez-Fuerte*, 428 U.S. 543 [1976]), searches of impounded vehicles (*Colorado* v. *Bertine*) and other personal items in need of inventorying (*Illinois* v. *Lafayette*, 462 U.S. 640 [1983]), and mandatory drug testing of public and private employees (*National Treasury Employees Union* v. *Von Raab*, 489 U.S. 656 [1989]; *Skinner* v. *Railway Labor Executives' Association*, 489 U.S. 602 [1989]). In *Skinner*, the Court observed,

> In light of the limited discretion exercised by the railroad employers under the [drug testing] regulations, the surpassing safety interest served by toxicological tests in this context, and the diminished expectation of privacy that attaches to information pertaining to the fitness of covered employees, we believe it is reasonable to conduct such tests

in the absence of a warrant or reasonable suspicion that any particular employee may be impaired. (p. 602)

It should be noted that the courts have placed significant restrictions on the scope of so-called administrative searches. For example, in *Marshall* v. *Barlow's, Inc.*, the Court ruled as unconstitutional searches based on the Occupational Safety and Health Act of businesses that had not been heavily regulated in the past. At the same time, administrative searches can give great latitude in terms of seizing contraband and evidence of a crime to whomever conducts the search. As stated in *New York* v. *Burger*, "The discovery of evidence of crimes in the course of an otherwise proper administrative inspection does not render that search illegal or the administrative scheme suspect" (p. 716).

Further, if the purpose of an administrative search is to detect evidence of criminal activity, probable cause is required. This was the decision reached in the recent Supreme Court case *City of Indianapolis* v. *Edmond* (531 U.S. 32 [2000]). In it, the Court decided whether a city's suspicionless checkpoints for detecting illegal drugs were constitutional. The Court held that stops such as those conducted during checkpoint operations require individualized suspicion. In addition, "because the checkpoint program's primary purpose [was] indistinguishable from the general interest in crime control" (p. 32), it was deemed in violation of the Fourth Amendment.

Moving on, the administrative search justification that has been applied to regulatory inspections has also been applied to situations involving "special needs beyond the normal need for law enforcement" (*Skinner* v. *Railway Labor Executives' Association*, p. 619). In *New Jersey* v. *TLO* (469 U.S. 325 [1985]), a student's purse was searched by an assistant principal, who suspected that the student was violating the school's policy against smoking. The search turned up marijuana, but according to the Supreme Court, "the schoolchild's legitimate expectation of privacy and the school's equally legitimate need to maintain an environment in which learning can take place" (p. 340) did not need a warrant or even probable cause. Similarly, in *O'Connor* v. *Ortega* (480 U.S. 709 [1987]), a case involving the warrantless search of a government employee's office, and in *Griffin* v. *Wisconsin* (483 U.S. 868 [1987]), a case in which a probation officer searched the home of a probationer under the officer's supervision, the Court invoked the logic of special needs beyond normal law enforcement to dispense with the warrant requirement.

Given the importance of administrative justification, a whole chapter (Chapter 7) is devoted to it later in this book. The actions supported by administrative justification are often called "special needs" and "regulatory" searches. In closing, see Figure 3–10 for a summary of the distinctions between administrative justification, reasonable suspicion, and probable cause.

Standard	Defined	When Required
Probable cause	More certain than not	• All arrests • All searches
Reasonable suspicion	Anywhere between probable cause and a hunch	• Stop and frisk • Vehicle stops • Certain detentions
Administrative justification	Balancing act between public interest and individual privacy expectations	• Administrative "searches" • Inspections • Regulatory actions

FIGURE 3–10 Standards of Justification Summarized.

Probable Cause to Search?

Officer Wheetley stopped Harris for an expired license plate. On approaching Harris's vehicle, Wheetley noticed that Harris was "visibly nervous" and unable to stop shaking. He also observed an open beer can in a cup holder. Wheetley asked for permission to search Harris's vehicle. Harris refused. Wheetley then went back to his cruiser and retrieved Aldo, a trained narcotics detection dog, and walked him around Harris's vehicle on a "free air sniff." Aldo alerted to the driver's side door handle. Harris then searched the truck, finding various items used in the manufacture of methamphetamine, but not the drug itself.

Harris moved to suppress the items, claiming that Aldo's "false positive" did not give Wheetley probable cause to search. In a hearing on the subject, Wheetley testified to Aldo's training record and training performance. On cross-examination, Harris's attorney focused not on Aldo's training, but on the dog's certification and performance in the field. Wheetley acknowledged that Aldo's certification had expired before he stopped Harris and also that he did not keep complete records on Aldo's field performance.

The trial court denied the motion and an intermediate state court affirmed. The Florida Supreme Court, however, reversed, holding that "the fact that the dog has been trained and certified is simply not enough to establish probable cause." It held the state must present "evidence of the dog's performance history," including records showing "how often the dog has alerted in the field without illegal contraband having been found." It further noted that without such records, Wheetley could never have probable cause to conclude Aldo was capable of reliably detecting contraband.

The U.S. Supreme Court took up the case and, in *Florida* v. *Harris* (568 U.S. ____ [2013]), decided that the state is not required to supply evidence of a drug dog's performance history in order to determine whether probable cause to search exists. The Court's rationale was as follows:

> In testing whether an officer has probable cause to conduct a search, all that is required is the kind of "fair probability" on which "reasonable and prudent [people] act." *Illinois* v. *Gates*, 462 U.S. 213, 235. To evaluate whether the State has met this practical and common-sensical standard, this Court has consistently looked to the totality of the circumstances and rejected rigid rules, bright-line tests, and mechanistic inquiries. *Ibid.* . . . The Florida Supreme Court flouted this established approach by creating a strict evidentiary checklist to assess a drug-detection dog's reliability. Requiring the State to introduce comprehensive documentation of the dog's prior hits and misses in the field, and holding that absent field records will preclude a finding of probable cause no matter how much other proof the State offers, is the antithesis of a totality-of-the-circumstances approach.

The Supreme Court's decision in this case raises certain questions:

1. What are the drawbacks and advantages of drug dogs?
2. To what extent should a drug dog's history of false positives and false negatives factor into questions concerning the admissibility of evidence?
3. Do you agree with the Supreme Court's decision?

Outline the history, purpose, and essential elements of the Fourth Amendment.

The Fourth Amendment to the U.S. Constitution reflects one of the primary grievances early American colonists had toward the Crown. It protects people from unreasonable searches and seizures. The key parts of the Fourth Amendment are the warrant clause and the reasonableness clause.

1. Explain the various perspectives on the relationship between the warrant and reasonable clauses of the Fourth Amendment.

2. When does the Fourth Amendment apply?

reasonableness clause The first part of the Fourth Amendment: "The right of the people to be secure in their persons, houses, papers, and effects, against unreasonable searches and seizures, shall not be violated. . . ."

warrant clause The second part of the Fourth Amendment: ". . . and no Warrants shall issue, but upon probable cause, supported by Oath or affirmation, and particularly describing the place to be searched, and the persons or things to be seized."

search For Fourth Amendment purposes, a government action that infringes on one's reasonable expectation of privacy.

seizure One of two government actions (the other being searches) restricted by the Fourth Amendment. Seizures can be of persons or property.

reasonableness When evaluating questionable police action, it is first necessary to determine whether the Fourth Amendment applies. If it does, then we ask, "Did the police act in line with Fourth Amendment requirements?" This question is concerned with the reasonableness of the action in question.

Define searches within the context of the Fourth Amendment.

A search occurs when government actors infringe on a legitimate expectation of privacy while looking for evidence.

Key Cases

Burdeau v. McDowell

United States v. Jacobsen

Katz v. United States

California v. Greenwood

Hoffa v. United States

United States v. On Lee

Oliver v. United States

United States v. Knotts

United States v. Jones

Kyllo v. United States

United States v. Place

1. When does a search occur?

2. When can private parties be considered government actors?

3. What cannot be done following a private-party search?

4. Explain the concept of reasonable expectation of privacy.

government action Action on the part of paid government officials, usually police officers. Government action is one of two requirements (the other being infringement on one's reasonable expectation of privacy) that must be in place for a Fourth Amendment search to occur.

reasonable expectation of privacy An expectation of privacy that society (through the eyes of a judge) is prepared to accept as reasonable. For a search to occur, a reasonable expectation of privacy must be infringed upon by a government actor.

curtilage The "area to which extends the intimate activity associated with the sanctity of a man's home and the privacies of life" (*Oliver* v. *United States*, 466 U.S. 170 [1984], p. 225).

open field Any unoccupied or undeveloped real property falling outside the curtilage of a home (*Oliver* v. *United States*, 466 U.S. 170 [1984], p. 170).

LEARNING OUTCOMES 3

Define seizures within the context of the Fourth Amendment.

Seizures of property occur when a meaningful possessory interest is interfered with. Seizures of persons occur when a reasonable person would believe he or she is not free to leave.

Key Cases

Soldal v. Cook County

California v. Hodari D.

1. What is a seizure?
2. Distinguish between seizure of a person and seizure of property.

seizure of property A seizure of property occurs when "there is some meaningful interference with an individual's possessory interest in that property" (*United States* v. *Jacobsen*, 466 U.S. 109 [1984]).

seizure of a person A seizure of a person occurs when a police officer—by means of physical force or show of authority—intentionally restrains an individual's liberty in such a manner that a reasonable person would believe that he or she is not free to leave (*Terry* v. *Ohio*, 392 U.S. 1 [1968]; *United States* v. *Mendenhall*, 446 U.S. 544 [1980]).

LEARNING OUTCOMES 4

Explain the concept of justification, including probable cause.

Justification requires that police must have cause before they can conduct a search or a seizure. There are three standards of justification necessary for searches and seizures. Probable cause falls between 51% and 100% certainty and is required for arrests and searches with and without warrants. Reasonable suspicion, which falls below 51% certainty but above a hunch, is required for stops and investigative detentions that fall short of arrests. Administrative justification is required in administrative and "special needs beyond law enforcement" searches.

Key Cases

Beck v. Ohio

Brinegar v. United States

Illinois v. Gates

Terry v. Ohio

Alabama v. White

1. What is justification and why is it important?
2. Compare and contrast probable cause, reasonable suspicion, and administrative justification.
3. What is the purpose of administrative justification?

justification Also known as *cause*, justification is necessary for the police to engage in actions that trigger the Fourth Amendment. Examples of justification include probable cause and reasonable suspicion.

probable cause More than bare suspicion; it exists when "the facts and circumstances within [the officers'] knowledge and of which they [have] reasonably trustworthy information [are] sufficient to warrant a prudent man in believing that the [suspect] had committed or was committing an offense" (*Beck* v. *Ohio*, 379 U.S. 89 [1964], p. 91). In practical terms, it refers to more than 50% certainty. The comparable civil standard is preponderance of evidence.

reasonable suspicion Justification that falls below probable cause but above a hunch. Reasonable suspicion is a Court-created justification; it is not mentioned in the Fourth Amendment. Reasonable suspicion is necessary for police to engage in stop-and-frisk activities.

articulable facts Events that are witnessed and can be explained. Contrast articulable facts with hunches and guesses. Articulable facts are necessary for establishing probable cause.

administrative justification A standard used to support certain regulatory and special needs searches. Created by the Supreme Court, it adopts a balancing approach, weighing the privacy interests of individuals with the interests of society in preserving public safety.

4

"Certain searches and arrests must be supported by warrants, and search and arrest warrants must be served properly, otherwise a guilty person may go free."

Searches and Arrests with Warrants

1 Summarize the activities governed by the Fourth Amendment.

2 Outline the components of search and arrest warrants.

3 Explain when arrest warrants are required and how they should be served.

4 Explain when search warrants are required and how they should be served.

5 Explain how bodily intrusions, the use of tracking devices, and electronic surveillance create "special circumstances" for Fourth Amendment purposes.

INTRO · A FOURTH AMENDMENT VIOLATION?

Following are the facts from a Supreme Court case (*Messerschmidt v. Millender*, 565 U.S. ___ [2012]):

> Shelly Kelly was afraid that she would be attacked by her boyfriend, Jerry Ray Bowen, while she moved out of her apartment. She therefore requested police protection. Two officers arrived, but they were called away to an emergency. As soon as the officers left, Bowen showed up at the apartment, yelled "I told you never to call the cops on me bitch!" and attacked Kelly, attempting to throw her over a second-story landing. After Kelly escaped to her car, Bowen pointed a sawed-off shotgun at her and threatened to kill her if she tried to leave. Kelly nonetheless sped away as Bowen fired five shots at the car, blowing out one of its tires.

> Kelly later met with Detective Curt Messerschmidt to discuss the incident. She described the attack in detail, mentioned that Bowen had previously assaulted her, that he had ties to the Mona Park Crips gang, and that he might be staying at the home of his former foster mother, Augusta Millender. Following this conversation, Messerschmidt conducted a detailed investigation, during which he confirmed Bowen's connection to the Millenders' home, verified his membership in two gangs, and learned that Bowen had been

arrested and convicted for numerous violent and firearm-related offenses. Based on this investigation, Messerschmidt drafted an application for a warrant authorizing a search of the Millenders' home for all firearms and ammunition, as well as evidence indicating gang membership.

DISCUSS Pay close attention to the evidence Messerschmidt was interested in searching for. Is his description of the items sought adequate? Why or why not?

▶ Introduction to Warrants

Five types of activities are governed by the Fourth Amendment: arrests with warrants, arrests without warrants, searches with warrants, searches without warrants, and the seizure of evidence (see Figure 4–1). This chapter's focus is on searches and arrests with warrants, which can include the seizure of evidence.

The Fourth Amendment seems fairly clear with respect to warrants: "and no Warrants shall issue, but upon probable cause, supported by Oath or affirmation, and particularly describing the place to be searched, and the persons or things to be seized." Despite this seemingly simple language, the Fourth Amendment's warrant requirement has been litigated extensively in the courts. The courts have focused on the meaning of *probable cause* as well as acceptable sources of information used to determine the presence of probable cause. Many decisions have also focused on the Fourth Amendment's requirement that warrants be supported by "oath or affirmation" and on the particularity requirement.

The Fourth Amendment's warrant requirement has been litigated extensively in the courts.

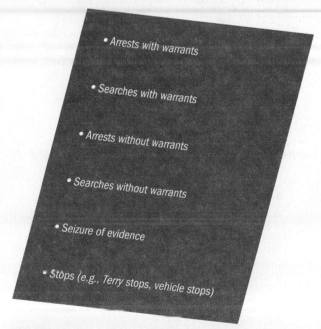

- Arrests with warrants
- Searches with warrants
- Arrests without warrants
- Searches without warrants
- Seizure of evidence
- Stops (e.g., Terry stops, vehicle stops)

FIGURE 4–1 Activities Governed by the Fourth Amendment.

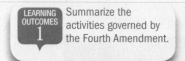

LEARNING OUTCOMES 1 Summarize the activities governed by the Fourth Amendment.

Generally, a search warrant is required for *any* type of search, regardless of where it is conducted, provided that (1) there are no exigent (that is, emergency) circumstances and (2) the search is not one justified on so-called administrative grounds. Even searches pursuant to arrest and searches under the automobile exception are justified in terms of exigencies. Arrest warrants, by contrast, are required for arrests in private places, provided exigent circumstances are absent.

▶ Warrant Components

An **arrest warrant** or a **search warrant** (see Figures 4–2 and 4–3 for examples) has three essential components (see Figure 4–4). First, it must be issued by a neutral and detached magistrate. Second, a showing of probable cause is required. Finally, it must conform to the Fourth Amendment's particularity requirement. The first requirement—a neutral and detached magistrate—is the same regardless of the type of warrant. The probable cause and particularity requirements differ depending on the type of warrant in question. These requirements are considered in the following subsections.

Neutral and Detached Magistrate

The logic for requiring a **neutral and detached magistrate** in the issuance of an arrest or a search warrant was described by the Supreme Court over 50 years ago in *Johnson* v. *United States* (333 U.S. 10 [1948]):

> The point of the Fourth Amendment . . . is not that it denies law enforcement the support of the usual inferences reasonable men draw from evidence. Its protection consists in requiring that those inferences be drawn by a neutral and detached magistrate instead of being judged by the officer engaged in the often competitive enterprise of ferreting out crime. (pp. 13–14)

Most judges are considered neutral and detached. Even so, the Supreme Court has focused, in a number of cases, on this first critical warrant requirement. In **Coolidge v. New Hampshire (403 U.S. 443 [1971])**, the Court declared that a state attorney general cannot issue a search warrant. State attorney generals are chief prosecutors and thus inclined to side with law enforcement officers. Similarly, in *United States* v. *United States District Court* (407 U.S. 297 [1972]), the Court decided that the president, acting through the attorney general of the United States, cannot authorize electronic surveillance without judicial approval. Justice Powell observed,

> The Fourth Amendment does not contemplate the executive officers of Government as neutral and detached magistrates. Their duty and responsibility is to enforce the laws, to investigate and to prosecute. . . . [T]hose charged with this investigative and prosecutorial duty should not be the sole judges of when to utilize constitutionally sensitive means in pursuing their tasks. The historical judgment, which the Fourth Amendment accepts, is that unreviewed executive discretion may yield too readily to pressures to obtain incriminating evidence and overlook potential invasions of privacy and protected speech. (p. 317)

There have also been some cases in which the Court has focused on the extent to which a judge can be viewed as neutral and detached. For example, in **Lo-Ji Sales, Inc. v. New York (442 U.S. 319 [1979])**, a magistrate issued a warrant for two obscene items, but he also authorized the police to seize any other items that they might find obscene upon examination of the location to be searched. The magistrate then accompanied the officers on the search, discovered items that he deemed to be obscene, and added them to the initial warrant. The items were then admitted as evidence against the defendants. The Supreme Court declared that the magistrate was not acting in a neutral and detached capacity: "[H]e was not acting as a judicial officer but as an adjunct law-enforcement officer" (p. 327).

Finally, if a magistrate has a financial interest in the issuance of warrants, he or she cannot be considered neutral and detached. This issue was presented to the Supreme Court in *Connally* v. *Georgia* (429 U.S. 245 [1977]). A Georgia statute authorized unsalaried magistrates to receive five dollars for each warrant issued but no money for warrant applications that were denied. The Court unanimously held that the statute violated the Constitution, citing that "judicial action by an officer of a court who has 'a direct, personal, substantial, pecuniary interest' in his conclusion to issue or to deny the warrant" (p. 250) cannot possibly be considered neutral and detached.

WARRANT OF ARREST ON COMPLAINT

(RCr 2.04,2.06)
(Caption)

TO ALL PEACE OFFICERS

You are hereby commanded to arrest _____

(Name of defendant)

and bring him forthwith before judge of the District Court (or, if he be absent or unable to act, before the nearest available magistrate) to answer a complaint made by _____ charging him with the offense of reckless driving.

Issued this _____ day of _____, 19_____.

_____
Judge

(Indorsement as to bail)

The defendant may give bail in the amount of $_____.

_____
Judge

(Amended October 14, 20___, effective January 1, 20___.)

FIGURE 4–2 Sample Arrest Warrant.

IN THE SUPERIOR COURT DISTRICT, EAST DESERT DIVISION
SUNNY COUNTY, STATE OF CALIFORNIA

SEARCH WARRANT
(PENAL CODE 1529)

THE PEOPLE OF THE STATE OF CALIFORNIA: To any Sheriff, Constable, Peace Officer or Policeman in Sunny County:

Proof, by Affidavit, having been this day made before me by:

JOHN SMITH
Deputy Sheriff
Sunny County Sheriff's Department

THAT THERE IS PROBABLE CAUSE FOR BELIEVING THAT:

There are narcotics, controlled substances and restricted substances records and documents which tend to show that a felony to wit, Transportation of Controlled Substances, in violation of Health and Safety Code Section 11379, Possession for Sales of Controlled Substances, in violation of Health and Safety Code Section 11378, Sales of Controlled Substances, in violation of Health and Safety Code Section 11379, is being committed in Sunny County, State of California.

YOU ARE THEREFORE COMMANDED at any time of the day or night _____ to make a search of:

PREMISES TO BE SEARCHED:

The premises located at:

123 MAIN STREET, #2A
TOWN OF PLEASANTVILLE
SUNNY COUNTY
STATE OF CALIFORNIA

The location is further described as a multi-unit apartment complex located on the east side of Main Street south of Oak Dr. The complex consists of numerous two-story buildings with each building having multiple apartments. Apartment 2A is located in building "F", which is located at the northwest corner of the complex. The exterior is tan stucco with grayish/blue trim and a gray composite shingle roof. Apartment 2A has the numbers "2A" which are black and approximately 4 inches tall, affixed to the wood trim to the right of the front door, which faces north.

And all rooms, attics, basements, cellars, safes, vaults, closed or locked containers, trash receptacles and other parts therein, surrounding grounds, garages, sheds, storage rooms, vehicles, campers, trailers and outbuildings of any kind located thereon.

And all persons located on or at the premises. And all vehicles belonging to or in the control of said persons.

And you are hereby authorized to answer all incoming telephone calls received at the premises and the vehicles to be searched and to further seize and record all the incoming telephonic pager numbers and messages received at the premises and the vehicles to be searched and to seize all telephonic "fax" messages received at the premises and the vehicles to be searched. And to determine if the aforementioned telephone calls, telephonic messages, or "faxed" messages are related to illegal activities.

FOR THE FOLLOWING PROPERTY:

Methamphetamine and paraphernalia commonly associated with the possession, packaging, and sale of methamphetamine such as scales, weighing devices and measuring devices; packaging materials including paper bindles, glass vials, plastic baggies, foil; processing materials including sifters, filters, screens and cutting agents; recordation of the purchase and/or sales of methamphetamine including ledgers, notebooks, pay/owe sheets, customer lists, video tapes and phone answering machine tape recordings, personal phone books; personal photographs which document the possession, sales and/or possession for sales of methamphetamine; and proceeds from the sales of methamphetamine consisting of currency.

Financial records including expenses incurred in obtaining chemicals and apparatus and income derived from sales of narcotics and other controlled substances as well as records showing legitimate income or the lack thereof and general living expenses.

Serial numbers, model numbers, identifying marks and descriptions of all personal property including, but not limited to, televisions, radios, stereo equipment, and other electrical devices, appliances, hand and power tools, firearms, bicycles, items of jewelry, silver, gold and coins which can be identified as stolen and/or evidence of the crime of Burglary and/or Possession of Stolen Property or property which is readily traded for narcotics in lieu of cash.

All articles of personal property which will identify persons in control of the premises, storage areas or containers where controlled substances may be found, including keys to those areas that may be locked, rental agreements and receipts, deeds of trust, documents or papers bearing names, canceled mail, paycheck stubs and other employment records, tax documents and personal identification.

AND IF YOU FIND THE SAME OR ANY PART THEREOF, to bring it forthwith before me at my courtroom

GIVEN UNDER MY HAND, and dated this *20th* day of August 2011.

Richard K. Griffin
Judge of the Superior Court
East Desert Division
Sunny County
State of California

FIGURE 4–3 Example of a Search Warrant.

Probable Cause Showing

LEARNING OUTCOMES 2 Outline the components of search and arrest warrants.

"Probable cause" was defined in Chapter 3. As such, there is no need to revisit the definition here, but it is important to point out that probable cause is required as a component of a valid warrant. Also, the meaning of probable cause—as opposed to the sources of information that give rise to it—differs, depending on whether an arrest or a search warrant is issued.

Probable Cause in an Arrest Warrant

The showing of probable cause in an arrest warrant is not particularly complex. The officer applying for the warrant must simply

> The meaning of probable cause—as opposed to the sources of information that give rise to it—differs, depending on whether an arrest or a search warrant is issued.

show probable cause that the person to be arrested committed the crime in question. When applying for an *arrest* warrant, the officer is not required to show probable cause that the suspect will be found at a particular location. In *Payton* v. *New York* (445 U.S. 573 [1980]), the majority stated, "If there is sufficient evidence of a citizen's participation in a felony to persuade a judicial officer that his arrest is justified, it is constitutionally reasonable to require him to open his doors to the officers of the law" (pp. 602–603).

Probable Cause in a Search Warrant

The showing of probable cause in a search warrant is twofold. First, the officer applying for the search warrant must show probable cause that the items to be seized are connected with criminal activity. Second, the officer must show probable cause that the items to be seized are in the location to be searched. Note that this second requirement does not apply to an arrest warrant.

Particularity

The Fourth Amendment expressly provides that warrants particularly describe the "place to be searched, and the persons or things to be seized." Not surprisingly, the **particularity**

Neutral and detached magistrate

Particularity (arrest warrant—description of person sought; search warrant—specify place to be searched and items sought)

Probable cause showing (arrest warrant—probable cause person sought committed the crime; search warrant—probable cause items sought are at a specific location and connected with a crime)

FIGURE 4–4 Warrant Requirements.

requirement differs, depending on the type of warrant issued. For an arrest warrant, the particularity requirement is easily satisfied. The particularity requirement for a search warrant, however, is far more complex.

Particularity in an Arrest Warrant

There are two ways to satisfy the Fourth Amendment's particularity requirement with regard to an arrest warrant. First, if the suspect's name is known, then simply supplying his or her name is enough to meet the particularity requirement. In some situations, however, the suspect's name is *not* known. Then, a specific description of the suspect is sufficient and a "John Doe" warrant will be issued. As long as other officers may locate the suspect with reasonable effort, the suspect's name is not required.

Arrest warrants are rarely issued without the suspect's name. This is not to suggest, however, that the police almost always know the suspect's name. Remember, there are many occasions involving warrantless arrests (for example, after a suspect is caught fleeing the bank he or she just robbed) in which an arrest can be made without knowledge of the suspect's name. As long as probable cause is in place, the name of the suspect is not essential (regardless of whether a warrant is issued).

Particularly in a Search Warrant

The particularity requirement for a search warrant is twofold. First, the warrant must specify the *place* to be searched. Next, the warrant must specify the *items* to be seized. The reason for this particularity requirement stems from the framers' concerns with so-called general warrants. *General warrants*, which were issued by the English Crown, permitted basically limitless searches for evidence of treason.

Contrary to popular belief, a search warrant does not need to state with absolute precision the place to be searched. It "is enough if the description is such that the officer with a search warrant can, with reasonable effort, ascertain and identify the place intended" (*Steele* v. *United States*, 267 U.S. 498 [1925],

Think About It…

Who Was That Bald Man? The police have in their possession the video from a security camera at a bank that was recently robbed. The suspect is a white male, six feet tall, with a mustache, a bald head, a scar on his left cheek, and a tattoo of a skull and crossbones on his neck. May the police apply for an arrest warrant based on this information, even if they never learn the suspect's name prior to applying for the warrant?

John Worrall

The particularity requirement for a search warrant is twofold. First, the warrant must specify the *place* to be searched. Next, the warrant must specify the *items* to be seized.

Think About It...

The Fourth Amendment's Particularity Requirement A police officer obtained a search warrant from a judge that authorized the seizure of "numerous marijuana plants and growing equipment" at 123 Main Street. Does this warrant comport with the Fourth Amendment's particularity requirement? What if the warrant also authorized the seizure of "stolen stereo equipment"?

Cavan Images, LLC/ Getty Images

p. 503). However, the items mentioned in the warrant should be described with sufficient specificity that a reasonable officer would know where to look for them.

In situations in which the warrant incorrectly specifies the place to be searched, the courts will focus on the reasonableness of the officers' mistake. For example, in **Maryland v. Garrison (480 U.S. 79 [1987])**, police officers obtained a warrant to search the person of Lawrence McWebb and the premises known as "2036 Park Avenue, third-floor apartment." They believed that McWebb's apartment occupied the entire third floor when, in fact, there were two apartments on that floor—one of which belonged to Garrison. The Court held that the warrant was valid for several reasons: It was based on information by a trusted informant, and the police had inquired with the local utility company and were given the impression that there was only one apartment on the third floor.

As for the items to be seized, the warrant must clearly specify what the police wish to seize. The case of *Lo-Ji Sales, Inc.* v. *New York* is again illustrative. Recall from the discussion about the neutral and detached magistrate requirement that the magistrate in *Lo-Ji Sales* issued a warrant that named two specific items but also permitted the police to seize anything the magistrate considered obscene. The Court unanimously held that the warrant failed to "particularly describe . . . the things to be seized" (p. 319).

Contrast *Lo-Ji Sales* with **Andresen v. Maryland (427 U.S. 463 [1976])**, in which the Court upheld a warrant that authorized the seizure of several items "together with other fruits, instrumentalities and evidence of crime at this [time] known" (p. 479). The Court noted that the crime in question was particularly complex and "could be proved only by piecing together many bits of evidence" (p. 482). This is a controversial decision, indeed, because it suggests that, under certain circumstances, the police can circumvent the Fourth Amendment's particularity requirement.

If the police have a hunch that an item is in a place to be searched but do not include the item in the application for a warrant, the item can be seized under the doctrine of plain view as long as the police are legally authorized (by obtaining a warrant) to be on the premises. Also, if a warrant does not particularly describe the items to be seized (or the place to be searched), then it is not automatically deemed in violation of the Fourth Amendment. If there is an objectively reasonable basis for the officers' mistaken belief, then the warrant will most likely be upheld (see *Massachusetts* v. *Sheppard*, 468 U.S. 981 [1981]). Also, just because an item is not listed in a warrant does not mean that it cannot be seized.

Challenging Warrants

Search warrants are challenged much more often than arrest warrants, mainly because there is so much potential for shortcomings in the affidavit of probable cause. This is especially true in the area of narcotics search warrants, as the evidence sought is often easy to move or dispose of. Following is a partial list of key mistakes/omissions that various courts have used to deny search warrants:

- Failure to state the time and/or time frame drugs were on the premises to be searched (e.g., *Nelms* v. *State*, 568 So. 2d 384 [1990]).

- Failure to connect the evidence sought to the property to be searched (e.g., *Garcia* v. *State*, 872 So. 2d 326 [FL 2004]).

- Reliance in the affidavit on conjecture and generalizations, such as "habitual users of drugs keep drugs and paraphernalia in their home" (*State* v. *Rangitch*, 700 P.2d 823 [WA 1985]).

- Too much reliance on officers' "training and experience."

The list could go on and is limited only by a good defense attorney's imagination. To shed more light on the subject, closely examine the language in Figure 4–5. It includes actual language from a probable cause affidavit, one in which a state supreme court reversed a man's conviction. The court held "there was no particularized nexus linking his home to evidence that he manufactured or sold drugs, and it did not matter that the police could not imagine where else defendant grew marijuana" (*State* v. *Thein*, 977 P.2d 582 [WA 1999]).

▶ Arrest Warrants

An **arrest** is the act of taking an individual into custody for the purpose of charging the person with a criminal offense (or, in the case of a juvenile, a delinquent act). Sometimes a stop (as in "stop-and-frisk," or a vehicle stop) can evolve into a *de facto* arrest in a number of circumstances. The courts will give weight to four factors in making their decision: (1) the purpose of the stop (for example, to question or interrogate a person), (2) the manner in which the stop takes place (for example, stopped by one officer or several), (3) the location in which the stop takes place (for example, stationhouse, street, or home), and (4) the duration of the stop. No single factor is necessarily determinative. If, however, a person is detained by several officers in a stationhouse for several days so as to be interrogated, then the

Based on my experience and training, as well as the corporate knowledge and experience of other fellow law enforcement officers, I am aware that it is generally a common practice for drug traffickers to store at least a portion of their drug inventory and drug related paraphernalia in their common residences. It is generally a common practice for drug traffickers to maintain in their residences records relating to drug trafficking activities, including records maintained on personal computers. Because drug traffickers will in many instances "front" (i.e., sell on consignment) controlled substances in full or partial quantities to their distributors or from their suppliers, such record keeping is necessary to keep track of amounts paid and owed. These records will also be maintained close at hand so as to readily ascertain current balances. Telephone/address listings of clients must be maintained and immediately available in order to efficiently conduct their drug trafficking business. Moreover, it is generally a common practice for traffickers to conceal at their residences large sums of money, either the proceeds of drug sales or to utilize either the proceeds of drugs sales or to utilized [sic] to purchase controlled substances. In this vein, drug traffickers typically make use of currency, wire transfers, cashiers checks and money orders to pay for controlled substances. Evidence of such financial transactions and records related to incoming expenditures of money and wealth in connection drug trafficking would also typically be maintained in residences.

I know from previous training and experiences that it is common practice for drug traffickers to maintain firearms, other weapons and ammunition in their residences for the purpose of protecting their drug inventory and drug proceeds[.] I am aware from my own experience and training that it is common practice for [sic] from law enforcement, but more commonly, from other drug traffickers who may attempt to "rip them off." Firearms and ammunition have been recovered in the majority of residence searches in the drug investigations in which I have been involved.

FIGURE 4–5 **A Flawed Probable Cause Affidavit.**

All four of these criteria should be considered together. For example, if a police/citizen encounter occurs at the stationhouse, the encounter may not be considered an arrest. However, if the encounter is overly lengthy and the citizen is not free to leave, then an arrest has taken place.

1. Purpose
   a. Intent to arrest = Arrest
   b. No intent to arrest = *Terry* stop or nonstop
2. Manner
   a. Person not free to leave = Arrest or *Terry* stop
   b. Person free to leave = Nonstop
3. Location
   a. At police station or in private = Arrest or *Terry* stop
   b. Public = Arrest, *Terry* stop, or nonstop
4. Duration
   a. Lengthy = Arrest
   b. Short = *Terry* stop or nonstop

FIGURE 4–6 **Factors Used to Distinguish Between an Arrest and a Stop.**

court will almost certainly consider such police activity tantamount to an arrest.

See Figure 4–6 for a summary of factors used to distinguish between an arrest and a stop. Also see Figure 4–7 for a summary of several Supreme Court decisions that have focused on the definition of arrest. As you can see, it is sometimes difficult to decide what law enforcement activity constitutes an arrest.

Justice Powell once stated that "a search may cause only an annoyance and temporary inconvenience to the law-abiding citizen, assuming more serious dimensions only when it turns up evidence of criminality [but an] arrest . . . is a serious personal intrusion regardless of whether the person seized is guilty or innocent" (*United States* v. *Watson*, 423 U.S. 411 [1976], p. 428).

Even so, an unconstitutional arrest has little significance by itself in criminal procedure. The reason for this is that the remedy for an illegal arrest is simply a release from custody. It is possible that a person unlawfully arrested may sue, but little recourse is generally available to a person who is unlawfully arrested. Why, then, focus attention on the constitutionality of arrests? The answer is that the constitutionality of an arrest is frequently critical in determining whether seized evidence is admissible in court.

Consider this example: Assume that a police officer arrests a defendant without probable cause. Such an arrest is automatically unconstitutional. Assume also that the officer finds an illegal firearm on the defendant and turns it over to the prosecutor, who decides to use it against the defendant at his trial on firearm charges. The defendant will almost certainly seek to have the firearm excluded as evidence on the grounds that it resulted from an unlawful arrest. In other words, the defendant will argue that the firearm is "fruit of the poisonous tree."

This hypothetical situation is the main reason it is important to study the law of arrest. It is not that the legality of an arrest matters by itself. What is important is that an unconstitutional arrest can lead to the exclusion of evidence. Virtually all arrest cases that make it to the Supreme Court have something in common: A convicted defendant is seeking to have his or her *arrest* declared unconstitutional so the evidence that led to his or her conviction will be suppressed and/or the conviction reversed.

An unconstitutional arrest can lead to the exclusion of evidence.

Henry v. *United States* (361 U.S. 98 [1959]): The Supreme Court found that an arrest occurred when the police stopped a car whose occupants were suspected of transporting illegal alcohol. According to the Court, "When the officers interrupted the two men and restricted their liberty of movement, the arrest, for purposes of this case, was complete."

Terry v. *Ohio* (392 U.S. 1 [1968]): The case that essentially altered the definition of arrest for all time. The Court ruled that a suspect's movements can be restricted without such activity being considered an arrest.

Davis v. *Mississippi* (394 U.S. 721 [1969]): Several youths, including Davis, were taken into custody and fingerprinted as part of a rape investigation. The officers did not have probable cause, and Davis was held for two days and interrogated throughout his detention. On the basis of his fingerprints and confession, Davis was charged, convicted, and sentenced to death. The Supreme Court reversed Davis's conviction on the grounds that detention was too long, too intrusive, and unsupported by probable cause.

Rawlings v. *Kentucky* (448 U.S. 98 [1980]): Several individuals were detained at a house where officers had served an arrest warrant but had failed to find the person named in the warrant. The Court declared that this type of detention amounted to an arrest because there was no probable cause to detain the individuals not named in the warrant. In addition, the detention lasted 45 minutes, which was unnecessarily long, under the circumstances.

Michigan v. *Summers* (452 U.S. 692 [1981]): The Supreme Court held that an individual *can* be detained during a search of his or her house, without such activity rising to the level of an arrest, as long as the police have a search warrant and even if there is no probable cause to arrest him or her.

Florida v. *Royer* (460 U.S. 491 [1983]): "An investigative detention must be temporary and last no longer than is necessary to effectuate the purpose of the stop. Similarly, the investigative methods employed should be the least intrusive means reasonably available to verify or dispel the officer's suspicion in a short period of time" (p. 500).

United States v. *Montoya de Hernandez* (473 U.S. 531 [1985]): The Supreme Court upheld law enforcement officials' 16-hour detention of a suspected drug "balloon swallower" while they waited for nature to take its course, so to speak.

FIGURE 4-7 **Various Supreme Court Cases Concerning the Definition of Arrest.**

When Arrest Warrants Are Required

Under common law, if an arresting officer had probable cause to believe that (1) a person was committing or had committed a felony or (2) a person was committing a certain misdemeanor in the officer's presence, then an arrest warrant was not required. This held true regardless of where the arrest took place, even if it was effected in someone's private home (for example, *Trupiano* v. *United States*, 334 U.S. 699 [1948]). The only real situation in which an arrest warrant *was* required was for a misdemeanor committed out of view of the arresting officer. The logic for this was set forth by the Supreme Court in *Carroll* v. *United States* (267 U.S. 132 [1925]):

> The reason for arrest for misdemeanors without warrant at common law was to promptly suppress breaches of the peace . . . while the reason for arrest without a warrant on a reliable report of a felony was because the public safety and the due apprehension of criminals charged with heinous offenses required that such arrests should be made at once without warrant. (p. 157)

Since 1925, the Supreme Court has stuck to the rule set forth in *Carroll*, subject to two exceptions. First, an arrest in someone's private home cannot be made without a warrant unless exigent circumstances are present. Second, an arrest in the home of a third party is impermissible without a warrant, again providing no exigent circumstances are in place. An example of a third-party situation is one in which the police seek to arrest a person who is visiting a friend's house.

Arrests in the Home

In the landmark decision of **Payton v. New York (445 U.S. 573 [1980])**, the Supreme Court held that the Fourth Amendment prohibits a warrantless, nonconsensual entry into a private home for the purpose of making an arrest. In that case, police officers, after two days of investigation, had assembled enough evidence to establish probable cause to believe that Payton had murdered the manager of a gas station. The officers went to Payton's apartment to arrest him. When no one answered the door, they used a crowbar to open the door and entered the apartment. They did not find Payton, but they did find, in plain view, a .30-caliber shell casing lying on the floor. They seized it and admitted it into evidence at Payton's trial. Payton ultimately surrendered to the police and was indicted for murder. The lower court admitted the shell casing into evidence, but the Supreme Court reversed, stating, "In terms that apply equally to seizures of property and to seizures of persons, the Fourth Amendment has drawn a firm line at the entrance to the house. Absent exigent circumstances, that threshold may

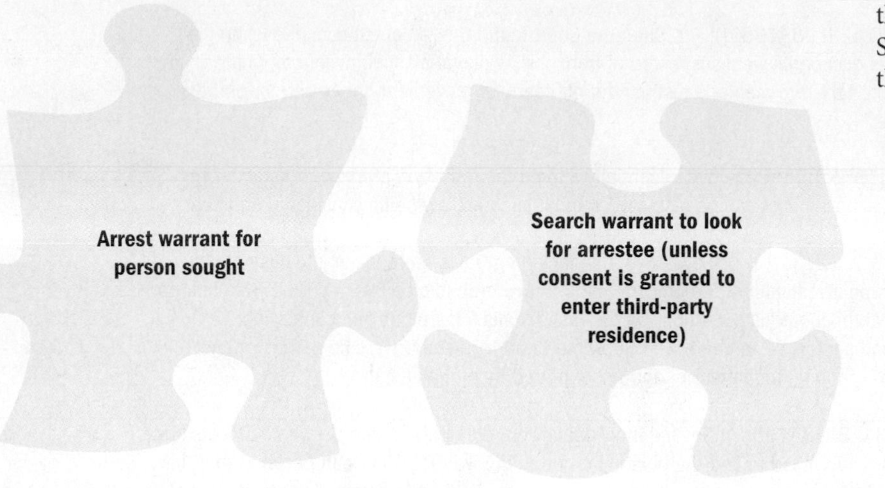

Arrest warrant for person sought

Search warrant to look for arrestee (unless consent is granted to enter third-party residence)

FIGURE 4–8 Third-Party Home Arrest Warrant Requirements.

not reasonably be crossed without a warrant" (p. 590). Justice Stevens also stated, citing an earlier case (*United States* v. *United States District Court*), that "physical entry of the home is the chief evil against which the wording of the Fourth Amendment is directed" (p. 585). In *Payton*, then, the Court handed down a bright-line rule: An arrest in the home must be accompanied by a warrant in the absence of exigent circumstances. The decision in *Kirk* v. *Louisiana* (536 U.S. 635 [2002]) reaffirmed this.

Arrests in Third-Party Homes

Not long after *Payton*, the Supreme Court decided **Steagald v. United States (451 U.S. 204 [1981])**. Justice Marshall expressed concern that although an arrest warrant may protect a person "from an unreasonable seizure, it [does] absolutely nothing to protect [a third party's] privacy interest in being free from an unreasonable invasion and search of his home" (p. 213). Accordingly, the Court decided that in such situations, the police must obtain not only an arrest warrant for the person they seek but also a *separate* warrant to search the third-party residence for the arrestee (see Figure 4–8).

> **LEARNING OUTCOMES 3** Explain when arrest warrants are required and how they should be served.

The facts in *Steagald* were as follows: Acting on an arrest warrant issued for a person by the name of Lyons, Drug Enforcement Administration (DEA) agents entered the home of Steagald. This entry was made without a warrant. While searching Steagald's home for Lyons, the agents found cocaine and other incriminating evidence, but they did not find Lyons. Steagald was arrested and convicted on federal drug charges. He appealed, and the Supreme Court eventually reversed Steagald's conviction. The Court offered the following in support of its position:

> Two distinct interests were implicated by the search in this case—Ricky Lyons' interest in being free from an unreasonable seizure and petitioner's [Steagald's] interest in being free from an unreasonable search of his home. Because the arrest warrant for Lyons addressed only the former interest, the search of petitioner's home was no more reasonable from petitioner's perspective that it would have been if conducted in the absence of any warrant. (p. 216)

The Court's decision in *Steagald* was not without opposition. Justices Rehnquist and White dissented, arguing that the police and judges "will, in their various capacities, have to weigh the time during which a suspect for whom there is an outstanding arrest warrant has been in the building, whether the dwelling is the suspect's home, how long he has lived there, whether he is likely to leave immediately, and a number of related and equally imponderable questions" (p. 213). The majority countered by pointing out that if the police did not need warrants to enter third-party residences, "[a]rmed solely with an arrest warrant for a single person, [the police] . . . could search all the homes of that individual's friends and acquaintances" (p. 215). Such a possibility would be controversial, indeed.

Thus, having an arrest warrant does *not* allow authorities to enter a third-party residence. A warrantless entry into a third-party residence violates the third party's rights. There are two exceptions to this rule, however. First, if the third party consents to a request by police, a search warrant won't be necessary (but the arrest warrant will still be necessary). Second, if there is an emergency, or "exigent circumstances," a warrant may not be required. See Figure 4–9 for a summary of situations in which an arrest warrant is required/not required.

Serving Arrest Warrants

Assuming a valid arrest warrant is in place, the police cannot use any means available to effect the arrest. For example, they cannot kick in a door without having any reason to do so. Similarly, they cannot use deadly force unless absolutely necessary and for the most dangerous of criminal offenders. In almost all

When an arrest warrant is required	**When an arrest warrant is not required**
• In a home/residence absent exigent circumstances	• The arrest is made in public
• In a third-party home; a separate search warrant is also required	• Exigent circumstances exist

FIGURE 4–9 Summary of Arrest Warrant Requirements.

Assuming a valid arrest warrant is in place, the police cannot use any means available to effect the arrest.

cases, the procedures for executing an arrest warrant are laid out in police department policy manuals.

The following subsections focus on four important issues with regard to the service of arrest warrants:

- When the police are required to "knock and announce" their presence
- Whether property damage is acceptable
- When deadly force can be used
- Media presence

The "Knock-and-Announce" Rule

Under common law, the police were entitled to break into a house to make an arrest after announcing their presence and their reason for being there. Today, the method of entry the police can use to serve warrants (arrest and search) is usually set forth in legislation. With regard to federal law enforcement, for example, 18 U.S.C. Section 3109 states that an officer "may break open any outer or inner door or window of a house. . . to execute a search warrant, if, after notice of his authority and purpose, he is refused admittance."

The law also generally requires that police officers announce their presence and state their authority (for example, "Police officers! Search warrant!"). Doing so is important for several reasons: (1) It helps avoid needless destruction of property, (2) it helps prevent violence resulting from unnecessary surprise, and (3) it helps preserve people's dignity and privacy. Of course, in certain situations, these reasons for a **"knock-and-announce" requirement** do not serve their intended purposes. In fact, the second reason can work oppositely from what is intended: If the police are required to announce their presence for all manner of suspects, such an announcement could *result* in violence, rather than reduce the possibility for it. It is thus preferable for police to announce their presence, but it is not constitutionally required (see, for example, **Hudson v. Michigan, 547 U.S. 586 [2006]**). See the accompanying timeline for a summary of key knock-and-announce decisions.

Property Damage

In *Sabbath v. United States* (391 U.S. 585 [1968]), the Supreme Court focused on the extent to which police officers can *break and enter* for the purpose of serving a warrant. In particular, the Court focused on the part of 18 U.S.C. Section 3109 that permits officers to "break open an outer door or window." In *Sabbath*, police officers enlisted the help of a man named Jones, whom they had caught trying to smuggle drugs into the country, to apprehend Sabbath, the man who was to receive the shipment of drugs. Jones agreed to deliver the drugs to Sabbath while the police looked on. After Jones entered the apartment, the officers knocked on the door. Not hearing a response, the officers opened the unlocked door, entered the apartment with guns drawn, and arrested Sabbath. The court of appeals affirmed Sabbath's conviction on the grounds that because the officers did not enter by force, the knock-and-announce rule of Section 3109 was not triggered.

The Supreme Court disagreed with this reasoning, however, and reversed Sabbath's conviction. According to the Court, "An unannounced intrusion into a dwelling—what Section 3109 basically proscribes—is no less an unannounced intrusion whether officers break down a door, force open a chain lock on a partially open door, open a locked door by use of a passkey, or, as here, open a closed but unlocked door" (p. 590). This case seems to suggest that whether physical damage is inflicted to the premises is immaterial. Instead, what is important is merely that officers knock and announce their presence.

In cases in which physical damage to the premises *is* significant, even excessive, the Fourteenth Amendment enters in. In *County of Sacramento* v. *Lewis* (523 U.S. 833 [1998]), a police officer ran over the passenger on a motorcycle, killing her, while pursuing the driver.

The Supreme Court held that because a stop had not occurred, the Fourth Amendment was not implicated. Instead, it held that the Fourteenth Amendment's due process clause was relevant because it protects citizens from arbitrary government action. The Court went on to note that had the police conduct in *Lewis* "shocked the conscience," then the police would have been liable. The Court also observed that "[w]hile prudence would have repressed the [officer's] reaction, the officer's instinct was to do his job as a law enforcement officer, not to induce [the driver of the motorcycle's] lawlessness, or to terrorize, cause harm, or kill" (p. 855).

TIMELINE

Timeline of Knock and Announce Cases

1995	1997	2003	2006
Wilson v. Arkansas, 514 U.S. 927 The knock and announce rule is relevant in determining the reasonableness of a search under the Fourth Amendment.	**Richards v. Wisconsin, 520 U.S. 358** There is no blanket exception to the knock and announce rule in felony drug cases, but a no knock entry may be warranted in certain circumstances (e.g., destruction of evidence).	**United States v. Banks, 540 U.S. 31** Officers must wait 15 to 20 seconds after announcing their presence before forcibly entering.	**Hudson v. Michigan, 547 U.S. 586** Evidence need not be excluded when police violate the knock and announce rule.

Applying *Lewis* to the service of warrants, complaints about excessively destructive police conduct during the service of warrants are also governed by the Fourteenth Amendment. If the police's conduct shocks the conscience, then they may be liable under the due process clause. But there is no easy way to define what conduct shocks the conscience. At least one case has suggested that when police officers show "deliberate or reckless indifference," their conduct can be seen as conscience shocking (see *Estelle* v. *Gamble*, 429 U.S. 97 [1976]).

Permissible Degree of Force

It is appropriate at this juncture to consider what level of force is permitted against people who are the targets of arrest warrants. Almost every state has a law or regulation concerning police use of force. The American Law Institute adopted just one such regulation, which resembles many others in place around the United States. Section 120.7 states that a police officer "may use such force as is reasonably necessary to effect the arrest, to enter premises to effect the arrest, or to prevent the escape from custody of an arrested person." Further, **deadly force** is authorized when the crime in question is a felony and when such force "creates no substantial risk to innocent persons," and the officer reasonably believes that there is a substantial risk that the fleeing felon will inflict harm on other people or police officers.

In **Tennessee v. Garner (471 U.S. 1 [1985])**—which involved the shooting death of a young, unarmed, fleeing felon—the Supreme Court adopted a rule similar to the American Law Institute's formulation. The result was the leading Supreme Court precedent concerning the use of deadly force to apprehend fleeing felons. The *Garner* decision declared unconstitutional a Tennessee statute that authorized police officers who give notice of the intent to arrest to "use all the necessary means to effect the arrest" if the suspect flees or resists.

The Court ruled that deadly force may be used when (1) it is necessary to prevent the suspect's escape and (2) the officer has probable cause to believe the suspect poses a serious threat of death or serious physical injury to other people or police officers. One would think that the Supreme Court would be unanimous in a decision such as this, but three justices dissented, noting that the statute struck down by the majority "assist[s] the police in apprehending suspected perpetrators of serious crimes and provide[s] notice that a lawful police order to stop and submit to arrest may not be ignored with impunity" (p. 28).

Four years after *Garner*, the Supreme Court decided the landmark case of **Graham v. Connor 490 U.S. 386 [1989])**, which set the standard for **nondeadly force**. The Court declared emphatically that *all* claims involving allegations of excessive force against police officers must be analyzed under the Fourth Amendment's reasonableness requirement. Further, the Court adopted a test of objective reasonableness to decide when excessive force is used. This requires focusing on what a *reasonable* police officer would do "without regard to [the officer's] underlying intent or motivation." In determining what a reasonable police officer would do, the Court looked to three factors: (1) the severity of the crime, (2) whether the suspect posed a threat, and (3) whether the suspect was resisting and/or attempting to flee the scene. Courts must, in focusing on these three factors, allow "for the fact that police officers are often forced to make

split-second judgments—about the amount of force that is necessary in a particular situation" (p. 386). Generally, then, if the crime in question is a serious one and the suspect is dangerous and resists arrest, then he or she will have difficulty succeeding with an excessive force claim.

Incidentally, both the *Garner* and *Graham* decisions resulted from Section 1983 lawsuits. Garner's surviving family members and Graham himself both sued on the grounds that their constitutional rights were violated. Whereas many of the cases examined in this book focus on the evidence of crimes (for example, weapons, drugs, confessions), *Garner* and *Graham* do not. How evidence was obtained was not at issue because there was none. Thus, the only remedy available to Garner's family and Graham was *civil litigation*.

Garner and *Graham* both are necessarily general. States, cities, and counties around the country have adopted more restrictive guidelines for their officers concerning the use of force. Police departments have their own use-of-force policies, as well.

Media Presence

In **Wilson v. Layne (526 U.S. 603 [1999])**, the Supreme Court decided whether the police can bring members of the media along during the service of an arrest warrant. The facts of the case are as follows: Early in the morning on April 16, 1992, deputy U.S. marshals and Montgomery County police officers entered the suspected home of Dominic Wilson. They were joined by a *Washington Post* reporter and a photographer as part of a marshals' service ride-along policy. Dominic's parents were asleep in bed when the officers arrived. They heard the officers enter the home and ran into the living room to investigate the disturbance. A verbal altercation ensued, and both the Wilsons were subdued. Dominic Wilson was never found. Even though the reporter observed what occurred and the photographer took pictures of what transpired, the story was never printed and the pictures were never published. The parents, Charles and Geraldine Wilson, nonetheless brought a *Bivens* action (the Section 1983 counterpart for lawsuits against *federal* officials) against the marshals, alleging the officers violated their Fourth Amendment rights by bringing the media into their home.

The case worked its way up through the courts and was ultimately heard by the Supreme Court, which decided that media presence during the service of arrest warrants violates the Fourth Amendment, as long as the presence serves no "legitimate law enforcement objectives." The Court declared that "it is a violation of the Fourth Amendment for police to bring members of the media or other third parties into a home during the execution of a warrant when the presence of the third parties in the home was not in aid of the execution of the warrant" (p. 614).

Chief Justice Rehnquist, writing for the majority, began by stating that the Fourth Amendment embodies the "centuries-old principle of respect for the privacy of the home" (p. 610). He went on to note that although the law enforcement officers were authorized to enter the Wilsons' home, "it does not necessarily follow that they were entitled to bring a newspaper reporter and photographer with them" (p. 611). The Court then considered whether the actions of both parties—the reporters and the police—were related to the objectives of the intrusion into the Wilsons' home. It ruled that they were not. Because the reporters were in the Wilsons' residence for their own purposes, they "were not present for any reason related to the justification for police entry into the home" (p. 611). However, if media presence *does* serve legitimate law enforcement objectives, then the Fourth Amendment will not be violated.

To many observers, the Court's decision in *Wilson* v. *Layne* seemed to sound the death knell for certain aspects of reality-based police television shows—and to an extent, it did. The police cannot take a camera crew with them when an arrest warrant is served. Media accompaniment is still permissible outside people's homes, however.

▶ Search Warrants

Searches with warrants are subjected to many of the same restrictions that arrests with warrants are. However, because the purpose of obtaining a search warrant is to search for something, as opposed to seizing a person, the courts have placed significant restrictions on what the police can do when searching for evidence with warrants. Just because a warrant is obtained does not mean that the police can look anywhere and take unlimited time to search for the item(s) named in the warrant.

When Search Warrants Are Required

Search warrants are required any time the police seek to search for evidence in a manner that is not governed by one of the well-established exceptions to the Fourth Amendment's warrant requirement. By way of preview, such exceptions include searches incident to arrest, hot pursuit, escape, endangerment, and destruction of evidence; automobile searches; plain-view searches; and searches performed

The courts have placed significant restrictions on what the police can do when searching for evidence with warrants.

when consent is obtained. In any other situation, a search warrant is necessary. Search warrants are also preferred any time they can be obtained, even if they are not formally *required*.

Serving Search Warrants

LEARNING OUTCOMES 4 — Explain when search warrants are required and how they should be served.

The knock-and-announce rules discussed earlier carry over to the service of search warrants. As indicated before, the police do not have to announce their presence if they have reasonable suspicion that exigent circumstances are present. Likewise, even if police do not "knock and announce," evidence seized cannot be excluded per *Hudson* v. *Michigan*.

Use of force is rarely an issue that arises during the service of a search warrant because, strictly speaking, a search warrant authorizes the police to look for evidence. If a person gets in the way during the service of a search warrant, however, he or she may be arrested and force may be applied if need be (that is, subject to the restrictions discussed earlier).

If the police mistakenly search the wrong residence, the search will not automatically be declared invalid. As pointed out earlier, as long as the mistake is a reasonable one, any evidence seized during a search of the wrong residence will be admissible in a criminal trial. The key, however, is that the mistake must be an *objectively reasonable* one, gauged from the standpoint of a reasonable officer.

Two other issues are relevant to the service of a search warrant. These do not necessarily apply in the case of arrest warrants. They are: (1) time restrictions, both for when the warrant can be served and for how long the police can look for evidence and (2) the scope and manner of the search (see Figure 4–10).

It is important to note that the police can sometimes request a search warrant with special instructions, which can include night service, no-knock authorization, and the like. Such warrants often require additional justification to convince a judge that special treatment is warranted.

Time Constraints

There are three means by which the courts impose time constraints on the police when it comes to the service of search warrants. First, the service of a search warrant should take place promptly after its issuance. Clearly, probable cause could dissipate if an excessive amount of time elapses between the time the warrant is issued and the time it is served. To avoid this

1. Time Constraints
   a. Search must be executed promptly after issuance.
   b. Search must be conducted during daylight hours if possible.
   c. Search must not last indefinitely.

2. Scope and Manner
   a. Search must be based on object sought.
   b. Search must avoid causing excessive and unnecessary property damage.
   c. Cannot search guests or third parties if probable cause to do so is lacking.

FIGURE 4–10 Summary of Search Warrant Restrictions.

potential problem, a warrant will sometimes specify that the search be conducted within a certain period of time.

A second time restriction that is occasionally imposed pertains to the time of day. Judges commonly restrict the service of warrants to the daytime hours or at least favor daytime service (see **Gooding v. United States, 416 U.S. 430 [1974]**). The Federal Rules of Criminal Procedure, for example, restrict the service of warrants to daytime hours, unless the issuing judge specifically authorizes execution at another time. *Daytime hours*, according to the Federal Rules, are between the hours of 6:00 a.m. and 10:00 p.m.

The third time restriction concerns how long the police can search for evidence. The general rule is that a search cannot last indefinitely. Once the item in the warrant has been discovered, the search must be terminated. If the police have difficulty finding the item or items named in the warrant, they can take as long as necessary to find them. If the police do not succeed in finding the evidence named in the warrant and then leave and come back later, they will be required to obtain another warrant. Steps should always be taken to avoid the appearance of arbitrariness, and people's Fourth Amendment privacy interests should always be respected.

Scope and Manner of the Search

Two additional restrictions with regard to the service of a search warrant concern the scope and manner of the search. *Scope* refers to where the police can look for evidence. *Manner* refers to the physical steps the police can take to find the evidence in question, including breaking down doors, forcibly opening locked cabinets, and so on.

The scope of the search must be reasonable, based on the object of the search. In other words, the police are restricted in looking for evidence insofar as they can only look where the item could reasonably be found. For example, assume the

The scope of the search must be reasonable, based on the object of the search.

evidence in question is a stolen diamond ring. Such an item is relatively small, so the police will be authorized to look almost anywhere for the ring. However, if the evidence in question is large in size—for example, a stolen big-screen television set—then the police cannot look in small places, where such an item could not possibly be found. The Supreme Court's statement in **Harris v. United States (331 U.S. 145 [1947])** provides further clarification: "[T]he same meticulous investigation which would be appropriate in a search for two small canceled checks could not be considered reasonable where agents are seeking a stolen automobile or an illegal still" (p. 152).

The police may also detain people as needed while serving a search warrant. According to the Court in **Michigan v. Summers (452 U.S. 692 [1981])**, "[A] warrant to search for contraband founded on probable cause implicitly carries with it the limited authority to detain the occupants of the premises while a proper search is conducted" (p. 704). The law enforcement interests at stake in that decision were officer safety, assistance with completion of the search, and prevention of flight.

This ruling was restricted by the 2013 decision in *Bailey* v. *United States* (568 U.S. ___ [2013]). In that case, as officers were preparing to execute a warrant, two detectives surveilled the property searched. They noticed two men leave the property, get in a car, and drive away. The detectives followed the men, stopped the car, ordered the men out, patted them down, and found incriminating evidence. The Supreme Court held that *Summers* did not apply in this context: "The rule in *Summers* is limited to the immediate vicinity of the premises to be searched and does not apply here, where Bailey was detained at a point beyond any reasonable understanding of the immediate vicinity of the premises in question."

Although the police may detain people who are on the premises to be searched, they cannot search the people unless probable cause exists (*Ybarra* v. *Illinois*, 444 U.S. 85 [1979]). A frisk is permissible, though, as long as the police have a reasonable suspicion that there is a risk to officer safety. If a person does not live on the premises, does not house personal belongings there, and is not a threat, he or she will probably be allowed to leave.

As discussed in the "Serving Arrest Warrants" section, federal law authorizes the police to break open doors and containers if they are refused admittance (18 U.S.C. Section 3109). Still, there are restrictions. The manner of the search must be limited to what is reasonably necessary to find the evidence in question. The Supreme Court has stated that "[e]xcessive or unnecessary destruction of property in the course of a search may violate the Fourth Amendment, even though the entry itself is lawful and the fruits of the search not subject to suppression" (*United States* v. *Ramirez*, 523 U.S. 65 [1998], p. 71). Additionally, the occupant of the place searched can be detained—even in handcuffs—for the duration of the search (*Muehler* v. *Mena*, 544 U.S. 93 [2005]).

▶ Special Circumstances

Added restrictions govern bodily intrusions. The same is true of tracking devices, recording instruments, and electronic surveillance in general. The following subsections touch on the special circumstances in each of these areas.

Search Warrants and Bodily Intrusions

LEARNING OUTCOMES 5 Explain how bodily intrusions, the use of tracking devices, and electronic surveillance create "special circumstances" for Fourth Amendment purposes.

The Supreme Court has been especially restrictive with regard to intrusions into the human body. The most well-known case that serves as an example is *Rochin* v. *California* (342 U.S. 165 [1952]). In that case, the police had information that a man was selling narcotics. They entered his home and forced their way into his bedroom. When the police asked the man about two capsules that were lying on his bed, he put the capsules in his mouth. The officers could not successfully remove the drugs from the man's mouth, so they took him to the hospital, where his stomach was pumped. Drugs were found and the man was convicted in California state court for possession of morphine. *Rochin* was decided in 1952, prior to when the exclusionary rule was applied to the states. As a result, the Court ruled that the way the police handled the man shocked the conscience, thereby violating his Fourteenth Amendment right to due process.

In another case, *Winston* v. *Lee* (470 U.S. 753 [1985]), the Supreme Court decided whether the government could require a bullet to be surgically removed from a suspected robber. The Court required not only that a warrant be obtained before allowing such an intrusion but also that the suspect's safety and privacy interests should be weighed against society's interest in capturing lawbreakers. The Court noted,

A compelled surgical intrusion into an individual's body for evidence . . . implicates expectations of privacy and security of such magnitude that the intrusion may be "unreasonable" even if likely to produce evidence of a crime. . . . The reasonableness of surgical intrusions beneath the skin depends on a case-by-case approach, in which the individual's interests in privacy and security are weighed against society's interests in conducting the procedure. In a given case, the question whether the community's need for evidence outweighs the substantial privacy interest at stake is a delicate one admitting of few categorical answers. (pp. 759–760)

The Court did not expressly decide what the appropriate procedure would be before surgery would be permitted, but it did cite a lower court decision, *United States* v. *Crowder* (543 F.2d 312 [1977]), in which the D.C. Circuit Court of Appeals decided that before surgery would be permissible (even if a warrant were obtained), an adversarial hearing with appellate review must occur. Thus, under certain circumstances, it would appear that certain types of bodily intrusions require more than a warrant.

Electronic Surveillance

The term *electronic surveillance* includes a variety of methods for spying on the activities of suspected criminals, including both conversations and suspected criminal actions. The methods used to spy on criminal suspects are quite diverse and include wiretapping, "bugging," hacking into computer transmissions, tracking movements of persons and equipment, video surveillance, and seeing through opaque surfaces using devices such as thermal imagers and "gun detectors."

Electronic surveillance law is exceedingly complex and rapidly changing, so a thorough introduction is beyond the scope of this text. However, by focusing some attention on legislative developments over time, sufficient familiarity can be gained with the general contours of the law in this important area of criminal procedure. The following subsections begin by looking at early legislative requirements in the area of electronic surveillance, then move into Title III of the Omnibus Crime Control and Safe Streets Act of 1968 (and its 1986 amendments), and finally consider the PATRIOT Act, which was passed following the September 11 terrorist attacks.

Most of the law in this area, especially Title III and the PATRIOT Act, restricts government interception of private communications. Thus, the bulk of the discussion that follows concerns the use of wiretaps and similar strategies to intercept communications. Other types of electronic surveillance—namely, the use of tracking devices, video recorders, and detection devices—are discussed in a separate subsection, as these types of activities are governed mostly by Supreme Court decisions.

Following *Katz* v. *United States*, 389 U.S. 347 (1967), the Supreme Court decided *Berger* v. *New York*, 388 U.S. 41 (1967), in which it considered a statute that permitted eavesdropping orders to be issued by magistrates if the police showed reasonable grounds that evidence of a crime would be discovered. The Court declared the statute unconstitutional, holding that a warrant supported by probable cause is necessary to secure permission to intercept people's communications. Importantly, though, *Katz* and *Berger* do not apply to the interception of communications that can be considered consensual, such as when the government plants a listening device on an informant.

Title III and the Electronic Communications Privacy Act

In 1968, Congress passed **Title III of the Omnibus Crime Control and Safe Streets Act** (18 U.S.C. §§2510–20). Then, in 1986, Congress amended the act by passing the **Electronic Communications Privacy Act (ECPA)** (Pub. L. No. 99–508 [1986]). Both acts govern law enforcement electronic surveillance activities at both the federal and state levels. They are of particular importance because they preempt state laws addressing electronic surveillance. That is, for electronic surveillance to conform to constitutional requirements, it must not only abide by state law but also by the 1968 and 1986 acts.

Both acts protect virtually all wire, oral, and electronic communications among private parties. Title III restricts the *interception* of "wire, oral or electronic communications," unless such interception is authorized by statute (see the act for definitions of each). The 1986 amendments to the act added *electronic communications* to the list of protected activities. The amendments also covered the electronic storage and processing of information. In short, in order for the government to intercept almost any wire, oral, and electronic communications among private parties, it must obtain a valid search warrant.

Unlike communications between private parties, communications among government employees and communications between private parties and the general public are not protected. For example, if an individual posts a message to the World Wide Web, it will not be protected in any way. Also, as discussed earlier, communications that are consensual in nature—such as between a suspect and a government informant—do not come under the protection of Title III or its amendments.

The requirements for obtaining a Title III warrant go beyond the requirements for obtaining a "typical" warrant. The application must contain:

- the identity of both the officer filing and the officer approving the application.
- "a full and complete statement of the facts and circumstances relied upon by the applicant to justify his belief that an order should be issued."
- "a particular description of the nature and location of the facilities from which or the place where the communication is to be intercepted."
- a "full and complete statement as to whether or not other investigative procedures have been tried and failed or why they reasonably appear to be unlikely to succeed if tried or to be too dangerous."
- "a statement of the period of time for which the interception is required to be maintained," including, if deemed necessary, "a particular description of facts establishing probable cause to believe that additional communications of the same type will occur" after "the described type of communication has been first obtained."
- "a full and complete statement of the facts concerning all previous applications . . . involving any of the same persons, facilities, or places specified in the application, and the action taken by the judge on each such application."
- "a statement setting forth the results thus far obtained from the interception, or a reasonable explanation of the failure to obtain such results."

When preparing to serve a Title III warrant, authorities can covertly enter the place where the interception is to take place (see *Dalia* v. *United States*, 441 U.S. 238 [1979]). The entry must be reasonable and not result in excessive property damage. Indeed, too much, if any, property damage would alert that suspect that an investigation is taking place. Also, if the circumstances of the interception change during the course of the investigation, the Title III warrant will need to be amended. For example, if when listening to conversations, the police are alerted to additional criminal conduct that they would like to hear about, they must seek an amendment to the original warrant.

If all Title III requirements are not met, the remedy is suppression of the evidence. That is, the exclusionary rule will apply. In fact, Title III has its own set of exclusionary rules, but they are more or less the same as the exclusionary rule introduced earlier. For example, if a Title III warrant fails to describe with particularity the communications to be intercepted, and assuming this is called to the attention of the court, any evidence resulting from the interception will be inadmissible in court. However, if authorities make a reasonable mistake, then the "good faith" exception announced in *United States* v. *Leon*, 468 U.S. 897 (1984) will apply. Also, in *United States* v. *Giordano*, 416 U.S. 505 (1974), the Court held that suppression of evidence is only required when the part of the act that has been violated "was intended to play a central role in the statutory scheme." In other words, trivial violations of the act will not likely result in suppression. For example, if fewer than all of the law enforcement officers involved in the investigation are identified in the warrant, then evidence will not be suppressed.

The Foreign Intelligence Surveillance Act

The **Foreign Intelligence Surveillance Act (FISA)**, passed in 1978, regulates electronic surveillance as it pertains to foreign intelligence gathering. In contrast, Title III and ECPA are mostly for domestic law enforcement purposes. FISA regulates a number of specific activities, including physical searches for intelligence-gathering purposes, the use of pen registers and so-called "trap-and-trace" devices, access to business records, and, of course, electronic surveillance. FISA also created the secretive **Foreign Intelligence Surveillance Court**, which hears requests for surveillance warrants. Before a warrant is issued, the court must find probable cause that:

- "the target of the surveillance is a foreign power or an agent of a foreign power . . .; and
- each of the facilities or places at which the electronic surveillance is directed is being used, or is about to be used, by a foreign power or an agent of a foreign power."

Electronic surveillance law continues to change at a feverish pace. What's more, when changes are made, they often incorporate "sunset" clauses that essentially terminate the legislation at a specified date. One example of this is the **Protect America Act**, signed into law on August 5, 2007. Among other things, the Act removed the warrant requirement for government surveillance of foreign intelligence targets. A sunset clause was included partly because of the controversy surrounding the legislation, but certain provisions have since been reauthorized more than once by federal legislation. Legislation in this area continues to face legal challenge, but with little success (for a recent example, see *Clapper* v. *Amnesty International USA*, 568 U.S. ___ [2013]).

Sneak-and-Peek Warrants?

The PATRIOT Act, passed in the wake of the 9/11 attacks on the World Trade Center towers and the Pentagon building in Washington, D.C., has brought to light a number of controversial law enforcement tools, including the so-called "sneak-and-peek" or "delayed-notice" search. A sneak-and-peek warrant can be served without notifying the party whose property is searched. This presumably gives law enforcement the upper hand and helps protect the covert nature of terrorism-related investigations. Brett Shumate, a law professor at Wake Forest University, describes the procedure in this way:

> These warrants allow a law enforcement agent to "enter, look around, photograph items and leave without seizing anything and without leaving a copy of the warrant." Agents often perform the search when the owner is absent, observe the interior, and confirm any suspicions about possible illegal activity. Agents will then seek a conventional search warrant to return to the property and seize evidence of criminal activity. In contrast with conventional search warrants, sneak-and-peek search warrants dispense with the notice and receipt requirements, at least temporarily. The dispensation of these requirements maintains the secrecy of the search and investigation.[1]

Note that this procedure is quite different from the search warrant process discussed early on in this chapter. In the typical situation, the party whose property is searched knows full well what is happening. He or she may not know exactly *when* a search is scheduled to occur, but it will certainly become clear once the warrant is actually served. Sneak-and-peek warrants are much more covert.

Sneak-and-peek warrants are not used just for terrorism investigations. Such warrants can be used in any federal investigation, with proper authorization. Pre–PATRIOT Act cases involving sneak and peek warrants include, but are not limited to, *United States* v. *Frietas* (856 F.2d 1425 [9th Cir. 1988]); *United States* v. *Rangburn* (983 F.2d 449 [2nd Cir. 1993]), and *United States* v. *Simons* (206 F.3d 392 [4th Cir. 2000]).

The main criticism of sneak-and-peek warrants is that they give law enforcement officials too much power. In March 2006, however, amendments to the PATRIOT Act were signed into law and certain portions of Section 213 were modified. For example, there are now time constraints for post-search notification of search. In general, the party searched must be notified within 30 days after the search that it occurred. Even so, this approach to uncovering evidence is still around and used commonly.

Sneak-and-peak warrants raise a number of constitutional questions, such as the following:

1. Should law enforcement be able to covertly enter and search a residence?
2. To what extent do Fourth Amendment warrant requirements, those introduced in this chapter, impede criminal investigations?

LEARNING OUTCOMES 1

Summarize the activities governed by the Fourth Amendment.

The key activities governed by the Fourth Amendment include arrests with warrants, searches with warrants, arrests without warrants, searches without warrants, the seizure of evidence, and certain stops.

1. What key activities are governed by the Fourth Amendment?

2. Why has the Fourth Amendment's warrant requirement been litigated extensively in the courts?

LEARNING OUTCOMES 2

Outline the components of search and arrest warrants.

A warrant has three required components: (1) a neutral and detached magistrate, (2) a showing of probable cause, and (3) particularity. The probable cause and particularity showings differ between search and arrest warrants.

Key Cases

> *Coolidge v. New Hampshire*
> *Lo-Ji Sales, Inc. v. New York*
> *Maryland v. Garrison*
> *Andresen v. Maryland*

1. Explain the three components of a valid warrant.

2. How does the showing of probable cause differ for an arrest warrant versus a search warrant?

3. How does particularity differ for an arrest warrant versus a search warrant?

arrest warrant An order issued by a judge directing a law enforcement officer to arrest an individual identified as one who has committed a specific criminal offense.

search warrant An order issued by a judge directing a law enforcement officer to search a particular location for evidence connected with a specific criminal offense.

neutral and detached magistrate One of the three elements of a valid warrant—any judge who does not have a conflict of interest or pecuniary interest in the outcome of a particular case or decision.

particularity The Fourth Amendment requirement that an arrest warrant name the person to be arrested (or provide a sufficiently detailed description) and that a search warrant describe the place to be searched and the things to be seized.

LEARNING OUTCOMES 3

Explain when arrest warrants are required and how they should be served.

Arrest warrants are required in two situations: (1) arrests in the home and (2) arrests in third-party homes. Arrests in public do not require warrants. During service of an arrest warrant, the police should announce their presence. Reasonable property damage is acceptable. Force can be used, but it is subject to legal constraints.

Key Cases

> *Payton v. New York*
> *Steagald v. United States*
> *Hudson v. Michigan*
> *Sabbath v. United States*
> *Tennessee v. Garner*
> *Graham v. Connor*
> *Wilson v. Layne*

1. When is an arrest warrant required?

2. When can the knock-and-announce rule be dispensed with?

3. What are the legal constraints on use of deadly and nondeadly force?

4. Explain the Supreme Court's view on media presence during the service of a search warrant.

arrest The act of taking an individual into custody for the purpose of charging the person with a criminal offense (or, in the case of a juvenile, a delinquent act).

"knock-and-announce" requirement The requirement that, before executing an arrest or search warrant, officers identify themselves and their intentions.

deadly force Force that is likely to cause death or serious bodily harm.

nondeadly force Force that is unlikely to cause death or serious bodily harm.

LEARNING OUTCOMES 4

Explain when search warrants are required and how they should be served.

Search warrants are required unless the method by which the search is conducted is one the Supreme Court has permitted to occur without a warrant. Search warrants should be served in the same careful manner as arrest warrants. Additional limitations focus on time restrictions, the scope and manner of the search, and media presence.

1. Briefly summarize the Supreme Court's view on time constraints for service of a search warrant.

2. Compare and contrast *Graham* v. *Connor* and *Tennessee* v. *Garner*.

3. In what ways are the scope and manner of a search pursuant to a warrant restricted?

Key Cases

Gooding v. *United States*

Harris v. *United States*

Michigan v. *Summers*

LEARNING OUTCOMES 5

Explain how bodily intrusions, the use of tracking devices, and electronic surveillance create "special circumstances" for Fourth Amendment purposes.

The traditional Fourth Amendment approach to determining constitutionality does not always work in the case of bodily intrusions or when tracking devices, video recordings, or detection devices are used. Additionally, the interception of communications, in particular, is governed by a restrictive body of law (for example, Title III of the Omnibus Crime Control and Safe Streets Act of 1968).

1. Explain the two leading Supreme Court cases that address bodily intrusion during the course of a search.

2. Summarize the rules surrounding the use of tracking devices.

3. What additional requirements (beyond the usual Fourth Amendment requirements) must be met for authorities to conduct electronic surveillance?

Title III of the Omnibus Crime Control and Safe Streets Act Federal legislation enacted in 1968 that set forth detailed guidelines on how authorities could intercept wire, oral, or electronic communications.

Electronic Communications Privacy Act (ECPA) Federal legislation enacted in 1986 that amended Title III of the Omnibus Crime Control and Safe Streets Act to include "electronic communications."

5

Searches and Arrests Without Warrants

"If it was not for exceptions to the warrant requirement, the Fourth Amendment would take substantially less effort to understand."

1 Summarize the issues involved in warrantless searches and seizures.

2 Explain the search incident to arrest doctrine.

3 Identify three types of exigent circumstances and how they operate as exceptions to the warrant requirement.

4 Summarize the special issues involved in automobile searches.

5 Summarize the plain-view doctrine.

6 Describe the situations in which warrantless arrests may be made.

7 Describe consent searches and the issues associated with them.

CELL PHONES AND THE FOURTH AMENDMENT

© Mikael Karlsson/Alamy

In *Riley v. California* (573 U.S. ___ [2014]), the Supreme Court was confronted with the question of whether a police officer's warrantless search of an arrestee's cell phone violated the Fourth Amendment. Riley was arrested for weapons violations following a traffic stop. A police officer then searched him, which is permissible under a popular exception to the Fourth Amendment's warrant requirement (search incident to arrest), discussed further later in this chapter. As part of the search, the officer also examined Riley's cell phone and found information linking him to a recent gang shooting. Later at the police station, a gang unit detective further examined the phone, confirming the arresting officer's suspicions that Riley was involved in the recent shooting.

Riley attempted to exclude the evidence obtained from his cell phone, arguing that the officers engaged in an unreasonable search. In a unanimous and somewhat unexpected decision, the Supreme Court agreed. It decided in part that "a search of digital information on a cell phone does not further . . . government interests . . . and implicates substantially greater individual privacy interests than a brief physical search." The *Riley* decision was heralded as a huge victory for privacy advocates, including the American Civil Liberties Union and other organizations concerned with potential overreach by authorities in a digital age.

DISCUSS **How might the Supreme Court's decision in this case extend to other technologies?**

► *Moving Beyond the Warrant Requirement*

If it were not for exceptions to the warrant requirement, the Fourth Amendment would take substantially less effort to understand. At the same time, however, the many exceptions to the Fourth Amendment's warrant requirement are what make it interesting. The so-called warrantless searches and seizures discussed in this chapter are based on Supreme Court decisions in which it was believed that to require a warrant would constitute an undue burden on law enforcement officials. Still, though, a warrant is always preferable; whenever circumstances permit, one should be obtained.

The exceptions to the Fourth Amendment's warrant requirement considered in this chapter are those requiring probable cause. This chapter's first main section covers warrantless searches, but warrantless arrests are also considered. There are other exceptions to the warrant requirement that do not require probable cause; they are discussed in the next two chapters. Chapter 6 examines the law of stop-and-frisk, and Chapter 7 looks at searches and seizures based on administrative justification (regulatory and special needs searches).

Broadly, there are five types of warrantless actions that require probable cause. They are called **exceptions to the warrant requirement** because the actions at issue do not need to be supported by a warrant. The five types of warrantless actions are (1) searches incident to (that is, following) arrest, (2) searches in the presence of exigent circumstances, (3) searches involving automobiles, (4) searches based on the "plain-view" doctrine, and (5) certain arrests, such as arrests made in public. Consent searches, introduced near the end of this chapter, require no warrant—or probable cause.

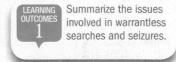

LEARNING OUTCOMES 1 Summarize the issues involved in warrantless searches and seizures.

► *Search Incident to Arrest*

Imagine a situation in which a police officer has lawfully (that is, with probable cause) arrested a suspect, is leading him away, and observes the suspect reach into his pocket. What would be going through the police officer's mind as he or she observed this behavior? Scenarios like this illustrate the reasoning behind the **search incident to arrest** exception. Namely, police officers must be permitted to engage in a search of a suspect incident to arrest (that is, following an arrest). It would be impractical, even dangerous, to wait for a warrant before conducting such a search incident to arrest.

The leading case in the area of incident searches is *Chimel v. California* (395 U.S. 752 [1969]). As the Supreme Court stated, a search incident to arrest is permitted "to remove any weapons that the [arrestee] might seek to use in order to resist arrest or effect his escape" and to "seize any evidence on the

It would be impractical, even dangerous, to wait for a warrant before conducting such a search incident to arrest.

arrestee's person in order to prevent its concealment or destruction" (p. 763). Also see Figure 5-1.

The most basic requirement concerning searches incident to arrest—and one that often goes overlooked—is that the arrest must be lawful. When the arrest itself is not lawful (that is, when it is not based on probable cause), any search that follows is unlawful (see *Draper* v. *United States*, 358 U.S. 307 [1959]).

Another important threshold issue with regard to searches incident to arrest concerns the nature of the offense. Courts have grappled with the question of whether a search should be permitted when the offense on which the arrest is based is not serious. Because the rationale of the exception is to provide officer safety, is officer safety likely to be compromised when a minor offense, as opposed to a serious offense, justifies the arrest?

Two important Supreme Court cases have sought to answer these questions. First, in *United States* v. *Robinson* (414 U.S. 218 [1973]), the Court reversed a lower court's decision that only a pat down of the suspect's outer clothing was permissible following an arrest for driving with a revoked license. And in a companion case to *Robinson*, *Gustafson* v. *Florida* (414 U.S. 260 [1973]), the Court upheld the search of a suspect after his arrest for failure to have his driver's license.

Thus, *any* arrest justifies a warrantless search incident to that arrest. A key restriction, however, is that the arrest must result in a person being *taken into custody*. This was the ruling from **Knowles v. Iowa (525 U.S. 113 [1998])**. In that case, a police officer stopped a person for speeding, and rather than arresting him (which the officer had justification to do), the officer issued him a citation. Then, the officer conducted a search of the car and found a marijuana pipe. The Court noted that traffic stops rarely pose the same threat to officer safety as arrests. This is not to suggest, however, that police officers cannot search people incident to lawful arrest for minor vehicle-related infractions. If the authority to arrest is present, an incident search is

permissible. The key restriction is that the person must actually be arrested and taken into custody. Otherwise, the search will not conform with Fourth Amendment requirements.

Timing of the Search

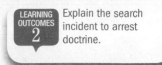

A key restriction pertaining to searches incident to arrest has to do with the timing of the search. Probable cause to arrest must *precede* the warrantless search (*Sibron* v. *New York*, 392 U.S. 40 [1968]). The reason for this is to restrict officers from engaging in "fishing expeditions," or searches based on less than probable cause that would presumably result in probable cause to make an arrest. Note, however, that if probable cause to arrest is in place, the officer is not required to formally arrest the suspect before engaging in the search (see *Rawlings* v. *Kentucky*, 448 U.S. 98 [1980]).

If the search follows an arrest, then it must take place *soon* after the arrest. In legal parlance, the search must be *contemporaneous* to the arrest. In **Preston v. United States (376 U.S. 364 [1964])**, the case that established this rule, Justice Black observed that the "justifications [for the search incident to arrest] are absent where a search is remote in time or place from the arrest" (p. 367). In *Preston*, police officers arrested the occupants of a car and took them to jail. After this, the officers searched the car, which had been towed to an impound lot. The Supreme Court noted that the possibilities of destruction of evidence and danger to the officers were no longer in place, as the suspects were no longer even present (see also *Chambers* v. *Maroney*, 399 U.S. 42 [1970]).

Note that although a noncontemporaneous search is not justified under the search incident to arrest exception, it is authorized under the automobile exception discussed later. Also, the Supreme Court authorizes inventory searches of automobiles that have been lawfully impounded. Inventory searches are discussed later, as well.

There is one significant exception to the contemporaneousness requirement. In *United States* v. *Edwards* (415 U.S. 800 [1974]), the Supreme Court, in a 5-to-4 decision, upheld the warrantless search and seizure of an arrestee's clothing ten hours after his arrest, during which time he was in jail. The Court noted that "searches and seizures that could be made on the spot at the time of arrest may legally be conducted later when the accused arrives at the place of detention" (p. 803). The Court did point out, however, that the taking of the individual's clothing at the time of the arrest would have been impractical because it "was late at night[,] no substitute clothing was then available for Edwards to wear, and it would certainly have been unreasonable for the police to have stripped respondent of his clothing and left him exposed in his cell throughout the night" (p. 805). Thus, the *Edwards* decision established the rule that a noncontemporaneous search incident to arrest is

The U.S. Supreme Court's Reasoning behind the Search Incident to Arrest Doctrine:

"It is scarcely open to doubt that the danger to an officer is far greater in the case of the extended exposure which follows the taking of a suspect into custody and transporting him to the police station than in the case of the relatively fleeting contact resulting from the typical *Terry*-stop."

"A police officer's determination as to how and where to search the person of a suspect whom he has arrested is necessarily a quick *ad hoc* judgment which the Fourth Amendment does not require to be broken down in each instance into an analysis of each step in the search."

FIGURE 5-1 Reasoning Behind Search Incident to Arrest Doctrine.

permissible when (1) an immediate search is nearly impossible and (2) the exigency still exists at the time of the later search.

Scope of the Search

The case of *United States* v. *Rabinowitz* (339 U.S. 56 [1950]) was the first to set limits on the scope of a search incident to arrest. In that case, the officers, armed with a valid arrest warrant, arrested a man and then conducted a warrantless search of his one-room business, including the desk, safe, and file cabinets. The Supreme Court upheld the search because the room "was small and under the immediate and complete control of the respondent" (p. 64).

Nearly 20 years after *Rabinowitz*, however, the Supreme Court voted to overturn its earlier decision. In the case of *Chimel* v. *California*, the Court argued that the *Rabinowitz* decision had been construed to mean that "a warrantless search 'incident to a lawful arrest' may generally extend to the area that is considered to be in the 'possession' or under the 'control' of the person arrested" (p. 759). Further, the Court noted that the *Rabinowitz* standard gave police "the opportunity to engage in searches not justified by probable cause, [but] by the simple expedient of arranging to arrest suspects at home rather than elsewhere" (p. 767). To get around this problem, Justice Stewart argued in favor of a new **armspan rule**. In the Court's words, a search incident to arrest would now be limited to the area "within [the] immediate control" of the person arrested—that is, "the area from within which he might have obtained either a weapon or something that could have been used as evidence against him" (p. 768).

An interesting twist on the aforementioned cases can be found in *Washington* v. *Chrisman* (455 U.S. 1 [1982]). In that case, an officer stopped a student on suspicion of drinking under age, an action that the Court considered an arrest. The officer asked the student for his identification and followed him to his dorm room, where the student's identification was presumably located. While at the student's room, the officer observed in plain view marijuana and drug paraphernalia. The officer

seized the evidence. The Supreme Court upheld the seizure of the evidence, stating that "[e]very arrest must be presumed to present a risk of danger to the arresting officer. . . . Moreover, the possibility that an arrested person will attempt to escape if not properly supervised is obvious" (p. 7). Thus, "it is not unreasonable, under the Fourth Amendment for an officer, as a matter of routine, to monitor the movements of an arrested person, as his judgment dictates, following the arrest" (p. 7).

The cases discussed thus far have focused narrowly on the scope of the incident search exception with reference to the arrestee. What if another person *besides* the arrestee poses a threat to the police? This concern has led to several exceptions to the armspan rule.

First, in *Maryland* v. *Buie* (494 U.S. 325 [1990]), the Supreme Court expanded the scope of the incident search in two ways. It held that the police may, as part of a search incident to arrest, look in areas immediately adjoining the place of arrest for other persons who might attack the officers; no justification is required. The key, however, is that such a search must occur incident to arrest. Next, the Court held that at any point up to the time the arrest is completed, the police may engage in a **protective sweep** (that is, "a cursory visual inspection of those places in which a person might be hiding"), but reasonable suspicion must exist for such a sweep to be justified. Thus, no justification is required *after* arrest, but reasonable suspicion is required to engage in a sweep up to the point of the arrest.

Aside from the possible danger to police officers from "confederates," there is the potential for such third parties to engage in the destruction of evidence. Only one Supreme Court case appears to address this issue: *Vale* v. *Louisiana* (399 U.S. 30 [1970]). In that case, police officers had warrants authorizing the arrest of the defendant. While engaged in surveillance of the house, the officers observed the defendant come out of the house and engage in what appeared to be a drug sale. They arrested the defendant outside the home but then went back inside and searched it, according to the officers, because two of the defendant's relatives had arrived at the house in the meantime and could have destroyed evidence. *Vale* was actually a case concerning exigent circumstances, and the Court reversed the Louisiana Supreme Court's decision that upheld the search. But, in fact, the Court's opinion was not particularly instructive. It stated, in relevant part, that "no reason, so far as anything before us appears, to suppose that it was impracticable for [the officers] to obtain a search warrant as well" (p. 35), but it did not expressly state that related searches would always be unconstitutional. Indeed, several lower courts have upheld warrantless searches of homes for evidence after arrest on less than probable cause (for example, *United States* v. *Hoyos*, 892 F.2d 1387 [9th Cir. 1989]; *United States* v. *Rubin*, 474 F.2d 262 [3rd Cir. 1973]).

Another type of warrantless search of a house following a lawful arrest has been authorized based on the need to secure the premises, usually pending the procurement of a search warrant. Thus, if the police believe another person or persons are in the house and could potentially destroy evidence, the house may be secured but not searched until a warrant has been obtained.

Think About It...

Proper Scope for a Search Incident to Arrest Two police officers arrived at Bobby Sheen's house with a valid warrant for his arrest. The officers were informed by a neighbor that two of Sheen's accomplices were in the house with him. The officers knocked, announced their presence, and entered the house. They encountered Sheen as he was descending the stairs. He was placed under arrest. Immediately after the arrest, one of the officers went upstairs and found drug paraphernalia on a nightstand. May this evidence be lawfully seized? What if the drug paraphernalia had been found in a drawer instead?

This was the decision reached in *Segura* v. *United States* (468 U.S. 796 [1984]). In that case, the Supreme Court, in another 5-to-4 decision, declared "that where officers, having probable cause, enter premises . . . , arrest the occupants . . . and take them into custody and, for no more than the period here involved [19 hours in this case], secure the premises from within to preserve the status quo while others, in good faith, are in the process of obtaining a warrant, they do not violate the Fourth Amendment's proscription against unreasonable seizures" (p. 798).

It is appropriate at this juncture to note that the Court has authorized the police to rely on the incident search exception to engage in searches well beyond the arrestee's armspan—and when no threat exists from people sympathetic to the arrestee. In particular, the Supreme Court has held that officers may engage in a warrantless, suspicionless search of a car and containers within it following the lawful arrest of the car's driver (*New York* v. *Belton*, 453 U.S. 454 [1981]), but "only if it is reasonable to believe that the arrestee might access the vehicle at the time of the search or that the vehicle contains evidence of the offense" in question (*Arizona* v. *Gant*, 556 U.S. 332 [2009]). The search incident to arrest rule does not extend to cell phones, however, as this chapter's opening vignette discussed (see *Riley* v. *California*, 573 U.S. ___ [2014]). See the accompanying timeline for a summary of key search incident to arrest cases.

▶ Exigent Circumstances

The exceptions to the search warrant requirement are premised on the impracticality of obtaining a warrant. Perhaps no exception illustrates this better than the **exigent circumstances** exception. Simply put, when the exigencies, or emergencies, of the

When the exigencies, or emergencies, of the situation require the police to act immediately at the risk of danger to themselves, danger to others, the destruction of evidence, or the escape of the suspect, it would be unreasonable to require the police to take time to obtain a warrant.

situation require the police to act immediately at the risk of danger to themselves, danger to others, the destruction of evidence, or the escape of the suspect, it would be unreasonable to require the police to take time to obtain a warrant.

Generally, three types of exigencies are recognized by the courts as authorizing the police to act without a warrant: (1) hot pursuit, (2) likelihood of escape or danger to others absent hot pursuit, and (3) evanescent evidence. Despite the fact that these exceptions allow the police to act without a warrant, probable cause is still required. For example, probable cause that the person being pursued is the suspect is required before the police can enter a home or building without a warrant to arrest him or her.

Hot Pursuit

The Supreme Court first recognized the **hot pursuit** exception in the case of ***Warden* v. *Hayden* (387 U.S. 294 [1967])**, in which the police were called by taxicab drivers who reported that their taxi company had been robbed. The police followed the suspect to a house, where they were granted entry by the suspect's wife. The suspect was upstairs in the house, pretending to be asleep. While searching the house for the suspect, the police found and seized clothing, a shotgun, and a pistol, all of which were used against the suspect at trial. The Court found the warrantless entry reasonable because the "exigencies of the situation made that course imperative" (p. 298). Several reasons were offered for the decision. First, Justice Brennan stated that "[t]he Fourth Amendment does not require police officers to delay in the course of an investigation if to do so would gravely danger their lives or the lives of others" (pp. 298–299). Also, "[s]peed . . . was essential, and only a thorough search of the house for persons and weapons could have insured that Hayden was the only man present and that the police had control of all weapons which could be used against them or to effect an escape" (p. 299). Despite the sweeping language from the *Hayden* decision, the Supreme Court has imposed several restrictions on searches and seizures premised on hot pursuit. Figure 5–2 summarizes additional restrictions concerning hot pursuit.

Escape and Endangerment to Others Absent Hot Pursuit

Hot pursuit is justified, as just discussed, when, among other things, the suspect may escape or inflict harm on police officers

TIMELINE

Scope of the Search Incident to Arrest over Time

1950	1969	1981	1982
***United States* v. *Rabinowitz*, 339 U.S. 561950** A full room search was sanctioned following an arrest.	***Chimel* v. *California*, 395 U.S. 752** The Court overruled Rabinowitz and the "armspan rule" was adopted. The arrestee can be searched, as can the arrestee's "grabbing area."	***New York* v. *Belton*, 453 U.S. 454** Officers may engage in a warrantless, suspicionless search of a car and containers within it following a lawful arrest of the car's driver.	***Washington* v. *Chrisman*, 455 U.S. 1** It is permissible to monitor the movements of an arrested person (in this case to his dorm to get his identification) and seize contraband found in plain view.

Restrictions on Hot Pursuit

- Hot pursuit permits warrantless entry only when, first, the police have probable cause to believe that the person they are chasing has committed a crime and is on the premises entered.
- The police are also required to have reason to believe the suspect will escape or that further harm, either to evidence or to other people, will occur if the suspect is not immediately apprehended.
- The police must begin hot pursuit from a lawful starting point. If, for example, officers are unlawfully on someone's private property, they will not succeed in claiming hot pursuit to justify any further warrantless action (e.g., *United States* v. *Santana*, 427 U.S. 38 [1976]).
- The hot pursuit doctrine applies only to serious offenses, including felonies and some misdemeanors (e.g., *Welsh* v. *Wisconsin*, 400 U.S. 740 [1984]).
- The scope of a search based on hot pursuit is broad: "The permissible scope of search must, at the least, be as broad as may reasonably be necessary to prevent the dangers that the suspect at large in the house may resist or escape" (*Warden* v. *Hayden*, p. 299). However, the search must be "prior to or immediately contemporaneous with" the arrest of the suspect. Also, officers may only search where the suspect or weapons might reasonably be found.

FIGURE 5–2 Restrictions on Hot Pursuit.

or others. In some situations, however, a suspect can potentially escape or inflict harm absent hot pursuit. In **Minnesota v. Olson (495 U.S. 91 [1990])**, for example, the prosecution sought to justify a warrantless entry and arrest of a suspect in a duplex that the police had surrounded. There was probable cause to believe that Olson, the man in the duplex, had been the driver of a getaway car involved in a robbery/murder the day before. The Supreme Court ruled that the officers acted unconstitutionally under the circumstances because Olson was only the driver, not the murder suspect, and the weapon had been recovered, which diminished the urgency of the situation. In addition, it was unlikely Olson would escape because the building was surrounded. On its face, then, this case is not useful on this point. However, the Court seemed to suggest that had Olson *not* been the driver (that is, had he been the murderer), had the weapon *not* been recovered, and had the building *not* been fully surrounded, the warrantless action would have been lawful.

A more recent case, *Brigham City* v. *Stuart* (547 U.S. 398 [2006]) brought clarification. In that case, police were called to a house that received complaints about a loud party. On arriving at the scene, officers witnessed a fight involving four adults and one juvenile. One of the adults hit the juvenile. The officers announced their presence, but they couldn't be heard above the commotion inside, so they entered without a warrant. In a unanimous decision, the Supreme Court held that such warrantless entries are constitutionally permissible so long as the police have an objectively reasonable basis to believe the occupant is "seriously injured or threatened with such injury."

Evanescent Evidence

In situations in which the search incident to arrest or hot pursuit exceptions do not apply, the Court has recognized an additional exception to the warrant requirement, one that permits warrantless searches for **evanescent evidence** (that is, disappearing evidence). This can include evidence inside a person or evidence that someone seeks or attempts to destroy.

LEARNING OUTCOMES 3 — Identify three types of exigent circumstances and how they operate as exceptions to the warrant requirement.

1984	**1990**	**2009**
Segura v. *United States*, 468 U.S. 796 Premises can be secured pending the procural of a search warrant. A **protective sweep** (cursory visual inspection of the places in which someone may be hiding) can be conducted if the police have reason to believe evidence may be destroyed by someone sympathetic to the arrestee.	*Maryland* v. *Buie*, 494 U.S. 325 The police may, as part of a search incident to arrest, conduct a protective sweep of the premises.	*Arizona* v. *Gant*, 556 U.S. 332 The rule in *Belton* v. *New York* is modified as follows: A search of the arrestee's vehicle is permissible "only if it is reasonable to believe that the arrestee might access the vehicle at the time of the search or that the vehicle contains evidence of the offense" in question.

Perhaps the best example of vanishing or disappearing evidence inside a person is alcohol in the blood. In *Breithaupt* v. *Abram* (352 U.S. 432 [1957]), the Court upheld the warrantless intrusion (via a needle) into a man's body for the purpose of drawing blood to see if he had been drinking. This decision was effectively overruled in a recent case. In **Missouri v. McNeely (569 U.S. ___ [2013])**, the Supreme Court ruled that the natural dissipation of alcohol in a person's bloodstream does not necessarily constitute an exigency justifying a warrantless search. The Court stopped short of deciding that *all* blood-draws must be supported by a warrant, but it certainly sent a message that a warrant should be obtained whenever practical. Part of the Court's reasoning for the decision was that it is much easier to obtain warrants these days than it was in the *Breithaupt* era.

The *Breithaupt* decision remains relevant, however, because it also established that warrantless searches for evanescent evidence are permissible only when (1) there is no time to obtain a warrant, (2) there is a "clear indication" that the search will result in obtaining the evidence sought, and (3) the search is conducted in a "reasonable manner." This three-prong approach remains more or less intact today.

In a later decision, *Schmerber* v. *California*, 384 U.S. 757 (1966), the Court offered the following reasoning in support of the reasonable manner requirement:

> The interests in human dignity and privacy which the Fourth Amendment protects forbid any such intrusions on the mere chance that desired evidence might be obtained. In the absence of a clear indication that in fact such evidence will be found, these fundamental human interest require law officers to suffer the risk that such evidence may disappear unless there is an immediate search.

In *Rochin* v. *California* (342 U.S. 165 [1952]), a case in which the *police* used a stomach pump to obtain evidence from a man's stomach, the Court declared that a due process violation occurred and that the officers' conduct shocked the conscience. The reason was that the police, not medical personnel, extracted the evidence. Another view is that the use of a stomach pump falls somewhat short of a routine medical procedure.

As for the clear indication requirement, the Court has been somewhat flexible. For example, in *United States* v. *Montoya de Hernandez* (469 U.S. 1204 [1985]), the Court treated the clear indication requirement from *Breithaupt* as being identical to the reasonable suspicion standard set forth in *Terry* v. *Ohio.* This case involved the detention for several hours of a woman who was suspected of smuggling narcotics in her alimentary canal.

Finally, it is important to remember that, like the hot pursuit exception, the exigency used to justify a warrantless search for evanescent evidence must be immediate. In other words, there must be good reason to believe that an immediate search will result in the seizure of the evidence in question. An example is **Cupp v. Murphy (412 U.S. 291 [1973])**. In that case, a man who had been informed of his wife's strangulation volunteered to come to the police station for questioning. While he was at the station, officers observed what appeared to be dried blood on the man's fingernails. The officers asked if they could take a scraping from his fingernails, and the man refused. He then started rubbing his hands behind his back and placing them in his pockets. At that point, the officers forcibly removed some of the material from under the man's fingernails. The Court upheld this action on the grounds that the police had probable cause to believe that "highly evanescent evidence" was in the process of being destroyed.

Recently, in *Kentucky* v. *King* (563 U.S. ___ [2011]), the Supreme Court held that police can make a forcible warrantless entry into a private residence if they have reason to believe evidence is being destroyed. In that case, officers smelled marijuana outside an apartment, knocked loudly, and announced their presence. They then heard what they believed was the sound of evidence being destroyed. They announced their intent to enter, kicked in the door, and found drugs in plain view—and other evidence—during the course of a protective sweep. The Supreme Court ruled that the evidence was admissible.

Offense Seriousness and Exigent Circumstances

The Supreme Court has also noted that the *seriousness* of the offense for which the warrantless arrest is to be made may be relevant in determining whether exigent circumstances are present. For example, in **Welsh v. Wisconsin (466 U.S. 740 [1984])**, a witness one night reported that an automobile was being driven erratically. Eventually, the car swerved off the road and stopped in a field. The driver walked away before police could arrive at the scene. When they did arrive, the police checked the registration of the car and found out it belonged to Welsh. They went

Think About It...

Immediacy and Evanescent Evidence A motor home that federal drug agents believed to contain a methamphetamine laboratory was parked in a secluded area near a river. The agents maintained visual surveillance throughout the afternoon. Around 4 p.m., one of the agents smelled chemicals "cooking." Shortly after that, the agents observed a man dash out of the motor home, gasping for air. In light of this incident, the agents decided to search the motor home. They ordered all of the occupants out of the motor home and placed them under arrest. The agents then entered the motor home to see if any other people were inside, to turn off any cooking apparatus, and to inventory the contents. They found a methamphetamine laboratory behind a drawn curtain at the back of the motor home. Was this action justified?

Michelle Marsan/Shutterstock

Hot Pursuit

Warrantless action based on a hot pursuit exigency is constitutional only if the police have probable cause to believe any of the following:
- The person they are pursuing has committed a serious offense.
- The person will be found on the premises the police seek to enter.
- The suspect will escape or harm someone or evidence will be lost or destroyed.
- The pursuit originates from a lawful vantage point.
- The scope and timing of the search are reasonable.

Evanescent (Disappearing) Evidence

A warrantless search for evanescent evidence is permissible when (1) there is probable cause to believe that evidence will be destroyed, lost, or devalued; (2) the procedures employed are reasonable; and (3) the exigency was not police created.

Danger to Others and/or Destruction of Evidence

A warrantless search In the absence of hot pursuit or the potential for damage to or destruction of evidence, a warrantless search is permissible if probable cause probable cause exists to believe a person on the premises is in imminent danger of death or serious bodily harm.

FIGURE 5–3 Summary of Exigent Circumstances.

to Welsh's house, gained entry, and arrested Welsh without a warrant. The Supreme Court held that the warrantless nighttime entry of a suspect's home to make an arrest for a *nonjailable* offense is a violation of the Fourth Amendment:

> Before government agents may invade the sanctity of the home, it must demonstrate exigent circumstances that overcome the presumption of unreasonableness that attaches to all warrantless home entries. An important factor to be considered when determining whether any exigency exists is the gravity of the underlying offense for which the arrest is being made . . . [A]pplication of the exigent circumstances exception in the context of home entry should rarely be sanctioned when there is probable cause that only a minor offense has been committed (p.750).

See Figure 5–3 for a summary of this and the preceding subsections. The figure outlines the basic rules concerning hot pursuit, evanescent evidence, and danger to others/destruction of evidence.

▶ Automobile Searches

In the landmark case of **Carroll v. United States (267 U.S. 132 [1925])**, the Supreme Court carved out an **automobile exception** to the Fourth Amendment's warrant requirement. The Court declared that the warrantless search of an automobile

The Court declared that the warrantless search of an automobile is permissible when (1) there is probable cause to believe the vehicle contains evidence of a crime and (2) securing a warrant is impractical.

is permissible when (1) there is probable cause to believe the vehicle contains evidence of a crime and (2) securing a warrant is impractical. *Carroll*, which was decided in 1925, resulted from the vehicle stop of a suspect who was known to have previously engaged in the sale of bootleg whiskey (that is, during Prohibition). A warrantless search of the car revealed 68 bottles of illegal liquor. The Supreme Court upheld the warrantless search on the grounds that the evidence would be lost if the police had been required to take the time to secure a warrant. Note that *Carroll* deals with vehicle *searches*, not stops. A different standard, namely, reasonable suspicion, is applied to vehicle stops.

Rationale

Three arguments can be offered in support of the automobile exception. First, because of the inherent mobility of vehicles, it is impractical to obtain warrants. According to the Court in *Carroll*,

> The guaranty (sic) of freedom from unreasonable searches and seizures by the Fourth Amendment has been construed, practically since the beginning of the Government, as recognizing a necessary difference between a search of a store, dwelling house or other structure in respect of which a proper official warrant readily may be obtained, and a search of a ship, motor boat, wagon or automobile, for contraband goods, where it is not practicable to secure a warrant because the vehicle can be quickly moved out of the locality in which the warrant must be sought. (p. 153)

The second reason for the automobile exception focuses on people's reasonable expectation of privacy. In particular, because vehicles are typically operated in public spaces, a lesser expectation of privacy is enjoyed. As the Court observed in *Cardwell* v. *Lewis* (417 U.S. 583 [1974]), people have a lesser expectation of privacy in an automobile because it serves a transportation function, not a privacy function; a car "seldom serves as one's residence or the repository of personal effects" (p. 590). Also, people have a lesser expectation of privacy in their automobiles because, by their very nature, automobiles travel "public thoroughfares where [their] occupants and [their] contents are in plain view" (p. 590).

The third reason for the automobile exception hinges on the government regulations to which vehicles are subjected. The old adage that "driving is a privilege, not a right" applies in this context. The Court's opinion in *United States* v. *Chadwick* (433 U.S. 1 [1977]) is illustrative. There, in deciding that the warrantless search of a man's footlocker, based on the automobile exception (because the footlocker was mobile), was unconstitutional,

Because vehicles are typically operated in public spaces, a lesser expectation of privacy is enjoyed.

the Court pointed to five issues concerning the regulated nature of automobiles: Automobiles (1) travel on public roads, (2) are subject to state regulations and licensing requirements, (3) are subject to other strict regulations, (4) are subject to periodic inspections, and (5) may be impounded for public safety reasons. Thus, the Court declared that the automobile exception should not apply to the warrantless search of personal items, despite their mobility.

Automobile Search Requirements

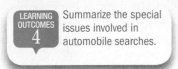
LEARNING OUTCOMES 4 Summarize the special issues involved in automobile searches.

Three general requirements must be met for a valid warrantless vehicle search: (1) the exception must only apply to automobiles; (2) with one exception, such a search must be premised on probable cause; and (3) it must be impractical to obtain a warrant (that is, the vehicle stop must be such that it is impractical, burdensome, or risky to take time to obtain a warrant). The third requirement is unresolved, as the courts have relied on lesser expectation of privacy analysis rather than an exigency argument to support warrantless searches of automobiles.

So far, the term *automobile* has been tossed around with wild abandon. Note, though, that *automobile* has a very specific meaning. In other words, precise types of vehicles are covered by the automobile exception. Cars, boats (for example, *United States* v. *Lee*, 274 U.S. 559 [1927]), and planes are all considered automobiles. However, what about the hybrid situation involving a vehicle serving the dual purpose of transportation and residence, such as a motor home or a tractor trailer with a sleeper cab? The Supreme Court was confronted with this question in the case of *California* v. *Carney* (**471 U.S. 386 [1985]**). Unfortunately, it refused to define explicitly the types of automobiles covered by the automobile exception and held that the test of whether a vehicle serves a transportation or residence function requires looking at the *setting* in which the vehicle is located. If the setting "objectively indicates that the vehicle is being used for transportation" (p. 386), then the automobile exception applies (see Figure 5–4).

In *Carroll*, the Court noted that "where seizure is impossible except without warrant, the seizing officer acts unlawfully and at his peril unless he can show the court probable cause" (p. 156). Simply put, despite the fact that a vehicle search is permissible without a warrant, the search must still be based on probable cause. Note, however, that probable cause to *search*

and probable cause to *arrest* are not one and the same. Although probable cause to search may exist, this does not automatically create probable cause to arrest. In *Carroll*, for example, the police had probable cause to search the vehicle but not probable cause to arrest the occupants. This distinction is important because it can bear on the admissibility of seized evidence. Indeed, there are other limitations placed on vehicle searches. Several are discussed in the accompanying "Evolution of *Carroll* v. *United States*" feature.

Similarly, probable cause to arrest does not authorize a full search of a vehicle, including the trunk, but it *can* authorize a search of the passenger compartment (**New York v. Belton, 453 U.S. 454 [1981]**; *Thoraton* v. *United States*, 541 U.S. 615 [2004]). However, in **Arizona v. Gant (556 U.S. 332 [2009])**, the Supreme Court restricted such searches. A man was arrested for driving on a suspended license. He was handcuffed and placed in a patrol car, then officers searched his car and found cocaine in the pocket of a jacket. He was convicted of drug offenses. The Supreme Court held that a *Belton*-type search is permissible "only if it is reasonable to believe that the arrestee might access the vehicle at the time of the search or that the vehicle contains evidence of the offense of arrest." Whereas *Belton* was a bright-line decision, *Gant* now makes it somewhat difficult to determine whether a search is sanctioned. It forces officers to decide whether the vehicle contains evidence of the offense in question.

Not long after *Gant*, the Court decided *Davis* v. *United States* (564 U.S. ___ [2011]). Davis was a passenger in a vehicle that was pulled over. He was arrested for giving police a false name. When he was seated in the back of the patrol car, officers searched the jacket he left in the vehicle. They found a gun, which Davis was not legally permitted to carry. Under *Gant*, the officers could not search the jacket because the search was not related to the arrest, but the Supreme Court sided with the police because at the time of the search (before the *Gant* decision was issued), their actions did not violate the Fourth Amendment. In other words, they acted in good faith.

There is one important exception to the rule that probable cause must be in place before a vehicle search can be conducted. In *New York* v. *Class* (475 U.S. 106 [1986]), the Court held in a 5-to-4 decision that the warrantless, suspicionless search of a car for the purpose of ascertaining the vehicle identification number (VIN) is permissible. All that is required is a valid traffic stop. This exception does not, however, authorize the police to enter cars at will, without any basis for a search. In support of its opinion, the Court pointed to the lesser expectation of privacy argument. Also, it noted that the search was minimally intrusive. The lower court in *Class* was not in agreement with the Supreme Court's decision: "The fact that certain information must be kept, or that it may be of a public nature, does not automatically sanction police intrusion into private space in order to obtain it" (p. 124).

A general rule concerning warrants is that they should be obtained whenever practical. However, given the circumstances surrounding most vehicle stops, it would seem foolish to require that the police obtain a warrant before engaging in the search of an

- Whether it is mobile or stationary

- Whether it is licensed

- Whether it is connected to utilities

- Whether it has convenient road access

FIGURE 5–4 Factors in Determining Whether a Vehicle Serves a Transportation Function.

automobile. As the Court observed in *Carroll*, in cases in which the securing of a warrant is reasonably practicable, a warrant must be used. In most situations involving the stop of an automobile, securing a warrant is not practical. In *Husty* v. *United States* (282 U.S. 694 [1931]), for example, a police officer followed up on a tip from an informant and found contraband in Husty's unattended car. Given that the car was unattended, one could argue that a warrant should have been secured, but the Court argued that the officer "could not know when Husty would come to the car or how soon it would be removed" (p. 701). Contrast *Husty* with *Coolidge* v. *New Hampshire* (403 U.S. 443 [1971]). In that case, the Court ruled that the automobile exception did not apply to a warrantless search and seizure of two cars located on the defendant's property because the police had probable cause to act more than two weeks before the search.

Husty and *Coolidge* suggest that the warrantless search of an automobile will only be upheld if it was impractical to obtain a warrant. This third requirement is unresolved, however. For example, in *Chambers* v. *Maroney* (399 U.S. 42 [1970]), the Court held that as long as the vehicle is readily mobile, a warrantless search is permissible, even if it is conducted away from the scene at the stationhouse. The actual search of the automobile in *Chambers* was made at the police station many hours after the car had been stopped on the highway, when the car was no longer movable. Furthermore, at that point, exigent circumstances no longer existed and a magistrate could have required a warrant. Yet the Court sanctioned the search (see also *Texas* v. *White*, 423 U.S. 67 [1975]).

One relatively recent case, *United States* v. *Johns* (469 U.S. 478 [1985]), seems to suggest that the rationale for the automobile exception is, at least in part, an exigency. In that case, the Court held that the warrantless search of an automobile is impermissible if it "adversely affect[s] a privacy [or] possessory interest" (p. 487). This argument seems to suggest that a search under the automobile exception needs to be premised on the urgency of the situation; otherwise, a warrant should be secured. Nevertheless, the Court in *Johns* did state that a three-day delay between the initial stop and the arrest was permissible, partly because the car's owner did not claim that the delay caused hardship.

So, what is the role of exigency in the automobile exception? A safe rule of thumb is that the presence or absence of exigent circumstances is irrelevant. Instead, a showing that the automobile was readily mobile is enough to justify a warrantless search

under the automobile exception (as long as probable cause is in place and the target of the search is, in fact, an automobile, as defined earlier).

Scope of the Automobile Search

Numerous court decisions have considered the scope of the search authorized under the automobile exception. Most of the decisions have focused on whether a container in an automobile can also be searched if probable cause to search the vehicle exists. In *Arkansas* v. *Sanders* (442 U.S. 753 [1979]), the Court ruled that the warrantless search of a suitcase was not permissible when the police waited for the suitcase to be placed in the vehicle. Similarly, in *Robbins* v. *California* (453 U.S. 420 [1981]), the Court held that a container discovered during a warrantless vehicle search can be seized but not searched until a warrant can be obtained.

Just one year after *Robbins*, the Court handed down its decision in *United States* v. *Ross* (456 U.S. 798 [1982]), which overturned *Robbins*. The Court declared that as long as the police have justification to conduct a warrantless vehicle search, they may conduct a search "that is as thorough as a magistrate could authorize in a warrant" (p. 800). The only limitation is "defined by the object of the search and the places in which there is probable cause to believe that it may be found" (p. 824). Accordingly, if the contraband sought is small (for example, a syringe), the scope of the vehicle search exception is almost limitless. Recently, the Supreme Court held that even passengers' personal belongings can be searched (*Wyoming* v. *Houghton*, 526 U.S. 295 [1999]).

Fewer cases have focused on precisely how far the police can go during a vehicle search in terms of inflicting damage to the vehicle. On the one hand, a due process violation may occur if the damage inflicted is excessive. On the other hand, it would appear that a certain degree of physical damage to an automobile is permissible. The *Carroll* decision, for example, was based on a warrantless search in which the police sliced open the vehicle's upholstery to look for contraband.

In another case, the Supreme Court considered whether allowing a drug dog to sniff a vehicle during a traffic stop violated the Fourth Amendment. In *Illinois* v. *Caballes* (543 U.S. 405 [2005]), an Illinois state trooper stopped a vehicle for speeding. During the ten-minute stop, while the trooper was going through all the usual motions associated with a traffic stop, another trooper arrived and allowed a drug dog to sniff the vehicle.

Level of Intrusion	Justification Required
Search of entire car, including containers	Probable cause to search
Search of passenger compartment and containers	Probable cause to arrest occupant
Weapons search of passenger compartment	Reasonable suspicion/fear for safety
Order occupants out of car	Reasonable suspicion to stop
Inventory search	Administrative

FIGURE 5-5 Levels of Justification for Automobile Searches.

The dog was alerted to the trunk. Marijuana was found, and the driver was arrested. The Supreme Court upheld the dog sniff, citing three factors: (1) the legality of the stop, (2) the short duration of the stop, and (3) the fact that no one can claim legal ownership to—and thereby assert a privacy interest in—contraband. This was a controversial decision, but one that clearly errs on the side of law enforcement. See Figure 5–5 for a summary of the levels of justification required to conduct various types of vehicle searches.

Other Actions in a Traffic Stop

Under current case law, the police are permitted wide latitude in conducting traffic stops. The police may stop a car based on the belief that a crime has been committed, which includes any traffic violation (*Whren* v. *United States*, 517 U.S. 806 [1996]). In addition, once a person has been stopped, the officer may order him or her to stand outside the vehicle without any justification (*Maryland* v. *Wilson*, 519 U.S. 408 [1997]). The police may also engage in searches with consent (*Ohio* v. *Robinette*, 519 U.S. 33 [1996]), seize items that are in plain view (*Horton* v. *California*, 496 U.S. 128 [1990]), frisk the driver and/or search the passenger compartment of the vehicle out of concerns for safety (*Michigan* v. *Long*, 463 U.S. 1032 [1983]), and search the entire car if probable cause to arrest and/or search is developed (*Belton*, 453 U.S. 454). Finally, police are not required to provide the *Miranda* warnings when asking questions pursuant to a routine vehicle stop (*Miranda* v. *Arizona*, 384 U.S. 436 [1966]).

Some questions have been raised concerning the constitutional protections afforded to passengers who happen to be riding in a vehicle that is stopped. For example, in *Brendlin* v. *California* (551 U.S. 249 [2007]), the Supreme Court was presented with the question of whether a passenger is considered "seized" within the meaning of the Fourth Amendment when the vehicle is stopped. It held that passengers, like drivers, are

seized in such situations. Why does this matter? Because the passenger was considered seized, he was able to challenge the constitutionality of the stop. He did so because police found contraband on his person.

What police *cannot* do during the course of a vehicle stop (or any other stop for that matter) is ascertain immigration status. In *Arizona* v. *United States*, 567 U.S. ___ (2012), the Supreme Court invalidated several parts of an Arizona law that required state officers to make a "reasonable attempt . . . to determine the immigration status" of any person stopped provided that "reasonable suspicion exists that the person is an alien and is unlawfully present in the United States." The Court held that "[d]etaining individuals solely to verify their immigration status would raise constitutional concerns."

See Figure 5–6 for a summary of the discussion in this section. Also see Figure 5–7, which calls attention to situations when other doctrines besides the automobile exception govern automobile searches.

► Plain-View Searches

Untrained observers frequently suggest that "plain view" applies in situations in which evidence can be seen without having to search for it. Although this may be a *literal* interpretation of what it means for something to be in plain view, it is not the interpretation the courts use. "Plain view" has a very specific meaning in criminal procedure, and the doctrine applies only in certain situations.

The **"plain-view" doctrine** first emerged in the Supreme Court's decision in *Coolidge* v. *New Hampshire* (**403 U.S. 443 [1971]**). The issue in *Coolidge* was whether evidence seized during a search of cars belonging to Coolidge was admissible. The police had a warrant to search the cars, but it was later deemed invalid, so the state argued that the evidence should still be admissible because the cars were in plain view from a public street

"Plain view" has a very specific meaning in criminal procedure, and the doctrine applies only in certain situations.

TIMELINE

Evolution of *Carroll* v. *United States*

1925	1970	1971
***Carroll* v. *United States*, 267 U.S. 132** Warrantless automobile search is permissible when there is probable cause to believe the vehicle contains evidence of a crime and securing a warrant is impractical.	***Chambers* v. *Maroney*, 399 U.S. 42** If the requirements for an automobile search are satisfied at the time the vehicle is first discovered, it can be searched later, such as at a police station or impound lot, without a warrant.	***Coolidge* v. *New Hampshire*, 403 U.S. 443** For a warrantless automobile search to be sanctioned, it must be impractical to obtain a warrant.

- Once a person has been stopped, the officer can order him or her to stand outside the vehicle without any justification (*Maryland v. Wilson*, 519 U.S. 408 [1997]; *Pennsylvania v. Mimms*, 434 U.S. 106 [1997]).
- Vehicle searches with consent are also permissible (*Ohio v. Robinette*, 519 U.S. 33 [1996]).
- Contraband located in plain view can be seized (*Horton v. California*, 496 U.S. 128 [1990]).
- An officer may frisk the driver and/or search the passenger compartment of the vehicle out of concerns for safety (*Michigan v. Long*, 463 U.S. 1032 [1983]).
- A *Belton/Gant*–type search is permissible if a proper arrest is made.
- A full search of the vehicle is permissible if probable cause develops.
- The police are not required to provide the *Miranda* warnings when asking questions pursuant to a routine vehicle stop (*Miranda v. Arizona*, 384 U.S. 436 [1966]).
- Passengers, like drivers, are considered "seized" for Fourth Amendment purposes during traffic stops (*Brendlin v. California*, 551 U.S. 249 [2007]), meaning they enjoy the same constitutional protections as drivers.

FIGURE 5–6 Other Actions Sanctioned in a Traffic Stop.

Automobile searches are governed by the automobile exception to the Fourth Amendment's warrant requirement, but by other doctrines in the following situations:
- Vehicle searches at international borders (administrative search rationale applies—see Chapter 7)
- Search incident to arrest (see *New York v. Belton* and *Arizona v. Gant*, discussed earlier in this chapter)
- Plain-view doctrine (see "Plain-View Searches" section in this chapter)
- Vehicle inventories (see Chapter 7)
- Consent searches (see end of this chapter)

FIGURE 5–7 When Other Doctrines Govern Automobile Searches.

and from the house in which Coolidge was arrested. The Court did not accept this argument, pointing out that just because the police could *see* the cars from where they were did not mean that they were permitted to seize the evidence in question. However, the Court did point out that had the police been *in* an area, such as a car or a house, evidence that was "immediately apparent as such" and was discovered "inadvertently" would have been admissible. In other words, part of the reason the evidence was not admissible in *Coolidge* was that the police officers were not lawfully in the cars when the evidence was seized.

To summarize, the Court decided in *Coolidge* that a plain-view seizure is authorized when (1) the police are lawfully in the area where the evidence is located, (2) the items are immediately apparent as subject to seizure, and (3) the discovery of the evidence is inadvertent. The first prong of the *Coolidge* ruling—the lawful access prong—has remained relatively stable over time. The second and third prongs, however, have undergone significant interpretation in recent years. The remainder of this section is therefore based on these three requirements.

The Lawful Access Requirement

For the plain-view doctrine to apply, the police must have **lawful access** to the object to be seized. As the Supreme Court decided in *Coolidge*,

> [P]lain view *alone* is never enough to justify the warrantless seizure of evidence. This is simply a corollary of the familiar principle . . . that no amount of probable cause can justify a warrantless search or seizure absent

1981	1906	2009
***New York* v. *Belton*, 453 U.S. 454** Vehicle passenger compartment can be searched following lawful arrest.	***New York* v. *Class*, 475 U.S. 106** A warrantless, suspicionless search of a car for the purpose of ascertaining the vehicle identification number (VIN) is permissible. A valid traffic stop is required, however.	***Arizona* v. *Gant*, 556 U.S. 332** The rule announced in *New York v. Belton* is modified as follows: A *Belton*-type search is permissible "only if it is reasonable to believe that the arrestee might access the vehicle at the time of the search or that the vehicle contains evidence of the offense of arrest."

"exigent circumstances." Incontrovertible testimony of the senses that an incriminating object is on premises belonging to a criminal suspect may establish the fullest possible measure of probable cause. But even where the object is contraband, this Court has repeatedly stated and enforced the basic rule that the police may not enter and make a warrantless seizure. (p. 468)

This excerpt from the Court's opinion in *Coolidge* reinforces the requirement that just because the police may *see* contraband does not necessarily mean they can *seize* it. If, for example, evidence is seen lying in a vacant lot or other public place, it may be seized. In such a situation, a search has not occurred. However, evidence that may be viewed from a public place but is, in fact, on private property cannot be seized unless a warrant is obtained or exigent circumstances are present. So, if a police officer on foot patrol observes a marijuana plant in the window of a private residence, he or she may not enter the premises and seize the plant, even though such observation establishes "the fullest possible measure of probable cause."

What is meant by *lawful vantage point*? There are four specific situations in which police officers can be found in a lawful vantage point for purposes of the plain-view doctrine. The first is during a warranted search. For example, if an officer comes upon an article during the execution of a valid search warrant, the plain-view doctrine may apply (subject to further restrictions described later). Second, officers are in a lawful vantage point during a valid arrest. This includes warrantless arrests in public, warrantless arrests based on exigent circumstances, and arrests with warrants. Third, when a warrantless search is conducted, the police officer is in a lawful vantage point—assuming, of course, that the warrantless search is based on probable cause. Finally, as illustrated in the previous paragraph, officers are always in a lawful vantage point during nonsearches.

The "Immediately Apparent" Requirement

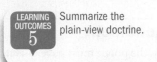 Summarize the plain-view doctrine.

In addition to the requirement that the police have lawful access to an object for the plain-view doctrine to apply, it must also be **immediately apparent** that the object is subject to seizure. *Immediately apparent* means that the officer has probable cause to seize the object.

This was the decision reached in **Arizona v. Hicks (480 U.S. 321 [1987])**. In that case, the police entered the defendant's apartment without a warrant because a bullet had been fired through his floor into the apartment below, injuring a person there. The warrantless entry was based on the exigency of looking for the shooter, for other potential victims, and for the weapon used in the incident. Once inside the apartment, the officer observed new stereo equipment that seemed out of place, given the surroundings. The officer suspected the stereo equipment was stolen, so he picked up a turntable in order to obtain its serial number. He then called in the information and confirmed that it was stolen. The Court held that this warrantless action did not satisfy the plain-view doctrine. It was not immediately apparent to the officer that the stereo equipment was stolen.

Remember that *probable cause to seize* and *immediately apparent* are one and the same. An officer does not need to be absolutely certain that the object is subject to seizure for the plain-view doctrine to apply. That was the decision reached in *Texas* v. *Brown* (460 U.S. 730 [1983]). In that case, Brown was stopped late at night at a routine driver's license checkpoint. When he opened the glove box in order to look for his license, an opaque balloon, knotted at the opening, fell out onto the floor of the passenger side of the vehicle. The officer making the stop observed what he perceived to be drug paraphernalia in the glove compartment and ultimately seized the balloon and its contents. The balloon was later proven to contain heroin. Brown was convicted of narcotics offenses. The Texas Court of Criminal Appeals reversed Brown's conviction, pointing out that the plain-view doctrine did not apply because the officer did not *know* incriminatory evidence was before him when he seized the balloon. A unanimous Supreme Court reversed the decision, stating, "The fact that [the officer] could not see through the opaque fabric of the balloon is all but irrelevant; the distinctive character of the balloon itself spoke volumes as to its contents—particularly to the trained eye of the officer" (p. 743).

The Role of Inadvertency

The role of *inadvertency* in the plain-view determination has received considerable attention. The original position of the Supreme Court in *Coolidge* v. *New Hampshire* was that an object seized under the plain-view doctrine must not have been anticipated by the police. For example, assume that a police

Think About It...

Considering the "Immediately Apparent" Requirement for Plain View Police officers have a warrant for the arrest of Randy Whitbeck, who is the suspect in a rape. They lawfully execute the warrant and arrest Whitbeck in his home. While there, one of the officers observes a rifle leaning up against the wall in an adjacent bedroom. With probable cause to suspect that it is an illegal assault weapon, she enters the room and seizes the gun. May the gun be introduced as evidence? Assume further that the gun is not connected in any way to the rape. Does it matter that the seizure of the gun is not connected with the rape? Finally, if the officers knew the rifle was contraband *prior* to serving the warrant and if the rifle was not named in the search warrant accompanying the arrest warrant, could they still seize it lawfully?

Arina P Habich/Shutterstock

officer obtains a warrant to search a suspect's home for the proceeds from a robbery. Assume further that the officer *expects* to find guns in the house but does not state in the warrant that guns will be sought. If, during the search, the officer finds guns, under the Supreme Court's old ruling, the guns will not be admissible, because the officers expected to find them. This restriction on the plain-view doctrine came to be known as the *inadvertency requirement*. The rationale for this restriction was that an officer who anticipates discovering evidence of a crime should seek prior judicial authorization (that is, a warrant). Further, the Fourth Amendment's particularity requirement would be compromised if general searches were permitted.

In *Horton* v. *California* **(496 U.S. 128 [1990])**, the Court declared that inadvertency, although a "characteristic of most legitimate 'plain view' seizures, . . . is not a necessary condition" of the doctrine (p. 130). The Court offered two reasons for abandoning the inadvertency requirement imposed in *Coolidge*. First, according to *Horton*, as long as a warrant particularly describes the places to be searched and the objects to be seized, the officer cannot expand the area of the search once the evidence has been found. In other words, it is unlikely that once officers have found the evidence listed in the warrant, they will go on a "fishing expedition," looking for evidence not listed in the warrant. According to the Court, the particularity requirement itself ensures that people's privacy is protected.

Second, the Court noted that "evenhanded law enforcement is best achieved by the application of objective standards of conduct, rather than standards that depend upon the subjective state of mind of the officer" (p. 138). An inadvertency requirement would force the courts to dwell on police officers' subjective motivations, which would be both time consuming and distracting. The Court went on to note that "[t]he fact that an officer is interested in an item of evidence and fully expects to find it in the course of a search should not invalidate its seizure if the search is confined in area and duration by the terms of the warrant or a valid exception to the warrant requirement" (p. 138).

► Warrantless Arrests

Just as there are a number of searches that can be conducted without a warrant, the Supreme Court has also sanctioned certain arrests that can be made without a warrant. They include arrests in the presence of exigent circumstances and arrests in public places. Generally, warrantless arrests are made in cases of serious offenses, but the police *are* authorized to make arrests for minor offenses (see Figure 5–8).

Arrests Based on Exigent Circumstances

Exigent (that is, emergency) circumstances justify warrantless entry into a private home for the purpose of making an arrest. The five exigencies identified earlier in this chapter justify warrantless entry for this purpose. In other words, a warrantless

Warrantless Arrests for Minor Offenses

Two U.S. Supreme Court Cases pertain to warrantless arrests for minor offenses:

Atwater v. *City of Lago Vista*, 532 U.S. 318 (2001):

"The Fourth Amendment does not forbid a warrantless arrest for a minor criminal offense, such as a misdemeanor seatbelt violation punishable only by a fine." In *Atwater*, the driver was arrested for failing to wear a seatbelt.

Virginia v. *Moore*, 553 U.S. 164 (2008):

Evidence seized during a postarrest vehicle search is admissible, even if state law forbids the officer to make an arrest in the situation. In *Moore*, the driver was stopped for driving with a suspended license. Virginia law required that the officer issue a citation and summons to appear in court, but the officer arrested the motorist.

FIGURE 5–8 **Warrantless Arrests for Minor Offenses.**

arrest, with probable cause, is permissible if any of the following is present: (1) hot pursuit, (2) danger to officers, (3) danger to third parties, (4) escape, and (5) destruction of evidence.

Arrests in Public Places

Unlike arrests made in the home (or in a third-party residence), arrests made in public do not require warrants. In *United States* v. *Watson* **(423 U.S. 411 [1976])**, the Supreme Court upheld the common-law rule that arrests made in public do not need to be predicated on a warrant. The Court expressed confidence in the ability of police officers to make probable cause determinations: "[W]e decline to transform [a] judicial preference [for arrest warrants] into a constitutional rule when the judgment of the Nation and Congress has for so long been to authorize warrantless public arrests on probable cause" (p. 423).

The court extended this decision to the curtilage of a home in *United States* v. *Santana* **(427 U.S. 38 [1976])**. In that case, the police, who had probable cause to arrest Santana, arrived at her house to find her standing in the opening of her front door. When she saw the officers approaching, she retreated into the house. The officers followed her into the house and made the arrest. The Supreme Court declared that the officers' actions were constitutional because when Santana was standing in the doorway, "[s]he was not in an area where she had any expectation of privacy" (p. 42). The entry into Santana's house was justified on exigent circumstances—namely, hot pursuit.

Watson and *Santana* therefore combine to permit another type of warrantless action authorized by the Fourth Amendment. As long as probable cause is in place, the police can make a warrantless arrest in a public place. A warrantless arrest in the curtilage of someone's home is also authorized. The key in *Santana*, though, was that the arrest was initiated by the police observing what they perceived to be criminal activity from a public place. This important qualification ensures that the police cannot just wander onto private property, looking for opportunities to make arrests. A crime must be

LEARNING OUTCOMES 6 Describe the situations in which warrantless arrests may be made.

Crime Report No. _____

CONSENT TO SEARCH

I, _____ give the San Bernardino Police Department
my consent to search the below listed property.

Address:_____ City_____
_____ Country _____
Address: _____ City _____
_____ Country _____
Vehicle/s: Make _____ Year _____ Veh. Lic. # _____
      Make _____ Year _____ Veh. Lic. # _____

Other:_____
_____
_____
_____
_____
_____

      Signed: _____
Date: _____ Time: _____
Witness _____ Witness _____

FIGURE 5–9   **Example Consent to Search Form.**

observed from a lawful vantage point; otherwise, a warrant will be required.

What if the offense takes place out of view of the officer? The courts have stated that if probable cause exists, the police can arrest anyone for any offense, as long as the arrest is made in a public place. It is useful, though, to distinguish between (1) various types of offenses and (2) whether the offense in question was committed in the presence of the officer. Generally, any offense committed in an officer's presence permits an arrest. Also, there is no requirement that the offense for which a person is arrested be "closely related" to the conduct that led to the confrontation between officer and suspect (*Devenpeck* v. *Alford*, 543 U.S. 146 [2004]). Additionally, serious offenses (felonies) committed *out* of the officer's view permit a warrantless, public arrest—provided that probable cause exists. Less clear is the issue of a warrantless, public arrest for a misdemeanor committed out of the officer's presence.

▶ Consent Searches

The general rule is that validly obtained consent justifies a warrantless search, with or without probable cause. However, for consent to be valid, it must be voluntary. Consent cannot be "the result of duress or coercion, express or implied" (**Schneckloth v. Bustamonte, 412 U.S. 218 [1973]**). When does duress or coercion take place? There is no clear answer to this question. Instead, the Court has opted for a *totality of circumstances* test. This test requires looking at the *surrounding circumstances* of the consent, including whether a show of force was made; whether the person's age, mental condition, or intellectual capacities inhibited understanding; whether the person is or was

in custody; and/or whether consent was granted "only after the official conducting the search [had] asserted that he possesses a warrant" (*Bumper* v. *North Carolina*, 391 U.S. 543 [1968]).

Importantly, consent to search may be valid even if the consenting party is unaware of the fact that he or she can refuse consent (*Schneckloth* v. *Bustamonte*, 412 U.S. 218 [1973]). As the Court stated in *Ohio* v. *Robinette* (519 U.S. 33 [1996]), "[J]ust as it 'would be thoroughly impractical to impose on the normal consent search the detailed requirements of an effective warning,' so too would it be unrealistic to require police officers to always inform detainees that they are free to go before a consent to search may be deemed involuntary" (pp. 39–40). This view was recently reaffirmed in *United States* v. *Drayton* (536 U.S. 194 [2002]), a case involving consent searches of bus passengers. Nevertheless, the issue of one's awareness of the right to refuse consent is still factored into the totality of circumstances analysis (for example, *United States* v. *Mendenhall*, 446 U.S. 544 [1980]), although ignorance of the right to refuse is not enough, in and of itself, to render consent involuntary.

To err on the side of constitutionality, many police departments have suspects complete "consent to search" forms. An example of one such form, from the San Bernardino, California, Police Department, is shown in Figure 5–9.

Scope Limitations

The *scope* of a consent search is limited to the terms of the consent. In other words, the person giving consent delineates the scope. This was the

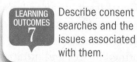

LEARNING OUTCOMES 7 Describe consent searches and the issues associated with them.

decision reached in the case of **Florida v. Jimeno (500 U.S. 248 [1991])**. For example, if a person tells the police "You may look around," it does not necessarily mean the police can look *anywhere* for evidence of criminal activity.

Another issue concerning the scope of a consent search is whether consent can be withdrawn once given. In *State* v. *Brochu* (237 A.2d 418 [Me. 1967]), the Maine Supreme Court held that a defendant's consent to search his house for evidence of his wife's murder did not extend to another search carried out the day after he was arrested as a suspect. Thus, although the man did not expressly request that the search be terminated, the Maine court still decided that consent had been terminated. The Supreme Court has not directly decided whether consent can be withdrawn, however.

Third-Party Consent

A handful of Supreme Court cases have focused on whether a third party (the third party being someone other than the authority asking for consent to search and the individual whose property he or she hopes to search) can give consent to have another person's property searched (for example, a landlord consenting to have a tenant's apartment searched; parents consenting to have their child's room searched). As far as the immediate family is concerned, there are several general rules: (1) Wives and husbands can give consent to have their partners' property searched and (2) parents can give consent to have their children's property searched, but (3) children cannot give consent to have their parents' property searched. The reason children cannot give consent is that they are considered incompetent to give voluntary consent, given their age.

More confusing is the situation of a roommate, former girlfriend, friend, or extended family member. Two important Supreme Court cases are relevant here. First, third-party consent can be given if (1) the third-party individual possesses "common authority" over the area to be searched and (2) the nonconsenting party (for example, the roommate) is not present (**United States v. Matlock, 415 U.S. 164 [1974]**). According to the Court, **common authority** rests on "mutual use of the property by persons generally having joint access or control for most purposes" (p. 172, n. 7). Thus, a third party could give consent to have a shared bathroom searched but not to have his or her roommate's bedroom searched. What happens, however, if the nonconsenting party is present and affirmatively objects to the search? The courts are divided on this issue.

There are some clear-cut situations in which two people possess common authority over a particular area, but what happens when it is not clear to officers at the scene whether common authority exists? In response to this question, the Supreme Court has held that the warrantless entry of private premises by police officers is valid if based on the **apparent authority** doctrine. In other words, a warrantless entry of a residence is valid if it is based on the consent of a person whom the police reasonably believe has authority to grant consent, even if their beliefs are ultimately erroneous (**Illinois v. Rodriguez, 497 U.S. 177 [1990]**). The test for reasonableness in this situation, according to the Court, is as follows: "[W]ould the facts available to the officer at the moment [of the entry] . . . warrant a man of reasonable caution in

the belief that the consenting party had authority over the premises?" (p. 179). *Rodriguez* involved consent given by a former girlfriend who possessed apparent authority to grant consent because she still had a key to her ex-boyfriend's apartment.

Still other cases have focused on whether third-party individuals can give consent. Most cannot. For example, a landlord cannot give consent to search property rented to another person (*Stoner* v. *California*, 376 U.S. 483 [1964]), one lessor cannot give consent to search the premises of another lessor (*United States* v. *Impink*, 728 F.2d 1228 [9th Cir. 1985]), hotel clerks cannot give consent to search guests' rooms (*Stoner* v. *California*), and college officials cannot give consent to search students' dormitories (*Piazzola* v. *Watkins*, 442 F.2d 284 [5th Cir. 1971]). Note, however, that consent given by the driver of a vehicle to search any part of the vehicle is valid, even if the driver is not the owner of the vehicle (*United States* v. *Morales*, 861 F.2d 396 [3rd Cir. 1988]).

What if both parties who have common authority are present when the police request consent, but one of them refuses consent and the other gives it? This issue came up in the case of *Georgia* v. *Randolph* (547 U.S. 103 [2006]), a case in which police were called to the scene of a domestic dispute. When the officers asked for consent to search, the husband unequivocally refused, but the wife readily consented. The officers took the wife up on her consent, searched the premises, and found cocaine. The husband sought to have the cocaine excluded from his subsequent trial, but a Georgia trial court denied his motion. The Georgia Supreme Court reversed and the U.S. Supreme Court affirmed, holding that "a physically present co-occupant's stated refusal to permit entry renders warrantless entry and search unreasonable and invalid" (p. 103).

The outcome will be different, however, if the nonconsenting party is no longer around. In *Fernandez* v. *California* (571 U.S. ____ [2014]), a male robbery suspect was arrested after refusing to let officers search his residence (it was the robbery, not his refusal to consent that prompted the arrest). After he was gone, the woman he shared the apartment with granted consent for officers to search. They found incriminating evidence, which the Supreme Court later declared admissible.

Think About It...

Scope of Consent Hector Lopez is stopped by the highway patrol for speeding. The officer who approaches his car asks if he will consent to a search of his vehicle. As reinforcements arrive, the officer states that they are concerned about drug smuggling on this stretch of freeway. Lopez gives consent and says, "Yes, you can search my car," and so the officers subject the car to an intensive search. They remove every bag and every moveable item from the vehicle and scrutinize each one carefully. They further check the spare tire compartment, engine compartment, glove box, and even the panels providing access to lighting, electrical, and so on. Have the officers exceeded the scope of Lopez's consent? What if, instead, Lopez stated, "Yes you can search my car, but I'm late for a doctor's appointment, so I have to leave in no more than five minutes"?

© Mikael Karlsson / Alamy

Did the Police Act Properly?

Two Drug Enforcement Administration (DEA) agents (Bryant and Keiffer) knocked on the door of a man (Munoz-Guerra) who they suspected was an armed and dangerous narcotics dealer. When Munoz-Guerra came to the door, the agents ordered him to place his hands on the glass door and then to slowly reach down and unlock it. He said he did not have a key and would need to go to another room to obtain one. Believing Munoz-Guerra would retrieve a gun from the other room, the agents kicked down the door and entered as the suspect retreated to another room. Once inside, they conducted a protective sweep of the apartment. During the course of the sweep, bales of marijuana were found. The Fifth Circuit Court of Appeals was confronted with the question of whether the entrance and the sweep were justified. Here is the court's answer:

> Agents Bryant and Keiffer knew when they knocked on the patio door that, once having made their presence known to Munoz-Guerra (and possibly to other occupants) it would be necessary to conduct a security search of the premises and to restrain the condominium's inhabitants. Warrantless entry was thus a foregone conclusion the instant the agents revealed themselves to Munoz-Guerra at the patio door. The question before this court, then, is whether exigent circumstances justified the agents' initial decision to approach the patio door. Our past opinions have consistently emphasized that without reason to believe that a criminal suspect was aware of police surveillance, the mere presence of firearms or destructible, incriminating evidence does not create exigent circumstances. . . . In the instant case, it was possible to secure the condominium covertly from the outside. There was no basis, on these facts, for believing that resort to a magistrate would have created risks of a greater magnitude than those which are present in any case where the police have probable cause but delay entry pending receipt of a warrant. . . . Had the [agents'] necessary efforts to secure the premises been visible to the inhabitants or had there been reason to believe that someone within the condominium was in need of immediate succor, the government's position would have merit. The government's argument that swift and immediate action may have minimized risks to human life and physical evidence, however, misses the mark. Our Fourth Amendment jurisprudence contemplates that protection of individual rights of privacy will be achieved at some cost to society's interest in public safety; and, in the ordinary case the risk that a criminal suspect will become aware of covert surveillance is deemed insignificant in contrast to the more substantial benefits we all derive from the procedural safeguards of judicial process. (*United States* v. *Munoz-Guerra*, 788 F.2d 295 [5th Cir. 1986], pp. 298–299)

In other words, the warrantless entry was not constitutional, according to the Fifth Circuit.

This case raises several interesting Fourth Amendment questions, including the following:

1. Do you agree with the court's decision in this case? Why or why not?
2. What could the agents have done differently?
3. What facts do we not know from the quick description? Would those facts have made any difference in the court's decision?

Summarize the issues involved in warrantless searches and seizures.

The Supreme Court has carved out several exceptions to the Fourth Amendment's warrant requirement. Although the exceptions vary considerably, a common thread runs through them: The Court has decided that it is not always practical to obtain a warrant.

Key Cases

Riley v. California

1. What are the main exceptions to the Fourth Amendment's warrant requirement?

2. What is the logic behind all the exceptions to the warrant requirement?

racial profiling The practice of stopping people based on race rather than legitimate criteria.

exceptions to the warrant requirement Law enforcement actions that do not require a warrant. Examples include searches incident to arrest, searches based on exigent circumstances, automobile searches, plain-view searches, arrests based on exigent circumstances, and arrests in public places.

Explain the search incident to arrest doctrine.

Searches incident to arrest are constitutionally permissible, but the arrest must, of course, be legal (that is, based on probable cause). Also, the arrest must result in someone being taken into custody. Next, the search must follow the arrest closely in time. Finally, the search incident to arrest is limited to (1) the person arrested and any containers discovered from that search and (2) the arrestee's immediate grabbing area.

Key Cases

Chimel v. California

Knowles v. Iowa

Preston v. United States

1. Summarize the requirements for a valid search incident to arrest.

search incident to arrest An exception to the Fourth Amendment's warrant requirement that allows officers to search a suspect following his or her arrest.

armspan rule Part of the search incident to arrest exception to the Fourth Amendment's warrant requirement that allows officers to search not only the suspect incident to arrest, but also his or her "grabbing area."

protective sweep A cursory visual inspection of those places in which a person might be hiding.

Identify three types of exigent circumstances and how they operate as exceptions to the warrant requirement.

Hot pursuit, threats to persons, and threats to evidence are exigent circumstances that also permit dispensing with the Fourth Amendment's warrant requirement. Warrantless searches and arrests based on hot pursuit are constitutional only if the police have probable cause to believe (1) that the person they are pursuing has committed a serious offense, (2) that the person will be found on the premises the police seek to enter, and (3) that the suspect will escape or harm someone or that evidence will be lost or destroyed.

Key Cases

Warden v. Hayden

Minnesota v. Olson

Missouri v. McNeely

Cupp v. Murphy

Welsh v. Wisconsin

1. What type of law enforcement activities fall under the banner of exigent circumstances?

2. When does the hot pursuit rule apply?

exigent circumstances Emergency circumstances, including hot pursuit, the possibility of escape, or evanescent evidence. When exigent circumstances are present, the police do not need to abide by the Fourth Amendment's warrant requirement.

hot pursuit An exigent circumstance that permits dispensing with the Fourth Amendment's warrant requirement. Hot pursuit applies only when the police have probable cause to believe (1) that the person they are pursuing has committed a serious offense, (2) that the person will be found on the premises the police seek to enter, and (3) that the suspect will escape or harm someone or that evidence will be lost or destroyed. Also, the pursuit must originate from a lawful vantage point and the scope and timing of the search must be reasonable.

evanescent evidence Evidence that is likely to disappear. An example is alcohol in a person's bloodstream.

Summarize the special issues involved in automobile searches.

For an automobile search to be constitutional, it must be (1) directed at a vehicle ready to serve a transportation function, (2) premised on probable cause to believe the vehicle contains evidence of a crime, and (3) completed without unnecessary delay.

Key Cases

Carroll v. United States

California v. Carney

New York v. Belton

Arizona v. Gant

1. What are the requirements for a valid automobile search?

2. What does the term *automobile* mean in the automobile search context?

automobile exception An exception to the Fourth Amendment's warrant requirement that permits police to search a vehicle without a warrant, so long as they have probable cause to do so.

Summarize the plain-view doctrine.

Items in plain view can be seized if the police have lawful access to the items and if it is immediately apparent that the items are contraband. The discovery of such items does not have to be inadvertent.

Key Cases

Coolidge v. New Hampshire

Arizona v. Hicks

Horton v. California

1. Why does the term *plain view* mean something different in criminal procedure than in everyday use?

2. Explain the lawful access prong of the plain-view doctrine.

3. Explain the immediately apparent prong of the plain-view doctrine.

"plain-view" doctrine An exception to the Fourth Amendment's warrant requirement that permits police to seize certain items in plain view.

lawful access One of the requirements for a proper plain-view seizure. The police must have lawful access to the item seized.

immediately apparent One of the requirements for a proper plain-view seizure. The police must have probable cause that the item is subject to seizure.

Describe the situations in which warrantless arrests may be made.

Two types of warrantless arrests have been authorized by the Supreme Court. First, if exigent circumstances are present, the police may make a warrantless arrest. Probable cause is required, however. Second, an arrest in public can be made without a warrant. Even certain minor offenses can support arrest in public places.

Key Cases

United States v. Watson

United States v. Santana

1. When is a warrantless arrest constitutionally permissible?

2. When is a warrantless arrest *not* constitutionally permissible?

LEARNING OUTCOMES 7

Describe consent searches and the issues associated with them.

Consent searches are constitutional, but consent must be voluntary, as determined by the totality of circumstances. The scope of a consent search is defined by the person giving consent. Third parties can give consent if they have actual or apparent authority over the premises or property to be searched.

Key Cases

Schneckloth v. *Bustamonte*

Florida v. *Jimeno*

United States v. *Matlock*

Illinois v. *Rodriguez*

1. What does "consent" mean in criminal procedure?
2. Why is consent a valuable law enforcement tool?
3. What are the rules concerning third-party consent?

common authority "Mutual use of the property by persons generally having joint access or control for most purposes" (*United States* v. *Matlock*, 415 U.S. 164 [1974], p. 172, n. 7).

apparent authority A person has apparent authority if the police *reasonably believe* he or she has authority to grant consent.

6

Stop-and-Frisk

1 Explain the Supreme Court's decision in *Terry* v. *Ohio*.

2 Summarize the rules concerning a "stop" in the stop-and-frisk context.

3 Summarize the rules concerning a "frisk" in the stop-and-frisk context.

4 Explain how stop-and-frisk law has expanded over time.

INTRO   STOP-AND-FRISK RUN AMOK?

On August 12, 2013, a federal district court judge found the City of New York liable for a pattern of unconstitutional stop-and-frisk activities by the New York Police Department (NYPD). The judge decided in part that

> the City adopted a policy of indirect racial profiling by targeting racially defined groups for stops based on local crime suspect data. This has resulted in the disproportionate and discriminatory stopping of blacks and Hispanics in violation of the Equal Protection Clause. Both statistical and anecdotal evidence showed that minorities are indeed treated differently than whites.

The following facts were uncontested in the case (i.e., both New York and the plaintiffs agreed to them):

- Between January 2004 and June 2012, the NYPD conducted over 4.4 million *Terry* stops.
- The number of stops per year rose sharply from 314,000 in 2004 to a high of 686,000 in 2011.
- Of all stops, 52% were followed by a protective frisk for weapons. A weapon was found after 1.5% of these frisks. In other words, in 98.5% of the 2.3 million frisks, no weapon was found.
- Of all stops, 8% led to a search into the stopped person's clothing, ostensibly based on the officer feeling an object during the frisk that he suspected to be a weapon, or immediately perceived to be contraband other than a weapon. In 9% of these searches, the felt object was in fact a weapon; 91% of the time, it was not. In 14% of these searches, the felt object was in fact contraband; 86% of the time it was not.
- Of all stops, 6% resulted in an arrest, and 6% resulted in a summons. The remaining 88% of the 4.4 million stops resulted in no further law enforcement action.
- In 52% of the 4.4 million stops, the person stopped was black, in 31% the person was Hispanic, and in 10% the person was white.

Spencer Platt/Getty Images

- In 2010, New York City's resident population was roughly 23% black, 29% Hispanic, and 33% white.
- In 23% of the stops of blacks, and 24% of the stops of Hispanics, the officer recorded using force. The number for whites was 17%.
- Weapons were seized in 1.0% of the stops of blacks, 1.1% of the stops of Hispanics, and 1.4% of the stops of whites.
- Contraband other than weapons was seized in 1.8% of the stops of blacks, 1.7% of the stops of Hispanics, and 2.3% of the stops of whites.
- Between 2004 and 2009, the percentage of stops where the officer failed to state a specific suspected crime rose from 1% to 36%.[1]

DISCUSS **Based on this information, do you agree with the judge's decision?**
For additional details on this case, which continues to develop, see http://ccrjustice.org/stopandfrisk.

▶ *Loosening the Fourth Amendment's Restraints*

Reasonable suspicion is defined as a lesser degree of certainty than probable cause but a greater degree of certainty than a hunch or unsupported belief. The term *reasonable suspicion* is found nowhere in the Constitution. Rather, reasonable suspicion is a standard created by the Supreme Court. The reason that the Court declared that certain confrontations between police and citizens can be based on reasonable suspicion is that crime control could not be accomplished without a lower standard than probable cause. If probable cause was always required, police officers would not even be able to question people about suspected involvement in criminal activity without a high degree of justification.

The law governing stop-and-frisk attempts to achieve a balance between due process and crime control. On the one hand, most people find it desirable for the police to control crime.

If crime ran rampant, people would curtail their activities by, for example, not going out at night. On the other hand, the Constitution is a highly prized guarantor of personal freedoms. Many people, despite their desire to see crime decline, would object to aggressive search-and-seizure tactics by the police. Reasonable suspicion is something of a compromise between the conflicting goals of crime control and due process; it can be seen as achieving a balance between having unrestricted law enforcement and being able to apprehend lawbreakers.

Reasonable suspicion is something of a compromise between the conflicting goals of crime control and due process.

When police activity does not constitute a search, the Fourth Amendment does not apply. By extension, then, when the Fourth Amendment does not apply, probable cause is not required. Much the same logic applies to a stop-and-frisk. If police conduct falls short of a stop or a frisk, the Fourth Amendment does not apply. Thus, when the Fourth Amendment does not apply, reasonable suspicion is not required. Additionally, if the police confront a person but such activity does not constitute a stop or a frisk, no justification is required. At the opposite extreme, though, if police conduct amounts to a more significant intrusion than a stop or a frisk, then a different standard of justification will be required—most likely, probable cause.

Terry v. Ohio: The Facts

***Terry* v. *Ohio* (392 U.S. 1 [1968])** forms the foundation for the law governing police actions that are based on reasonable suspicion. Because it is of critical importance, its facts are worth considering in some depth:

> . . . while he was patrolling in plain clothes in downtown Cleveland at approximately 2:30 in the afternoon of October 31, 1963, [Officer McFadden's] attention was attracted by two men, Chilton and Terry, standing on the corner of Huron Road and Euclid Avenue. He had never seen the two men before, and he was unable to say precisely what first drew his eye to them. However, he testified that he had been a policeman for 39 years and a detective for 35, and that he had been assigned to patrol this vicinity of downtown Cleveland for shoplifters and pickpockets for 30 years. He explained that he had developed routine habits of observation over the years, and that he would "stand and watch people or walk and watch people at many intervals of the day." He added: "Now, in this case, when I looked over, they didn't look right to me at the time."

> His interest aroused, Officer McFadden took up a post of observation in the entrance to a store 300 to 400 feet away from the two men. "I get more purpose to watch them when I seen their movements," he testified. He saw one of the men leave the other one and walk southwest on Huron Road, past some stores. The man paused for a moment and looked in a store window, then walked on a short distance, turned around and walked back toward the corner, pausing once again to look in the same store window. He rejoined his companion at the corner, and the two conferred briefly. Then the second man went through the same series of motions, strolling down Huron Road, looking in the same window, walking on a short distance, turning back, peering in the store window again, and returning to confer with the first man at the corner. The two men repeated this ritual alternately between five and six times apiece—in all, roughly a dozen trips. At one point, while the two were standing together on the corner, a third man approached them and engaged them briefly in conversation. This man then left the two others and walked west on Euclid Avenue. Chilton and Terry resumed their measured pacing, peering, and conferring. After this had gone on for 10 to 12 minutes, the two men walked off together, heading west on Euclid Avenue, following the path taken earlier by the third man.

> By this time, Officer McFadden had become thoroughly suspicious. He testified that after observing their elaborately casual and oft-repeated reconnaissance of the store window on Huron Road, he suspected the two men of "casing a job, a stick-up," and that he considered it his duty as a police officer to investigate further. He added that he feared "they may have a gun." Thus, Officer McFadden followed Chilton and Terry and saw them stop in front of Zucker's store to talk to the same man who had conferred with them earlier on the street corner. Deciding that the situation was ripe for direct action, Officer McFadden approached the three men, identified himself as a police officer and asked for their names. At this point, his knowledge was confined to what he had observed. He was not acquainted with any of the three men by name or by sight, and he had received no information concerning them from any other source. When the men "mumbled something" in response to his inquiries, Officer McFadden grabbed petitioner Terry, spun him around so that they were facing the other two, with Terry between McFadden and the others, and patted down the outside of his clothing. In the left breast pocket of Terry's overcoat, Officer McFadden felt a pistol. He reached inside the overcoat pocket, but was unable to remove the gun. At this point, keeping Terry between himself and the others, the officer ordered all three men to enter Zucker's store. As they went in, he removed Terry's overcoat completely, removed a .38-caliber revolver from the pocket and ordered all three men to face the wall with their hands raised. Officer McFadden proceeded to pat down the outer clothing of Chilton and the third man, Katz. He discovered another revolver in the outer pocket of Chilton's overcoat, but no weapons were found on Katz. The officer testified that he only patted the men down to see whether they had weapons, and that he did not put his hands beneath the outer garments of either Terry or Chilton until he felt their guns. So far as appears from the record, he never placed his hands beneath Katz' outer garments. Officer McFadden seized Chilton's gun, asked the proprietor of the store to call a police wagon, and took all three men to the station, where Chilton and Terry were formally charged with carrying concealed weapons.

The Supreme Court sanctioned the stops, pat downs, and subsequent weapon seizures on the grounds that requiring a warrant could threaten officer safety or the safety of others.

Stop and Frisk: Two Separate Acts

A *stop* is separate from a *frisk*. A stop always precedes a frisk, but a stop *does not* give a police officer permission to conduct

A *stop* is separate from a *frisk*.

a frisk. Rather, the officer must have separate justification for each act. Reasonable suspicion is required to stop a person, and it is also required to frisk a person.

In *Terry*, the Supreme Court ruled that in addition to the suspicion required to justify a stop, the officer must have reasonable suspicion that the person stopped is *armed* and *dangerous* in order to conduct a frisk. In support of this position, the Court used a balancing test: Each intrusion by the government must be justified by a legitimate objective. In other words, no legitimate law enforcement objective is served when a police officer frisks a person whom the officer does not perceive as threatening.

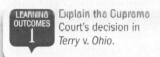

For example, assume a police officer observes two men in an area with much drug traffic activity, whispering to each other and passing items back and forth. Arguably, the officer would have reasonable suspicion that criminal activity is afoot, thus permitting him or her to question the men. However, if the officer does not perceive that either suspect is armed and dangerous, then a frisk would be inappropriate.

Between Reasonable Suspicion and Stop-and-Frisk

In *Terry*, the Supreme Court also held that before a frisk can take place, the officer must identify him- or herself as a police officer. However, if exigent circumstances exist, the identification may not be necessary. In *Adams* v. *Williams* (407 U.S. 143 [1972]), an officer, acting on a tip that a man in a nearby car had a gun at his waist, approached the car and asked the man to open the door. When the suspect rolled down his car window instead of opening the door, the officer reached into the car and removed a gun from the man's waistband. The officer did not identify himself, but the Supreme Court ruled that the seizure of the weapon was reasonable in light of the circumstances.

In addition to requiring that an officer identify himself or herself, the Court in *Terry* also required an officer to make a "reasonable inquiry." Few cases have addressed the definition of *reasonable inquiry*, but as will be considered in the later discussion of confession and interrogation law, if the officer's questions become too accusatory, they may fall outside the type permitted during the course of a *Terry* stop.

▶ The Stop

In many situations it is clear when a police officer has stopped someone. For instance, when a patrol officer legally pulls a motorist over, it is safe to say that such activity constitutes a stop. Similarly, if a police officer handcuffs a suspect, that person has clearly been stopped (and arrested). But what about a simple confrontation between a foot patrol officer and a pedestrian? If the officer directs general questions—such as "What is your name?"—at the pedestrian, can this be considered a stop? Given that there are many situations such as this, the definition of a *stop* must be given special attention.

Definition of a Stop

Generally speaking, a **stop** is the detention of a person by a law enforcement officer for the purpose of investigation. Why does the definition of a stop matter? Remember, if the police officer's activities do not amount to a stop, then the Fourth Amendment does not apply. This is because a stop is the same thing as a seizure of a person. As the Court observed in *Terry* v. *Ohio*, "[W]henever a police officer accosts an individual and restrains his freedom to walk away, he has 'seized' that person" (p. 16).

In *Terry*, the Supreme Court stated that "obviously not all personal intercourse between policemen and citizens involves seizures of persons" (p. 20, n. 16). Instead, the Fourth Amendment applies only "when the officer, by means of physical force or show of authority, has in some way restrained the liberty of [a] citizen" (p. 20, n. 16). Thus, there is an important distinction to be drawn between (1) a forcible seizure or a stop and (2) a less intrusive type of confrontation in which, for example, the officer merely questions a person who is free to ignore the officer and leave. The seizure or stop requires reasonable suspicion (provided it is considered a *Terry* stop and not an arrest), but the simple questioning requires no justification.

There is no easy way to distinguish a *stop* from a *nonstop*, but the Supreme Court has attempted to clarify the differences with an objective test. In **United States v. Mendenhall (446 U.S. 544 [1980])**, the Court observed,

> [A] person has been "seized" within the meaning of the Fourth Amendment only if, in view of all the circumstances surrounding the incident, a *reasonable person would have believed that he was not free to leave*. Examples of circumstances that might indicate a seizure, even where the person did not actually attempt to leave, would be the threatening presence of several officers, the display of a weapon by an officer, some physical touching of the person of the citizen, or the use of language or tone of voice indicating that compliance with the officer's request might be compelled. (p. 554, emphasis added)

The Court's decision in *Mendenhall* stemmed from a confrontation between plainclothes Drug Enforcement Agency (DEA) agents and a 22-year-old African American woman in the Detroit airport. The agents had asked the woman for her ticket and identification, and she complied. When they realized the name on the ticket did not match her name, the agents asked the woman to accompany them into a nearby private room. The Court did not actually decide whether the woman had been stopped, but it did create the objective test described in the previous quote. Figure 6–1 lists several criteria used to distinguish between a stop and a consensual encounter.

Florida v. *Royer* (460 U.S. 491 [1983]) was the first case to apply the test set forth in *Mendenhall* in order to determine the conditions under which a seizure or stop may take place.

If the police officer's activities do not amount to a stop, then the Fourth Amendment does not apply.

FIGURE 6–1 Factors Used to Distinguish Between a Stop and Consensual Encounter.

The facts in *Royer* were virtually identical to the facts in *Mendenhall*, except that the officers did not return the detained individual's plane ticket or driver's license. The Supreme Court held, in a 5-to-4 decision, that given the circumstances, when the officers did not indicate that the individual was free to leave, a seizure had taken place. The Court wrote,

> The predicate permitting seizures on suspicion short of probable cause is that law enforcement interests warrant a limited intrusion on the personal security of the suspect. The scope of the intrusion permitted will vary to some extent with the particular facts and circumstances of each case. This much, however, is clear: *an investigative detention must be temporary and last no longer than is necessary to effectuate the purpose of the stop. Similarly, the investigative methods employed should be the least intrusive means reasonably available to verify or dispel the officer's suspicion in a short period of time.* (p. 500, emphasis added)

The detained individual was subjected to the functional equivalent of an arrest, and as a result, the agents needed probable cause to detain him for as long as they did (which, incidentally, was only about 15 minutes). Moving the subject from a public location to a private location was one of the key factors that helped turn the encounter from a stop into an arrest.

Contrast *Royer* with the Supreme Court's decision in *Florida* v. *Rodriguez* (469 U.S. 1 [1984]). In that case, the Court ruled that a seizure had *not* taken place when a plainclothes officer approached a man in an airport, displayed his badge, asked permission to talk with the man, and requested that he move approximately 15 feet to where the man's companions were standing with other police officers. The Court described this type of confrontation as "clearly the sort of consensual encounter that implicates no Fourth Amendment interest" (p. 5). It seems, therefore, at least in the airport context, that certain confrontations that take place in common areas do not amount to stops within the meaning of the Fourth Amendment.

In another case, *Michigan* v. *Chestnut* (486 U.S. 567 [1988]), police officers in their car followed a man who fled on foot when he spotted their patrol car. The officers did not activate their siren or lights, display weapons, ask the man to stop, or attempt to block the suspect's path. The Court acknowledged that this type of conduct can be "somewhat intimidating," but it ruled,

nevertheless, that the act of police officers following the man did not amount to a stop. The situation would have been different, however, if the police officers had visibly chased the defendant. In the Court's words, "[W]hat constitutes a restraint on liberty prompting a person to conclude that he is not free to leave will vary, not only with the particular police conduct at issue, but also with the setting in which the conduct occurs" (p. 573).

Yet another case has applied the objective test set forth in *Mendenhall*. The case of **California v. Hodari D. (449 U.S. 621 [1991])** involved the apprehension of an individual who was chased by the police on foot. The Court ruled that the individual had not been seized at the time he threw away a rock of cocaine, because the police had not yet caught up with him. The individual argued that he was "stopped" when he was being pursued by the police officers because the chase was sufficient to cause a reasonable person to believe he was not free to leave. In other words, he argued that he was subjected to a "show of authority" stop. Accordingly, the individual argued in court that the cocaine should not be admissible as evidence. Rejecting his argument, the Court ruled that the seizure of a person during a pursuit occurs only when there is an application of force by the police or the suspect submits to police authority (that is, gives up).

Another case seeks to give meaning to the definition of a *stop*. In **Florida v. Bostick (501 U.S. 429 [1991])**, police officers approached a passenger on a bus and asked to inspect his ticket and identification and also his luggage. Both actions were conducted pursuant to a policy that permitted police officers to conduct suspicionless *Terry* stops for the purpose of detecting drug activity. The Supreme Court refused to adopt the Florida Supreme Court's analysis, which held that such drug sweeps were seizures, implicating the Fourth Amendment. Instead, the Court ruled that "in order to determine whether a particular encounter constitutes a seizure, a court must consider all the circumstances surrounding the encounter to determine whether the police conduct would have communicated to a reasonable person that the person was not free to decline the officer's requests or otherwise terminate the encounter" (p. 439). The Supreme Court remanded the case back to the Florida Supreme Court, instead of reversing it. Nevertheless, a portion of Justice O'Connor's opinion suggests that the majority was not satisfied with the Florida court's decision: The bus passenger's perception of not being free to leave was, according to O'Connor, "the natural result of his decision to take the bus."

In *United States* v. *Drayton* (536 U.S. 194 [2002]), the U.S. Supreme Court held that *Bostick*-like bus detentions are permissible and that passengers need not be advised of their right to deny consent to search. Another recent decision requires suspects to provide identification if an officer so requests it (*Hiibel* v. *Sixth Judicial District of Nevada*, 5YZ U.S. 177 [2004]).

Figure 6–2 contains a summary of the cases discussed in this section, namely, those concerned with the definition of a stop.

- -

Duration of a Stop

What is the proper duration of a stop? Better yet, when does a stop evolve into an arrest because it takes too long? There

LEARNING OUTCOMES **2** Summarize the rules concerning a "stop" in the stop-and-frisk context.

Supreme Court Cases Relevant to the Definition of "Stop" (aka, seizure)

United States v. *Mendenhall*, 446 U.S. 544 (1980):

"[A] person has been 'seized' within the meaning of the Fourth Amendment only if, in view of all the circumstances surrounding the incident, a *reasonable person would have believed that he was not free to leave.*"

Florida v. *Royer*, 460 U.S. 491 (1983):

"...an investigative detention must be temporary and last no longer than is necessary to effectuate the purpose of the stop. Similarly, the investigative methods employed should be the least intrusive means reasonably available to verify or dispel the officer's suspicion in a short period of time." (p. 500)

Florida v. *Rodriquez*, 469 U.S. 1 (1984):

A stop did not occur when a plainclothes officer approached a man in an airport, displayed his badge, asked permission to talk with the man, and requested that he move approximately 15 feet to where the man's companions were standing with other police officers.

Michigan v. *Chestnut*, 486 U.S. 567 (1988):

"[W]hat constitutes a restraint on liberty prompting a person to conclude that he is not free to leave will vary, not only with the particular police conduct at issue, but also with the setting in which the conduct occurs." (p. 573)

California v. *Hodari D.*, 499 U.S. 621 (1991):

The suspect was not seized at the time he threw away a rock of cocaine because the police had not yet caught up to him.

Florida v. *Bostick*, 501 U.S. 429 (1991):

"[I]n order to determine whether a particular encounter constitutes a seizure, a court must consider all the circumstances surrounding the encounter to determine whether the police conduct would have communicated to a reasonable person that the person was not free to decline the officer's requests or otherwise terminate the encounter." (p. 439)

FIGURE 6–2 Cases Relevant to the Definition of "Stop."

are no easy answers. In *Florida* v. *Royer*, discussed earlier, the Supreme Court held that a 15-minute detention exceeded the bounds of a proper stop—and became a *de facto* arrest. Yet, in certain exceptional circumstances, the Supreme Court has permitted detentions lasting much longer. For example, in *United States* v. *Sharpe* (470 U.S. 675 [1985]), officers followed two vehicles suspected of involvement in drug trafficking. One vehicle was stopped and the driver was detained for 40 minutes while the officers sought and stopped the second car and its driver. The Court did not establish a bright-line rule for what time period is considered permissible, but it did state that "in evaluating whether an investigative detention is unreasonable, common sense and ordinary human experience must govern over rigid criteria" (p. 685). Thus, the 40 minute detention of the driver of the first car was permissible.

In another case, **United States v. Montoya De Hernandez (473 U.S. 531 [1985])**, a woman who was traveling from Colombia was detained for 16 hours in an airport because she was suspected of being a "balloon swallower" (that is, a person who smuggles narcotics by hiding them in his or her alimentary canal). This was actually a very controversial case. The woman was given two options: (1) to return on the next available flight to Colombia or (2) to remain in detention until she was able to produce a monitored bowel movement. She chose the first option, but officials were unable to place her on the next flight, and she refused to use toilet facilities. Officials then obtained a court order to conduct a pregnancy test (she claimed to be pregnant), an X-ray exam, and a rectal exam. The exams revealed 88 cocaine-filled balloons in her alimentary canal. She was convicted of numerous federal drug offenses, but the court of appeals reversed that decision, holding that her detention violated the Fourth Amendment. The Supreme Court, in turn, reversed the court of appeals decision and ruled that the 16-hour detention was permissible. According to the Court, "The detention of a traveler at the border, beyond the scope of a routine customs search and inspection, is justified at its inception if customs

agents, considering all the facts surrounding the traveler and her trip, reasonably suspect that the traveler is smuggling contraband in her alimentary canal" (p. 541).

In another case, *Courson* v. *McMillian* (939 F.2d 1479 [11th Cir. 1991]), the Eleventh Circuit Court ruled that an officer's act of stopping a car and holding the occupants at gunpoint for 30 minutes was not illegal because most of the time was spent waiting for backup to arrive. Citing *Adams* v. *Williams*, the court observed,

> The Fourth Amendment does not require a policeman who lacks the precise level of information necessary for probable cause to arrest to simply shrug his shoulders and allow a crime to occur or criminal to escape. On the contrary, *Terry* recognizes that it may be the essence of good police work to adopt an intermediate response. A brief stop of a suspicious individual, in order to determine his identity or to maintain the status quo momentarily while obtaining more information, may be most reasonable in light of the facts known to the officer at the time (pp. 145–146).

Contrast the decision reached in *Courson* v. *McMillian* with that reached in *United States* v. *Luckett* (484 F.2d 89 [9th Cir. 1973]). In *Luckett*, the Second Circuit Court declared a jaywalker's detention invalid because it was based on a hunch that there was a warrant for the jaywalker's arrest. The court ruled that the stop effectively turned into an arrest, not just because of the duration of the stop but because there was no basis for an arrest at the time of the stop.

Are there any clear answers, then, as to what the appropriate duration of a stop is? Unfortunately, no, but the Supreme Court has stated that "the reasonableness of a stop turns on the facts and circumstances of each case." In particular, the Court has emphasized "(1) the public interest served by the seizure, (2) the nature and scope of the intrusion, and (3) the objective facts upon

The reasonableness of a stop turns on the facts and circumstances of each case.

which the law enforcement officer relied in light of his knowledge and expertise" (*United States* v. *Mendenhall*, p. 561). Moreover, the Court has ruled that "the use of a particular method to restrain a person's freedom of movement does not necessarily make police action tantamount to an arrest" and that "police may take reasonable action, based upon the circumstances, to protect themselves . . . or to maintain the status quo" (*United States* v. *Kapperman*, 764 F.2d 786 [11th Cir. 1985], p. 790, n. 4).

Figure 6–3 summarizes the meaning of "stop" in the stop-and-frisk context.

▶ *The Frisk*

As indicated, the additional step of frisking a suspect is a Fourth Amendment intrusion that requires justification apart from that required to stop the person. Specifically, in order to conduct a **frisk** (a superficial examination by the officer of the

---

A *Terry* stop/seizure is characterized by two specific events:

(1) The police question a person or communicate with him or her.

(2) A reasonable person would believe that he or she is not free to leave. Reasonable suspicion is required in order to make a *Terry* stop conform to Fourth Amendment requirements. Conversely, if an officer detains a person in such a manner that a reasonable person would believe he or she *is* free to leave, the protections of the Fourth Amendment do not apply, and reasonable suspicion is not required. If the officer wishes to conduct a frisk—a separate act from a stop—he or she must have reasonable suspicion that the suspect is armed and dangerous, not just reasonable suspicion, as required for a *Terry* stop. There are no clear answers as to what is the appropriate duration for a stop. However, as the Supreme Court suggested in *United States* v. *Mendenhall*, a lengthy stop is constitutionally permissible when

(a) the public interest is served by the seizure,

(b) the nature and scope of the intrusion are not excessive, and

(c) the officer possesses enough in the way of objective facts to justify the stop (p. 561).

Thus, if a person is stopped and detained for a long time based on an officer's hunch but poses no threat to public safety, the stop will probably be declared illegal. In such a situation, the stop would need to be justified by probable cause because it would amount to a *de facto* arrest.

FIGURE 6–3 Summary of "Stop" in Stop-and-Frisk.

person's body surface or clothing to discover weapons or items that could be used to cause harm), the officer needs reasonable suspicion that the suspect is armed and dangerous. This is in addition to the reasonable suspicion required to stop the person for questioning.

Permissible Grounds for a Frisk

Although *Terry* held that a frisk is permissible only when an officer reasonably fears for his or her safety, there is still considerable dispute over the situations in which a frisk is appropriate. What does it mean, in other words, to *fear for one's safety*? Numerous court decisions have wrestled with this question.

For example, in **Pennsylvania v. Mimms (434 U.S. 106 [1977])**, police officers observed a man driving a vehicle with expired plates. The officers stopped the vehicle in order to issue the man a traffic summons. When the officers asked the man to step out of the car, the officers observed a large bulge in the pocket of his jacket. Fearing that the bulge might be a weapon, one of the officers frisked the man. It turned out that the bulge was a .38-caliber revolver. The man claimed at his trial that the gun was seized illegally, but the Supreme Court upheld the frisk. Even though a bulge in one's pocket does not necessarily indicate he or she has a weapon, the Court granted some latitude in its decision to law enforcement personnel.

However, in **Ybarra v. Illinois (444 U.S. 85 [1979])**, the Court ruled that officers did not have grounds to frisk 12 bar patrons during a search of the bar itself. Justice Stewart stated in *Ybarra* that "[t]he 'narrow scope' of the *Terry* exception does not permit a frisk for weapons on less than reasonable belief or suspicion directed at the person to be frisked, even though that person happens to be on premises where an authorized narcotics search is taking place" (p. 94). Thus, just because someone happens to be in an area in which criminal activity is supposedly taking place does not make him or her eligible for a frisk.

Despite the limitations on frisks imposed by the *Ybarra* decision, the Court has since gone back somewhat on its decision in that case. In **Minnesota v. Dickerson (508 U.S. 366 [1993])**, police officers observed a man leaving a "crack" house. As he approached and saw the officers, he turned and began walking in the opposite direction. The officers stopped and frisked him and found drugs on him. The frisk was conducted without reasonable suspicion or any other level of justification. The Court ruled that the police exceeded the bounds of a valid frisk when they found drugs on the man's person, but the Court did *not* rule that the frisk was unconstitutional. It would seem, then, that under certain circumstances, a frisk is permissible on less than reasonable suspicion. Apparently, the act of leaving a "crack" house and acting evasively was sufficient justification to conduct a frisk, even though the police went too far in doing so.

In *Arizona v. Johnson* (No. 07-1122 [2009]), the Court further expanded the frisk doctrine. In that case, gang task force officers were patrolling and stopped a vehicle for a traffic violation. The officers had no reason to suspect the vehicle's occupants of criminal activity, but they nevertheless ordered them out of the car. One of them was frisked and a weapon was found. The Court sanctioned this activity, noting that "a passenger's motivation to use violence during the stop to prevent apprehension for a crime more grave than a traffic violation is just as great as that of the driver."

So, are there any clear rules that establish when an officer can reasonably fear for his or her safety? The answer is no. Ultimately, the determination of a potential threat is a subjective one. Almost without exception, the courts will defer to the judgment of the officer, assuming that he or she is able to articulate some specific facts that contributed to reasonable suspicion that the suspect was armed and dangerous. Figure 6–4 summarizes the circumstances as to when a frisk is permissible.

Scope of a Frisk

Certain cases have focused specifically on the permissible scope of a frisk. Two issues have been raised: (1) the definition of a *frisk*—that is, what the officer can physically do to a person that does not rise to the level of a search, and (2) the items that can be felt for during the course of a frisk.

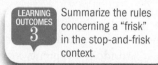

LEARNING OUTCOMES 3 — Summarize the rules concerning a "frisk" in the stop-and-frisk context.

With regard to the first issue, the Supreme Court in *Terry* described a *frisk* as "a carefully limited search of the outer clothing . . . in an attempt to discover weapons which might be used to assault [a police officer]" (p. 30). In **Sibron v. New York (392 U.S. 40 [1968])**, the Court offered additional clarification by declaring that the act of reaching into a suspect's pockets is impermissible when the officer makes "no attempt at an initial limited exploration for arms" (p. 65). Generally, then, a frisk is little more than an open-handed pat down of someone's outer clothing. Only if the officer feels something that resembles a weapon can he or she then reach into the suspect's pocket (or other area used to conceal it) to determine what the item is. As the Supreme Court observed in *United States* v. *Richardson* (949 F.2d 851 [6th Cir. 1991]), "When actions by the police exceed the bounds permitted by reasonable suspicion, the seizure becomes an arrest and must be supported by probable cause" (p. 856).

With regard to the second issue, or the items that can be felt for during the course of a frisk, the Supreme Court in *Ybarra* v. *Illinois* emphasized that frisks must be directed at discovering weapons, not criminal evidence. In *Ybarra*, one of the police officers had removed what he described as a "cigarette pack with objects in it" from the suspect. The Court basically decided that the officer's actions were too intrusive; the package could not have been considered a threat to the safety of the officers conducting the search. Significantly, the Court did not declare the seizure illegal because the officer was not looking for weapons but because the officer did not have reasonable suspicion to frisk every patron in the bar. Nevertheless, a frisk should not

---

1. When the person has a reputation for dangerousness
2. When the person is suspected of having committed a dangerous felony
3. When visual cues suggest the presence of a weapon or similar dangerous instrument
4. When the suspect makes suggestive or furtive gestures

FIGURE 6–4 When a Frisk Is Permissible.

The Permissible Scope of a Frisk Two police officers were approached by a person (previously unknown to them) who stated that Jack Smith was in the Valley Grill on First Street and that he had several bags of cocaine for sale. The person provided detailed information concerning Smith and described the clothing he was wearing. The officers went to the Valley Grill and found no one of that description. After the officers left the bar, however, they observed a person walking on the sidewalk who matched the description they had been given. The officers approached him, blocked his path, and asked for his identification. The man's identification revealed that his name was Jack Smith. At that point, the officers ordered Smith to remove his shoes. He did so as the officers continued to ask him questions. Was this action appropriate?

© Michael Matthews - Police Images/Alamy

be used as a "fishing expedition" to see if some kind of usable evidence can be found on the person.

Two additional points concerning the scope of a frisk need to be underscored at this juncture. First, just because the Supreme Court has declared that a frisk should be conducted based on the motive to preserve officer safety does not mean that the officer cannot seize contraband found during the course of a lawful frisk. This issue is discussed in the section on plain touch and feel later in this chapter. What is important now, though, is that a frisk is supposed to be *motivated* by the desire to remove weapons and other instruments of potential harm from a criminal suspect.

Second, remember that a valid frisk can always evolve into a Fourth Amendment search, provided that probable cause develops along the way. For example, assume that a Chicago police officer frisks a suspect because she fears he may be carrying a gun. If it turns out that the suspect is carrying a pistol, which is illegal in the city of Chicago, she could arrest the suspect and conduct a full search incident to arrest. In this example, though, the object seized during the frisk (that is, the gun) must be immediately apparent to the officer for the seizure to be legal. As the Supreme Court stated in *Minnesota* v. *Dickerson*,

> Although the officer was lawfully in a position to feel the lump in respondent's pocket, because *Terry* entitled him

to place his hands upon respondent's jacket, the court below determined that the incriminating character of the object was not immediately apparent to him. Rather, the officer determined that the item was contraband only after conducting a further search, one not authorized by *Terry* or by any other exception to the warrant requirement. (p. 379)

In the example, then, had the seizure followed careful manipulation of the object by the officer, a seizure based on the frisk would not conform to Fourth Amendment requirements. Figure 6–5 provides additional examples of proper and improper frisks.

Figure 6–6 summarizes the meaning of "frisk" in the stop-and-frisk context.

▶ *Expansion of Stop-and-Frisk*

In *Terry* v. *Ohio*, the Supreme Court created an exception to the Fourth Amendment's requirement that probable cause is required for searches by holding that police officers can stop and frisk people based on reasonable suspicion. In the wake of *Terry*, significant and controversial Supreme Court decisions

Proper	Improper
An officer observes a large "bulge" in the front waistband of a suspicious individual's pants and frisks him for a weapon.	A man is sitting in a car waiting to pick up a friend. An officer orders him out of the car and frisks him.
Two officers observe a man "casing" a convenience store. When they confront him, he becomes argumentative. They frisk him for a weapon.	An officer confronts a suspicious individual who is in an area that has been experiencing a number of daytime burglaries. He reaches into the man's pockets looking for weapons and/or contraband.
An officer stops a speeding vehicle. The driver gives the officer false identification, whereupon the officer orders him out and frisks him.	Several men are waiting in line for a nightclub. Officers approach them, block their path, and reach into each individual's jacket feeling for weapons and/or contraband.

FIGURE 6–5 Examples of Proper and Improper Frisks.

A frisk is permissible when an officer reasonably fears for his or her safety. However, there is no easy way to discern the facts that would cause an officer to reasonably fear for his or her safety. If an officer can offer no facts or testimony to support the frisk, it will probably be declared unconstitutional. On the other hand, if the officer possesses some objective information that served as the basis for a frisk (for example., observing a bulge in a suspect's pocket), the frisk will probably be legal.

A number of cases have focused on the permissible scope of a frisk, and three important restrictions have been imposed. First, a frisk can be nothing more than a patdown of someone's outer clothing. Groping or squeezing is not permissible. Second, a frisk must be motivated by the desire to promote officer safety, not by the desire to seek out any form of contraband. That is, the sole purpose of a *Terry* patdown is to protect the officer from weapons that might be used by the suspect during the encounter. Finally, for an officer to legally seize an item during the course of a frisk, that item must be immediately apparent to the officer as contraband.

FIGURE 6–6 Summary of "Frisk" in Stop-and-Frisk.

Significant and controversial Supreme Court decisions have modified the scope of the stop-and-frisk exception to the Fourth Amendment's probable cause requirement.

have modified the scope of the stop-and-frisk exception to the Fourth Amendment's probable cause requirement. Illustrative cases fall into five categories:

- Vehicle stops and weapons searches of automobiles
- Protective sweeps of residences
- Plain touch and feel
- Profiling
- Investigative detentions

Vehicle Stops

Automobile searches were covered earlier, but it is appropriate to mention here, during the discussion of stop-and-frisk, what police officers can do with automobiles in the presence of reasonable suspicion. **Delaware v. Prouse (440 U.S. 648 [1979])** set forth the rule that police officers can stop and detain motorists in their vehicles so long as the officers have "at least articulable and reasonable suspicion" that the motorists are violating the law. For example, if a police officer observes a driver run a stop sign, the officer is justified in pulling the person over and detaining him or her because reasonable suspicion is present. The decision in *Pennsylvania* v. *Mimms* also authorizes a police officer to order a driver out of a car. The logic is that doing so is a minimal intrusion that can be justified by safety concerns. These decisions (as well as *Terry*) also permit a police officer to frisk a motorist who has been pulled over if the officer reasonably fears for his or her safety.

Interestingly, if a police officer orders a driver (or a passenger, or both) out of the car, is reasonably suspicious that the

driver is armed and dangerous, and frisks the driver, the officer may also search the area of the interior of the car within the suspect's immediate control. Such a search is permissible even when the driver has already been ordered to step out of the vehicle. The case that established this ruling was *Michigan* v. *Long* (463 U.S. 1032 [1983]). In *Long*, police officers saw a car swerve into a ditch and after stopping to investigate, they observed that the driver was intoxicated and that there was a large hunting knife on the floor of the vehicle. The Supreme Court ruled that the officers were justified in searching the passenger compartment and frisking the driver.

Michigan v. *Long* is an important decision because a search almost always requires probable cause. Note, however, that the scope of the search in this case was limited to the vehicle occupant's grabbing area, which included the whole of the interior of the car. Neither containers inside the car nor any in the trunk of the car (if any) can be searched during the course of a vehicle weapons search based on reasonable suspicion.

Protective Sweeps

Another decision that essentially expands *Terry* is **Maryland v. Buie (494 U.S. 325 [1990])**—a case that was already discussed in the search incident to arrest section of the previous chapter. If police lawfully make an arrest in a person's residence, a protective sweep of the home is permitted based on the *Terry* rationale.

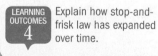

LEARNING OUTCOMES 4 — Explain how stop-and-frisk law has expanded over time.

A *sweep* is when one or more officers disperse throughout the home with the intent of looking for other people that could pose a threat to the officers making the arrest. In the Court's words, a *protective sweep* is a "quick and limited search of the premises, incident to arrest, and conducted to protect the safety of police officers or others" (p. 325). This protective sweep, which requires reasonable suspicion, should be distinguished from the automatic but more limited sweep that is permitted incident to a lawful arrest.

According to the Supreme Court, a sweep is permitted if the officer possesses "a reasonable belief based on specific and

articulable facts that an area to be swept harbors an individual posing a danger to those at the arrest scene" (p. 337). In addition, a sweep "may extend only to a cursory inspection of those spaces where a person may be found" and may last only as long as is necessary to eliminate the suspicion of danger. The case of *Maryland* v. *Buie* thus expands *Terry* in the sense that police officers can do more than just frisk a person who is arrested in a private residence. Note, however, that this case does not permit officers to *search* but only to *sweep* the area. A search would have to be supported by probable cause. However, items in plain view can be seized.

The Court's decision in *Maryland* v. *Buie* is not without its critics, however—the dissenters in the case being perhaps the most vocal. Consider Justice Brennan's observations in the dissent he wrote:

> *Terry* and its early progeny permitted only brief investigative stops and extremely limited searches based on reasonable suspicion . . . but this Court more recently has applied the rationale underlying *Terry* to a wide variety of more intrusive searches and seizures prompting my continued criticism of the emerging tendency on the part of the Court to convert the *Terry* decision from a narrow exception into one that swallows the general rule that [searches] are reasonable only if based on probable cause. (p. 339)

The exception Justice Brennan refers to is *Terry's* exception to the Fourth Amendment's requirement that reasonable searches be supported by probable cause. In a sense, *Terry* chipped away at the Fourth Amendment. Brennan's concern in this case, then, is that the Fourth Amendment continues to be weakened in cases that continue to uphold police actions that would otherwise be considered searches, but for the Court's decision in *Terry* v. *Ohio*.

This is an important area of law about which to remain informed. No doubt, the Supreme Court will continue to decide cases that involve the relationship among probable cause, reasonable suspicion, and the police activities that each permits.

Plain Touch and Feel

In *Minnesota* v. *Dickerson*, discussed earlier in this chapter, the ruling was that police officers exceeded the bounds of *Terry* when they frisked the suspect because the officer "squeezed, slid, and otherwise manipulated the packet's content" before learning that it was cocaine. Despite that decision, *Dickerson* is considered by many to be the case that officially recognized the doctrine known as *plain touch* (sometimes called *plain feel*). The Supreme Court has long recognized that the items in plain view fall outside Fourth Amendment protections because they are in plain view to the police. *Dickerson* is something of a cross between a *Terry*-based frisk and the plain-view doctrine. According to one source, "[I]f the officer, while staying within the narrow limits of a frisk for weapons, feels what he has probable cause to believe is a weapon, contraband or evidence, the officer may expand the search or seize the object."[2]

The reason the Supreme Court frowned on the frisk conducted by the police in *Dickerson* was that it was not immediately apparent to the officers that the suspect had contraband in his pocket. Thus, for the plain-feel doctrine to apply, two conditions must be met: (1) Police must have reasonable suspicion to frisk, *and* (2) contraband must be immediately apparent for it to be lawfully seized. Stated more formally, "[T]he police may seize contraband detected solely through the officer's sense of touch, if, as with the plain-view doctrine, the officer had a right to touch the object in question (lawful vantage point and lawful access) and, upon tactile observation, the object's identity as contraband was immediately apparent."[3] Figure 6–7 presents examples of proper seizures based on plain view, feel, and touch during stop-and-frisk situations.

Example 1: An officer conducts a pat down of a man who seems intoxicated and smells like marijuana. When he feels a bulge in the man's jacket, the officer reaches into his pocket and finds a "bong."

Example 2: While serving an arrest warrant, an officer frisks a suspect and feels a bulge in his pocket. Upon reaching into the suspect's pocket, the officer feels two baggies full of rock-like objects. He seizes the items, which turn out to be crack cocaine.

Example 3: An officer responds to a complaint and notices a large bulge in the suspect's pocket. He reaches in the suspect's pocket and withdraws a bottle.

FIGURE 6-7 Examples of Proper Seizures Based on Plain View, Feel, and Touch.

Profiling

An especially controversial variety of *Terry*-like investigative stops includes those based on so-called drug courier profiles. This chapter gives detailed attention to **drug courier profiling** not just because it is a controversial criminal justice topic but also because it is an appropriate topic for a chapter on stop-and-frisk. Almost without exception, drug courier profiling occurs in the stop-and-frisk context—that is, when a person is stopped and questioned because he or she appears suspicious in some way. Drug courier profiling is most common in airports but also occurs on U.S. highways and elsewhere.

Indeed, profiling of offenders occurs for other offenses, as well. Law enforcement officials have developed profiles of a number of other varieties of offenders, including car thieves (*People v. Martinez*, 12 Cal. Rptr. 2d 838 [Cal. Ct. App. 1992]), child abusers (*Flanagan v. State*, 586 So.2d 1085 [Fla. Dist. Ct. App. 1991]), child batterers (*Commonwealth v. Day*, 569 N.E.2d 397 [Mass. 1991]), sexual abusers (*State v. McMillan*, 590 N.E.2d 23 [Ohio Ct. App. 1990]), and, of course, terrorists (see the case study at the end of this chapter), among others.

> **Drug courier profiling occurs in the stop-and-frisk context—that is, when a person is stopped and questioned because he or she appears suspicious in some way.**

The carrying of controlled substances by airline passengers is a common way that drugs enter the United States from foreign countries. Law enforcement agents *could* conceivably search every person who passes through an airport, but such an effort would be costly, time consuming, unacceptable to passengers, and almost certainly unconstitutional. Warrantless searches that are based on no articulable justification are always unreasonable under the Fourth Amendment, unless one of a few "specifically established and well-delineated exceptions" applies (*Katz v. United States*, 389 U.S. 347 [1967], p. 357). In other words, such searches violate the Fourth Amendment because they are not based on probable cause, as the amendment requires.

Given that suspicionless searches are illegal, the police are left with two options when it comes to confronting people suspected of being drug couriers. These two options are "consensual encounters in which contact is initiated by a police officer without any articulable reason whatsoever and the citizen is briefly asked some questions [and] a temporary involuntary detention . . . which must be predicated on 'reasonable suspicion'" (*United States v. Bueno*, 21 F.3d [1978]). Both consensual encounters and investigative detentions are not considered searches, so they fall outside the Fourth Amendment's probable cause requirement.

When a person gives consent to the police to conduct a search or ask questions, the Fourth Amendment does not apply. Assuming the citizen remains free to decline the officer's request to conduct a search, the officer can legally ask a person for permission to look in his or her car, bag, house, or other area. The logic behind consent searches was touched on in *Terry v. Ohio*, in which the Supreme Court stated that "there is nothing in the Constitution which prevents a policeman from addressing questions to anyone on the streets" (p. 27). There is one significant restriction, though, for a consent search (or stop) to be truly consensual, and it goes directly to the definition of *stop* covered earlier in this chapter: "[T]he Fourth Amendment permits police officers to approach individuals at random in airport lobbies and other public places to ask them questions and to request consent to search their luggage, so long as a reasonable person would understand that he or she could refuse to cooperate" (*Florida v. Bostick*, p. 431). In other words, the constitutionality of a consent search is premised on the requirement

Think About It...

Putting It All Together Deputy Smith was on patrol in his police cruiser when he heard a report over the radio that a bank had just been robbed and that four male perpetrators had fled in a blue 1976 Ford pickup without license plates. Several minutes later, Smith observed a vehicle matching the description given over the radio except that it *had* license plates. He followed the truck and, after turning on his flashers, ordered the driver of the truck to pull over to the side of the road, which he did. Smith approached the truck and observed three men and a woman inside, each of whom appeared nervous and upset by the fact that they had been pulled over. After Smith ordered the occupants out of the car, he observed a bulge in the driver's pocket. He frisked the driver and found a weapon. Was Smith justified in stopping the vehicle and frisking the driver?

© Ryan McGinnis/Alamy

that the person is truly free to decline when asked by a police officer to allow a search.

Perhaps more common in the practice of drug courier profiling is the use of investigative detentions, or *Terry* stops. *Terry*, as addressed throughout the bulk of this chapter, permits police officers to stop people based on reasonable suspicion that criminal activity is afoot. *Terry* stops occur in airports and elsewhere when a person is involuntarily detained. For this type of stop to occur, however, the officer needs to show that there is, in fact, reasonable suspicion that the person is a drug courier. The primary question that makes drug courier profiling a controversial topic is "What characteristics must a person display for reasonable suspicion to be established?"

Clearly, not every person walking through an airport can be stopped. Thus, law enforcement officials must look for specific characteristics of drug couriers. As the Supreme Court observed in *United States* v. *Mendenhall*, "Much . . . drug traffic is highly organized and conducted by sophisticated criminal syndicates. . . . And many drugs . . . may be easily concealed. As a result, the obstacles to detection . . . may be unmatched in any other area of law enforcement" (pp. 545–546). Further, one of the most significant impediments in the war on drugs is the "extraordinary and well-documented difficulty of identifying drug couriers" (*Florida* v. *Royer*, p. 519).

The drug courier profile is generally attributed to Paul Markonni, a Drug Enforcement Administration (DEA) agent who identified a number of suspicious characteristics of likely drug couriers when he was assigned to a drug interdiction unit at the Detroit airport. That profile has since been described as an "informally compiled abstract of characteristics thought typical of persons carrying illicit drugs" (*United States* v. *Mendenhall*, p. 547). There is no single, nationally recognized drug courier profile or set of characteristics indicative of drug courier profiling. Instead, specific cases must be considered to ascertain which types of characteristics fit the drug courier profile.

The first drug courier profile case of note, *United States* v. *Van Lewis* (409 F. Supp. 535 [E.D. Mich. 1976]), listed several characteristics to be used in identifying drug couriers: (1) the use of small denominations of currency for ticket purchase, (2) travel to and from major drug import centers, (3) the absence of luggage or use of empty suitcases on trips that normally require extra clothing, and (4) travel under an alias. In a similar case, the Fifth Circuit Court, in *Elmore* v. *United States* (595 F.2d 1036 [5th Cir. 1979]), described these common characteristics of drug couriers:

(1) arrival from or departure to an identified source city; (2) carrying little or no luggage; (3) unusual itinerary, such as rapid turnaround time for a very lengthy airplane trip; (4) use of an alias; (5) carrying unusually large amounts of currency in the many thousands of dollars, usually on their person, or in briefcases or bags; (6) purchasing airline tickets with a large

amount of small denomination currency; and (7) unusual nervousness beyond that ordinarily exhibited by passengers. (p. 1039, n. 3)

Some secondary characteristics of drug couriers were also identified in *Elmore* v. *United States*, including "(1) the almost exclusive use of public transportation, particularly taxicabs, in departing from the airport; (2) immediately making a phone call after deplaning; (3) leaving a false or fictitious call-back telephone number with the airline being utilized; and (4) excessively frequent travel to source or distribution cities" (p. 1039, n. 3).

Still other characteristics of drug couriers include unusual dress, age between 25 and 35, and extreme paleness consistent with being extremely nervous.[4] Another study points to characteristics such as "not checking bags at the airport, not using identification tags on luggage, purchasing tickets on the day of a flight, exiting first or last from the plane, visually scanning the terminal for law enforcement, making no eye contact with airport personnel, walking quickly through the terminal while continuously checking over one's shoulder, and quickly leaving the airport on arrival."[5] See Figure 6–8 for a fairly comprehensive list of the typical characteristics of drug couriers.

Reid v. Georgia (448 U.S. 438 [1980]) was one of the first Supreme Court cases to address drug courier profiling. The petitioner, Reid, arrived at the Atlanta airport on an early morning flight. A narcotics agent on duty at the time observed that Reid repeatedly looked over his shoulder at another man and that both were carrying shoulder bags. As the two men left the airport, the narcotics officer approached them and asked them for identification and to consent to a search. Reid tried to run away and, in doing so, left his bag behind, which turned out to contain cocaine. He was later apprehended and brought to trial on drug possession charges. He attempted to have the cocaine thrown out under the exclusionary rule, claiming that he had been unconstitutionally detained as he was leaving the airport with the other man.

1. Use small denominations of currency for ticket purchases
2. Travel to and from major drug import centers
3. Have no luggage or use empty suitcases on trips that normally require extra clothing
4. Travel under an alias
5. Have an unusual itinerary, such as a rapid turnaround time for a very lengthy airplane trip
6. Carry unusually large amounts of currency (that is, many thousands of dollars)
7. Display unusual nervousness beyond that ordinarily exhibited by passengers
8. Use public transportation almost exclusively upon departing the airport
9. Immediately make a phone call after deplaning
10. Leave a false or fictitious call-back telephone number with the airline
11. Dress in an unusual manner
12. Are between 25 and 35 years old
13. Are extremely pale (consistent with being extremely nervous)
14. Do not use identification tags on luggage
15. Purchase tickets on the day of the flight
16. Exit first or last from the plane
17. Walk quickly through the terminal while continuously checking over their shoulders
18. Quickly leave the airport on arrival

FIGURE 6–8 **Typical Characteristics of Drug Couriers.**

The trial court granted Reid's motion to suppress the cocaine; however, the Georgia Court of Appeals reversed the lower court's decision and ruled that the narcotics agent had performed a permissible stop based on the so-called drug courier profile. In its decision, the Georgia Court of Appeals noted that Reid (1) had arrived from Fort Lauderdale, Florida, a place of origin for drugs; (2) was traveling at an unusual hour; (3) was attempting to conceal that fact that he was traveling with another person; and (4) was not traveling with any luggage, other than the shoulder bag (p. 441).

The U.S. Supreme Court granted *certiorari*, holding that "the judgment of the appellate court cannot be sustained insofar as it rests on the determination that the DEA agent lawfully seized the petitioner when he approached him" (p. 441). The Court went on to note that the agent "could not . . . have reasonably suspected the petitioner of criminal activity on the basis . . . that the petitioner preceded another person and occasionally looked backward at him" (p. 441). The other reasons for stopping Reid were also criticized by the Court because the unusual hour, lack of luggage, and place of origin "describe a very large category of presumably innocent travelers, who would be subject to virtually random seizures were the Court to conclude that as little foundation as there was in this case could justify the seizure" (p. 441). The Court declared that the DEA agent did not have reasonable suspicion to detain Reid.

In **United States v. Sokolow (490 U.S. 1 [1989])**, DEA agents stopped Sokolow upon his arrival at Honolulu International Airport and found a large quantity of cocaine in his carry-on luggage. In support of the stop, the agents noted that Sokolow (1) had paid $2,100 for his airline ticket with a roll of $20 bills; (2) traveled under an assumed name; (3) had flown in from a major "source city," Miami; (4) had stayed in Miami for only 48 hours; (5) appeared nervous; and (6) did not check any luggage. The district court denied Sokolow's motion to suppress the drugs, finding that the agents had reasonable suspicion to stop him in the airport. However, the court of appeals declared that the stop was illegal, a violation of the Fourth Amendment. The court relied on a two-pronged test to assess the legality of the stop. It required a showing that (1) there was "ongoing criminal activity" and that there were (2) "personal characteristics" of drug courier profiles. Although the second prong would seem to have been met in this case, the appeals court decided that the first prong had not been met because the government did not offer "empirical documentation that the combination of facts at issue did not describe the behavior of significant numbers of innocent persons" (p. 2). In other words, the court of appeals found no evidence of ongoing criminal activity and thus ruled that the stop was in violation of the Fourth Amendment. The U.S. Supreme Court reversed the appeals court decision. It held that the agents *did* have reasonable suspicion that Sokolow was engaged in the transportation of narcotics. In criticizing the two-pronged test used by the appeals court, the Supreme Court noted that the test "created unnecessary difficulty in

dealing with one of the relatively simple concepts embodied in the Fourth Amendment" (p. 3). In reference to the suspicious conduct observed by the agents, the Court went on to note that "although each of these factors [e.g., paying $2,100 for a plane ticket with small denomination bills] is not by itself proof of illegal conduct and is quite consistent with innocent travel, taken together they amount to reasonable suspicion that criminal activity was afoot" (p. 4).

Investigative Detentions

The Supreme Court has held that certain police station detentions are justifiable on less than probable cause. One type of **investigative detention**, a stationhouse detention, is less intrusive than an arrest but more intrusive than a *Terry* stop. Stationhouse detentions are used in many locations for such purposes as obtaining fingerprints and photographs, ordering lineups, administering polygraph examinations, and securing other types of evidence.

In *Davis* v. *Mississippi* (394 U.S. 721 [1969]), the Court excluded fingerprint evidence obtained from 25 rape suspects, but it did note that detention for fingerprinting could have been permissible if "narrowly circumscribed procedures" were in place. In other words, the Court suggested that to justify the detention, there had to be some objective basis for detaining a person, a clear investigation underway, and a court order stating that adequate evidence exists. In another case, *Hayes* v. *Florida* (470 U.S. 811 [1985]), the Court stated,

> Our view continues to be that the line is crossed when the police, without probable cause or a warrant, forcibly remove a person from his home or other place in which he is entitled to be and transport him to the police station, where he is detained, although briefly, for investigative purposes. We adhere to the view that such seizures, at least where not under judicial supervision, are sufficiently like arrests to invoke the traditional rule that arrests may constitutionally be made only on probable cause. (p. 816)

The key in *Hayes*, however, is that the detention was not consensual. In cases in which consent is obtained, probable cause is not necessary. In short, a stationhouse detention for the purpose of fingerprinting is permissible when (1) there is reasonable suspicion to believe the suspect has committed a crime, (2) there is a reasonable belief that the fingerprints will inculpate or exculpate the suspect, and (3) the procedure is carried out promptly. (Note that the Supreme Court has not addressed stationhouse detentions *not* involving fingerprinting.)

The Supreme Court has held that certain police station detentions are justifiable on less than probable cause.

Profiling in the War on Terror

In 2004, two Arab gentlemen, Tarik Farag and Amro Elmasry, traveled from San Diego to New York's JFK airport on American Airlines Flight 236. As soon as they deplaned at JFK, they were met by no fewer than ten armed agents in SWAT gear with guns and police dogs. They were ordered to raise their hands and were frisked, handcuffed, and whisked off to an interrogation room. The investigation yielded no evidence of wrongdoing. The men sued, arguing that their arrests were unjustified, but the government cited the following as justification for the airport detention (note that these facts were reported to the captain by two counterterrorism agents who were on the flight):

- At the beginning of the flight, despite sitting on opposite sides of the aisle, plaintiffs spoke to each other over the heads of other passengers in a mixture of Arabic and English.

- Elmasry made an allegedly "unusual" initial seat change "from a window seat . . . to a middle seat . . . between two other male passengers."

- After Elmasry changed seats, he and Farag talked to each other "loudly" over the heads of other passengers in a mixture of Arabic and English.

- Elmasry looked at his watch when the plane took off, when the plane landed, and at other points during the flight.

- After the meal service, Elmasry "got out of his seat . . ., went into the aisle, leaned over to Farag, and spoke a 'very short sentence' to Farag in a mixture of Arabic and English."

- Immediately thereafter, plaintiffs moved together to the back of the plane, and did not take their carry-on luggage with them.

- Plaintiffs got up to return to the front of the cabin at the very end of the flight, after the "fasten seatbelt" indicator was lit.

- Upon returning to the front of the plane, Farag did not sit in his original seat (17E), but rather, in Elmasry's original seat (18A), which was located directly behind Smith.

- After the plane landed, Elmasry took out his cellular phone and deleted five or six numbers. (*Farag* v. *United States*, 2008 U.S. Dist. LEXIS 95331 [2008], pp. 23–24)

This case raises interesting questions about the intersection between profiling and the war on terror.

1. Is there merit to the government's argument?
2. Compare and contrast terrorist profiling and drug courier profiling.
3. Is profiling a valuable law enforcement asset or a threat to civil liberties? Defend your answer.

LEARNING OUTCOMES 1

Explain the Supreme Court's decision in *Terry* v. *Ohio*.

A person can be stopped if an officer has reasonable suspicion that criminal activity is afoot and frisked if an officer has reasonable suspicion that the person is armed and dangerous.

Key Case

Terry v. *Ohio*

1. Why is it important to view stop-and-frisk as two separate acts?
2. How does stop-and-frisk loosen the Fourth Amendment's restraints?

LEARNING OUTCOMES 2

Summarize the rules concerning a "stop" in the stop-and-frisk context.

A stop, defined as a brief detention, is usually permissible (1) when the officer observes a person engaging in unusual activity, (2) when the officer receives information from an informant who is reliable, and/or (3) when the officer receives a communication from another police department that the person to be stopped is suspected of involvement in criminal activity.

Key Cases

United States v. *Mendenhall*

California v. *Hodari D.*

Florida v. *Bostick*

United States v. *Montoya De Hernandez*

1. Define *stop*.
2. Why is the duration of a stop important?
3. At what point does a stop evolve into an arrest?

stop Sometimes called an "investigative stop" or an "investigative detention," a brief nonconsensual encounter between a law enforcement officer and a citizen that does not rise to the level of an arrest; the detention of a person by a law enforcement officer for the purpose of investigation.

LEARNING OUTCOMES 3

Summarize the rules concerning a "frisk" in the stop-and-frisk context.

Frisks are limited. If one is authorized because the officer reasonably fears for his or her safety, it is limited to a pat down of the person's outer clothing. Above all else, the frisk must be motivated by an officer's concern for safety.

Key Cases

Pennsylvania v. *Mimms*

Ybarra v. *Illinois*

Minnesota v. *Dickerson*

Sibron v. *New York*

1. Summarize the permissible grounds for a frisk.
2. What is the proper scope of a frisk?
3. Describe a situation in which a stop is justified but a frisk is not.

frisk A superficial examination by the officer of the person's body surface or clothing to discover weapons or items that could be used to cause harm.

Explain how stop-and-frisk law has expanded over time.

Stop-and-frisk law has expanded as a result of Supreme Court decisions in the areas of vehicle stops, protective sweeps, plain touch and feel, profiling (typically drug courier profiling), and investigative detentions.

Key Cases

Delaware v. *Prouse*

Maryland v. *Buie*

Reid v. *Georgia*

United States v. *Sokolow*

1. Summarize the means by which stop-and-frisk law has been expanded over the years.

2. What is drug courier profiling?

3. Describe the characteristics of a person who fits the drug courier profile.

drug courier profiling A crime-detection process that makes use of what is known about the likely and observable characteristics of drug couriers. Drug courier profiling usually occurs in stop-and-frisk situations.

investigative detention Also called a stationhouse detention, a less intrusive detention than an arrest but more intrusive than a *Terry* stop. Stationhouse detentions are used in many locations for such purposes as obtaining fingerprints and photographs, ordering lineups, administering polygraph examinations, and securing other types of evidence.

"Special needs and regulatory searches strike a balance between the interests of public safety and personal freedom."

7

Special Needs and Regulatory Searches

1 Explain the importance of administrative justification.

2 Summarize the rules surrounding inventory searches.

3 Distinguish between several types of inspections.

4 Distinguish between legal and illegal checkpoints.

5 Explain when school disciplinary searches are permissible.

6 Explain when searches of government employees' offices are permissible.

7 Summarize the Supreme Court's view on drug and alcohol testing.

8 Summarize the Supreme Court's view on probation and parole searches.

One week after a hit-and-run accident that resulted in the death of a bicyclist, Illinois highway patrol officers set up a checkpoint at approximately the same location and time of night as the accident. Their purpose was to obtain information from drivers passing through the area about the hit-and-run. Each passing vehicle was stopped for 10 to 15 seconds and occupants were asked whether they had seen anything happen at that location the previous week. One driver who approached the checkpoint swerved and nearly hit an officer. The officer smelled alcohol on the driver's breath and directed him to a side street where another officer administered a field sobriety test. The driver was convicted of driving under the influence. Did the officers' actions conform to Fourth Amendment requirements? The U.S. Supreme Court was tasked with answering this question. It decided,

> . . . information-seeking highway stops are less likely to provoke anxiety or to prove intrusive, since they are likely brief, the questions asked are not designed to elicit self-incriminating information, and citizens will often react positively when police ask for help. The law also ordinarily permits police to seek the public's voluntary cooperation in a criminal investigation. That the importance of soliciting the public's assistance is offset to some degree by the need to stop a motorist— which amounts to a "seizure" in Fourth Amendment terms, [is not enough to render the stop unconstitutional]. (*Illinois* v. *Lidster*, 540 U.S. 419 [2004], pp. 4–6)

© ZUMA Press, Inc./Alamy

Checkpoints of the type in *Lidster* are the topic of this chapter, as are a number of other law enforcement activities that generally fall short of a full-blown search, arrest, or stop. At issue here are administrative and special needs–type searches.

DISCUSS If a checkpoint like this one was sanctioned by the Supreme Court, what other types of checkpoints, if any, should be authorized?

▶ *Casting Off the Fourth Amendment's Restraints*

Actions based on administrative justifications are those in which the primary purpose is noncriminal. They resemble searches because they intrude on people's privacy—and can lead to the discovery of evidence. Technically, however, they are not searches. Instead of being based on probable cause or reasonable suspicion, administrative actions invoke a balancing test, weighing citizens' privacy interests against the interest to ensure public safety. When the latter outweighs the former, an administrative "search" is allowed, subject to certain limitations. Such limitations are often spelled out in agency policy documents.

LEARNING OUTCOMES 1 Explain the importance of administrative justification.

The Supreme Court has authorized numerous varieties of actions under the administrative justification exception to the Fourth Amendment's probable cause and warrant requirements. Sometimes they are described as *special needs beyond law enforcement searches*; other times, they are called *regulatory searches*. They include (1) inventories, (2) inspections, (3) checkpoints, (4) school discipline, (5) "searches" of government employees' offices, (6) drug and alcohol testing, and (7) parole and probation supervision (see Figure 7–1). Note that when the term "search" appears in quotes, it is because although a particular action may look like a search, it is not the same as a true Fourth Amendment search.

- Inventories
- Inspections
- Checkpoints
- School discipline
- Government employee office searches
- Drug/alcohol testing
- Parole/probation supervision

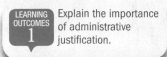

FIGURE 7–1 Common Varieties of Regulatory and Special Needs Searches.

An inventory can be of a vehicle and/or
of a person's personal items.

▶ Inventories

Like seizures based on plain view, inventories can be viewed as another fallback measure. An inventory can be of a vehicle and/or of a person's personal items. Usually, a search occurs under the automobile exception (in the case of an automobile) or a search incident to arrest (when a person is involved), and an inventory is taken after the fact for the purpose of developing a record of what items have been taken into custody. Both types of inventories are fallbacks in the sense that they often occur *after* an earlier search.

Vehicle Inventories

A **vehicle inventory** occurs in a number of situations, usually after a car has been impounded for traffic or parking violations. In *South Dakota v. Opperman* **(428 U.S. 364 [1976])**, the Supreme Court held that a warrantless inventory is permissible on administrative/regulatory grounds. However, it must (1) follow a *lawful* impoundment; (2) be of a routine nature, following standard operating procedures; and (3) not be a "pretext concealing an investigatory police motive." Thus, even though an inventory can be perceived as a fallback measure, which permits a search when probable cause is lacking, it cannot be used in lieu of a regular search requiring probable cause.

Why did the Court opt for another standard besides probable cause for the inventory, despite the fact that it is still a "search" in the conventional sense of the term? The Court noted that the probable cause requirement of the Fourth Amendment is "unhelpful" in the context of administrative care-taking functions (for example, inventories) because the concept of probable cause is linked to criminal investigations. Probable cause is irrelevant with this type of administrative action, "particularly when no claim is made that the protective procedures are a subterfuge for criminal investigations" (p. 371). See Figure 7–2 for more on the reasoning behind the Supreme Court's decision to permit vehicle inventories.

Note that inventories include containers. That is, the police may examine *any* container discovered during the course of a vehicle inventory, but this should be mandated by departmental

procedures. This was the decision reached in *Colorado v. Bertine* **(479 U.S. 367 [1987])**. That decision also helped the police insofar as the Court refused to alter the vehicle inventory exception to the Fourth Amendment when secure impound facilities are accessible. As the Court stated, "[T]he security of the storage facility does not completely eliminate the need for inventorying; the police may still wish to protect themselves or the owners of the lot against false claims of theft or dangerous instrumentalities" (p. 373).

In *Bertine*, the Court also rejected an argument that car owners should be able to make their own arrangements if their vehicles are impounded (for example, have it towed by a private company, have a friend drive it home). The Court stated, "The reasonableness of any particular governmental activity does not necessarily or invariably turn on the existence of alternative 'less intrusive' means" (p. 374).

Reading *Opperman* and *Bertine* would suggest that inventories are relatively standard and intended mainly to take note of a car's contents. However, in *Michigan v. Thomas* (458 U.S. 259 [1982]), the Supreme Court concluded that the police could go even further. In that case, officers found a loaded .38 revolver in one of the impounded vehicle's air vents. The Court upheld the officers' actions because marijuana had been found in the vehicle shortly before the gun was detected.

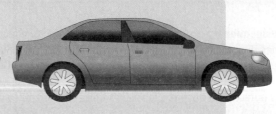

- Protect owner's property while it is in custody

- Protect the police against claims of lost or stolen property

- Protect the police and the public from dangerous items

FIGURE 7–2 Reasons for Vehicle Inventories.

In conclusion, two important issues must be understood with regard to vehicle inventories:

- If during the course of a valid inventory, the police discover evidence that gives rise to probable cause to search, then a more extensive search is permissible.

- Despite the Supreme Court's apparent willingness to give police wide latitude with vehicle inventories, what makes them constitutional is clear guidelines as to how the inventory should be conducted. In other words, the Court has authorized inventories without probable cause or a warrant only if, in addition to the other requirements discussed, it is conducted in accordance with clear departmental policies and procedures. Requiring the police to follow appropriate policies minimizes discretion and the concern that inventories may be used for criminal investigation purposes.

Person Inventories

LEARNING OUTCOMES 2
Summarize the rules surrounding inventory searches.

The inventory exception to the Fourth Amendment's warrant requirement applies in the case of a **person inventory**, as well. The action permitted is often called an *arrest inventory*. The general rule is that the police may search an arrestee and his or her personal items, including containers found in his or her possession, as part of a routine inventory incident to the booking and jailing procedure. As decided in **Illinois v. Lafayette (462 U.S. 640 [1983])**, neither a search warrant nor probable cause is required. According to the Court,

> Consistent with the Fourth Amendment, it is reasonable for police to search the personal effects of a person under lawful arrest as part of the routine administrative procedure at a police station incident to booking and jailing the suspect. The justification for such searches does not rest on probable cause, and hence the absence of a warrant is immaterial to the reasonableness of the search. Here, every consideration of orderly police administration—protection of a suspect's property, deterrence of false claims of theft against the police, security, and identification of the suspect—benefiting both the police and the public points toward the appropriateness of the examination of respondent's shoulder bag. (pp. 643–648)

It is important to understand that an inventory of person must follow a lawful arrest, so the requirement for probable cause to search is essentially satisfied at the arrest stage.

The Supreme Court's decision in *Opperman*, discussed in the vehicle inventories section, has essentially been extended to person inventories. That is, as part of inventorying a person's possessions pursuant to a valid arrest, the police may also examine containers. The Court felt that it would be unduly burdensome on the police to require them to distinguish between which containers may or may not contain evidence of criminal activity.

▶ Inspections

Various **inspections** are permissible without a warrant or probable cause. For all practical purposes, they are "searches." Even so, the courts have continually stressed that the justification for such searches is the "invasion versus need" balancing act—that is, the benefits of some inspections outweigh the costs of inconveniencing certain segments of the population. Most of these exceptions to the warrant requirement are based on the Court's decision in **Camara v. Municipal Court (387 U.S. 523 [1967])**, where it was concluded that "there can be no ready test for determining reasonableness other than by balancing the need to search against the invasion which the search entails" (pp. 536–537).

Home Inspections

Two types of home inspection have been authorized by the Court. The first concerns health and safety inspections of residential buildings, such as public housing units. In *Frank* v. *Maryland* (359 U.S. 360 [1959]), for example, the Court upheld the constitutionality of a statute designed to punish property holders for failing to cooperate with warrantless health and safety inspections. The Court noted that such inspections "touch at most upon the periphery of the important interests safeguarded by the Fourteenth Amendment's protection against official intrusion" (p. 367). In 1967, however, the Court overruled the *Frank* decision in *Camara v. Municipal Court* (387 U.S. 523 [1967]).

Various *inspections* are permissible without a warrant or probable cause.

Picsfive/Shutterstock

Think About It...

Business Inspections Komfortable Kitty Drug Company manufactures and packages veterinary drugs. Several times during a one-year period, Federal Drug Administration (FDA) agents inspected the company's premises to ensure compliance with the Food, Drug, and Cosmetic Act (actual legislation). The agents cited Komfortable Kitty for several violations. Drugs that were allegedly in violation of the act were seized pursuant to an *in rem* arrest warrant (that is, a warrant authorizing the arrest of property). Altogether, over $100,000 worth of drugs and equipment was seized. Komfortable Kitty has contested the constitutionality of the seizure. Does the company have a valid case?

In *Camara*, the Court noted that nonconsensual administrative inspections of private residences amount to a significant intrusion upon the interests protected by the Fourth Amendment. Today, a warrant is required for authorities to engage in a home inspection. However, the meaning of *probable cause* in such a warrant differs from that discussed earlier. The Court has stated that if an area "as a whole" needs inspection, based on factors such as the time, age, and condition of the building, then the probable cause requirement will be satisfied. The key is that probable cause in the inspection context is not *individualized* as in the typical warrant. That is to say, inspections of this sort are geared toward buildings, not persons.

A second type of home inspection is a welfare inspection. In **Wyman v. James (400 U.S. 309 [1971])**, the Supreme Court upheld the constitutionality of a statute that allowed welfare case workers to make warrantless visits to the homes of welfare recipients. The purpose of such inspections is to ensure that welfare recipients are conforming with applicable guidelines and rules. The Court declared that welfare inspections are not searches within the meaning of the Fourth Amendment, which means they can be conducted without a warrant *or* probable cause. Of course, such inspections should be based on neutral criteria and should not mask intentions to look for evidence of criminal activity.

Business Inspections

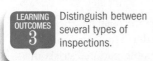
LEARNING OUTCOMES 3 — Distinguish between several types of inspections.

Compared to home inspections, far more case law exists in the arena of business inspections. *See v. City of Seattle* (387 U.S. 541 [1967]), a companion case to *Camara*, was one of the first to focus on the constitutionality of business inspections. *See* involved a citywide inspection of businesses for fire code violations. The Court noted that "[t]he businessman, like the occupant of a residence, has a constitutional right to go about his business free from unreasonable official entries upon his private commercial property" and therefore warrants were required for business inspections.

However, soon after *See*, the Court created what came to be known as the **closely regulated business** exception to the warrant requirement set forth in *Camara* and *See*. Specifically, in **Colonnade Catering Corp. v. United States (397 U.S. 72 [1970])**, the Court upheld a statute criminalizing the refusal to allow warrantless entries of liquor stores by government inspectors. According to the Court:

We agree that Congress has broad power to design such powers of inspection under the liquor laws as it deems necessary to meet the evils at hand. The general rule laid down in *See v. City of Seattle* . . . —"that administrative entry, without consent, upon the portions of commercial premises which are not open to the public may only be compelled through prosecution or physical force within the framework of a warrant procedure"—is therefore not applicable here. In *See*, we reserved decision on the problems of "licensing programs" requiring inspections, saying they can be resolved "on a case-by-case basis

under the general Fourth Amendment standard of reasonableness," . . . What we said in *See* reflects this Nation's traditions that are strongly opposed to using force without definite authority to break down doors. We deal here with the liquor industry long subject to close supervision and inspection. As respects that industry, and its various branches including retailers, Congress has broad authority to fashion standards of reasonableness for searches and seizures. (pp. 76–77)

Additional business inspection cases are featured in the accompanying timeline.

Fire and International Mail Inspections

In **Michigan v. Tyler (436 U.S. 499 [1978])**, the Supreme Court authorized the warrantless inspection of a burned building/residence (that is, fire inspection) immediately after the fire has been put out. The key is that the inspection must be contemporaneous, not several days or weeks after the fire. The justification offered by the Court was that it is necessary to determine the cause of a fire as soon as possible after it has been extinguished. A warrant in such an instance, felt the Court, would be unduly burdensome.

In a related case, *Michigan v. Clifford* (464 U.S. 287 [1984]), the Court decided on the constitutionality of a warrantless arson-related inspection that was conducted five hours after the fire was extinguished. Although the inspection began as just that, when evidence of arson was found, a more extensive search was conducted. The Court required a warrant because the officials engaging in the search admitted it was part of a criminal investigation.

Interestingly, in *Clifford*, the Court stated that "the home owner is entitled to reasonable advance notice that officers are going to enter his premises for the purposes of ascertaining the cause of the fire" (p. 303), which suggests that notice, but not a warrant, is required for the typical fire inspection. More extensive searches, however, still require warrants supported by probable cause.

The Supreme Court has permitted government officials to open incoming international mail. For example, in **United States v. Ramsey (431 U.S. 606 [1977])**, customs agents opened mail that was coming into the United States from Thailand, a known source of drugs. Further, the agents felt that a specific envelope was heavier than what would have been considered usual. Considering these factors, the Supreme Court upheld the warrantless search:

The border-search exception is grounded in the recognized right of the sovereign to control, subject to substantive limitations imposed by the Constitution, who and what may enter the country. It is clear that there is nothing in the rationale behind the border-search exception which suggests that the mode of entry will be critical. It was conceded at oral argument that customs officials could search, without probable cause and without a warrant, envelopes carried by an entering traveler, whether in his luggage or on his person. . . . Surely no different constitutional standard should apply simply

1967

***See v. City of Seattle*, 387 U.S. 541** A warrant is required for the unconsented administrative entry and inspection of a commercial business.

1970

***Collonnade Catering Corp.* v. *United States*, 397 U.S. 72** A statute criminalizing refusal to allow warrantless entry and inspection of liquor stores is upheld. The **closely-regulated business** doctrine is created, meaning that certain businesses (liquor stores, firearms dealerships) can be subjected to warrantless inspections because they are closely regulated and there is a need to ensure compliance with applicable laws.

because the envelopes were mailed, not carried. The critical fact is that the envelopes cross the border and enter this country, not that they are brought in by one mode of transportation rather than another. It is their entry into this country from without it that makes a resulting search "reasonable." (p. 620)

▶ Checkpoints

Several types of **checkpoints** are constitutionally permissible without warrants. A checkpoint is a means of investigating a large number of people and should be distinguished from an inspection. Whereas an *inspection* targets particular homes and/or businesses, a *checkpoint* possesses an element of randomness— or total predictability. Either *everyone* is stopped or every *n*th person (for example, every tenth person) is stopped. A checkpoint is similar to an investigation insofar as its purpose is not criminal in the sense that a typical search is. And to the extent that some checkpoints border on looking for evidence of crime (for example, illegal immigrants), they are often justified because they are not based on individualized suspicion.

> To the extent that some checkpoints border on looking for evidence of crime (for example, illegal immigrants), they are often justified because they are not based on individualized suspicion.

Border and Immigration Checkpoints

In *Carroll* v. *United States* (267 U.S. 132 [1925]), the Supreme Court stated that brief border detentions are constitutionally permissible. Further, it is in the interest of "national self protection" to permit government officials to require "one entering the country to identify himself as entitled to come in . . ." (p. 154). More recently, in *United States* v. *Montoya de Hernandez* (473 U.S. 531 [1985]), the Court reaffirmed the need for warrantless border inspections: "Routine searches of the persons and effects of entrants [at the border] are not subject to any requirement of reasonable suspicion, probable cause, or a warrant. . . . [O]ne's expectation of privacy [is] less at the border" (p. 538). The Court wrote,

> [This case reflects] longstanding concern for the protection of the integrity of the border. This concern is, if anything, heightened by the veritable national crisis in law enforcement caused by smuggling of illicit narcotics . . . and in particular by the increasing utilization of alimentary canal smuggling. This desperate practice appears to be a relatively recent addition to the smugglers' repertoire of deceptive practices, and it also appears to be exceedingly difficult to detect. (pp. 538–539)

In **United States v. Martinez-Fuerte (428 U.S. 543 [1976])**, the Court upheld the decision of the Immigration and Naturalization Service (INS—now called ICE, for Immigration and Customs Enforcement) to establish roadblocks near the Mexican border for the purpose of discovering illegal aliens. The Court offered a number of reasons for its decision. First, "[t]he degree of intrusion upon privacy that may be occasioned by a

Think About It...

Detecting Illegal Aliens The U.S. Border Patrol relies on checkpoints north of the Mexican border to look for illegal aliens. (In California, these can be found as far as 90 miles north of the border.) These checkpoints are often stationed in the middle of major freeways, where every car must slow down and, at a minimum, be waved through by one of several agents standing between the lanes. In addition, there is little, if any, opportunity to exit the freeway in order to avoid the checkpoints. Can these checkpoints be considered administrative? What if, instead of having the cars slow down, the border patrol required all vehicles to *stop*, at which point they would briefly search the trunk, cargo compartment (that is, for a pickup truck, van, or tractor trailer), and so on in an effort to detect illegal aliens? Could they legally do this?

James Steidl/ Shutterstock

1972	**1981**	**1987**
***United States* v. *Biswell*, 406 U.S. 311** The warrantless inspection of a firearms dealership during normal business hours does not violate the Fourth Amendment.	***Donovan* v. *Dewey*, 452 U.S. 494** The closely-regulated business doctrine is modified. In addition to demonstrating that the business is closely regulated, it is necessary that (1) the government have a "substantial" interest in the activity at stake, (2) warrantless inspections are necessary to ensure compliance with the law, and (3) the inspection protocol provides a "constitutionally adequate substitute for a warrant."	***New York* v. *Burger*, 482 U.S. 691** Vehicle junkyard inspections are upheld under the *Dewey* criteria.

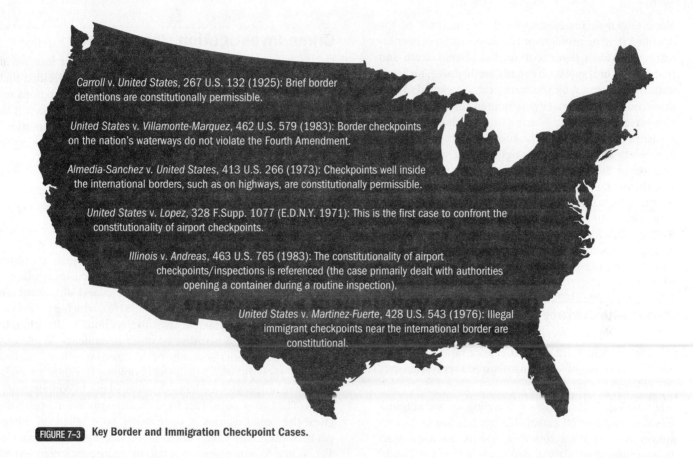

Carroll v. *United States*, 267 U.S. 132 (1925): Brief border detentions are constitutionally permissible.

United States v. *Villamonte-Marquez*, 462 U.S. 579 (1983): Border checkpoints on the nation's waterways do not violate the Fourth Amendment.

Almeida-Sanchez v. *United States*, 413 U.S. 266 (1973): Checkpoints well inside the international borders, such as on highways, are constitutionally permissible.

United States v. *Lopez*, 328 F.Supp. 1077 (E.D.N.Y. 1971): This is the first case to confront the constitutionality of airport checkpoints.

Illinois v. *Andreas*, 463 U.S. 765 (1983): The constitutionality of airport checkpoints/inspections is referenced (the case primarily dealt with authorities opening a container during a routine inspection).

United States v. *Martinez-Fuerte*, 428 U.S. 543 (1976): Illegal immigrant checkpoints near the international border are constitutional.

FIGURE 7–3 Key Border and Immigration Checkpoint Cases.

search of a house hardly can be compared with the minor interference with privacy resulting from the mere stop for questioning as to residence" (p. 565). Second, motorists could avoid the checkpoint if they so desired. Third, the Court noted that the traffic flow near the border was heavy, so individualized suspicion was not possible. Fourth, the location of the roadblock was not decided by the officers in the field "but by officials responsible for making overall decisions" (p. 559). Finally, a requirement that such stops be based on probable cause "would largely eliminate any deterrent to the conduct of well-disguised smuggling operations, even though smugglers are known to use these highways regularly" (p. 557). It is important to note that law enforcement officers must have justification to examine the bags and personal effects of individuals who are stopped

at immigration checkpoints (or during any immigration check) (*Bond* v. *United States*, 529 U.S. 334 [2000]). See Figure 7–3 for a summary.

Sobriety Checkpoints

 **LEARNING OUTCOMES 4** Distinguish between legal and illegal checkpoints.

In ***Michigan Dept. of State Police* v. *Sitz* (496 U.S. 444 [1990])**, the Court upheld a warrantless, suspicionless checkpoint designed to detect evidence of drunk-driving. In that case, police checkpoints at which all drivers were stopped and briefly (approximately 25 seconds) observed for signs of intoxication were set up.

If such signs were found, the driver was detained for sobriety testing, and if the indication was that the driver was intoxicated, an arrest was made. The Court weighed the magnitude of the governmental interest in eradicating the drunk-driving problem against the slight intrusion to motorists stopped briefly at such checkpoints. Key to the constitutionality of Michigan's checkpoint was two additional factors: (1) evenhandedness was ensured because the locations of the checkpoints were chosen pursuant to written guidelines, and every driver was stopped; and (2) the officers themselves were not given discretion to decide whom to stop. Significantly, the checkpoint was deemed constitutional even though motorists were *not* notified of the upcoming checkpoint *or* given an opportunity to turn around and go the other way. According to the Court,

> No one can seriously dispute the magnitude of the drunken driving problem or the State's interest in eradicating it. Media reports of alcohol-related death and mutilation on the Nation's roads are legion. The anecdotal is confirmed by the statistical. . . . For decades, this Court has "repeatedly lamented the tragedy." . . . Conversely, the weight bearing on the other scale—the measure of the intrusion on motorists stopped briefly at sobriety checkpoints—is slight. . . . In sum, the balance of the State's interest in preventing drunken driving, the extent to which this system can reasonably be said to advance that interest, and the degree of intrusion upon individual motorists who are briefly stopped, weighs in favor of the state program. We therefore hold that it is consistent with the Fourth Amendment. (pp. 451–455)

License and Safety Checkpoints

In *Delaware* v. *Prouse* (440 U.S. 648 [1979]), the Supreme Court held that law enforcement officials cannot randomly stop drivers for the purpose of checking their drivers' licenses. The Court's reasoning is interesting:

> An individual operating or traveling in an automobile does not lose all reasonable expectation of privacy simply because the automobile and its use are subject to government regulation. Automobile travel is a basic, pervasive, and often necessary mode of transportation to and from one's home, workplace, and leisure activities. Many people spend more hours each day traveling in cars than walking on the streets. Undoubtedly, many find a greater sense of security and privacy in traveling in an automobile than they do in exposing themselves by pedestrian or other modes of travel. Were the individual subject to unfettered governmental intrusion every time he entered an automobile, the security guaranteed by the Fourth Amendment would be seriously circumscribed. . . . Accordingly, we hold that except in those situations in which there is at least articulable and reasonable suspicion that a motorist is unlicensed or that an automobile is not registered, or that either the vehicle or an occupant is otherwise subject to seizure for violation of the law, stopping an automobile and detaining the driver in

order to check his driver's license and the registration of the automobile are unreasonable under the Fourth Amendment. (pp. 662–663)

The Court did note, however, that "this holding does not preclude the State of Delaware or other States from developing methods for spot checks that involve less intrusion or that do not involve the unconstrained exercise of discretion" (p. 663). In particular, "Questioning of all oncoming traffic at roadblock-type stops is one possible alternative" (p. 663). If officers stopped every 5th, 10th, or 20th vehicle, then this action would probably conform to the Court's requirement that roadblocks and checkpoints restrict individual officers' discretion to the fullest extent possible.

Crime Investigation Checkpoints

In *Illinois* v. *Lidster* (540 U.S. 419 [2004]), the case featured at the beginning of this chapter, the Supreme Court decided that checkpoints are also authorized for officers to ask questions related to crimes that had occurred earlier at the same area. The key in that case, however, was that officers asked questions about a crime that occurred *earlier*. They were not looking to detect criminal activity at that very moment.

Other Types of Checkpoints

Still other types of checkpoints have come to the Supreme Court's attention. In *United States* v. *Villamonte-Marquez*, for example, the Court distinguished stops of boats on water from stops of vehicles on land. In that case, customs officers stopped and boarded a person's boat to inspect documents in accordance with 19 U.S.C. Section 1581(a), which permits officers to board any vessel, at any time, without justification, to examine the vessel's manifest or other documents. While onboard the defendant's boat, one of the customs officers smelled what he thought was marijuana. Looking through an open hatch, the officer spotted bales that turned out to contain marijuana. The Court noted that fixed checkpoints are not possible, given the expansiveness of open water, so it relied on different reasoning. The Court noted that boardings such as that in *Villamonte-Marquez* are essential to ensure enforcement of the law in waters, "where the need to deter or apprehend drug smugglers is great" (p. 593). Key restrictions the Court *did* impose, though, were that such detentions be brief and limited to the inspection of documents. The reason the seizure of the marijuana was upheld in *Villamonte-Marquez* was that the contraband was in plain view.

Airport checkpoints are also authorized, and there is no need for probable cause or reasonable suspicion in such situations. According to the Ninth Circuit, "The need to prevent airline hijacking is unquestionably grave and urgent. . . . A pre-boarding screening of all passengers and carry-on articles sufficient in scope to detect the presence of weapons or explosives is reasonably necessary to meet the need" (*United States* v. *Davis*, 482 F.2d 893 [9th Cir. 1973]). Another court reached a similar conclusion (*United States* v. *Lopez*, 328 F. Supp. 1077 [E.D.N.Y. 1971]). And the Fifth Circuit's opinion in

United States v. *Skipwith* (482 F.2d 1272 [5th Cir. 1971]) is particularly helpful:

[T]he intrusion which the airport search imposes on the public is not insubstantial. It is inconvenient and annoying, in some cases it may be embarrassing, and at times it can be incriminating. There are several factors, however, which make this search less offensive to the searched person than similar searches in other contexts. One such factor is the almost complete absence of any stigma attached to being subjected to search at a known, designated airport search point. . . . In addition, the offensiveness of the screening process is somewhat mitigated by the fact that the person to be searched must voluntarily come to and enter the search area. He has every opportunity to avoid the procedure by not entering the boarding area. Finally, the circumstances under which the airport search is conducted make it much less likely that abuses will occur. Unlike searches conducted on dark and lonely streets at night where often the officer and the subject are the only witnesses, these searches are made under supervision and not far from the scrutiny of the traveling public. Moreover, the airlines, which have their representatives present, have a definite and substantial interest in assuring that their passengers are not unnecessarily harassed. The officers conducting the search under these circumstances are much more likely to be solicitous of the Fourth Amendment rights of the traveling public than in more isolated, unsupervised surroundings. (pp. 1275–1276)

Note that airport screenings are now conducted by *public* as opposed to *private* actors. Prior to the September 11, 2001, terrorist attacks on the World Trade Center and the Pentagon, airport inspections were conducted by private security companies. Now, they are conducted by Transportation Safety Administration (TSA) officials, who are employed by the federal government. This change is of no consequence to the constitutionality of airport screenings, however, even though such inspections are today sometimes more intrusive than prior to 9/11 (for example, "shoe searches" and searches at the boarding gate in addition to at the main security checkpoint).

Unconstitutional Checkpoints

The administrative rationale is *not* acceptable, by comparison, to detect evidence of criminal activity. This was the decision reached in **City of Indianapolis v. Edmond (531 U.S. 32 [2000])**, a case in which the Supreme Court decided whether a city's suspicionless checkpoints for detecting illegal drugs were constitutional. Here is how the Supreme Court described the checkpoints:

The city of Indianapolis operated a checkpoint program under which the police, acting without individualized suspicion, stopped a predetermined number of vehicles at roadblocks in various locations on city roads for the primary purpose of the discovery and interdiction of illegal narcotics. Under the program, at least one officer would (1) approach each vehicle, (2) advise the driver

that he or she was being stopped briefly at a drug checkpoint, (3) ask the driver to produce a driver's license and the vehicle's registration, (4) look for signs of impairment, and (5) conduct an open-view examination of the vehicle from the outside. In addition, a narcotics-detection dog would walk around the outside of each stopped vehicle. (p. 32)

The Court held that stops such as those conducted during Indianapolis's checkpoint operations require individualized suspicion. In addition, "because the checkpoint program's primary purpose [was] indistinguishable from the general interest in crime control" (p. 44), it was deemed in violation of the Fourth Amendment.

▶ School Discipline

Public school administrators and teachers may "search" a student without a warrant if they possess reasonable suspicion that the action will yield evidence that the student has violated the law or is violating the law or rules of the school. However, such **school disciplinary "searches"** must not be "excessively intrusive in light of the age and sex of the students and the nature of the infraction" (p. 381). This was the decision reached in **New Jersey v. T.L.O. (469 U.S. 325 [1985])**. In *T.L.O.*, a high school student was caught smoking in a school bathroom (in violation of school policy) and was sent to the vice principal. When the vice principal searched the student's purse for cigarettes, he also found evidence implicating the student in the sale of marijuana. The Court held that the evidence was admissible because the administrator had sufficient justification to search the purse for evidence concerning the school's antismoking policy.

In support of its decision in *T.L.O.*, the Court noted that a warrant requirement "would unduly interfere with the maintenance of the swift and informal disciplinary procedures needed in the schools . . .[and] . . . the substantial need of teachers and administrators for freedom to maintain order in the schools" (p. 376). The majority further stated that the reasonableness test for school disciplinary "searches" involves a twofold inquiry: "First, one must consider 'whether the . . . action was justified at its inception . . .' second, one must determine whether the search as actually conducted 'was reasonably related in scope to the circumstances which justified the interference in the first place'" (p. 341).

There are important limits on school discipline searches, especially in light of the Supreme Court's decision in *Safford Unified School District* v. *Redding* (No. 08-479 [2009]). In that case, Savana Redding, an eighth grader, was "strip searched"

Public school administrators and teachers may "search" a student without a warrant if they possess reasonable suspicion that the action will yield evidence that the student has violated the law or is violating the law or rules of the school.

by school officials on a belief that she was in possession of certain nonprescription medications, in violation of school policy. Writing for the majority, Justice Souter found that the search violated the Fourth Amendment because there was no "indication of danger to the students from the power of the drugs or their quantity, nor any reason to suppose that (Redding) was carrying pills in her underwear." More than just reasonable suspicion is necessary, then, to support particularly intrusive searches of this nature—for school discipline, but also in the workplace.

Note that *T.L.O.* concerns students in kindergarten through grade 12. A different story emerges in the context of public and private universities. The courts have generally held that the Fourth Amendment is applicable at the university level. That is, for university personnel to conduct searches of students' dorm rooms, lockers, and so on, some level of justification is required.

Locker Checks and Drug Dog "Sniffs"

LEARNING OUTCOMES 5 Explain when school disciplinary searches are permissible.

A handful of lower court decisions concern inspections of public school students' lockers as well as drug dog "sniffs" for the purpose of detecting illicit drugs. First, random, suspicionless locker inspections are generally permissible, assuming the students have been given some notification in advance that their lockers are subject to inspection at any time (see *Commonwealth* v. *Cass*, 709 A.2d 350 [Pa. 1998]). However, "searches" of *specific* lockers would still be subject to the reasonableness test set forth in *T.L.O.*

With regard to the use of drug dogs, the Fifth Circuit held that so-called "sniffs" of lockers and cars in public schools are constitutional (*Horton* v. *Goose Creek Independent School District*, 690 F.2d 470 [5th Cir. 1982]). The court reasoned that lockers and cars were inanimate objects located in a public place.

Then there is the Seventh Circuit's controversial holding in *Doe* v. *Renfrow* (631 F.2d 91 [7th Cir. 1980]) that the exploratory sniffing of *students* (as opposed to their property) was not a search. The Seventh Circuit affirmed the lower federal court's observation that "the presence of the canine team for several minutes was a minimal intrusion at best and not so serious as to invoke the protections of the Fourth Amendment" (*Doe* v. *Renfrow*, 475 F. Supp. 1012 [1979], p. 1020). In another appellate court case, though, the Ninth Circuit held that dog sniffs of students' possessions implicate the Fourth Amendment and require probable cause (*B.C.* v. *Plumas Unified School District*, 192 F.3d 1260 [9th Cir. 1999]). This is a disagreement between federal circuits that is ripe for some Supreme Court resolution.

▶ "Searches" of Government Employee Offices

In a case very similar to *T.L.O.*, although not involving a public school student, the Court held that neither a warrant nor probable cause was required to "search" a government employee's office, but the "search" must be "a noninvestigatory work-related intrusion or an investigatory search for evidence of suspected work-related employee misfeasance" (**O'Connor v. Ortega, 480**

U.S. 709 [1987]). Justice O'Connor summarized the Court's reasoning: "[T]he delay in correcting the employee misconduct caused by the need for probable cause rather than reasonable suspicion will be translated into tangible and often irreparable damage to the agency's work, and ultimately to the public interest" (p. 724). It is important to note, however, that the Court was limiting its decision strictly to work-related matters: "[W]e do not address the appropriate standard when an employee is being investigated for criminal misconduct or breaches of other nonwork-related statutory or regulatory standards" (p. 729). The Court further noted in *Ortega* that the appropriate standard by which to judge such "searches" is *reasonableness*:

> We hold, therefore, that public employer intrusions on the constitutionally protected privacy interests of government employees for noninvestigatory, work-related purposes, as well as for investigations of work-related misconduct, should be judged by the standard of reasonableness under all the circumstances. Under this reasonableness standard, both the inception and the scope of the intrusion must be reasonable. (pp. 725–726)

Recently, the Supreme Court was confronted with the question of whether a police officer's employer could examine the content of messages sent via a pager. Ontario, California, police officers were given department-issued pagers. When some of them exceeded the number of allotted monthly messages, the department acquired transcripts of the officers' messages, learned that some of them were sexually explicit, and then disciplined the officers accordingly. They sued under Section 1983, alleging their Fourth Amendment rights were violated. The Supreme Court disagreed, holding that the department's "search" of the pager message contents was reasonable (*City of Ontario* v. *Quon*, No. 08-1332 [2010]).

LEARNING OUTCOMES 6 Explain when searches of government employees' offices are permissible.

At the risk of confusing matters, it should be pointed out that *reasonableness* in the context of public school student and government employee "searches" is not the same as *reasonable suspicion*. The latter refers to a certain level of suspicion, whereas the former focuses on the procedural aspects of the actions in question (for example, Did authorities go too far in looking for evidence?). The distinction between *reasonableness* and *reasonable suspicion* is a subtle but important one—hence, the reason for discussing disciplinary and work-related "searches" in the section on administrative justification.

Perhaps more important, none of the foregoing applies to individuals employed in *private* companies. The reason for this should be fairly clear: Private employees work for private employers, the latter not being bound by the strictures of the Fourth Amendment. Stated simply, private employers can search private employees' lockers, desks, and the like without infringing on any constitutional rights.

Private employers can search private employees' lockers, desks, and the like without infringing on any constitutional rights.

of a parolee" (p. 843). What was the Court's logic for this decision? It stated, "Parolees, who are on the 'continuum' of state-imposed punishments, have fewer expectations of privacy than probationers, because parole is more akin to imprisonment than probation is" (p. 843).

Police/Probation Partnerships

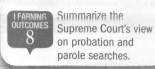

LEARNING OUTCOMES 8 — Summarize the Supreme Court's view on probation and parole searches.

A controversial practice closely connected to searches of probationers comes in the form of **police/probation partnerships**, a cutting-edge law enforcement strategy now being experimented with across the country. An example of one such approach is Boston's Operation Night Light. The program began in 1992 as an informal collaboration between probation officers and Boston's Anti-Gang Violence Unit. Teams composed of one probation officer and two police officers serving as backup make surprise visits to the homes, schools, and worksites of high-risk youth probationers, mostly during the hours of 7 p.m. to midnight. The program grew to the extent that 50 police officers and 50 probation officers worked together like this seven nights a week.

Another example of a police/probation partnership in action is the IMPACT project in San Bernardino, California. The program was virtually identical to Boston's. One difference was that the teams consisted of one San Bernardino police officer and one San Bernardino County probation officer. (Probation is a county-level function in California.) Also, *all* new probationers were under scrutiny.

What makes these and other police/probation partnerships interesting from a Fourth Amendment standpoint are the search-and-seizure implications. On one hand, these partnerships may be highly effective crime-reduction mechanisms. On the other hand, critics of police/probation partnerships claim that they are little more than a method of circumventing the Fourth Amendment's probable cause and warrant requirements. In other words, critics claim that police officers use probation officers as "stalking horses" to skirt the Fourth Amendment. The California Supreme Court's *Bravo* decision, for example, permits warrantless, suspicionless searches of probationers, even by police officers.

Here again, due process and crime control collide. Police/probation partnerships may effectively reduce crime, but they may also compromise due process. Someday, the constitutionality of these partnerships will be decided in court. Most likely, the U.S. Supreme Court will decide on the matter in the near future. The Fourth Amendment implications are simply too serious to ignore.

Andrea Church/Shutterstock

Think About It...

Searches of Government Employees Federal law enforcement agents suspected that several employees in a government agency were engaged in criminal wrongdoing. Several of the agency's records were subpoenaed. To ensure that the records were being prepared in accordance with the subpoena, the agents visited the government agency. During the course of their visit, the director of the agency was asked to open an employee's office. Upon looking in the employee's office, the agents found incriminating documents and seized them. They also searched the employee's file cabinet and found more incriminating documents, which were also seized. Is this a valid search of a government employee's office, as authorized by *O'Connor* v. *Ortega* (480 U.S. 709 [1987])?

▶ Drug and Alcohol Testing

The Supreme Court has, especially recently, decided on the constitutionality of **drug and alcohol testing** programs. Three lines of cases can be discerned: (1) employee testing, (2) hospital patient testing, and (3) school student testing. Cases involving drug and alcohol testing of each of these three groups are reviewed in the following subsections.

Drug and Alcohol Testing of Employees

The Supreme Court has permitted warrantless, suspicionless drug and alcohol testing of employees. In **Skinner v. Railway Labor Executives' Association (489 U.S. 602 [1989])** and *National Treasury Employees Union* v. *Von Raab* (489 U.S. 656 [1989]), the Court upheld the constitutionality of certain regulations that permit drug and alcohol testing, citing two reasons for its decision. The first was deterrence; without suspicionless drug testing, there would be no deterrent to employees to stay off drugs. The second reason was that drug testing promotes businesses' interest in obtaining accurate information about accidents and who is responsible. In *Skinner*, Justice Stevens made this observation:

> Most people—and I would think most railroad employees as well—do not go to work with the expectation that they may be involved in a major accident, particularly one causing such catastrophic results as loss of life or the release of hazardous material requiring an evacuation. Moreover, even if they are conscious of the possibilities that such an accident might be a contributing factor, if the risk of serious personal injury does not deter their use of these substances, it seems highly unlikely that the additional threat of loss of employment would have any effect on their behavior. (p. 634)

Two interesting limitations should be noted about both of these cases. The first is that the Court did not decide whether warrantless, suspicionless drug testing could be used for *law enforcement* purposes. Rather, such testing was held to be constitutional for *regulatory* reasons. Second, both cases focused on federal regulations: Federal Railroad Administration guidelines in *Skinner* and U.S. Customs Service Policy in *National Treasury Employees Union*. Left open was the question of private

business policy. Nevertheless, the courts have since upheld drug and alcohol testing of teachers, police officers, and several other groups.[1]

This line of cases would seem to suggest that employee drug testing is becoming increasingly common across the United States. Although it is certainly true that more employees are subject to drug testing now than in the past, the Supreme Court has clearly stated that certain drug testing policies are unconstitutional. For example, in *Chandler* v. *Miller* (520 U.S. 305 [1997]), the Court struck down a Georgia statute that required every person seeking nomination or election to undergo a test for illegal drugs.

Drug and Alcohol Testing of Hospital Patients

LEARNING OUTCOMES 7 — Summarize the Supreme Court's view on drug and alcohol testing.

In a recent case, **Ferguson v. Charleston (532 U.S. 67 [2001])**, the Supreme Court addressed the constitutionality of drug testing of hospital patients. In the fall of 1988, staff at a Charleston, South Carolina, public hospital became concerned over the apparent increase in the use of cocaine by patients who were receiving prenatal treatment. Staff at the hospital approached the city and agreed to cooperate in prosecuting pregnant mothers who tested positive for drugs. A task force was set up, consisting of hospital personnel, police, and other local officials. The task force formulated a policy for how to conduct the tests, preserve the evidence, and use it to prosecute those who tested positive. Several women tested positive for cocaine. The question before the Supreme Court was whether the Fourth Amendment was violated when hospital personnel, working with the police, tested pregnant mothers for drug use without their consent. Not surprisingly, the Court answered with a "yes":

> Because the hospital seeks to justify its authority to conduct drug tests and to turn the results over to police without the patients' knowledge or consent, this case differs from the four previous cases in which the Court considered whether comparable drug tests fit within the closely guarded category of constitutionally permissible suspicionless searches. . . . Those cases employed a

Think About It...

Drug Testing of Students The school board approved a policy prohibiting a high school student from participating in any extracurricular activities or driving to and from school unless the student and his or her parent or guardian consented to and the student passed tests for drugs, alcohol, and tobacco in random, unannounced urinalysis examinations. (Extracurricular activities include not only athletic teams but also organizations such as the student council, foreign language clubs, and so on.) When consent for testing had been given and the individuals had taken and passed the tests, then participation in the extracurricular organizations or driving to and from school would be permitted. The testing was to be conducted by Acme Toxicology Services, which would collect the samples, and the local hospital's laboratory services division, which would perform the tests. Can this type of random, suspicionless drug testing be considered an administrative search?

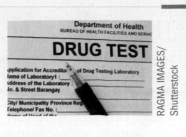

balancing test weighing the intrusion on the individual's privacy interest against the "special needs" that supported the program. The invasion of privacy here is far more substantial than in those cases. In previous cases, there was no misunderstanding about the purpose of the test or the potential use of the test results, and there were protections against the dissemination of the results to third parties. Moreover, those cases involved disqualification from eligibility for particular benefits, not the unauthorized dissemination of test results. The critical difference, however, lies in the nature of the "special needs" asserted. In each of the prior cases, the "special need" was divorced from the State's general law enforcement interest. Here, the policy's central and indispensable feature from its inception was the use of law enforcement to coerce patients into substance abuse treatment. (pp. 77–78)

Drug and Alcohol Testing of School Students

The Supreme Court has recently extended its drug testing decisions to include public school students. Specifically, in **Vernonia School District 47J v. Acton (515 U.S. 646 [1995])**, the Court upheld a random drug testing program for school athletes. The program had been instituted because the district had been experiencing significant student drug use. Under the program, all students who wished to play sports were required to be tested at the beginning of the season and then retested randomly later in the season. The Court noted that athletes enjoy a lesser expectation of privacy, given the semipublic nature of locker rooms, which is where the testing took place. Also, athletes are often subject to other intrusions, including physical exams, so drug testing involved a "negligible" privacy intrusion, according to the Court.

Even more recently, the Supreme Court affirmed *Vernonia School District*. The case of **Board of Education v. Earls (536 U.S. 822 [2002])** dealt with another student drug testing policy. The Student Activities Drug Testing Policy, implemented by the Board of Education of Independent School District

no. 92 of Pottawatomie County, required students who participate in extracurricular activities to submit to random, suspicionless drug tests. Urine tests were intended to detect the use of illegal drugs. Together with their parents, two students, Lindsay Earls and Daniel James, brought a Section 1983 lawsuit against the school district, alleging that the drug testing policy violated the Fourth Amendment, as incorporated to the states through the due process clause of the Fourteenth Amendment. The district court found in favor of the school district, but the Tenth Circuit Court reversed the decision, holding that the policy violated the Fourth Amendment. It concluded that random, suspicionless drug tests would only be permissible if there were some identifiable drug abuse problem. However, the Supreme Court held that random, suspicionless drug testing of students who participate in extracurricular activities "is a reasonable means of furthering the School District's important interest in preventing and deterring drug use among its schoolchildren and does not violate the Fourth Amendment" (p. 822).

▶ Probation and Parole Supervision

A person on probation enjoys a lesser expectation of privacy than the typical citizen. In **Griffin v. Wisconsin (483 U.S. 868 [1987])**, the Supreme Court held that a state law or agency rule permitting probation officers to search a probationer's home without a warrant and based on reasonable suspicion was constitutional. The majority (of only five justices) concluded that probation supervision "is a 'special need' of the State permitting a degree of impingement upon privacy that would not be constitutional if applied to the public at large" (p. 875). See Figure 7-4 for a list of common federal probation conditions. Note in particular condition number 23, which pertains to searches.

A person on probation enjoys a lesser expectation of privacy than the typical citizen.

1. support his dependents and meet other family responsibilities;
2. make restitution to a victim of the offense under section 3556 (but not subject to the limitation of section 3663 (a) or 3663A (c)(1)(A));
3. give to the victims of the offense the notice ordered pursuant to the provisions of section 3555;
4. work conscientiously at suitable employment or pursue conscientiously a course of study or vocational training that will equip him for suitable employment;
5. refrain, in the case of an individual, from engaging in a specified occupation, business, or profession bearing a reasonably direct relationship to the conduct constituting the offense, or engage in such a specified occupation, business, or profession only to a stated degree or under stated circumstances;
6. refrain from frequenting specified kinds of places or from associating unnecessarily with specified persons;
7. refrain from excessive use of alcohol, or any use of a narcotic drug or other controlled substance, as defined in section 102 of the Controlled Substances Act (21 U.S.C. 802), without a prescription by a licensed medical practitioner;
8. refrain from possessing a firearm, destructive device, or other dangerous weapon;
9. undergo available medical, psychiatric, or psychological treatment, including treatment for drug or alcohol dependency, as specified by the court, and remain in a specified institution if required for that purpose;
10. remain in the custody of the Bureau of Prisons during nights, weekends, or other intervals of time, totaling no more than the lesser of one year or the term of imprisonment authorized for the offense, during the first year of the term of probation or supervised release;
11. reside at, or participate in the program of, a community corrections facility (including a facility maintained or under contract to the Bureau of Prisons) for all or part of the term of probation;
12. work in community service as directed by the court;
13. reside in a specified place or area, or refrain from residing in a specified place or area;
14. remain within the jurisdiction of the court, unless granted permission to leave by the court or a probation officer;
15. report to a probation officer as directed by the court or the probation officer;
16. permit a probation officer to visit him at his home or elsewhere as specified by the court;
17. answer inquiries by a probation officer and notify the probation officer promptly of any change in address or employment;
18. notify the probation officer promptly if arrested or questioned by a law enforcement officer;
19. remain at his place of residence during nonworking hours and, if the court finds it appropriate, that compliance with this condition be monitored by telephonic or electronic signaling devices, except that a condition under this paragraph may be imposed only as an alternative to incarceration;
20. comply with the terms of any court order or order of an administrative process pursuant to the law of a State, the District of Columbia, or any other possession or territory of the United States, requiring payments by the defendant for the support and maintenance of a child or of a child and the parent with whom the child is living;
21. be ordered deported by a United States district court, or United States magistrate judge, pursuant to a stipulation entered into by the defendant and the United States under section 238(d)(5) of the Immigration and Nationality Act, except that, in the absence of a stipulation, the United States district court or a United States magistrate judge, may order deportation as a condition of probation, if, after notice and hearing pursuant to such section, the Attorney General demonstrates by clear and convincing evidence that the alien is deportable;
22. satisfy such other conditions as the court may impose or;
23. if required to register under the Sex Offender Registration and Notification Act, submit his person, and any property, house, residence, vehicle, papers, computer, other electronic communication or data storage devices or media, and effects to search at any time, with or without a warrant, by any law enforcement or probation officer with reasonable suspicion concerning a violation of a condition of probation or unlawful conduct by the person, and by any probation officer in the lawful discharge of the officer's supervision functions.

 **Common Federal Probation Conditions.**
Source: 18 U.S.C. Section 3563.

The Court has also ruled that evidence seized by parole officers during an illegal search and seizure need not be excluded at a parole revocation hearing (see *Pennsylvania Board of Probation and Parole* v. *Scott*, 524 U.S. 357 [1998]). This latter decision can be interpreted to mean that the exclusionary rule does not apply in parole revocation hearings. A warrant requirement, the Court noted, "would both hinder the function of state parole systems and alter the traditionally flexible, administrative nature of parole revocation proceedings" (p. 364).

More recently, in *United States* v. *Knights* (534 U.S. 112 [2001]), the Supreme Court held that warrantless searches of probationers are permissible not only for probation-related purposes (for example, to ensure that probation conditions are being conformed with) but also for investigative purposes. In that case, a probationer was suspected of vandalizing utility

company facilities. A police detective searched the probationer's residence and found incriminating evidence. The Supreme Court held that "[t]he warrantless search of Knights, supported by reasonable suspicion and authorized by a probation condition, satisfied the Fourth Amendment" (p. 112).

Needless to say, all three of the aforementioned decisions do not provide a great deal of guidance to probation officers on the streets. *Griffin*, for example, dealt with the constitutionality of one statute in one state. This means that probation officers are mostly forced to turn to state-level supreme court decisions for guidance.

In **Samson v. California (547 U.S. 843 [2006])**, the Supreme Court extended its earlier probation decision to parole supervision. It held that "[t]he Fourth Amendment does not prohibit a police officer from conducting a suspicionless search

THE CASE

A Proper Checkpoint?

Here are the facts from an actual case:

During the spring and summer of 1992, street crime, including four drive-by shootings, escalated in the Soundview neighborhood of the Bronx. In response, the 43rd precinct instituted the so-called Watson Avenue Special Operation. This involved a temporary vehicular checkpoint in an eight square-block narcotics-ridden area where most of the drive-by shootings had taken place. The checkpoint was to be active three days a week on a random basis and for approximately six hours a day, primarily in the evening hours. When the checkpoint was in operation, officers manning the barricade were to stop every vehicle seeking to enter the area in order to ascertain the driver's connection to the neighborhood. Drivers who approached the checkpoint were to be allowed to avoid questioning by driving around the area or by parking their cars and entering the area on foot. Area residents and commercial vehicles were to be allowed into the neighborhood. Officers manning the barricades were verbally instructed that they could also allow cars dropping off small children or visiting the local church to enter the area. Other than that, vehicles were not permitted beyond the barricades. The operation was in effect for six weeks, between August 26 and October 10, 1992. (*Maxwell* v. *City of New York,* 102 F.3d 664 [2d Cir. 1996], p. 665)

Answer the following questions with respect to the checkpoint in this case:

1. If you were tasked with ruling on the constitutionality of the checkpoint, what would your decision be?
2. What factors make the checkpoint described different than a checkpoint with a general crime-control focus?
3. Should more or fewer of these types of checkpoints be used? Why?

LEARNING OUTCOMES 1

Explain the importance of administrative justification.

The term *administrative justification* is something of a euphemism. It is not really *justification* at all. Actions based on administrative justification require that the government's interest in protecting public safety outweighs individual privacy interests.

1. In what ways do actions based on administrative justification get around the requirements of the Fourth Amendment?

2. What interests are balanced in the administrative/regulatory/special needs search context?

LEARNING OUTCOMES 2

Summarize the rules surrounding inventory searches.

Inventories fall into two categories: (1) vehicle inventories and (2) person inventories. A vehicle inventory must follow a lawful impoundment, be of a routine nature, follow department policy, and not be used as a pretext concealing an investigative police motive. A person inventory is justified on similar grounds, except that it must be preceded by a lawful arrest.

Key Cases

South Dakota v. *Opperman*

Colorado v. *Bertine*

Illinois v. *Lafayette*

1. What types of inventories have been sanctioned by the U.S. Supreme Court?

2. Explain the limitations on each type of constitutional inventory.

vehicle inventory A procedure used to take record of a vehicle's contents after it has been lawfully impounded. Vehicle inventories do not invoke the Fourth Amendment and do not require probable cause.

person inventory A procedure used to take record of a person's personal possessions after he or she has been lawfully arrested. Person inventories do not invoke the Fourth Amendment and do not require probable cause—but they can only occur after a lawful arrest (that is, one satisfying Fourth Amendment requirements).

LEARNING OUTCOMES 3

Distinguish between several types of inspections.

Four types of inspections have been recognized and sanctioned by the U.S. Supreme Court: welfare compliance inspections, closely regulated business inspections, fire inspections, and international mail inspections.

Key Cases

Camara v. *Municipal Court*

Wyman v. *James*

Colonnade Catering Corp. v. *United States*

Michigan v. *Tyler*

United States v. *Ramsey*

1. What types of inspections have been sanctioned by the U.S. Supreme Court?

2. Explain the limitations on each type of constitutional inspection.

inspection An exception to the Fourth Amendment's warrant requirement that permits certain authorities to inspect a closely regulated business.

closely regulated business A type of business subject to warrantless, suspicionless inspections. Examples include liquor stores and firearm dealerships.

LEARNING OUTCOMES 4

Distinguish between legal and illegal checkpoints.

For a checkpoint to conform to constitutional requirements, it must be minimally intrusive, brief, and not directly tied to a criminal investigation. Examples of legal (that is, constitutional) checkpoints are border checkpoints, illegal immigrant checkpoints, and sobriety checkpoints. Checkpoints conducted for the sole purpose of detecting criminal activity are unconstitutional.

Key Cases

United States v. *Martinez-Fuerte*

Michigan Dept. of State Police v. *Sitz*

Illinois v. *Lidster*

City of Indianapolis v. *Edmond*

1. Distinguish between border checkpoints and illegal immigrant checkpoints.

2. What criteria make a checkpoint pass constitutional muster?

checkpoints Brief detentions that do not require probable cause or a warrant. Their purpose should *not* be to detect evidence of criminal conduct, such as narcotics trafficking. Examples include border checkpoints, illegal immigrant checkpoints, sobriety checkpoints, license and safety checkpoints, crime-investigation checkpoints, and airport checkpoints.

LEARNING OUTCOMES 5

Explain when school disciplinary searches are permissible.

School disciplinary "searches" are constitutionally permissible, but they must be reasonable. Random, suspicionless locker inspections are permissible but only with ample notice to students.

Key Cases

New Jersey v. T.L.O.

1. What are school discipline searches?
2. What justification, if any, is required for officials to conduct a school discipline search?

school disciplinary "searches" Although they are not "searches" in the traditional Fourth Amendment sense, school officials can search (K–12) students' possessions without a warrant or probable cause for evidence of activity in violation of school policy.

LEARNING OUTCOMES 6

Explain when searches of government employees' offices are permissible.

"Searches" of government employees' offices are permissible with neither a warrant nor probable cause but must amount to noninvestigatory work-related intrusions or investigatory searches for evidence of suspected work-related employee misconduct.

Key Cases

O'Connor v. Ortega

1. Under what circumstances are suspicionless searches of government employees' offices constitutional?

LEARNING OUTCOMES 7

Summarize the Supreme Court's view on drug and alcohol testing.

Employees and public school students can be screened for substance use but only by properly trained individuals following appropriate policies (for example, nurses). Hospital patients, however, cannot be subjected to drug and alcohol testing.

Key Cases

Skinner v. Railway Labor Executives' Assoc.

Ferguson v. Charleston

Vernonia School District 47J v. Acton

Board of Education v. Earls

1. Summarize U.S. Supreme Court case law involving drug testing.
2. When does drug testing go too far? Cite specific case law.

drug and alcohol testing A procedure of testing for drug or alcohol use, usually via urinalysis. Employees and school students can be subjected to warrantless, suspicionless drug and alcohol testing, but hospital patients cannot—if the evidence is turned over to law enforcement authorities.

LEARNING OUTCOMES 8

Summarize the Supreme Court's view on probation and parole searches.

Probation supervision permits warrantless searches premised on reasonable grounds. The same applies to parolee searches.

Key Cases

Griffin v. Wisconsin

Samson v. California

1. Explain the Supreme Court's decision in *Griffin* v. *Wisconsin*.
2. Explain the Supreme Court's decision in *Samson* v. *California*.

police/probation partnerships A practice of teaming probation officers with police officers for the purpose of crime control or prevention. Such partnerships are controversial because police officers can effectively skirt the Fourth Amendment's requirements when they team with probation officers who have more latitude to conduct searches of probationers.

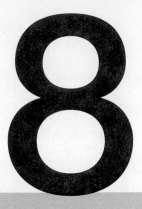

8

Interrogation and Confessions

"The courts have imposed a litany of restrictions on what law enforcement officials can do in order to elicit incriminating statements from suspected criminals."

1 Identify the three methods by which the constitutionality of interrogations and confessions is analyzed.

2 Summarize how due process and voluntariness impact interrogations and confessions.

3 Summarize how the Sixth Amendment impacts interrogations and confessions.

4 Explain *Miranda* rights and how they impact interrogations and confessions.

5 Explain how the exclusionary rule operates in the confessions/interrogations context.

A LEGITIMATE PUBLIC SAFETY EXCEPTION?

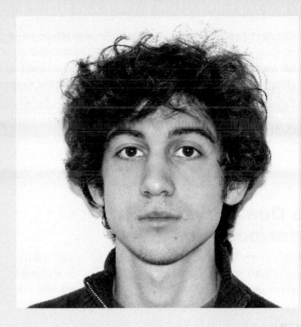

© FBI Photo/Alamy

Dzhokhar Tsarnaev and his older brother, Tamerlan, allegedly detonated two homemade explosive devices at the finish line of the 2013 Boston Marathon. Three people were killed and more than 200 were injured in the incident. Tamerlan was killed during the ensuing manhunt, but Dzhokhar, who survived bullet wounds and two gun battles with law enforcement officers, was captured and charged by federal authorities with using and conspiring to use a weapon of mass destruction and malicious destruction of property with an explosive device. Conviction of either charge could result in the death penalty. As of this writing, the case still has not gone to trial.

The *Miranda* rule, an important part of this chapter, requires police officers to advise a criminal suspect of his or her constitutional rights prior to any questioning—especially the rights to remain silent and to be afforded an attorney. However, the Supreme Court has also approved a public safety exception to *Miranda*, which permits dispensing with the warnings in certain situations. The exception assumes circumstances can arise in which the need for police questioning takes on special urgency. So it was in the wake of the Boston bombing. Police invoked the public safety exception and questioned Dzhokhar without advising him of his *Miranda* rights. He was eventually notified of his constitutional right not to incriminate himself.

Although the courts have supported the need for urgent questioning in special cases, the announcement by authorities that Dzhokhar would not be advised of his rights prior to questioning—even though he had been hospitalized for hours after arrest and the immediate danger of more bombs seemed to have passed—surprised legal experts. Interrogators, however, argued that the need for urgency still existed, as he might have conspired with collaborators who continued to work on carrying out other attacks as he lay immobilized.

 DISCUSS Should the public safety exception to *Miranda* have been invoked in the case of Dzhokhar Tsarnaev? Why or why not?

▶ *Getting Suspects to Talk*

This chapter turns to the law of confessions and interrogations. The Fifth Amendment is what protects suspects from improper interrogation procedures and from being forced to supply illegally obtained confessions, but it is not the *only* protection offered to suspects in the confession context. Other amendments, such as the Sixth and the Fourteenth, also apply, but the Fifth is most applicable. The very fact that *three* amendments place restrictions on what the government can do in order to obtain confessions suggests that the U.S. Constitution places a high degree of value on people's rights to be free from certain forms of questioning.

The very fact that *three* amendments place restrictions on what the government can do in order to obtain confessions suggests that the U.S. Constitution places a high degree of value on people's rights to be free from certain forms of questioning.

LEARNING OUTCOMES 1 Identify the three methods by which the constitutionality of interrogations and confessions is analyzed.

Most of the law concerning confessions and admissions has arisen in the context of police interrogation. The courts have imposed a litany of restrictions on what law enforcement officials can do in order to elicit incriminating statements from suspected criminals. Certain protections discussed in this chapter, such as the Sixth Amendment right to counsel, also extend beyond police interrogation to the trial phase and beyond.

It is worthwhile, before continuing, to define the terms *confession* and *admission*. A **confession** occurs when a person implicates him- or herself in criminal activity following police questioning and/or interrogation. An **admission**, by contrast, need not be preceded by police questioning; a person can simply admit to involvement in a crime without any police encouragement. Despite these differences, a confession and an admission will be treated synonymously throughout the remainder of this chapter.

Police Conduct and Voluntariness A suspect was interrogated by five officers who, with their guns drawn, stood over him as he lay handcuffed on the ground, semi-conscious from a gunshot he had received earlier (a wound that was not inflicted by the officers). The officers did not threaten to shoot the suspect if he failed to confess. Rather, they simply pointed their guns at him. Assuming the suspect confessed, would his confession be considered involuntary under the Fourteenth Amendment?

▶ *The Due Process Voluntariness Approach*

One approach to confessions and admissions can be termed the **due process voluntariness approach**. In general, when a suspect makes an involuntary statement, his or her statement will not be admissible in a criminal trial (or, as indicated earlier, in any other criminal proceeding) to prove his or her guilt.

At one time, the Fifth and Sixth Amendments did not apply to the states. An illustrative case is **Brown v. Mississippi (297 U.S. 278 [1936])**. Police officers had resorted to whippings and other brutal methods in order to obtain confessions from three African-American defendants who were later convicted based on their confessions alone. The Supreme Court analyzed this case under the Fourteenth Amendment's due process clause and found the convictions invalid because the interrogation techniques had been so offensive.

When, then, is a confession involuntary? As decided in *Fikes* v. *Alabama* (352 U.S. 191 [1957]), the answer is when, under the "totality of circumstances that preceded the confessions," the defendant is deprived of his or her "power of resistance" (p. 198). This answer, unfortunately, does not provide any uniform criteria for determining voluntariness. Instead, the courts take a case-by-case approach to determining voluntariness. Usually, this requires focusing on two issues: (1) the police conduct in question and (2) the characteristics of the accused.

Police Conduct

It has been made patently clear that physical brutality to coerce a confession violates the Fourteenth Amendment. As Justice Douglas stated in **Williams v. United States (341 U.S. 97 [1951])**, "Where police take matters into their own hands, seize victims, and beat them until they confess, they deprive the victims of rights under the Constitution" (p. 101).

In many other situations, however, the police conduct in question may not rise to the level of torture but may still be questionable. For example, in *Rogers* v. *Richmond* (365 U.S. 534

[1963]), a man confessed after the police told him they were going to take his wife into custody. And in *Lynumm* v. *Illinois* (372 U.S. 528 [1963]), a defendant confessed after being promised leniency. Both confessions were found to be coerced. This is not to suggest that deception on the part of the police necessarily gives rise to an involuntary confession but only that it is one of several considerations in determining voluntariness.

It is safe to conclude that psychological pressures, promises of leniency, and deception are rarely *by themselves* enough to render a statement involuntary, but two or more such acts (especially if coupled with physical force) will more than likely result in an involuntary confession.

Characteristics of the Accused

 LEARNING OUTCOMES 2 Summarize how due process and voluntariness impact interrogations and confessions.

As far as characteristics of the accused are concerned, conditions such as disabilities and immaturity have resulted in excluded confessions. For example, in *Haley* v. *Ohio* (332 U.S. 596 [1948]), the Supreme Court reversed a 15-year-old boy's confession. In the Court's words, "Mature men possibly might stand the ordeal from midnight to 5 a.m. but we cannot believe that a lad of tender years is a match for the police in such a contest" (pp. 599–600).[1]

In some instances, fatigue and pain (for example, as the result of an injury) can also render an accused's statement involuntary; however, such a result usually requires some questionable conduct on the part of the officials engaged in questioning of the accused (see *Ashcraft* v. *Tennessee*, 322 U.S. 143 [1944]; *Mincey* v. *Arizona*, 437 U.S. 385 [1978]; and *Beecher* v. *Alabama*, 408 U.S. 234 [1972]).

As a general rule, voluntariness is overcome when (1) the police subject the suspect to coercive conduct and (2) the conduct is sufficient to overcome the will of the suspect. The second requirement involves looking at the totality of circumstances to determine if the suspect's vulnerabilities and condition, coupled with the police conduct, led to giving an involuntary confession (see **Colorado v. Connelly, 479 U.S. 157 [1986]**). See Figure 8–1 for a list of factors used to determine whether a confession is voluntary. Also see Figure 8–2 for a summary of various Supreme Court cases concerned with the voluntariness of confessions.

Physical brutality to coerce a confession violates the Fourteenth Amendment.

Police Behavior

- Psychological pressure by the police
- Promises of leniency
- Deception
- Length of detention
- Duration of questioning
- Intensity of questioning
- Deprivation of access to family, friends, nourishment, and counsel
- Whether the suspect was advised of his or her rights

Characteristics of the Suspect

- Disability
- Immaturity
- Intoxication
- Fatigue
- Pain
- Age
- Level of education
- Familiarity with the criminal process

FIGURE 8–1 Factors Considered in Determining Voluntariness.

Supreme Court Cases Pertaining to the Voluntariness of Confessions

Chambers v. *Florida*, 309 U.S. 227 (1940): "Confessions of murder procured by repeated inquisitions of prisoners without friends or counselors present, and under circumstances to inspire terror, held compulsory."

Ashcraft v. *Tennessee*, 322 U.S. 143 (1944): The suspect was questioned for 38 hours with only one 5-minute break. The confession was deemed involuntary.

Leyra v. *Denno*, 347 U.S. 556 (1954): Police relied on a psychiatrist who posed as a doctor in order to give the accused relief from a sinus problem. The psychiatrist used subtle forms of questions and ultimately obtained a statement from the accused. The Court felt that the suspect was unable to resist the psychiatrist's subtle questioning.

Payne v. *Arkansas*, 356 U.S. 560 (1958): A mentally challenged 19-year-old was held incommunicado for three days without counsel and given little food. His resulting confession was deemed involuntary.

Spano v. *New York*, 360 U.S. 315 (1959): Detectives relied on a police officer who was a friend of the accused to question him. The officer falsely stated that his job would be in jeopardy if he did not get a statement from the accused. The Supreme Court concluded that the false statement, including the sympathy thereby obtained, was sufficient to render the accused's statement involuntary.

Frazier v. *Cupp*, 394 U.S. 731 (1969): The Supreme Court held that a police officer's false statement that a co-defendant implicated the accused was not sufficient to produce an involuntary statement.

FIGURE 8–2 Defining Voluntariness in the Confession Context.

▶ The Sixth Amendment Approach

The Sixth Amendment also places restrictions on what the police can do to obtain confessions and admissions from criminal suspects. In particular, the Supreme Court's decision in **Massiah v. United States (377 U.S. 201 [1964])** led to the rule that the Sixth Amendment's guarantee to counsel in all "formal criminal proceedings" is violated when the government "deliberately elicits" incriminating responses from a person. The two key elements to the Sixth Amendment approach are deliberate elicitation and formal criminal proceedings (see Figure 8–3). The following subsections define each element.

Deliberate Elicitation

In the *Massiah* case, the defendant was released on bail pending a trial for violations of federal narcotics laws and subsequently made an incriminating statement in the car of a friend who had allowed the government to install a radio designed to eavesdrop on the conversation. Justice Stewart, writing for the majority, argued that if the Sixth Amendment's right to counsel is "to have any efficacy it must apply to indirect and surreptitious interrogations as well as those conducted in the jailhouse" (p. 206). Furthermore, "Massiah [the defendant] was more seriously imposed upon . . . because he did not even know that he was under interrogation by a government agent" (p. 206). These are issues

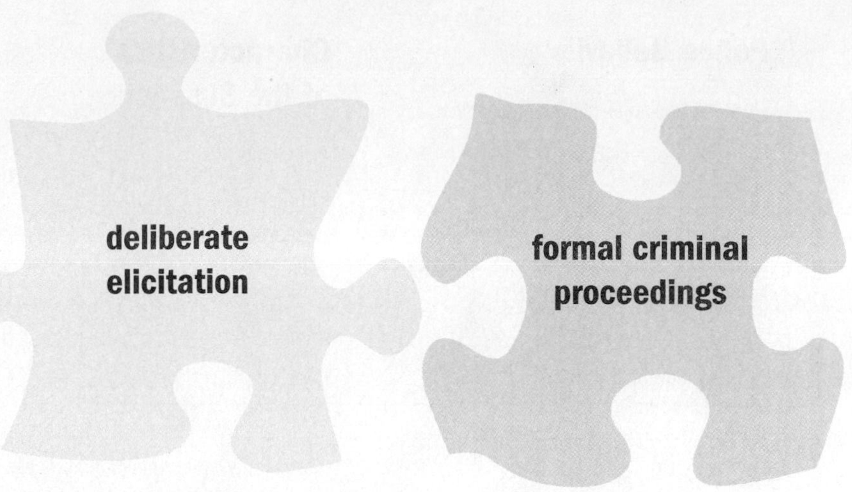

deliberate elicitation   **formal criminal proceedings**

FIGURE 8–3 Sixth Amendment and Confessions.

of **deliberate elicitation**, in which police officers create a situation likely to induce a suspect into making an incriminating statement.

In another Sixth Amendment case, **Brewer v. Williams (430 U.S. 387 [1977])**, a defendant was suspected of killing a 10-year-old girl. Before he was to be taken by police officers to another city, his attorneys advised him not to make any statements during the trip. The attorneys were also promised by the police officers that they would not question the defendant during the trip. Nevertheless, during the trip, one of the officers suggested that the girl deserved a "Christian burial." The officer further mentioned that an incoming snowstorm would make it difficult to find the girl's body. The officer then stated, "I do not want you to answer me. I don't want to discuss it further. Just think about it as we're riding down the road" (p. 432). Shortly thereafter, the defendant admitted to killing the girl and directed the police to her body. The Court reversed the defendant's conviction, arguing that the officer had "deliberately and designedly set out to elicit information from Williams [the defendant] just as surely as—and perhaps more effectively than—if he had formally interrogated him" (p. 399).

In a related case, **United States v. Henry (447 U.S. 264 [1980])**, the Supreme Court focused on whether the officers "intentionally creat[ed] a situation likely to induce Henry [the defendant] to make incriminating statements without the assistance of counsel" (p. 274). In that case, a man named Nichols, who was in jail with Henry, was enlisted by the police to be alert to any statements Henry made concerning a robbery. The police did not ask Nichols to start a *conversation* with Henry, only to be alert to what he said. The Supreme Court found that the officers created a situation likely to elicit an incriminating response but only because Nichols was a paid informant.

However, when law enforcement officers place an informant who is not paid but is working closely with the police in the same cell as the defendant, deliberate elicitation does not necessarily occur. This was the decision reached in *Kuhlmann* v. *Wilson* (477 U.S. 436 [1986]). Kuhlmann, the informant, did not ask the defendant any questions concerning the crime for which the defendant was charged but instead listened to (and later reported on) the defendant's "spontaneous" and "unsolicited" statements.

Clearly, the line between these two cases is thin. The only distinction appears to be that Nichols, the informant in *Henry*, had worked with the police in the past and was being paid.

Formal Criminal Proceedings

LEARNING OUTCOMES **3** Summarize how the Sixth Amendment impacts interrogations and confessions.

A case closely related to *Massiah* (and decided shortly after it) is *Escobedo* v. *Illinois* (378 U.S. 478 [1964]). Escobedo was arrested for murder, questioned, and released. Then, ten days later, an accomplice implicated Escobedo and he was rearrested. He requested to consult with his attorney, but that request was denied. Escobedo was convicted of murder, based partly on the statement provided by his accomplice. The Supreme Court reversed this decision, however:

> We hold . . . that where, as here, the investigation is no longer a general inquiry into an unsolved crime but has begun to focus on a particular suspect, the suspect has been taken into police custody, the police carry out a process of interrogations that lends itself to eliciting incriminating statements, the suspect has requested and been denied an opportunity to consult with his lawyer, and the police have not effectively warned him of his absolute constitutional right to remain silent, the accused has been denied "the Assistance of Counsel" in violation of the Sixth Amendment . . . and that no statement elicited by the police during the interrogation may be used against him at a criminal trial. (pp. 490–491)

Unfortunately, *Escobedo* was cause for some confusion. In *Massiah*, the Court held that the Sixth Amendment right to counsel applies once formal proceedings have begun (for example, a preliminary hearing, trial, or anything in between). However, in *Escobedo*, the Court seemed to broaden the scope of the Sixth Amendment by holding that it also applies once the accused becomes the focus of an investigation by the police. This left a significant question unanswered: When does a person become an accused? That is, when do formal criminal proceedings commence?

Think About It...

Suspect Characteristics and Voluntariness Ed Hornby approached a police officer on the street and said that he had killed someone and wanted to talk about it. He later confessed to an unsolved murder that had occurred several years earlier. Prior to trial, Hornby sought to have his confession excluded, arguing that it was involuntary. At trial, a psychiatrist testified for the defense that Hornby suffered from *command auditory hallucinations*, a condition that rendered him unable to resist what the "voices in his head" told him to do. How should the court decide? What if, instead, Hornby had become hesitant to talk and his confession had been preceded by a lengthy middle-of-the-night interrogation, during which he had been denied food and a desperately needed trip to the restroom?

Massiah was indicted, so many courts have concluded that **formal criminal proceedings** begin with indictment (for example, *United States ex rel. Forella v. Follette*, 405 F.2d 680 [2nd Cir. 1969]). However, eight years after *Massiah* (and after *Miranda*), the Supreme Court decided *Kirby v. Illinois* (406 U.S. 682 [1972]), holding that the Sixth Amendment is implicated whenever the "adverse positions of the government and defendant have solidified" so that "a defendant finds himself faced with the prosecutorial forces of organized society, and immersed in the intricacies of substantive and procedural criminal law" (p. 689). The Court clarified this statement by noting that the Sixth Amendment applies "whether by way of *formal charge, preliminary hearing, indictment, information, or arraignment*" (p. 689, emphasis added). This was echoed in *Rothgery v. Gillespie County* (554 U.S. 1 [2008]), wherein the Court held that the Sixth Amendment right to counsel can attach at the initial appearance.

Massiah does not apply simply because a suspect or arrestee has retained the services of counsel. In *Moran v. Burbine* (475 U.S. 412 [1986]), the Supreme Court held that what is important in determining whether the Sixth Amendment right to counsel applies is whether "the government's role [has] shift[ed] from investigation to accusation" (p. 430). Similarly, in *Maine v. Moulton* (474 U.S. 159 [1985]), the Court held that "to exclude evidence pertaining to charges as to which the Sixth Amendment right to counsel had not attached at the time the evidence was obtained, simply because other charges were pending at that time, would unnecessarily frustrate the public's interest in the investigation of criminal activities" (p. 180).

It should be noted that the Sixth Amendment approach to interrogations and confessions is offense specific. This was reiterated by the Supreme Court in *Texas v. Cobb* (531 U.S. 162 [2001]), where it was decided that a man's confession to a crime

The Sixth Amendment approach to interrogations and confessions is offense specific.

with which he had not been charged did not violate the Sixth Amendment. The defendant was indicted for burglary and given access to counsel, which obviously prohibits deliberate elicitation of incriminating information. However, he confessed to murdering the woman and child who lived in the home he allegedly burglarized. He later sought to have his confession excluded, but the Supreme Court disagreed, in essence finding that the burglary charge did not trigger the Sixth Amendment protection for the murder charge.

Waiver of the Sixth Amendment Right to Counsel

One's Sixth Amendment right to counsel can be waived in the confession context. In *Michigan v. Jackson* (475 U.S. 625 [1986]), the Supreme Court held that once an accused individual has asserted his or her Sixth Amendment right to counsel, any statements obtained from subsequent questioning would be inadmissable at trial unless the accused initiated the communication.

This decision was overturned, however, in *Montejo v. Louisiana* (556 U.S. 778 [2009]). Unbeknownst to police, Montejo had been appointed an attorney, but he was encouraged by a detective to write a letter of apology to the wife of the man he killed. Before doing so, he was advised of his *Miranda* rights (discussed in detail in the next section), but again, he had been appointed counsel—it was just that police did not know this. The prosecution introduced the apology letter at trial. Montejo sought to have it excluded because his attorney was not present when it was written. The Supreme Court disagreed. It felt that *Miranda* and other decisions offer sufficient protection. Also, had Montejo asserted his right to counsel, the outcome would have likely been different.

What is the practical meaning of the *Montejo* decision? Law enforcement is now allowed, after reading a suspect the *Miranda* rights and receiving a voluntary waiver of the right to counsel, to interrogate a suspect who has been appointed counsel, provided that the suspect (1) has not previously asserted

Miranda protection or (2) has previously asserted *Miranda* protection and susequently waives it. The decision is beneficial to law enforcement because it offers more opportunities for them to secure incriminating statements from criminal suspects.

▶ The Miranda Approach

In a very important yet frequently overlooked case, *Malloy* v. *Hogan* (378 U.S. 1 [1964]), the Supreme Court held that the Fifth Amendment's self-incrimination clause applies to the *states*. In announcing that ruling some 40 years ago, the Court said that "today the admissibility of a confession in a state criminal prosecution is tested by the same standard applied in federal prosecution since 1897" (p. 7).

Not long after that decision, the Supreme Court moved beyond *Massiah*, *Escobedo*, and the due process voluntariness approaches to interrogation law, focusing instead on the Fifth Amendment. In **Miranda v. Arizona (384 U.S. 436 [1966])**, the Court announced the following important rule: "[T]he prosecution may not use statements, whether exculpatory or inculpatory, stemming from *custodial interrogation* of the defendant unless it demonstrates the use of procedural safeguards effective to secure the privilege against self-incrimination" (p. 444, emphasis added). This wording clearly established that the Fifth Amendment should serve as the basis for determining the constitutionality of a confession. Pertinent facts from *Miranda* are as follows:

> On March 13, 1963, petitioner, Ernesto Miranda, was arrested at his home and taken in custody to a Phoenix police station. He was there identified by the complaining witness. The police then took him to "Interrogation Room No. 2" of the detective bureau. There he was questioned by two police officers. The officers admitted at trial that Miranda was not advised that he had a right to have an attorney present. Two hours later, the officers emerged from the interrogation room with a written confession signed by Miranda. At the top of the statement was a typed paragraph stating that the confession was made voluntarily, without threats or promises of immunity and "with full knowledge of my legal rights, understanding any statement I make may be used against me."

It is important to note that the Sixth and Fourteenth Amendments still apply to interrogations and confessions in certain situations. For example, if the police conduct in question is not a custodial interrogation (as in *Miranda*) but formal charges have been filed, the Sixth Amendment will apply. Similarly, if custody and interrogation do not take place *and* formal charges are not filed, the due process voluntariness test can still be relevant for the purpose of determining the constitutionality of a confession or admission. In fact, think of the Fourteenth Amendment's due process clause, in particular, as being something of a fallback. If no other constitutional protections apply, the guarantee of due process almost always does.

Miranda is often interpreted as requiring a code of conduct for police interrogation (see Figure 8–4 for a proper set

Minimum required *Miranda* Warnings

"You have the right to remain silent. Anything you say can and will be used against you in a court of law. You also have the right to an attorney. If you cannot afford an attorney, one will be provided to you at no cost."

FIGURE 8–4 Minimum Required *Miranda* Warnings.

The failure to give *Miranda* warnings does not, by itself, constitute a violation of constitutional rights.

of *Miranda* warnings). However, and very important, it is only a rule governing the admissibility of evidence. The judiciary is forbidden under the separation of powers doctrine from setting policy for the executive branch. As the Supreme Court observed in *United States* v. *Patane* (542 U.S. 630 [2004]), "the police do not violate a suspect's constitutional rights (or the *Miranda* rule) by negligent or even deliberate failures to provide full *Miranda* warnings. Potential violations occur, if at all, only upon the admission of unwarned statements into evidence." In other words, the failure to give *Miranda* warnings does not, by itself, constitute a violation of constitutional rights. It only impacts the admissibility of statements given by the defendant.

It should also be underscored that a key component of *Miranda* is that the questioning (and detention) must be conducted by government actors. If the people engaged in questioning cannot be considered government actors, then Fifth Amendment protections do not apply. However, when a private individual conducts a custodial interrogation as an agent of (working for) the police, *Miranda* applies.

It is also critical to note that when neither custody nor interrogation (or both) occur, *Miranda* does not apply. So when a suspect who was not in custody or "interrogated" answered an officer's questions about a murder, but then fell silent when asked more detailed questions, and the prosecution used the suspect's silence as proof of guilt at his trial, the Supreme Court approved (*Salinas* v. *Texas*, 570 U.S.—[2013]). In support of its decision, the Court noted " . . . that petitioner's Fifth Amendment claim fails because he did not expressly invoke the privilege in response to the officer's question."

Because the Supreme Court limited its decision in *Miranda* to *custodial interrogations*, it is important to understand the definitions of these two important terms: *custody* and *interrogation*.

Custody

 LEARNING OUTCOMES 4 — Explain *Miranda* rights and how they impact interrogations and confessions.

Many people believe that *Miranda* rights apply whenever the police begin to question a person. This is not the case; if the person being questioned is not in *custody*, *Miranda* rights do not apply. Simple police questioning, or even a full-blown interrogation, is not enough to trigger the protections afforded by the Fifth Amendment.

For *Miranda* protection to apply, the person subjected to such questioning must be in police custody.

For *Miranda* protection to apply, the person subjected to such questioning must be in police custody.

What is **custody?** The Court announced that *Miranda* applies when "a person has been taken into custody or otherwise deprived of his freedom of action in any significant way." An arrest is a clear-cut case of police custody, but what about a lesser intrusion? Unfortunately, there is no easy answer to this question. Instead, the courts have chosen to focus on the circumstances surrounding each individual case. The Court has stated, however, that "the only relevant inquiry [in analyzing the custody issue] is how a reasonable man in the suspect's position would have understood his situation" (**Berkemer v. McCarty, 468 U.S. 420 [1984]**, p. 442).

In the absence of a full-blown arrest, the courts have focused on six types of police/citizen encounters in determining whether custody exists for purposes of *Miranda*: (1) traffic and field stops, (2) questioning in the home, (3) questioning at the police station or equivalent facility, (4) questioning of juveniles, (5) questioning between a probation officer and probationer, and (6) questioning for minor crimes. Also see Figure 8–5 for examples of custodial and noncustodial situations.

First, custody does not take place in the typical traffic stop. This was the decision reached in *Berkemer v. McCarty*, cited earlier. There, a motorist was stopped for weaving in and out of traffic. After he admitted to drinking and smoking marijuana, the officer arrested him. The motorist argued that he should have been advised of his right to remain silent, but the Supreme Court disagreed, noting that vehicle stops are "presumptively temporary and brief" and sufficiently public to avoid the appearance of being coercive. The Court added, "From all that appears in the stipulation of facts, a single police officer asked [the defendant] a modest number of questions and requested him to perform a simple balancing test at a location visible to passing motorists" (p. 442) and thus did not violate the Fifth Amendment.

The same applies to stops not involving vehicles. *Miranda* permits law enforcement officers to engage in "[g]eneral on-the-scene questioning as to facts surrounding a crime or other general questioning of citizens in the factfinding process" (p. 477). With regard to *Terry* stops in particular, "[t]he comparatively nonthreatening character of [investigative] detentions explains the absence of any suggestion in our opinions that *Terry* stops are subject to the dictates of *Miranda*" (p. 440). But what if an investigative stop becomes more intrusive than a *Terry* stop, say, by taking place over a long period of time and/or in a private setting? Then, the Fifth Amendment's self-incrimination clause, made known to suspects through the *Miranda* warnings, will usually apply.

Second, it is possible for questioning in one's home to rise to the level of custody. In *Orozco v. Texas* (394 U.S. 324 [1969]), the Supreme Court declared that custody existed when four police officers woke a man in his own home and began questioning him. However, in contrast to *Orozco* is *Beckwith v. United States* (425 U.S. 341 [1976]). There, Internal Revenue Service (IRS) agents interviewed a man in his home, an action that the Supreme Court declared noncustodial. The man argued that because he was the focus of a criminal investigation, he should have been advised of his right to remain silent. However, Chief Justice Burger noted that "*Miranda* specifically defined 'focus,' for its purposes, as 'questioning initiated by law enforcement officers *after* a person has been taken into custody or otherwise deprived of his freedom of action in any significant way'" (p. 347).

Third, questioning at the police station or an equivalent facility can also rise to the level of custody. However, not all stationhouse questioning can be considered custodial. Consider what the Supreme Court said in *Oregon v. Mathiason* (429 U.S. 492 [1977]), a case involving a man who voluntarily agreed to meet officers at the police station for questioning. He admitted to involvement in a crime but later argued that his visit to the stationhouse was custodial because of its inherently coercive nature. The Court said,

> Any interview of one suspected of a crime by a police officer will have coercive aspects to it, simply by virtue of the fact that the police officer is part of a law enforcement system which may ultimately cause the suspect to be charged with a crime. But police officers are not required to administer *Miranda* warnings to everyone whom they question. Nor is the requirement of warnings to be imposed simply because the questioning takes place in the stationhouse, or because the questioned person is one whom the police suspect. (p. 495)

In a later case, **California v. Beheler (463 U.S. 1121 [1983])**, the Court offered some clarification concerning its decision in *Mathiason*. It pointed out that *Miranda* is not implicated "if the suspect is not placed under arrest, voluntarily comes to the police station, and is allowed to leave unhindered by the police after a brief interview" (p. 1121). Interesting

Custodial Situation	Noncustodial Situation
Police questioning in a person's home (*Orozco v. Texas*, 394 U.S. 324 [1969])	Traffic stop (*Berkemer v. McCarty*, 468 U.S. 420 [1984])
Suspect is arrested and forced to go to police station for questioning	*Terry* stop (*Terry v. Ohio*, 392 U.S. 1 [1968])
	Suspect voluntarily goes to police station for questioning and is free to leave (*California v. Beheler*, 463 U.S. 1121 [1983])

FIGURE 8–5 Custodial and Noncustodial Situations Under Miranda.

is that the *Beheler* decision seems to hold even if a person is pressured to come to the police station for questioning (see, for example, *Yarborough* v. *Alvarado*, 541 U.S. 652 [2004]).

Fourth, if the person questioned is a juvenile, the police need to tread carefully. As the Court noted in *J.D.B.* v. *North Carolina* (564 U.S.—[2011]), "a reasonable child subjected to police questioning will sometimes feel pressured to submit when a reasonable adult would feel free to go." Police in that case had questioned a boy in a school conference room about his alleged involvement in the theft of a digital camera. He confessed, but the Supreme Court reversed his conviction.

Fifth, custody questions have come up in the context of probation officer/probationer meetings. In *Minnesota* v. *Murphy*, 465 U.S. 420 (1984), a probationer was ordered to meet with his probation officer for questioning. During the meeting, the probationer confessed to a rape and a murder. He later argued that he should have been advised of his *Miranda* rights, but the Court disagreed, holding that Murphy's "freedom of movement [was] not restricted to the degree associated with formal arrest." Furthermore, while "[c]ustodial arrest is said to convey to the suspect a message that he has no choice but to submit to the officers' will and to confess . . . [i]t is unlikely that a probation interview, arranged by appointment at a mutually convenient time, would give rise to a similar impression." The Court commented further in *Murphy*:

> Many of the psychological ploys discussed in *Miranda* capitalize on the suspect's unfamiliarity with the officers and the environment. Murphy's regular meetings with his probation officer should have served to familiarize him with her and her office and to insulate him from psychological intimidation that might overbear his desire to claim the privilege. Finally, the coercion inherent in custodial interrogation derives in large measure from an interrogator's insinuation that the interrogation will continue until a confession is obtained . . . . Since Murphy was not physically restrained and could have left the office, any compulsion he might have felt from the possibility that terminating the meeting would have led to revocation of probation was not comparable to the pressure on a suspect who is painfully aware that he literally cannot escape a persistent custodial interrogator. (p. 433)

Finally, the Supreme Court has had occasion to determine whether *Miranda* applies—specifically, whether people can be considered in custody for minor offenses. Again, *Berkemer* was

a case involving a traffic stop. The second issue before the Court in that case was whether an exception to *Miranda* should exist for relatively minor crimes, such as misdemeanors. The Court declared that no distinction should be drawn between types of crimes as far as *Miranda* is concerned. Instead, the only relevant issue is whether a person is in custody (and, of course, interrogated). Even for a misdemeanor, the incentive for police to try to induce the defendant to incriminate him- or herself may well be significant.

Figure 8–6 provides a list of factors that are used to distinguish custodial from noncustodial encounters.

Interrogation

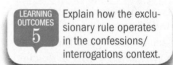
LEARNING OUTCOMES 5 — Explain how the exclusionary rule operates in the confessions/interrogations context.

The second major component of *Miranda* is interrogation. Custody by itself is not enough to require that the *Miranda* warnings be given. For a person to be afforded Fifth Amendment protection—and particularly, to be advised of his or her right to remain silent—he or she must be subjected to interrogation.

Miranda defined **interrogation** as "questioning initiated by law enforcement officers." Then, in ***Rhode Island* v. *Innis* (446 U.S. 291 [1980])**, the Court noted that interrogation "must reflect a measure of compulsion above and beyond that inherent in custody itself" (p. 300). Thus, any questions that tend to incriminate—that is, those that are directed toward an individual about his or her suspected involvement in a crime—are considered interrogation.

Unfortunately, many *questions* are not readily identifiable as such. In *Innis*, the Supreme Court noted that in addition to "express questioning," the "functional equivalent" of a question is also possible. The **functional equivalent of a question** includes "any words or actions on the part of the police (other than those normally attendant to arrest and custody) that the police should know are reasonably likely to elicit an incriminating response from the suspect" (p. 302, n. 8).

In *Innis*, while police officers were driving the defendant to the police station after his arrest for armed robbery, they engaged in a conversation about the danger the missing robbery weapon posed to schoolchildren with disabilities. Apparently in response to the conversation, the defendant directed the officers to the location of the weapon. Interestingly, though, the Supreme Court held that the officers' conversation did not constitute interrogation: It was "nothing more than a dialogue between the two officers to which no response from the

Custodial Situation	Noncustodial Situation
Arrest	Typical traffic stop
Excessively lengthy confrontation	General on-the-scene questioning
Not free to leave	Free to leave
Involuntary encounter	Voluntary encounter
Private place, such as a police station	Public place, where movement is not restricted

FIGURE 8–6 Distinguishing Between Custodial and Noncustodial Situations.

respondent was invited" (p. 315). The majority assumed implicitly that suspects will not respond to "indirect appeals to . . . humanitarian impulses," but Justice Stevens dissented and argued that such an assumption "is directly contrary to the teachings of police interrogation manuals, which recommend appealing to a suspect's sense of morality as a standard and often successful interrogation technique" (p. 315).

Even though *Innis* did not ultimately involve the functional equivalent of a question, the Court essentially expanded the definition of *questioning*. Namely, a mere conversation between police officers designed to elicit an incriminating response—even if the conversation is not directed toward the suspect—can require giving the *Miranda* warnings. Of course, the person must also be in custody for the *Miranda* warnings to apply. Figure 8–7 lists some of the factors considered when distinguishing between interrogation and general questioning.

- -

Other *Miranda* Issues

A number of important Supreme Court cases have hinged on (1) the substance and adequacy of the *Miranda* warnings and (2) waivers of *Miranda*. If, for example, the *Miranda* warnings are not given adequately, the police risk having a confession being thrown out of court. Also, like many rights, those provided by *Miranda* can be waived. That is, suspects can elect *not* to remain silent. Finally, suspects are not required to be advised of their *Miranda* rights when doing so could compromise public safety. These and other *Miranda* issues are considered in the subsections that follow.

Substance and Adequacy of the Warnings

There is a long line of cases involving people who have sought to have their confessions excluded at trial because all or some of the *Miranda* warnings were not read adequately. For example, in **California v. Prysock (453 U.S. 355 [1981])**, the juvenile

Interrogation	General Questioning
Guilt-seeking questions	Information-gathering questions
Conversation intended to elicit a response	Conversation not intended to elicit a response

FIGURE 8–7 Distinguishing Between Interrogation and General Questioning.

defendant was told, "You have the right to talk to a lawyer before you are questioned, have him present with you while you are being questioned, and all during the questioning" (p. 359). The defendant was then told that he had the right to a court-appointed lawyer but not that one would be provided for him if he was indigent.

The defendant challenged his conviction, but the Court concluded that the warnings given to him were sufficient and that *Miranda* itself indicates that no talismanic incantation was required to satisfy its strictures" (p. 359).

In another interesting case, *Duckworth* v. *Eagan* (492 U.S. 192 [1989]), the following warnings were given:

Before we ask you any questions, you must understand your rights. You have the right to remain silent. Anything you say can be used against you in court. You have the right to talk to a lawyer for advice before we ask you any questions, and to have him with you during questioning. You have this right to the advice and presence of a lawyer even if you cannot afford to hire one. We have no way of giving you a lawyer, but one will be appointed for you, if you wish, if and when you go to court. If you wish to answer questions now without a lawyer present, you have the right to stop answering questions at any time. You also have the right to stop answering at any time until you've talked to a lawyer. (p. 198)

Even though the warnings in this version suggested that counsel would only be provided at court, the Supreme Court held, in a 5-to-4 decision, that these warnings "touched all the bases required by *Miranda*" (p. 203). Thus, as long as all the essential *Miranda* information is communicated, simple departures will not render a confession thereby obtained inadmissible in a criminal trial.

Another factor involving the substance and adequacy of the *Miranda* warnings concerns the role of additional, unnecessary information. If more information than the original *Miranda* warnings is provided to a suspect, will any subsequent confession be inadmissible? For example, must the defendant be advised of the consequences of deciding to answer questions? The case of *Colorado* v. *Spring* (479 U.S. 564 [1987]) is a useful point of departure. There, the defendant was arrested and questioned on suspicion of transporting stolen firearms. He was also questioned about a homicide. He admitted that he had been given his *Miranda* warnings and that he understood them; however, he argued that the statements he made about the homicide were not admissible because he had not been informed that he was going to be questioned about the homicide (that is, he was arrested on suspicion of transporting stolen firearms). Unfortunately for the defendant, the majority held that "a suspect's awareness of all the possible subjects of questioning in advance of interrogation is not relevant to determining whether the suspect voluntarily, knowingly, and intelligently waived his Fifth Amendment privilege" (p. 577).

A similar issue came up in *Florida* v. *Powell* (559 U.S. [2010]), a case in which the following was added to the *Miranda* warning: "You have the right to use any of these rights at any time you want during this interview." The Supreme Court held that advising a

Were the *Miranda* Rights Read Properly? William Wentworth was interrogated while in police custody. He wore an expensive suit, lavish jewelry, and otherwise exhibited an aura of financial success. Before being interrogated, he was read the following rights: "You have the right to remain silent. Anything you say can and will be used against you in court. You have the right to talk with an attorney, either retained by you or appointed by the court, before giving a statement, and to have your attorney present when answering any questions." Wentworth made an incriminating statement during the interrogation and later moved to suppress it on the grounds that he was not informed that counsel would be provided if he was indigent. How should the court decide?

Mike Flippo/Shutterstock

To ensure that the *Miranda* warnings are read properly, most police departments have a policy describing in detail their wording.

suspect that he or she has the right to talk with an attorney before answering any questions *and* that the suspect can invoke that right at any time during questions conformed with *Miranda*.

To ensure that the *Miranda* warnings are read properly, most police departments have a policy describing in detail their wording. Figure 8–8 provides an example of one such policy from the San Bernardino, California, Police Department.

Waiver of Miranda

In *Miranda*, the Supreme Court stated that if a person talks after he or she has been read the warnings, "a heavy burden rests on the government to demonstrate that the defendant knowingly and intelligently waived his privilege against self-incrimination and his right to retained or appointed counsel" (p. 475). Furthermore, "a valid waiver will not be presumed simply from the silence of the accused after warnings are given or simply from the fact that a confession was in fact eventually obtained" (p. 475). According to the Supreme Court,

> Whatever the testimony of the authorities as to waiver of rights by an accused, the fact of lengthy interrogation or incommunicado incarceration before a statement is made

---

STANDARD OPERATING PROCEDURE PROCEDURE FOR MIRANDA ADVISEMENT	CHAPTER #15 (Revised)	PROCEDURE #1 10-26-88

PURPOSE
To ensure uniformity when advising persons of their Miranda rights.

PROCEDURE
It is <u>not</u> necessary that the defendant sign a written waiver of his rights. The law only requires that the waiver be free, intelligent, and voluntary.

The Miranda warning should always be <u>read</u> to the suspect rather than relying on memory, using the following wording:
1. You have the right to remain silent.
2. Anything you say can and will be used against you in court.
3. You have the right to talk with an attorney and to have an attorney present before and during any questioning.
4. If you cannot afford an attorney, one will be appointed free of charge to represent you before and during any questioning.

After the warning and in order to secure a waiver, the following questions should be asked and an affirmative reply secured to each question. The officer should always make a record of the <u>exact words</u> used by the defendant when he answers each of the following questions.
1. Do you understand the rights I have just explained to you?
2. With these rights in mind, do you wish to talk to me/us now?

When the person being advised of his Miranda rights speaks only Spanish, the following waiver shall be read:
1. Usted tiene el derecho de no decir nada.
2. Cualquier cosa que usted diga puede usarse contra usted y se usara contra usted en una corte de leyes.
3. Usted tiene el derecho de hablar on un abogado, y de tener un abogado presente antes y durante cualquier interrogacion.
4. Si usted no puede pagarle a un abogado, uno le sera nombrado gratis para que le represente a usted antes ye durante la interrogacion.

Renucia
1. ¿Entiende usted cada uno de los derechos que acabo de explicarle a usted? ¿Si o no?
2. ¿Teniendo en cuenta estos derechos suyos, desea usted hablar on nosotros ahora? ¿Si o no?

FIGURE 8–8 *Miranda* Advisement Policy.

is strong evidence that the accused did not validly waive his rights. In these circumstances the fact that the individual eventually made a statement is consistent with the conclusion that the compelling influence of the interrogation finally forced him to do so. It is inconsistent with any notion of a voluntary relinquishment of the privilege. Moreover, any evidence that the accused was threatened, tricked, or cajoled into a waiver will, of course, show that the defendant did not voluntarily waive his privilege. (p. 476)

In recent years, the courts have interpreted this language loosely. That is, whereas *Miranda* declared that a waiver should be viewed with considerable caution, later decisions have suggested that the burden of demonstrating a valid waiver is not difficult to meet. For example, in *Colorado v. Connelly*, the Court held that the government need only show the validity of a waiver by a "preponderance of evidence." And in *Fare v. Michael C.*, the Court held that the "totality of the circumstances approach is adequate to determine whether there has been a waiver" (p. 725). A similar conclusion was reached in *Berghuis v. Thompkins* (560 U.S. 370 [2010]) when the Supreme Court held that "where the prosecution shows that a *Miranda* warning was given and that it was understood by the accused, an accused's uncoerced statement establishes an implied waiver of the right to remain silent."

Before moving on, it is worth mentioning that in addition to the requirement that a valid *Miranda* waiver must be knowing and intelligent, it must also be voluntary. The test for voluntariness is similar to the due process voluntariness test discussed earlier in this chapter. Threats, physical force, and the like can lead to defendants issuing involuntary confessions. However, in *Fare v. Michael C.*, the Court held that the confession obtained from a 16-year-old was not involuntary. In a strongly worded dissent, Justice Powell argued that the juvenile in this case "was immature, emotional, and uneducated, and therefore was likely to be vulnerable to the skillful, two-on-one, repetitive style of interrogation to which he was subjected" (p. 733). A safe rule is that the police must engage in seriously questionable conduct for the voluntariness requirement of a *Miranda* waiver to be violated.

In addition to the requirement that a valid *Miranda* waiver must be knowing and intelligent, it must also be voluntary.

Again, to be safe, many police departments require that each suspect completes a *Miranda* waiver before interrogation commences. Doing so helps ensure that the waiver is documented. An example of a *Miranda* waiver form, from the San Bernardino, California, Police Department, is reprinted in Figure 8–9.

Questioning After Assertion of One's Right to Remain Silent

As a general rule, questioning must cease once the accused asserts his or her right to remain silent. However, there is at least one circumstance in which the police can question a suspect after he or she has asserted the *Miranda* rights. In *Michigan v. Mosley* (423 U.S. 96 [1975]), the Supreme Court permitted questioning after an assertion of *Miranda*. In that case, two hours after the defendant had stated that he did not want to talk, a different police officer confronted him in a different room about another crime and read him the *Miranda* rights for a second time. After this, the man made incriminating statements. In a 7-to-2 decision, the Court held that the suspect's *Miranda* rights had been "scrupulously honored." The Court said that the second officer's actions were acceptable because "the police here immediately ceased the interrogation, resumed questioning only after the passage of a significant period of time and the provision of a fresh set of warnings, and restricted the second interrogation to a crime that had not been a subject of the earlier interrogation" (p. 106).

In *Bobby v. Dixon* (565 U.S.—[2011]), police did not warn Dixon of his *Miranda* rights before questioning him about his suspected involvement in a forgery case. In a subsequent interrogation during which he *was* informed of his *Miranda* rights, Dixon confessed to a murder. Both crimes arose out the same act (Dixon and an acquaintance were accused of burying a man alive and stealing his identity), but Dixon was questioned separately about his involvement in each. Dixon's conviction was upheld. The Court stated: "Dixon received *Miranda* warnings before confessing to Hammer's murder; the effectiveness of those warnings was not impaired by the sort of 'two-step interrogation technique' . . . " used in the investigation.

The common thread running throughout the last two cases is that the second set of questions either involved a separate crime or led to a confession to a second crime. What if police had continued to ask questions about the same crime? Had they done so immediately, the questioning would have been inappropriate. But the issue is less than black and white according to the Supreme Court's recent decision in **Maryland v. Shatzer (559 U.S. 98 [2010]).** In that case, police (albeit a different officer) resumed questioning about the same crime more than *two weeks* after the suspect was released following initial questioning. The suspect was re-read his *Miranda* rights, which he then waived. He confessed to various crimes of sex abuse. The Supreme Court decided that his confession

WAIVER

I HAVE BEEN ADVISED THAT:
1. I HAVE THE ABSOLUTE RIGHT TO REMAIN SILENT.
2. ANYTHING I SAY CAN AND WILL BE USED AS EVIDENCE AGAINST ME IN COURT.
3. I HAVE THE RIGHT TO BE REPRESENTED BY AN ATTORNEY AND TO CONSULT WITH HIM BEFORE MAKING ANY STATEMENT OR ANSWERING ANY QUESTIONS AND I HAVE THE RIGHT TO HAVE AN ATTORNEY PRESENT DURING ANY QUESTIONING.
4. IF I CANNOT AFFORD AN ATTORNEY, ONE WILL BE APPOINTED BY THE COURT, FREE OF CHARGE, TO REPRESENT ME BEFORE ANY QUESTIONING, IF I DESIRE.

I UNDERSTAND THESE RIGHTS. THESE RIGHTS HAVE BEEN EXPLAINED TO ME. WITH THESE RIGHTS IN MIND, I AM WILLING TO TALK TO OFFICERS ABOUT THE CHARGES AGAINST ME.

DATE _____   SIGNED _____
WITNESS _____   WITNESS _____

FIGURE 8–9 *Miranda* Waiver Form.

If public safety is in jeopardy, no *Miranda* warnings are required—at least in the short term.

was admissible, in part because "[h]is change of heart [was] . . . likely attributable to the fact that further deliberation in familiar surroundings [had] caused him to believe (rightly or wrongly) that cooperating with the investigation [was] in his interest."

The Public Safety Exception to Miranda

On some occasions, custodial interrogation is permissible without the *Miranda* warnings. Specifically, if public safety is in jeopardy, no *Miranda* warnings are required—at least in the short term. This was the decision reached in **New York v. Quarles (467 U.S. 649 [1984])**. There, the Court held that the warnings need not be given if the suspect could have endangered public safety.

The facts from *Quarles* are as follows: After receiving information that a man with a gun had just entered a supermarket, Officer Kraft, along with three other officers, entered the store. Kraft spotted the defendant, drew his gun, and ordered the man to stop and put his hands over his head. When the officers frisked the man, they found an empty shoulder holster on him. When they asked where the man had put the gun, he replied, "The gun is over there." Officer Kraft retrieved the revolver and then placed the man under arrest and read him the *Miranda* warnings. The trial court and the lower appellate courts excluded the gun on the grounds that it was obtained in violation of *Miranda* (that is, the man had not been advised of his right to remain silent at the time the gun was found).

The Supreme Court disagreed. Justice Rehnquist wrote the majority opinion, arguing that rigid application of *Miranda* is not always warranted, particularly when public safety is a concern:

> [T]he need for answers to questions in a situation posing a threat to public safety outweighs the need for the prophylactic rule protecting the Fifth Amendment's privilege against self-incrimination. We decline to place officers such as Officer Kraft in the untenable position of having to consider, often in a matter of seconds, whether it best serves society for them to ask the necessary questions without the *Miranda* warnings and render whatever probative evidence they uncover inadmissible, or

for them to give the warnings in order to preserve the admissibility of evidence they might uncover but possibly damage or destroy their ability to obtain that evidence and neutralize the volatile situation confronting them. (pp. 657–658)

The Court also made it clear that the appropriate test for determining whether a threat to public safety exists is an objective one—that is, one based on what a reasonable person in the same circumstances would believe: "[W]here spontaneity rather than adherence to a police manual is necessarily the order of the day, the application of the [public safety] exception . . . should not be made to depend on *post hoc* findings at a suppression hearing concerning the subjective motivation of the arresting officer" (p. 656). The majority in *Quarles* apparently believed that an objective threat to public safety existed. Insofar as the officers did not know where the gun was located, not knowing "obviously posed more than one danger to the public safety: an accomplice might make use of it [or] a customer or employee might later come upon it" (p. 657).

The *Quarles* decision is a controversial one. As Justice O'Connor noted in disagreement with the newly issued public safety exception to *Miranda* (although not with the majority's ultimate decision),

> *Miranda* has never been read to prohibit the police from asking questions to secure the public safety. Rather, the critical question *Miranda* addresses is who shall bear the cost of securing the public safety when such questions are asked and answered: the defendant or the state. *Miranda*, for better or worse, found the resolution of that question implicit in the prohibition against compulsory self-incrimination and placed the burden on the State. (p. 664)

Quarles, by contrast, appears to place the burden on the defendant. It does so, in Justice O'Connor's view, not by ensuring that public safety is preserved but by creating a *Miranda* loophole that helps ensure that otherwise inadmissible evidence can be used against the defendant.

Challenging Miranda

The *Miranda* decision was not without controversy. In 1968, shortly after the decision was announced, Congress passed a Crime Control Act that, among other things, attempted

TIMELINE

The Evolution of *Miranda* v. *Arizona*

1966	**1978**	**1980**	**1981**
***Miranda* v. *Arizona*, 384 U.S. 436** Any person subjected to custodial interrogation must be advised of his or her Fifth Amendment right to be free from compelled self-incrimination and to have the assistance of counsel.	***Fare* v. *Michael C.*, 439 U.S. 1310** The *Miranda* warning applies only to the right to have an attorney present. The suspect cannot demand to speak to a priest, a probation officer, or any other official.	***Rhode Island* v. *Innis*, 446 U.S. 291** Interrogation "must reflect a measure of compulsion above and beyond that inherent in custody itself" and can include the functional equivalent of a question, or "any words or actions on the part of the police (other than those normally attendant to arrest and custody) that the police should know are reasonably likely to elicit an incriminating response from the suspect."	***California* v. *Prysock*, 453 U.S. 355** No "talismanic incantation" is required to satisfy *Miranda*; subtle deviations in the wording of the warnings will not render a confession unconstitutional.

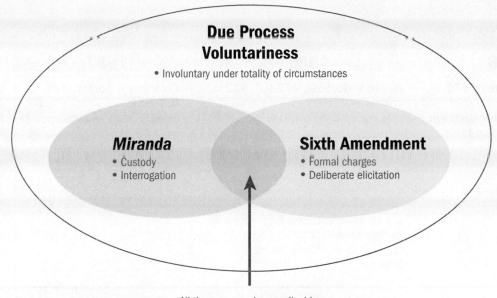

Due Process
Voluntariness
• Involuntary under totality of circumstances

Miranda
• Custody
• Interrogation

Sixth Amendment
• Formal charges
• Deliberate elicitation

All three approaches applicable

FIGURE 8–10 Relationship Between the Various Approaches to Confession Law.

to overrule the *Miranda* decision. The statute, codified as **18 U.S.C. Section 3501**, states that in any federal prosecution, a confession "shall be admissible in evidence if it is voluntarily given." Under the law, suspects are not required to be advised of their right to counsel, their right not to incriminate themselves, and so on.

For several years, Section 3501 remained dormant. The U.S. attorneys general have known that to utilize the statute would be to challenge the authority of the U.S. Supreme Court. But critics of *Miranda* were looking for an opportunity to bring Section 3501 before the Court. That opportunity arose in 2000: Charles Dickerson was indicted for bank robbery and related crimes. He moved to suppress a statement he made to Federal Bureau of Investigation (FBI) agents on the grounds that he had not received his *Miranda* warnings. The district court granted Dickerson's motion to suppress but also noted that the confession was voluntary, despite the apparent *Miranda* violation.

Then, the Court of Appeals for the Fourth Circuit held (in a 2-to-1 decision) that "Congress, pursuant to its power

to establish the rules of evidence and procedure in the federal courts, acted well within its authority in enacting Section 3501, [and] Section 3501, rather than *Miranda*, governs the admissibility of confession in federal court" (*United States* v. *Dickerson*, 166 F.3d 667 [4th Cir. 1999], p. 671). The case then went before the Supreme Court. In a 7-to-2 opinion, Chief Justice Rehnquist wrote for the Court,

> We hold that *Miranda*, being a constitutional decision of this Court, may not be in effect overruled by an Act of Congress, and we decline to overrule *Miranda* ourselves. We therefore hold that *Miranda* and its progeny in this Court govern the admissibility of statements made during custodial interrogation in both state and federal courts. (***Dickerson*** v. ***United States*, 530 U.S. 428 [2000]**, p. 431)

See Figure 8–10 for a summary of the interrogation/confession issues discussed thus far. Also see the accompanying timeline for a summary of several key Supreme Court decisions since *Miranda*.

1983	1984	1984	1985
***California* v. *Beheler*, 463 U.S. 1121** *Miranda* is not implicated "if the suspect is not placed under arrest, voluntarily comes to the police station, and is allowed to leave unhindered by the police after a brief interview."	***Berkemer* v. *McCarty*, 468 U.S. 420** Roadside questioning of a motorist following a legitimate traffic stop does not amount to custodial interrogation for *Miranda* purposes.	***New York* v. *Quarles*, 467 U.S.649** A suspect can be questioned in the field without a *Miranda* warning if the information the police seek is needed to protect public safety. For example, in an emergency, suspects can be asked where they hid their weapons.	***Oregon* v. *Elstad*, 470 U.S. 298** Admissions made in the absence of *Miranda* warnings are not admissible at trial, but *post-Miranda* voluntary statements are admissible. A *post-Miranda* voluntary statement is admissible even if an initial incriminating statement was made in the absence of *Miranda* warnings.

1986	1986	1987	2000
Colorado v. *Connelly, 479 U.S. 157* The admissions of mentally impaired defendants can be admitted in evidence as long as the police acted properly and there is a preponderance of the evidence that the defendants understood the meaning of *Miranda.*	*Moran* v. *Burbine, 475 U.S. 412* An attorney's request to see the defendant does not affect the validity of the defendant's waiver of the right to counsel. Police misinformation to an attorney does not affect waiver of *Miranda* rights. For example, a suspect's statements may be used if they are given voluntarily, even though his family has hired an attorney and the statements were made before the attorney arrived. Only the suspect can request an attorney, not his friends or family.	*Colorado* v. *Spring, 479 U.S. 564* Suspects need not be aware of all the possible outcomes of waiving their rights for the *Miranda* warning to be considered properly given.	*Dickerson* v. *United States, 530 U.S. 428* *Miranda* may not be overruled by an act of Congress, as was attempted with the passage of 18 U.S.C. Section 3501.

▶ The Exclusionary Rule and Confessions

It is important to focus on the role of the *exclusionary rule* in the confession analysis. It is often said that the exclusionary rule applies only to the Fourth Amendment. Part of the reason for this is that the Fifth Amendment essentially contains its own exclusionary rule by prohibiting compulsion of testimony. Whatever view one takes, the debate is largely semantic. In the end, evidence obtained in violation of *any* constitutional amendment will not be admissible in a criminal trial.

Generally speaking, a confession obtained in violation of *Miranda* or some constitutional provision will be excluded. However, just because a confession is obtained illegally does not mean that any subsequently obtained evidence will automatically be excluded. In fact, illegally obtained statements are themselves considered admissible in certain instances. Accordingly, the following subsections focus on two lines of cases involving confessions and the exclusionary rule: (1) impeachment cases and (2) "fruit of the poisonous tree" cases.

Confessions and Impeachment

One situation in which improperly obtained incriminating statements may be admissible is when such statements are used for purposes of impeachment (that is, attacking the credibility of a witness in court). A key restriction on this rule, however, is that the statement must be obtained voluntarily in the due process sense. Also, the rules vary depending on whether it is a *Miranda* case or Sixth Amendment right-to-counsel case.

For an example of a *Miranda* case, consider **Harris v. New York (401 U.S. 222 [1971])**. The prosecution sought to introduce an out-of-court statement that was inconsistent with the defendant's in-court testimony, even though the out-of-court statement was obtained in violation of *Miranda*. The Supreme Court held that the out-of-court-statement was admissible—only for impeachment purposes, not to be used as evidence against Harris. The Court noted further that such a statement must be obtained voluntarily, which it was in Harris's case (see also *Oregon* v. *Hass*, 420 U.S. 714 [1975]; *New Jersey* v. *Portash*, 437 U.S. 385 [1978]).

Note that for a statement obtained in violation of *Miranda* to be admissible for impeachment purposes, the statement must, in fact, be an oral communication. The prosecution cannot introduce evidence of an accused's out-of-court *silence* for impeachment purposes. This issue arose in the case of *Doyle* v. *Ohio* (426 U.S. 610 [1976]), in which after the defendant's in-court exculpatory story, the prosecution sought to introduce evidence that the defendant did not offer the same explanation to the police. The Supreme Court held that the defendant's silence was not admissible for purposes of impeachment (see also *Wainwright* v. *Greenfield*, 474 U.S. 284 [1986]).

As for the Sixth Amendment approach, in *Michigan* v. *Harvey* (494 U.S. 344 [1990]), the Supreme Court held that a statement obtained in violation of the right to counsel (police questioned the defendant after he invoked his right to counsel and later waived

Think About It...

Should the Exclusionary Rule Apply? Assume the police have Jack Richter in custody and are interrogating him about his suspected involvement in a gruesome murder. They do not advise him of his *Miranda* rights. Further, one of the officers, who is notorious for his aggressive interrogation techniques, holds a .357 revolver (loaded with one round) to Richter's head and plays "Russian roulette" in order to obtain a confession. Richter succumbs to the pressure and admits to the murder. He also points the police to the location of the murder weapon. Obviously, his statement will not be admissible. What about the murder weapon?

© FRANCK CAMHI/ Alamy

Chavez v. Martinez, 538 U.S. 760 Failure to give a suspect a *Miranda* warning is not illegal unless the case becomes a criminal one.

United States v. Patane, 542 U.S. 630 A voluntary statement given in the absence of a *Miranda* warning can be used to obtain evidence that can be used at trial. Failure to give the warning does not make seizure of evidence illegal per se.

Florida v. Powell, 559 U.S. The *Miranda* warnings do not require that the suspect be advised that he or she has the right to have an attorney present during questioning. It is sufficient to advise the suspect that he or she has the right to talk with a lawyer before questioning and to consult a lawyer at any time during questioning.

Maryland v. Shatzer, 559 U.S. 98 *Miranda* protections do not apply if a suspect is released from police custody for at least 14 days and then questioned. However, if the suspect is re-arrested, then *Miranda* warnings must be read.

it) could be admitted for impeachment purposes. Recently, in *Kansas* v. *Ventris* (556 U.S.—[2009]), the Supreme Court reached a similar conclusion. In that case police relied on an informant to obtain a statement from Ventris—after Ventris had been formally charged with a crime. It admitted the statement, but for impeachment purposes, not as part of the government's case in chief, even though the incriminating statement was obtained in violation of the Sixth Amendment. The difference is subtle, but important.

Confessions and "Fruit of the Poisonous Tree"

As you know by now, unconstitutionally obtained derivative evidence is not admissible under the "fruit of the poisonous tree" doctrine. However, the Supreme Court has not been so quick to apply the same rule in the case of illegally obtained confessions. It has held that physical evidence obtained in violation of *Miranda* is admissible, as long as the information supplied by the accused is voluntary in the due process sense.

The first case of note concerning the derivative evidence doctrine in the confession context was **United States v. Bayer (331 U.S. 532 [1947])**, a case decided well before the *Miranda* decision was handed down. There, the Court held that the Fourth Amendment "fruit of the poisonous tree" doctrine did not control the admissibility of improperly obtained confessions.

Then, in *Michigan* v. *Tucker* (417 U.S. 433 [1974]), a case decided after *Miranda* but involving an interrogation that took place before *Miranda*, the Court suggested that it had not changed its position. In *Tucker*, a suspect was questioned about a rape without being advised of his right to counsel. Tucker claimed he was with a friend at the time of the crime. The police then obtained incriminating evidence against Tucker from the friend. Although this information was clearly fruit of the initial interrogation, the Court stated that "[t]he police conduct at issue here did not abridge respondent's constitutional privilege against compulsory self-incrimination, but departed only from the prophylactic standards later laid down by this Court in *Miranda* to safeguard this privilege" (p. 446). In other words, the Court saw no reason to exclude the friend's statement.

In *Oregon* v. *Elstad* (470 U.S. 298 [1985]), the Court reaffirmed its *Tucker* decision, making clear that it would continue to treat *Miranda* as a prophylactic rule, at least insofar as it governs the admissibility of derivative evidence. What's more, derivative evidence obtained from a violation of *Miranda* is admissible but only if voluntarily obtained. In sum, these decisions govern derivative evidence, not the initial incriminating statements (such as Tucker's claim that he was with a friend). The latter are inadmissible when obtained in violation of the Fifth Amendment.

TIMELINE

The Evolution of *Miranda* v. *Arizona*, continued

Berghuis v. Thompkins, 560 U.S. 370 Unless a suspect asserts his or her *Miranda* rights, any subsequent voluntary statements given after the warnings are admissible in court. Simply remaining silent does not imply that a suspect has invoked *Miranda* protection.

J.D.B. v. North Carolina, 564 U.S. Children may be more prone to confessing to crimes they did not commit, and this needs to be taken into consideration in deciding whether a police interrogation is also custodial. In other words, the suspect's age factors in to the *Miranda* custody analysis.

THE CASE

Does *Miranda* Apply When There Are No Criminal Charges?

In *Chavez* v. *Martinez* (538 U.S. 760 [2003]), a police officer interrogated a man while he was receiving treatment for a gunshot wound. The man was *not* advised of his *Miranda* rights and made incriminating statements. He was never charged with a crime, but later sued under 42 U.S.C. Section 1983 (introduced in Chapter 2), arguing that his constitutional rights were violated. The Supreme Court disagreed because the man was not compelled to be a "witness" against himself in a "criminal case." This decision would seem to suggest *Miranda* warnings are never required unless statements obtained without the warnings are actually used against the accused in a criminal case. Chavez did not know his statements would not be admissible at trial.

This case illustrates an important point: Because there was no criminal case against Chavez, the question of whether his statements should have been admissible was immaterial. Even so, does that mean no other remedies should have been available? He sued because he felt his rights were violated by the interrogation even though criminal charges were not filed. What if, as an alternative, a motorist is stopped without sufficient justification, consents to a search, and is sent on her way because nothing was found and then misses her long-scheduled flight out of the country? What recourse, if any, should be available to the motorist in this instance? There are no easy answers to questions like these, but they underscore the point that constitutional remedies apply in fairly narrow circumstances.

This case raises a number of interesting questions, as the decision was somewhat controversial:

1. Do you agree with the Supreme Court's decision in *Chavez* v. *Martinez*? Why or why not?
2. Are available remedies equipped to deal with situations like that which Chavez experienced?
3. Describe a hypothetical situation in which an available remedy (exclusionary rule, civil litigation, complaint, etc.) does not work or cannot be effective.

CHAPTER 8 Interrogation and Confessions

LEARNING OUTCOMES 1

Identify the three methods by which the constitutionality of interrogations and confessions is analyzed.

The admissibility of confessions hinges on compliance with the Fifth Amendment (self-incrimination), the Sixth Amendment (right to counsel), and the Fourteenth Amendment (due process voluntariness approach).

1. In what ways are confessions constitutionally protected?

2. What are the consequences of an improperly obtained confession?

confession When a person implicates him- or herself in criminal activity following police questioning and/or interrogation.

admission When a person simply admits to involvement in a crime without any police encouragement.

LEARNING OUTCOMES 2

Summarize how due process and voluntariness impact interrogations and confessions.

An involuntarily obtained confession violates due process.

Key Cases

Brown v. *Mississippi*

Williams v. *United States*

Colorado v. *Connelly*

1. Summarize the due process voluntariness approach to interrogations and confessions.

2. What factors affect the voluntariness of a confession?

due process voluntariness approach The requirement that any confession be voluntary under the "totality of circumstances."

LEARNING OUTCOMES 3

Summarize how the Sixth Amendment impacts interrogations and confessions.

Confessions are also governed by the Sixth Amendment's right-to-counsel clause but only when formal charges have been filed. If the police deliberately elicit information from a person who has already been charged with a crime, the charged individual has the right to have counsel present during questioning.

Key Cases

Massiah v. *United States*

Brewer v. *Williams*

United States v. *Henry*

1. What is deliberate elicitation?

2. What, for purposes of the Sixth Amendment approach to interrogations and confessions, are formal criminal proceedings?

deliberate elicitation In the Sixth Amendment right-to-counsel context, deliberate elicitation occurs when police officers create a situation likely to induce a suspect into making an incriminating statement.

formal criminal proceeding In the Sixth Amendment right-to-counsel context, either a formal charge, a preliminary hearing, indictment, information, or arraignment.

LEARNING OUTCOMES 4

Explain *Miranda* rights and how they impact interrogations and confessions.

A confession will be thrown out, as was the decision in *Miranda* v. *Arizona*, if a suspect's incriminating statement is a result of custodial interrogation in which the suspect was not advised of his or her constitutional right to have counsel present. Before custodial interrogation can commence, suspects must be advised of their so-called *Miranda* rights.

Key Cases

Miranda v. *Arizona*

Berkemer v. *McCarty*

California v. *Beheler*

Rhode Island v. *Innis*

California v. *Prysock*

Maryland v. *Shatzer*

New York v. *Quarles*

Dickerson v. *United States*

1. What are the *Miranda* warnings?

2. When are *Miranda* warnings required?

3. Distinguish between custody and interrogation.

4. Explain the public safety exception to *Miranda*.

5. What are the requirements for a valid *Miranda* waiver?

custody Typically an arrest. Custody is important in the *Miranda* context because *Miranda* warnings do not need to be read if a person is not in custody.

interrogation Express questioning (for example, Where were you on the night of the crime?) or the functional equivalent of a question (see definition). The definition of interrogation is important in the *Miranda* context because *Miranda* warnings do not need to be read if a person is not technically interrogated.

functional equivalent of a question "[A]ny words or actions on the part of the police (other than those normally attendant to arrest and custody) that the police should know are reasonably likely to elicit an incriminating response from the suspect (*Rhode Island* v. *Innis*, 446 U.S. 291 [1980], p. 302, n. 8).

18 U.S.C. Section 3501 A federal statute enacted in the wake of the *Miranda* decision providing that any confession "shall be admissible in evidence if it is voluntarily given." The statute was deemed unconstitutional in *Dickerson* v. *United States* (530 U.S. 428 [2000]).

LEARNING OUTCOMES 5

Explain how the exclusionary rule operates in the confessions/interrogations context.

Just because a confession is obtained illegally does not mean that any subsequently obtained evidence will automatically be excluded. In fact, illegally obtained statements are themselves considered admissible in certain instances. One situation in which improperly obtained incriminating statements may be admissible is when such statements are used for purposes of impeachment (that is, attacking the credibility of a witness in court). Physical evidence obtained in violation of *Miranda* is admissible, as long as the information supplied by the accused is voluntary in the due process sense.

Key Cases

Harris v. *New York*
United States v. *Bayer*

1. Explain how the exclusionary rule operates in the confession/interrogation context.

2. How does the "fruit of the poisonous tree" doctrine operate in the confessions/interrogations context?

"... witnesses to crime are frequently inaccurate in their descriptions."

9

Identifications

1 Summarize suspects' rights during identification procedures.

2 Outline pretrial suspect identification techniques.

3 Describe flaws in identification procedures and strategies for minimizing mistakes.

4 Explain how the exclusionary rule operates in the identification context.

IDENTIFICATION AND A WRONGFUL CONVICTION

Consider the following account:

> On a September night in 1983, a woman walking to a bus stop was confronted by a man in a vehicle who offered to give her a ride home. She accepted and gave the man directions. Instead of exiting where she told him, however, the man drove the woman to an isolated parking lot and raped her on the hood of his car, again in the backseat of the car, and yet again after he drove to another location. He then drove her to a house where he unlocked the door and forced the woman inside, raping her a fourth time. On the way to the house, the woman took note of two street signs and remembered them. After she was able to escape to a friend's house, the woman reported the incident to the police. She then rode with police to the house she remembered as the location of the attack. Billy Wayne Miller, who was sleeping in what turned out to be his father's house, was identified by the woman as the rapist. He was arrested, charged, convicted, and subsequently sentenced to 22 years in prison. However, he was not the perpetrator.[1] DNA evidence later cleared him, but not until after he spent a substantial amount of his life behind bars.

Unfortunately, stories like Miller's are not isolated. In the vigorous pursuit to secure criminal convictions,

© Janine Wiedel Photolibrary/Alamy

authorities have sometimes relied on rather shaky identification procedures. In Miller's case, he was sent to prison for more than two decades primarily because of one witness's account of the events. Identification procedures, including their limitations, flaws, and fixes, are the topic of this chapter.

DISCUSS Are wrongful convictions like Billy Wayne Miller's a significant problem today?

▶ Dealing With Witnesses to Crime

Identification procedures include those systems and activities that allow witnesses of crimes to identify suspected perpetrators. The three most common types of identification procedures are lineups, showups, and photographic arrays. In a **lineup**, the suspect is placed alongside several other people (sometimes called "fillers," "foils," or "distractors") who resemble him or her, and the witness (or victim) picks the suspect out of the lineup. The fillers may be jail inmates, actors, or volunteers. In a **showup**, the suspect is brought before the witness alone, so the witness can be asked whether that person is the perpetrator. Finally, in a **photographic array** (or photographic display), several photographs, including one of the suspect, are shown to a witness or victim, and he or she is asked to pick out the perpetrator.

Identification procedures fall into two broad categories: (1) out of court and (2) in court. The three identification procedures just described—lineups, showups, and photographic arrays—occur *out of court* and prior to trial. There are, however, many occasions in which the prosecution may wish to have a witness identify the suspect *in court* and during trial. Of course, not all witnesses recollect accurately and/or can be trusted with regard to a suspect's identification. It is therefore important to consider the *witness examination process* with an eye toward witness identification.

Naturally, it is in the prosecution's interest to introduce evidence that a witness or victim picked the perpetrator out of a lineup. However, it is not as simple as demonstrating that a witness identified the perpetrator. The identification procedure must be fair as well as conform to constitutional requirements. Those constitutional requirements place restrictions on what officials can do in terms of arranging lineups, showups, and photographic arrays. These restrictions are critical because witnesses to crimes are frequently inaccurate in their descriptions.

Accordingly, this chapter begins with a discussion of the constitutional restrictions that govern the identification process. The three main identification procedures are then introduced. The chapter concludes with a look at the flaws associated with identification procedures—and some fixes.

Constitutional Limitations on Identification Procedures

Identification procedures have been challenged on several grounds, stemming from the Fourteenth Amendment's due process clause, the Fifth Amendment's self-incrimination clause, and the Sixth Amendment's right-to-counsel clause. People have also challenged the constitutionality of identification

Identification procedures have only been successfully challenged on right-to-counsel and due process grounds.

procedures on Fourth Amendment grounds. Identification procedures have only been successfully challenged on right-to-counsel and due process grounds.

Right to Counsel

In **United States v. Wade (388 U.S. 218 [1967])**, a defendant was placed in a police lineup, without his attorney present, *after* he had been indicted for a crime. The Supreme Court held that this violated the Sixth Amendment because a postindictment lineup is a "critical stage" in the criminal process. Further, "the presence of counsel [at postindictment lineups] is necessary to preserve the defendant's basic right to a fair trial" (p. 227). Indeed, the right to counsel extends well beyond the identification stage.

The key in *Wade* was that the lineup was postindictment—that is, conducted after charges had been filed. Had charges *not* been filed, a different decision would have probably resulted. Another important feature of the *Wade* decision was that it distinguished lineups from "various other preparatory steps, such as systematized or scientific analyzing of the accused's fingerprints, blood sample, clothing, hair and the like" (p. 227). Counsel is not required for these types of activities because

> [k]nowledge of the techniques of science and technology is sufficiently available, and the variables in techniques few enough, that the accused has the opportunity for a meaningful confrontation of the Government's case at trial through the ordinary processes of cross-examination of the Government's expert witnesses and the presentation of the evidence of his own experts. (pp. 227–228)

Recently, the Supreme Court has extended the Sixth Amendment right to counsel to include other hearings, such as preliminary hearings and arraignments (see, for example, *Kirby v. Illinois*, 406 U.S. 682 [1972]).

Due Process

The Supreme Court has also clearly stated that the Fourteenth Amendment's due process clause bears on the constitutionality of identification procedures. For example, in **Stovall v. Denno (388 U.S. 293 [1967])**, the Court held that the accused is entitled to protection against procedures "so unnecessarily suggestive and conducive to irreparable mistaken identification" (p. 293) as to amount to a due process violation. In general, for an identification procedure to satisfy the due process clause, it must be (1) reliable and (2) minimally suggestive.

Whether an identification procedure is *reliable* is determined in light of the facts and circumstances surrounding the case. The following factors are used in determining whether an identification procedure is reliable:

> The opportunity of the witness to view the criminal at the time of the crime, the witness's degree of attention,

Think About It...

Counsel During a Lineup Sam Linde has been arrested and charged with burglarizing Paul's Appliance Store. Authorities also suspect that Linde has burglarized several other appliance stores in the area, including John's Appliance Store. Suppose the police want to place Linde in a lineup for a witness who saw him leave John's Appliance Store in the middle of the night. Must counsel be present?

the accuracy of the witness's prior description of the criminal, the level of certainty demonstrated by the witness at the confrontation, and the length of time between the crime and the confrontation. (*Neil v. Biggers*, 409 U.S. 188 [1972], p. 199)

Indeed, the Court stated in *Biggers* that reliability is more important than *suggestiveness*. In the Court's words, it is "the likelihood of misidentification which violates a defendant's right to due process" (p. 199). This position was reaffirmed in the case of **Manson v. Braithwaite (432 U.S. 98 [1977])**, in which the Court held that the totality of circumstances determines whether an identification procedure is unreliable.

Suggestiveness has also been important in determining whether an identification procedure violates the due process clause. If the procedure is set up such that the witness or victim is almost guaranteed to pick the perpetrator, it is unnecessarily suggestive and violates due process. If, for example, an offender is six feet tall and placed in a lineup with several others who are considerably shorter, then the procedure will be considered suggestive.

The Supreme Court has been fairly judicious in terms of due process violations during witness identification, and has set the bar very high for challenging identifications on this basis. In *Perry v. New Hampshire* (565 U.S. [2012]), police were interviewing a woman in her apartment who had reported that a man was breaking into cars in the parking lot. When the woman was asked to describe the man, she pointed out the window and said the culprit was standing right next to one of the police officers outside. Barion Perry, the man she pointed to, was arrested. He sought exclusion of the woman's identification, but the Supreme Court, in an 8-to-1 decision, concluded that happenstance was responsible for the identification procedure. It was not by design: "The Due Process Clause does not require a preliminary judicial inquiry into the reliability of an eyewitness

If the procedure is set up such that the witness or victim is almost guaranteed to pick the perpetrator, it is unnecessarily suggestive and violates due process.

identification when the identification was not procured under unnecessarily suggestive circumstances *arranged* by law enforcement" (emphasis added).

Self-Incrimination

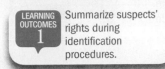

The Fifth Amendment's self-incrimination clause has been invoked with regard to identification procedures. In particular, some defendants have argued that being forced to participate in a lineup or photographic array is itself incriminating and, as such, violates the Fifth Amendment. However, in *United States* v. *Wade*, the Court held that the privilege against self-incrimination does not limit the use of identification procedures.[2] The reason the Court offered is that even though incriminating information can result from identification procedures, such evidence is physical or real as opposed to testimonial. In *Wade*, the Court decided on the constitutionality of an identification procedure, in which the accused was required to utter words that were presumably uttered by the perpetrator. The Court concluded that this type of identification procedure was valid because the defendant's voice was used as an identifying characteristic, not as a means to get him to express his guilt. Thus, the Fifth Amendment does not apply to identification procedures.

The Fourth Amendment

Last, identification procedures have been challenged on Fourth Amendment grounds. Like the Fifth Amendment, the Fourth Amendment has yet to be successfully invoked with regard to identification procedures. According to the Supreme Court, no one enjoys a reasonable expectation of privacy in characteristics that are exposed to the public. For example, if an offender is viewed by a witness, the witness's identification of the offender will be admissible in court, even though the identification is incriminating. The offender/defendant may argue that the act of being viewed by the witness is incriminating, but the courts consider this sort of knowing exposure as beyond constitutional protection.

One of the leading cases in this area is **Schmerber v. California (384 U.S. 757 [1966])**. There, a sample of the defendant's blood was taken by a doctor in a hospital following the defendant's arrest. The sample was used as evidence in the defendant's trial for drunk driving. The defendant argued that the blood sample was incriminating and should be excluded from trial. The Supreme Court disagreed:

> Particularly in a case such as this, where time had to be taken to bring the accused to a hospital and to investigate the scene of the accident, there was no time to seek out a magistrate and secure a warrant. Given these special facts, we conclude that the attempt to secure evidence of blood-alcohol content in this case was an appropriate incident to petitioner's arrest. (pp. 770–771)

Obviously, if the police want to seize a person so as to obtain fingerprints, a voice exemplar, or some other form of evidence, they are bound by Fourth Amendment restrictions. As noted elsewhere in this book, probable cause is required before the police can seize a person. Assuming a seizure is justified, however, any real or physical evidence obtained by the police will be admissible.

There is at least one exception to the Fourth Amendment's probable cause requirement as it pertains to identification procedures. In **Hayes v. Florida (470 U.S. 811 [1985])**, the Court stated,

> There is . . . support in our cases for the view that the Fourth Amendment would permit seizures for the purpose of fingerprinting, if there is reasonable suspicion that the suspect has committed a criminal act, if there is a reasonable basis for believing that fingerprinting will establish or negate the suspect's connection with that crime, and if the procedure is carried out with dispatch. (p. 817)

However, if conducted in the home, such a seizure must be preceded by judicial authorization. See Figure 9–1 for a summary of the constitutional restrictions on identification procedures.

- **Fourth Amendment:** The Fourth Amendment protects from an unlawful search or seizure conducted for the purpose of securing an identification. There is an exception, however: A witness can identify a suspect who is wrongfully seized if the identification is sufficiently independent of the illegal seizure.
- **Fifth Amendment:** Technically, the Fifth Amendment does not apply to identification procedures. This is true even if a suspect is asked to supply a voice exemplar, if this is done for the purpose of identification (and not a confession or admission).
- **Sixth Amendment:** The Sixth Amendment right to counsel exists in the context of making an identification but only in limited circumstances. First, the right to counsel only applies if formal adversarial charges have commenced. Second, a suspect in a photographic array does not enjoy Sixth Amendment protection, regardless of whether charges have been filed.
- **Fourteenth Amendment:** The Fourteenth Amendment's due process clause always applies to identification procedures. In particular, if an identification procedure is too suggestive, it will violate the Fourteenth Amendment.

FIGURE 9–1 **Summary of Constitutional Issues in Identification Procedures.**

▶ Pretrial Identification Techniques

As described earlier, there are three types of pretrial identification techniques: lineups, showups, and photographic arrays. Each of these identification procedures is described in a following section, with particular focus on how the constitutional restrictions already discussed apply to it.

Lineups

Suspects can be forced to participate in lineups because lineups exhibit physical characteristics, not testimonial evidence. Indeed, suspects placed in lineups can also be required to supply voice exemplars but solely for identification purposes, not as a confession. If a suspect refuses to participate in a lineup, he or she can be cited with contempt (*Doss* v. *United States*, 431 F.2d 601 [9th Cir. 1970]), and the prosecutor can comment at trial about the suspect's refusal to cooperate (*United States* v. *Parhms*, 424 F.2d 152 [9th Cir. 1970]).

Steps to Minimize Suggestiveness

As noted earlier, the due process clause restricts identification procedures. In particular, an overly **suggestive lineup** violates due process. In *United States* v. *Wade*, the Supreme Court noted that a lineup becomes suggestive when, for instance,

> all in the lineup but the suspect were known to the identifying witness, . . . the other participants in a lineup were grossly dissimilar in appearance to the suspect, . . . only the suspect was required to wear distinctive clothing which the culprit allegedly wore, . . . the suspect is pointed out before or during a lineup, and . . . the participants in the lineup are asked to try on an article of clothing which fits only the suspect. (p. 233)

There are several steps a police department might take to minimize the suggestiveness in a lineup:

- Include five or more people in the lineup.
- Ensure all lineup participants have the same physical build/makeup.
- Let the suspect choose his or her place in the lineup.
- Require all persons in the lineup to take the same requested action, such as utter a certain word or phrase.
- All lineup participants should conduct themselves such that the actual suspect is not singled out.
- Ideally, the lineup participants do not know who the suspect is.

An important restriction concerning lineups is that people cannot be indiscriminately picked off the street for participation. If a person is *not* already in custody, the police must have reasonable suspicion that he or she has committed the crime in question (see *Hayes* v. *Florida*). However, if the person *is* in custody prior to the lineup, then he or she can be forced to stand in a lineup without any judicial authorization (see *United States* v. *Anderson*, 490 F.2d 785 [D.C. Cir. 1974]).

Showups

A showup is a one-on-one victim/offender confrontation, usually conducted outside the courtroom setting. Specifically, a showup is usually held when 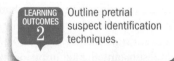 the suspect has been apprehended shortly after having committed the crime and the witness is still at or near the scene of the crime. A lineup is always preferable to a showup (because a lineup consists of several potential suspects); however, a showup is necessary under certain circumstances.

For example, when a witness is immobile and cannot be present at a lineup, a showup is an effective alternative. In

LEARNING OUTCOMES 2 — Outline pretrial suspect identification techniques.

Suspects can be forced to participate in lineups because lineups exhibit physical characteristics, not testimonial evidence.

A showup is a one-on-one victim/offender confrontation, usually conducted outside the courtroom setting.

Think About It...

Altering the Suspect's Appearance On December 24, the Toy Emporium was robbed. The suspect escaped before security guards and police could capture him, but store security cameras and several witnesses indicated that the crime was committed by a white male who was 6 feet, 3 inches tall; approximately 270 pounds; and between 25 and 30 years of age, and who was wearing a green trench coat and had long hair. Two hours after the robbery, a man was arrested in a nearby town because he fit the general description of the robber. However, he was bald and wearing a brown trench coat. A lineup was conducted, in which the suspect was required to wear a wig resembling the long hair of the perpetrator. He was positively identified by several witnesses. Does the act of requiring the suspect to alter his appearance conform to constitutional requirements?

What Constitutes a Valid Showup? The police believe that Anna Delgado was involved in a hit-and-run car accident in which a man was killed. They do not have the reasonable suspicion required to seize Delgado for appearance in a lineup, but they do have a witness to the accident. The police decide to take the witness to Delgado's place of work to make an identification. Delgado is identified at her place of employment. Is this type of showup valid?

Mark Aplet/Shutterstock

Stovall v. *Denno*, the Supreme Court noted, "Faced with the responsibility for identifying the attacker, with the need for immediate action and with the knowledge that [the victim] could not visit the jail, the police followed the only feasible procedure and took [the accused] to the hospital room" (p. 295). In a similar vein, a showup is preferable when the *suspect* is immobile (see *Jackson* v. *United States*, 412 F.2d 149 [D.C. Cir. 1969]).

A showup is sometimes desirable to facilitate prompt identification when time is of the essence. If the witness is required to wait for a lineup, for instance, misidentification is more likely to result. A showup conducted more than 60 minutes after the crime, however, will usually not be upheld (see *United States* v. *Perry*, 449 F.2d 1026 [D.C. Cir. 1971]). But in at least one case, the Supreme Court upheld a stationhouse showup in which no emergency existed. In *Neil* v. *Biggers* **(409 U.S. 188 [1972])**, the Court sanctioned an arranged one-on-one showup, even though it took place well after the point at which the crime in question was committed. The Court noted, given the facts, that there was "no substantial likelihood of misidentification" (p. 201). This was because the witness had an opportunity to view the suspect for almost 30 minutes, under good lighting, prior to the showup.

The same constitutional provisions that govern lineups also govern showups. Specifically, the Sixth Amendment right to counsel applies but only after adversarial proceedings have commenced (see *Moore* v. *Illinois*, **434 U.S. 220 [1977]**). Due process protections also exist. If the showup is unnecessarily suggestive under a totality-of-circumstances analysis, any identification that comes from it will not be admissible in court.

In-Court Showups

What happens when a witness identifies the accused for the first time in *court*? This has happened on occasion and is best described as an **in-court showup**. The key feature of an in-court showup is that the witness has *not* identified the suspect, either in a lineup or related procedure, prior to trial. How do the courts deal with this? The answer is important because an in-court identification is highly suggestive. Namely, the suspect has already been identified by virtue of having been charged with the crime.

The leading case dealing with in-court showups is *Moore* v. *Illinois*, although the focus of the case was on the preliminary hearing, not the trial. The Court's decision would be expected to apply to criminal trials as well as other adversarial proceedings, however. Here are the facts from that case, as described by the Supreme Court:

> After petitioner had been arrested for rape and related offenses, he was identified by the complaining witness as her assailant at the ensuing preliminary

hearing, during which petitioner was not represented by counsel nor offered appointed counsel. The victim had been asked to make an identification after being told that she was going to view a suspect, after being told his name and having heard it called as he was led before the bench, and after having heard the prosecutor recite the evidence believed to implicate petitioner. Subsequently, petitioner was indicted, and counsel was appointed, who moved to suppress the victim's identification of petitioner. The Illinois trial court denied the motion on the ground that the prosecution had shown an independent basis for the victim's identification. At trial, the victim testified on direct examination by the prosecution that she had identified petitioner as her assailant at the preliminary hearing, and there was certain other evidence linking petitioner to the crimes. He was convicted and the Illinois Supreme Court affirmed. (p. 220)

Notwithstanding the clear violation of the Sixth Amendment in this case (which the Supreme Court also pointed out), the Court pointed to the suggestiveness that occurs when a witness identifies a suspect for the first time at a formal hearing:

> It is difficult to imagine a more suggestive manner in which to present a suspect to a witness for their critical first confrontation than was employed in this case. The victim who had seen her assailant for only 10 to 15 seconds, was asked to make her identification after she was told that she was going to view a suspect, after she was told his name and heard it called as he was led before the bench, and after she heard the prosecutor recite the evidence believed to implicate petitioner. Had petitioner been represented by counsel, some or all of this suggestiveness could have been avoided. (pp. 229–230)

What message is to be gleaned from *Moore* v. *Illinois*? In general, law enforcement officials should have witnesses identify suspects via lineups, showups, or photographic arrays *prior* to the point at which adversarial proceedings commence. Any of these identification procedures would result in a less suggestive identification than would be likely at trial. Clearly, though, lineups, showups, and photographic arrays can also be suggestive.

Photographic Identifications

The last type of identification procedure to be considered in this chapter is the photographic identification array. It involves displaying a picture of the suspect along with pictures of several other people to a victim or witness for the purpose of identification.

Photographic identification procedures approximate real-life lineups by including several people, but they are not subjected to the same constitutional restrictions that lineups are. In particular, there is no Sixth Amendment right to counsel during a photographic identification. However, due process protections *do* apply.

To minimize due process problems, several photographs of like individuals should be shown to the witness or victim so as to minimize unnecessary suggestiveness. In **Simmons v. United States (390 U.S. 377 [1968])**, the Supreme Court shed some light on the importance of a carefully constructed photographic array:

> Despite the hazards of initial identification by photograph, this procedure has been used widely and effectively in criminal law enforcement, from the standpoint both of apprehending offenders and of sparing innocent suspects the ignominy of arrest by allowing eyewitnesses to exonerate them through scrutiny of photographs. The danger that use of the technique may result in convictions based on misidentification may be substantially lessened by a course of cross-examination at trial which exposes to the jury the method's potential for error. We are unwilling to prohibit its employment, either in the exercise of our supervisory power or, still less, as a matter of constitutional requirement. Instead, we hold that each case must be considered on its own facts, and that convictions based on eyewitness identification at trial following a pretrial identification by photograph will be set aside on that ground only if the photographic identification procedure was so impermissibly suggestive as to give rise to a very substantial likelihood of irreparable misidentification. (p. 384)

As indicated, to conform to due process requirements, multiple photographs of like individuals are ideal for a photographic array. However, in one case, the Supreme Court sanctioned a photographic array consisting of one picture. In *Manson v. Braithwaite* (432 U.S. 98 [1977]), introduced earlier, the Court sanctioned an in-court identification based on an earlier identification from a single photograph because it was reliable based on the totality of circumstances. The reasons the Court cited are illustrative. In particular, the Court described how Glover, the witness, who was also a police officer, arrived at his conclusion that the suspect (referred to in the following case excerpt as the *vendor* of illegal drugs) in the photograph was, in fact, the perpetrator. Here are the criteria on which the Court focused:

Photographic identification procedures approximate real-life lineups by including several people, but they are not subjected to the same constitutional restrictions that lineups are.

- *The opportunity to view.* Glover testified that for two to three minutes he stood at the apartment door, within two feet of the respondent. The door opened twice, and each time the man stood at the door. The moments passed, the conversation took place, and payment was made. Glover looked directly at his vendor. It was near sunset, to be sure, but the sun had not yet set, so it was not dark or even dusk or twilight. Natural light from outside entered the hallway through a window. There was natural light, as well, from inside the apartment.

- *The degree of attention.* Glover was not a casual or passing observer, as is so often the case with eyewitness identification. Trooper Glover was a trained police officer on duty—and specialized and dangerous duty—when he called at the third floor of 201 Westland in Hartford on May 5, 1970. . . . It is true that Glover's duty was that of ferreting out narcotics offenders and that he would be expected in his work to produce results. But it is also true that, as a specially trained, assigned, and experienced officer, he could be expected to pay scrupulous attention to detail, for he knew that subsequently he would have to find and arrest his vendor. In addition, he knew that his claimed observations would be subject later to close scrutiny and examination at any trial.

- *The accuracy of the description.* Glover's description was given to D'Onofrio [a backup officer] within minutes after the transaction. It included the vendor's race, his height, his build, the color and style of his hair, and the high cheekbone facial feature. It also included clothing the vendor wore. No claim has been made that respondent did not possess the physical characteristics so described. D'Onofrio reacted positively at once. Two days later, when Glover was alone, he viewed the photograph D'Onofrio produced and identified its subject as the narcotics seller.

- *The witness's level of certainty.* There is no dispute that the photograph in question was that of respondent.

- *The time between the crime and the identification.* Glover's description of his vendor was given to D'Onofrio within minutes of the crime. The photographic identification took place only two days later. We do not have here the passage of weeks or months between the crime and the viewing of the photograph. (pp. 114–116)

Taken together, these five considerations led the Court to this conclusion:

> These indicators of Glover's ability to make an accurate identification are hardly outweighed by the corrupting effect of the challenged identification itself. Although identifications arising from single-photograph displays may be viewed in general with suspicion, see *Simmons v. United States*, 390 U.S., at 383, we find in the instant case little pressure on the witness to acquiesce in the suggestion that such a display entails. D'Onofrio had left the photograph at Glover's office and was not present when Glover first viewed it two days after the event. There thus was little urgency and Glover could view the photograph at his leisure.

And since Glover examined the photograph alone, there was no coercive pressure to make an identification arising from the presence of another. The identification was made in circumstances allowing care and reflection (p. 116).

The *Manson* decision suggests that single-photograph arrays are constitutionally permissible, but understand that the witness in this case was a police officer and that the facts were somewhat unusual. It is doubtful that the Supreme Court would uphold a similar identification today. It is always preferable to place multiple pictures of like individuals in a photographic array.

To summarize the points made thus far, see Figure 9–2. It contains the Gallatin, Tennessee, Police Department's policy for the use of showups, lineups, and photographic arrays.

9.29 Showup, Lineup, and Photographic Identification

9.29.1 Showup

A showup is the presentation of a suspect to an eyewitness a short time after the commission of a crime. Many courts have suppressed evidence from a showup due to the inherent suggestiveness of the event. Because of this, a lineup is preferred over a showup when possible. However, when exigent circumstances require the use of a showup, the following guidelines will be used:

1. A showup will not be conducted when the suspect is in a cell, restrained, or dressed in jail clothing;
2. A showup will not be conducted with more than one witness present at a time. Witnesses will not be allowed to communicate with each other regarding the identification of the suspect;
3. The same suspect will not be presented to the same witness more than once;
4. The suspect will not be required to put on clothing worn by the perpetrator, speak words uttered by the perpetrator, or perform other actions of the perpetrator; and
5. Officers will not say or do anything that might suggest to the witness that the suspect is or may be the perpetrator.

9.29.2 Photographic Identification

In conducting a photographic identification, an officer must use multiple photographs shown individually to a witness or simultaneoulsy in a book or array. Additionally, an officer will adhere to the following guidelines when conducting a photographic identification:

1. Use at least six photographs of individuals who are reasonably similar in age, height, weight, and general appearance and of the same sex and race;
2. Whenever possible, avoid mixing color and black and white photos, use photos of the same size and basic composition, and never mix mug shots with other snapshots or include more than one photo of the same suspect;
3. Cover any portions of mug shots or other photographs that provide identifying information on the subject, and similarly cover those used in the array;
4. Show the photo array to only one witness at a time;
5. Never make suggestive statements that may influence the judgement or perception of the witness; and
6. Preserve the photo array, together with full information about the identification process, for future reference.

9.29.3 Lineup

A lineup is the live presentation of at least five individuals to a victim. In conducting a lineup, an officer will schedule the lineup on a date and at a time that is convenient for all concerned parties. Additionally, the officer must fulfill necessary legal requirements for the transfer of a subject to the lineup location should he/she be incarcerated at a detention center; make timely notice to the detention center concerning the pickup; and make arrangements for picking up the prisoner. Finally, the officer must make arrangements to have at least four other persons act as "fill ins" at the lineup who are of the same race, sex, and approximate height, weight, age, and physical appearance and who are similarly clothed.

The officer in charge of conducting the lineup will ensure that the following requirements are adhered to:

1. Ensure that the prisoner has been informed of his/her right to counsel if formal charges have been made against him/her, and also ensure that he/she has the opportunity to retain counsel or request that one be provided;
2. Obtain a written waiver on the prescribed departmental form should the prisoner waive his/her right to counsel;
3. Allow counsel representing the accused an opportunity to observe the manner in which the lineup is conducted;
4. Advise the accused that he/she may take any position in the lineup which he/she prefers and may change positions prior to summoning a new witness;
5. Ensure that all persons in the lineup are numbered consecutively and are referred to only by number;
6. Ensure that a complete written, audio, and video record of the lineup proceedings are made and retained when possible;
7. Ensure that witnesses are not permitted to see nor are they to be shown any photographs of the accused immediately prior to the lineup;
8. Ensure that not more than one witness views the lineup at a time and that they are not permitted to speak with one another during lineup proceedings; and
9. Scrupulously avoid using statements, clues, casual comments, or providing unnecessary or irrelevant information that in any manner may influence the witnesses' decision-making process or perception.

FIGURE 9–2 Identification Policy From the Gallatin, Tennessee, Police Department.

▶ *Identification Procedures: Flaws and Fixes*

Nearly every suspect identification procedure can be flawed in some fashion, some more than others. Consider showups. No matter what steps police take to ensure fairness, showups are prone to mistaken identification.

Experiences like that of Billy Wayne Miller, featured at the outset of this chapter, could be less common if authorities relied exclusively on lineups and photographic identification procedures. However, even lineups and photographic arrays can be flawed. The Innocence Project, an organization that works to exonerate wrongfully convicted inmates, claims that "eyewitness misidentification is the single greatest cause of wrongful convictions nationwide."[3] Several examples of flawed witness identification appear in Figure 9–3.

Some might take issue with the Innocence Project's arguments, but many researchers have also found that identification procedures can be problematic, so much so that in May of 1998, then–U.S. Attorney General Janet Reno organized a working group of prosecutors, defense attorneys, police officers, and other experts who were tasked with creating a set of "best practices" for identification procedures. The working group's findings were echoed in an article published by a group of psychologists at around the same time. They identified "four simple rules of procedure that follow from the scientific literature that we argue could largely relieve the criminal justice system of its role in contributing to eyewitness identification problems."[4]

The rules are paraphrased as follows:

- Officers who conduct lineups and photographic identifications should not know who the suspect is.

- Witnesses should be told (1) that the suspect may not be in the lineup and (2) that the officer conducting it does not know who the suspect is.

Nearly every suspect identification procedure can be flawed in some fashion, some more than others.

- Care should be taken to ensure the suspect does not "stand out" in the lineup such that the witness can easily identify him or her.

- The police should obtain a statement from the witness confirming his or her identification of the suspect.[5]

Double-Blind Lineups

When the investigator conducting a lineup knows who the suspect is, he or she can unintentionally (and even intentionally) influence the witness and thereby taint the identification procedure. For example, the investigator may say to the witness, "Why don't you take another look at number three." Assuming the suspect is in the number three position in a lineup, clearly this comment could sway the witness in the direction the investigator prefers.

A **double-blind lineup** is one in which the investigator conducting the lineup (or assembling a photo array) does not know who the suspect is. This helps ensure that the investigator will not lead the witness in a particular direction. Studies indeed show that double-blind procedures reduce the risks of mistaken identifications.[6] Here is a summary of the findings from one of the most recent studies in this area:

> Administrator knowledge had the greatest effect on identifications of the suspect for simultaneous photo-spreads paired with biased instructions, with single-blind administrations increasing identifications of the suspect. When biased instructions were given, single-blind administrations produced fewer foil identifications than double-blind administrations. Administrators exhibited a greater proportion of biasing behaviors during single-blind administrations than during double-blind administrations.[7]

Virtual Officer Lineups

A problem with double-blind lineups is that they are resource intensive. They require at least two investigators instead of the usual one—one to know the

LEARNING OUTCOMES 3 · Describe flaws in identification procedures and strategies for minimizing mistakes.

- A witness in a rape case was shown a photo array in which only one photo—of the person police suspected was the perpetrator—was marked with an "R."
- Witnesses substantially changed their description of a perpetrator (including key information such as height, weight and presence of facial hair) after they learned more about a particular suspect.
- Witnesses only made an identification after multiple photo arrays or lineups—and then made hesitant identifications (saying they "thought" the person "might be" the perpetrator, for example), but at trial the jury was told the witnesses did not waver in identifying the suspect.

FIGURE 9–3 **Examples of Flawed Witness Identifications.**
Source: www.innocenceproject.org/understand/Eyewitness-Misidentification.php (accessed November 19, 2013).

The Photo Array Revisited What if, for purposes of having several of a suspected rapist's victims identify him in a photographic lineup, the police tell the second witness who the first witness identified, the third witness who the first and second witnesses identified, and so on? What if, instead, the police show five different photographic arrays to a single witness, but the suspected rapist appears once in each array?

John Worrall

identity of the suspect and another to administer the lineup without knowing the suspect's real identity. One solution to this problem is to use a "virtual officer" to conduct the procedure.[8] One team of researchers has gone so far as to develop software in which a virtual officer (called "Officer Garcia") conducts a photographic display. Because the virtual officer does not know the identity of the suspect or his or her placement in the array, the procedure is not susceptible to investigator influence. A YouTube demonstration is available online.[9]

▶ The Exclusionary Rule and Identifications

When identification procedures violate constitutional protections, the results from such procedures cannot be considered admissible in a criminal trial. Generally, there are two means by which identifications will be excluded: (1) when an in-court identification is tainted by an out-of-court identification and (2) when a suspect is searched and/or seized improperly and then identified by a witness.

Tainted Identifications

In-court identifications are viewed cautiously. In most such situations, the defendant is sitting in the courtroom, not surrounded by anyone else matching his or her description (as in a lineup), and sometimes looking sinister or even guilty (e.g., wearing prison coveralls). Furthermore, given the fact that the defendant has been identified—at least, for trial purposes— as the one suspected of having committed a crime, witnesses often jump to the conclusion that the defendant is the one who should be held responsible.

Nevertheless, courts routinely permit in-court identifications. But if an in-court identification is tainted by an out-of-court identification, it may be excluded. This is known as a **tainted identification**.

Unfortunately, it is not always easy to decide whether an in-court identification is "fruit of the poisonous tree." In *United States* v. *Wade*, the Supreme Court held that an illegally conducted lineup does not invalidate later identifications resulting from an "independent source." The independent source in this context does not have to be another person. Instead, if the witness had plenty of time to view the perpetrator prior to the

police lineup, showup, or photographic array, then his or her in-court identification may be admissible. Some factors that are considered include

the prior opportunity to observe the alleged criminal act, the existence of any discrepancy between any pre-lineup description and the defendant's actual description, any identification prior to lineup of another person, the identification by picture of the defendant prior to the lineup, failure to identify the defendant on a prior occasion, and the lapse of time between the alleged act and the lineup identification. (p. 241)

Also, if the witness did not experience intense anxiety or pressure during the criminal act (and thus had plenty of opportunity to absorb what was occurring), it is likely that his or her in-court identification will not be tainted by questionable police conduct during a lineup (see *United States* v. *Johnson*, 412 F.2d 753 [1st Cir. 1969], *cert. denied*, 397 U.S. 944 [1970]).

Identifications Resulting from Illegal Searches and Seizures

What happens if a person is wrongfully arrested—say, based on less than probable cause— and then placed in a lineup and identified by a witness? Can the witness's identification be considered admissible in a criminal trial? What if, further, the lineup is nonsuggestive and otherwise abides by constitutional requirements? Unfortunately, the Supreme Court has offered few answers to these questions.

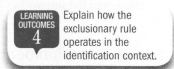

LEARNING OUTCOMES 4 — Explain how the exclusionary rule operates in the identification context.

Davis v. *Mississippi* (394 U.S. 721 [1969]) is a worthwhile point of departure. In *Davis*, the fingerprint identification of a rape suspect was deemed inadmissible because it was the product of an illegal arrest. However, in **United States v. Crews (445 U.S. 463 [1980])**, the Supreme Court decided otherwise. In that case, Crews was illegally arrested and photographed and then his photograph was shown to a witness, who identified him as the perpetrator. He was tried and convicted based, in part, on the witness's identification. The Supreme Court agreed with the trial court that the arrest was illegal but still upheld Crews's conviction. Three members of the majority justified this decision by arguing that the "fruit" was gathered at the point of the illegal arrest, as opposed to later, so the derivative evidence doctrine

When Is an In-Court Identification Tainted? Joan Vines heard noises emanating from Sarah Locklear's apartment and minutes later saw two men, one with black gloves and a brown paper bag, exit from the basement of the building and leave in a green 1956 Plymouth. Vines left her apartment immediately to check on things. She found the door to the Locklear apartment open, and she located a piece of stereo equipment just outside the building. Suddenly, the Plymouth returned, so Vines retreated to her apartment. Through her window, she watched the same two men put the piece of stereo equipment into the car. The men left again in the car, but not before Vines jotted down the license plate number. She later gave it to the police, together with physical descriptions of the two men. Vines was then brought to the station for the purpose of identifying one of the suspects. She was taken to a room in which the suspect was seated. The suspect was requested to stand and turn around, which he did. Vines identified him as one of the two participants in the burglary of Locklear's apartment. Vines later identified the man at his trial for burglary. Will the in-court identification be tainted by the stationhouse identification?

should not apply. The Court further noted that the identification had not "'been come at by exploitation' of the violation of the defendant's Fourth Amendment rights" (p. 471).

Inasmuch as *Crews* was decided well after *Davis* v. *Mississippi*, it would seem that an identification resulting from an illegal search and/or seizure would be admissible. Think back, as well, to how the exclusionary rule applies in the *Miranda* context. The Supreme Court held in *United States* v. *Bayer* (331 U.S. 532 [1947]) that the "fruit of the poisonous tree" doctrine does not control the admissibility of physical evidence obtained from illegal confessions. These decisions, taken together, chip away at the exclusionary rule and reinforce the notion that the "fruit of the poisonous tree" doctrine applies in limited circumstances—primarily, when an illegal search and/or seizure (as opposed to an improper confession or identification) results in the subsequent seizure of tangible evidence.

A Valid Identification?

Read the following facts from an actual case (*State v. Chen*, 27 A.3d 930 [N.J. 2011]):

Late in the evening on January 23, 2005, Johann Christian Kim (JC) received a phone call from his ex-girlfriend, defendant Cecilia X. Chen. The two had not spoken since June 2000, around the time their relationship ended. During the call, defendant told JC that she was not doing well and had recently broken up with her boyfriend. She apologized for having taken JC for granted and wondered aloud how things might have turned out had they remained together. JC stated that he was happily married and expecting a child. Defendant cried at times before the conversation ended.

Three days after that phone call, JC's wife, Helen, was home alone recovering from surgery. At 4:00 in the afternoon, she received a phone call from an unknown woman who asked for Mr. Kim. The woman explained that she was calling about a second mortgage with Bank of America, but the Kims had no such mortgage. The caller ID listed a liquor store located in Neptune City. The Kims lived nearby in Ocean Township. A short time later Helen was disturbed by loud knocking on the front door. A young woman who Helen did not know, but who Helen later identified as defendant, was at the door. The woman explained that her car had broken down and asked to use a phone and the bathroom. Helen let the woman into the house, but called JC to tell him about the strange phone call and woman. While they were speaking, the woman returned from the bathroom, grabbed Helen, and stabbed her with a kitchen knife in the back of the shoulder. Helen fought back. A neighbor who lived across the street, Lori Schoch, heard Helen's screams and saw part of the struggle on the front porch. Schoch called the police. Helen was able to disarm her attacker, and the woman ran off.

Helen described her assailant to police as an Asian or Filipino woman who was about 5′4″, twenty to twenty-five years old, and wearing black frame glasses. Schoch provided a similar description to the police within about two hours of the attack. Helen drew a picture of her assailant that night. She showed it to JC who thought it looked familiar. Between the drawing and the unusual phone call, JC thought that perhaps it might be defendant. JC had access to defendant's personal website and showed Helen five to ten pictures of defendant on the computer. When she saw one picture, Helen "just jumped" and was "ninety percent positive" that defendant was her attacker . . .

On April 17, 2006, defendant was indicted on charges of aggravated assault, armed robbery, and weapons offenses. Nearly twenty-two months after the attack, on November 14, 2006, the police presented a photo array to Helen and Schoch for the first time. A detective testified that one of the reasons the police waited to show the photo array was out of concern that the website pictures might have prejudiced Helen. Helen and Schoch separately selected defendant's picture.

Answer the following questions concerning this case:

1. Should the April 17 identification have been excluded?
2. What was the court's decision in the case? You will need to read the full case, which can be found here: http://tinyurl.com/muzuqzk (accessed November 19, 2013).
3. Is it possible to define an ideal maximum amount of time that should pass between a criminal act and a victim or witness's identification of the perpetrator?

CHAPTER 9 | Identifications

LEARNING OUTCOMES 1

Summarize suspects' rights during identification procedures.

Suspects enjoy the right counsel in postindictment lineups. All identification procedures must conform to due process requirements and not be unnecessarily suggestive.

Key Cases

United States v. Wade

Stovall v. Donno

Manson v. Braithwaite

Schmerber v. California

Hayes v. Florida

1. Explain how due process applies in the identification context.

2. Explain how the Sixth Amendment right to counsel applies in the identification context.

lineup An identification procedure in which the suspect is placed alongside several other people who resemble him or her. The intent of the procedure is to ensure that a witness or victim picks the suspect out of the lineup.

showup An identification procedure in which the suspect is brought before the witness (or victim) alone, so the witness can be asked whether that person is the perpetrator.

photographic array A procedure in which several photographs, including one of the suspect, are shown to a witness or victim, and he or she is asked to pick out the perpetrator.

LEARNING OUTCOMES 2

Outline pretrial suspect identification techniques.

Identification procedures are of three types: (1) lineups, (2) showups, and (3) photographic identifications or arrays. Lineups consist of several like-looking individuals placed in a line so the victim or witness can identify the suspected perpetrator. Showups are one-on-one victim/witness–suspect identification. Photographic arrays, also called mug books, are the photographic equivalent of in-person lineups.

Key Cases

Neil v. Biggers

Moore v. Illinois

Simmons v. United States

1. Explain the three types of pretrial identification procedures.

2. What is an in-court showup?

3. What would a constitutionally valid photographic array look like?

suggestive lineup A flawed lineup that almost ensures that the victim or witness will identify the suspect. For example, if the suspect is male and the other lineup participants are female, this would be a suggestive lineup.

in-court showup A procedure in which a witness identifies the perpetrator in court. This sometimes occurs when a prosecutor asks a testifying witness to point to the perpetrator.

LEARNING OUTCOMES 3

Describe flaws in identification procedures and strategies for minimizing mistakes.

Witnesses are prone to mistaken identification, especially in show-up situations. Even lineups and photo arrays can result in mistaken identification. As such, various procedures have been developed to improve identification procedures. Two recent examples include double-blind lineups and virtual officer lineups.

1. What are some of the flaws associated with identification procedures?

2. What can be done to improve identification procedures?

double-blind lineup A lineup procedure in which neither the witness nor the investigator staging the lineup knows who the suspect is.

LEARNING OUTCOMES 4

Explain how the exclusionary rule operates in the identification context.

An identification, whether occurring during trial or prior to trial, can be excluded as evidence. First, if an in-court identification is tainted by an improper out-of-court identification, it will be inadmissible. Similarly, if an identification takes place following the illegal arrest and/or search of a suspect, it can be excluded as well. There are exceptions to these rules, however. Usually, if the identification is sufficiently divorced from any prior illegality, it will be admissible at trial.

Key Cases

United States v. Crews

1. In what ways does the exclusionary rule apply in the identification context?

2. What is a tainted identification?

3. Why is the concept of a tainted identification important in the criminal procedure context?

tainted identification An identification that would not have taken place but for some earlier unconstitutional activity.

"... trials in the United States are carefully choreographed events with few unpredictable twists and turns."

10

The Pretrial Process

1 Explain the purpose and process of the initial appearance.

2 Explain the purpose and process of the probable cause hearing.

3 Summarize bail and other types of pretrial release.

4 Explain the purpose and process of the preliminary hearing.

5 Summarize the arraignment process.

6 Summarize the discovery process.

RICHARD F. TOO...
JUDGE

SHOULD THE CONVICTED HAVE ACCESS TO DNA EVIDENCE?

William Osborne was convicted in Alaska of kidnapping, assault, and sexual assault. After he was convicted, he sought access to the state's DNA evidence that was used to convict him. His intent was to use DNA testing that was not available at the time of his 1994 trial. The district attorney denied his request, so Osborne sued, claiming that his due process rights were violated. Eventually, the U.S. Supreme Court took up the case and was tasked with answering the question of whether a convicted individual has a constitutional right—after criminal proceedings have concluded—to access the government's DNA evidence. In *District Attorney* v. *Osborne* the Court answered with a "no." Here is an excerpt from the Court's opinion:

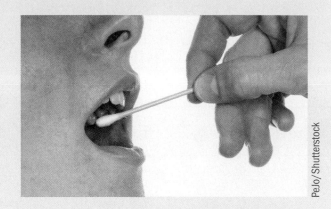

PeJo/Shutterstock

> DNA testing has an unparalleled ability both to exonerate the wrongly convicted and to identify the guilty. The availability of new DNA testing technologies, however, cannot mean that every criminal conviction, or even every criminal conviction involving biological evidence, is suddenly in doubt. The task of establishing rules to harness DNA's power to prove innocence without unnecessarily overthrowing the established criminal justice system belongs primarily to the legislature. . . . Forty-six states and the federal government have already enacted statutes dealing specifically with access to evidence for DNA testing. These laws recognize the value of DNA testing but also the need for conditions on accessing the State's evidence. Alaska is one of a handful of States yet to enact specific DNA testing legislation, but Alaska

courts are addressing how to apply existing discovery and postconviction relief laws to this novel technology. (*District Attorney* v. *Osborne*, No. 08-6 [2009], pp. 8–11)

The Court thus left it to the Alaska legislature to decide whether Osborne should gain access to the DNA evidence. Although Osborne's appeal occurred in the posttrial phase, the case is important because it touches on the issue of discovery, the extent to which the prosecution and defense must share evidence in their possession. Discovery is addressed at the end of the chapter. First, we consider other steps in the pretrial phase of the criminal process.

DISCUSS **Do you agree with the Supreme Court's decision in this case?**

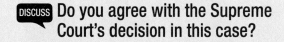

▶ *The Road to Trial*

Once a person has been arrested, be it with or without a warrant, he or she will be booked at the arresting officer's police station or the sheriff's station (that is, sheriffs usually run jails). **Booking** consists of filling out paperwork about who was arrested, the time of the arrest, and the offense involved. Next, the arrestee's personal items are inventoried. The arrestee may also be photographed and fingerprinted, depending on the offense and the jurisdiction involved. Finally, the arrestee is placed in a holding cell, jail cell, or similar confinement facility and allowed to contact counsel, family, friends, and other individuals, as needed. (Contrary to popular depictions, more than one phone call is typically allowed.)

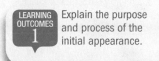

LEARNING OUTCOMES 1 — Explain the purpose and process of the initial appearance.

Once arrested and booked, the suspect is then brought before a magistrate or judge in what is known as the **initial appearance**. Not all jurisdictions require an initial appearance (also referred to as *presentment*), but for those that do, the suspect must be brought before

a judge in a relatively short period of time. Delays of more than six hours are usually unacceptable; they may be necessary on occasion, however, if the time of arrest precludes appearance before a judge (for example, 1:00 a.m. on Monday).

The initial appearance is designed to serve a number of purposes. In a misdemeanor case, such as minor in possession, the trial may take place at this stage. In a more serious case, however, the accused will be advised of

- the reason he or she is being detained (notification of formal charges often comes later at arraignment),

Not all jurisdictions require an initial appearance (also referred to as *presentment*), but for those that do, the suspect must be brought before a judge in a relatively short period of time.

- his or her protection against self-incrimination, and
- his or her right to appointed counsel, if need be. The judge may also set bail at the initial appearance, but the bail determination often requires a separate hearing. For ease of exposition, this chapter treats the bail determination as its own hearing, independent of the initial appearance.

The initial appearance is usually swift and subject to few procedural constraints. In fact, only one Supreme Court decision has dealt explicitly with the initial appearance. In *Rothgery v. Gillespie County* (554 U.S. 191 [2008]), the Court held that the Sixth Amendment right to counsel applies at the initial appearance. In contrast, the probable cause, bail, and preliminary hearings have received much more of the Court's attention.

▶ *The Probable Cause Hearing*

In **Gerstein v. Pugh** (420 U.S. 103 [1975]), the Supreme Court held that the Fourth Amendment requires a so-called **probable cause hearing** either before or promptly after arrest.[1] A probable cause hearing *before* an arrest usually results in an arrest warrant being issued. Recall that an arrest warrant is issued based on a judge's determination as to whether probable cause is in place. No hearing to determine probable cause after such an arrest is necessary, because it would be redundant. However, when an arrest is made *without* a warrant, a probable cause determination must often be made. The purpose of the probable cause hearing is, in essence, to determine whether there is probable cause to keep a person detained.

The *Gerstein* decision challenged the preliminary hearing system in Florida. Probable cause was determined at preliminary hearings in that state, but those hearings were not required until 30 days after arrest. Basically, a person could be held following a warrantless arrest for 30 days, sometimes longer. The Court held that such a lengthy detention required a judicial determination of probable cause *early on*:

> [W]hile the State's reasons for taking summary action subside, the suspect's need for a neutral determination of probable cause increases significantly. The consequences of prolonged detention may be more serious than the interference occasioned by arrest. Pretrial confinement may imperil the suspect's job, interrupt his source of income, and impair his family's relationship. . . . When the stakes are this high, the detached judgment of a neutral magistrate is essential if the Fourth Amendment is to furnish meaningful protection from unfounded interference with liberty. (p. 114)

The Court decided, in essence, that the prosecutor's decision to charge is not in itself enough to satisfy the probable cause requirement. However, the Court also noted that a probable cause hearing is *not* required after every arrest. An arrest

When an arrest is made *without* a warrant, a probable cause determination must often be made.

with a warrant, as noted, need not be followed by a probable cause hearing. Likewise, when an arrest is based on a grand jury indictment, a probable cause hearing is not required, either. The logic for this is that the grand jury performs an investigative function, makes its probable cause determination, and then issues its indictment. Finally, if the detention in question is relatively short, such as when a preliminary hearing follows shortly after arrest, a probable cause hearing will not be required.

Procedural Issues Surrounding the Hearing

The lower court's decisions leading up to the Supreme Court's decision in *Gerstein* required that a probable cause hearing resemble an adversarial trial, complete with counsel, compulsory process, and the like. The Supreme Court reversed the lower courts' decisions as to these issues, declaring that the probable cause hearing is a not a "critical stage" of the criminal process. In support of its decision, the Court observed,

LEARNING OUTCOMES 2 — Explain the purpose and process of the probable cause hearing.

> Criminal justice is already overburdened by the volume of cases and the complexities of our system. The processing of misdemeanors, in particular, and the early stages of prosecution generally are marked by delays that can seriously affect the quality of justice. A constitutional doctrine requiring adversary hearings for all persons detained pending trial could exacerbate the problem of pretrial delay. (p. 122, n. 23)

Timing of the Hearing

The Court, in *Gerstein*, required that if it is to be held, the probable cause hearing must take place "promptly after arrest." It did not define what was meant by *promptly*, but in **Riverside County v. McLaughlin** (500 U.S. 44 [1991]), the Court offered some clarification. In a 5-to-4 decision, the Court held that a hearing that takes place within 48 hours of arrest conforms with Fourth Amendment requirements:

> In order to satisfy *Gerstein*'s promptness requirement, a jurisdiction that chooses to combine probable cause determinations with other pretrial proceedings must do so as soon as is reasonably feasible, but in no event later than 48 hours after arrest. Providing a probable cause determination within that time frame will, as a general matter, immunize such a jurisdiction from systemic challenges. Although a hearing within 48 hours may nonetheless violate *Gerstein* if the arrested individual can prove that his or her probable cause determination was delayed unreasonably, courts evaluating the reasonableness of a delay must allow a substantial degree of flexibility, taking into account the practical realities of pretrial procedures. Where an arrested individual does not receive a probable cause determination within 48 hours, the burden of proof shifts to the government to demonstrate the existence of a bona fide emergency

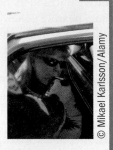
or other extraordinary circumstance, which cannot include intervening weekends or the fact that in a particular case it may take longer to consolidate pretrial proceedings. (p. 44)

Acceptable excuses for delay include "unavoidable delays in transporting arrested persons from one facility to another, handling late-night bookings where no magistrate is readily available, [and] obtaining the presence of an arresting officer who may be busy processing other suspects or securing the premises of an arrest" (p. 57). Unacceptable reasons for delay, by contrast, include the need to gather additional evidence to support the arrest in hindsight and issues of bad faith, such as to inconvenience an individual and make him or her wait for no legitimate reason.

▶ Pretrial Release

Once a person has been arrested, the question as to whether he or she should be temporarily released (either via bail or on his or her own recognizance) invariably comes up. On the one hand, if the arrestee does not pose a significant risk of flight and has been arrested for a relatively minor offense, **pretrial release** seems a sensible approach. On the other hand, if the arrestee is likely to fail to appear in later proceedings, he or she should probably be jailed pending additional court proceedings.

The Eighth Amendment states, "Excessive bail shall not be required." This simply means that bail cannot be set ridiculously high. Not everyone enjoys a constitutional right to bail, however. In capital cases, for example, bail has always been denied. Consider what the Supreme Court stated in *Carlson* v. *Landon* (342 U.S. 524 [1952]): "In England, [the Bail] clause has never been thought to accord a right to bail in all cases, but merely to provide that bail shall not be excessive in those cases where it is proper to grant bail. When this clause was carried over into our Bill of Rights, nothing was said that indicated any different concept" (p. 545).

The Eighth Amendment prohibition against excessive bail *has not* been incorporated to the states.

Critics of some courts' decisions to deny bail have argued that because the U.S. criminal justice system presumes innocence, everyone should be released. After all, a defendant cannot be considered guilty until the state proves his or her guilt beyond a reasonable doubt. However, in *Bell* v. *Wolfish* (441 U.S. 520 [1979]), the Supreme Court stated that the presumption of innocence is merely "a doctrine that allocates the burden of proof in criminal trials" (p. 533).[2]

It is also important to point out that the Eighth Amendment prohibition against excessive bail *has not* been incorporated to the states. For example, in *Murphy* v. *Hunt* (455 U.S. 478 [1982]), a detainee sued under Section 1983, claiming that his Eighth Amendment right was violated. The Supreme Court held that his suit was moot because he was convicted in Nebraska state court. This important decision, coupled with the realization that the Eighth Amendment's excessive bail provision has not been incorporated, explains some of the discrepancies in bail decisions.

The Constitution does not specify whether bail should be set in a separate hearing, but numerous Court decisions seem to suggest a separate hearing is warranted. For example, in **Stack v. Boyle (342 U.S. 1 [1951])**, the Court stated that as part of the bail determination, the judge should consider "the nature and circumstances of the offense charged, the weight of the evidence against [the accused], [and] the financial ability of the defendant to give bail and the character of the defendant" (p. 6, n. 3).

Assuming a bail hearing is required, it is also not clear whether a simple probable cause–type hearing is all that is needed or if a more adversarial proceeding is necessary. Because bail is set once charges have already been filed, it would seem that, at a minimum, counsel should be provided. In fact, in *United States* v. *Salerno* (481 U.S. 739 [1987]), the Court concluded that a federal preventive detention statute that provided for counsel, evidence presentation, and cross-examination was acceptable, but it did not state whether such rights should be afforded to the accused in every bail hearing. Thus, the question of what type of bail hearing is required, if any, remains unanswered. In some situations (and in certain jurisdictions), the bail decision is made during another hearing, such as the initial appearance.

The Pretrial Release Decision

The pretrial release decision has traditionally taken one of three forms. The first, and most common, results in release on bail. This is when the court collects a deposit from the individual being released in order to ensure that he or she will appear for later hearings. Second, some arrestees are released on their own recognizance, which means they simply promise to show up when required. Finally, in recent years, the courts have adopted a policy of preventive

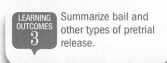

LEARNING OUTCOMES **3** Summarize bail and other types of pretrial release.

detention for certain individuals, which involves a calculation as to the arrestee's level of dangerousness and flight risk. Release is denied to those individuals likely to pose a threat to others or not likely to appear at their scheduled hearings.

Release on Bail

Pretrial release with **bail** is a common practice. Indeed, 18 U.S.C. Section 3142 provides that "upon all arrests in criminal cases, bail shall be admitted, except where the punishment may be death." Most states have adopted similar language in their constitutions. California's constitution, for example, provides that "all persons shall be bailable by sufficient sureties, unless for capital offenses when the proof is evidence or the presumption great" (Cal. Const. Art. I, Section 6). There is variability from state to state, however, because, once again, the Eighth Amendment's excessive bail provision has not been incorporated to the states through the due process clause of the Fourteenth Amendment.

The bail decision is sometimes problematic. More often than not, a judge sets bail according to the nature of the offense in question, not according to the accused's ability to pay.[3] The frequent result of this is that indigent defendants—no matter what they are accused of—languish in jail cells until their court dates because they cannot afford to post bail.

In response to many defendants' inability to post bail, the professional **bail bond agent** has stepped in.[4] These individuals collect a fee from the accused, usually a percentage of bail, and then post a bond so the accused can be released. If the accused shows up at trial, the agent collects his or her fee and gets his or her money back from the court. If the accused fails to show up, then the agent loses the amount posted. In order to avoid such an eventuality, bail bonds agents employ *bounty hunters*, whose job it is to catch the accused and bring him or her before the court. There is a misperception, however, that bail bonds agents can, with impunity, do whatever it takes to apprehend those who "skip" bail. Indeed, in response to concerns that such agents have been given too much authority, some states have adopted legislation to restrict their activities. Texas is perhaps most restrictive. Figure 10–1 reprints a Texas statute that sets forth the procedures bail bond agents must follow to re-arrest those who skip bail.

It is important to note an important flaw inherent in the bail bond agent system. The problem is that the agents, not the courts, gain a certain degree of power. Regardless of what amount the court sets as bail, bonds agents can then decide who gets released or who stays in jail based on the accused's ability to pay. Those who can pay the fee effectively buy their freedom, if only temporarily. Those who cannot pay stay in jail. The courts sit on the sidelines, essentially, while the whole bail bond process plays out. As described in the decision for *Pannell* v. *United States* (320 F.2d 698 [D.C.Cir. 1963]),

> Certainly the professional bondsman system as used in this District is odious at best. The effect of such a system is that the professional bondsmen hold the keys to the jail in their pockets. They determine for whom they will act as surety—who in their judgment is a good risk. The bad risks, in the bondsmen's judgment, and the ones who are unable to pay the bondsmen's fees, remain in jail. The court and the commissioner are relegated to the relatively unimportant chore of fixing the amount of bail. The result of this system in the District of Columbia is that most defendants, for months on end, languish in jail unable to make bond awaiting disposition of their cases. Instead of being allowed the opportunity of obtaining worthwhile employment to support their families, and perhaps to pay at least in part for their defense, almost 90 per cent of the defendants proceed in forma pauperis, thus casting an unfair burden on the members of the bar of this community who are required to represent these defendants without pay. (p. 699)

Release on One's Own Recognizance

Even though release on bail is the most common form of pretrial release, the courts have experimented with releasing people on their own recognizance. **Release on recognizance (ROR)** means that the accused is released with the assumption that he or she will show up for scheduled court hearings. Naturally, then, this method of pretrial release is reserved for those individuals who pose a minimal risk of flight.

New York City's Manhattan Bail Project was the first significant effort to explore the possibilities of ROR. This program, administered by the Vera Institute, focused on indigent defendants who, according to carefully set criteria, posed a minimal flight risk. Among the criteria considered were previous convictions, the nature of the offense, whether the accused was employed, and whether the accused had roots in the community (for example, a family to go back to). The program was a resounding success: Only 1.6% of those individuals recommended for ROR intentionally failed to appear at court.

The results of the Manhattan Bail Project prompted other cities around

---

(a) Any [bail bond agent], desiring to [apprehend] his [bond recipient] and after notifying the [bond recipient's] attorney, if the [bond recipient] is represented by an attorney, in a manner provided by Rule 21a, Texas Rules of Civil Procedure, of the [bail bond agent's] intention to surrender the [bond recipient], may file an affidavit of such intention before the court or magistrate before which the prosecution is pending. The affidavit must state:

(1) the court and cause number of the case;

(2) the name of the defendant;

(3) the offense with which the defendant is charged;

(4) the date of the bond;

(5) the cause for the [apprehension]; and

(6) that notice of the [bail bond agent's] intention to surrender the [bond recipient] has been given as required by this subsection.

FIGURE 10–1 Example of Bail Agent Re-Arrest Procedure.

the United States to adopt similar programs. In 1984, Congress passed the federal Bail Reform Act, which provided that any person charged with a noncapital offense "be ordered released pending trial on his personal recognizance or upon the execution of an unsecured appearance bond in an amount specified by the judicial officer, unless the officer determines . . . that such a release will not reasonably assure the appearance of the person as required" (18 U.S.C. Sections 3146–3152).

An important feature of this new legislation was that bail was to be considered only as one of many options to ensure the accused's appearance at trial. Among the other options were restrictions on travel and association, along with other conditions that would ensure the appearance of the accused (see 18 U.S.C. Section 3146[a]). The Bail Reform Act also provided that when bail was to be used, the money should be deposited with the court, not with a bail bond agent.

Although the federal government and many states still release people on their own recognizance, this practice is not regularly relied on for serious offenses. In fact, when the offense in question is serious and the accused presents a significant risk of flight, bail may be altogether denied, as the following subsection attests.

Preventive Detention: Denying Pretrial Release

Growing concern over crimes committed by defendants out on pretrial release prompted some reforms. In 1970, for example, the District of Columbia passed the first **preventive detention** statute, which authorized denial of bail to dangerous persons charged with certain offenses for up to 60 days (D.C. Code 1970 Section 23-1322). Then, Congress passed the federal Bail Reform Act of 1984 (18 U.S.C. Sections 3141–3150), which authorized judges to revoke pretrial release for firearms possession, failure to comply with curfew, and failure to comply with other conditions of release. The act also permitted detention for up to ten days of an individual who "may flee or pose a danger to any other person or the community" (Section 3142[d]).

Somewhat controversially, the Bail Reform Act of 1984 permitted pretrial detention for *more than* ten days of certain individuals. Thus, according to the act, if it is deemed that no pretrial release condition "will reasonably assure the appearance of the person as required and the safety of any other person and the community," then indefinite detention is acceptable. For a detention of this nature to conform to Fourth and Eighth Amendment restrictions, a hearing must be held to determine whether the case "involves a serious risk that the person will flee; [or] a serious risk that the person will obstruct or attempt to obstruct justice, or threaten, injure, or intimidate, a prospective witness or jury" (Section 3142[f]).

Criteria for Release

As indicated already, the Constitution does not guarantee the right to bail. Some people are denied bail, and others are granted bail. What criteria influence a judge's decision? Three factors are typically considered: (1) the accused's

Think About It...

Amount of Bail Mike Rhodes has been arrested for the crime of robbery, which carries a possible life sentence. The judge sets bail in the amount of $100,000. Rhodes has $12 to his name and no assets. (He rides the bus and lives with his parents.) As such, he cannot even afford the 10% deposit typically required to secure a bail bond. His only recourse is to sue under 42 U.S.C. Section 1983, claiming that his Fourteenth Amendment right to equal protection was violated when the judge set bail well beyond his means. Should his lawsuit succeed?

© Chris Howes/Wild Places Photography/Alamy

flight risk, (2) the level of dangerousness of the accused, and (3) the accused's financial status (see Figure 10–2).

Flight Risk

In *Stack* v. *Boyle*, the Supreme Court declared that the purpose of bail is to ensure the accused's appearance at trial:

Like the ancient practice of securing the oaths of responsible persons to stand as sureties for the accused, the modern practice of requiring a bail bond or the deposit of a sum of money subject to forfeiture serves as additional assurance of the presence of an accused. . . . Since the function of bail is limited, the fixing of bail for any individual defendant must be based upon standards

Flight Risk
The higher the flight risk, the higher the bail.

Dangerousness
The greater the defendant's perceived dangerousness, the higher the bail.

Financial Status
Bail, if granted, should not be set beyond the defendant's means.

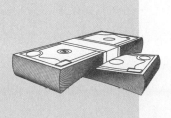

FIGURE 10–2 **Criteria for Release on Bail.**

relevant to the purpose of assuring the presence of that defendant. (p. 5)

This does not mean, though, that a judge can set an unrealistic bail amount, in light of the Eighth Amendment's admonition:

> Admission to bail always involves a risk that the accused will take flight. That is a calculated risk which the law takes as the price of our system of justice. . . . In allowance of bail, the duty of the judge is to reduce the risk by fixing an amount reasonably calculated to hold the accused available for trial and its consequence. But the judge is not free to make the sky the limit, because the Eighth Amendment to the Constitution says: "Excessive bail shall not be required." (p. 8)

In short, a delicate balance needs to be struck to ensure the accused's appearance at trial. Bail should be set at an amount designed to minimize the risk of flight, yet the amount set should not be so much that the accused cannot reasonably afford to pay it, either by cash or by bond.

Dangerousness

Aside from the obvious risk of flight, some defendants are particularly dangerous individuals. Thus, the courts sometimes see fit either to deny bail or to set the amount relatively high because of perceived dangerousness. In *United States* v. *Salerno*, the Supreme Court dealt with a challenge to the Bail Reform Act of 1984 that, among other things, dangerousness cannot be considered. In the Court's words,

> Nothing in the text of the Bail Clause [of the Eighth Amendment] limits permissible government considerations solely to questions of flight. The only arguable substantive limitation of the Bail Clause is that the Government's proposed conditions of release or detention not be "excessive" in light of the perceived evil. . . . [W]hen the government has admitted that its only interest is in preventing flight, bail must be set by a court at a sum designed to ensure that goal, and no more. . . . We

believe that when Congress has mandated detention on the basis of a compelling interest other than prevention of flight, as it has here, the Eighth Amendment does not require release on bail. (p. 754)

The issue of dangerousness, as it pertains to the bail decision, also came up in the case of *Schall* v. *Martin* **(467 U.S. 253 [1984])**. There, the Supreme Court upheld a statute that provided for detention of a juvenile who posed a serious risk of committing a crime while on release. The statute was criticized as essentially amounting to punishment without trial, but the Court decided that *punishment* only exists when the government's *intent* is to punish. And because the purpose of the state's detention policy was not to punish but rather to protect the community from a dangerous individual, it was deemed constitutional. Of course, given the problems inherent in predicting criminal behavior, the Court's argument is somewhat specious.

Financial Status

The courts usually take into account the accused's financial status in making a bail decision. Failure to do so can lead to irrational bail determinations. For example, if bail is set at a fixed amount, a poor individual will have a considerably more difficult time coming up with the required funds than a wealthy individual. Perhaps more important, if the wealthy individual views the amount as a "drop in the bucket," then he or she may not be motivated to show up for trial.

Surprisingly, bail can be denied simply because the accused is unable to pay it. In *Schilb* v. *Kuebel* **(404 U.S. 357 [1971])**, the Supreme Court took it upon itself to decide on the constitutionality of a state statute that provided that a criminal defendant who was not released on his or her own recognizance could (1) deposit 10% of the amount of set bail with the court, 10% of which would be forfeited to the court as *bail bond costs*, or (2) pay the full amount of bail, all of which would be refunded if the accused showed up at court. The defendant argued that the statute unfairly targeted indigent individuals because they were forced to choose the first option. However, the Supreme Court upheld the statute because "[i]t should be obvious that the poor man's real hope and avenue for relief is the personal recognizance provision" (p. 369). Furthermore, in the words of the Court, "[I]t is by no means clear that [the second option, paying the full amount,] is more attractive to the affluent defendant" (p. 370).

▶ The Preliminary Hearing

The **preliminary hearing** is distinguished from the initial appearance, the probable cause hearing, and the pretrial release hearing. It almost always takes place after one of these hearings as well as after the charging decision. According to the decision

The preliminary hearing is distinguished from the initial appearance, the probable cause hearing, and the pretrial release hearing.

in *Thies* v. *State* (178 Wis. 98 [1922]), the preliminary hearing is intended to prevent "hasty, malicious, improvident, and oppressive prosecutions" and to ensure that "there are substantial grounds upon which a prosecution may be based" (p. 103). Finally, the preliminary hearing resembles a criminal trial in that it is usually adversarial.

Just as the Constitution does not require a bail hearing, neither is a preliminary hearing required. This was the decision reached in **Lem Woon v. Oregon (229 U.S. 586 [1913])** and reaffirmed in *Gerstein* v. *Pugh*. Thus, it is up to each state to determine if such a hearing is warranted.

Fortunately, most states, as well as the federal government, require preliminary hearings, at least to a certain extent. Whether a preliminary hearing is required typically depends on a jurisdiction's method of filing criminal charges. In grand jury indictment jurisdictions (that is, those that *require* that charges be filed in the form of a grand jury indictment), if the prosecutor secures an indictment within a specified time period, no preliminary hearing is required. However, if a prosecutor proceeds by information, then the defendant will usually be entitled to a preliminary hearing before the charges are filed.

Whether a jurisdiction proceeds by indictment or information has important implications concerning the defendant's rights. The defendant does *not* enjoy the right to counsel during a grand jury proceeding. The defendant does not even enjoy the right to challenge the state's case. In a preliminary hearing, however, both rights exist. Thus, a zealous prosecutor in a jurisdiction that provides for either an indictment or an information-charging decision may opt for indictment because the accused will enjoy fewer rights. Of course, this issue may be moot because accused individuals can and often do waive their right to a preliminary hearing.

The Probable Cause Requirement

Assuming a preliminary hearing is required, the prosecutor has the burden of proving that the case should be *bound over* (that is, handed over) to a grand jury or go to trial. The standard of proof is *probable cause*. Invariably, this step is confused with the probable cause hearing. The two hearings can be distinguished as follows: A probable cause hearing dwells on the justification to arrest, whereas a preliminary hearing dwells on whether probable cause exists to proceed with a trial. This is a critical distinction and is often responsible for holding separate probable cause and preliminary hearings in certain states.

The reason for setting probable cause as the appropriate standard for a preliminary hearing is that setting a *higher* standard would essentially make trial pointless. To require proof beyond a reasonable doubt, for example, would make holding a later criminal trial redundant. On the other hand, some people favor having more proof than probable cause because once a probable cause hearing has taken place, the preliminary hearing seems somewhat redundant. To minimize some of the confusion, one court observed that "probable cause to arrest does not automatically mean that the Commonwealth has sufficient competent legal evidence to justify the costs both to the defendant and to the Commonwealth of a full trial" (*Myers* v. *Commonwealth*, 363 Mass. 843 [1973], p. 849).

Basically, the prosecutor needs to convince the judge that there is enough evidence to proceed with a trial. More specifically, there must be enough evidence to make a judge or jury contemplate which case is more convincing: that of the prosecution or the defense. If it is clear that the state has no case but perhaps had probable cause for arrest, the court will order that the would-be defendant be released.

Procedural Issues

Because a preliminary hearing is adversarial in nature, it seems sensible that the right to counsel should apply. According to the Supreme Court in **Coleman v. Alabama (399 U.S. 1 [1970])**, it does, and the state must provide counsel if the accused is indigent. The Court declared that the preliminary hearing is a critical stage of the criminal process: "Plainly the guiding hand of counsel at the preliminary hearing is essential to protect the indigent accused against an erroneous and improper prosecution" (p. 9).

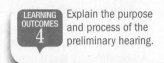

LEARNING OUTCOMES 4 — Explain the purpose and process of the preliminary hearing.

Evidence procedures in a preliminary hearing are markedly different than those in a criminal trial. First, the Federal Rules of Criminal Procedure allow hearsay evidence in preliminary hearings, although not explicitly.[5] By contrast, *hearsay evidence* (that is, what one person previously heard and then repeats while testifying in court) is restricted in a criminal trial. Also, the exclusionary rule does not technically apply in preliminary hearings. Actually, it is not so much that the rule does not apply but rather that the preliminary hearing is an inappropriate stage of the criminal process in which to object to evidence. As the Federal Rules of Criminal Procedure also state, the defendant "may not object to evidence on the ground that it was unlawfully acquired."[6] (Note that the Federal Rules of Criminal Procedure apply to federal courts, not state courts. So some states may maintain different procedures.)

Another procedural matter in the preliminary hearing concerns the right to cross-examine witnesses as well as to use compulsory process to require their appearance. Although these rights exist at criminal trials, preliminary hearings restrict them somewhat. In fact, the Supreme Court stated that there is no constitutional right to cross-examine at the preliminary hearing (*Goldsby* v. *United States*, 160 U.S. 70 [1895]). The court has discretion over the extent of cross-examination, but the bulk of it is reserved for trial.

Some have expressed concern that too much cross-examination at a preliminary hearing may turn it into a full-blown criminal trial. But one court has stated that "past experience indicates that trial strategy usually prevents such a result as both the prosecution and the defense wish to withhold as much of their case as possible" (*Myers* v. *Commonwealth*). Furthermore, "defense tactics usually mitigate against putting the defendant on the stand or presenting exculpatory testimony at the preliminary hearing unless defense counsel believes this evidence is compelling enough to overcome the prosecution's case" (pp. 856–857).

▶ The Arraignment

Once a person has been formally charged, he or she will be arraigned. The purpose of the **arraignment** is to formally notify the defendant of the charge lodged against him or her. Also at the arraignment, the defendant enters one of three pleas: (1) **guilty**, (2) **not guilty**, or (3) *nolo contendere*. A plea of guilty is an admission by the defendant of every allegation in the indictment or information. Such a plea may be entered for a number of reasons. For example, the defendant may simply elect to be honest and admit responsibility. The defendant may also plead guilty after having made a plea agreement with the prosecution.

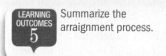

A plea of not guilty is fairly self-explanatory. The defendant formally contends that he or she did not commit the crime in question. A plea of not guilty will result in a full-blown criminal trial, especially for a serious crime. Finally, a plea of *nolo contendere* means "I do not desire to contest the action." It resembles a guilty plea but is different in the sense that it may not be used against the defendant in any later civil litigation that arises from the acts that led to the criminal charge. Also, in some jurisdictions, if the defendant enters a plea of *nolo contendere*, the court may not ask the defendant whether he or she committed the crime in question. But with a guilty plea, the defendant is required to allocute. **Allocution** is when the defendant explains to the judge exactly what he or she did and why. The allocution is documented in court records and can be used against the defendant in related civil proceedings.

See Figure 10–3 for a summary of the pretrial procedure discussed thus far.

▶ Discovery

Criminal (as well as civil) trials in the United States are carefully choreographed events with few unpredictable twists and turns. In fact, as many a litigator will attest, most criminal trials are relatively boring and predictable. Even the most celebrated criminal trial of the 1990s, the O. J. Simpson trial, put the most attentive of observers to sleep at times.

Trials in this country are rarely exciting for several reasons. First, most prosecutors and defense attorneys are not great orators. And second, given the process of *discovery*, each side *knows* what evidence the other side will present, with few exceptions.

Discovery is the process by which each party to a case learns of the evidence that the opposition will present. The Federal

The purpose of the arraignment is to formally notify the defendant of the charge lodged against him or her.

Most criminal trials are relatively boring and predictable.

Probable Cause Hearing

The probable cause hearing is not *required* by the Constitution. Nevertheless, a probable cause determination needs to be made at some stage of the criminal process. If the arrest is by warrant, the hearing is not necessary. If the arrest is warrantless, then a probable cause hearing is necessary but only if a preliminary hearing is not set to take place immediately. Also, if the arrest is premised on a grand jury indictment, a probable cause hearing will not be necessary. The purpose of the probable cause hearing is to avoid unnecessarily lengthy detention unsupported by probable cause.

Pretrial Release

A few court decisions seem to suggest that a separate pretrial release hearing is required, but the Supreme Court has offered no clarification on this matter. As a practical matter, it is sometimes worthwhile to make the bail decision in another hearing, such as the initial appearance. Today, whether a bail hearing is required hinges on the jurisdiction in question and the nature of the offense.

Preliminary Hearing

The preliminary hearing is required but only in limited circumstances and for certain offenses—usually felonies. If a prosecutor obtains a grand jury indictment within a short period of time, a preliminary hearing may not be necessary. On the other hand, if the prosecutor proceeds with information, then a preliminary hearing may be required.

Arraignment

Once a person has been charged with a crime, he or she will be arraigned. At the arraignment, the defendant will be notified of the charges against him or her and be allowed to enter a formal plea of guilty, not guilty, or *nolo contendere*.

FIGURE 10–3 Summary of Pretrial Proceedings.

Rules of Criminal Procedure provide that the defendant may, upon request, *discover* from the prosecution

- any written statements or transcriptions of oral statements made by the defendant that are in the prosecution's possession,

- the defendant's prior criminal record, and

- documents, photographs, tangible items, results from physical and mental evaluations, and other forms of real evidence considered *material* to the prosecution's case.[7]

Evidence is considered *material* if it is consequential to the case or, more simply, capable of influencing the outcome of the case. If the defense requests items in the second or third categories, the prosecution will be granted *reciprocal discovery*, where it learns of the defense's evidence.

Rule 16 of the Federal Rules of Criminal Procedure seems to permit a great deal of discovery, but it is actually restrictive. Several states permit even more discovery, such as the names and addresses of all persons known to have any information concerning the case. This means that the prosecution must provide the defense with a list of *all* individuals likely to give testimony at trial—and vice versa.

Discovery ends where strategy begins. That is, although both sides are given great latitude in terms of learning what evidence the opposition intends to use, strategy does not need to be shared. For example, the method of argument that the prosecution wishes to use in order to convince the jury of a particular fact is not subject to discovery. Similarly, the order in which the defense seeks to call witnesses need not be communicated to the prosecution. Strategy is also referred to as *work product*. Work product is not part of the discovery process.

The sections that follow focus on discovery by the prosecution, discovery by the defense, and constitutional issues raised in the discovery process. Be reminded that, consistent with the title of this chapter, discovery is part of the *pretrial process*. It takes place in the hours and days leading up to the criminal trial. But if, for example, a new witness becomes available during the course of a trial, discovery can take place later in the criminal process, as well.

Discovery by the Prosecution

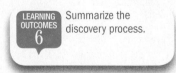
LEARNING OUTCOMES 6 · Summarize the discovery process.

Discovery by the prosecution is relatively limited because of the constitutional rights enjoyed by criminal defendants. For example, the defense cannot be compelled to provide the prosecution with incriminating information, particularly in the form of statements and admissions. The scope of prosecutorial discovery has been addressed repeatedly in the courts via the Fifth and Sixth Amendments.

Fifth Amendment Restrictions

What if the defense wishes to present an alibi at trial or to assert a defense to criminal liability? Should the prosecutor be

Discovery ends where strategy begins.

Discovery by the prosecution is relatively limited because of the constitutional rights enjoyed by criminal defendants.

permitted to discover this information? The Supreme Court faced the alibi issue in **Williams v. Florida (399 U.S. 78 [1970])**. Florida had a *notice of alibi statute*, which provided that the defendant had to permit discovery of alibi defenses coupled with a list of witnesses who would support them. The Court found that this type of discovery does not violate the Fifth Amendment because it is not self-incriminating. In fact, the purpose of an alibi defense is to exculpate (that is, clear) the defendant. According to the Court, "Nothing in the Fifth Amendment privilege entitles a defendant as a matter of constitutional right to await the end of the State's case before announcing the nature of his defense, any more than it entitles him to await the jury's verdict on the State's case-in-chief before deciding whether or not to take the stand himself" (p. 85).

The *Williams* decision extends to other defenses, as well. For example, if the defense intends to argue that the defendant is not guilty by reason of insanity, then the prosecutor needs to be notified in advance of this intention. Alternatively, if the defense intends to argue that the defendant acted in self-defense, then the prosecution should be notified. The reason for requiring this notification is that it provides the prosecutor with an opportunity to plan its argument to the contrary.

Sixth Amendment Restrictions

The Sixth Amendment provides, in relevant part, that the accused enjoys the right "to have compulsory process for obtaining witnesses in his favor." As such, some constitutional challenges to the discovery process have been raised on these grounds.

For example, in **United States v. Nobles (422 U.S. 225 [1975])**, the defense attempted to call to the stand a private investigator whose testimony would have cast doubt on the prosecution's case. The trial judge ruled that the investigator could not testify until the prosecution received portions of the investigator's pretrial investigative report. The Supreme Court upheld this decision. The defense argued that this decision infringed on the accused's right to compulsory process—namely, to call the investigator to the stand. But according to the Court, "The Sixth Amendment does not confer the right to present testimony free from the legitimate demands of the adversarial system; one cannot invoke the Sixth Amendment as a justification for presenting what might have been a half-truth" (p. 241). The defense further argued that being forced to supply information from the investigator's report violated attorney/client privilege, but the Court countered by concluding that attorney/client privilege was basically waived when the defense decided to have the investigator testify about the contents of his report.

A second Sixth Amendment issue that has been raised with regard to discovery is whether, if the defense does not inform the prosecution that a particular witness will testify, that testimony can be excluded. In *Taylor* v. *Illinois* (484 U.S. 400 [1988]), the defense called a witness who had not been on a witness list supplied to the prosecution before trial. The trial court excluded

the witness's testimony, citing a violation of discovery procedure. The defendant appealed, arguing that exclusion of the witness's testimony violated the compulsory process clause of the Sixth Amendment. However, the Supreme Court ruled that exclusion of the testimony was appropriate and did not violate the Sixth Amendment. The purpose of discovery, the Court noted, is to "minimize the risk that fabricated testimony will be believed" (p. 413). (Also see *Michigan* v. *Lucas*, 500 U.S. 145 [1991], for further attention to the relationship between certain Sixth Amendment rights and the discovery process.)

In summary, *Nobles* and *Taylor* suggest that it is relatively difficult to infringe on a defendant's Sixth Amendment rights, as far as discovery is concerned. If the defense takes steps to secure a tactical advantage over the prosecution, either by failing to supply a complete list of witnesses or the documents about which witnesses will testify, then the Sixth Amendment right to compulsory process will not be violated. Thus, this particular Sixth Amendment right is a qualified one. Compulsory process must be preceded by granting the prosecution appropriate discovery.

Discovery by the Defense

Naturally, discovery should benefit the *defense* more than the *prosecution*. After all, the prosecution presents the state's case against the defendant; it is only sensible that the defense should learn the nature of the prosecution's case. Generally, though, the prosecution has the most information of both parties because it has to prove *beyond* a reasonable doubt that the defendant committed the crime. The defense, by contrast, only needs to raise reasonable doubt in the minds of the jurors that the defendant did *not* commit the crime.

It was already pointed out that in *Williams* v. *Florida* the Supreme Court required the defense to notify the prosecution as to any defenses, alibi or otherwise, it would assert as well as a list of witnesses who would testify in support of those defenses. In **Wardius v. Oregon (412 U.S. 470 [1973])**, the Court declared that this type of discovery must be *reciprocal*. That is, the Court

held that the prosecution must provide the defense with a list of witnesses who will testify in rebuttal to the defendant's alibi or defense:

> [I]n the absence of a strong showing of state interests to the contrary, discovery must be a two-way street. The State may not insist that trial be run as a "search for truth" so far as defense witnesses are concerned, while maintaining "poker game" secrecy for its own witnesses. It is fundamentally unfair to require a defendant to divulge the details of his own case while at the same time subjecting him to the hazard of surprise concerning refutation of the very pieces of evidence which he disclosed to the State. (pp. 475–476)

A key feature of the *Wardius* decision is that it applies only to evidence that is truly reciprocal. More specifically, if the defense supplies the prosecution with a list of witnesses who will testify, the prosecution is not necessarily required to supply the defense with something wholly disconnected from a witness list. This was the decision reached in *United States* v. *Armstrong* (517 U.S. 456 [1996]), in which the Supreme Court held that the prosecution need only supply the defense with evidence that is "material to the preparation of the defendant's case" (p. 462).

Basically, if the evidence the defense wants to discover is a "shield," or used to refute the state's case, access will be granted. If, by contrast, the evidence is a "sword," or intended to challenge prosecutorial conduct, access will not be granted.

In *State* v. *Eads* (166 N.W.2d 766 [Iowa 1969]), one court summarized the restrictions on defense discovery even for "shield" purposes. If a *state interest* is likely to be compromised, then the prosecution is not required to disclose evidence to the defense, even if such evidence is intended to be used by the defense to challenge or refute the state's case. State interest precludes discovery by the defense under these circumstances:

> (1) It would afford the defendant increased opportunity to produce perjured testimony and to fabricate evidence to meet the State's case; (2) witnesses would be subject to bribe, threat and intimidation; (3) since the State cannot compel the defendant to disclose ... evidence [protected by the Fifth Amendment], disclosure by the State would afford the defendant an unreasonable advantage at trial; and (4) disclosure is unnecessary in any event because of the other sources of information which defendant has under existing law. (p. 769)

In the wake of *Eads*, several states have imposed restrictions on defense discovery when certain state interests have been called into question. For example, many states prohibit discovery of the identities of prosecution witnesses until after they have testified so as to prevent defense from tampering with (or threatening of) prosecution witnesses.

The Prosecution's Duty to Disclose Exculpatory Evidence

As a matter of due process, the prosecution has a constitutional duty to reveal exculpatory evidence to the defense. If the prosecution obtains evidence suggesting that the defendant is

1963

Brady v. Maryland, 373 U.S. 83 The prosecution is required to disclose exculpatory evidence to the defense. Failure to do so violates due process.

1976

United States v. Agurs, 427 U.S. 97 "A prosecutor does not violate the constitutional duty of disclosure unless his omission is sufficiently significant to result in the denial of the defendant's right to a fair trial."

not guilty, it needs to inform the defense of this fact. This requirement is an ongoing duty, both before and during trial. However, if the evidence clearly establishes factual innocence, it should be disclosed before the trial (*Unites States* v. *Ruiz*, 536 U.S. 622 [2002]). Numerous Supreme Court cases have emphasized this important requirement (see the accompanying timeline for a summary).

In *Mooney* v. *Holohan* (294 U.S. 103 [1935]), the prosecution knowingly used perjured testimony to convict the defendant. The Court held that due process is violated when the prosecution "has contrived a conviction through the pretense of a trial which in truth is but used as a means of depriving a defendant of liberty through a deliberate deception of court and jury by the presentation of testimony known to be perjured." In *Mooney*, the prosecution *arranged* to have a witness give false testimony. Later, the Court applied the rule in *Mooney* to cases where perjured testimony is *not* arranged by the prosecution but, rather, given by a witness on his or her own volition. If the prosecution later learns that the testimony is false, it is bound to notify the defense (*Alcorta* v. *Texas*, 355 U.S. 28 [1957]).

In *Napue* v. *Illinois* (360 U.S. 264 [1959]), the Supreme Court held that the prosecution is also bound to disclose its knowledge of false testimony that affects the credibility of a witness. In that case, a witness testified falsely that the prosecution had not promised him leniency for his willingness to cooperate. Because the prosecutor knew the witness's testimony was false and did nothing to correct it, the defendant's conviction was reversed, as "[t]he jury's estimate of the truthfulness and reliability of a given witness may well be determinative of guilt or innocence, and it is upon such subtle factors as the possible interest of the witness in testifying falsely that a defendant's life or liberty may depend."

In **Brady v. Maryland (373 U.S. 83 [1963])**, perhaps the most important case in this area of law, the Supreme Court drastically altered its previous decisions concerning the prosecution's duty to disclose exculpatory evidence. The Court held that "the suppression by the prosecution of evidence favorable to an accused upon request violates due process where the evidence is *material either to guilt or to punishment*, irrespective of the

good faith or bad faith of the prosecution" (emphasis added). The Court also eloquently stated:

> Society wins not only when the guilty are convicted but when criminal trials are fair; our system of the administration of justice suffers when any accused is treated unfairly. An inscription on the walls of the Department of Justice states the proposition candidly for the federal domain: "The United States wins its point whenever justice is done its citizens in the courts." . . . A prosecution that withholds evidence on demand of an accused which, if made available, would tend to exculpate him or reduce the penalty helps shape a trial that bears heavily on the defendant. That casts the prosecutor in the role of an architect of a proceeding that does not comport with standards of justice, even though, as in the present case, his action is not "the result of guile." (pp. 87–88)

Whether evidence is *material* is not entirely clear, but in *United States* v. *Agurs* (427 U.S. 97 [1976]), the Supreme Court offered some clarification. The defendant stabbed and killed a man with the victim's knife. She claimed self-defense but was nevertheless found guilty. The defense argued that because the prosecution had not disclosed that the victim had a prior criminal record, the conviction should be reversed. The Court disagreed, stating that the victim's prior criminal record was not material enough to the question of guilt or innocence. Important to this decision is the fact that the defense did not request information about the victim's prior criminal record at trial, only on appeal. Had the defense explicitly requested such information at trial, a different decision probably would have resulted.

An obvious problem is posed by the *Agurs* decision: If the defense does not know what exculpatory evidence the prosecution has, it cannot request that evidence. Does this mean that the defense should be denied access to exculpatory evidence if it does not request it? In *United States* v. *Bagley* (473 U.S. 667 [1985]), the Court sought to answer this question but, unfortunately, offered little clarification. The defense had posed a broad request to the prosecution for discovery of "any deals, promises or inducements made to [prosecution] witnesses in exchange for their testimony." The prosecution failed to disclose some of

1985	1995
United States v. Bagley, 473 U.S. 667 "Nondisclosed evidence at issue is material only if there is a reasonable probability that, had the evidence been disclosed to the defense, the result of the proceeding would have been different." A 'reasonable probability' is a probability sufficient to undermine confidence in the outcome.	**Kyles v. Whitley, 514 U.S. 419** The Supreme Court outlines four factors that should be considered in determining the meaning of "reasonable probability" under *Bagley*.

the requested information, but on appeal, the Supreme Court held that this action did not constitute a due process violation. According to the Court, there was no "reasonable probability" that the exculpatory evidence would have influenced the outcome of the case.

What amounts to a "reasonable probability" that the outcome of the case may be altered by failure to disclose exculpatory evidence? In **Kyles v. Whitley (514 U.S. 419 [1995])**, the Court identified four elements that should be considered. First, reasonable probability does not mean a preponderance of evidence but something less. Second, when exculpatory evidence is included, the reasonable probability standard does not require the defense to show that the other evidence presented by the prosecution is insufficient to prove guilt. Third, once the defense demonstrates a reasonable probability of a different outcome, its job is done; the appellate court cannot decide that the prosecution's failure to disclose evidence amounted to a harmless error. Finally, although the prosecution is not required to present every shred of evidence that may prove helpful to the defense, it "must be assigned the consequent responsibility to gauge the likely net effect of all such evidence and make disclosure when the point of 'reasonable probability' is reached."

In summary, the prosecution's constitutional duty to disclose exculpatory evidence hinges on whether such evidence would have a reasonable probability of changing the outcome of the case. Who makes the decision as to what constitutes a reasonable probability that the outcome of a case will be changed if exculpatory evidence is not disclosed? Depending on the case, it is usually the judge or the prosecutor who makes the decision.

Access to DNA Evidence

In *District Attorney* v. *Osborne* (557 U.S. 52 [2009]), featured in this chapter's opening story, the Supreme Court was confronted with the question of whether the due process clause requires the state to turn over DNA evidence to those found guilty of criminal activity. It decided that there is no such duty and that legislatures are the proper forum to set appropriate rules governing the release of DNA evidence. This decision makes clear, then, that there is no constitutional duty to disclose possibly exculpatory evidence *after* trial. "After trial" means post-sentencing.

In 2011, the Supreme Court decided another DNA-related case (*Skinner* v. *Switzer*, 562 U.S. [2011]). Convicted inmates who seek access to DNA evidence to prove their innocence may file Section 1983 lawsuits, but not proceed via petitioning for habeas corpus relief. So, although the Court seemed to close the door on DNA access in *Osborne*, it cracked it open again in *Skinner*. Federal courts may hear inmates' claims that their state DNA testing procedures are flawed, but the mechanism for doing so is via filing a Section 1983 civil rights lawsuit.

Access to Eyewitness Statements

In *Smith* v. *Cain* (565 U.S. [2012]), the Supreme Court decided whether disclosure to the defense of police files containing eyewitness statements was material, where such statements are the only evidence linking the defendant to the crime in question. It held in part: ". . . the eyewitness's testimony was the *only* evidence linking Smith to the crime, and the eyewitness's undisclosed statements contradicted his testimony. The eyewitness's statements were plainly material, and the State's failure to disclose those statements to the defense thus violated *Brady*."

The Prosecution's Duty to Preserve Evidence

Just as it is bound to share exculpatory evidence, the prosecution is also constitutionally bound to *preserve* evidence. Simply put, the prosecution cannot destroy exculpatory evidence in an effort to gain a conviction. To do so would be a violation of due process. For the defense to convince the court that the prosecution has destroyed exculpatory evidence, it must demonstrate three facts: (1) that the evidence was expected to "play a significant role in the suspect's defense," (2) that the evidence was of "such a nature that the defendant would be unable to obtain comparable evidence by other reasonably available means," and (3) that the destruction of the evidence was a result of "official animus toward [the defendant]or . . . a conscious effort to suppress exculpatory evidence" (*California* v. *Trombetta*, 467 U.S. 479 [1984]).

A case that offers some clarification concerning these three requirements is **Arizona v. Youngblood (488 U.S. 51 [1988])**.

Disclosure of Exculpatory Evidence Leonard Baum was convicted of first-degree murder and sentenced to death. In preparing an appeal, Baum's attorney learned that the state never disclosed certain evidence favorable to Baum. That evidence included eyewitness statements taken by the police following the murder, statements made to the police by an informant who was never called to testify, and a list of the license numbers of cars parked at the crime scene on the night of the murder, which did not include Baum's car. Baum argues that had this evidence been disclosed at his trial, there would have been a reasonable probability that he would not have been found guilty. Should Baum be granted a new trial?

© Andrew Rubtsov/Alamy

There, the Supreme Court stated that "unless a criminal defendant can show bad faith on the part of the police [or prosecution], failure to preserve potentially useful evidence does not constitute due process of law" (p. 58).

Not only must prosecutors preserve evidence but so, too, must police. Without a proper **chain of custody** (and sometimes even with one), the defense will allege that the evidence was tampered with or tainted in such away that it cannot prove the defendant's involvement in a crime. As such, prosecutors' offices and police departments are very concerned with maintaining a proper chain of custody.

A Meritorious Brady Claim?

Read the following facts from a real case (*United States* v. *Rodriguez*, 489 Fed.Appx. 528 [3d Cir. 2012]):

> In September 2007, Philadelphia plainclothes police officers on patrol in an unmarked car observed Stanley Rodriguez conversing with the driver of a car stopped in the middle of the street. In plain view, Rodriguez passed a rolled up book bag to the driver, who placed two rectangular objects wrapped in green tape into the bag and returned it to Rodriguez. One of the officers identified the objects as kilogram packages of cocaine from their shape and wrapping, and the officers followed Rodriguez. Alerted by a bystander to the presence of the police, Rodriguez fled on foot, throwing the book bag onto the roof of a nearby garage. The officers apprehended Rodriguez, and then retrieved the book bag containing the two green-wrapped objects. Laboratory analysis subsequently determined the packages contained two kilograms of cocaine.
>
> Rodriguez was subsequently indicted [for drug offenses]. Prior to trial, the government informed Rodriguez that several officers involved in his arrest had been subject to complaints unrelated to his case [and were being] investigated by the Philadelphia Police Internal Affairs Division (IAD). The government subsequently informed Rodriguez that most of the investigations involved Officer Norman, whose credibility had been undermined in the course of an investigation and against whom one investigation remained open, but that allegations of improper search [activities] had resulted in a finding of departmental violation against Officers Reynolds and Walker and remained open against Officers Betts, O'Malley, and McGrory. Rodriguez filed a motion for...review of the internal affairs files concerning the open investigations, which the government opposed, noting in its brief that it did not intend to call Officer Norman. The District Court denied the motion, holding the IAD investigation into an alleged improper search was neither material nor exculpatory as required under *Brady*.

Consider the following questions about this case:

1. Is the *Brady* claim in this case meritorious?
2. Should Rodriguez have been allowed to call as witnesses the officers involved in arresting him?
3. What if Officer Norman had been convicted of a crime for his misconduct? Would that have altered the *Brady* inquiry?

LEARNING OUTCOMES 1

Explain the purpose and process of the initial appearance.

The pretrial process typically begins with an initial appearance. This is where, at a minimum, the accused is advised of the charges against him or her. In a misdemeanor case, the trial may take place at this stage. Also, the accused may be advised of his or her privilege against self-incrimination as well as the right to appointed counsel, if he or she is indigent.

1. What is booking?

2. What is the initial appearance and what is its purpose?

booking The process by which an arrest is officially documented and the arrestee is placed into custody. During booking, the arrestee's personal items will be inventoried and he or she will be fingerprinted and/or photographed.

initial appearance The first appearance of an accused person before a judge. Trial may occur for misdemeanors.

LEARNING OUTCOMES 2

Explain the purpose and process of the probable cause hearing.

If the defendant is arrested without a warrant, a separate court hearing may be held to determine whether probable cause to arrest existed. This determination can be made independent of any other hearing. The probable cause hearing, if required, needs to be held promptly after arrest, usually within 48 hours.

Key Cases

Gerstein v. Pugh

Riverside County v. McLaughlin

1. What is the probable cause hearing?

2. When is a probable cause hearing not required?

probable cause hearing A hearing in which a judge decides whether there was probable cause for arrest. If the arrest was with a warrant, the probable cause hearing is not necessary. Also called a *Gerstein* hearing (for the Supreme Court's decision in *Gerstein* v. *Pugh*).

LEARNING OUTCOMES 3

Summarize bail and other types of pretrial release.

The accused may be released on bail, in which case he or she deposits a certain amount of money with the court (possibly through a bail bond agent) as an incentive to show up for later hearings. Failure to show up will result in, among other things, forfeiture of the bail money. A defendant can also be released on his or her own recognizance (ROR). At the other extreme, a defendant who is presumed to pose a significant risk of flight may be held without bail. This tactic is known as preventive detention.

Key Cases

Stack v. Boyle

Schall v. Martin

Schilb v. Kuebel

1. What methods of pretrial release are available? Define each.

2. Explain the criteria for pretrial release.

pretrial release One of several methods to release a defendant prior to his or her trial date.

bail A process by which a defendant pays a certain amount of money in order to be released from jail prior to his or her trial date. Defendants who appear for trial receive their money back. Those who fail to appear for trial forfeit the bail amount.

bail bond agent A professional who posts the defendant's bail in exchange for a fee.

release on recognizance (ROR) The accused is released with the assumption that he or she will show up for scheduled court hearings.

preventive detention The act of denying bail to certain defendants who are either dangerous or pose a high flight risk.

Explain the purpose and process of the preliminary hearing.

The preliminary hearing differs from the other hearings already discussed in that it is intended to be a check on the prosecution's charging decision. A preliminary hearing is generally not required, however, if (1) the defendant waives it or (2) the prosecutor proceeds by indictment. In the latter instance, the grand jury essentially serves as an appropriate check on the charging decision.

Key Cases

Lem Woon v. *Oregon*

Coleman v. *Alabama*

1. What is the purpose of the preliminary hearing?
2. When is the preliminary hearing required?
3. What rights does the defendant enjoy during the preliminary hearing?

preliminary hearing A hearing that serves as a check on the prosecutor's charging decision. The standard of proof is probable cause, and the main inquiry in the hearing is whether there is probable cause to take the case to trial. The preliminary hearing is to be distinguished from the initial appearance, the probable cause hearing, and the pretrial release hearing. It almost always takes place after one of these hearings as well as after the charging decision.

Summarize the arraignment process.

After the preliminary hearing (or grand jury indictment), the arraignment is held. At this stage, the defendant is formally notified of the charges against him or her. In addition, he or she enters a plea of guilty, not guilty, or *nolo contendere.*

1. What occurs at the arraignment stage?
2. How does arraignment differ from the preliminary hearing and the probable cause hearing?

arraignment A hearing in which the defendant is formally notified of the charge lodged against him or her. The defendant also enters one of three pleas: (1) guilty, (2) not guilty, or (3) *nolo contendere.*

guilty A plea in which the defendant claims responsibility for the crime with which he or she has been charged.

not guilty A plea in which the defendant does not claim responsibility for the crime with which he or she has been charged. A not guilty plea is not the same as a plea of innocent. There is no plea of innocent.

nolo contendere A plea similar to guilty with a literal meaning of "I do not desire to contest the action." It resembles a guilty plea but is different in the sense that it may not be used against the defendant in any later civil litigation that arises from the acts that led to the criminal charge.

allocution When the defendant explains to the judge exactly what he or she did and why. The defendant is usually required to allocute when he or she pleads guilty.

Summarize the discovery process.

Discovery is the process whereby the prosecution advises the defense of the evidence it will use to secure a conviction. The defense must also disclose the evidence it intends to use to exonerate the defendant. Discovery tips in favor of the defense.

Key Cases

Williams v. *Florida*

United States v. *Nobles*

Wardius v. *Oregon*

Brady v. *Maryland*

Kyles v. *Whitley*

Arizona v. *Youngblood*

1. What is discovery?
2. Who benefits most from discovery and why?
3. Summarize the prosecutor's duty to disclose exculpatory evidence.

discovery The process by which each party to a case learns of the evidence that the opposition will present.

chain of custody A chronological documentation (or paper trail) showing how seized evidence has been preserved, transferred, analyzed, and disposed of. It is mainly a record of the individuals who have had physical possession of the evidence at any point during the criminal process.

11

"The constitution imposes a number of important restrictions on prosecutors, grand juries, and the right to counsel."

Prosecutors, Grand Juries, and Defense Attorneys

1 Describe the prosecutor's role, prosecutorial discretion, and the issues surrounding prosecutorial misconduct.

2 Explain the purpose, functions, and powers of the grand jury.

3 Outline the development of the right to counsel.

INTRO A DEFENSE ATTORNEY CONCEDES GUILT

Joe Elton Nixon was charged with murder. His defense attorney said the following as part of his opening statements at trial:

> In this case, there won't be any question, none whatsoever, that my client, Joe Elton Nixon, caused Jeannie Bickner's death. . . . [T]hat fact will be proved to your satisfaction beyond any doubt. . . . This case is about the death of Joe Elton Nixon and whether it should occur within the next few years by electrocution or maybe its natural expiration after a lifetime of confinement.
>
> Now, in arriving at your verdict, in your penalty recommendation, for we will get that far, you are going to learn many facts . . . about Joe Elton Nixon. Some of those facts are going to be good. That may not seem clear to you at this time. But, and sadly, most of the things you learn of Joe Elton Nixon are not going to be good. But, I'm suggesting to you that when you have seen all the testimony, heard all the testimony and the evidence that has been shown, there are going to be reasons why you should recommend that his life be spared.

Would an effective defense attorney admit at the outset of a trial that his or her client is guilty? That is precisely what Nixon's attorney did. This case, *Florida* v. *Nixon* (543 U.S. 175 [2004]), went to the U.S. Supreme Court, which was tasked with determining whether what the defense attorney did violated Nixon's Sixth Amendment

Chris Ryan/Getty Images

right to counsel. It decided, interestingly, that there was no violation, that Nixon's attorney was effective. The Court said that in certain cases, "Mounting a 'defendant did not commit the crime' defense risks destroying counsel's penalty phase credibility and may incline the jury against leniency for the defendant." Nixon's attorney tried to spare Nixon's life because he realized there was not much else he could do.

DISCUSS Do you think Nixon's defense attorney was effective?

▶ The Prosecutor

The prosecutor performs a valuable function in reinforcing the notion that a crime is an offense against the state. In fact, Article II, Section 3, of the U.S. Constitution states that the executive branch of the federal government "shall take Care that the Laws be faithfully executed." This constitutionally mandated duty to execute the law usually falls on prosecutors. Of course, police officers, as part of the executive branch, do their part to execute the laws, but a strong argument can be made that prosecutors possess even more authority because of their ability to decide whether to bring formal charges against suspected criminals.

Just as police officers have the discretion to decide whether to make an arrest, so, too, do prosecutors have enormous discretion. As the Supreme Court noted in *Bordenkircher* v. *Hayes* (434 U.S. 357 [1978]), "[S]o long as the prosecutor has probable cause to believe that the accused committed an offense defined by statute, the decision whether or not to prosecute, and what charge to file or bring before a grand jury, generally rests entirely on his discretion" (p. 364). Figure 11–1 presents portions of a federal prosecutor's charging document (aka, "information").

Prosecutors do not have *unlimited* discretion, however. There are important restrictions on their decision to charge. Some stem from the Constitution, whereas others stem from statutes and other related sources.

The Charging Decision

The prosecutor generally has the authority to decide whether to proceed with charges. This is known as **prosecutorial discretion**. He or she can elect not to charge for a number of reasons, even over strenuous objection on the part of the complainant or victim. The prosecutor's discretion can be further manifested by the act of *plea bargaining*; that is, he or she can accept a guilty plea for a lesser offense than the one charged. Finally, prosecutors sometimes have to answer to authorities that mandate, or at least strongly encourage, prosecution.

Deciding Not to Prosecute

The most obvious reason for nonprosecution is lack of evidence. The prosecutor may determine that, based on the evidence presented to him or her by the police, the suspect is innocent. In such an event, there would be no point in proceeding to trial on the slight chance that a conviction would be obtained. Even if the prosecutor *believes* the suspect is guilty, if there is not enough *evidence* to obtain a conviction, he or she will likely elect not to prosecute.

There are other reasons not to prosecute, as well. For example, even if the state's case is strong, there may be an incentive

UNITED STATES DISTRICT COURT
NORTHERN DISTRICT OF ILLINOIS
EASTERN DIVISION

UNITED STATES OF AMERICA	)	
	)	
v.	)	No.________
	)	
ANTHONY MATTHEWS	)	Violations: Title 18, United States Code,
	)	Section 1343

<u>COUNT ONE</u>

The UNITED STATES ATTORNEY charges:

1. At times material to this information:
   a. Defendant ANTHONY MATTHEWS owned and controlled Express Mortgage, a licensed Illinois mortgage brokerage located on Wabash Street and on Western Boulevard in Chicago, Illinois.
   b. Bank One was a financial institution, the deposits of which were insured by the Federal Deposit Insurance Corporation ("FDIC"). Wells Fargo Home Mortgage was a subsidiary of Wells Fargo Bank.
   c. MIT Lending and St. Francis Mortgage were mortgage companies engaged in the business of issuing mortgage loans for the purchase of residential property.
2. Beginning no later than 2003 and continuing through at least 2006, at Chicago, in the Northern District of Illinois, Eastern Division, and elsewhere,

ANTHONY MATTHEWS,

defendant herein, together with other co-schemers known to the United States Attorney, devised, intended to devise, and participated in a scheme to defraud and to obtain money by means of materially false and fraudulent pretenses, representations, and promises, which scheme affected financial institutions. More specifically, defendant schemed to fraudulently obtain over $1 million in mortgage loan proceeds from various banks and mortgage lending institutions, including Bank One, Wells Fargo Bank, MIT Lending, St. Francis Mortgage and Wells Fargo Home Mortgage, among others (hereinafter referred to collectively as "lenders"), as described below.

FIGURE 11–1 Portions of a Federal Prosecutor's Charging Document (Information).

not to prosecute. In particular, if it appears the defense's case is *stronger*, it may behoove the prosecutor to proceed with charges against a different individual.

Nonetheless, prosecutors are human and, as such, can be influenced by the facts of a particular case. Say, for instance, that a law mandates life in prison for growing in excess of 1,000 marijuana plants. Assume further that a suspect apprehended for violating such a law has a spotless record, is married, and has four children. Would life in prison be the best punishment for such an individual, or would a fine, community service, or other sanction be more appropriate? This decision is up to the prosecutor, and depending on the nature of the case, he or she may elect not to proceed with charges.

As another example, California's "three strikes" law requires life in prison for third-time felons. The first two felonies that qualify as "strikeable" under California's law can only be of certain varieties; typically, they are serious offenses. However, the third felony can be of *any* type. Critics of California's "three strikes" law often point to the man who was sentenced to prison for life for stealing a slice of pizza. Had the prosecutor who charged this individual been more sensible in exercising his or her discretion, then public outcry may not have been so significant.

Another reason for not charging traces to economic concerns. Simply put, it is not possible, given the resource restrictions that exist in most prosecutors' offices, to proceed with charges against every criminal suspect. Not having the time to build a case because of a high caseload may effectively force a prosecutor to be lenient with certain individuals.

Challenging the Decision Not to Prosecute

A prosecutor's decision not to press charges is rarely challenged, but on occasion higher authorities may get involved when they disagree with a prosecutor's decision. Failure to press charges can sometimes

It is not possible, given the resource restrictions that exist in most prosecutors' offices, to proceed with charges against every criminal suspect.

Think About It…

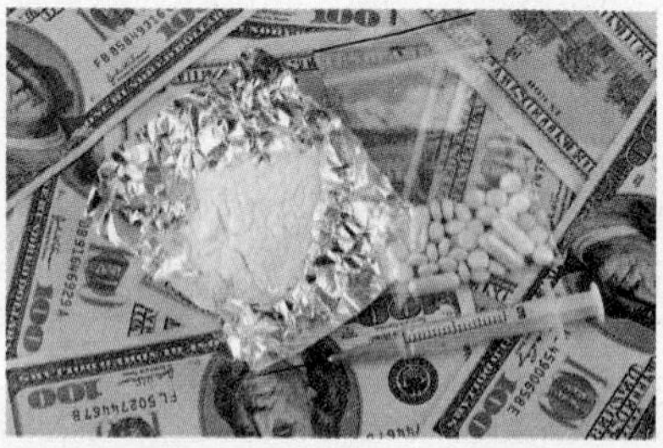

buradaki/Shutterstock

Reasons for Nonprosecution A controversial reason for nonprosecution is a by-product of the United States' so-called war on drugs. Civil asset forfeiture statutes permit the forfeiture of money and property tied to criminal activity—most frequently, the illicit drug trade. Many asset forfeiture statutes permit forfeited proceeds to go to the executive branch, which usually means the police but sometimes prosecutors. Some have argued that when there is not enough evidence to proceed with a criminal case, prosecutors can opt to pursue civil forfeiture, for which the burden of proof is generally lower. And as an added bonus, if a forfeiture action succeeds and a person's property is forfeited to the state, the prosecutor may reap a financial reward for selecting a civil proceeding instead of a criminal one. Is the possibility of civil asset forfeiture a legitimate reason not to prosecute? That is, if a prosecutor chooses not to press criminal charges against someone, instead opting for forfeiture, should the decision be considered constitutional?

FIGURE 11-2 Portions of the Federal *Code of Conduct for Judicial Employees*.

be questioned by a court, which can provide relief to individuals who disagree with the prosecutor's decision (for example, *NAACP* v. *Levi*, 418 F. Supp. 1109 [D.D.C. 1976]). Other times, a prosecutor's supervisor or other high-ranking officials may step in. According to one source, "Many states by statute confer upon the attorney general the power to initiate prosecution in cases where the local prosecutor has failed to act. In practice, however, attorneys general have seldom exercised much control over local prosecuting attorneys."[1]

Another way of preventing prosecutors from abusing their discretion (that is, by failing to act) is to require them to abide by standards of conduct. These standards help prosecutors decide which cases are worthy of prosecution as well as what charges to pursue, all the while ensuring that they act in accordance with the law. Figure 11-2 presents portions of the *Code of Conduct for Judicial Employees*, published by the Administrative Office of the U.S. Courts.

Some U.S. jurisdictions require court approval of a prosecutor's decision not to pursue charges. The prosecutor is typically required to explain to the court in writing his or her reasons for failing to prosecute. Although this approach may seem sensible on its face, the Supreme Court has been somewhat critical of judicial review of prosecutorial decisions. In *Wayte* v. *United States* (470 U.S. 598 [1985]), the Court gave this reason for avoiding judicial oversight: "Such factors as the strength of the case, the prosecution's general deterrence value, the Government's overall enforcement plan are not readily susceptible to the kind of analysis the courts are competent to make" (p. 606).

In general, if the prosecutor's decision not to press charges stems from legitimate factors, such as lack of evidence or case backlog, then the decision should be honored. The prosecutor's decision should be honored even if he or she agrees to dismiss criminal charges if the defendant agrees not to file a civil suit.

Restrictions on Bringing Charges

LEARNING OUTCOMES 1 Describe the prosecutor's role, prosecutorial discretion, and the issues surrounding prosecutorial misconduct.

This section turns to situations in which charges are filed but for inappropriate reasons. In other words, whereas the previous sections considered situations in which the prosecutor *fails* to bring charges, this section considers situations in which the prosecutor *cannot* bring charges.

There are two primary reasons a prosecutor cannot bring charges against an accused individual: (1) if the prosecution is unfair and selective (that is, targets a certain individual unfairly) and (2) if the prosecution is pursued for vindictive reasons. The following subsections focus in detail on these situations.

Unfair and Selective Prosecution

If the prosecutor's decision to press charges is *discriminatory* in nature, the Fourteenth Amendment's equal protection clause can be violated. For example, in *Yick Wo* v. *Hopkins* (118 U.S. 356 [1886]), the Supreme Court stated,

> Though the law itself be fair on its face and impartial in appearance, yet, if it is applied and administered by public authority with an evil eye and an unequal hand, so as practically to make unjust and illegal discriminations between persons in similar circumstances, material to their rights, the denial of equal justice is still within the prohibition of the Constitution. (pp. 373–374)

Simply put, if an individual is targeted for prosecution merely because he or she falls into a certain group (for example, a minority group), then his or her constitutional rights will be violated. This is known as **selective prosecution**.

Since *Yick Wo*, the Court has become more specific as to what constitutes selective prosecution. In **Oyler v. Boles (368 U.S. 448 [1968])**, the Court held that prosecution becomes selective and in violation of the equal protection clause only when it is intentional and is intended to target "a certain class of cases . . . or specific persons." In that case, the defendant presented evidence that he was the only individual of six sentenced under a particular statute. The Court held that this was not discriminatory because the defendant was unable to demonstrate intent by the prosecutor or provide evidence that he fit the group targeted for prosecution.

Since the *Oyler* decision, the courts have imposed a three-pronged test for determining whether prosecution violates equal protection. It must be shown that (1) similarly situated individuals were not prosecuted, (2) the prosecutor intended for this to happen, and (3) the decision resulted from an arbitrary, rather than rational, classification scheme. An *arbitrary* classification scheme would be based on, for example, race or sex. A *rational* classification scheme would be one that considers the evidence against each individual without regard to the color of

If the prosecutor's decision to press charges is discriminatory in nature, the Fourteenth Amendment's equal protection clause can be violated.

his or her skin, country of origin, religious preference, sex, or other such criterion.

One method by which prosecutors can open themselves to allegations of unfair and selective prosecution is through what is known as **pretextual prosecution**. This occurs when the prosecutor lacks the evidence to charge someone with a particular crime and so charges him or her with a lesser crime. However, prosecutors are rarely chastised for this type of conduct. For example, in *United States* v. *Sacco* (428 F.2d 164 [9th Cir. 1970]), a court noted that allowing a prosecutor to pursue lesser charges when the evidence to mount a more serious charge does not exist is perfectly acceptable.

Vindictive Prosecution

If a prosecutor's charging decision is motivated by revenge, then the resulting charge violates the due process clause of the Fourteenth Amendment. Specifically, if a prosecutor charges an individual simply because he or she is exercising his or her constitutional rights, such charges will not be allowed. This is known as **vindictive prosecution**.

In **Blackledge v. Perry (417 U.S. 21 [1974])**, the defendant was convicted in a lower court for misdemeanor assault with a deadly weapon. After the defendant filed an appeal with the county superior court, the prosecutor obtained an indictment charging the offender with *felony* assault for the same conduct.

The defendant pled guilty to this offense and was sentenced to five to seven years. The Supreme Court concluded that "vindictiveness against a defendant for having successfully attacked his first conviction must play no part in the sentence he receives after a new trial" (p. 33). The Court concluded further that such punishment after the fact must be overturned, unless the prosecutor can explain the increase in charges.

The Supreme Court's decision in *Blackledge* applies only in limited contexts, a point that cannot be overemphasized. Namely, it applies only after (1) the charged individual exercises his or her legal rights and (2) the prosecutor increases the charges after the first trial. With regard to the latter restriction, this means that if the prosecutor threatens the defendant with more serious charges during the pretrial phase, the Fourteenth Amendment will not be violated. New evidence that may legitimately warrant a more serious charge could come along during this phase.

However, in *United States* v. *Goodwin* (457 U.S. 368 [1982]), the Supreme Court noted that it is possible for a prosecutor to act vengefully during the pretrial phase. It is possible, the Court noted, that "a defendant in an appropriate case might prove objectively that the prosecutor's [pretrial] charging decision was motivated by a desire to punish him for doing something that the law plainly allowed him to do" (p. 384). Furthermore, although "the defendant is free to tender evidence to the court to support a claim that enhanced charges are a direct and unjustifiable penalty for the exercise of a procedural right . . . only in rare cases [will] a defendant be able to overcome the presumptive validity of the prosecutor's actions through such a demonstration" (p. 384). In other words, if the more serious charging decision is made prior to trial, it is presumed that the prosecutor is not acting in a vindictive fashion, and the defendant must prove otherwise.

Dealing with Overzealous Prosecutors

By charging offenders, prosecutors serve as advocates for the government. In this capacity, they are immune from suit for charging suspects with crimes.[2] This is reasonable because imagine what would happen to the criminal process if prosecutors could be sued at every turn for charging offenders!

Prosecutors also act as advocates when they argue the government's case, and they can do almost anything in this capacity

to secure a conviction without fear of being held liable. Prosecutors have been shielded from such actions as using false statements at pretrial hearings (*Burns* v. *Reed*, 500 U.S. 478 [1991]), using false testimony at trial (*Imbler* v. *Pachtman*, 424 U.S. 409 [1976]), failing to disclose exculpatory evidence (*Kalina* v. *Fletcher*, 522 U.S. 118 [1997]), fabricating evidence, influencing witnesses, and even breaching plea agreements.

In a recent case, *Connick* v. *Thompson*, (563 U.S. [2011]), the Supreme Court held that a district attorney's office may not be held liable for failing to train its prosecutors in the event of a single failure by one prosecutor to disclose exculpatory evidence to the defense. This and decisions before it have set the bar to prove prosecutorial misconduct quite high.

Recourse

Despite the immunity they enjoy, there is recourse for dealing with overzealous prosecutors. Such recourse generally comes in one of four varieties:

- Private admonition or reprimand
- Public reprimand
- Suspension from law practice
- Permanent disbarment

Prosecutors' supervisors and state bar associations can take the first three actions. The fourth action, disbarment, is usually taken by bar associations alone. How often are prosecutors punished for their wrongdoing? Not very often. According to the Center for Public Integrity, out of more than 11,000 cases of prosecutorial misconduct, only two prosecutors were disbarred.[3] Reprimand was the most common sanction.

The story of Mike Nifong, the prosecutor in the infamous Duke lacrosse case (in which three white Duke University lacrosse players were accused of rape by an African American stripper), sheds some light on the problem of prosecutorial misconduct. He was the prototypical overzealous prosecutor. For example, he repeatedly made statements to the press that were unsupported and controversial. He also continued to pursue criminal charges, even as new evidence came to light that would have made securing a conviction difficult. The state bar association filed complaints against Nifong. He was ultimately disbarred and held in contempt of court. Also, because some of Nifong's actions may not have been consistent with the role of an "advocate," his immunity may have been "qualified" rather than absolute. He was sued by the wrongfully accused lacrosse players and their families. As of this writing, Nifong has claimed bankruptcy and the fate of the lawsuit is unclear.

Joinder

Joinder refers to a situation in which the prosecutor either (1) brings multiple charges against the same individual in the same trial or (2) brings charges against multiple individuals in the same trial. In determining whether either is appropriate, two questions must be asked: First, based on the jurisdiction in question, is joinder appropriate? Second, if joinder is appropriate, will it be unfairly prejudicial? An answer of "no" to the first question and "yes" to the second requires what is known as a **severance**.

The question of whether joinder is appropriate is best resolved prior to trial, but sometimes joinder is not addressed until *after* trial. Assume, for example, that a single defendant is charged in the same trial for assault and robbery. Assume further that he is convicted on both counts. If he later claims that joinder was inappropriate (which, incidentally, means the burden of proof falls on him) and succeeds with this argument, what will the result be? According to the Supreme Court in **United States v. Lane (474 U.S. 438 [1986])**, if this joinder has "a substantial and injurious effect or influence in determining the jury's verdict" (p. 449), new and separate trials must be held.

Multiple Charges Against the Same Individual

According to the Federal Rules of Criminal Procedure, multiple charges can be brought against the same individual under the following circumstances: when the charges arise out of (1) the same criminal event (for example, robbery of a convenience store and assault when fleeing the scene), (2) two separate criminal acts that are tied together in some fashion (for example, a convenience store robbery to obtain cash to buy and sell illegal drugs), or (3) two criminal acts that are the same or similar in character.[4] This latter circumstance is somewhat vague, but an example should clarify: If a serial killer uses the same modus operandi against his victims, he or she may be tried for several homicides in the same criminal trial.

When the defense argues against joinder, there are a number of motivating concerns. First, there is the concern that the jury (or the judge, if a bench trial is held) will not consider the criminal acts for which the accused is charged separately. Another concern is that the jury will view all the evidence against the accused in a cumulative, rather than a separate, fashion. Say, for example, that the prosecution presents eyewitness testimony against a defendant accused of robbery. Also assume that the prosecution presents a murder weapon allegedly used by the defendant on the victim of the robbery. The jury may consider together the eyewitness testimony and the murder weapon and arrive at the conclusion that the accused is guilty. But if the robbery and homicide were tried separately, the jury may not arrive at this conclusion so easily. Finally, another defense argument against joinder is that by trying an individual on several charges in the same trial, he or she will have difficulty asserting separate defenses to the criminal acts at issue.

An obvious problem with joinder is the possibility of double jeopardy. When a prosecutor tries a person on several related crimes in the same trial, he or she must do so carefully. In short, the criminal acts alleged must be similar but not identical. Double jeopardy is considered in Chapter 13, but for now, an example may prove helpful: If the prosecutor charges an individual for first-degree as well as second-degree murder of the same victim in the same trial and the individual is convicted of both offenses, it will be deemed unconstitutional.

Charges Against Multiple Defendants

The second form of joinder is when multiple defendants are charged in the same criminal trial. The Federal Rules of Criminal Procedure state, "Two or more defendants may be charged in the same indictment or information if they are alleged to have participated in the same act or transaction or in the same series of acts or transactions constituting an offense or offenses."[5] In other words, joinder of defendants is reserved in most instances for crimes of conspiracy (that is, crimes in which two or more individuals plot during a criminal act).

As with joinder of *charges*, joinder of *defendants* raises a number of concerns. For instance, the jury may get confused as to who, if anyone, is guilty and simply convict all of the defendants. Or the jury may convict one defendant who is perhaps less guilty than another defendant who is clearly guilty simply because they associated together. Also, it is conceivable that one defendant may testify against another but then refuse to answer questions on cross-examination, citing self-incrimination concerns.

There are clearly arguments against joinder, concerning both charges and defendants. However, there is one clear argument in favor of joinder—namely, efficiency. Allowing prosecutors to join charges and defendants reduces court backlog and speeds up the administration of justice.

▶ The Grand Jury

According to the Fifth Amendment, "No person shall be held to answer for a capital, or otherwise infamous crime, unless on a presentment or indictment of a grand jury." This part of the Fifth Amendment cannot be fully appreciated without considering the time in which it was written. The framers favored **grand jury** indictments in certain situations for fear that the prosecutor, a representative of government, could become too powerful in terms of making charging decisions. Indeed, the framers shared a clear sentiment that government should be kept in check, and the grand jury was one method of ensuring this.

Despite that intent, the grand jury is no longer so independent. Instead, the grand jury is now highly dependent on the actions of the prosecutor. Grand juries still perform important investigative functions, and they are quite powerful in terms of, for instance, being able to subpoena witnesses and records. But their role today is tied closely to the prosecutor. In fact, almost every state makes the prosecutor the main legal adviser of the grand jury and requires him or her to be present during all grand jury sessions. However, in some states, the grand jury functions independently of the prosecutor.

Even though the Fifth Amendment suggests that indictment by grand jury is guaranteed for certain offenses, this right has not been incorporated. In the 1884 decision of **Hurtado v. California (110 U.S. 516 [1884])**, the Supreme Court stated that indictment by a grand jury is not a right guaranteed by the due process clause of the Fourteenth Amendment. The Court stated,

> [W]e are unable to say that the substitution for a presentment or indictment by a grand jury of [a] proceeding by information after examination and commitment by a magistrate, certifying to the probable guilt of the defendant, with the right on his part to the aid of counsel, and

to the cross-examination of the witnesses produced for the prosecution, is not due process of law. (p. 538)

It should be emphasized that the right to grand jury indictment not being incorporated to the states does not mean that states do not require this method of prosecution. Several states do require that, for the most part, felonies are to be prosecuted only by grand jury indictment. The same is true for the federal system. Most states, however, permit prosecution by indictment or information. See Figure 11–3 for an overview of the mechanisms for filing serious charges in each state.

So, because most states permit indictment or information, under what circumstances is one or the other method used? Typically, grand jury indictment will be the charging mechanism of choice when (1) the case is of great public and/or political significance, (2) the investigative power of the grand jury is useful, (3) the grand jury may be able to issue an indictment more quickly compared to holding a preliminary hearing and then issuing an information indictment, or (4) one or more witnesses is hesitant to speak in open court, preferring the secrecy surrounding grand jury proceedings.

How a Grand Jury Is Constructed

A grand jury can be *impaneled* either by the court or by the prosecutor. Usually, the court has this responsibility, but prosecutors are becoming increasingly able to decide whether a grand jury is necessary.

The term *grand jury* should not be construed as singular; in larger jurisdictions, several grand juries may be acting at the same time. One or more could be performing investigative functions, and one or more others could be working on specific cases.

Duration

Once a grand jury has been convened, its members serve for a specified period of time. A term can last from one to three months but sometimes less, if the court or prosecutor believes that further deliberation is unnecessary. Under the Federal Rules of Criminal Procedure, a regular grand jury cannot serve for a period longer than 18 months, unless the court extends the service "upon a determination that such extension is in the public interest."[6] Fortunately, people selected for grand juries do not have to meet every day; usually, a grand jury meets several days a month.

Size

Grand juries are larger than ordinary trial juries. In the past, grand juries consisting of 24 or so people were not uncommon. Today, grand juries are usually smaller, in the neighborhood of 16 to 20 people. One state, Tennessee, permits a grand jury of 13 individuals, but the voting requirements in that state are fairly restrictive.

Voting Requirements

Grand jury voting requirements also vary by state. The most common voting requirement is that 12 grand jury members must agree on an indictment. However, one state, Virginia,

The grand jury is now highly dependent on the actions of the prosecutor.

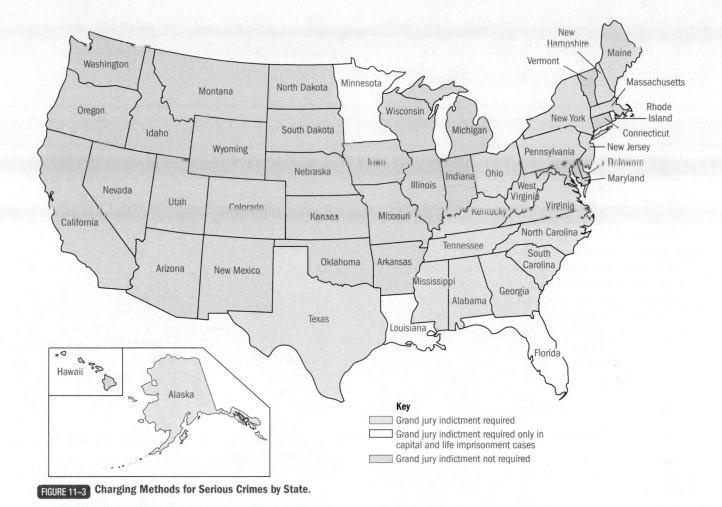

Key

▨	Grand jury indictment required
☐	Grand jury indictment required only in capital and life imprisonment cases
▨	Grand jury indictment not required

FIGURE 11–3 Charging Methods for Serious Crimes by State.

requires only four votes for issuance of a *true bill*, which is the endorsement made by a grand jury when it finds sufficient evidence to warrant a criminal charge. Texas, for example, requires a vote of 9 out of 12.

As with a *petit jury* (trial jury), a grand jury is headed by a foreperson, who is charged with, among other duties, signing the indictment and keeping track of the votes of each member.

Selection of Members

People are selected for a grand jury in the same way they are selected for an ordinary trial (i.e., petit) jury: They are subpoenaed. In some states, grand jury members are selected from a list of eligible voters. In others, they are selected from a list of licensed drivers. Still other states select grand jury members from a list of tax returns, telephone directories, and so on. Most people do not get the opportunity to serve on a grand jury because grand juries are not convened that frequently.

The grand jury selection process usually involves two stages. First, a list of potential grand jury members is compiled by any of the methods (or others) just described. This list of grand jury members is known as the *venire*. Next, people are selected from the list to serve on the grand jury. At both stages, constitutional complications can arise.

First, special steps need to be taken to ensure that the list of potential grand jurors, like that for a typical petit jury, is fair and impartial. In particular, the defendant can raise constitutional challenges to the grand jury selection process if it is *not* fair and impartial. One such challenge is based on the *equal protection clause*. This requires showing that there is a significant disparity between a group's representation in the community and its representation on the grand jury (see *Casteneda* v. *Partida*, 430 U.S. 482 [1977]).

Another constitutional challenge against the composition of the grand jury pool stems from the *fair cross-section requirement* announced in *Taylor* v. *Louisiana* (419 U.S. 522 [1975]). The Court in that case held that "systematic exclusion" of a "large distinct group" from the pool from which the (petit) jury is chosen violates the Sixth Amendment. The same logic carries over to the grand jury. If, for example, a grand jury consists of all white members and 40% of the community is black, the fair cross-section requirement will have been violated. By contrast, if the grand jury does not contain a snake handler, a militant feminist, a rabbi, or some such specific type of individual, the fair cross-section requirement will not have been violated because these and other individuals do not constitute large, distinct groups.

As for the selection of grand jury members from the pool, similar constitutional concerns can be raised. If, for instance, the grand jury pool is representative of a fair cross-section of the community, it is still possible that people could be excluded from the jury on a systematic basis. In *Rose* v. *Mitchell* (443 U.S. 545 [1979]), the Court held that the "right to equal protection of the laws [is] denied when [the defendant] is indicted from a grand jury from which members of a racial group purposefully have been excluded" (p. 556).

Secrecy of Grand Jury Proceedings

Grand jury proceedings are intensely secret. In *United States* v. *Rose* (215 F.2d 617 [1954]), the Third Circuit Court of Appeals announced several reasons for this:

(1) to prevent the escape of those whose indictment may be contemplated; (2) to insure the utmost freedom to the grand jury in its deliberations, and to prevent persons subject to indictment or their friends from importuning the grand jurors; (3) to prevent subornation of perjury or tampering with the witnesses who may testify before the grand jury and later appear at the trial of those indicted by it; (4) to encourage free and untrammeled disclosures by persons who have information with respect to the commission of crimes; [and] (5) to protect the innocent accused who is exonerated from disclosure of the fact that he has been under investigation, and from the expense of standing trial where there was no probability of guilt. (pp. 628–629)

Rights of Witnesses Testifying Before Grand Juries

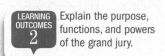
LEARNING OUTCOMES 2 Explain the purpose, functions, and powers of the grand jury.

Grand juries rely heavily on witness testimony. However, the rights afforded to grand jury witnesses differ significantly from those afforded to witnesses in other settings (for example, at trial). Also, the rights afforded to the individuals targeted by grand jury investigations differ from those afforded to criminal defendants.

The cases in this area revolve around three issues: (1) the right of the individual targeted by a grand jury investigation to testify, (2) whether grand jury witnesses are required to be advised of their right not to testify, and (3) the right to counsel as applied in grand jury proceedings.

Right to Testify

It is well known that the defendant in a criminal trial has a constitutional right to testify or not testify in his or her own defense. In contrast, someone who is the target of a grand jury investigation usually *does not* enjoy the right to testify. Indeed, several states do not even grant the target of a grand jury investigation the right to be present. This restriction is justified on the same secrecy grounds discussed earlier. Also, because many grand jury proceedings are investigative, there may not be a specific target until the proceedings have reached a close. In such a situation, it would be cumbersome to allow all potential targets to be present in order to give testimony in their defense.

Being Advised of the Right Not to Testify

When witnesses appear before grand juries, they enjoy the Fifth Amendment's privilege against self-incrimination. This is no different than in a criminal trial. However, a question has

arisen in the courts over whether grand jury witnesses must be *told* that they can remain silent. In other words, the courts have grappled with whether the *Miranda* warnings should apply in the grand jury context.

As noted earlier in this book, the *Miranda* warnings are only required during custodial interrogation. Therefore, one must ask, "Are grand jury proceedings akin to custodial interrogations?" At least one decision suggests that *Miranda* does not apply in the grand jury context because the proceedings are not as "inherently coercive" as traditional custodial interrogations (for example, *Gollaher* v. *United States*, 419 F.2d 520 [9th Cir. 1969]). However, some states require by law that the targets of grand jury investigations, as well as grand jury witnesses, be advised of their right not to testify. The Supreme Court has yet to rule on this issue.

Right to Counsel

Should grand jury witnesses and the targets of grand jury investigations be provided with counsel? The Supreme Court has answered "no" to this question in at least two cases: *In re Groban's Petition* (352 U.S. 330 [1957]) and **United States v. Mandujano (425 U.S. 564 [1976])**. A person who has already been charged may have a right to counsel before a grand jury proceeding, but such an individual is rarely the target of such a proceeding (see, for example, *Kirby* v. *Illinois*, 406 U.S. 682 [1972]). The typical grand jury witness is someone called upon to shed light on a particular case. Such witnesses do not enjoy the right to counsel in grand jury proceedings, but they can of course assert Fifth Amendment protection and refuse to incriminate themselves. As we will see shortly, though, the grand jury may offer a grant of immunity in exchange for a witness's testimony.

The Supreme Court has stated that grand jury proceedings take place before the initiation of adversarial criminal proceedings and, as such, are outside the scope of the Sixth Amendment's right to counsel. There are also several additional reasons for not allowing counsel to be present during grand jury proceedings: (1) The investigation could be delayed if the witness repeatedly confers with his or her attorney; (2) the investigation could be disrupted if the witness raises objections and arguments; and, of course; (3) secrecy could be compromised.

By way of summary, the rights of witnesses and those targeted by grand jury investigations appear in Figure 11–4.

Investigative Powers of the Grand Jury

One of the main duties of a grand jury is to investigate alleged wrongdoing in order to determine whether an indictment should be issued. Because of this function, a grand jury has a great deal of investigative power. For example, as decided in **United States v. Calandra (414 U.S. 338 [1974])**, a grand jury

One of the main duties of a grand jury is to investigate alleged wrongdoing in order to determine whether an indictment should be issued.

1961	**1963**		**1966**	**1967**	
Hamilton v. Alabama, 368 U.S. 52 Due process is violated when counsel is not made available to the accused at arraignment.	**Douglas v. California, 372 U.S. 353** The right to counsel extends to convicted indigents for appeals of right (that is, appeals to which the individual is legally entitled—see Chapter 13).	**White v. Maryland, 373 U.S. 59** Due process is violated when a suspect enters a guilty plea before a judge without the presence of counsel.	**Miranda v. Arizona, 384 U.S. 436** Suspects must be advised of their right to have counsel present during custodial interrogations.	**United States v. Wade, 388 U.S. 218** A "critical stage" test is articulated for determining when the right to counsel applies. A postindictment lineup is a critical stage of the criminal process, and the accused should be afforded counsel.	**Gilbert v. California, 388 U.S. 263** The right to counsel does not apply in the taking of handwriting exemplars (that is, samples).

Right to Testify

Someone who is the target of a grand jury investigation usually *does not* enjoy the right to testify. Indeed, several states do not even grant the target of a grand jury investigation the right to be present.

Right to Counsel

Grand jury witnesses and the targets of grand jury investigations need not be provided with counsel (*In re Groban's Petition*, 352 U.S. 330 [1957]; *United States* v. *Mandujano*, 425 U.S. 564 [1976]). A person who has already been charged may have a right to counsel before a grand jury proceeding, but such an individual is rarely the target of such a proceeding (see, for example, *Kirby* v. *Illinois*, 406 U.S. 682 [1972]).

FIGURE 11–4 Constitutional Rights of Grand Jury Witnesses and Those Targeted by Grand Jury Investigations.

"may compel the production of evidence or the testimony of witnesses as it considers appropriate, and its operation generally is unrestrained by the technical procedural and evidentiary rules governing the conduct of criminal trials" (p. 343). In this vein, a grand jury can subpoena witnesses and evidence. However, it can also extend grants of immunity to certain individuals in exchange for their testimony, and it can find people in contempt for failing to cooperate with an investigation.

Subpoenas

Two types of subpoenas are available to grand juries: (1) a **subpoena *ad testificandum*** and (2) a **subpoena *duces tecum***. The former compels a witness to appear before the grand jury, and the latter compels the production of tangible evidence (for example, a suspected murder weapon). The power of the grand jury to utilize both of these mechanisms is virtually unrestricted; however, there have been a few constitutional objections to their use.

First, some have argued that a subpoena to appear before the grand jury amounts to a seizure within the meaning of the Fourth Amendment. The Supreme Court acknowledged in

United States v. *Dioniso* (410 U.S. 1 [1973]) that being forced to appear before a grand jury may be inconvenient but not in comparison to the "historically grounded obligation of every person to appear and give his evidence before the grand jury" (pp. 9–10). Furthermore, Fourth Amendment restrictions on the grand jury's subpoena power "would assuredly impede its investigation and frustrate the public's interest in the fair and expeditious administration of the laws" (p. 17).

As for tangible evidence, the Supreme Court has likewise held that a subpoena *duces tecum* does not amount to a Fourth Amendment seizure. However, according to the Court in **Hale v. Henkel (201 U.S. 43 [1906])**, such a subpoena must comport with the Fourth Amendment's particularity requirement. In *United States* v. *Gurule* (437 F.2d 239 [10th Cir. 1970]), the Tenth Circuit announced a three-prong test for ensuring that a grand jury subpoena satisfies the Fourth Amendment's reasonableness requirement: "(1) the subpoena may command only the production of things relevant to the investigation being pursued; (2) specification of things to be produced must be made with reasonable particularity; and (3) production of records covering only a reasonable period of time may be required" (p. 241).

Grants of Immunity

Even though witnesses appearing before the grand jury enjoy the Fifth Amendment privilege against self-incrimination, the grand jury can get around this. In particular, the grand jury can extend *grants of immunity* to witnesses in exchange for their testimony. A grant of transactional immunity prohibits future prosecution on the acts for which the witness testifies. In contrast, so-called use and derivative use immunity only bar the use of the witness's testimony against him or her in the future.

1967	**1970**	**1972**	**1973**	
***Mempa* v. *Rhay*, 389 U.S. 128** The preliminary hearing is a critical stage of the criminal process—counsel must be provided.	***Coleman* v. *Alabama*, 399 U.S. 1** The sentencing hearing is a critical stage of the criminal process—counsel must be provided.	***Kirby* v. *Illinois*, 406 U.S. 682** The *Wade* decision is limited by the Court's decision that criminal prosecution does not begin until indictment, formal charge, or the "initiation of adversary proceedings."	***United States* v. *Ash*, 413 U.S. 300** The Court abandons the critical stage analysis and focuses instead on whether "trial-like confrontations" necessitate counsel.	***Gagnon* v. *Scarpelli*, 411 U.S. 778** Indigents are entitled to counsel at probation and parole revocation hearings but only on a case-by-case basis.

If evidence is obtained after the fact, independent of the witness's testimony before the grand jury, then he or she can be charged (see *Kastigar* v. *United States*, 406 U.S. 441 [1972]).

Findings of Contempt

When someone is subpoenaed to appear before the grand jury but does not show up, the jury's **contempt power** can be utilized. That is, the grand jury can impose civil and criminal sanctions on the individual. For example, an individual who refuses to appear before the grand jury can be jailed until he or she agrees to appear. Note that the grand jury's contempt power is limited to compelling the presence of the witness, not his or her testimony. The witness who *does* appear can still invoke the Fifth Amendment privilege and not make a statement.

▶ The Defense Attorney

The Sixth Amendment to the U.S. Constitution provides "in all criminal prosecutions, the accused shall enjoy the right . . . to have the Assistance of Counsel for his defense." This right was applied to the states in the landmark decision of **Gideon v. Wainwright (372 U.S. 335 [1963])**. Although on its face this portion of the Sixth Amendment seems straightforward, it has actually given rise to two important questions: (1) What constitutes a *criminal prosecution*? and (2) what does *assistance of counsel* mean?

Answers to these two questions are provided in the subsections that follow. Waiver of counsel and the right to counsel of one's own choice are also addressed, as is effective assistance of counsel.

The Right to Counsel in a Criminal Prosecution

Prior to *Gideon*, the right to counsel did not exist for all individuals. Usually, counsel was provided only for defendants who could afford it. There were occasions prior to the 1960s, however, in which counsel was provided to criminal defendants who could *not* afford it. For example, the constitutional right of an indigent defendant to be represented by counsel was first announced in **Powell v. Alabama (287 U.S. 45 [1932])**. In that case, the Supreme Court reversed the convictions of several indigent defendants who were not represented by counsel at trial. Significantly, though, the Court based its decision on the Fifth Amendment's due process clause, not the Sixth Amendment:

> The right to be heard would be, in many cases, of little avail if it did not comprehend the right to be heard by counsel. Even the intelligent and educated layman has small and sometimes no skill in the science of law. If charged with crimes, he is incapable, generally, of determining for himself whether the indictment is good or bad. He is unfamiliar with the rules of evidence. Left without aid of counsel he may be put on trial without a proper charge, and convicted upon incompetent evidence, or evidence irrelevant to the issue or otherwise inadmissible. He lacks both the skill and knowledge adequately to prepare his defense, even though he may have a perfect one. He requires the guiding hand of counsel at every step in the proceedings against him. Without it, though he be not guilty, he faces the danger of conviction because he does not know how to establish his innocence. (pp. 68–69)

However, the right to counsel announced in *Powell* was not without limitations. It applied only to "capital case[s], where the defendant is unable to employ counsel, and is incapable adequately of making his own defense because of ignorance, feeblemindedness, illiteracy, or the like" (p. 71).

The Contemporary Sixth Amendment Approach

In *Johnson* v. *Zerbst* (304 U.S. 458 [1938]), the Court recognized the Sixth Amendment right to counsel in all federal prosecutions, stating that the Sixth Amendment "embodies a realistic recognition of the obvious truth that the average defendant does not have the professional legal skill to protect himself" (pp. 462–463).

But the Sixth Amendment's right to counsel was still not extended to the states. In *Johnson*, the Court refused to apply its decision to the states, and this holding was reaffirmed a few years later in the case of *Betts* v. *Brady* (316 U.S. 455 [1942]). There, the Court held that "[t]he Due Process Clause of the Fourteenth Amendment does not incorporate, as such, the specific guarantees found in the Sixth Amendment" (pp. 461–462). It would not be until the 1963 decision in *Gideon* v. *Wainwright* that the Sixth Amendment right to counsel became incorporated. In that case, the Court recognized that "lawyers in criminal courts are necessities, not luxuries" (p. 344).

1974	1975	1981	1987	2008
Ross v. Moffitt, 417 U.S. 600 The right to counsel does not necessarily exist so that indigent convicts can prepare petitions for *discretionary appeals* (that is, those that the reviewing court gets to decide it wants to hear).	**Gerstein v. Pugh**, 420 U.S. 103 There is no right to counsel during a probable cause hearing.	**Estelle v. Smith**, 451 U.S. 454 There is no right to have counsel present during a psychiatric evaluation.	**Pennsylvania v. Finley**, 481 U.S. 551 The right to counsel does not exist so that convicted criminals can prepare *habeas corpus* petitions.	**Rothgery v. Gillespie County**, No. 07-440 The initiation of "adversary proceedings" starts at the initial appearance.

Gideon dealt with a felony, which led the Supreme Court to conclude that the Sixth Amendment right to counsel applies only in felony proceedings. However, in *Argersinger* v. *Hamlin* (407 U.S. 25 [1972]), the Court held that the right to counsel applies in misdemeanor cases, also. According to the Court, "The requirement of counsel may well be necessary for a fair trial even in petty-offense prosecution. We are by no means convinced that legal and constitutional questions involved in a case that actually leads to imprisonment even for a brief period are any less complex than when a person can be sent off for six months or more" (p. 33).

This decision was then clarified in *Scott* v. *Illinois* (440 U.S. 367 [1979]), in which the Court held that the right to counsel does not apply where loss of liberty is merely a *possibility*. In short, when there is no possibility of confinement, the Sixth Amendment right to counsel does not apply. A twist on the *Scott* decision was recently handed down in *Alabama* v. *Shelton* (535 U.S. 654 [2002]), in which the Court held that "[a] suspended sentence that may 'end up in the actual deprivation of a person's liberty' may not be imposed unless the defendant was accorded 'the guiding hand of counsel' in the prosecution for the crime charged" (p. 654). *Shelton* differed from *Scott* because Shelton was placed on probation; Scott was not.

Note that the right to counsel also extends to other stages of the criminal process, both in the period leading up to trial and well beyond. The right to counsel at other stages of the criminal process is summarized in the accompanying timeline.

Waiver of the Right to Counsel

LEARNING OUTCOMES 3 — Outline the development of the right to counsel.

Although the Sixth Amendment provides for the right to counsel, accused individuals sometimes prefer to represent themselves. Indeed, according to the Supreme Court, criminal defendants have a constitutional right to represent themselves at trial (*Faretta* v. *California*, 422 U.S. 806 [1975]). This is known as a pro se **defense**. In reaching this decision, the Court noted that the Sixth Amendment only guarantees the *assistance* of counsel, not necessarily *representation* by counsel:

The language and spirit of the Sixth Amendment contemplate that counsel, like the other defense tools

Although the Sixth Amendment provides for the right to counsel, accused individuals sometimes prefer to represent themselves.

guaranteed by the Amendment, shall be an aid to a willing defendant—not an organ of State interposed between an unwilling defendant and his right to defend himself personally. . . . An unwanted counsel "represents" the defendant only through a tenuous and unacceptable legal fiction. Unless the accused has acquiesced in such representation, the defense presented is not the defense guaranteed him by the Constitution, for in a very real sense, it is not his defense. (pp. 820–821)

The Court also emphasized in *Faretta* that the framers viewed the "inestimable worth of free choice" as more important

Think About It...

Right to Counsel in the Pretrial Phase—A man was arrested without a warrant when a police officer caught him robbing the First Street branch of American Bank. Four hours later, the man was brought before a judge for a probable cause hearing. The judge decided that the officer had probable cause to arrest. The man was convicted of the crime and sentenced to prison. He is now appealing his conviction, claiming that he should have been given access to counsel at the probable cause hearing. Is he right?

The Image Bank/Getty Images

Bell v. Cone, 535 U.S. 68 Defense counsel's failure to present any mitigating evidence or to make a closing statement at the defendant's capital sentencing hearing was not ineffective. Among the reasons for the Court's decision was that the mitigating evidence that was not presented during the sentencing hearing *was* presented at trial, so the jury did have an opportunity to review it.

Florida v. Nixon, 543 U.S. 175 Defense counsel was permitted to acknowledge—in open court—his client's guilt and instead focus the defense on reasons why the defendant's life should be spared. The evidence was so clearly indicative of the defendant's guilt that the Supreme Court did not feel the defense attorney's strategy was ineffective.

Rompilla v. Beard, 545 U.S. 374 Defense counsel is bound to make reasonable efforts to obtain and review material that it knows the prosecution will probably rely on as part of its case.

than the right to counsel. Also, "[t]o force a lawyer on a defendant can only lead [the defendant] to believe that the law contrives against him" (p. 834).

Not every defendant who wishes to proceed without counsel is allowed to do so, however. In **Johnson v. Zerbst (304 U.S. 458 [1938])**, the Supreme Court stated that a defendant may only waive counsel if the waiver is "competent and intelligent." According to the Court in *Carnley* v. *Cochran* (369 U.S. 506 [1962]), "the record must show, or there must be an allegation and evidence must show, that an accused was offered counsel but intelligently and understandingly rejected the offer. Anything less is not a waiver" (p. 516). The Court elaborated further in *Von Moltke* v. *Gillies* (332 U.S. 708 [1948]):

> To be valid such waiver must be made with an apprehension of the nature of the charges, the statutory offenses included within them, the range of allowable punishments thereunder, possible defenses to the charges and circumstances in mitigation thereof, and all other facts essential to a broad understanding of the whole matter. A judge can make certain that an accused's professed waiver of counsel is understandingly and wisely made only from a penetrating and comprehensive examination of all the circumstances. (p. 724)

What constitutes a knowing and intelligent waiver is not always clear. However, in *Massey* v. *Moore* (348 U.S. 105 [1954]), the Court offered clarification by stating that "[o]ne might not be insane in the sense of being incapable of standing trial and yet lack the capacity to stand trial without benefit of counsel" (p. 108). But in *Godinez* v. *Moran* (509 U.S. 389 [1993]), a case decided some years later, the Court held that a person who is competent to stand trial is also competent to waive counsel at trial and for pleading purposes. This decision all but reversed an earlier decision in which the Court held that competence to stand trial could be interpreted as competence to waive counsel (see *Westbrook* v. *Arizona*, 384 U.S. 150 [1966]).

In certain circumstances, while permitting waiver of counsel, the court can require that *standby counsel* be available to the defendant—that is, an attorney who is standing by in order to assist the accused, if necessary. This was the decision reached in *McKaskle* v. *Wiggins* (465 U.S. 168 [1984]), in which the Court held that a judge can appoint standby counsel "to relieve the judge of the need to explain and enforce basic rules

of courtroom protocol or to assist the defendant in overcoming routine obstacles that stand in the way of the defendant's achievement of his own clearly indicated goals" (p. 184). When waiver of counsel is knowing and intelligent, a judge's decision to appoint standby counsel will not be unconstitutional as long as (1) the defendant retains control over the case and (2) the jury understands that the defendant represents him- or herself.

In 2004, the Supreme Court decided that waiver of the right to counsel is one that the defendant takes, potentially, at his or her own peril. In *Iowa* v. *Tovar* (541 U.S. 77 [2004]), the Court decided that a trial court was not required to warn the accused that waiving the right to counsel at a plea hearing involves two risks: (1) the possibility that valid defenses will be overlooked and (2) that the accused will be deprived of advice as to whether a guilty plea is warranted. At the same time, though, the Constitution does not prohibit a court from insisting on representation of counsel for criminal defendants who are competent to stand trial but who also suffer from serious mental illness that would compromise their ability to put on an effective defense (*Indiana* v. *Edwards*, 554 U.S. 164 [2008]).

Indigent Versus Nonindigent Defendants' Right to Counsel of Their Choice

Clearly, the defendant who is not indigent can hire counsel of his or her choosing. What's more, the wealthier the defendant, the better counsel he or she can afford. Unfortunately, the indigent defendant does not have such a choice. The Sixth Amendment right to counsel does not guarantee the indigent defendant permission to *choose* counsel; rather, counsel will be *provided*. Usually, counsel will be a public defender. If, however, an indigent can show good cause that the attorney appointed to represent him or her is not doing so adequately, another attorney can be appointed. What constitutes *inadequate representation* is discussed in the next section.

Surprisingly, there are situations in which defendants, if they can afford representation, cannot hire counsel of their choice. If, for example, the defendant's choice of an attorney poses serious conflict-of-interest problems, the defendant may be forced to hire another attorney (for example, *Wheat* v. *United States*, 486 U.S. 153 [1988]). If the defendant's attorney is not qualified to practice law, then another attorney may be required (for example, cf. *Leis* v. *Flynt*, 439 U.S. 438 [1979]). And, somewhat controversially, if a defendant's assets are frozen pursuant to a

2007	**2008**	**2011**
***Schriro* v. *Landrigan*, 550 U.S.** A defense attorney was not ineffective when his client instructed him not to present mitigating evidence during the death penalty sentencing phase.	***Wright* v. *Van Patten*, 552 U.S.** If the defense attorney participates in a plea hearing by speakerphone, rather than in person, it does not mean he or she provided ineffective assistance.	***Harrington* v. *Richter*, 562 U.S.** Defense counsel was not ineffective when it failed to utilize the testimony of its own blood evidence expert who could have testified to the defendant's account of the events. Blood evidence was not central to the case, and it was apparent that even the defense attorney questioned the defendant's account of the crime for which he was on trial.

civil forfeiture statute and he or she cannot afford counsel of his or her choosing, then a less expensive attorney may be required or a public defender may be appointed (see *Caplin & Drysdale* v. *United States*, 491 U.S. 617 [1989]).

On the other hand, if a defendant with means has his or her eye on a particular attorney who is qualified to practice law and does not have any conflicts of interest, the defendant must be able to hire the attorney. If a judge wrongfully prohibits the defendant from hiring the attorney of his or her choice, the defendant's ensuing conviction must be overturned (*United States* v. *Gonzalez-Lopez*, 548 U.S. 140 [2006]).

An issue related to counsel of one's choice is whether indigent defendants can retain expert witnesses of their own choosing. In *Ake* v. *Oklahoma* (470 U.S. 68 [1985]), the Supreme Court held that an indigent defendant enjoys a constitutional right to an expert witness when his or her sanity is at issue. However, the Court limited its holding to provide for only one expert (and that expert must be state employed). States vary in their rules concerning expert witnesses for indigent defendants. Often there are price caps that limit how much an indigent defendant's expert can be paid. At a point, it becomes necessary to assume that the *state*'s experts (for example, ballistics experts) present objective and accurate testimony that is not prejudicial to the accused.

Effective Assistance of Counsel

If the Sixth Amendment's right to counsel provision was extended to indigent defendants with a blind eye, then some defendants would be convicted and others acquitted because of varying levels of competence among attorneys. All attorneys are not the same. Some, although authorized to practice law, prove to be totally ineffective in their duties. As such, the courts have grappled with what constitutes **effective assistance of counsel**.

The Meaning of "Effective Assistance"

So, what constitutes effective assistance of counsel? The lower courts are somewhat divided in terms of how to answer this question, so it is necessary to focus on the Supreme Court's standard for deciding whether defense counsel's assistance is or is not effective. Before getting to the cases, however, Figure 11–5 reprints portions of the *Code of Conduct for Federal Public*

Canon 1: A federal public defender employee should uphold the integrity and independence of the office.

Canon 2: A federal public defender employee should avoid impropriety and the appearance of impropriety in all activities.

Canon 3: A federal public defender employee should adhere to appropriate standards in performing the duties of the office.

Canon 4: A federal public defender employee may engage in activities to improve the law, the legal system, and the administration of justice.

Canon 5: A federal public defender employee should regulate extra-official activities to minimize the risk of conflict with official duties.

Canon 6: A federal public defender employee should regularly file reports of compensation received for all extra-official activities.

Canon 7: A federal public defender employee should refrain from inappropriate political activity.

FIGURE 11–5 Portions of the *Code of Conduct for Federal Public Defender Employees*.

2011

Premo v. Moore , 562 U.S.
Defense counsel was not ineffective for failing to seek suppression of the defendant's unconstitutionally obtained confession.

Missouri v. Frye, 566 U.S.
Defense counsel must inform the defendant of formal plea offers that contain favorable terms and conditions. Defense counsel in this case failed to notify the defendant of a prosecutor's favorable plea agreement and the agreement subsequently expired.

2012

Lafler v. Cooper, 566 U.S.
Flawed advice leading to the rejection of a plea offer can form the basis of an ineffective assistance claim. Defense counsel in this case advised his client to reject a plea agreement on the mistaken belief that the defendant could not be convicted of assault with intent to murder.

Maples v. Thomas, 565 U.S. If defense counsel "abandons" the defendant, causing him or her to miss a key appellate deadline, a second chance to appeal the conviction must be given.

Defender Employees, published by the Administrative Office of the U.S. Courts. Public defenders are defense attorneys for indigent individuals, but the Code is informative nevertheless.

In the first case, *McMann v. Richardson* (397 U.S. 759 [1970]), the Court held that counsel is effective when his or her legal advice is "within the range of competence demanded of attorneys in criminal cases" (p. 771). This is something of a vague standard, so the Court created a new test in **Strickland v. Washington (466 U.S. 668 [1984])**. There, the Court held that a two-prong test must be applied in order to determine whether counsel is ineffective:

> First, the defendant must show that counsel's performance was deficient. This requires showing that counsel made errors so serious that counsel was not functioning as the "counsel" guaranteed the defendant by the Sixth Amendment. Second, the defendant must show that the deficient performance prejudiced the defense. This requires showing that counsel's errors were so serious as to deprive the defendant of a fair trial, a trial whose result is unreliable. (p. 687)

The two prongs announced in this case are now known as the *performance* prong and the *prejudice* prong. With regard to the former, "The proper measure of attorney performance remains simply reasonableness under prevailing professional norms" (p. 688). Defense counsel's performance will be considered adequate if he or she avoids conflicts of interest, serves as an advocate for the defendant's case, and brings to bear "such skill and knowledge as will render the trial a reliable adversarial testing process" (p. 688). And with regard to the prejudice prong, the defendant must prove that "there is a reasonable probability that, but for counsel's unprofessional errors, the result of the proceeding would have been different" (p. 694). In other words, the burden falls on the defendant to show that the outcome of the case hinged on the ineffective assistance provided by his or her defense attorney. If defense counsel acted ineffectively but such actions did not influence the outcome of the case, then a *Strickland* claim cannot succeed.

Several cases decided in the wake of *Strickland* are summarized in the accompanying timeline. They shed light on the meaning of effective assistance, according to the U.S. Supreme Court.

The burden falls on the defendant to show that the outcome of the case hinged on the ineffective assistance provided by his or her defense attorney.

Think About It...

Effective Assistance of Counsel? A woman has been convicted of check fraud. On appeal, she claims that she was denied access to effective counsel. She argues that her attorney, a young public defender, had never tried a jury case and did not have enough time to prepare an adequate defense. Will her appeal succeed?

Anton Gvozdikov/ Shutterstock

A Case of Nonprosecution

Following are the facts reported by the U.S. District Court for the District of Columbia in *NAACP* v. *Levi*, a classic case discussed earlier in this chapter:

On May 31, 1971, Carnell Russ, a 24-year-old black man, while operating his motor vehicle on an Arkansas highway, was arrested for an alleged speeding violation by Jerry Mac Green, a white state trooper. Russ was accompanied by his wife, their minor children, and an adult cousin. The trooper directed him to the county courthouse. Russ complied and upon arrival, parked his vehicle and was escorted into the courthouse by the arresting trooper and two other white law enforcement officers, Charles Ratliff and Norman Draper. Minutes later, Russ returned to the vehicle where his family awaited. He requested and received from his wife sufficient money to post the necessary collateral. He then joined the three officers who were close by observing his actions. The four retraced their steps with Russ again in custody. A short time thereafter, Mrs. Russ first observed two of the officers leave and minutes later an ambulance depart from the rear of the courthouse area where her husband had just entered in the officers' custody. She later learned that Mr. Russ, while under detention, had been shot in the center of his forehead by Ratliff and then transported to a hospital. Green and Draper were the sole witnesses to the shooting. Her husband died from the gunshot wound within hours. (p. 1112)

Ratliff was indicted and found not guilty of voluntary manslaughter pursuant to an investigation by the state police. Criminal charges were not brought against the other two officers, and the case was closed. The National Association for the Advancement of Colored People (NAACP) learned of the prosecutor's decision not to charge the other two officers and sued (under several federal statutes), offering up several legal arguments, among them that the officers ". . . acted in an arbitrary, capricious and discriminatory manner by failing to investigate the Russ shooting to determine if his constitutional rights and Federal statutes had been violated by Arkansas law enforcement authorities" (p. 1113). The decision reached by the court was that the defendants' motion to dismiss the cases should not be granted and, further, that the plaintiffs should have an opportunity to present their case in a civil trial. This is an important example of a court stepping in and providing a remedy for those who disagree with the nonprosecution of a certain individual or individuals.

This case presents some questions with respect to nonprosecution:

1. Should courts be permitted to provide a remedy for nonprosecution?
2. For what other reasons might a court intervene in a nonprosecution situation?

Describe the prosecutor's role, prosecutorial discretion, and the issues surrounding prosecutorial misconduct.

A prosecutor's decision whether to charge is rarely challenged; however, prosecutors' charging decisions are subject to certain constitutional restrictions. Unfair and selective prosecutions are inappropriate and violate the equal protection clause of the Fourteenth Amendment. Vindictive prosecutions violate due process. Prosecutors generally enjoy absolute immunity for their charging decisions.

Key Cases

   Oyler v. Boles

   Blackledge v. Perry

   United States v. Lane

1. What is the role of the prosecutor?

2. Identify reasons for nonprosecution.

3. What are the limitations on prosecutorial discretion?

prosecutorial discretion   A prosecutor's authority to decide whether to proceed with criminal charges against a particular suspect.

selective prosecution   When an individual is targeted for prosecution merely because he or she falls into a certain group (for example, a minority group).

pretextual prosecution   When the prosecutor lacks the evidence to charge someone with a particular crime and so charges him or her with a lesser crime.

vindictive prosecution   Prosecution based on revenge.

joinder   When the prosecutor either (1) brings multiple charges against the same individual in the same trial or (2) brings charges against multiple individuals in the same trial.

severance   The opposite of joinder. For example, severance occurs when separate trials are held for different charges against the same defendant.

Explain the purpose, functions, and powers of the grand jury.

Grand juries are useful when the case in question is of great public and/or political significance, when its extensive investigative powers are helpful, when time is of the essence, and when one or more witnesses is hesitant to speak in open court, preferring the secrecy that surrounds grand jury proceedings. Grand jury proceedings are secretive. Targets of grand jury investigations do not enjoy the same rights as criminal defendants. Grand juries also have extensive investigative powers.

Key Cases

   Hurtado v. California

   United States v. Mandujano

   United States v. Calandra

   Hale v. Henkel

1. Summarize important Supreme Court decisions concerning the secrecy of grand jury proceedings.

2. Explain the investigative powers of the grand jury.

grand jury   A body of people selected to hear evidence against an accused person (or persons) and determine whether there is sufficient evidence to bring the case to trial.

subpoena *ad testificandum*   A subpoena that compels a witness to appear before the grand jury.

subpoena *duces tecum*   A subpoena that compels the production of tangible evidence (for example, a suspected murder weapon).

contempt power   The grand jury's authority to hold people in contempt of court for failing to appear before it. Civil and criminal sanctions can be imposed.

Outline the development of the right to counsel.

Criminal defendants enjoy the Sixth Amendment right to counsel once adversarial criminal proceedings have commenced. Like many constitutional rights, the right to counsel can be waived, but the trial court can appoint standby counsel in certain circumstances. Counsel is ineffective when specific errors are made that are prejudicial to the defendant's case.

Key Cases

Gideon v. *Wainwright*

Powell v. *Alabama*

Johnson v. *Zerbst*

Strickland v. *Washington*

1. Summarize the development of the right to counsel.

2. What are the requirements for a valid waiver of the right to counsel?

3. What is meant by "effective assistance of counsel"?

pro se defense When a defendant waives his or her Sixth Amendment right to counsel and defends him- or herself.

effective assistance of counsel The requirement that a defense attorney must effectively represent his or her client. In *Strickland* v. *Washington* (466 U.S. 668 [1984]), the Supreme Court held that a two-prong test must be applied in order to determine whether counsel is ineffective: "First, the defendant must show that counsel's performance was deficient. This requires showing that counsel made errors so serious that counsel was not functioning as the 'counsel' guaranteed the defendant by the Sixth Amendment. Second, the defendant must show that the deficient performance prejudiced the defense" (p. 687).

12

"Obtaining a guilty plea as the result of plea bargaining is the most common method of securing a conviction."

Plea Bargaining and Guilty Pleas

1 Define *plea bargaining* and summarize the arguments for and against its use.

2 Summarize the plea-bargaining process and the effects of plea bargaining.

3 Outline the elements of a valid guilty plea.

© SuperStock/Alamy

Sergio Robles, a diagnosed schizophrenic, was convicted of killing a Pasadena, California, police officer during a 2009 shootout. Robles, who would have likely faced the death penalty under ordinary circumstances, pleaded guilty to murder in exchange for a 40-year prison sentence. The plea agreement came after two years of investigation and three separate mental evaluations to determine Robles's state of mind. Two doctors determined he was insane during the shooting; one determined he was not. The prosecutor agreed to the bargain after realizing that putting dueling experts in front of a trial jury could have been too risky. Had jurors sided with the two doctors who determined Robles was insane, he may have been found not guilty by reason of insanity.

The Robles case calls attention to the controversy surrounding guilty pleas. On the one hand, he was sentenced to a lengthy prison term. On the other hand, it is clear that his victim's family and the slain officer's colleagues were not entirely content with the agreement. Indeed, the widow of the officer Robles killed said at the

Kellie L Folkerts/Shutterstock

sentencing hearing that "I hope your life is so miserable that you look forward to death."[1]

DISCUSS **Should plea bargains be allowed in cases like this?**

▶ An Alternative to Trial

Obtaining a guilty plea as the result of plea bargaining is the most common method of securing a conviction. The overwhelming majority—90%, by some estimates—of criminal convictions in the United States result from guilty pleas, rather than trials. Moreover, these pleas usually derive from some bargaining between the defense attorney and the prosecutor. This is known as **plea bargaining**. Both parties stand to gain something from a guilty plea: The prosecutor obtains a conviction, and the defense attorney usually succeeds in getting lenient treatment for his or her client.

Plea bargaining is essential to the administration of justice. If every defendant demanded his or her right to a jury trial and succeeded in such a demand, the criminal justice system would literally collapse. In this vein, arguments against plea bargaining are really like thought exercises; nothing can be done to eliminate plea bargaining because there are just too many criminals and not enough prosecutors, courts, and prisons.

At the same time, critics' views should not be dismissed. Consistent with what Americans are all taught, many people believe that judges and juries should determine guilt and that prosecutors and defense attorneys should only play a secondary role in this process. Plea bargaining essentially permits attorneys to decide the outcome of a case without ever going to trial. Additionally, it is well known that when two defendants face the same charge, the one who plea bargains invariably receives a lesser sentence than the one who does not.

Understand, though, that plea bargaining is not the only way to arrive at a guilty plea. Many defendants plead guilty to the charges against them even when no bargaining takes place.

The bulk of this chapter focuses on plea bargaining; however, the section "Guilty Pleas" is especially important for both types of guilty pleas: those that follow bargaining and those that do not. A sample of the plea form that is submitted to the court is presented in Figure 12–1.

The History and Rise of Plea Bargaining

Plea bargaining supplants trial by jury. At what point in history did the practice of plea bargaining gain acceptance? This section looks at the history of plea bargaining, reasons for its rise, and arguments for and against it, in addition to attempts to restrict the practice. It also looks at the Supreme Court's view on plea bargaining.

Historical Origins

One of the earliest reported cases addressing plea bargaining was decided in the early 1800s. In that case, *Commonwealth* v. *Battis* (1 Mass. 95 [1804]), a court was hesitant to permit a guilty plea by a defendant charged with a capital crime. The court gave the defendant time to contemplate his plea and even "examined, under oath, the sheriff, the jailer and justice (before whom the examination of the prisoner was had [sic] previous to commitment), as to the sanity of the prisoner; and whether there had been tampering with him, either by promises, persuasions, or hopes of pardon if he would plead guilty" (p. 96).

Following *Battis*, other cases involving some degree of plea bargaining were reported. One court's opinion focused on a Michigan statute that set forth specific requirements necessary

PLEA FORM

STATE OF TEXAS   §   IN THE MUNICIPAL COURT

VS.   §   CITY OF _____

_____   §   _____ COUNTY, TEXAS

CAUSE NUMBER:

PLEA OF *NOLO CONTENDERE*

I, the undersigned, do hereby enter my appearance on the complaint of the offense, to wit: _____

_____

charged in Municipal Court Cause Number _____. I have been informed of my right to a jury trial and that my signature on this plea of nolo contendere (meaning "no contest") will have the same force and effect as a plea of guilty on the judgment of the Court. I do hereby plead nolo contendere to said offense as charged, waive my right to a jury trial or hearing by the Court, and agree to pay the fine and costs the judge assesses. I understand that my plea may result in a conviction appearing on either a criminal record or a driver's license record.

_____   _____

Date   Defendant's Signature

                                                               _____

                                                                 Address

PLEA OF GUILTY

I, the undersigned, do hereby enter my appearance on the complaint of the offense, to wit: _____

_____

charged in Municipal Court Cause Number _____. I have been informed of my right to a jury trial and that my signature to this plea of guilty will have the same force and effect as a judgment of the Court. I do hereby plead guilty to the offense as charged, waive my right to a jury trial or hearing by the Court, and agree to pay the fine and costs the judge assesses. I understand that my plea may result in a conviction appearing on either a criminal record or a driver's license record.

_____   _____

Date   Defendant's Signature

                                                                 _____

                                                                 Address

PLEA OF NOT GUILTY

I, the undersigned, do hereby enter my appearance on the complaint of the offense, to wit: _____

_____

charged in Municipal Court Cause Number _____. I plead not guilty.

Initial One:

_____ I want a jury trial.

_____ I waive my right to a jury trial and request a trial before the Court.

_____   _____

Date   Defendant's Signature

                                                                  _____

                                                                  Address

FIGURE 12–1   Sample Plea Form.

for a valid guilty plea. The court expressed concern that some of what could be called *plea bargaining* was taking place without the approval of the courts (*Edwards* v. *People*, 39 Mich. 760 [1878]). The court observed that Michigan passed the statute "for the protection of prisoners and of the public" in response "to serious abuses caused by [prosecutors] procuring prisoners to plead guilty when a fair trial might show they were not guilty, or might show other facts important to be known" (p. 761). The court also found it "easy to see that the Legislature thought there was danger that prosecuting attorneys . . . would procure prisoners to plead guilty by assurances [that] they have no power to make[,] of influence in lowering the sentence, or by bringing some other unjust influence to bear on them" (p. 762). These claims suggest that plea bargaining was a somewhat common practice by the second half of the nineteenth century.

Plea bargaining became even more common in the early to middle 1900s. Many states had, by then, impaneled commissions to study the workings of their criminal justice systems. An example of one such commission was the New York State Crime Commission, which was impaneled in 1927. The studies published by these commissions reported an increase in the practice of plea bargaining. For example, the Georgia Department of Public Welfare reported that the rate of pleading guilty increased 70% from 1916 to 1921.[2] Similarly, statistics in New York revealed that between 1839 and 1920, the guilty plea rate rose to some 90% of all cases.[3]

Reasons for the Rise

Why the apparent rise in plea bargaining? Historical accounts show that in the early days of English criminal justice, a jury would hear 12 to 20 felony cases in a single day.[4] Trials played out in a similar fashion in U.S. courts during the 1800s. One historian points out that many early trials in the United States were carried out without lawyers for the defendant and even, in some cases, for the government.[5] As the U.S. legal system began to mature and lawyers became regular participants, trials slowed down and guilty plea rates increased out of necessity. According to one source, "[P]lea bargaining should be viewed as a natural outgrowth of a progressively adversarial criminal justice system."[6]

Despite its apparent necessity, plea bargaining was criticized extensively by early commentators. Some called it an "incompetent, inefficient, and lazy method of administering justice."[7] Others suggested that plea bargaining was just a means of avoiding trials for individuals charged with committing criminal acts. The following section considers some of these criticisms in depth.

- -

Arguments For and Against Plea Bargaining

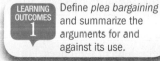

Define *plea bargaining* and summarize the arguments for and against its use.

There are several arguments in support of plea bargaining, and given that plea bargaining is a widely accepted practice in the U.S. justice system, these arguments have clearly won out.

Plea bargaining is a widely accepted practice in the U.S. justice system.

- Plea bargaining is widely accepted because, despite certain drawbacks, it benefits all members of the courtroom work group: the judge, the prosecutor, and the defense attorney (not to mention the defendant). Thus, the arguments in support of plea bargaining are really arguments concerning the *benefits* of reaching plea agreements. Each of these arguments needs to be viewed in context, however. In some situations, such as highly celebrated cases, the costs of plea bargaining may outweigh the benefits.

- Plea bargaining benefits the prosecutor because it provides him or her with a greater ability to dispose of a busy case load. District attorneys are often faced with limited resources and, as such, cannot prosecute every case that comes before them. Specifically, a district attorney may opt to pursue charges on cases that have a highly public element and/or are likely to result in guilty convictions. Cases that do not look promising may be prime candidates for plea bargaining. According to one observer, plea bargaining may be favored by the prosecution simply because it allows the courtroom work group to further its "mutual interest in avoiding conflict, reducing uncertainty, and maintaining group cohesion."[8]

- Defense attorneys also benefit from plea bargaining. Public defenders, who are the most common type of counsel in criminal trials, face resource constraints similar to those of prosecutors. Thus, plea bargaining benefits public defenders by allowing quick disposition of cases. It also allows them to focus on cases that they perceive as being worthy of trial. Bargaining also benefits privately retained counsel because it speeds up the process, which translates into "more money for less work." This is not to suggest, however, that this is the prime motivation of defense attorneys. Many zealously guard the interests of their clients.

- Plea bargaining benefits the defendant perhaps more than the prosecutor or the defense attorney. The obvious reason for this is that the defendant generally receives a lesser sentence (or charge, which also affects the ultimate punishment) as a result of plea bargaining. On another level, as will be discussed later, the defendant loses his or her chance at an acquittal and, sometimes, important rights, including the right to a trial by jury. But the Supreme Court has said that these costs may be outweighed by the benefits of "avoiding the anxieties and uncertainties of trial" (*Blackledge* v. *Allison*, 431 U.S. 63 [1977], p. 71).

- The court also benefits from plea bargaining. The prompt disposition of cases saves judicial resources, as researching a plea bargain takes less time than holding a full-blown trial. In fact, to the chagrin of many, the victims of crime

Arguments for	Arguments against
Contributes to cohesion in the courtroom work group	Behooves the prosecutor to choose the most serious charge from which to begin bargaining
Helps the prosecutor dispose of a busy case load	Contributes to inefficiency
Helps the public defender dispose of a busy case load	Wastes time; most defendants plead guilty anyway
Benefits the defendant by providing a reduction in charges and/or a favorable sentencing recommendation	Undermines the integrity of the justice system
Saves on judicial resources by avoiding the costs of going to trial	Decides the defendant's guilt without having a trial
May give the victim the satisfaction of having a prompt resolution of the case	Allows the criminal to get away with his or her crime
May benefit the victim who does not wish to testify at trial	An innocent individual may be coerced to plead guilty (that is, legal versus factual guilt)

FIGURE 12–2 Arguments For and Against Plea Bargaining.

may even benefit from plea bargaining. A quickly reached plea bargain may give the victim the satisfaction of having the case closed sooner rather than later. Moreover, the victim may also not want to testify or risk the possibility that the prosecution will not succeed in obtaining a conviction.[9] Figure 12–2 summarizes the arguments for and against plea bargaining.

Apart from the obvious concern with the prosecutor and defense attorney effectively deciding a defendant's guilt, there are other problems posed by plea bargaining.

- In an effort to secure a conviction, the prosecutor will start with the most serious charge and work down. That is, the prosecutor may *overcharge* as a first step in the bargaining process. This negotiation process is much like that of buying a used car at a dealership, in which the dealer usually starts with a ridiculously high price but is willing to negotiate. In the end, however, few buyers end up purchasing a car for its fair market value. The concern with plea bargaining, then, is that the defendant will be encouraged to plead guilty to an offense that is more serious than that for which he or she would be convicted at trial.

- Plea bargaining may contribute to *inefficiency*. As one researcher observed, "[D]efense attorneys commonly devise strategies whose only utility lies in the threat they pose to the court's and prosecutor's time."[10]

In an effort to secure a conviction, the prosecutor will start with the most serious charge and work down.

- Critics further contend that not only is plea bargaining inefficient, but it also wastes time. They claim that plea bargaining is not necessary to obtain guilty pleas and that most defendants plead guilty anyway, if they think it is highly likely that going to trial will result in a verdict of guilty.[11]

- Plea bargaining may undermine the integrity of the criminal justice system. Throughout this book, discussion has examined the complex rules of criminal procedure set forth by the U.S. Constitution and interpreted by the Supreme Court. Critics of plea bargaining claim that the practice circumvents these "rigorous standards of due process and proof imposed during trials."[12] In response to these concerns, some jurisdictions have attempted to place restrictions on plea bargaining (see Figure 12–3).

- Another reason that plea bargaining may undermine the criminal process is that it effectively decides the defendant's guilt without having a trial, an exhaustive investigation, or the presentation of evidence and witness testimony. As mentioned earlier in this section, the defendant's guilt is effectively decided by the prosecutor. One critic has argued that plea-bargaining decisions result from improper considerations:

  One mark of a just legal system is that it minimizes the effect of tactical choices upon the outcome of its processes. In criminal cases, the extent of an offender's punishment ought to turn primarily upon what he did and, perhaps, upon his personal characteristics rather than upon a postcrime, postarrest decision to exercise or not to exercise some procedural option.[13]

- Plea bargaining may also allow criminals to get away with their crimes—or at least to receive lenient sentences. Further, critics claim that providing reduced sentences may

Ban Plea Bargaining

The state of Alaska once banned the practice of plea bargaining altogether. In 1975, the Alaska attorney general banned all forms of plea bargaining.

Set Cutoff Dates for Plea Bargaining

Some jurisdictions have banned plea bargaining if it occurs a certain number of days (for example, 60 days) after formal charge or indictment. Plea bargaining is acceptable prior to the deadline.

Ban Bargaining for Certain Offenses

Some jurisdictions have also experimented with banning plea bargaining for certain offenses. For example, the Bronx County (New York) District Attorney once enacted a ban on plea bargaining whenever a grand jury returned a felony indictment.

Jury Waiver

The *jury waiver* approach gives the defendant the opportunity to engage in plea negotiations in exchange for giving up his or her right to a jury trial. This process has come to be known as the *slow plea of guilty*, insofar as it does not result in the disposition of a case prior to trial.

Impose Other Restrictions

- California: Voters passed a referendum in 1982 that provided for no plea bargaining in any case involving (1) a serious felony, (2) a felony in which a firearm was used, or (3) the offense of driving under the influence.
- El Paso County, Texas: In 1987, two state district judges adopted a policy of prohibiting all plea negotiations in their courts as a method of ensuring equal treatment for similarly situated defendants.
- Maricopa County, Arizona: In 1995, five Maricopa County Superior Court judges adopted a policy that prohibited plea agreements based on stipulated (that is, agreed upon) sentences.

FIGURE 12–3 Attempts to Limit Plea Bargaining Throughout History.

reduce the deterrent effect of harsh punishment. In both cases, plea bargaining may give the impression that defendants can negotiate their way out of being adequately punished for their crimes.

- Innocent individuals may be coerced to plead guilty. In such a situation, a plea bargain amounts to an admission of legal guilt, when, in fact, the defendant may not be factually guilty. An example of the pressure on innocent defendants to plead guilty is found in *North Carolina* v. *Alford* (400 U.S. 25 [1970]). In that case, the defendant, facing the death penalty if he was convicted, pled guilty to the crime, but did not admit to all elements of it. His plea (and other similar pleas) was promptly dubbed the ***Alford* plea**. Certain jurisdictions permit Alford pleas (also called "best-interests pleas"). A defendant who makes an *Alford* plea does not allocute, which means he or she does not—and indeed is not required to—explain the details of the offense for the judge.

The Supreme Court's View on Plea Bargaining

Notwithstanding the competing views on plea bargaining, the Supreme Court has essentially laid the debate to rest by upholding the validity of the practice. In ***Brady* v. *United States* (397 U.S. 742 [1970])**, for example, the Court stated, "Of course, that the prevalence of guilty pleas is explainable does not necessarily validate those pleas or the system which produces them. But we cannot hold that it is unconstitutional for the State to extend a benefit to a defendant who in turn extends a substantial benefit to the State" (pp. 752–753). Next, in the case of *Santobello* v. *New York* (404 U.S. 257 [1971]), the Court offered the following argument in support of plea bargaining: "The disposition of criminal charges by agreement between the prosecutor and the accused, sometimes loosely called 'plea bargaining,' is an essential component of the administration of justice. Properly administered, it is to be encouraged" (p. 260).

How, then, is plea bargaining to be properly administered? The following sections seek to answer this question. First, the plea-bargaining process is described, and then the effects of plea bargaining, the rules concerning plea bargaining, and situations in which guilty pleas can be challenged are all discussed. The reader will develop an understanding of the complex practice of plea bargaining as it has been interpreted through the courts—most notably, the U.S. Supreme Court.

The Plea-Bargaining Process

The prosecutor can make several different offers in order to secure a guilty plea. The most straightforward and common method is to reduce the charge or charges against the defendant. Other alternatives include dismissing other pending charges and promising to recommend a particular sentence.

Assuming that what is offered by the prosecution is acceptable to the defendant, he or she can make one of two pleas: a simple plea of guilty or a plea of *nolo contendere*. The former is akin to saying "I am guilty," and the latter is akin to saying "I do not contest this." Both pleas are effectively the same. The only difference is that the *nolo* plea cannot be used as an admission of guilt in a subsequent civil case.

Rights During Plea Bargaining

The Sixth Amendment right to counsel applies during plea bargaining because charges have already been filed before bargaining commences. According to the Supreme Court in *Kirby* v. *Illinois* (406 U.S. 682 [1972]), the right to counsel attaches when, after charges have been filed, the "defendant finds himself faced with the prosecutorial forces of organized society, and immersed in the intricacies of substantive and procedural criminal law" (p. 689). This means that the prosecutor cannot bargain directly with the defendant unless counsel has been waived.

The Sixth Amendment also requires that defense counsel be effective during the plea-negotiation process. This means that the defense attorney must, at a minimum, investigate the case so as to make an informed decision with regard to what sentences and charges are offered by the prosecution. To be effective, counsel must also ensure that his or her client understands the consequences of the plea-bargaining process. In addition, defense counsel must share with his or her client any and all plea offers presented by the prosecution (*Missouri v. Frye*, 566 U.S. ___ [2012]).

Next, the defendant enjoys the right to be informed of exculpatory evidence in possession of the prosecution. That is, if the prosecutor has evidence that casts doubt on the accused's guilt, he or she must inform the defense of that evidence. For evidence to be considered *exculpatory*, it must have a reasonable probability of affecting the outcome of the case. Evidence that is inconsequential to the question of guilt, which is clearly rare, need not be provided to the defense (*United States* v. *Bagley*, 473 U.S. 667 [1985]).

As will be discussed in the next chapter, the defendant enjoys the right to be present at his or her own trial. However, this right does not apply in the context of plea bargaining. That is to say, no court has required that a criminal defendant be provided a constitutional right to be present during plea bargaining. This could change, but for now, all that is required is that the defense effectively communicates to his or her client the nature of the sentence or charges offered by the prosecution.

In *United States* v. *Ruiz* (536 U.S. 622 [2002]), the Supreme Court decided that the defendant *does not* have the right to impeachment information relating to informants and other witnesses, nor does he or she have the right to information supporting any affirmative defense that he or she might raise if the case went to trial. Thus, there are limitations to the defendant's rights during the plea-bargaining process.

Types of Inducements

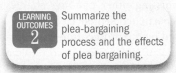

Summarize the plea-bargaining process and the effects of plea bargaining.

The Constitution places few restrictions on offers the prosecution may make during the bargaining process, which are known as **prosecutorial inducements**. Because *Brady* v. *United States* (397 U.S. 742 [1970]) was the first Supreme Court case to condone plea bargaining, it is a fitting point of departure before considering the offers prosecutors can make. The defendant in *Brady* was charged with kidnapping under a statute that permitted (1) a jury to recommend the death penalty if it saw fit *or* (2) a judge to sentence the defendant to life in prison, if guilt was determined via a bench trial. The defendant opted for a jury trial but then changed his plea to guilty and was sentenced to 30 years. He then argued that the statute effectively compelled him to plead guilty because of fear of the death penalty. The Supreme Court rejected this claim.

The reasoning the Court offered for its decision is somewhat complicated but important. Justice White emphasized that the statute in *Brady caused* the guilty plea but did not *coerce* it. He then emphasized that coercion is possible only when physical force or mental pressure is applied. This means that if "Brady was so gripped by fear of the death penalty or hope of leniency that he did not or could not, with the help of counsel, rationally weigh the advantages of going to trial against the advantages of pleading guilty" (p. 750), then his argument would have succeeded. However, Justice White found that the statute at most *influenced* Brady and that the coercion argument was exaggerated. In further support of his opinion, Justice White quoted an appellate court decision dealing with plea bargaining, *Shelton* v. *United States* (246 F.2d 571 [5th Cir. 1957]):

> [A] plea of guilty entered by one fully aware of the direct consequences, including the actual value of any commitments made to him by the court, prosecutor, or his own counsel, must stand unless induced by threats (or promises to discontinue improper harassment), misrepresentation (including unfulfilled or unfulfillable promises), or perhaps by promises that are by their nature improper as having no proper relationship to the prosecutor's business (for example, bribes). (p. 572)

In short, a guilty plea resulting from an inducement from the prosecution, like a confession obtained in a police interrogation room, should be voluntary. A guilty plea will be considered involuntary when it results from prosecutorial coercion (for example, physical force or strong psychological pressuring). If, by contrast, the prosecutor causes a guilty plea simply because the accused thinks that pleading as such is his or her best way of avoiding a long prison term, then the defendant cannot succeed by claiming such a plea is involuntary.

What, then, offers/inducements can the prosecution properly make? *Brady* answered this question only insofar as the Court held that the prosecutor cannot coerce a guilty plea. In **Bordenkircher v. Hayes (434 U.S. 357 [1978])**, the Court attempted to offer a clearer answer. In that case, the defendant was indicted by a grand jury for forging a check for $88.30. The range of punishment was two to ten years in prison. The prosecutor offered to recommend a five-year sentence but threatened to seek an indictment under a habitual criminal statute if the defendant did not accept the offer. Because the defendant had two prior felony convictions, a conviction under the habitual criminal statute could have resulted in life in prison. Somewhat controversially, in a 5-to-4 decision, the Supreme Court upheld the defendant's conviction under the habitual criminal statute on the theory that it resulted from a choice among known alternatives. Basically, the Court said that the defendant had the choice to accept five years in prison and neglected to take the opportunity. The defendant argued that his second conviction

© Simon Balson/Alamy

was vindictive, citing *North Carolina* v. *Pierce* (395 U.S. 711 [1969]). But the Court countered by stating that "the imposition of these difficult choices [is] an inevitable—'and permissible'— attribute of any legitimate system which tolerates and encourages the negotiation of pleas" (*Bordenkircher* v. *Hayes*, p. 364).

Reduced to its most fundamental elements, the Court's opinion in *Bordenkircher* thus implies that the prosecution has great latitude in terms of being able to persuade the defendant to accept a plea, as long as the higher charges are authorized by law and are openly presented to the defense. This suggests, as well, that the prosecution may offer a charge or sentencing concession in exchange for the defendant agreeing not to appeal or claim that some constitutional right has been violated. The Court stated further,

> There is no doubt that the breadth of discretion that our country's legal system vests in prosecuting attorneys carries with it the potential for both individual and institutional abuse. And broad though that discretion may be, there are undoubtedly constitutional limits upon its exercise. We hold only that the course of conduct engaged in by the prosecutor in this case, which no more than openly presented the defendant with the unpleasant alternatives of forgoing trial or facing charges on which he was plainly subject to prosecution, did not violate the Due Process Clause of the Fourteenth Amendment. (p. 365)

In a related case, **United States** v. **Goodwin (457 U.S. 368 [1982])**, the Court reached a similar decision. In that case, the defendant was indicted on additional charges after plea negotiations broke down. The Court held that the prosecutor could file additional charges if an initial expectation that the defendant would plead guilty to a lesser charge proved unfounded. The Court refused to accept the defendant's argument that this prosecution was vindictive and, once again, gave broad authority to prosecutors in the plea-bargaining process.

Nonetheless, certain prosecutorial inducements are *not* permissible. For example, the Supreme Court has stated that "a prosecutor's offer during plea bargaining of adverse or lenient treatment for some person *other* than the accused . . . might pose a greater danger of inducing a false guilty plea by skewing the assessment of the risks a defendant must consider" (*Bordenkircher* v. *Hayes*, p. 365, n. 8). Also, if the prosecutor flagrantly deceives the accused or fabricates evidence and/or starts rumors concerning the accused's level of involvement in the offense, a resulting guilty plea will be deemed unconstitutional.

Questionable Inducements

Judge Joseph A. Colquitt has used the term **ad hoc plea bargaining** to refer to some of the strange concessions that defendants agree to make as part of prosecutors' decisions to secure guilty pleas.[14] There are five types of these ad hoc bargains:

1. unusual probation condition
2. quid pro quo agreement
3. unauthorized form of punishment
4. unauthorized benefit
5. pleading guilty to an unrelated or nonexistent crime

Colquitt also states that ad hoc plea bargaining "may involve neither a plea nor a sentence. For example, if a defendant charged with public intoxication seeks to avoid a statutorily mandated minimum sentence of 10 days in the county jail, the prosecutor might agree to dismiss the charges if the defendant agrees to make a monetary contribution to a local driver's education program" (p. 711).

Getty Images

1. Charitable contributions in lieu of fines or jail terms: *State* v. *Stellato* (523 A.2d 1345 [Conn. App. Ct. 1987]); *Ratliff* v. *State* (596 N.E.2d 241 [Ind. Ct. App. 1992])
2. Relinquished property ownership: *United States* v. *Thao Dinh Lee* (173 F.3d 1258 [10th Cir. 1999])
3. Agreement to surrender a professional license or not work in a particular profession: *United States* v. *Hoffer* (129 F.3d 1196 [11th Cir. 1997])
4. Voluntary agreement to undergo sterilization: *State* v. *Pasicznyk* (1997 WL 79501 [Wash. Ct. App. Feb. 25, 1997])
5. Voluntary agreement to undergo surgical castration: *ACLU* v. *State* (5 S.W.2d 418 [Ark. 1999])
6. Agreement to enter the army on a four-year enlistment: *State* v. *Hamrick* (595 N.W.2d 492 [Iowa 1999])
7. Agreement not to appeal: *People* v. *Collier* (641 N.Y.S.2d 181 [App. Div. 1996])
8. Shaming punishments, such as bumper stickers for convicted DUI offenders: *Ballenger* v. *State* (436 S.E.2d 793 [Ga. Ct. App. 1993])
9. Agreement to seal the records of a case: *State* v. *Campbell* (21 Media L. Rep. 1895 [Wash. Super. Ct. 1993])
10. Ordering offenders to surrender profits, such as from books written about their crimes: *Rolling* v. *State ex rel. Butterworth* (741 So. 2d 627 [Fla. Dist. Ct. App. 1999])
11. Banishment to another location: *State* v. *Culp* (226 S.E.2d 841 [N.C. Ct. App. 1976]); *Phillips* v. *State* (512 S.E.2d 32 [Ga. Ct. App. 1999])
12. Pleading guilty to nonexistent crimes (that is, crimes that are not prohibited by law): *Bassin* v. *Isreal* (335 N.E.2d 53 [Ill. App. Ct. 1975])

FIGURE 12–4 **Examples of Ad Hoc Plea Bargaining Concessions.**

Judges can even get involved in ad hoc plea bargaining. Colquitt points to one shocking example of this method of bargaining run amok. The case, *Ryan* v. *Comm'n on Judicial Performance* (754 P.2d 724 [Cal. 1988]), involved a woman who was required to participate in a drug treatment program as a result of several narcotics convictions. The probation officer asked to have the woman removed from the program because she supposedly failed to follow program guidelines. At a hearing to decide on the matter, the woman, "who was wearing a low-cut sweater, bent over several times to remove documents from her purse. Thereafter the judge dismissed all criminal charges against her. When his clerk asked why the charges had been dropped, [the judge] replied, 'she showed me her boobs'" (p. 734). The judge was subsequently removed from the bench. Some less extreme examples of ad hoc plea concessions, as well as some relevant cases, are described in Figure 12–4.

Statutory and Judicial Inducements

So far, the discussion has considered only what the prosecution can and cannot do as far as inducing the defendant to plead guilty. There have also been some interesting cases dealing with statutory and judicial inducements. **Statutory inducements** refer to laws that provide lenient sentences in exchange for guilty pleas. **Judicial inducements** include actions by judges that influence the bargaining process.

With regard to statutory inducements, an illustrative case is **Corbitt v. New Jersey (439 U.S. 212 [1978])**. In that case, the defendant was convicted of first-degree murder and sentenced to life in prison, as required by the state statute with which he was charged. However, the statute provided that if he decided to plead guilty to the crime, he could be sentenced either to life imprisonment or to a term of 30 years. The defendant claimed that the statute violated due process, but the Supreme Court

The judge is usually not part of the negotiation process.

upheld it in the spirit of consistency. That is, the Court stated that it could not permit prosecutorial bargaining as in *Bordenkircher* "and yet hold that the legislature may not openly provide for the possibility of leniency in return for a plea" (p. 221).

Traditionally, plea bargaining results from the prosecution and the defense reaching an agreement; the judge is usually not part of the negotiation process. Today, however, certain jurisdictions permit a degree of judicial involvement in the plea-bargaining process. For example, the American Bar Association standards regarding guilty pleas permit judicial participation when it is requested but only for the purpose of clarifying acceptable charges and sentences. The judge cannot at any point, "either directly or indirectly, [communicate] to the defendant or defense counsel that a plea agreement should be accepted or that a guilty plea should be entered."[15]

- -
Effects of Plea Bargaining

A plea bargain ultimately affects four separate parties: (1) the court, (2) the prosecutor, (3) the defendant (most often through the defense attorney), and (4) the victim. How plea bargaining affects these individual parties is discussed in the subsections that follow.

Effects on the Court

The court is not directly bound by a plea agreement. In deciding whether to accept the bargain, the court weighs the sometimes competing interests of the agreement and the public interest. Thus, if accepting a plea agreement poses a significant risk to the public—say, because a dangerous criminal will be spared prison and placed on probation (an unlikely event)—then the court has the discretion to deny it.

An illustrative case is *United States* v. *Bean* (564 F.2d 700 [5th Cir. 1977). The facts were as follows: Bean was charged on October 22, 1976, with theft of property (that is, a car) and with burglary of a habitation, in violation of state law. At the initial arraignment, Bean pleaded not guilty to both counts. On November 30, another arraignment was held on Bean's request. At this time, the court was informed that a plea bargain had been reached between the government prosecutor and Bean and his counsel. Bean would plead guilty to the theft count and

In deciding whether to accept the bargain, the court weighs the sometimes competing interests of the agreement and the public interest.

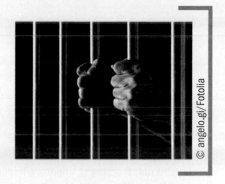
cooperate with the prosecutor in investigating others involved in the burglary. In return, the prosecutor would move for a dismissal of the burglary charge. Judge Spears rejected the plea because the offense of entering a home at night where people were sleeping was a much more serious offense than the theft of an automobile. The Fifth Circuit Court of Appeals upheld Judge Spears's decision, stating,

> Without deciding what unusual circumstances may result in the refusal of a plea bargain being an abuse of discretion, we find that Judge Spears' action in this case was well within the scope of his discretion. A decision that a plea bargain will result in the defendant's receiving too light a sentence under the circumstances of the case is a sound reason for a judge's refusing to accept the agreement.... In this case, Judge Spears was faced with a man who was charged with burglarizing at night a home on Fort Sam Houston in Texas, while Lieutenant Colonel Robert W. Oppenlander, his wife, two daughters and one son were asleep inside. In addition, the presentence report indicated that Bean had previously been committed to four years in the Texas Department of Corrections for state charges of burglary and theft of a business at nighttime. Bean had also served twenty days for unlawfully carrying a weapon in San Antonio. Given this information Judge Spears was reluctant to accept a plea bargain that would allow Bean to plead guilty to only the theft of an automobile. (p. 704)

Effects on the Prosecutor

The consequences of plea bargaining are of far greater magnitude for the prosecutor than for the court. Assuming the court accepts a plea bargain, whether it is a charge or sentence reduction, then the prosecutor must fulfill his or her part of the agreement. Note, however, that the prosecutor is not strictly obligated to fulfill his or her promises early in the plea-bargaining process. More specifically, the prosecutor is not bound by the plea bargain prior to the point at which it is accepted by the court.

A case dealing with the extent to which a prosecutor must uphold his or her end of the bargain prior to the point at which

The prosecutor is not bound by the plea bargain prior to the point at which it is accepted by the court.

the court accepts it is *Mabry* v. *Johnson* **(467 U.S. 504 [1984])**. In that case, the defense attorney called the prosecutor to accept a plea offer, but the prosecutor told him that the offer was a mistake and withdrew it. The prosecutor then offered a more harsh offer in its place, one that would have resulted in a longer prison term. The Supreme Court upheld this practice, arguing that the plea agreement was reached with full awareness on the part of the defendant and "was thus in no sense the product of governmental deception; it rested on no 'unfulfilled promise' and fully satisfied the test for voluntariness and intelligence" (p. 510). In an analogous decision, the prosecution agreed to a plea agreement, but then reneged when it became clear the defendant had aided a fellow inmate in another crime while awaiting sentencing. The Supreme Court sided with the prosecution (*Puckett* v. *United States*, No. 07-9712 [2009]).

As for the time *after* the court accepts the bargain, an illustrative case is *Santobello* v. *New York* **(404 U.S. 257 [1971])**. The defendant was indicted for two felonies. He first entered a plea of not guilty on each count. After subsequent negotiations, however, the prosecutor agreed to allow the defendant to plead guilty to a lesser offense. The defendant then withdrew his pleas of not guilty and agreed to plead guilty to the lesser offense. The court accepted the plea. At sentencing, however, a new prosecutor, who was unaware of what had transpired earlier, requested the maximum sentence. The defense objected on the grounds that the previous prosecutor promised not to make any particular sentencing recommendation. The judge then stated that he was not influenced by the second prosecutor's sentencing recommendation and imposed the maximum sentence. In response to this turn of events, the Supreme Court declared that the sentence should be declared unconstitutional as a matter of due process. The Court stated that "when a plea rests in any significant degree on a promise or agreement of the prosecutor, so that it can be said to be part of the inducement or consideration, such promise must be fulfilled" (p. 262).

Some years after *Santobello*, in the case of *United States* v. *Benchimol* **(471 U.S. 453 [1985])**, the Supreme Court seemed to change its opinion with regard to a prosecutor's breach of a plea agreement after the court has accepted it. In *Benchimol*, the prosecutor agreed to recommend a sentence of probation with restitution, but the presentence report mentioned nothing of the agreement. The defense attorney pointed out the error, and the prosecution agreed that an agreement had been reached. Even so, the court sentenced the defendant to six years. The defendant then sought to have his sentence vacated, and the court of

Think About It...

Judicial Inducements Judge Dubois has before her the prosecutor, defense attorney, and defendant in one of the cases slated to be heard in her court. The defense attorney and prosecutor tell the judge that they have reached a plea agreement and that Charles Down, the defendant, has agreed to plead guilty to manslaughter instead of first-degree murder. Judge Dubois then questions Down to ensure that the plea is voluntary, intelligent, and based in fact. During the questioning, Down begins to express reservations about the plea agreement and says, "On second thought, I don't want to plead guilty." Judge Dubois then looks at Down and says, "You should really plead guilty, because from the looks of things, you're going to get the chair if you don't." Down agrees to plead guilty but later appeals, arguing that his plea was not voluntary. How should the court rule?

© Jim West/Alamy

appeals agreed. However, the Supreme Court reversed, holding that unless the prosecution supports a recommendation "enthusiastically" or sets forth its reasons for a lenient recommendation, the court is under no obligation to honor the agreement. According to the Supreme Court,

> It may well be that the Government in a particular case might commit itself to "enthusiastically" make a particular recommendation to the court, and it may be that the Government in a particular case might agree to explain to the court the reasons for the Government's making a particular recommendation. But respondent does not contend, nor did the Court of Appeals find, that the Government had in fact undertaken to do either of these

things here. The Court of Appeals simply held that as a matter of law such an undertaking was to be implied from the Government's agreement to recommend a particular sentence. But our view of Rule 11(e) [of the *Federal Rules of Evidence*, which sets forth procedures for plea bargaining] is that it speaks in terms of what the parties in fact agree to, and does not suggest that such implied-in-law terms as were read into this agreement by the Court of Appeals have any place under the Rule. (p. 455)

Effects on the Defendant

The defendant who accepts an offer to plead guilty often faces consequences besides a reduced sentence or charge. Important rights are often waived, such as the right to appeal, the right to a jury trial, and privilege against self-incrimination. Also, if the defendant supplies inaccurate information during the course of plea negotiations, he or she may not benefit from lenient treatment. Furthermore, in exchange for pleading guilty, the prosecution may require that the defendant testifies against a codefendant.

A significant Supreme Court case dealing with the latter consequence—that is, possible testimony against a codefendant—is **Ricketts v. Adamson (483 U.S. 1 [1987])**. In that case, the defendant testified against both of his codefendants in exchange for a reduction in the charge he was facing. He was then sentenced on the reduced charge. After that, the codefendants' convictions were overturned on appeal. The prosecution then retried the codefendants, but the original defendant refused to testify at the second trial, claiming that his duty had been fulfilled. The prosecution then filed an information charging him with first-degree murder. The Supreme Court did not bar the first-degree murder prosecution because the original agreement contained a clause to the effect that the agreement would be void if the defendant refused to testify against his codefendants. Justice Brennan did acknowledge, however, that the defendant could have construed the plea agreement only to require his testimony at the first trial. The Court noted that the proper procedure, if such a situation would arise in the future, would be to submit a disagreement over the plea to the court that accepted the plea. That way, the expense of a further trial and appeals could be avoided.

At the other extreme, the defendant can sometimes *preserve* certain rights following a plea agreement. These types of arrangements are known as *conditional guilty pleas*. For example, New York law provides that an order denying a motion to suppress evidence alleged to have been obtained as a result of unlawful search and seizure "may be reviewed on appeal from a judgment of conviction notwithstanding the fact that such judgment of conviction is predicated upon a plea of guilty" (N.Y. Crim. Proc. Law §§ 710.20 [1], 710.70 [2]). These types of agreements are rare, however. In *Tollett v. Henderson* (411 U.S. 258 [1973]), the Supreme Court stated that "[w]hen a criminal defendant has solemnly admitted in open court that he is in fact guilty of the offense with which he is charged, he may not thereafter raise independent claims relating to the deprivation

The defendant who accepts an offer to plead guilty often faces consequences besides a reduced sentence or charge.

of constitutional rights that occurred prior to the entry of the guilty plea" (p. 267).

Effects on the Victim

Although plea bargaining mainly occurs between the prosecution and defense, it is important not to leave out the victim. Victims are affected by plea bargaining in at least two respects. First, a plea agreement may give the victim a measure of closure relatively quick. On the other hand, a plea agreement may be viewed by the victim as lenient. That is, he or she may feel the offender was not adequately "punished" for the offense in question. To address this problem, several states have laws that require victim involvement or input during the bargaining process.[16]

▶ Guilty Pleas

Assuming the prosecutor offers an acceptable inducement to the defendant and assuming the defendant agrees to plead guilty in exchange for leniency, the judge still must determine that the defendant understands the plea. This is in addition to the need to determine that the plea conforms to statutory and other requirements, as discussed earlier. In *Boykin* v. *Alabama* (395 U.S. 238 [1969]), the Supreme Court held that it would be unconstitutional "for the trial judge to accept [a] guilty plea without an affirmative showing that it is intelligent and voluntary" (p. 242). In order to determine that the plea is voluntary, the judge usually questions the defendant. As the Court noted in *McCarthy* v. *United States* (394 U.S. 459 [1969]),

> By personally interrogating the defendant, not only will the judge be better able to ascertain the plea's voluntariness, but he also will develop a more complete record to support his determination in a subsequent post-conviction attack. . . . Both of these goals are undermined in proportion to the degree the district court judge resorts to "assumptions" not based upon recorded responses to his inquiries. (p. 468)

For a guilty plea to be valid, it must conform to three requirements: (1) it must be intelligent; (2) it must be voluntary, not coerced; and (3) it must be based in fact. That is, if the defendant pleads guilty to a crime he or she did not commit, then technically the plea will be invalid. The following subsections consider the case law regarding these three important requirements.

Intelligence

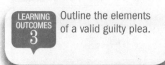
LEARNING OUTCOMES 3 — Outline the elements of a valid guilty plea.

In general, for a plea to be *intelligent* (that is, understood), it must conform to specific requirements. The defendant must understand (1) the nature of the charge or charges of which he or she is accused, (2) the

If the defendant pleads guilty to a crime he or she did not commit, then technically the plea will be invalid.

possible sentence or sentences associated with the charges, and (3) the rights he or she may waive if a guilty plea is entered (see Figure 12–5). A person whose mental capacity is called into question may be declared incompetent at a pretrial hearing and treated in order to restore his or her competency.

Understanding the Charge

In **Henderson v. Morgan (426 U.S. 637 [1976])**, the defendant was charged with first-degree murder. However, he pleaded guilty to second-degree murder following an offer by the prosecution. Several years later, he sought to have his conviction voided on the grounds that at the time he entered his plea, he did not understand that one of the elements of second-degree murder was intent to cause death. The Supreme Court held that "since respondent did not receive adequate notice of the offense to which he pleaded guilty, his plea was involuntary and the judgment of conviction was entered without due process of law" (p. 647). The element of intent in second-degree murder (that is, the *mens rea*) was viewed as critical, which meant it should have been explained to the defendant.

It is not clear based on *Henderson* whether the *judge* must explain the elements of the offense to the defendant or whether this is the job of *counsel*. The Court intimated that if defense counsel explains the offense to the accused, then little else is needed: "[I]t may be appropriate to presume that in most cases defense counsel routinely explain the nature of the offense in sufficient detail to give the accused notice of what he is being asked to admit" (p. 647). Nevertheless, the judge should at least inquire as to whether the defendant understands the charge.

Understanding Possible Sentences

There are virtually no Supreme Court cases dealing with the defendant's understanding of the possible sentences that could result from a plea bargain. However, Rule 11 of the *Federal Rules of Criminal Procedure* requires that the defendant understand the consequences of the plea. This includes an understanding of the minimum and maximum sentences as well as applicable sentencing guidelines that the judge might be required to abide by.

Whether other consequences attendant to plea bargaining and sentencing have to be explained depends on the situation. On the one hand, at least one lower court has held that the defendant does not need to be informed of the loss of the right to vote (for example, *People v. Thomas*, 41 Ill.2d 122 [1968]). On the other hand, failure to tell the defendant that deportation is a possible consequence of a guilty plea may result in a decision that such a plea is invalid (see, for example, *Padilla v. Kentucky*, No. 08-651 [2010]).

Understanding of Rights Waived as a Result of Pleading Guilty

The rights *waived* as a result of plea bargaining are different than the rights *denied* as a result of plea bargaining. For example, loss of the right to vote is not a loss due to voluntary waiver; it is a consequence tied to being convicted (even if by guilty plea) of a serious crime. The rights *waived* are those the defendant would otherwise be granted by the Constitution but that are essentially given up in exchange for lenient treatment.

Understanding Possible Sentences

The accused must understand the minimum and maximum sentences as well as applicable sentencing guidelines that the judge might be required to abide by. For example, failure to tell the defendant that deportation is a possible consequence of a guilty plea may result in a decision that such a plea is invalid (see, for example, *Padilla* v. *Kentucky*, No. 08-651 [2010]).

Understanding the Charge

The accused must understand the elements of the crime to which he or she is pleading guilty (***Henderson*** v. ***Morgan***, **426 U.S. 637 [1976]**).

Understanding of Rights Waived as a Result of Pleading Guilty

The rights *waived* are those the defendant would otherwise be granted by the Constitution but are essentially given up in exchange for lenient treatment. The constitutional rights typically waived through plea bargaining are the right to trial by jury, the privilege against self-incrimination, and the right to confront adverse witnesses.

FIGURE 12–5 Elements of the "Intelligence" Component of a Guilty Plea.

The constitutional rights typically waived through plea bargaining are the right to trial by jury, the privilege against self-incrimination, and the right to confront adverse witnesses. By pleading guilty, the defendant forgoes having a trial, which is when these rights are frequently applicable. The privilege against self-incrimination, however, still applies outside the trial context, such as in pretrial custodial interrogations. Regardless, the defendant must be clearly informed of the constitutional rights that are waived as a result of plea bargaining. According to the Supreme Court in ***Boykin*** v. ***Alabama*** **(395 U.S. 238 [1969])**, there can be no presumption of "a waiver of these three important federal rights from a silent record" (p. 243).

Think About It…

A Valid Guilty Plea? Bill Dover, a federal prisoner, filed an appeal claiming that his guilty plea was not knowing and intelligent because of ineffective assistance of counsel. Specifically, Dover claimed that his attorney mistakenly advised him that if he pleaded guilty, he would become eligible for parole after serving one-third of his prison sentence. In actuality, because Dover was a second-time offender, he was required under state law to serve one-half of his sentence before being eligible for parole. In other words, Dover claimed that he was not advised of the actual sentence that would result from his plea bargaining. Should he succeed with his petition?

© Jim Lane/Alamy

Voluntariness

In addition to the requirement that a plea be understood, it also must be voluntary. Even though a plea may be understood, it may have resulted from coercion, threats, physical abuse, or the like. Thus, the Federal Rules of Criminal Procedure require that a plea be "voluntary and not the result of force or threats or of promises (other than promises in the agreement)."[17]

Factual Basis

For a plea bargain to be valid, the plea must result from conduct that has a basis in fact. In other words, a defendant cannot (that is, according to the courts anyway) plead guilty to a crime he or she did not commit. This means that the court should inquire about the crime in question by, perhaps, having the accused describe the conduct giving rise to his or her guilty plea. This does not always occur, but according to the Supreme Court in **McCarthy v. United States (394 U.S. 459 [1969])**,

> Requiring this examination of the relation between the law and the acts the defendant admits having committed is designed to "protect a defendant who is in the position of pleading voluntarily with an understanding of the nature of the charge but without realizing that his conduct does not actually fall within the charge." (p. 467)

Importantly, the Court in *McCarthy* did not state that a factual basis for the plea bargain is a *constitutional* requirement, only that there should be one.

The Court elaborated on this matter in a similar case, in which the defendant pleaded guilty but insisted on his innocence. The Court stated that "an express admission of guilt . . . is not a constitutional requisite to the imposition of a prison sentence even if he is unwilling or unable to admit his participation in the acts constituting the crime" (*North Carolina* v. *Alford*, 400 U.S. 25 [1970]). The Court upheld the man's plea but also pointed out the following:

> Because of the importance of protecting the innocent and of insuring that guilty pleas are a product of free and intelligent choice, various state and federal court decisions properly caution that pleas coupled with claims of innocence should not be accepted unless there is a factual basis for the plea . . . and until the judge taking the plea has inquired into and sought to resolve the conflict between the waiver of trial and the claim of innocence. (p. 38, n. 10)

Thus, although there appears to be no constitutional basis for requiring that a guilty plea be tied to specific criminal acts, the courts—including the Supreme Court—prefer to avoid guilty pleas accepted from otherwise innocent defendants. Unfortunately, it would be purely conjecture to estimate how many innocent criminal defendants plead guilty in order to "play the odds" and avoid potentially lengthy prison terms.

Prosecutorial Obligations During Plea Bargaining

A plea bargain was reached between Prosecutor 1 and the defendant, in which the defendant agreed to plead guilty to less serious charges.

Three months later, at the defendant's sentencing hearing, a different prosecutor, Prosecutor 2, represented the state. The following exchange took place between the judge and Prosecutor 2:

Prosecutor 2: At this time, Your Honor, the government calls for sentencing the case of the *United States of America* v. *Defendant.*

Judge: Anything you wish to say, Mr. Prosecutor 2?

Prosecutor 2: Well, Your Honor, in light of the plea-bargaining agreement, the government, at this time, is recommending three years' incarceration. We also recommend that, if possible, the defendant be incarcerated at a minimum-security prison.

Judge: Why?

Prosecutor 2: Well, Your Honor, that was part of the plea bargain.

Judge: Not because you believe in it?

Prosecutor 2: Well, Your Honor, I do have some problems with that, but this is the way I understand it.

Judge: Anything else?

Prosecutor 2: Nothing further.

The defendant was then sentenced to four years in prison at a different institution. He appealed his sentence.

In this actual case, *United States* v. *Brown* (500 F.2d 375 [4th Cir. 1974]), the court held that the prosecution failed to fulfill its end of the bargain and that the case should be remanded so a different judge could determine the appropriate sentence. In the court's words,

[W]e believe that the government failed to keep its bargain. We have no occasion to consider the propriety of sentence, or recommendation as to sentence, as an element of a plea bargain, but it is manifest that the consideration which induced defendant's guilty plea was not simply the prospect of a formal recitation of a possible sentence, but rather the promise that an Assistant United States Attorney would make a recommendation on sentencing. This could reasonably be expected to be the sound advice, expressed with some degree of advocacy, of a government officer familiar both with the defendant and with his record and cognizant of his public duty as a prosecutor for the United States. (p. 377)

Cases like this raise a number of interesting questions, such as the following:

1. Should more than one prosecutor be involved in a single case like this?
2. What possible problems may occur if multiple prosecutors are responsible for different stages of the same criminal case?
3. What advantages are there to having multiple prosecutors involved in the same case?

Define *plea bargaining* and summarize the arguments for and against its use.

Plea bargaining occurs when the prosecution offers some concession to the defendant in exchange for a guilty plea. Supporters of the practice claim that bargaining is necessary to ensure the orderly and prompt flow of criminal cases. Critics claim, among other things, that defendants are forced to give up important constitutional rights as a result of the plea-bargaining process.

Key Cases

    Brady v. *United States*

1. What is plea bargaining?

2. Describe a situation in which a defendant pleads guilty without plea bargaining.

3. Summarize the arguments in favor of plea bargaining.

4. Summarize the arguments against plea bargaining.

plea bargaining "The defendant's agreement to plead guilty to a criminal charge with the reasonable expectation of receiving some consideration from the state. [10]

***Alford* plea** A plea in which a defendant does not allocute, which means he or she does not—and indeed is not required to—explain the details of the offense to the judge.

Summarize the plea-bargaining process and the effects of plea bargaining.

During bargaining, the defendant must be represented by counsel and that counsel must be effective. The defendant also has the right to be informed by the prosecution of exculpatory evidence in the state's possession. Finally, the prosecution can offer a wide range of inducements to the defense in order to secure a guilty plea, but those inducements cannot be coercive in nature. Plea bargaining affects the court, prosecutor, defendant, and victim in a number of important ways.

Key Cases

    Bordenkircher v. *Hayes*

    United States v. *Goodwin*

    Corbitt v. *New Jersey*

    Mabry v. *Johnson*

    Santobello v. *New York*

    United States v. *Benchimol*

    Ricketts v. *Adamson*

1. Explain the accused's constitutional rights during plea bargaining.

2. Explain ad hoc plea bargaining.

3. What are the effects of plea bargaining on the court? The prosecutor? The defendant? The victim?

prosecutorial inducements Offers made by the prosecution to the defendant.

ad hoc plea bargaining A term used to describe some of the strange concessions that defendants agree to make as part of prosecutors' decisions to secure guilty pleas.

statutory inducements Statutes that offer incentives for pleading guilty.

judicial inducements When a judge offers something to the defendant in exchange for a guilty plea. Most judicial inducements are prohibited.

Outline the elements of a valid guilty plea.

All plea agreements must be valid; that is, they must be knowing and intelligent, voluntary, and based in fact. A knowing and intelligent waiver is one in which the defendant understands the charge, the possible sentences, and the rights waived as a result of bargaining. A voluntary plea is one that is not coerced by the state. Finally, a plea agreement should be based in fact—that is, premised on conduct that actually took place.

Key Cases

    Henderson v. *Morgan*

    Boykin v. *Alabama*

    McCarthy v. *United States*

1. What does "intelligence" mean in terms of a guilty plea?

2. What does "factual basis" mean in terms of a guilty plea?

13

Trial and Beyond

"Constitutional protections for the defendant extend through and well beyond trial."

1 Describe the defendant's rights at trial.

2 Summarize how sentences are determined and the offender's rights during sentencing.

3 Describe the various types of appeals and the offender's constitutional rights during the appellate stage.

4 Summarize the right to and restrictions on *habeas corpus*.

MCT via Getty Images

INTRO DEALING WITH A DEADLOCKED JURY

In the event a jury becomes hopelessly deadlocked during its deliberations, a court may give the jury a so-called "*Allen* charge," after the Supreme Court's decision in *Allen v. United States*, 164 U.S. 492 (1896). The text of the "*Allen* charge" may read like this:

> You have informed the Court of your inability to reach a verdict in this case.
>
> At the outset, the Court wishes you to know that although you have a duty to reach a verdict, if that is not possible, the Court has neither the power nor the desire to compel agreement upon a verdict.
>
> The purpose of these remarks is to point out to you the importance and the desirability of reaching a verdict in this case, provided, however, that you as individual jurors can do so without surrendering or sacrificing your conscientious scruples or personal convictions.
>
> You will recall that upon assuming your duties in this case each of you took an oath. The oath places upon each of you as individuals the responsibility of arriving at a true verdict upon the basis of your opinion and not merely upon acquiescence in the conclusions of your fellow jurors.
>
> However, it by no means follows that opinions may not be changed by conference in the jury room. The very object of the jury system is to reach a verdict by a comparison of views and by consideration of the proofs with your fellow jurors.
>
> During your deliberations you should be open-minded and consider the issues with proper deference to and respect for the opinions of each other and you should not hesitate to re-examine your own views in the light of such discussions.
>
> You should consider also that this case must at some time be terminated; that you are selected in the same manner and from the same source from which any future jury must be selected; that

Junial Enterprises/Shutterstock

> there is no reason to suppose that the case will ever be submitted to twelve persons more intelligent, more impartial or more competent to decide it, or that more or clearer evidence will ever be produced on one side or the other.
>
> You may retire now, taking as much time as is necessary for further deliberations upon the issues submitted to you for determination.[1]

DISCUSS Could a set of judge's instructions like this be construed as coercive? See, for example, *United States v. Ybarra* (No. 08-3137 [8th Cir. 2009]).

▶ *Rights at Trial*

Assuming a defendant does not plea bargain, a trial will probably result. Thus, it is important to focus on constitutional rights during the trial stage. The main rights the defendant enjoys at trial are as follows: (1) the right to a speedy trial, (2) the right to a public trial, (3) the right to an impartial judge, (4) the right to an impartial jury, (5) the right to confrontation, (6) the right to compulsory process, (7) the right to double-jeopardy protection, and (8) the right to assert an entrapment defense.

Speedy Trial

The Sixth Amendment provides, in part, "In all criminal prosecutions, the accused shall enjoy the right to a speedy trial." The federal "Speedy Trial Act" (18 U.S.C. Sections 3161–3174) plus statutes in every state also set forth a right to a **speedy trial**.

Somewhat surprisingly, it was not until 1966 that the Supreme Court addressed the Sixth Amendment's speedy trial provision. In *United States v. Ewell* (383 U.S. 116 [1966]), the Court identified three advantages associated with having a speedy trial:

- It prevents excessive incarceration.
- It minimizes the anxiety experienced by the accused as a result of a publicized accusation.
- It prevents damage to the defendant's case resulting from too much delay.

Not only does the defense benefit from a speedy trial, but so do the government and even society at large. First, having a speedy trial provides the opportunity for a guilty verdict to be secured quickly (assuming, of course, that the defendant is guilty). Also, having a speedy trial minimizes the opportunity for an individual out on bail to commit additional crimes while awaiting trial. However, if the accused is kept in detention prior to trial, too much delay can take a financial toll on the government.

For the reasons just set forth, having a speedy trial can prove advantageous. However, this can be a double-edged sword. Having a speedy trial may promote efficiency, but too much efficiency may damage the defense's case. That is, if the defense is not given adequate time to prepare, then an erroneous guilty verdict could result. In *Ewell*, the Court stated that "[t]he essential ingredient is orderly expedition and not mere speed" (p. 120).

When the Right to a Speedy Trial Applies

In **United States v. Marion (404 U.S. 307 [1971])**, the defendants sought to dismiss the indictment against them by arguing that the government had known of their identities for three years prior to the indictment. More specifically, they argued that their Sixth Amendment right to a speedy trial had been violated because the government had known of them prior to the point at which they had been indicted. Their argument failed miserably; the Court held that the Sixth Amendment's guarantee to a speedy trial attaches only *after* the person (or persons) has been accused of a crime. The Court further stated that being accused of a crime did not necessarily mean that formal charges had to be filed. Namely, "[T]he actual restraints imposed by arrest and holding to answer on a criminal charge" (pp. 327–328) can be sufficient to amount to an accusation. This has since come to be known as the **accusation rule**.

Consequences of Violating the Right to a Speedy Trial

Assuming prosecution is delayed to an unconstitutional degree, what is the appropriate remedy? This question was answered in **Strunk v. United States (412 U.S. 434 [1973])**. In that case, the defendant was found guilty of a crime in a federal district court after a ten-month delay between indictment and arraignment. The Seventh Circuit Court of Appeals held that the defendant was denied a speedy trial but only remanded the case for a reduction in the defendant's sentence. The U.S. Supreme Court reversed, holding that dismissal is the *only* remedy. Thus, any time a defendant's right to a speedy trial is denied, the charges against him or her will be dismissed altogether.

Public Trial

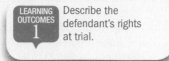

LEARNING OUTCOMES 1 — Describe the defendant's rights at trial.

In *In re Oliver* (333 U.S. 257 [1948]), the Supreme Court stated, "The knowledge that every criminal trial is subject to contemporaneous review in the forum of public opinion is an effective restraint on possible abuse of power. . . . Without publicity, all other checks are insufficient; in comparison of publicity, all other checks are of small account" (p. 271). Furthermore, "the presence of interested spectators may keep [the defendant's] triers keenly alive to a sense of their responsibility and to the importance of their functions" (p. 271, n. 25). This is what is meant by a **public trial**: It is one that is open to the public.

Oliver dealt expressly with criminal trials, but the Supreme Court has held that openness also applies to other hearings. For example, suppression hearings should be open to the public (**Waller v. Georgia, 467 U.S. 39 [1984]**), as should *voir dire* (*Presley* v. *Georgia*, No. 09-5270 [2010]). By extension, most other hearings—with the exception of grand jury proceedings, which are traditionally carried out in secret—should be considered public, as well.

Closing Trials

Most, but not all, trials are open to the public. Indeed, the defendant, whose interest is frequently served by openness, may want the trial closed to the public. This could be in an effort to minimize negative publicity, especially when the trial is for a heinous crime. **Sheppard v. Maxwell (384 U.S. 333 [1966])** illustrates the occasional conflict that can arise with the negative effects of trial publicity. In that case, the courtroom was packed with members of the public and media for all nine weeks of the trial. This made if difficult for people to hear one another. The press also handled and took pictures of evidentiary exhibits. The Supreme Court reversed the defendant's conviction, citing the "carnival atmosphere" of the trial in its decision.[2]

The government can also seek to close a trial to the public. In *Waller* v. *Georgia* (467 U.S. 39 [1984]), the Supreme Court created a test for determining when the government will succeed

> The defendant, whose interest is frequently served by openness, may want the trial closed to the public.

Think About It...

When the Defendant Is Responsible for the Delay Charles Pitt escaped from jail while awaiting his trial on narcotics offenses. He was apprehended by the police nine months later. He was then tried, convicted, and sentenced to prison for ten years. He has appealed his conviction, claiming that his Sixth Amendment right to a speedy trial was denied because of the nine-month delay. How should the appellate court rule?

© Imagestate Media Partners Limited/Alamy

in closing a trial to the public. The government must show (1) that there is an overriding interest, such as protection of certain witnesses; (2) that the closure is no broader than absolutely necessary; and (3) that reasonable alternatives have been considered.

Impartial Judge

It is important to note that the Sixth Amendment speaks only of juries (in addition to other important provisions), not judges. But the Supreme Court has held that the due process clause of the Fourteenth Amendment guarantees a criminal defendant the right to trial by an **impartial judge**. This right applies in two situations:

- A *bench trial*, in which the judge decides the defendant's fate instead of a jury, and
- A *jury trial*, in which the judge acts solely as a trier of law (that is, makes legal decisions, not factual ones).

The discussion begins with the right to an impartial judge and then moves into the more complicated issue of the right to trial by an impartial jury.

The Supreme Court first decided on the matter of an impartial judge in **Tumey v. Ohio (273 U.S. 510 [1927])**. In that case, the judge of a municipal court was also the city mayor. In addition, he received the fines and fees that he levied against those convicted in his courtroom. The Supreme Court concluded that due process is violated when the judge "has a direct, personal, substantial pecuniary interest in reaching a conclusion against him in his case" (p. 523).

Another impartial judge case was **Ward v. Monroeville (409 U.S. 57 [1972])**, in which the fees/fines collected by the judge did not go to the mayor/judge but instead to the town's budget. The amount of money collected was apparently substantial. The

Court concluded, again, that due process was violated, this time stating that "the mayor's executive responsibilities for village finances may make him partisan to maintain the high level of contribution from the mayor's court" (p. 59). Contrast this decision with that of *Dugan* v. *Ohio* (277 U.S. 61 [1928]). There, the Supreme Court held that due process was *not* violated because the mayor/judge was one of several members of a city commission and, as such, did not have substantial control over the city's funding sources.

Impartial Jury

As noted in the previous section, it is fairly easy to determine when a judge is impartial. After all, a judge is one person. Deciding on what constitutes an **impartial jury** is far more difficult and complex.

The right to a jury trial has always been recognized in the federal courts, but this right was not extended to the states until 1968 in the case of *Duncan* v. *Louisiana* (391 U.S. 145 [1968]). The Court noted in that case that the right to a jury trial is "an inestimable safeguard against the corrupt or overzealous prosecutor and against the compliant, biased, or eccentric judge" (p. 156). The right to a jury trial has therefore been incorporated, but subsequent decisions have restricted this right. The following subsections describe how.

Limitations on the Right

First, there is no Sixth Amendment constitutional right to a jury trial in noncriminal proceedings. More specifically, there is no right to a jury trial in noncriminal proceedings that are nevertheless part of the "criminal" process. This excludes civil trials, which of course are by jury. This has come to be known as the **noncriminal proceeding rule**. The reason for this should be fairly

obvious: The Sixth Amendment states, "In all *criminal prosecutions*, the accused shall enjoy the right to a...trial, by an impartial jury" (emphasis added). Juvenile delinquency proceedings are not considered "criminal" in the Sixth Amendment sense (*McKeiver* v. *Pennsylvania* (403 U.S. 528 [1971]).

The Supreme Court has also carved out a *petty crime exception* to the Sixth Amendment right to a jury trial. In *Duncan*, mentioned earlier, the Court expressly forbade jury trials for petty offenses, and in **Baldwin v. New York (399 U.S. 66 [1970])**, the Court announced its reasoning for this. It argued that the "disadvantages, onerous though they may be," of denying a jury trial for a petty crime are "outweighed by the benefits that result from speedy and inexpensive nonjury adjudication" (p. 73).

What exactly is a *petty crime*? Unfortunately, there are no easy answers to this question, either. *Duncan* failed to define a *petty* offense, but in *Baldwin*, the Court concluded that any crime that can bring punishment of more than six months is no longer a petty one. This has come to be known as the **six-month imprisonment rule**; thus, defendants do not enjoy a right to jury trial when the punishment they face is less than six months in jail or prison.

Jury Size and Voting Requirements

Many juries consist of 12 members, but the Supreme Court has stated that this is not a requirement. In *Williams* v. *Florida* (399 U.S. 78 [1970]), the Court stated that the 12-member jury was a "historical accident" and "unnecessary to effect the purposes of the jury system" (p. 102). The Court noted that a six-member jury would even provide "a fair possibility for obtaining a representative cross-section of the community, ...[a]s long as arbitrary exclusions of a particular class from the jury rolls are forbidden" (p. 102).

However, in *Ballew* v. *Georgia* (435 U.S. 223 [1978]), the Court concluded that a five-member jury was unconstitutional and found it unlikely that such a small group could engage "in meaningful deliberation, . . . remember all the facts and arguments, and truly represent the common sense of the entire community" (p. 241). Thus, the appropriate size for a jury is anywhere between 6 and 12 members.

As for voting requirements, a unanimous decision is not always required. In two companion cases, **Johnson v. Louisiana**

> **Defendants do not enjoy a right to jury trial when the punishment they face is less than six months in jail or prison.**

(406 U.S. 356 [1972]) and *Apodaca* v. *Oregon* (406 U.S. 404 [1972]), the Court upheld a Louisiana statute that permitted 9-to-3 jury verdicts as well as an Oregon statute permitting 10-to-2 decisions. According to the Court,

> In our view, disagreement of three jurors does not alone establish reasonable doubt, particularly when such a heavy majority of the jury, after having considered the dissenters' views, remained convinced of guilt. . . . That want of jury unanimity is not to be equated with the existence of reasonable doubt emerges even more clearly from the fact that when a jury in a federal court, which operates under the unanimity rule and is instructed to acquit a defendant if it has a reasonable doubt, . . . cannot agree unanimously upon a verdict, the defendant is not acquitted, but is merely given a new trial. (p. 363)

In short, guilt can be determined by less than an unanimous jury in certain jurisdictions. This is somewhat controversial, however, because according to the dissent in *Johnson* and *Apodaca*, permitting a less-than-unanimous decision diminishes reliability. Namely, jurors may not debate as fully as they may if a unanimous decision is required; that is, people may succumb to group pressure.

Waiving the Right to a Jury Trial

Based on the discussion thus far, it appears that the Supreme Court has somewhat reduced the Sixth Amendment right to a jury trial. This may seem somewhat unfair to those concerned with the defendant's civil liberties. Nevertheless, there are occasions on which the defendant wishes to waive his or her right to a jury trial. If the case is particularly inflammatory or one with which the community is intimately familiar, then obtaining a fair jury may be difficult. In such a situation, the defendant may opt for a *bench trial*, in which the judge decides the question of guilt.

The leading case dealing with waiver of the right to a jury trial is *Patton* v. *United States* (281 U.S. 276 [1930]). In that case, the defendants argued that their decision to waive the right to a jury trial was invalid because they lacked the authority to do so. The Supreme Court disagreed and stated that the right to a jury trial can be waived at the request of the defendant. The waiver must, however, be "express and intelligent." The waiver must also be voluntary, not a product of government coercion (see *United States* v. *Jackson*, 390 U.S. 570 [1968]).

It is important to note that waiver of the right to a jury trial can be vetoed. That is, the judge can *require* a jury trial, even if the defendant desires otherwise. Often, such a veto comes at the request of the prosecutor. In *Singer* v. *United States* (380 U.S. 24

Think About It...

Small Jury Voting Requirements A man was charged with the offense of obscenity and convicted in a state trial court before a six-person jury. A poll of the jury after the verdict indicated that the jury had voted 5 to 1 to convict. The man appealed his conviction, claiming that his right to trial by jury under the Sixth Amendment was violated when the state permitted a less-than-unanimous verdict by a six-member jury. How should the appellate court decide?

moodboard/Alamy

[1965]), the Court upheld a federal statute permitting vetoes of this nature. According to the Court, refusal to grant the defendant a waiver merely subjects the defendant to "the very thing that the Constitution guarantees him" (p. 36)—namely, a jury trial. In describing some reasons for a veto, the Court stated further, "The Constitution recognizes an adversary system as the proper method of determining guilt, and the Government, as a litigant, has a legitimate interest in seeing that cases in which it believes a conviction is warranted are tried before the tribunal which the Constitution regards as most likely to produce a fair result" (p. 36). Thus, if the government feels that a jury trial is preferable, in the sense that it will produce a fairer result than a bench trial, then a veto of the defendant's waiver of a jury trial is constitutionally permissible.

Selection of Potential Jurors

The process behind selecting an impartial jury is rather complicated. To begin, a list of potential, or prospective, jurors must be compiled. The creation of this list is critical, for without an impartial list, the final jury will not reflect a fair cross-section of the community. Once a list has been put together, then a panel of jurors is selected. This is when individuals are selected, usually randomly, for *jury duty*.

Thus, think of jury selection as a three-stage process: (1) a list of potential jurors is compiled, (2) potential jurors are selected from that list, and (3) the jury itself is chosen. This section addresses the first and second stages; the third stage, *voir dire*, is addressed later.

The list of potential jury members can be called the *jury pool, master jury wheel,* or *jury list*. For simplicity, the term **jury list** will be used here. The jury list can be compiled from a number of sources. One of the most common methods is to draw from voter registration lists. The federal courts, the state of Washington, and several other states rely on this method. Another method of compiling the list is via driver's license registration lists. California currently uses this method. Some states even use telephone directory lists. Still other states rely on jury commissioners: individuals, appointed by a judge, who are responsible for compiling jury lists.

To be on the jury list, potential jurors usually have to possess important traits. For example, they must be of a certain age—usually, over 18. They must also be U.S. citizens and free of felony convictions. The requirements to serve on a jury vary considerably from one state to the next.

Once the jury list has been compiled, people are selected from the list for service. Individuals selected from the jury list are called a *panel* or *venire*. The term **jury panel** will be used here.

Anyone who has been called on for jury duty has, at one time, been part of a jury panel. As most people know, there are several means by which one can be excused from a jury panel. Examples of people typically exempted from jury service are aliens, individuals unable to speak English, those under 18, those charged with a felony or who are serving a sentence, and those for whom jury service could cause severe hardship. People in law enforcement positions or who work in so-called critical occupations, such as the military and government, are typically exempted, as well.

Voir dire is concerned with the selection of jury members who can be impartial, as the Sixth Amendment requires.

The Voir Dire Process

Once the jury panel has been chosen, *voir dire* commences.

Voir dire is the process of selecting a jury from a jury panel. It is important to understand that once *voir dire* commences, the concern is *not* to ensure that the jury represents a fair cross-section of the community. Instead, *voir dire* is concerned with the selection of jury members who can be *impartial*, as the Sixth Amendment requires. The term *voir dire* means "to see what is said." Thus, at this stage, the judge, prosecutor, and defense have an opportunity to review potential jurors for evidence of bias.

Voir dire can be simple or complicated. In some jurisdictions, the judge decides who will serve on the jury. The prosecution and defense merely suggest questions to the judge in these jurisdictions. Doing so speeds up the process and also helps ensure that jurors do not develop preconceived ideas about the case in question.

Usually, however, it is the attorneys who do the questioning. This process can take from a few hours to a few weeks. *Voir dire* at O. J. Simpson's criminal trial took several weeks. *Voir dire* can also take time because nothing precludes the attorneys from investigating jurors' backgrounds, interviewing their acquaintances, and even hiring social scientists who are experts in anticipating prospective jurors' probable decisions.

Voir dire usually begins with the judge asking questions—for instance, dealing with potential jurors' familiarity with the case, attitudes toward one or the other party to the case, demographic information, and so on. In high-profile cases, prospective jurors are often asked to complete a questionnaire intended to divulge information that might lead to their disqualification or excusal. This is often done to guide the attorneys in their *voir dire* questioning. The Supreme Court has upheld this type of questioning, noting that it is perfectly acceptable for the judge to question jurors about their knowledge and opinions concerning the case (*Mu'Min* v. *Virginia*, 500 U.S. 415 [1991]).

The prosecution and defense are given unlimited opportunities to make **challenges for cause**. Convincing reasons can be found for the exclusion of potential jurors, some of which even have statutory origins. For example, if a member of the jury panel is related to the defendant, a challenge for cause will almost certainly succeed. Also, if the potential juror served on a past jury in a case dealing with a similar crime, a challenge for cause will probably succeed. If a potential juror stands to benefit financially from the outcome of the case, he or she will probably be excused based on a challenge for cause.

Peremptory challenges, by contrast, call for removal of potential jurors *without* any type of argument. Think of a peremptory challenge as a fallback measure. If, say, the defense fails with a challenge for cause to exclude a potential juror who it believes will be biased against the defendant, a peremptory challenge can be used. In fact, a peremptory challenge can be used to exclude a potential juror for nearly any reason. As the Supreme Court stated in *Swain* v. *Alabama* (380 U.S. 202 [1965]), the

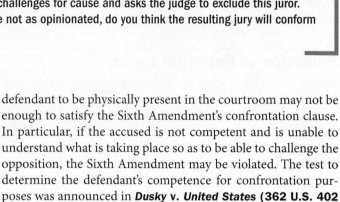
Think About It...

Strong Opinions on the Death Penalty Assume that, during *voir dire*, the following exchange takes place between a defense attorney and a potential juror:

Defense Attorney: Do you have any reservations against the death penalty?

Potential Juror: No, of course not. I firmly support capital punishment. I think we should execute all criminals.

Defense Attorney: Do you think you can set aside your personal convictions for the purposes of this trial and make an objective decision based on the evidence?

Potential Juror: I suppose so. I think I could probably keep an open mind.

Now, assume that the defense attorney seeks to exercise one of her challenges for cause and asks the judge to exclude this juror. The judge denies the request. Assuming that the remaining jurors are not as opinionated, do you think the resulting jury will conform to the Sixth Amendment requirements discussed thus far?

peremptory challenge "is often exercised upon the 'sudden impressions and unaccountable prejudices we are apt to conceive upon the bare looks and gestures of another,' upon a juror's 'habits and associations,' or upon the feeling that the 'bare questioning [of a juror's] indifference may sometimes provoke a resentment'" (pp. 242–243). Peremptory challenges are numbered. How many are available depends on the state and the type of offense (see Figure 13–1).

It is generally unacceptable for the prosecution (and the defense) to exclude a juror based on race or ethnicity. In *Batson* v. *Kentucky* (476 U.S. 79 [1986]), the Court decided that prosecutors can be called on to explain their use of peremptory challenges to exclude minorities. If the defense makes the showing, then the prosecutor will be required to explain his or her reasons for excluding jurors based on race and ethnicity. However, this explanation does not need to be as convincing as one that would accompany a challenge for cause. It simply needs to be what the Court calls *race neutral*.

Confrontation

The Sixth Amendment's provision that an accused person enjoys the right to be "confronted with the witnesses against him" is manifested in three ways. The first method of **confrontation** is to allow the defendant to appear at his or her own trial. In fact, in *Illinois* v. *Allen* (397 U.S. 337 [1970]), the Supreme Court expressly stated that "[o]ne of the most basic of rights guaranteed by the Confrontation Clause is the accused's right to be present in the courtroom at every state of his trial" (p. 338). The other two methods of confrontation extended to the defendant are to require the live testimony of witnesses before the defendant and to permit him or her to challenge witnesses' statements in open court. Each of these methods of confrontation is considered in a following section.

The Defendant's Right to Be Present

The Supreme Court's opinion in *Illinois* v. *Allen* seems eminently sensible. Certainly, the defendant would be seriously hampered in his or her ability to confront adverse witnesses if he or she was not allowed to attend the trial. But allowing the defendant to be physically present in the courtroom may not be enough to satisfy the Sixth Amendment's confrontation clause. In particular, if the accused is not competent and is unable to understand what is taking place so as to be able to challenge the opposition, the Sixth Amendment may be violated. The test to determine the defendant's competence for confrontation purposes was announced in *Dusky* v. *United States* (362 U.S. 402 [1960]). The test assesses whether the defendant "has sufficient present ability to consult with his lawyer with a reasonable degree of rational understanding—and whether he has a rational as well as factual understanding of the proceedings against him" (p. 402). The burden of proving *incompetence* falls on the defendant (*Medina* v. *California*, 505 U.S. 437 [1992]).

It is important to understand that this test for competency is different from the insanity defense often discussed in criminal law texts. *Competency to stand trial*—the type of competency considered here—deals with the defendant's ability to understand what is happening at trial (as well as at pretrial hearings, etc.). The *insanity defense* deals with the defendant's competence at the time he or she committed the crime. The issue of competency to stand trial is narrowly concerned with the defendant's ability to understand what is happening and communicate with counsel.

The Defendant's Right to Live Testimony

The Sixth Amendment's mention of confrontation includes, according to the Supreme Court, the defendant's right to **live testimony**. That is, he or she enjoys the right to have witnesses physically appear in the courtroom to give their testimony. Even so, this right may be qualified for certain reasons. In fact, over 100 years ago, the Supreme Court stated in *Mattox* v. *United States* (156 U.S. 237 [1895]) that the defendant's right to live testimony is "subject to exceptions, recognized long before the adoption of the Constitution" (p. 243). One such exception is a statement from a deceased witness relayed through another individual. Obviously a dead person cannot testify in person!

A number of Supreme Court cases have addressed questions of whether witnesses should have been present to give testimony. A summary of some recent decisions appears in Figure 13–2.

State	Number of Peremptory Challenges					
	Criminal					
	Capital		Felony		Misdemeanor	
	State	Defense	State	Defense	State	Defense
Alabama	12	12	6	6	3	3
Alaska	N/A	N/A	10	10	3	3
Arizona	10	10	6	6	6	6
Arkansas	10	12	6	8	3	3
California	20	20	20/10	20/10	10/6	10/6
Colorado	10	10	5	5	3	3
Connecticut	25	25	15/6	15/6	3	3
Delaware	12	20	6	6	6	6
District of Columbia	N/A	N/A	10	10	3	3
Florida	10	10	10/6	10/6	3	3
Georgia	10	20	6	12	2	4
Hawaii	N/A	N/A	12/3	12/3	3	3
Idaho	10	10	10/6	10/6	4	4
Illinois	14	14	7	7	5	5
Indiana	20	20	10	10	5	5
Iowa	N/A	N/A	10/6	10/6	4	4
Kansas	12	12	12/8/6	12/8/6	3	3
Kentucky	8	8	8	8	3	3
Louisiana	12	12	12/6	12/6	6	6
Maine	N/A	N/A	10/8	10/8	4	4
Maryland	10	20	5	10	4	4
Massachusetts	N/A	N/A	12/4	12/4	4	4
Michigan	N/A	N/A	12/5	12/5	5	5
Minnesota	N/A	N/A	9/3	15/5	3	5
Mississippi	12	12	6	6	6	6
Missouri	9	9	6	6	2	2
Montana	8	8	6/3	6/3	6/3	6/3
Nebraska	12	12	6	6	3	3
Nevada	8	8	4	4	4	4
New Hampshire	10	20	15/3	15/3	3	3
New Jersey	12	20	12	20	10	10
New Mexico	8	12	3	5	3	5
New York	20	20	20/15/	20/15/10	10	10
North Carolina	14	14	6	6	6	6
North Dakota	N/A~	N/A	6/4	6/4	6/4	6/4
Ohio	6	6	4	4	3	3
Oklahoma	9	9	5	5	3	3
Oregon	12	12	6	6	6/3	6/3
Pennsylvania	20	20	7	7	5	5
Puerto Rico	N/A	N/A	10/5	10/5	5	5
Rhode Island	N/A	N/A	6	6	3	3
South Carolina	5	10	5	10	5	5
South Dakota	20	20	20/10	20/10	3	3
Tennessee	15	15	8	8	3	3
Texas	15	15	10	10	5	5
Utah	10	10	4	4	3	3
Vermont	N/A	N/A	6	6	6	6
Virginia	4	4	4	4	3	3
Washington	12	12	6	6	3	3
West Virginia	N/A	N/A	2	6	4	4
Wisconsin	N/A	N/A	6/4	6/4	4	4
Wyoming	12	12	8	8	4	4

Note: The following states do not have a death penalty statute: Alaska, District of Columbia, Hawaii, Iowa, Maine, Massachusetts, Michigan, Minnesota, North Dakota, Puerto Rico, Rhode Island, Vermont, West Virginia, and Wisconsin.

FIGURE 13–1 Peremptory Challenges by State.

- *Melendez-Diaz* v. *Massachusetts*, 557 U.S. _____ (2009). A state forensic analyst's laboratory report was testimonial and, as such, the defendant should have been permitted to question its preparer.
- *Bullcoming* v. *New Mexico*, 564 U.S. _____ (2011). Confrontation was violated when prosecutors offered a crime-lab report analyzing Bullcoming's blood sample and called the lab's supervisor to the witness stand rather than the technician who conducted the test. In other words, the lab report could not be admitted without also calling the analyst to the witness stand for cross-examination.
- *Michigan* v. *Bryant*, 562 U.S. _____ (2011). A shooting victim informed police that Bryant had shot him. The victim died shortly thereafter, but the statement was introduced at trial through the testimony of the officer who heard it and used it to establish Bryant's guilt. The Court ruled that the victim's statements were "not testimonial . . . because they had a 'primary purpose . . . to enable police assistance to meet an ongoing emergence.'"
- *Williams* v. *Illinois*, 567 U.S. _____ (2012). In a bench trial for rape, the defendant's right to confrontation was not violated when a state crime-lab representative testified that the defendant's DNA profile produced by the state matched the DNA profile produced by an outside laboratory using vaginal swabs taken from the victim. The Court held in part that "[a]n expert witness may voice an opinion based on facts concerning the events at issue even if the expert lacks first-hand knowledge of those facts."

FIGURE 13–2 **Recent Confronation Cases.**

The Defendant's Right to Challenge Witness Testimony

Part of the defendant's right to confrontation is the ability to challenge witnesses in the courtroom. This ability is manifested when each witness physically appears in court before the defendant. This type of confrontation permits questioning by the defense and is intended to submit the witness's account to relevant scrutiny.

Also, the Court has held that the defendant can be limited in terms of the nature of the confrontation, which is usually accomplished through questioning—specifically, *cross-examination*. Each of these limitations is discussed in a following subsection. First, the order of questioning in a typical criminal trial is considered. Then, the focus moves to when face-to-face contact is required and what Supreme Court case law addresses the defendant's right to cross-examine witnesses.

In *Coy v. Iowa* **(487 U.S. 1012 [1988])**, the Supreme Court considered the constitutionality of a state law that permitted the placement of a large opaque screen between the defendant and two young girls who testified that he had sexually assaulted them. The Court declared that the statute was unconstitutional because "the Confrontation Clause guarantees the defendant a face-to-face meeting with witnesses appearing before the trier of fact" (p. 1016).

Contrast *Coy* with *Maryland* v. *Craig* (497 U.S. 836 [1990]). In *Craig*, the Court considered whether a statute permitting a witness's testimony via closed-circuit television was constitutional. The statute provided for such a procedure in cases in which the judge determined that face-to-face testimony would "result in the child suffering serious emotional distress such that the child cannot reasonably communicate" (p. 836). The Court upheld the statute, claiming that it did not violate the confrontation clause. It stated that a central concern of the confrontation clause "is to ensure the reliability of the evidence against a criminal defendant by subjecting it to rigorous testing in the context of an adversary proceeding before the trier of fact" (p. 845). Further, it held that the statute in question did "not impinge upon the truth-seeking or symbolic purposes of the Confrontation Clause" (p. 852).

Compulsory Process

The compulsory process clause of the Sixth Amendment provides that the defendant can use subpoenas to obtain witnesses, documents, and other objects that are helpful to his or her defense. The right to **compulsory process** was incorporated to the states in **Washington v. Texas (388 U.S. 14 [1967])**, in which the Supreme Court stated that compulsory process protects "[t]he right to offer the testimony of witnesses, and to compel their attendance" (p. 19). Further, the Court stated,

> We hold that the petitioner in this case was denied his right to have compulsory process for obtaining witnesses in his favor because the State arbitrarily denied him the right to put on the stand a witness who was physically and mentally capable of testifying to events that he had personally observed, and whose testimony would have been relevant and material to the defense. The Framers of the Constitution did not intend to commit the futile act of giving to a defendant the right to secure the attendance of witnesses whose testimony he had no right to use. The judgment of conviction must be reversed. (p. 23)

At least two Supreme Court cases have considered aspects of the defendant's right to compulsory process. In particular, questions as to constitutional rights violations have been posed in instances in which the defense has been denied the right to subpoena a witness. For example, in *Roviaro* v. *United States* (353 U.S. 53 [1957]), the prosecution refused to provide the defense with the identity of a police informant. The Court recognized that the government had a significant interest in concealing the identity of the informant, mainly to further its efforts in combating the trafficking of illicit drugs. But the Court also found that the defendant's right to confrontation was denied by the prosecution's refusal to release the witness's identity. The informant was the only witness to the drug transaction for which the defendant was charged, so the defense clearly would have had a difficult time mounting an effective case without this witness.

Next, in *United States* v. *Valenzuela-Bernal* (458 U.S. 858 [1982]), the defendant was charged with transporting illegal narcotics. He was arrested along with three other individuals who were unlawfully in the United States. Immigration officials concluded that two of the three aliens were not needed for the prosecution, so it deported them. The defendant then argued that his right to compulsory process was violated by the deportation. Surprisingly, the Court held that the government's interest in deporting illegal aliens and minimizing overcrowding in detention facilities outweighed the defendant's interest in mounting an effective defense. The Court concluded that the defendant did not offer a valid reason why the two deported witnesses were necessary for his defense.

Double-Jeopardy Protection

The constitutionally guaranteed protection against **double jeopardy** is designed to ensure that a person who has been convicted or acquitted of a crime is not tried or punished for the same offense twice. Double jeopardy occurs when, for the same offense, a person is (1) reprosecuted after acquittal, (2) reprosecuted after conviction, or (3) subjected to separate punishments for the same offense. Double jeopardy does not apply, however, to prosecutions brought by separate sovereigns. The federal government, each state government, and each Native American tribe is considered a separate sovereign.

Early English common law contains the foundations of the modern-day protection against double jeopardy. The rule of *autrefois acquit* prohibited the retrial of a defendant who was found not guilty. The rule of *autrefois convict*, on the other hand, prohibited the retrial of a defendant who *was* found guilty. These rules were adopted by the American colonies.

Today, every state provides double-jeopardy protection because of the Supreme Court's decision in **Benton v. Maryland (395 U.S. 784 [1969])**, in which the Court declared that the Fifth Amendment's protection against double jeopardy is a fundamental right.

When Double Jeopardy Protection Applies

The Fifth Amendment suggests that double jeopardy occurs when a person's "life or limb" is threatened. This language has been taken to mean that double jeopardy applies in all criminal proceedings. Determining whether a proceeding is criminal, however, is not always easy. Courts will often look to the legislature's intent in writing the statute that is the basis for prosecution. For example, in **Kansas v. Hendricks (521 U.S. 346 [1997])**, the Supreme Court found that a statute providing for a

Constitutionally guaranteed protection against double jeopardy is designed to ensure that a person who has been convicted or acquitted of a crime is not tried or punished for the same offense twice.

"sexual predator" proceeding, in addition to a criminal proceeding, did not place the defendant in double jeopardy, because it provided for *civil* confinement.

The Blockburger Rule

A rather complicated issue in double-jeopardy jurisprudence concerns the definition of **same offense**. In **Blockburger v. United States (284 U.S. 299 [1932])**, the Supreme Court developed a test that states that "[w]here the same act or transaction constitutes a violation of two distinct statutory provisions, the test to be applied to determine whether there are two offenses or only one, is whether each requires proof of an additional fact which the other does not" (p. 304). This test came to be known as the **Blockburger rule**.

According to the *Blockburger* rule, an offense is considered the same offense if two separate statutes that define the offense both contain elements A, B, and C. Moreover, if one crime contains elements A, B, and C and the other has elements A and B, both are considered the same offense because neither statute requires proof of a fact that the other does not. For example, assume that the offense of first-degree murder contains elements A (premeditated), B (deliberate), and C (killing) and that the offense of second-degree murder contains elements B (deliberate) and C (killing). Both offenses are considered the same for double-jeopardy purposes because second-degree murder does not require proof of another element that first-degree murder does not. If a person is convicted of first-degree murder, then, according to this example, he or she cannot be charged with second-degree murder.

Separate offenses can be identified when, for example, one crime contains elements A, B, and C and the other contains elements A, B, and D. Both crimes require proof of an additional element that the other does not. For example, assume that the offense of joyriding contains elements A (unlawful taking), B (of an automobile), and C (the intent to *temporarily* deprive the owner of possession). Assume also that the offense of car theft contains elements A (unlawful taking), B (of an automobile), and D (the intent to *permanently* deprive the owner of possession). These are considered separate offenses because each offense requires proof of an element that the other does not. Thus, a person who is found guilty of joyriding can also be charged with the crime of car theft (see *Brown* v. *Ohio*, 432 U.S. 161 [1977]).

Entrapment

A person tried for a crime can assert any of numerous defenses to criminal liability, including self-defense, insanity, involuntary intoxication, and others. Criminal law texts cover these in detail. One defense that straddles the line between criminal law and criminal procedure is the *entrapment defense*. It is a defense in the criminal law sense, but it is one of the only defenses that calls into question law enforcement's role in the instigation of a crime. Hence, it is almost always brought up in the realm of criminal procedure. The defendant can assert entrapment prior to trial, but for simplicity's sake, it will be discussed here. Entrapment is an affirmative defense, which means it can easily be raised at trial.

The heading of this section suggests that the defendant enjoys the *right* to assert an entrapment defense. It is important to note, however, that the Constitution does not provide this right. It is a right only in the sense that the Supreme Court has decided that an accused person can assert an entrapment defense.

The **entrapment defense** is based on the belief that someone should not be convicted of a crime that the government instigated. In its simplest form, the entrapment defense arises when government officials "plant the seeds" of criminal intent. That is, if a person commits a crime that he or she otherwise would not have committed but for the government's conduct, he or she will probably succeed with an entrapment defense.

The first Supreme Court case recognizing the entrapment defense was *Sorrells* v. *United States* **(287 U.S. 435 [1932]).** In that case, Chief Justice Hughes stated, "We are unable to conclude that… [the] …processes of detection or enforcement should be abused by the instigation by government officials of an act on the part of persons otherwise innocent in order to lure them to its commission and to punish them" (p. 448). This reasoning underlies the treatment of the entrapment defense in U.S. courts to this day.

Despite its apparent simplicity, the entrapment defense has been a contentious one. In particular, there has been some disagreement in the courts over the relevance of the offender's predisposition and how far the government can go in order to lure a person into criminal activity. When an entrapment decision is based on the offender's predisposition, this is known as a *subjective inquiry*. By contrast, a focus on the government conduct presumably responsible for someone's decision to commit a crime is known as an *objective inquiry*.

The American Law Institute's *Model Penal Code* takes an objective approach with regard to the entrapment defense: If the government "employ[ed] methods of persuasion or inducement which create a substantial risk that such an offense will be committed by persons other than those who are ready to commit it,"[3] then the defense is available regardless of the offender's initial willingness to offend. The Supreme Court, however, has opted to focus on the subjective predisposition of the offender instead the government's role in instigating the crime in question (for example, *Hampton* v. *United States*, 425 U.S. 484 [1976]).

See Figure 13–3 for a summary of constitutional rights the defendant enjoys at trial.

- speedy trial
- public trial
- impartial judge
- impartial jury
- confrontation
- compulsory process
- double jeopardy protection
- right to assert an entrapment defense

FIGURE 13–3 **Summary of Key Trial Rights.**

▶ *Sentencing*

Once a person has been convicted at trial, he or she must be sentenced. A **sentence** is the penalty received. Sentencing occurs at a separate, post-trial hearing but rarely for misdemeanor

The entrapment defense arises when government officials "plant the seeds" of criminal intent.

convictions. Individuals charged with misdemeanors are often tried and sentenced in the same hearing.

Several sentencing options are available to the judge. The judge may impose a sentence and then suspend it, pending good behavior on the part of the defendant. The judge may also require the defendant to pay a fine or, in more extreme cases, to serve a term in prison. Probation or another method of supervised release is a possibility, as well. In any case, the type of sentence can hinge on the judge's own goal of sentencing—that is, his or her view as to the most important purpose of sentencing. The following section considers leading goals of criminal sentencing.

Determining the Appropriate Sentence

Determining the appropriate sentence almost always involves considering both the seriousness of the offense and the offender's prior record. Other factors that are considered include the defendant's possible threat to the community and his or her degree of remorse for committing the crime. Even age, family ties, employment status, and other demographic factors can come into play. Moreover, the defendant who pleads guilty may receive a different sentence than the defendant who is found guilty in a trial. A guilty plea suggests that the defendant is willing to admit what he or she did and, as such, should be treated more leniently.

Sentencing can also be determined by the number of separate crimes growing out of a single criminal act. If, for instance, a defendant is convicted of killing another person with a handgun, he or she may be sentenced for the killing as well as for unlawful possession of a handgun, if the law permits the latter. In such a situation, the judge may sentence the defendant to consecutive or concurrent sentences. With a *concurrent sentence*, the defendant serves time for both crimes at once. *Consecutive sentences*, by contrast, are served separately, one after another. In the murder example, the defendant would serve time in prison for the killing, and then when that term was completed, he or she would begin serving the sentence for possession.

Indeed, sentencing can be influenced by the defendant's degree of cooperation with the police. In *Roberts* v. *United States* **(445 U.S. 552 [1980]),** the Court held that the sentencing judge was permitted to consider the defendant's refusal to cooperate with the police in investigating his crime. Still other factors, such as the offender's mental status, can be considered. In fact, it has been determined that a mentally ill individual can be held in custody, such as in a mental institution, for a longer term than a traditional prison sentence for the crime charged (for example, *Jones* v. *United States*, 103 S.Ct. 3043 [1983]). This often happens following an insanity plea.

Most jurisdictions have what is known as the "going rate" for a criminal offense.[4] Usually, this is an unwritten, informal agreement between members of a courtroom work group (that is, a judge, defense attorney, and prosecutor) as to what sentence a typical case merits. Usually, if the seriousness of the offense and the offender's background characteristics are known, one can predict with a fair degree of accuracy what sentence will be imposed.

A judge's sentencing decisions can also be influenced by *victim impact statements*. For example, Proposition 8, adopted by California voters in 1982, provides that "the victim of any crime, or the next kin of the victim . . . has the right to attend all sentencing proceedings . . . [and] to reasonably express his or her views concerning the crime, the person responsible, and the need for restitution."[5] The Supreme Court has decided that testimony in the form of a victim impact statement is admissible (*Payne* v. *Tennessee*, 501 U.S. 808 [1991]).

The judge is then required to take the victim's or next of kin's statement into account when deciding on a sentence for the offender.

Constitutional Rights During Sentencing

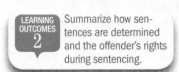

Summarize how sentences are determined and the offender's rights during sentencing.

A convicted criminal enjoys several important constitutional rights during the sentencing process. For example, the double-jeopardy provision of the Fifth Amendment, as discussed earlier, applies. Further, the defendant is entitled to a reasonable punishment for his or her crime. Namely, the punishment should reflect the seriousness of the crime. For example, in *Solem* v. *Helm* (463 U.S. 277 [1983]), the Court held that a life sentence for the defendant's seventh nonviolent offense was unconstitutional. The Court prohibited the sentence, stating that the defendant "received the penultimate sentence for relatively minor criminal conduct" (p. 305).

The defendant also has the right to participate in the sentencing process. With the possible exception of misdemeanor sentencing, which may take place out of the presence of the defendant, the defendant has the right to be present during sentencing. Also, the defendant should be advised of his or her right to appeal. The defendant also has the right to have counsel present at the sentencing hearing to argue on his or her behalf. The Sixth Amendment right to counsel operates essentially the same way at sentencing as it does at trial.

The defendant also has the right to ask the sentencing judge to ignore past convictions that were obtained in violation of the right to counsel. For example, in **United States v. Tucker (404 U.S. 443 [1972])**, the Supreme Court invalidated an individual's 25-year sentence because the sentencing judge arrived at the sentence by considering the defendant's past convictions, for which he was not afforded counsel. The Court stated,

The government is…on solid ground in asserting that a sentence imposed by a federal district judge, if within statutory limits, is generally not subject to review. …But these general propositions do not decide the case before us. For we deal here not with a sentence imposed in the informed discretion of a trial judge, but with a sentence founded at least in part upon misinformation of constitutional magnitude. As in *Townsend* v. *Burke*, 334 U.S. 736 (1690), "this prisoner was sentenced on the basis of assumptions concerning his criminal record which were materially untrue." The record in the present case makes evident that the sentencing judge gave specific consideration to the respondent's previous convictions before imposing sentence upon him. Yet it is now clear that two of those convictions were wholly unconstitutional under *Gideon* v. *Wainwright*, 372 U.S. 335 (1963). (p. 446)

In summary, a defendant enjoys at least three important constitutional rights during the sentencing process: (1) the right not to be put twice in jeopardy, (2) the right to a sentence that conforms with the Eighth Amendment's proscription against cruel and unusual punishment, and (3) the right to counsel at sentencing-related hearings, regardless of his or her ability to afford representation.

A number of Supreme Court decisions have addressed questions about the constitutionality of various sentencing practices. The accompanying timeline offers a summary.

▶ Appeals

An **appeal** occurs when an appellate court, such as one of the federal courts of appeal, examines a lower court's decision in order to determine whether the proper procedure was followed or the correct law was applied. In other words, when a defendant appeals, he or she is claiming that the court made an error. Thus, the appeal guarantees that a defendant who is found guilty can challenge his or her conviction. Further, the appeal guarantees that another judge or panel of judges, disconnected from the initial trial, will make the relevant decision.

Although appealing convictions is an important part of the criminal process, the Supreme Court has never held that doing so is constitutionally permissible. That is, nowhere does the U.S. Constitution specify that a certain number of appeals will be granted to each convicted criminal. In *McKane* v. *Durston* (153 U.S. 684 [1894]), the Supreme Court stated, "A review by an appellate court of the final judgment in a criminal case, however grave the offense of which the accused is convicted, was not at common law, and is not now, a necessary element of due process of law" (p. 687).

Most appeals are post-trial in nature and filed by the defense, which is why this topic is being discussed at the end of this book. However, in some situations, the defense appeals a court's decision, such as on a motion to suppress evidence, during the trial. And in some instances, the prosecution can even file an appeal.

1972	**1976**		**1982**	**1991**	**1997**
Furman v. Georgia, **408 U.S. 238** The death penalty, as carried out in the United States, amounts to cruel and unusual punishment, in violation of the Eighth Amendment.	*Gregg v. Georgia,* **428 U.S. 153** Death penalty is reinstated.	*Woodson v. North Carolina,* **428 U.S. 280** Mandatory death penalty laws—that is, those that do not take aggravating and mitigating circumstances into account—are unconstitutional.	*Enmund v. Florida,* **458 U.S. 782** It is unconstitutional to impose death on a person who participates in a felony that results in murder without considering the participant's level of intent.	*Harmelin v. Michigan,* **501 U.S. 957** A life sentence without the possibility of parole for a first-time, nonviolent drug offender does not constitute cruel and unusual punishment.	*Kansas v. Hendricks* **521 U.S. 346** Civil commitment was upheld for convicted child molesters who have served their sentences under the state's Sexually Violent Predators Act.

Types and Effects of Appeals

Despite the Supreme Court's view that appealing one's conviction is not constitutionally guaranteed, every state and the federal government has rules providing a certain number of appeals to a convicted criminal. At both the state and federal levels, a convicted criminal is usually granted at least one **direct appeal** (also known as an appeal of right).

An appeal of right, or a direct appeal, is automatically granted to the defendant by law. That is, an appeal of right *must* be heard by an appellate court. It is not up to the appellate court to decide whether to hear such an appeal. By contrast, the appellate court can decide, at its own discretion, whether to hear a **discretionary appeal**. Also, appeals of right are limited, but discretionary appeals can be filed several times, provided they are not redundant.

When a defendant appeals a decision, there are a number of possible consequences. In the typical appeal, the defendant seeks to correct a decision by the lower court that he or she perceives to be in error. In such an instance, the appellate court will either affirm or reverse the lower court's decision. It may also remand (that is, send back) the case for further proceedings, consistent with its opinion.

Another consequence of an appeal can be a **trial *de novo***. When the defendant appeals for a trial *de novo*, he or she is essentially requesting a new, independent trial at the appellate level. Trials *de novo* are rare. Further, they are usually limited to appeals of decisions arising from misdemeanor courts of limited jurisdiction. Rarely, if ever, will a convicted felon succeed in obtaining a trial *de novo* in an appellate court. The primary reason for this is that an appellate court interprets the *law*, not the *facts*. It is the job of the trial court to determine guilt based on the facts.

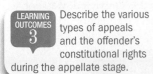

LEARNING OUTCOMES 3 Describe the various types of appeals and the offender's constitutional rights during the appellate stage.

Whether the defendant seeks a new trial or simply a review of the trial court's decision on some matter, he or she will not necessarily go free if a decision is returned in his or her favor. If, for example, the appellate court considers a lower court's decision not to exclude evidence and decides that the lower court's decision should be reversed, this means the evidence should

Rarely does an appellate court decide guilt; its job is to interpret the law and review the conduct of the trial court.

have been excluded, not that the defendant should be acquitted. For example, in the famous *Miranda* case (*Miranda* v. *Arizona*, 384 U.S. 436 [1966]), the Supreme Court did not free Ernesto Miranda. Instead, it remanded his case for a new trial. He was subsequently found guilty and sentenced to more than 20 years in prison. It is, therefore, important when reading cases to understand precisely what the reviewing court is deciding. Rarely does an appellate court decide guilt; its job is to interpret the law and review the conduct of the trial court.

What happens to convicted defendants while they are appealing? In almost all cases, they serve out the conditions of their sentences. Assume, for example, that a defendant appeals his guilty conviction on the grounds that he was denied counsel at trial. Assume further that the defendant's appeal has merit. If he was sentenced to prison following trial, he will remain there until the appeal is heard, if it ever is. However, for a select few convicts, the judge will issue a *stay*, which means the convicted individual will not serve time before the appeal is heard. This is a rare situation and usually involves an individual who poses a low flight risk. The fact that most convicted criminals are considered flight risks further explains why stays of imprisonment are rarely granted.

Constitutional Rights During the Appellate Process

Even though the Supreme Court has held that appealing one's conviction is not constitutionally required, it has held, on a number of occasions, that when an appeal is permissible, the government must follow certain procedures. Specifically, the government must ensure that the defendant has (1) access to trial transcripts, (2) the right to counsel, and (3) the right to be free from government retaliation for a successful appeal. Before these procedural issues can be considered, though, the defendant must file *notice of an appeal*. An example of such a notice, from the U.S. District Court for the Southern District of California, is presented in Figure 13–4.

Apprendi v. New Jersey, 530 U.S. 466 Any fact, other than prior conviction, that increases the penalty for a crime beyond that allowed by statute must be submitted to a jury and proven beyond a reasonable doubt.

Atkins v. Virginia, 122 S. Ct. 2242 The execution of a mentally retarded person violates the Eighth Amendment.

Roper v. Simmons, 543 U.S. 551 The execution of offenders who committed their capital crime under the age of 18 violates the Eighth Amendment.

Deck v. Missouri, 544 U.S. 622 The constitution forbids the use of visible shackles during a capital trial's penalty phase.

United States District Court for the _____

District of _____

File Number _____

)
v.   )   Notice of Appeal
)
)

Notice is hereby given that _____ (plaintiffs) (defendants) in the above named case,* hereby appeal to the United States Court of Appeals for the _____ Circuit (from the final judgment) (from the order (describing it)) entered in this action on the _____ day of _____, 20 _____.

(s)_____

Attorney for _____

Address:_____

_____

* See Rule 3(c) for permissible ways of identifying appellants.

FIGURE 13–4 Example of a Notice of Appeal.

Ensuring That the Defendant Has Access to Trial Transcripts

In **Griffin v. Illinois (351 U.S. 12 [1956])**, the Supreme Court considered whether an Illinois appellate procedure that required the defendant to produce transcripts of the trial—even if he or she could not afford to do so—violated the Constitution. The Court struck down the procedure, claiming that the government cannot impose a restriction on the right to appeal "in a way that discriminates against some convicted defendants on account of their poverty" (p. 18). In a related case, *Entsminger* v. *Iowa* (386 U.S. 748 [1967]), decided some time later, the Court invalidated a state procedure that allowed defense counsel, rather than an indigent defendant, to decide whether an appeal could continue with an incomplete trial transcript.

Ensuring the Defendant's Right to Counsel During Appeals

As has been discussed at some length in this text, criminal defendants enjoy the Sixth Amendment right to counsel under a number of circumstances. However, the Sixth Amendment expressly states that this right only applies in *criminal prosecutions*. Even so, the Supreme Court has required that counsel be provided to indigent defendants *on appeal* as a matter of either equal protection or due process. Interestingly, though, the Court has also said that there is no right to self-representation at the appellate stage (see *Martinez* v. *Court of Appeal*, 528 U.S. 152 [2000]).

The first case discussing the right to counsel during the appellate stage was **Douglas v. California (372 U.S. 353 [1963])**. There, the Court concluded that the government must provide an indigent defendant with counsel to assist in his or her appeals of right. The Court stated that "where the merits of the *one and only* appeal an indigent has as of right are decided without benefit of counsel…an unconstitutional line has been drawn between rich and poor" (p. 357). The Court has also held that the Constitution requires counsel—particularly, effective counsel—for a nonindigent defendant in his or her appeals of right (see *Evitts* v. *Lucey*, 469 U.S. 387 [1985]).

Both *Douglas* and *Evitts* dealt with the right to counsel in appeals of right. By contrast, the Supreme Court has held that counsel is not constitutionally guaranteed in *discretionary appeals*. Specifically, in *Ross* v. *Moffitt* (417 U.S. 600 [1974]), the Court held,

A defendant in respondent's circumstances is not denied meaningful access to the State Supreme Court simply because the State does not appoint counsel to aid him in seeking review in that court, since at that stage, under North Carolina's multitiered appellate system, he will have, at the very least, a transcript or other record of the trial proceedings, a brief in the Court of Appeals setting forth his claims of error, and frequently an opinion by that court disposing of his case, materials which, when supplemented by any *pro se* submission that might be

2005

United States v. Booker, 543 U.S. 220 Federal sentencing guidelines are advisory, not mandatory.

Oregon v. Guzek, 546 U.S. 517 The Constitution does not permit defendants facing the death penalty to present new evidence during the sentencing phase.

2006

Carey v. Musladin, 549 U.S. 70 It was not unfairly prejudicial for trial spectators to wear buttons depicting the murder victim.

2008

Baze v. Rees, 553 U.S. 35 A three-drug lethal-injection protocol does not violate the Eighth Amendment's prohibition of cruel and unusual punishment.

Think About It...

Constitutional Rights During the Appeals Process
Judge Lawson has before him two convicted criminals who are giving notice of their intent to appeal their convictions for robbery. The two are indigent and thus pursuing their appeals without the assistance of counsel. They request access to the trial transcripts, but Judge Lawson rules against them, claiming that because, in his view, their appeals are frivolous, it would be a waste of taxpayer funds to supply them with the trial transcripts. Is this action constitutional?

© Marmaduke St. John/ Alamy

made, would provide the Supreme Court with an adequate basis for its decision to grant or deny review under its standards of whether the case has "significant public interest," involves "legal principles of major significance," or likely conflicts with a previous Supreme Court decision. (pp. 614–615)

- -

▶ Habeas Corpus

The most common method of challenging one's conviction is to appeal. However, filing an appeal or several appeals is not the only avenue of redress for a person who is wrongfully convicted. Another avenue is by means of a **habeas corpus** petition filed with the federal courts. This is known as a *collateral attack* and is a constitutional right.[6]

Habeas corpus plays out as follows: First, the accused individual petitions one of the federal district courts and asks the court to issue a *writ of habeas corpus*, which literally means "you have the body." Then, if the court decides to issue the writ, the petitioner is brought before the court so the constitutionality of his or her confinement can be reviewed.

Given that the Supreme Court hears a limited number of cases each term, it is unlikely that it will issue a writ. This leaves the defendant with the option of petitioning the federal district court. Also, it is important to remember that a *habeas corpus* petition must be limited to a constitutional claim. Finally, it is totally within the discretion of the court that is petitioned to decide whether the writ will be issued. The Constitution provides that the "privilege of the Writ of Habeas Corpus shall not be suspended," but this has been interpreted to mean that a defendant can *submit habeas petitions*, not that the defendant will necessarily get his or her day in court.

On several occasions, the Supreme Court has emphasized the importance of the writ. For example, in **Sanders v. United States (373 U.S. 1 [1963])**, the Court emphasized that "[c]onventional notions of finality of litigation have no place where life or liberty is at stake and infringement of constitutional rights is alleged" (p. 8). Similarly, in *Kaufman v. United States* (394 U.S. 217 [1969]), the Court held that the writ is necessary to provide "adequate protection of constitutional rights" (p. 226).

However, more recently, the Court has intimated that a *habeas corpus* review should be qualified. In particular, it has held that writs should not be liberally issued for claims arising from state courts. As the Court stated in **Stone v. Powell (428 U.S. 465 [1976])**, "Despite differences in institutional environment and the unsympathetic attitude to federal constitutional claims of some state judges in years past, we are unwilling to assume that there now exists a general lack of appropriate sensitivity to constitutional rights in the trial and appellate courts of the several States" (p. 494, n. 35).

These conflicting perspectives have influenced a number of important Supreme Court cases addressing the constitutional

It is totally within the discretion of the court that is petitioned to decide whether the writ will be issued.

Graham v. Florida, 560 U.S. Juvenile offenders cannot be sentenced to life in prison for nonhomicide offenses.

United States v. Comstock, 560 U.S. 126 It is constitutionally permissible for the federal government to use civil commitment to keep a sexually dangerous federal prisoner confined beyond the date of scheduled release.

Miller v. Alabama, 567 U.S. Life in prison without parole for juvenile homicide offenders is cruel and unusual punishment, in violation of the Eighth Amendment.

Alleyne v. United States, 570 U.S. Any element of a crime that increases the mandatory minimum punishment must be submitted to a jury and proven beyond a reasonable doubt.

right to *habeas corpus*. Recently, the Court has placed limitations on the scope of the writ. Also, the Antiterrorism and Effective Death Penalty Act of 1996 has had important effects on *habeas corpus*. The following sections focus on some of these restrictions and modifications.

Restrictions on the Right to *Habeas Corpus*

LEARNING OUTCOMES 4 — Summarize the right to and restrictions on *habeas corpus*.

The Supreme Court has restricted the right to *habeas corpus* in a number of ways. First, it has limited the types of claims that can succeed (for example, *Teague v. Lane*, 489 U.S. 288 [1989]). Second, the Court has held that *habeas* review may not be granted if the petitioner fails to submit a claim within the time frame specified by state law (for example, *Kuhlmann v. Wilson*, 477 U.S. 436 [1986]). Third, it is generally necessary for a convicted individual to exhaust all state remedies before a federal *habeas* review will be granted (for example, *Ex parte Hawk*, 321 U.S. 114 [1944]).

Finally, restrictions have been imposed in situations in which a prisoner filed multiple *habeas* petitions (for example, *Magwood v. Patterson*, No. 09-158 [2010]).

The Right to Counsel in the *Habeas Corpus* Context

The Supreme Court has guaranteed the right to counsel in direct appeals of right, but not in discretionary appeals. Because *habeas corpus* is purely discretionary, the Supreme Court has held that no right to counsel exists, unless, of course, the prisoner can afford representation (see *Ross v. Moffitt*, 417 U.S. 600 [1974]). The Court has held, however, that federal prisoners have a "constitutional right of access to the courts" (*Bounds v. Smith*, 430 U.S. 817 [1977]).

The Supreme Court has also held that a state cannot prohibit prisoners from helping each other prepare and submit *habeas corpus* petitions (*Johnson v. Avery*, 393 U.S. 483 [1969]). Moreover, the Court has held that an indigent *habeas corpus* petitioner is entitled to a free transcript of his or her trial to assist in preparing the appropriate paperwork (see *Griffin v. Illinois*).

What Is the Goal of Sentencing?

Four broad goals of sentencing can be identified: (1) *rehabilitation*, or reformation; (2) *retribution*; (3) *incapacitation*; and (4) *deterrence*, either general or specific. *Specific deterrence* refers to discouraging the offender from committing additional crimes. *General deterrence* refers to discouraging all would-be offenders from committing crimes.

The differences among these four goals of punishment have been well described in a famous case heard by the Pennsylvania Supreme Court, *Commonwealth v. Ritter* 13, Pa. D. & C. 285 (1930):

- As far as the principle of reformation is concerned, however important it may be in the general run of cases, it obviously has little or no application to such a case as the present. Whichever be the penalty here inflicted, the defendant will not again be in contact with society, and since secular law is concerned with one's relation to the community and not primarily with his inward moral development, the spiritual regeneration of a defendant is not, in such a case as this, a dominant factor. In other words, it would not be a practical consideration weighing in favor of life imprisonment that thereby the defendant might be susceptible of moral reformation, whereas the opportunity for this would be denied to him if the death penalty were inflicted.

- The second theory, which has been urged as a basis for the imposition of penalties, is that of retribution. This may be regarded as the doctrine of legal revenge, or punishment merely for the sake of punishment. It is to pay back the wrongdoer for his wrongdoing, to make him suffer by way of retaliation even if no benefit results thereby to himself or to others. This theory of punishment looks to the past and not to the future and rests solely upon the foundation of vindictive justice. It is this idea of punishment that generally prevails, even though those who entertain it may not be fully aware of their so doing. Historically, it may be said that the origin of all legal punishments had its root in the natural impulse of revenge. At first, this instinct was gratified by retaliatory measures on the part of the individual who suffered by the crime committed, or, in the case of murder, by his relatives. Later, the state took away the right of retaliation from individuals, and its own assumption of the function of revenge really constituted the beginning of criminal law. The entire course, however, of the refinement and humanizing of society has been in the direction of dispelling from penology any such theory. Indeed, even in classical times moralists and philosophers rejected the idea entirely. Plato puts into the mouth of Protagoras the words: "No one punishes those who have been guilty of injustice solely because they have committed injustice, unless indeed he punishes in a brutal and unreasonable manner. When any one makes use of his reason in inflicting punishment, he punishes, not on account of the fault that is past, for no one can bring it about that what has been done may not have been done, but on account of a fault to come, in order that the person punished may not again commit the fault and that his punishment may restrain from similar acts those persons who witness the punishment.". . . .

- Rejecting, therefore, the theory of retribution as a proper basis upon which to impose the penalty of law, we come to the third principle which has been advocated, namely, the restraint of the wrongdoer in order to make it impossible for him to commit further crime. Here we arrive not only at a justifiable basis for action but at one which is vital to the protection of society. To permit a man of dangerous criminal tendencies to be in a position where he can give indulgence to such propensities would be a folly which no community should suffer itself to commit, any more than it should allow a wild animal to range at will in the city streets. If, therefore, there is danger that a defendant may again commit crime, society should restrain his liberty until such danger be past, and, in cases similar to the present, if reasonably necessary for that purpose, to terminate his life. Admittedly, restraint by imprisonment can never be as wholly effectual as execution, and there are, from time to time, cases where imprisonment may not be sufficient for the protection of society. It is on this ground that it is pertinent to take testimony in regard to the history of a defendant and of the circumstances attending his commission of crime. If his record shows that he is of a dangerous type, or that he habitually commits grave crimes, or that he has a homicidal tendency, or that he is hopelessly depraved, or that he has a savage nature, or that he has committed murder under circumstances of such atrocity and inhuman brutality as to make his continued existence one of likely danger to society, then, in my opinion, the sentence of death is both justifiable and advisable. The community may not be safe with such a man in existence even though he be serving a term of life imprisonment; he may again commit murder within the prison walls, or may escape and again make innocent victims his prey, or may even, by cunning simulation of repentance, obtain a pardon from governmental authorities. . . .

- This brings us to the final and what must be fairly regarded as one of the most important objectives of punishment, namely, the element of deterrence—the theory which regards the penalty as being not an end in itself but the means of attaining an end, namely, the frightening of others who might be tempted to imitate the criminal. From this angle, a penalty is a cautionary measure, aimed at the prevention of further crime in the community. There has been much controversy and an enormous amount of literature on the subject as to whether the death penalty does or does not act as a deterrent. With that controversy, we have nothing to do. As stated before, the law of Pennsylvania retains the death penalty as an optional alternative. The real question is not as to whether the death penalty is in general a deterrent, but as to the particular kinds of murder cases in which execution would or would not be most likely to effect deterrence. It becomes a problem of determining the basis upon which to make such classification.

This case raises interesting questions about sentencing:

1. Which goal of sentencing do you feel is most important and why?
2. What sentencing goal(s) is/are prioritized by the U.S. criminal justice system?

LEARNING OUTCOMES 1

Describe the defendant's rights at trial.

Constitutional rights enjoyed by the defendant at trial include speedy trial, public trial, impartial judge, impartial jury, confrontation, compulsory process, double-jeopardy protection, and the right to assert an entrapment defense. Each right is limited in one or more key respects.

Key Cases

United States v. Marion
Strunk v. United States
In re Oliver
Waller v. Georgia
Sheppard v. Maxwell
Tumey v. Ohio
Ward v. Monroeville
Baldwin v. New York
Johnson v. Louisiana
Batson v. Kentucky
Illinois v. Allen
Dusky v. United States
Mattax v. United States
Coy v. Iowa
Washington v. Texas
Benton v. Maryland
Kansas v. Hendricks
Blockburger v. United States
Sorrells v. United States

1. Summarize the main rights at trial.
2. What trial right is the most important and why?
3. What makes entrapment straddle the lines between criminal law and criminal procedure?

speedy trial A trial that meets with the Sixth Amendment's requirement for a speedy trial. A trial is no longer "speedy" when there is intentional delay that is prejudicial to the defendant's case.

accusation rule The requirement that a person must first be accused (i.e., charged) for the Sixth Amendment's speedy trial provision to apply.

public trial A trial that is open to the public and/or complies with the Sixth Amendment's public trial provision. Courts can sometimes limit public access and the proceedings will still be considered public.

impartial judge A judge who is capable of basing his or her decisions on the law and who has no conflict of interest or pecuniary stake in the outcome of the case. There is no constitutional right to an impartial judge. This right is a Supreme Court creation.

impartial jury A jury that is capable of making a decision based solely on the facts of the case.

noncriminal proceeding rule The rule that limits juries to criminal trials. The rule is a bit of a misnomer because civil trials are by jury.

The noncriminal proceeding applies to steps of the criminal process that are not themselves considered "criminal." Examples are juvenile adjudicatory hearings and civil commitment hearings.

six-month imprisonment rule The rule that limits jury trials to cases in which more than six-months' incarceration in jail or prison is possible.

jury list The master list from which prospective jurors are subpoenaed. Examples include lists of those with drivers' licenses or voter registration lists.

jury panel The list of individuals drawn from the jury list. The jury panel consists of those individuals subpoenaed for jury service.

voir dire The process of selecting jurors for service. *Voir dire* proceeds through three stages: questioning by the judge, challenges for cause, and peremptory challenges.

challenge for cause A means of excluding prospective jurors who cannot be impartial. Prosecutors and defense attorneys have an unlimited number of challenges for cause in criminal cases.

peremptory challenge A means of excluding prospective jurors with no reason offered. Peremptory challenges are limited depending on the case type and the jurisdiction. Peremptory challenges cannot be used to excuse prospective jurors based on race.

confrontation The defendant's Sixth Amendment right to be present at his or her trial, hear live testimony of adverse witnesses, and challenge such witnesses' statements in open court.

live testimony The confrontation requirement that adverse witnesses provide live testimony.

compulsory process The Sixth Amendment requirement that criminal defendants enjoy the right to compel the production of witnesses and evidence. This is often accomplished via subpoena.

double jeopardy The Fifth Amendment requirement that a person cannot be reprosecuted after acquittal, reprosecuted after conviction, or subjected to separate punishments for the same offense.

same offense For double-jeopardy purposes, the same offense is one that has the same elements as another offense. For example, first- and second-degree murders are considered the "same offense" for double-jeopardy purposes. First-degree murder is defined as the premeditated deliberate killing of another person. Second-degree murder is the same offense, less the premeditation requirement. A person cannot be convicted of both offenses; otherwise, a double-jeopardy violation occurs.

Blockburger rule A rule stemming from *Blockburger* v. *United States* (284 U.S. 299 [1932]) that helps courts determine what constitutes the "same offense" for double jeopardy purposes: "[w]here the same act or transaction constitutes a violation of two distinct statutory provisions, the test to be applied to determine whether there are two offenses or only one, is whether each requires proof of an additional fact which the other does not" (p. 304).

entrapment defense A criminal defense based on the belief that someone should not be convicted of a crime that the government instigated. It is a defense in the criminal law sense, but it is one of the only defenses that calls into question law enforcement's role in the instigation of a crime. This is why entrapment is important in criminal procedure.

Summarize how sentences are determined and the offender's rights during sentencing.

There are numerous constitutional restrictions, stemming from the Eighth Amendment, on the types of sentences judges can hand down. Also, the offender enjoys the right to double-jeopardy protection, to participate in the sentencing process, to have counsel present, and to receive a reasonable punishment.

Key Cases

Roberts v. United States

Furman v. Georgia

Gregg v. Georgia

United States v. Tucker

1. How is the appropriate sentence determined?
2. What constitutional rights exist during sentencing?
3. In what ways has the Supreme Court limited the types of sentences that can be handed down? Be specific and cite cases.

sentence The penalty received by a person convicted at trial.

Describe the various types of appeals and the offender's constitutional rights during the appellate stage.

An appeal occurs when an appellate court, such as one of the federal courts of appeal, examines a lower court's decision in order to determine whether the proper procedure or law was followed. Direct appeals are automatically granted by law. Discretionary appeals are not guaranteed; it is up to the reviewing court to decide whether it will hear the appeal.

Key Cases

Griffin v. Illinois

Douglas v. California

1. What is the purpose of an appeal?
2. What type of appeal is most likely to succeed?
3. What happens to a person who successfully appeals?

appeal The practice of asking an appellate court to examine a lower court's decision in order to determine whether the proper procedure was followed or the correct law was applied.

direct appeal An appeal that is authorized by law.

discretionary appeal An appeal that will be heard only if the reviewing court agrees to do so.

trial *de novo* A type of appeal in which the appellate court holds a new trial as if the prior trial never occurred.

Summarize the right to and restrictions on *habeas corpus*.

Habeas corpus is another method challenging one's conviction. The Supreme Court has limited the types of claims that can succeed. It has also held that a *habeas corpus* review may not be granted if the petitioner fails to submit a claim within the time frame specified by state law. Third, it is generally necessary for a convicted individual to exhaust all state remedies before a federal *habeas* review will be granted. Finally, restrictions have been imposed in situations in which prisoners have filed multiple *habeas* petitions.

Key Cases

Sanders v. United States

Stone v. Powell

1. Compare and contrast *habeas corpus* and appeals.
2. What restrictions exist with respect to *habeas corpus*?

habeas corpus A means of challenging the constitutionality of one's confinement, best viewed as an alternative to appealing. *Habeas corpus* is a constitutional right (Article I, Section 9, Clause 2).

Appendix

The Constitution of the United States of America

We the People of the United States, in Order to form a more perfect Union, establish Justice, insure domestic Tranquility, provide for the common defence, promote the general Welfare, and secure the Blessings of Liberty to ourselves and our Posterity, do ordain and establish this Constitution for the United States of America.

Article I

Section 1 All legislative Powers herein granted shall be vested in a Congress of the United States, which shall consist of a Senate and House of Representatives.

Section 2 The House of Representatives shall be composed of Members chosen every second Year by the People of the several States, and the Electors in each State shall have the Qualifications requisite for Electors of the most numerous Branch of the State Legislature.

No person shall be a Representative who shall not have attained to the Age of twenty five Years, and been seven Years a Citizen of the United States, and who shall not, when elected, be an Inhabitant of that State in which he shall be chosen.

Representatives and direct Taxes shall be apportioned among the several States which may be included within this Union, according to their respective Numbers which shall be determined by adding to the whole Number of free Persons, including those bound to Service for a Term of Years, and excluding Indians not taxed, three fifths of all other Persons. The actual Enumeration shall be made within three Years after the first Meeting of the Congress of the United States, and within every subsequent Term ten Years, in such Manner as they shall by Law direct. The Number of Representatives shall not exceed one for every thirty Thousand, but each State shall have at Least one Representative; and until such enumeration shall be made, the State of New Hampshire shall be entitled to chuse three, Massachusetts eight, Rhode-Island and Providence Plantations one, Connecticut five, New York six, New Jersey four, Pennsylvania eight, Delaware one, Maryland six, Virginia ten, North Carolina five, South Carolina five, and Georgia three.

When vacancies happen in the Representation from any State, the Executive Authority thereof shall issue Writs of Election to fill such Vacancies.

The House of Representatives shall chuse their speaker and other Officers; and shall have the sole Power of Impeachment.

Section 3 The Senate of the United States shall be composed of two Senators from each State chosen by the Legislature thereof, for six Years; and each Senator shall have one Vote.

Immediately after they shall be assembled in Consequence of the first Election, they shall be divided as equally as may be into three Classes. The Seats of the Senators of the first Class shall be vacated at the Expiration of the second year, of the second Class at the Expiration of the fourth Year, and of the third Class at the Expiration of the sixth Year, so that one third may be chosen every second Year and if Vacancies happen by Resignation, or otherwise, during the Recess of the Legislature of any State, the Executive thereof may make temporary Appointments until the next Meeting of the Legislature, which shall then fill such Vacancies.

No Person shall be a Senator who shall not have attained to the Age of thirty Years, and been nine Years a Citizen of the United States, and who shall not, when elected, be an Inhabitant of that State for which he shall be chosen.

The Vice President of the United States shall be President of the Senate, but shall have no Vote, unless they be equally divided.

The Senate shall chuse their other Officers, and also a President pro tempore, in the Absence of the Vice President, or when he shall exercise the Office of President of the United States.

The Senate shall have the sole Power to try all Impeachments. When sitting for that Purpose, they shall be on Oath or Affirmation. When the President of the United States is tried, the Chief Justice shall preside: And no Person shall be convicted without the Concurrence of two thirds of the Members present.

Judgment in Cases of Impeachment shall not extend further than to removal from Office, and disqualification to hold and enjoy any Office of honor, Trust or Profit under the United States; but the Party convicted shall nevertheless be liable and subject to Indictment, Trial, Judgment and Punishment, according to Law.

Section 4 The Times, Places and Manner of holding Elections for Senators and Representatives, shall be prescribed in each State by the Legislature thereof; but the Congress may at any time by law make or alter such Regulations, except as to the Places of chusing Senators.

The Congress shall assemble at least once in every Year, and such Meeting shall be on the first Monday in December, unless they shall by Law appoint a different Day.

Section 5 Each House shall be the Judge of the Elections, Returns and Qualifications of its own Members, and a Majority of each shall constitute a Quorum to do Business; but a smaller Number may adjourn from day to day, and may be authorized to compel the Attendance of absent Members, in such Manner, and under such Penalties as each House may provide.

Each House may determine the Rules of its Proceedings, punish its Members for disorderly Behaviour, and with the Concurrence of two thirds, expel a Member.

Each House shall keep a journal of its Proceedings, and from time to time publish the same, excepting such Parts as may in their judgment require Secrecy; and the Yeas and Nays of the Members of either House on any question shall, at the Desire of one fifth of those present, be entered on the Journal.

Neither House, during the Session of Congress, shall, without the Consent of the other, adjourn for more than three days, nor to any other Place than that in which the two Houses shall be sitting.

Section 6 The Senators and Representatives shall receive a Compensation for their Services, to be ascertained by Law, and paid out of the Treasury of the United States. They shall in all Cases, except Treason, Felony and Breach of the Peace, be privileged from Arrest during their Attendance at the Session of their respective Houses, and in going to and returning from the same; and for any Speech or Debate in either House, they shall not be questioned in any other Place.

No Senator or Representative shall, during the Time for which he was elected, be appointed to any civil Office under the Authority of the United States, which shall have been created, or the Emoluments whereof shall have been encreased during such time; and no Person holding any Office under the United States, shall be a Member of either House during his Continuance in Office.

Section 7 All Bills for raising Revenue shall originate in the House of Representatives; but the Senate may propose or concur with Amendments as on other Bills.

Every Bill which shall have passed the House of Representatives and the Senate, shall, before it become a Law, be presented to the President of the United States; If he approves he shall sign it, but if not he shall return it, with his Objections to that House in which it shall have originated, who shall enter the Objections at large on their journal, and proceed to reconsider it. If after such Reconsideration two thirds of that House shall agree to pass the Bill, it shall be sent, together with the Objections, to the other House, by which it shall likewise be reconsidered, and if approved by two thirds of that House, it shall become a Law. But in all such Cases the Votes of both Houses shall be determined by Yeas and Nays, and the Names of the Persons voting for and against the Bill shall be entered on the Journal of each House respectively. If any Bill shall not be returned by the President within ten Days (Sundays excepted) after it shall have been presented to him, the Same shall be a Law, in like Manner as if he had signed it, unless the Congress by their Adjournment prevent its Return, in which Case it shall not be a Law.

Every Order, Resolution, or Vote to which the Concurrence of the Senate and House of Representatives may be necessary (except on a question of Adjournment) shall be presented to the President of the United States; and before the Same shall take Effect, shall be approved by him, or being disapproved by him, shall be repassed by two thirds of the Senate and House of Representatives, according to the Rules and Limitations prescribed in the Case of a Bill.

Section 8 The Congress shall have Power To lay and collect Taxes, Duties, Imposts and Excises, to pay the Debts and provide for the common Defence and general Welfare of the United States; but all Duties, Imposts and Excises shall be uniform throughout the United States;

To borrow Money on the credit of the United States;

To regulate Commerce with foreign Nations, and among the several States, and with the Indian Tribes;

To establish a uniform Rule of Naturalization, and uniform Laws on the subject of Bankruptcies throughout the United States;

To coin Money, regulate the Value thereof, and of foreign Coin, and fix the Standard of Weights and Measures;

To provide for the Punishment of counterfeiting the Securities and current Coin of the United States;

To establish Post Offices and post Roads;

To promote the Progress of Science and useful Arts, by securing for limited Times to Authors and Inventors the exclusive Right to their respective Writings and Discoveries;

To constitute Tribunals inferior to the supreme Court;

To define and punish Piracies and Felonies committed on the high Seas, and Offences against the Law of Nations;

To declare War, grant Letters of Marque and Reprisal, and make Rules concerning Captures on Land and Water;

To raise and support Armies, but no Appropriation of Money to that Use shall be for a longer Term than two Years;

To provide and maintain a Navy;

To make Rules for the Government and Regulation of the land and naval Forces;

To provide for calling forth the Militia to execute the Laws of the Union, suppress Insurrections and repel Invasions;

To provide for organizing, arming, and disciplining, the Militia, and for governing such Part of them as may be employed in the Service of the United States, reserving to the States respectively, the Appointment of the Officers, and the Authority of training the Militia according to the discipline prescribed by Congress;

To exercise exclusive Legislation in all Cases whatsoever, over such District (not exceeding ten Miles square) as may, by Cession of particular States, and the Acceptance of Congress, become the Seat of the Government of the United States, and to exercise like Authority over all Places purchased by the Consent of the Legislature of the State in which the Same shall be for the Erection of Forts, Magazines, Arsenals, dock-Yards, and other needful Buildings;—And

To make all Laws which shall be necessary and proper for carrying into Execution the foregoing Powers, and all other Powers vested by this Constitution in the Government of the United States, or in any Department or Officer thereof.

Section 9 The Migration or Importation of such Persons as any of the States now existing shall think proper to admit, shall not be prohibited by the Congress prior to the Year one thousand eight hundred and eight, but a Tax or duty may be imposed on such Importation, not exceeding ten dollars for each Person.

The Privilege of the Writ of Habeas Corpus shall not be suspended, unless when in Cases of Rebellion or Invasion the public Safety may require it.

No Bill of Attainder or ex post facto Law shall be passed.

No Capitation, or other direct, Tax shall be laid, unless in Proportion to the Census or Enumeration herein before directed to be taken.

No Tax or Duty shall be laid on Articles exported from any State.

No Preference shall be given by any Regulation of Commerce or Revenue to the Ports of one State over those of another; nor shall Vessels bound to, or from, one State, be obliged to enter, clear, or pay Duties in another.

No Money shall be drawn from the Treasury, but in Consequence of Appropriations made by Law; and a regular Statement and Account of the Receipts and Expenditures of all public Money shall be published from time to time.

No Title of Nobility shall be granted by the United States: And no Person holding any Office of Profit or Trust under them, shall, without the Consent of the Congress, accept of any present, Emolument, Office, or Title, of any kind whatever, from any King, Prince, or foreign State.

Section 10 No state shall enter into any Treaty, Alliance, or Confederation; grant Letters of Marque and Reprisal; coin Money; emit Bills of Credit; make any Thing but gold and silver Coin a Tender in Payment of Debts; pass any Bill of Attainder, ex post facto Law, or Law impairing the Obligation of Contracts, or grant any Title of Nobility.

No State shall, without the Consent of the Congress, lay any Imposts or Duties on Imports or Exports, except what may be absolutely necessary for executing its inspection Laws: and the net Produce of all Duties and Imposts, laid by any State on Imports or Exports, shall be for the Use of the Treasury of the United States, and all such Laws shall be subject to the Revision and Controul of the Congress.

No State shall, without the Consent of Congress, lay any Duty of Tonnage, keep Troops, or Ships of War in time of Peace, enter into any Agreement or Compact with another State, or with a foreign Power, or engage in War, unless actually invaded, or in such imminent Danger as will not admit of delay.

Article II

Section 1 The executive Power shall be vested in a President of the United States of America. He shall hold his Office during the Term of four Years, and, together with the Vice President, chosen for the same Term, be elected as follows.

Each State shall appoint, in such Manner as the Legislature thereof may direct, a Number of Electors, equal to the whole Number of Senators and Representatives to which the State may be entitled in the Congress; but no Senator or Representative, or Person holding an Office of Trust of Profit under the United States, shall be appointed an Elector.

The Electors shall meet in their respective States, and vote by Ballot for two Persons, of whom one at least shall not be an Inhabitant of the same State with themselves. And they shall make a List of all the Persons voted for, and, of the Number of Votes for each; which List they shall sign and certify, and transmit sealed to the Seat of the Government of the United States, directed to the President of the Senate. The President of the Senate shall, in the Presence of the Senate and House of Representatives, open all the Certificates, and the Votes shall then be counted. The Person having the greatest Number of Votes shall be the President, if such Number be a Majority of the whole Number of Electors appointed; and if there be more than one who have such Majority, and have an equal Number of Votes, then the House of Representatives shall immediately chuse by Ballot one of them for President; and if no Person have a Majority, then from the five highest on the List the said House shall in like Manner chuse the President. But in chusing the President, the Votes shall be taken by States, the Representation from each State having one Vote; A quorum for this Purpose shall consist of a Member or Members from two thirds of the States, and a Majority of all the States shall be necessary to a Choice. In every Case, after the Choice of the President, the Person having

the greatest Number of Votes of the Electors shall be the Vice President. But if there should remain two or more who have equal Votes, the Senate shall chuse from them by Ballot the Vice President.

The Congress may determine the Time of chusing the Electors, and the Day on which they shall give their Votes; which Day shall be the same throughout the United States.

No Person except a natural born Citizen, or a Citizen of the United States, at the time of the Adoption of this Constitution, shall be eligible to the Office of President; neither shall any Person be eligible to that Office who shall not have attained to the Age of thirty five Years, and been fourteen Years a Resident within the United States.

In Case of the Removal of the President from Office, or of his Death, Resignation, or Inability to discharge the Powers and Duties of the said Office, the Same shall devolve on the Vice President, and the Congress may by Law provide for the Case of Removal, Death, Resignation or Inability, both of the President and Vice President, declaring what Officer shall then act as President, and such Officer shall act accordingly, until the Disability be removed, or a President shall be elected.

The President shall, at stated Times, receive for his Services, a Compensation, which shall neither be encreased nor diminished during the Period for which he shall have been elected, and he shall not receive within that Period any other Emolument from the United States, or any of them.

Before he enter on the Execution of his Office, he shall take the following Oath or Affirmation—"I do solemnly swear (or affirm) that I will faithfully execute the Office of President of the United States, and will to the best of my Ability, preserve, protect and defend the Constitution of the United States."

Section 2 The President shall be Commander in Chief of the Army, and Navy of the United States, and of the Militia of the several States, when called into the actual Service of the United States; he may require the Opinion, in writing, of the principal Officer in each of the executive Departments, upon any Subject relating to the Duties of their respective Offices, and he shall have Power to grant Reprieves and Pardons for Offences against the United States, except in Cases of Impeachment.

He shall have Power, by and with the Advice and Consent of the Senate, to make Treaties, provided two thirds of the Senators present concur; and he shall nominate, and by and with the Advice and Consent of the Senate, shall appoint Ambassadors, other public Ministers and Consuls, Judges of the supreme Court, and all other Officers of the United States, whose Appointments are not herein otherwise provided for, and which shall be established by Law: but the Congress may by Law vest the Appointment of such inferior Officers, as they think proper, in the President alone, in the Courts of Law, or in the Heads of Departments.

The President shall have Power to fill up all Vacancies that may happen during the Recess of the Senate, by granting Commissions which shall expire at the end of their next Session.

Section 3 He shall from time to time give to the Congress Information of the State of the Union, and recommend to their Consideration such Measures as he shall judge necessary and expedient; he may, on extraordinary Occasions, convene both Houses, or either of them, and in Case of Disagreement between them, with Respect to the Time of Adjournment, he may adjourn them to such Time as he shall think proper; he shall receive Ambassadors and other public Ministers; he shall take Care that the Laws be faithfully executed, and shall Commission all the Officers of the United States.

Section 4 The President, Vice President and all civil Officers of the United States, shall be removed from Office on Impeachment for, and Conviction of, Treason, Bribery, or other high Crimes and Misdemeanors.

Article III

Section 1 The judicial Power of the United States, shall be vested in one supreme Court, and in such inferior Courts as the Congress may from time to time ordain and establish. The Judges, both of the supreme and inferior Courts, shall hold their Offices during good Behaviour, and shall, at stated Times, receive for their Services, a Compensation, which shall not be diminished during their Continuance in Office.

Section 2 The judicial Power shall extend to all Cases, in Law and Equity, arising under this Constitution, the Laws of the United States, and Treaties made, or which shall be made, under their Authority;—to all Cases affecting Ambassadors, other public Ministers and Consuls;—to all Cases of admiralty and maritime Jurisdiction;—to Controversies to which the United States shall be a Party;—to Controversies between two or more States;—between a State and Citizens of another State;—between Citizens of different States,—between Citizens of the same State claiming Lands under Grants of different States,—and between a State, or the Citizens thereof, and foreign States, Citizens of Subjects.

In all Cases affecting Ambassadors, other public Ministers and Consuls, and those in which a State shall be Party, the supreme Court shall have original Jurisdiction. In all the other Cases before mentioned, the supreme Court shall have appellate Jurisdiction, both as to Law and Fact, with such Exceptions, and under such Regulations as the Congress shall make.

The Trial of all Crimes, except in Cases of Impeachment, shall be by Jury; and such Trial shall be held in the State where the said Crimes shall have been committed; but when not committed within any State, the Trial shall be at such Place or Places as the Congress may by Law have directed.

Section 3 Treason against the United States, shall consist only in levying War against them, or in adhering to their Enemies, giving them Aid and Comfort. No Person shall be convicted of Treason unless on the Testimony of two Witnesses to the same overt Act, or on Confession in open Court.

The Congress shall have Power to declare the Punishment of Treason, but no Attainder of Treason shall work Corruption of Blood, or Forfeiture except during the Life of the Person attainted.

Article IV

Section 1 Full Faith and Credit shall be given in each State to the public Acts, Records, and judicial Proceedings of every other State. And the Congress may by general Laws prescribe the Manner in which such Acts, Records and Proceedings shall be proved, and the Effect thereof.

Section 2 The Citizens of each State shall be entitled to all Privileges and Immunities of Citizens in the several States.

A Person charged in any State with Treason, Felony, or other Crime, who shall flee from Justice, and be found in another State, shall on Demand of the executive Authority of the State from which he fled, be delivered up, to be removed to the State having Jurisdiction of the Crime.

No Person held to Service or Labour in one State under the Laws thereof, escaping into another, shall, in Consequence of any Law or Regulation therein, be discharged from such Service or Labour, but shall be delivered up on Claim of the Party to whom such Service or Labour may be due.

Section 3 New States may be admitted by the Congress into this Union; but no new State shall be formed or erected within the Jurisdiction of any other State; nor any State be formed by the Junction of two or more States, or Parts of States, without the Consent of the Legislatures of the States concerned as well as of the Congress.

The Congress shall have Power to dispose of and make all needful Rules and Regulations respecting the Territory or other Property belonging to the United States; and nothing in this Constitution shall be so construed as to Prejudice any Claims of the United States, or of any particular State.

Section 4 The United States shall guarantee to every State in this Union a Republican Form of Government, and shall protect each of them against Invasion, and on Application of the Legislature, or of the Executive (when the Legislature cannot be convened) against domestic Violence.

Article V

The Congress, whenever two thirds of both Houses shall deem it necessary, shall propose Amendments to this Constitution, or, on the Application of the Legislatures of two thirds of the several States, shall call a Convention for proposing Amendments, which, in either Case, shall be valid to all Intents and Purposes, as Part of this Constitution, when ratified by the Legislatures of three fourths of the several States, or by Conventions in three fourths thereof, as the one or the other Mode of Ratification may be proposed by the Congress; Provided that no Amendment which may be made prior to the Year One thousand eight hundred and eight shall in any Manner affect the first and fourth Clauses in the Ninth Section of the first Article; and that no State, without its Consent, shall be deprived of its equal Suffrage in the Senate.

Article VI

All Debts contracted and Engagements entered into, before the Adoption of this Constitution, shall be as valid against the United States under this Constitution, as under the Confederation.

This Constitution, and the laws of the United States which shall be made in Pursuance thereof; and all Treaties made, or which shall be made, under the Authority of the United States, shall be the supreme Law of the Land; and the Judges in every State shall be bound thereby, any Thing in the Constitution or Laws of any State to the Contrary notwithstanding.

The Senators and Representatives before mentioned, and the Members of the several State Legislatures, and all executive and judicial Officers, both of the United States and of the several States, shall be bound by Oath or Affirmation, to support this Constitution; but no religious Test shall ever be required as a Qualification to any Office or public Trust under the United States.

Article VII

The Ratification of the Conventions of nine States, shall be sufficient for the Establishment of this Constitution between the States so ratifying the Same.

Done in Convention by the Unanimous Consent of the States present the Seventeenth Day of September in the Year of our Lord one thousand seven hundred and Eighty seven and of the Independence of the United States of America the Twelfth. In witness whereof we have hereunto subscribed our Names,

Go. WASHINGTON
Presid't. and deputy from Virginia

Attest
WILLIAM JACKSON
Secretary

DELAWARE
Geo. Read
Gunning Bedford jun
John Dickinson
Richard Basset
Jaco. Broom

MASSACHUSETTS
Nathaniel Gorham
Rufus King

CONNECTICUT
Wm. Saml. Johnson
Roger Sherman

NEW YORK
Alexander Hamilton

NEW JERSEY
Wh. Livingston
David Brearley
Wm. Paterson
Jona. Dayton

PENNSYLVANIA
B. Franklin
Thomas Mifflin
Robt. Morris
Geo. Clymer
Thos. FitzSimons
Jared Ingersoll
James Wilson
Gouv. Morris

NEW HAMPSHIRE
John Langdon
Nicholas Gilman

MARYLAND
James McHenry
Dan of St. Thos. Jenifer
Danl. Carroll

VIRGINIA
John Blair
James Madison, Jr.

NORTH CAROLINA
Wm. Blount
Richd. Dobbs Spaight
Hu. Williamson

SOUTH CAROLINA
J. Rutledge
Charles Cotesworth Pinckney
Charles Pinckney
Pierce Butler

GEORGIA
William Few
Abr. Baldwin

Articles in addition to, and amendment of the Constitution of the United States of America, proposed by Congress and ratified by the Legislatures of the several states, pursuant to the Fifth Article of the original Constitution.

(The first ten amendments were passed by Congress on September 25, 1789, and were ratified on December 15, 1791.)

Amendment I

Congress shall make no law respecting an establishment of religion, or prohibiting the free exercise thereof; or abridging the freedom of speech, or of the press; or the right of the people peaceably to assemble, and to petition the Government for a redress of grievances.

Amendment II

A well regulated Militia, being necessary to the security of a free State, the right of the people to keep and bear Arms, shall not be infringed.

Amendment III

No Soldier shall, in time of peace be quartered in any house, without the consent of the Owner, nor in time of war, but in a manner to be prescribed by law.

Amendment IV

The right of the people to be secure in their persons, houses, papers, and effects, against unreasonable searches and seizures, shall not be violated, and no warrants shall issue, but upon probable cause, supported by Oath or affirmation, and particularly describing the place to be searched, and the persons or things to be seized.

Amendment V

No person shall be held to answer for a capital, or otherwise infamous crime, unless on a presentment or indictment of a Grand Jury, except in cases arising in the land or naval forces, or in the Militia, when in actual service in time of War or public danger; nor shall any person be subject for the same offence to be twice put in jeopardy of life or limb; nor shall be compelled in any criminal case to be a witness against himself, nor be deprived of life, liberty, or property, without due process of law;

nor shall private property be taken for public use, without just compensation.

Amendment VI

In all criminal prosecutions, the accused shall enjoy the right to a speedy and public trial, by an impartial jury of the State and district wherein the crime shall have been committed, which district shall have been previously ascertained by law, and to be informed of the nature and cause of the accusation; to be confronted with the witnesses against him; to have compulsory process for obtaining witnesses in his favor, and to have the Assistance of Counsel for his defence.

Amendment VII

In Suits at common law, where the value in controversy shall exceed twenty dollars, the right of trial by jury shall be preserved, and no fact tried by a jury, shall be otherwise re-examined in any Court of the United States, than according to the rules of the common law.

Amendment VIII

Excessive bail shall not be required, nor excessive fines imposed, nor cruel and unusual punishments inflicted.

Amendment IX

The enumeration in the Constitution, of certain rights, shall not be construed to deny or disparage others retained by the people.

Amendment X

The powers not delegated to the United States by the Constitution, nor prohibited by it to the States, are reserved to the States respectively, or to the people.

Amendment XI

(Ratified on February 7, 1795)

The Judicial power of the United States shall not be construed to extend to any suit in law or equity, commenced or prosecuted against one of the United States by Citizens of another State, or by Citizens or Subjects of any Foreign State.

Amendment XII

(Ratified on June 15, 1804)

The Electors shall meet in their respective states, and vote by ballot for President and Vice-President, one of whom, at least, shall not be an inhabitant of the same state with themselves; they shall name in their ballots the person voted for as President, and in distinct ballots the person voted for as Vice-President, and they shall make distinct lists of all persons voted for as President, and of all persons voted for as Vice-President, and of the number of votes for each, which lists they shall sign and certify, and transmit sealed to the seat of the government of the United States, directed to the President of the Senate;—The President of the Senate shall, in the presence of the Senate and House of Representatives, open all the certificates and the votes shall then be counted;—The person having the greatest number of votes for President, shall be the President, if such number be a majority of the whole number of Electors appointed; and if no person have such majority; then from the persons having the highest numbers not exceeding three

on the list of those voted for as President, the House of Representatives shall choose immediately, by ballot, the President. But in choosing the President, the votes shall be taken by states, the representation from each state having one vote; a quorum for this purpose shall consist of a member or members from two-thirds of the states, and a majority of all the states shall be necessary to a choice. And if the House of Representatives shall not choose a President whenever the right of choice shall devolve upon them, before the fourth day of March next following, then the Vice-President shall act as President, as in the case of the death or other constitutional disability of the President.—The person having the greatest number of votes as Vice-President, shall be the Vice-President, if such number be a majority of the whole number of Electors appointed, and if no person have a majority, then from the two highest numbers on the list, the Senate shall choose the Vice-President; a quorum for the purpose shall consist of two-thirds of the whole number of Senators, and a majority of the whole number shall be necessary to a choice. But no person constitutionally ineligible to the office of President shall be eligible to that of Vice-President of the United States.

Amendment XIII

(Ratified on December 6, 1865)

Section 1 Neither slavery nor involuntary servitude, except as a punishment for crime whereof the party shall have been duly convicted, shall exist within the United States, or any place subject to their jurisdiction.

Section 2 Congress shall have power to enforce this article by appropriate legislation.

Amendment XIV

(Ratified on July 9, 1868)

Section 1 All persons born or naturalized in the United States, and subject to the jurisdiction thereof, are citizens of the United States and of the State wherein they reside. No State shall make or enforce any law which shall abridge the privileges or immunities of citizens of the United States; nor shall any State deprive any person of life, liberty, or property, without due process of law; nor deny to any person within its jurisdiction the equal protection of the laws.

Section 2 Representatives shall be apportioned among the several States according to their respective numbers, counting the whole number of persons in each State, excluding Indians not taxed. But when the right to vote at any election for the choice of electors for President and Vice President of the United States, Representatives in Congress, the Executive and Judicial officers of a State, or the members of the Legislature thereof, is denied to any of the male inhabitants of such State, being twenty-one years of age, and citizens of the United States, or in any way abridged, except for participation in rebellion, or other crime, the basis of representation therein shall be reduced in the proportion which the number of such male citizens shall bear to the whole number of male citizens twenty-one years of age in such State.

Section 3 No person shall be a Senator or Representative in Congress, or elector of President and Vice President, or hold any office, civil or military, under the United States, or under any State, who, having previously taken an oath, as a member of Congress, or as an officer of the United States, or as a member of any State legislature, or as an executive or judicial officer of any State, to support the Constitution of the United States, shall have engaged in insurrection or rebellion against the same, or given aid or comfort to the enemies thereof. But Congress may by a vote of two-thirds of each House, remove such diability.

Section 4 The validity of the public debt of the United States, authorized by law, including debts incurred for payment of pensions and bounties for services in suppressing insurrection or rebellion, shall not be questioned. But neither the United States nor any State shall assume or pay any debt or obligation incurred in aid of insurrection or rebellion against the United States, or any claim for the loss or emancipation of any slave, but all such debts, obligations and claims shall be held illegal and void.

Section 5 The Congress shall have power to enforce, by appropriate legislation, the provisions of this article.

Amendment XV

(Ratified on February 3, 1870)

Section 1 The right of citizens of the United States to vote shall not be denied or abridged by the United States or by any State on account of race, color, or previous condition of servitude.

Section 2 The Congress shall have power to enforce this article by appropriate legislation.

Amendment XVI

(Ratified on February 3, 1913)

The Congress shall have power to lay and collect taxes on incomes, from whatever source derived, without apportionment among the several States, and without regard to any census or enumeration.

Amendment XVII

(Ratified on April 8, 1913)

The Senate of the United States shall be composed of two Senators from each State, elected by the people thereof, for six years; and each Senator shall have one vote. The electors in each State shall have the qualifications requisite for electors of the most numerous branch of the State legislatures.

When vacancies happen in the representation of any State in the Senate, the executive authority of such State shall issue writs of election to fill such vacancies: Provided, That the legislature of any State may empower the executive thereof to make temporary appointments until the people fill the vacancies by election as the legislature may direct.

This amendment shall not be so construed as to affect the election or term of any Senator chosen before it becomes valid as part of the Constitution.

Amendment XVIII

(Ratified on January 16, 1919)

Section 1 After one year from the ratification of this article the manufacture, sale, or transportation of intoxicating liquors within, the importation thereof into, or the exportation thereof from the United States and all territory subject to the jurisdiction thereof for beverage purposes is hereby prohibited.

Section 2 The Congress and the several States shall have concurrent power to enforce this article by appropriate legislation.

Section 3 This article shall be inoperative unless it shall have been ratified as an amendment to the Constitution by the legislatures of the several States, as provided in the Constitution, within seven years from the date of the submission hereof to the States by the Congress.

Amendment XIX

(Ratified on August 18, 1920)

The right of citizens of the United States to vote shall not be denied or abridged by the United States or by any State on account of sex.

Congress shall have power to enforce this article by appropriate legislation.

Amendment XX

(Ratified on February 6, 1933)

Section 1 The terms of the President and Vice President shall end at noon on the 20th day of January, and the terms of Senators and Representatives at noon on the 3rd day of January, of the years in which such terms would have ended if this article had not been ratified; and the terms of their successors shall then begin.

Section 2 The Congress shall assemble at least once in every year, and such meeting shall begin at noon on the 3rd day of January, unless they shall by law appoint a different day.

Section 3 If, at the time fixed for the beginning of the term of the President, the President elect shall have died, the Vice President elect shall become President. If a President shall not have been chosen before the time fixed for the beginning of his term, or if the President elect shall have failed to qualify, then the Vice President elect shall act as President until a President shall have qualified; and the Congress may by law provide for the case wherein neither a President elect nor a Vice President elect shall have qualified, declaring who shall then act as President, or the manner in which one who is to act shall be selected, and such person shall act accordingly until a President or Vice President shall have qualified.

Section 4 The Congress may by law provide for the case of the death of any of the persons from whom the House of Representatives may choose a President whenever the rights of choice shall have devolved upon them, and for the case of the death of any of the persons from whom the Senate may choose a Vice President whenever the right of choice shall have devolved upon them.

Section 5 Sections 1 and 2 shall take effect on the 15th day of October following the ratification of this article.

Section 6 This article shall be inoperative unless it shall have been ratified as an amendment to the Constitution by the legislatures of three-fourths of the several States within seven years from the date of its submission.

Amendment XXI

(Ratified on December 5, 1933)

Section 1 The eighteenth article of amendment to the Constitution of the United States is hereby repealed.

Section 2 The transportation or importation into any State, Territory, or possession of the United States for delivery or use therein of intoxicating liquors, in violation of the laws thereof, is hereby prohibited.

Section 3 This article shall be inoperative unless it shall have been ratified as an amendment to the Constitution by conventions in the several States, as provided in the Constitution, within seven years from the date of the submission hereof to the States by the Congress.

Amendment XXII

(Ratified on February 27, 1951)

No person shall be elected to the office of the President more than twice, and no person who has held the office of President, or acted as President, for more than two years of a term to which some other person was elected President shall be elected to the office of the President more than once. But this Article shall not apply to any person holding the office of President when this Article was proposed by the Congress, and shall not prevent any person who may be holding the office of President, or acting as President, during the term within which this Article becomes operative from holding the office of President or acting as President during the remainder of such term.

Amendment XXIII

(Ratified on March 29, 1961)

Section 1 The District constituting the seat of Government of the United States shall appoint in such manner as the Congress may direct:

A number of electors of President and Vice President equal to the whole number of Senators and Representatives in Congress to which the District would be entitled if it were a State, but in no event more than the least populous State; they shall be in addition to those appointed by the States, but they shall be considered, for the purposes of the election of President and Vice President, to be electors appointed by a State; and they shall meet in the District and perform such duties as provided by the twelfth article of amendment.

Section 2 The Congress shall have power to enforce this article by appropriate legislation.

Amendment XXIV

(Ratified on January 23, 1964)

Section 1 The right of citizens of the United States to vote in any primary or other election for President or Vice President, for electors for President or Vice President, or for Senator or Representative in Congress, shall not be denied or abridged by the United States or any State by reason of failure to pay any poll tax or other tax.

Section 2 The Congress shall have power to enforce this article by appropriate legislation.

Amendment XXV

(Ratified on February 10, 1967)

Section 1 In case of the removal of the President from office or of his death or resignation, the Vice President shall become President.

Section 2 Whenever there is a vacancy in the office of the Vice President, the President shall nominate a Vice President who shall take office upon confirmation by a majority vote of both Houses of Congress.

Section 3 Whenever the President transmits to the President pro tempore of the Senate and the Speaker of the House of Representatives his written declaration that he is unable to discharge the powers and duties of his office, and until he transmits to them a written declaration to the contrary, such powers and duties shall be discharged by the Vice President as Acting President.

Section 4 Whenever the Vice President and a majority of either the principal officers of the executive departments or of such other body as Congress may by law provide, transmit to the President pro tempore of the Senate and the Speaker of the House of Representatives their written declaration that the President is unable to discharge the powers and duties of his office, the Vice President shall immediately assume the powers and duties of the office as Acting President.

Thereafter, when the President transmits to the President pro tempore of the Senate and the Speaker of the House of Representatives his written declaration that no inability exists, he shall resume the powers and duties of his office unless the Vice President and a majority of either the principal officers of the executive department or of such other body as Congress may by law provide, transmit within four days to the President pro tempore of the Senate and the Speaker of the House of Representatives their written declaration that the President is unable to discharge the powers and duties of his office. Thereupon Congress shall decide the issue, assembling within forty-eight hours for that purpose if not in session. If the Congress, within twenty-one days after receipt of the latter written declaration, or, if Congress is not in session, within twenty-one days after Congress is required to assemble, determines by two-thirds vote of both Houses that the President is unable to discharge the powers and duties of his office, the Vice President shall continue to discharge the same as Acting President; otherwise, the President shall resume the powers and duties of his office.

Amendment XXVI

(Ratified on July 1, 1971)

Section 1 The right of citizens of the United States, who are eighteen years of age or older, to vote shall not be denied or abridged by the United States or by any State on account of age.

Section 2 The Congress shall have power to enforce this article by appropriate legislation.

Amendment XXVII

(Ratified on May 7, 1992)

No law varying the compensation for the services of Senators and Representatives shall take effect until an election of Representatives shall have intervened.

Glossary

18 U.S.C. Section 242 A federal statute used to hold police officers (and other government actors) criminally liable for actions that cause violations of people's constitutional or other federally protected rights.

18 U.S.C. Section 3501 A federal statute enacted in the wake of the *Miranda* decision providing that any confession "shall be admissible in evidence if it is voluntarily given." The statute was deemed unconstitutional in *Dickerson* v. *United States* (530 U.S. 428 [2000]).

42 U.S.C. Section 1983 A federal statute that provides a remedy in federal court for the "deprivation of any rights...secured by the Constitution and laws" of the United States. Also called "Section 1983."

accusation rule The requirement that a person must first be accused (i.e., charged) for the Sixth Amendment's speedy trial provision to apply.

ad hoc plea bargaining A term used to describe some of the strange concessions that defendants agree to make as part of prosecutors' decisions to secure guilty pleas.

adjudication The process by which a court arrives at a decision in a case.

administrative justification A standard used to support certain regulatory and special needs searches. Created by the Supreme Court, it adopts a balancing approach, weighing the privacy interests of individuals with the interests of society in preserving public safety.

admission When a person simply admits to involvement in a crime without any police encouragement.

Alford plea A plea in which a defendant does not allocute, which means he or she does not—and indeed is not required to—explain the details of the offense to the judge.

allocution When the defendant explains to the judge exactly what he or she did and why. The defendant is usually required to allocute when he or she pleads guilty.

apparent authority A person has apparent authority if the police *reasonably believe* he or she has authority to grant consent.

appeal The practice of asking an appellate court to examine a lower court's decision in order to determine whether the proper procedure was followed or the correct law was applied.

armspan rule Part of the search incident to arrest exception to the Fourth Amendment's warrant requirement that allows officers to search not only the suspect incident to arrest, but also his or her "grabbing area."

arraignment A hearing in which the defendant is formally notified of the charge lodged against him or her. The defendant also enters one of three pleas: (1) guilty, (2) not guilty, or (3) *nolo contendere*.

arrest warrant An order issued by a judge directing a law enforcement officer to arrest an individual identified as one who has committed a specific criminal offense.

arrest The act of taking an individual into custody for the purpose of charging the person with a criminal offense (or, in the case of a juvenile, a delinquent act).

articulable facts Events that are witnessed and can be explained. Contrast articulable facts with hunches and guesses. Articulable facts are necessary for establishing probable cause.

automobile exception An exception to the Fourth Amendment's warrant requirement that permits police to search a vehicle without a warrant, so long as they have probable cause to do so.

bail bond agent A professional who posts the defendant's bail in exchange for a fee.

bail A process by which a defendant pays a certain amount of money in order to be released from jail prior to his or her trial date. Defendants who appear for trial receive their money back. Those who fail to appear for trial forfeit the bail amount.

Blockburger rule A rule stemming from *Blockburger* v. *United States* (284 U.S. 299 [1932]) that helps courts determine what constitutes the "same offense" for double jeopardy purposes: "[w]here the same act or transaction constitutes a violation of two distinct statutory provisions, the test to be applied to determine whether there are two offenses or only one, is whether each requires proof of an additional fact which the other does not" (p. 304).

booking The process by which an arrest is officially documented and the arrestee is placed into custody. During booking, the arrestee's personal items will be inventoried and he or she will be fingerprinted and/or photographed.

bright-line decisions A decision in which a court hands down a *specific rule*, one subject to very little interpretation.

case-by-case adjudication The reality that some cases cannot result in bright-line rules. Courts often look to the "totality of circumstances" when taking a case-by-case approach.

chain of custody A chronological documentation (or paper trail) showing how seized evidence has been preserved, transferred, analyzed, and disposed of. It is mainly a record of the individuals who have had physical possession of the evidence at any point during the criminal process.

challenge for cause A means of excluding prospective jurors who cannot be impartial. Prosecutors and defense attorneys have an unlimited number of challenges for cause in criminal cases.

checkpoints Brief detentions that do not require probable cause or a warrant. Their purpose should *not* be to detect evidence of criminal conduct, such as narcotics trafficking. Examples include border checkpoints, illegal immigrant checkpoints, sobriety checkpoints, license and safety checkpoints, crime-investigation checkpoints, and airport checkpoints.

civil litigation The same as a lawsuit.

civilian input A method of citizen input into the complaint review process in which a civilian panel receives and investigates a complaint, leaving adjudication and discipline with the department itself.

civilian monitor The weakest method of citizen input that leaves investigation, adjudication, and discipline inside the department. A civilian is allowed to review the adequacy and impartiality of the process.

civilian review The strongest method of citizen input in which a civilian panel investigates, adjudicates, and recommends punishment to the police chief.

closely regulated business A type of business subject to warrantless, suspicionless inspections. Examples include liquor stores and firearm dealerships.

color of law One of two requirements for a successful Section 1983 lawsuit. An official acts under color of law when he or she acts in an official capacity.

common authority "Mutual use of the property by persons generally having joint access or control for most purposes" (*United States* v. *Matlock*, 415 U.S. 164 [1974], p. 172, n. 7).

compulsory process The Sixth Amendment requirement that criminal defendants enjoy the right to compel the production of witnesses and evidence. This is often accomplished via subpoena.

confession When a person implicates him- or herself in criminal activity following police questioning and/or interrogation.

confrontation The defendant's Sixth Amendment right to be present at his or her trial, hear live testimony of adverse witnesses, and challenge such witnesses' statements in open court.

contempt power The grand jury's authority to hold people in contempt of court for failing to appear before it. Civil and criminal sanctions can be imposed.

courts of general jurisdiction The main trial courts at the state level. They are usually located at the county level and are often called "superior courts."

courts of limited jurisdiction Courts that have jurisdiction over relatively minor offenses and infractions. An example of a limited jurisdiction court is a traffic court.

crime-control perspective A perspective that emphasizes the importance of controlling crime, perhaps to the detriment of civil liberties.

criminal procedure A vast set of rules and guidelines that describe how suspected and accused criminals are to be handled and processed by the justice system.

curtilage The area between a "house" and undeveloped real property. It is usually considered the area immediately surrounding a residence in which a reasonable expectation of privacy exists.

custody Typically an arrest. Custody is important in the *Miranda* context because *Miranda* warnings do not need to be read if a person is not in custody.

damage suit A lawsuit in which one or more parties seek monetary compensation.

deadly force Force that is likely to cause death or serious bodily harm.

deliberate elicitation In the Sixth Amendment right-to-counsel context, deliberate elicitation occurs when police officers create a situation likely to induce a suspect into making an incriminating statement.

direct appeal An appeal that is authorized by law.

discovery The process by which each party to a case learns of the evidence that the opposition will present.

discretionary appeal An appeal that will be heard only if the reviewing court agrees to do so.

distinguish An appellate court's decision to treat a case before it as sufficiently distinct that it cannot be decided by looking to past rulings. In other words, the set of facts is unique and never before considered by an appellate court.

district court Federal trial courts. There are 94 federal district courts in the United States, including 89 district courts in the 50 states and 1 each in Puerto Rico, the Virgin Islands, the District of Columbia, Guam, and the Northern Mariana Islands.

double jeopardy The Fifth Amendment requirement that a person cannot be reprosecuted after acquittal, reprosecuted after conviction, or subjected to separate punishments for the same offense.

double-blind lineup A lineup procedure in which neither the witness nor the investigator staging the lineup knows who the suspect is.

drug and alcohol testing A procedure of testing for drug or alcohol use, usually via urinalysis. Employees and school students can be subjected to warrantless, suspicionless drug and alcohol testing, but hospital patients cannot—if the evidence is turned over to law enforcement authorities.

drug courier profiling A crime-detection process that makes use of what is known about the likely and observable characteristics of drug couriers. Drug courier profiling usually occurs in stop-and-frisk situations.

due process perspective A general concern with people's rights and liberties. The due process perspective is closely aligned with a liberal political orientation.

due process voluntariness approach The requirement that any confession be voluntary under the "totality of circumstances."

effective assistance of counsel The requirement that a defense attorney must effectively represent his or her client. In *Strickland* v. *Washington* (466 U.S. 668 [1984]), the Supreme Court held that a two-prong test must be applied in order to determine whether counsel is ineffective: "First, the defendant must show that counsel's performance was deficient. This requires showing that counsel made errors so serious that counsel was not functioning as the 'counsel' guaranteed the defendant by the Sixth Amendment. Second, the defendant must show that the deficient performance prejudiced the defense" (p. 687).

Eighth Amendment Part of the U.S. Constitution, which states, "Excessive bail shall not be required, nor excessive fines imposed, nor cruel and unusual punishments inflicted."

Electronic Communications Privacy Act (ECPA) Federal legislation enacted in 1986 that amended Title III of the Omnibus Crime Control and Safe Streets Act to include "electronic communications."

entrapment defense A criminal defense based on the belief that someone should not be convicted of a crime that the government instigated. It is a defense in the criminal law sense, but it is one of the only defenses that calls into question law enforcement's role in the instigation of a crime. This is why entrapment is important in criminal procedure.

evanescent evidence Evidence that is likely to disappear. An example is alcohol in a person's bloodstream.

exceptions to the warrant requirement Law enforcement actions that do not require a warrant. Examples include searches incident to arrest, searches based on exigent circumstances, automobile searches, plain-view searches, arrests based on exigent circumstances, and arrests in public places.

exclusionary rule The Supreme Court–created rule requiring that evidence obtained in violation of the Constitution cannot be used in a criminal trial to prove guilt.

exigent circumstances Emergency circumstances, including hot pursuit, the possibility of escape, or evanescent evidence. When exigent circumstances are present, the police do not need to abide by the Fourth Amendment's warrant requirement.

extralegal remedies Remedies conducted outside the legal process, such as a personal vendetta.

Federal Rules of Criminal Procedure The rules that govern the conduct of all criminal proceedings brought in federal courts.

Fifth Amendment Part of the U.S. Constitution, which states, "No person shall be held to answer for a capital, or otherwise infamous crime, unless on a presentment or indictment of a Grand Jury, except in cases arising in the land or naval forces, or in the Militia, when in actual service in time of War or public danger; nor shall any person be subject for the same offense to be twice put in jeopardy of life or limb; nor shall be compelled in any criminal case to be a witness against himself, nor be deprived of life, liberty, or property, without due process of law; nor shall private property be taken for public use, without just compensation."

formal criminal proceeding In the Sixth Amendment right-to-counsel context, either a formal charge, a preliminary hearing, indictment, information, or arraignment.

Fourteenth Amendment Part of the U.S. Constitution, which states, "All persons born or naturalized in the United States, and subject to the jurisdiction thereof, are citizens of the United States and of the State wherein they reside. No State shall make or enforce any law which shall abridge the privileges or immunities of citizens of the United States, nor shall any State deprive any person of life, liberty, or property, without due process of law; nor deny to any person within its jurisdiction the equal protection of the laws."

Fourth Amendment Part of the U.S. Constitution, which states, "The right of the people to be secure in their persons, houses, papers, and effects, against unreasonable searches and seizures, shall not be violated, and no Warrants shall issue, but upon probable cause, supported by Oath or affirmation and particularly describing the place to be searched, and the persons or things to be seized."

frisk A superficial examination by the officer of the person's body surface or clothing to discover weapons or items that could be used to cause harm.

"fruit of the poisonous tree" doctrine An extension of the exclusionary rule. The poisonous tree is the initial unconstitutional search or seizure. Anything obtained from the tree is considered forbidden fruit and is not admissible at trial.

functional equivalent of a question "[A]ny words or actions on the part of the police (other than those normally attendant to arrest and custody) that the police should know are reasonably likely to elicit an incriminating response from the suspect (*Rhode Island* v. *Innis*, 446 U.S. 291 [1980], p. 302, n. 8).

"good faith" exception An exception to the exclusionary rule providing that when an honest mistake is made during the course of a search or seizure, any subsequently obtained evidence will be considered admissible.

government action Action on the part of paid government officials, usually police officers. Government action is one of two requirements (the other being infringement on one's reasonable expectation of privacy) that must be in place for a Fourth Amendment search to occur.

grand jury A body of people selected to hear evidence against an accused person (or persons) and determine whether there is sufficient evidence to bring the case to trial.

guilty A plea in which the defendant claims responsibility for the crime with which he or she has been charged.

habeas corpus A means of challenging the constitutionality of one's confinement, best viewed as an alternative to appealing. *Habeas corpus* is a constitutional right (Article I, Section 9, Clause 2).

hot pursuit An exigent circumstance that permits dispensing with the Fourth Amendment's warrant requirement. Hot pursuit applies only when the police have probable cause to believe (1) that the person they are pursuing has committed a serious offense, (2) that the person will be found on the premises the police seek to enter, and (3) that the suspect will escape or harm someone or that evidence will be lost or destroyed. Also, the pursuit must originate from a lawful vantage point and the scope and timing of the search must be reasonable.

immediately apparent One of the requirements for a proper plain-view seizure. The police must have probable cause that the item is subject to seizure.

impartial judge A judge who is capable of basing his or her decisions on the law and who has no conflict of interest or pecuniary stake in the outcome of the case. There is no constitutional right to an impartial judge. This right is a Supreme Court creation.

impartial jury A jury that is capable of making a decision based solely on the facts of the case.

impeachment exception An exception to the exclusionary rule providing that evidence considered inadmissible at one trial can be used in a later trial to impeach (that is, cast doubt on the credibility of) the defendant.

in-court showup A procedure in which a witness identifies the perpetrator in court. This sometimes occurs when a prosecutor asks a testifying witness to point to the perpetrator.

incorporation The Supreme Court's practice of using the Fourteenth Amendment's due process clause, which holds that no state shall "deprive any person of life, liberty, or property, without due process of law," to make certain protections specified in the Bill of Rights applicable to the states.

independent source An exception to the fruit of the poisonous tree doctrine that permits the introduction of evidence if it has arrived via an independent source, such as a party disconnected from the case at hand.

inevitable discovery exception An exception to the fruit of the poisonous tree doctrine that permits the introduction of evidence if it would have been discovered anyway.

initial appearance The first appearance of an accused person before a judge. Trial may occur for misdemeanors.

injunctive relief A court-ordered prohibition against a certain act or condition.

inspection An exception to the Fourth Amendment's warrant requirement that permits certain authorities to inspect a closely regulated business.

intermediate appellate courts At the state level, courts to which verdicts from courts of general jurisdiction are appealed.

internal review A nonjudicial remedy in which the police investigate on their own complaints against officers.

interrogation Express questioning (for example, Where were you on the night of the crime?) or the functional equivalent of a question (see definition). The definition of interrogation is important in the *Miranda* context because *Miranda* warnings do not need to be read if a person is not technically interrogated.

investigative detention Also called a stationhouse detention, a less intrusive detention than an arrest but more intrusive than a *Terry* stop. Stationhouse detentions are used in many locations for such purposes as obtaining fingerprints and photographs, ordering lineups, administering polygraph examinations, and securing other types of evidence.

joinder When the prosecutor either (1) brings multiple charges against the same individual in the same trial or (2) brings charges against multiple individuals in the same trial.

judicial inducements When a judge offers something to the defendant in exchange for a guilty plea. Most judicial inducements are prohibited.

jury list The master list from which prospective jurors are subpoenaed. Examples include lists of those with drivers' licenses or voter registration lists.

jury panel The list of individuals drawn from the jury list. The jury panel consists of those individuals subpoenaed for jury service.

justification Also known as *cause*, justification is necessary for the police to engage in actions that trigger the

Fourth Amendment. Examples of justification include probable cause and reasonable suspicion.

"knock-and-announce" requirement The requirement that, before executing an arrest or search warrant, officers identify themselves and their intentions.

lawful access One of the requirements for a proper plain-view seizure. The police must have lawful access to the item seized.

legal remedies Remedies made available by the law, by a court decision, or by a police agency policy or procedure.

lineup An identification procedure in which the suspect is placed alongside several other people who resemble him or her. The intent of the procedure is to ensure that a witness or victim picks the suspect out of the lineup.

live testimony The confrontation requirement that adverse witnesses provide live testimony.

mediation A method of alternative dispute resolution in which a neutral third party renders disciplinary decisions.

neutral and detached magistrate One of the three elements of a valid warrant—any judge who does not have a conflict of interest or pecuniary interest in the outcome of a particular case or decision.

nolo contendere A plea similar to guilty with a literal meaning of "I do not desire to contest the action." It resembles a guilty plea but is different in the sense that it may not be used against the defendant in any later civil litigation that arises from the acts that led to the criminal charge.

noncriminal proceeding rule The rule that limits juries to criminal trials. The rule is a bit of a misnomer because civil trials are by jury. The noncriminal proceeding applies to steps of the criminal process that are not themselves considered "criminal." Examples are juvenile adjudicatory hearings and civil commitment hearings.

nondeadly force Force that is unlikely to cause death or serious bodily harm.

not guilty A plea in which the defendant does not claim responsibility for the crime with which he or she has been charged. A not guilty plea is not the same as a plea of innocent. There is no plea of innocent.

ombudsman A term used to describe the neutral third party who conducts mediation.

open field Any unoccupied or undeveloped real property falling outside the curtilage of a home (*Oliver* v. *United States*, 466 U.S. 170 [1984], p. 170).

particularity The Fourth Amendment requirement that an arrest warrant name the person to be arrested (or provide a sufficiently detailed description) and that a search warrant describe the place to be searched and the things to be seized.

peremptory challenge A means of excluding prospective jurors with no reason offered. Peremptory challenges are limited depending on the case type and the jurisdiction. Peremptory challenges cannot be used to excuse prospective jurors based on race.

person inventory A procedure used to take record of a person's personal possessions after he or she has been lawfully arrested. Person inventories do not invoke the Fourth Amendment and do not require probable cause—but they can only occur after a lawful arrest (that is, one satisfying Fourth Amendment requirements).

photographic array A procedure in which several photographs, including one of the suspect, are shown to a witness or victim, and he or she is asked to pick out the perpetrator.

"plain-view" doctrine An exception to the Fourth Amendment's warrant requirement that permits police to seize certain items in plain view.

plea bargaining "The defendant's agreement to plead guilty to a criminal charge with the reasonable expectation of receiving some consideration from the state."[i]

police/probation partnerships A practice of teaming probation officers with police officers for the purpose of crime control or prevention. Such partnerships are controversial because police officers can effectively skirt the Fourth Amendment's requirements when they team with probation officers who have more latitude to conduct searches of probationers.

post-conviction review process The process, which consists of appeals and *habeas corpus* petitions, that begins when a person is committed to prison or sentenced to death.

precedent A rule of case law (that is, a decision by a court) that is binding on all lower courts and the court that issued it.

preliminary hearing A hearing that serves as a check on the prosecutor's charging decision. The standard of proof is probable cause, and the main inquiry in the hearing is whether there is probable cause to take the case to trial. The preliminary hearing is to be distinguished from the initial appearance, the probable cause hearing, and the pretrial release hearing. It almost always takes place after one of these hearings as well as after the charging decision.

pretextual prosecution When the prosecutor lacks the evidence to charge someone with a particular crime and so charges him or her with a lesser crime.

pretrial release One of several methods to release a defendant prior to his or her trial date.

pretrial The period between arrest and trial.

preventive detention The act of denying bail to certain defendants who are either dangerous or pose a high flight risk.

probable cause hearing A hearing in which a judge decides whether there was probable cause for arrest.

If the arrest was with a warrant, the probable cause hearing is not necessary. Also called a *Gerstein* hearing (for the Supreme Court's decision in *Gerstein* v. *Pugh*).

probable cause More than bare suspicion; it exists when "the facts and circumstances within [the officers'] knowledge and of which they [have] reasonably trustworthy information [are] sufficient to warrant a prudent man in believing that the [suspect] had committed or was committing an offense" (*Beck* v. *Ohio*, 379 U.S. 89 [1964], p. 91). In practical terms, it refers to more than 50 percent certainty. The comparable civil standard is preponderance of evidence.

procedural due process Protection of significant life, liberty, or property interests, sometimes described as "procedural fairness."

prosecutorial discretion A prosecutor's authority to decide whether to proceed with criminal charges against a particular suspect.

prosecutorial inducements Offers made by the prosecution to the defendant.

pro se defense When a defendant waives his or her Sixth Amendment right to counsel and defends him- or herself.

protective sweep A cursory visual inspection of those places in which a person might be hiding.

public duty defense A defense that shields police officers from criminal liability when performing certain official functions, such as using deadly force.

public trial A trial that is open to the public and/or complies with the Sixth Amendment's public trial provision. Courts can sometimes limit public access and the proceedings will still be considered public.

"purged taint" exception An exception to the fruit of poisonous tree doctrine that permits the introduction of evidence if it has become attenuated to the extent that it dissipated the taint of the initial unconstitutional act.

qualified immunity Immunity from suit that applies some of the time and in certain situations. Sometimes qualified immunity serves as an "affirmative defense," meaning that it is raised at trial—if the case goes that far. If a criminal justice official acts on a reasonably mistaken belief, as gauged from the standpoint of a reasonable officer, then qualified immunity can be granted.

racial profiling The practice of stopping people based on race rather than legitimate criteria.

reasonable expectation of privacy An expectation of privacy that society (through the eyes of a judge) is prepared to accept as reasonable. For a search to occur, a reasonable expectation of privacy must be infringed upon by a government actor.

reasonable suspicion Justification that falls below probable cause but above a hunch. Reasonable suspicion is

a Court-created justification; it is not mentioned in the Fourth Amendment. Reasonable suspicion is necessary for police to engage in stop-and-frisk activities.

reasonableness clause The first part of the Fourth Amendment: "The right of the people to be secure in their persons, houses, papers, and effects, against unreasonable searches and seizures, shall not be violated...."

reasonableness When evaluating questionable police action, it is first necessary to determine whether the Fourth Amendment applies. If it does, then we ask, "Did the police act in line with Fourth Amendment requirements?" This question is concerned with the reasonableness of the action in question.

release on recognizance (ROR) The accused is released with the assumption that he or she will show up for scheduled court hearings.

remedy A method of rectifying wrongdoing.

rule of four The requirement that four U.S. Supreme Court justices must agree to hear a case before it goes before the full Court.

same offense For double-jeopardy purposes, the same offense is one that has the same elements as another offense. For example, first- and second-degree murders are considered the "same offense" for double-jeopardy purposes. First-degree murder is defined as the premeditated deliberate killing of another person. Second-degree murder is the same offense, less the premeditation requirement. A person cannot be convicted of both offenses; otherwise, a double-jeopardy violation occurs.

school disciplinary "searches" Although they are not "searches" in the traditional Fourth Amendment sense, school officials can search (K–12) students' possessions without a warrant or probable cause for evidence of activity in violation of school policy.

search incident to arrest An exception to the Fourth Amendment's warrant requirement that allows officers to search a suspect following his or her arrest.

search warrant An order issued by a judge directing a law enforcement officer to search a particular location for evidence connected with a specific criminal offense.

search For Fourth Amendment purposes, a government action that infringes on one's reasonable expectation of privacy.

seizure of a person A seizure of a person occurs when a police officer—by means of physical force or show of authority—intentionally restrains an individual's liberty in such a manner that a reasonable person would believe that he or she is not free to leave (*Terry* v. *Ohio*, 392 U.S. 1 [1968]; *United States* v. *Mendenhall*, 446 U.S. 544 [1980]).

seizure of property A seizure of property occurs when "there is some meaningful interference with an individual's possessory interest in that property" (*United States v. Jacobsen*, 466 U.S. 109 [1984]).

seizure One of two government actions (the other being searches) restricted by the Fourth Amendment. Seizures can be of persons or property.

selective prosecution When an individual is targeted for prosecution merely because he or she falls into a certain group (for example, a minority group).

sentence The penalty received by a person convicted at trial.

sentencing The process by which the guilty party may be sentenced to death (for a capital crime), committed to prison, fined, placed on probation, or subjected to a host of other possible sanctions.

severance The opposite of joinder. For example, severance occurs when separate trials are held for different charges against the same defendant.

showup An identification procedure in which the suspect is brought before the witness (or victim) alone, so the witness can be asked whether that person is the perpetrator.

"silver platter" doctrine A practice prior to *Elkins* v. *United States* (364 U.S. 206 [1960]) that permitted the use of evidence in *federal* court that had been obtained illegally by *state* officials.

six-month imprisonment rule The rule that limits jury trials to cases in which more than six-months' incarceration in jail or prison is possible.

Sixth Amendment Part of the U.S. Constitution, which states, "In all criminal prosecutions, the accused shall enjoy the right to a speedy and public trial, by an impartial jury of the State and district wherein the crime shall have been committed, which district shall have been previously ascertained by law, and to be informed of the nature and cause of the accusation; to be confronted with the witnesses against him; to have compulsory process for obtaining witnesses in his favor, and to have the Assistance of Counsel for his defence."

speedy trial A trial that meets with the Sixth Amendment's requirement for a speedy trial. A trial is no longer "speedy" when there is intentional delay that is prejudicial to the defendant's case.

stare decisis A Latin term that means to abide by or to adhere to decided cases. Most courts adhere to the principle of *stare decisis.*

state supreme courts The highest courts at the state level.

statutory inducements Statutes that offer incentives for pleading guilty.

stop Sometimes called an "investigative stop" or an "investigative detention," a brief nonconsensual encounter between a law enforcement officer and a citizen that does not rise to the level of an arrest; the detention of a person by a law enforcement officer for the purpose of investigation.

subpoena *ad testificandum* A subpoena that compels a witness to appear before the grand jury.

subpoena *duces tecum* A subpoena that compels the production of tangible evidence (for example, a suspected murder weapon).

substantive due process Protection from arbitrary and unreasonable action on the part of state officials.

suggestive lineup A flawed lineup that almost ensures that the victim or witness will identify the suspect. For example, if the suspect is male and the other lineup participants are female, this would be a suggestive lineup.

superior courts The most common name for state-level courts of general jurisdiction.

tainted identification An identification that would not have taken place but for some earlier unconstitutional activity.

Title III of the Omnibus Crime Control and Safe Streets Act Federal legislation enacted in 1968 that set forth detailed guidelines on how authorities could intercept wire, oral, or electronic communications.

totality of circumstances All the facts and circumstances surrounding the case. In case-by-case adjudication, these must be examined in order to determine whether a constitutional rights violation has taken place.

trial *de novo* A type of appeal in which the appellate court holds a new trial as if the prior trial never occurred.

U.S. courts of appeals At the federal level, courts to which verdicts from the district courts are appealed.

U.S. Supreme Court The highest court in the federal court system.

vehicle inventory A procedure used to take record of a vehicle's contents after it has been lawfully impounded. Vehicle inventories do not invoke the Fourth Amendment and do not require probable cause.

vindictive prosecution Prosecution based on revenge.

voir dire The process of selecting jurors for service. *Voir dire* proceeds through three stages: questioning by the judge, challenges for cause, and peremptory challenges.

warrant clause The second part of the Fourth Amendment: "…and no Warrants shall issue, but upon probable cause, supported by Oath or affirmation, and particularly describing the place to be searched, and the persons or things to be seized."

writ of certiorari An order by the court requiring the lower court to send the case and a record of its proceedings to the U.S. Supreme Court for review.

References

Chapter 1, Introduction to Criminal Procedure

1. http://www.faa.gov/uas/ (accessed August 19, 2014).

2. Seattle is one such city. See http://www.slate.com/articles/technology/future_tense/2013/02/domestic_surveillance_drone_bans_are_sweeping_the_nation.html (accessed November 6, 2013).

3. *Federal Rules of Criminal Procedure.* http://www.law.cornell.edu/rules/frcrmp (accessed August 19, 2014).

4. Some scholars believe that the Ninth Amendment to the U.S. Constitution (also referred to as the *penumbra clause*) implies that all of the rights not specifically spelled out in the Constitution are automatically protected nonetheless. But to demonstrate this, a court would have to recognize a particular right as fundamental in case law. Privacy could be considered one such right.

5. Packer, H. L. (1968). *The limits of the criminal sanction.* Palo Alto, CA: Stanford University Press.

6. Ibid., p. 163.

7. Note that references to the federal-level Supreme Court are always capitalized (for example, *the U.S. Supreme Court, the Supreme Court,* and even *the Court*), whereas those to state-level supreme courts are not (that is, except in citing a particular state court, such as the *Florida Supreme Court*).

Chapter 2, The Exclusionary Rule and Other Remedies

1. *Herring* v. *United States,* 555 U.S. 135 (2009).

2. Courts often use the term *derivative evidence* in lieu of *fruit of the poisonous tree.* The former refers simply to evidence *derived* from a previous unconstitutional search or seizure.

3. Birzer, M. L. (2001). Crimes committed by police officers. In M. J. Palmiotto (Ed.), *Police misconduct* (pp. 171–178). Upper Saddle River, NJ: Prentice Hall.

4. Police Executive Research Forum. (1981).Three ways police themselves can implement effective complaint procedures. In Police Executive Research Forum *Police agency handling of officer misconduct: A model policy statement* (p. 1). Washington, DC: Author. Reprinted by permission.

5. Walker, S., & Bumphus, V. W. (1992). *Civilian review of the police: A national survey of the 50 largest cities.* Omaha: University of Nebraska at Omaha.

6. Walker, S., & Wright, B. (1997). Varieties of citizen review: The relationship of mission, structure, and procedures to police accountability. In R. G. Dunham & G. P. Alpert (Eds.), *Critical issues in policing: Contemporary readings* (3rd ed., p. 322). Prospect Heights, IL: Waveland.

7. West, P. (1987). *Investigations of complaints against the police: Summary findings.* Washington, DC: Police Executive Research Forum.

8. Geller, W. A. (1985). *Police leadership in America.* New York: Praeger, pp. 157–198.

9. Technically there is a difference between arbitration and mediation, but for our purposes it is safe to treat them as more or less identical.

10. Whitebread, C. H., & Slobogin, C. (2000). *Criminal procedure* (4th ed.). New York: Foundation Press, p. 65.

Chapter 3, Introduction to the Fourth Amendment

1. See http://www.starchase.com (accessed August 19, 2014).

2. Whitebread, C. H., & Slobogin, C. (2000). *Criminal procedure* (4th ed.). New York: Foundation Press, pp. 120–125.

Chapter 4, Searches and Arrests with Warrants

1. Shumate, B. A. (2006/2007). From "sneak and peek" to "sneak and steal": Section 213 of the USA Patriot Act. *Regent University Law Review, 19,* 203–204.

Chapter 6, Stop-and-Frisk

1. *Floyd* v. *City of New York,* 08 Civ. 1034 (SAS), decided August 12, 2013.

2. Emanuel, S. L., & Knowles, S. (1998). *Emanuel law outlines: Criminal procedure.* Larchmont, NY: Emanuel, p. 129.

3. Dressler, J. (1977). *Law outlines: Criminal procedure.* Santa Monica, CA: Casenotes, pp. 12–15.

4. Wilson, B. (1994). The war on drugs: Evening the odds through the use of the airport drug courier profile. *Boston University Public Interest Journal, 6,* 202–232.

5. Williams, C. R., & Arrigo, B. A. (1999). Discerning the margins of constitutional encroachment: The drug courier profile in the airport milieu. *American Journal of Criminal Justice, 24,* 31–46.

Chapter 7, Special Needs and Regulatory Searches

1. Bookspan, P. T. (1988). Jar wars: Employee drug testing, the Constitution, and the American drug problem. *American Criminal Law Review, 26,* 359–400.

Chapter 8, Interrogation and Confessions

1. Note that *Haley* dealt with due process, not *Miranda.* The Court held in *Fare* v. *Michael C.* (442 U.S. 707 [1979]) that juveniles are not to be treated differently than adults in the *Miranda* context.

Chapter 9, Identifications

1. McGonigle, S., & Emily, J. (2008, October 13). DNA exoneree fell victim to "drive-by" identification. *Dallas Morning News*, http://www.public.iastate.edu/~nscentral/mr/08/1017/exoneration.html.

2. Note that the Fifth Amendment would apply if a defendant in a lineup was forced to answer questions from the police or witnesses.

3. http://www.innocenceproject.org/understand/Eyewitness-Misidentification.php (accessed November 19, 2013).

4. Wells, G. L., Small, M., Penrod, S., Malpass, R. S., Fulero, S. M., & Brimacombe, C. A. E. (1998). Eyewitness identification procedures: Recommendations for lineups and photospreads. *Law and Human Behavior*, 22, 603–647.

5. Ibid., pp. 627–635.

6. See, for example, Greathouse, S. M., & Kovera, M. B. (2009). Instruction bias and lineup presentation moderate the effects of administrator knowledge on eyewitness identification. *Law and Human Behavior*, 33, 70–82; Haw, R. M., & Fisher, R. P. (2004). Effects of administrator-witness contact on eyewitness identification accuracy. *Journal of Applied Psychology*, 89, 1106–1112; and Russano, M. B., Dickinson, J. J., Greathouse, S. M., & Kovera, M. B. (2006). Why don't you take another look at number three: Investigator knowledge and its effects on eyewitness confidence and identification decisions. *Cardozo Public Law, Policy, and Ethics Journal*, 4, 355–379.

7. Greathouse, S. M., & Kovera, M. B. (2009). Instruction bias and lineup presentation moderate the effects of administrator knowledge on eyewitness identification. *Law and Human Behavior*, 33, 70–82.

8. MacLin, O. H., Zimmerman, L. A., & Malpass, R. S. (2005). PC-eyewitness and the sequential superiority effect: Computer-based lineup administration. *Law and Human Behavior*, 29, 303–321.

9. http://www.youtube.com/watch?v=SEhcLQmwtjQ (accessed November 19, 2013); see also Cutler, B. L., Daugherty, B., Babu, S., Hodges, L., & Van Wallendael, L. (2009). Creating blind photoarrays using virtual human technology: A feasibility test. *Police Quarterly*, 12, 289–300.

Chapter 10, The Pretrial Process

1. Probable cause hearings are not required in certain jurisdictions.

2. Note that some states have preset bail schedules for low-level offenses. For these states, some of the following discussion is not applicable.

3. See, for example, Paulsen, M. (1966). Pre-trial release in the United States. *Columbia Law Review, 66*, 109–125, 113.

4. Not all states have bail bond agents.

5. The hearsay language was removed from the Federal Rules in 2002, but the Advisory Committee notes make it clear that hearsay can still be admitted. See http://www.law.cornell.edu/rules/frcrmp/NRule5_1.htm (accessed May 30, 2011).

6. Federal Rules of Criminal Procedure, Rule 5.1(e).

7. Ibid., Rule 16.

Chapter 11, Prosecutors, Grand Juries, and Defense Attorneys

1. Kamisar, Y., LaFave, W., & Israel, J. (1999). *Modern criminal procedure* (9th ed.). St. Paul, MN: West, p. 894.

2. Johns, M. Z. (2005). Reconsidering absolute prosecutorial immunity. *Brigham Young University Law Review*, 53–154.

3. Center for Public Integrity. (n.d.). *Harmful error: Investigating America's local prosecutors*, http://www.publicintegrity.org/accountability/harmful-error (accessed November 20, 2013).

4. Federal Rules of Criminal Procedure, Rule 8.

5. Ibid.

6. Ibid., Rule 6.

Chapter 12, Plea Bargaining and Guilty Pleas

1. Rogers, B. (2011, May 13). Officer's killer gets 40 years in plea bargain. *Houston Chronicle*, A1.

2. Georgia Department of Public Welfare. (1924). Crime and the Georgia courts. *Journal of the American Institute of Criminal Law and Criminology*, 16, 16.

3. Moley, R. (1928). The vanishing jury. *Southern California Law Review*, 2, 97–127, 107.

4. Langbein, J. H. (1978). The criminal trial before lawyers. *University of Chicago Law Review*, 45, 263–316, 277.

5. Friedman, L. M. (1993). *Crime and punishment in American history*. New York, NY: Basic Books, p. 235.

6. Guidorizzi, D. D. (1998). Should we really "ban" plea bargaining? The core concerns of plea bargaining critics. *Emory Law Journal*, 47, 753, 760.

7. Alschuler, A. W. (1979). Plea bargaining and its history. *Law and Society Review*, 13, 211–245, 211 (quoting the *Chicago Tribune*, April 27, 1928, p. 1).

8. Weninger, R. A. (1987). The abolition of plea bargaining: A case study of El Paso County, Texas. *UCLA Law Review*, 35, 265–313, 267, n. 5.

9. Demarest, C. E. (1994, April 15). Plea bargaining can often protect the victim. *New York Times*, p. A30.

10. Alschuler, A. W. (1968). The prosecutor's role in plea bargaining. *University of Chicago Law Review*, 36, 50–112, 54.

11. Arenella, P. (1983). Rethinking the functions of criminal procedure: The Warren and Burger courts' competing ideologies. *Georgetown Law Journal*, 72, 185–248, 216–19.

12. Worden, A. P. (1990). Policymaking by prosecutors: The uses of discretion in regulating plea bargaining. *Judicature*, 73, 335–340, 336.

13. Alschuler, A. W. (1981). The changing plea bargaining debate. *California Law Review*, 69, 652–730, 652.

14. Colquitt, J. A. (2001). Ad hoc plea bargaining. *Tulane Law Review*, 75, 695–776, 695.

15. American Bar Association. (1986). Standard 14-3.3[d] from *Standards for Criminal Justice* (2nd ed.), supp., vol. 3. Washington, DC: American Bar Association.

16. U.S. Department of Justice. (2002). *Victim input into plea agreements*. Washington, DC: Author. Retrieved November 7, 2008, from https://www.ncjrs.gov/ovc_archives/bulletins/legalseries/bulletin7/ncj189188.pdf (accessed November 19, 2013).

17. Federal Rules of Criminal Procedure, Rule 11.

18. Miller, H. S., McDonald, W. F., & Cramer, J. A. (1978). *Plea bargaining in the United States*. Ann Arbor, MI: Inter University Consortium for Political and Social Research, pp. 1–2.

Chapter 13, Trial and Beyond

1. http://www.courtswv.gov/supreme-court/docs/fall2005/32693.htm (accessed November 21, 2013).

2. Although the defense in *Sheppard* did not directly seek closure of the trial, it did make requests for a continuance, a change of venue, and a mistrial.

3. American Law Institute, *Model Penal Code* 2.13(1)(b) (1985).

4. Walker, S. (2001). *Sense and nonsense about crime and drugs* (5th ed.). Belmont, CA: Wadsworth, p. 41.

5. California Penal Code, Section 1191.1 (1996).

6. U.S. Constitution, Article I, Section 9, Clause 2.

Cases Index

Note: Cases in **bold** indicate Key Cases; page numbers in **bold** indicate primary discussions of Key Cases. Page numbers followed by *f* and *t* indicate figures and tables, respectively.

Subject Index

Note: Page numbers in **bold** indicate pages on which definitions appear; page numbers followed by *f* and *t* indicate figures and tables, respectively.

A

Abandoned property, 50–51
Accuracy of description, 161
Accusation rule, 222
Accused, characteristics of, 138
Actual possession, 53
Ad hoc plea bargaining, **211–212**, 212*f*
Adjudication, **18**
Administrative justification, 59–60, 120
Airport checkpoint, 126–127
Alford plea, 209
Allocution, **177**
Alternative remedy
    civil litigation, 33–37
    criminal law, 33
    exclusionary rule and, 27*f*
    nonjudicial, 37–41
Anderson, Mark, 24
Antiterrorism and Effective Death Penalty Act of 1996, 235
Apparent authority, **97**
Appeal
    defined, **231**
    notice of, 233*f*
    rights during appellate process, 232–234
    types and effects of, 232
Appellate court dispositions, 14*f*
A priori, 54
Armspan rule, **85**
Arraignment, 17–18, **177**
Arrest. *See also* Arrest warrant
    defined, 69, 71*f*
    inventory, 122
    search incident to, 83–86
    warrantless, 95–96
Arrest warrant. *See also* Warrants
    defined, **66**
    example, 66*f*
    overview, 69–70

particularity in, 68
probable cause in, 67
requirements for, 71–72, 72*f*
serving, 72–75

Article VI of U.S. Constitution, 3
Assembly line metaphor, 9
Attenuation, 31
Automatic appeal, 18
Automobile exception, **89**
Automobile search
    levels of justification for, 92*t*
    rationale for, 89–90
    requirements for, 90–91
    warrantless search of, 89
Automobile stop, 111
Autrefois convict, rule of, 229

B

Bail, **173**
    bond agent, **173**
    bond agent re-arrest procedure, 173*f*
    determination, 18
Bail Reform Act of 1984, 174
Bench trial, 18, 223
Bill of Rights, 4
Bivens action, 74
Blockburger rule, **229**
Bodily intrusions, 77
Booking, 17
Border checkpoint, 124–125
Bound over, 176
Bounty hunter, 173
Bright-line decision, **16**
Business inspection, 124–125*t*

C

Case-by-case adjudication, **16**
Case citations, 13*f*
Chain of custody, 182
Challenge for cause, **225**

269

Charge(s/ing)

bargaining, 207

decision, 187–189

document, 188f

joinder of, 191–192

methods for serious crimes, by state, 193f

understanding of, 215

Checkpoint

border and immigration, 124–125

crime investigation, 126

defined, **124**

license and safety, 126

other, 126–127

sobriety, 125–126

unconstitutional, 127

Civilian input, **40**

Civilian monitor, **40**

Civilian review, 38, **40**

Civil lawsuit, stages of, 35f

Civil litigation, 33–37, **34**

Civil proceedings and exclusionary rule, 26–28

Civil Rights Act of 1964, Title VII, 3

Closely-regulated business, **124**, 125t

Closing trial to public, 199f, 222

Code of Conduct for Federal Public Defender Employees, 199

Code of Conduct for Judicial Employees, 189f

Coercion in plea bargaining, 210

Collateral attack, 18, 234

Color of law, **34**, **36**, 36f

Colquitt, Joseph A., 211–212

Common authority, **97**

Competency to stand trial, 226

Competing concerns, 8–10

Complaint investigation process, 40f

Compulsory process, **228**–229

Concurrent sentence, 230

Conditional guilty plea, 214

Confession

due process voluntariness approach, 138–139

exclusionary rule and, 150–151

factors determining voluntariness, 139f

Confrontation, **226**–228

Consecutive sentences, 230

Consent search, 96–97, 113

Constitutional procedure

defined, 2

remedies for rights violations, 24–25

Constitutional rights. *See also* Right to counsel; Trial, rights at; Waiver; specific amendments to Constitution

during appellate process, 232–234

to challenge witness testimony, 228

to cross-examine witnesses, 176

habeas corpus, 18, 234, 235

to impartial jury, 223–225

incorporation, 4–6, 5f

to live testimony, 226

Miranda, 3, 194

during plea bargaining, 210

to be present, 226

of relevance in criminal procedure, 3–4

remedies for violations of, 24–25

during sentencing process, 231

sources of, 3

Constructive possession, 53

Contempt power, **196**

Controlled Substances Act, 131f

Counsel. *See* Defense attorney; Right to counsel

County liability under Section 1983, 36

Court cases. *See also* Cases Index

parties to, 14f

publications, 13–14, 13f

tracing progress of, 14–16

websites, 13–14

Courts

effects of plea bargaining on, 212–213

of general jurisdiction, **10**

jurisdictions, 12f

of limited jurisdiction, **10**

military, 11

system, structure of, 10–13, 10f, 11f

tribal, 11

Crime-control perspective, **9–10**

Crime investigation checkpoint, 126

Criminal law, 33

Criminal procedure, **2**

theory versus reality, 7–8

Criminal process

adjudication, 18

overview, 16, 16f

post-conviction review process, 18

pretrial, 18

sentencing, 18

Curtilage, 51–52, 51t

Custody, 142–144, **143**

F

Factual basis of guilty plea, 217
Factual guilt, 8
False friends, 50
Farag, Tarik, 116
Federal court structure, 10
Federalism, **3**, 5, 177–178, 191–192, 215
Federal Rules of Criminal Procedure, 176
    confessions, admissions, and, 138–139
    in criminal procedure, **3**
    discovery and, 178
    grand jury and, 192
    self-incrimination clause, 142
    text of, 4*t*
    Fifth Amendment, *Miranda* rights and, 3
Financial status and pretrial release, 175
Fire inspection, 123–124
First Amendment, 3
Firsthand knowledge and probable cause, 57
Flawed witness identifications, 163
Flight risk and pretrial release, 174–175
Foreign Intelligence Surveillance Act (FISA), 78
Formal criminal proceeding, **139**, 140–141
42 U.S.C. Section 1983
    county and municipal liability under, 35–36
    criminal statutes compared to, 33
    individual liability under, 38*f*
    overview, 3, **35–36**
Fourteenth Amendment
    in criminal procedure, **4**, 4*t*
    incorporation, 4–6, 4*f*
    interrogations and confessions and, 142
Fourth Amendment
    analysis of, 47
    applicability of exclusionary rule beyond, 26
    basic terminology, 46–47
    cell phones and, 83
    in criminal procedure, 3, 7
    exclusionary rule, 25
    identification procedures and, 158
    justification doctrine, 54–60
    purpose and elements of, 46
    search within meaning of, 47–53
    seizures in violation of, 3
    seizures under, 53–54
    text of, **4**, 4*t*

    violation of, 65
    warrants and, 65
Frisk. *See also* Stop and frisk
    defined, **108**–109
    permissible grounds for, 109
    proper and improper, 110*f*
    scope of, 109–110
    as separate from stop, 104–105
"Fruit of the poisonous tree" doctrine
    confessions and, 151
    identifications and, 164–165
    overview, **30**–32
Functional equivalent of question, **144**–145
Fundamental rights, 6

G

"Good faith" exception to exclusionary rule, 10, **29**–30
Government action and search, **48**–49
Government employee office, search of, 128
Government officials, defined, 48–49, 49*t*
GPS tracking, 46
Grand jury
    construction of, 192–194
    defined, **192**
    indictment by, 18
    investigation by and exclusionary rule, 26, 28
    investigative powers of, 194–196
    rights of witnesses testifying before, 194
    role of, 192–194
    secrecy of proceedings of, 194
Guilty plea
    conditional, 214
    defined, **177**, **230**
    factual basis of, 217
    intelligence component of, 215–216
    restrictions on right of, 235
    right of, 18, 231, 232
    right to counsel and, 232
    validity of, 215
    voluntariness of, 217

H

Health and safety inspection, 122
Hearsay evidence, 176
Herring, Bennie Dean, 24

Home
  arrests in, 71–72
  inspection, 122–123
Hot pursuit, **86**
House, definition, 47
Hypothetical independent source exception, 32

I

Identification procedures
  constitutional limitations on, 156–158
  exclusionary rule and, 164–165
  flaws and fixes, 163–164
  policy example, 163*f*
  pretrial, 159–162
  types of, 156
Immediately apparent requirement for search, **94**
Immigration checkpoint, 124–125
Immunity, grants of by grand jury, 194–196
IMPACT project (San Bernardino), 132
Impartial judge, **223**
Impartial jury, **223**–225
Impeachment exception, **30**, 150–151
Inadequate representation, 198
Inadvertency in plain-view search, 94
Incorporation, 4–6
In-court showup, **160**
Independent source, **32**
Indigent defendant and right to counsel, 198–199
Inevitable discovery exception, **32**
Informant cases, 57*t*
Initial appearance, **170**–171
Injunctive relief, **34**
Innocence Project, 163
Insanity defense, 226
Inspection
  defined, **122**
  fire and international mail, 123–124
  home and business, 122–123, 124–125*t*
Intelligence component of guilty plea, 215–216
Intermediate appellate courts, **10**
Internal review, **38**, 40*f*
International mail inspection, 123–124
  defined, **144**
  general questioning compared to, 145*f*
Inventories
  person, 122
  vehicle, 121–122

Investigative detention, **115**
Investigative powers of grand jury, 194–196
Interrogation, *Miranda* approach, 144–145

J

Joinder, **191**–192
Judicial inducements, **212**
Jury
  grand. *See* Grand jury
  list, **225**
  panel, **225**
  right to impartial, 223–225
  trial. *See* Jury trial
  waiver approach, 209*f*
Jury trial
  defined, 223
  selection of potential jurors, 225
  waiving right to, 224–225
Justification
  other standards, 57–60
  probable cause, 47, 54–57

K

"Knock and announce" requirement, **73**, 73*t*, 75

L

Lawful access, **93**–94
  requirement for search, 93–94
Legal guilt, 8
Legal remedy, **24**
Level of certainty, 161
Lexis Nexis database, 14
License checkpoint, 126
Lineup, **156**, 159, 162*f*
Live testimony, **226**
Locker checks in schools, 128

M

Manhattan Bail Project, 173–174
Manner of search, 76
Material evidence, 178
Means, concern with, 9
Media presence when serving arrest warrants, 74–75

Pretextual prosecution, **190**

Pretrial

    arraignment, 177

    defined, 16

    discovery, 177–182

    identification techniques. *See* Pretrial identification techniques

    preliminary hearing, 175–176

    probable cause hearing, **171**–172

    release. *See* Pretrial release

Pretrial identification techniques

    lineups, 159

    photographic identifications, 160–162

    showups, 159–160

Pretrial release

    criteria for, 174–175

    decision, 173–174

    defined, **172**

    overview, 177*f*

Preventive detention, **174**

Prima facie case, 18

Private individuals as government agents, 49

Private search as government search, 49

Probable cause

    in arrest warrant, 67

    factors in, 56*f*

    hearing, **171**–172, 177*f*

    in home inspections, 122–123

    immediately apparent compared to, 94

    as justification, 47, 54–57

    preliminary hearings and, 176

    warrants and, 65, 67

Probation supervision, 130–132

Procedural due process, **4**

Profiling

    drug courier, 113–115

    in war on terror, 116

Progress of cases, tracing, 14–16

Property damage when serving arrest warrants, 73–74

Property, seizure of, **53**

Prosecution

    discovery by, 178–179

    duty to disclose exculpatory evidence, 179–181

    duty to preserve evidence, 181–182

Prosecutor

    charging decisions, 187–189

    effects of plea bargaining on, 213–214

    joinder, 191

    overzealous, 190–191

    restrictions on bringing charges, 189–190

    role of, 187

Prosecutorial discretion, **187**

Prosecutorial inducements, **210**

Pro se defense, **197**

Protect America Act, 78

Protective sweep, **85**, 111–112

Prudent man notion, 54

Public defender, 18

Public duty defense, **33**

Public place, arrest in, 95–96

Public safety exception to *Miranda*, 148

Public trial, **221**, 222–223

"Purged taint" exception, **31**

Pursuit, seizure by, 54

Q

Qualified immunity, **37**

R

Reasonable expectation of privacy, **50**–53

Reasonable inquiry, 105

Reasonableness

    clause, **46**

    defined, **47**

    reasonable suspicion compared to, 128

Reasonable suspicion

    factors giving rise to, 58*f*

    as justification, **57**–59

    reasonableness compared to, 128

    stop-and-frisk and, 103–104

Reciprocal discovery, 178

Regulatory search

    checkpoints, 124–127

    drug and alcohol testing, 129–130

    government employee offices, 128

    inspections, 122–124

    inventories, 121–122

    probation and parole supervision, 130–132

    school discipline, 127–128

Release

    on bail, 173, 174

    on recognizance, **173**–174

Reliability of identification procedure, 157

Remedy, **24**. *See also* Alternative remedy; Exclusionary rule; Nonjudicial remedies

Reno, Janet, 163

Right(s)

constitutional. *See* Constitutional rights

fundamental, 6

Miranda, 3, 194

to remain silent, 17–18, 194

at trial. *See* Trial, rights at

Right to counsel

during appeals, 233–234

in criminal prosecution, 196–197

habeas corpus and, 232

indigent versus nonindigent defendants, 198–199

at lineups, 157

at stages of criminal process, 195–197*t*

waiver of, 141–142, 197–198

of witnesses testifying before grand juries, 194

Robles, Sergio, 205

Rule of four, **16**

S

Safety checkpoint, 126

Same offense, **229**

School disciplinary search, **127**–128

Scope of frisk, 109–110

Scope of search

of automobiles, 91–92

consent search, 96

defined, 76

incident to arrest, 85–86

Search. *See also* Regulatory search; Scope of search; Search warrant; Warrantless search

automobile, 89–92, 92*t*

defined, **46**

elements of, 48

government action and, 48–49

illegal, identifications resulting from, 164–165

reasonable expectation of privacy and, 50–53

unreasonable, 3, 46

Search warrant. *See also* Warrants

bodily intrusions and, 77

defined, **66**

example, 67*f*

particularity in, 68–69

probable cause in, 67

requirements for, 75

serving, 75–76, 77

Secrecy of grand jury proceedings, 194

Seizure

based on plain view, feel, and touch, 113*f*

defined, **47**

illegal, identifications resulting from, 164–165

of persons, **53**–54

of property, **53**

unreasonable, 3, 46

Selection of potential jurors, 225

Selective incorporation, 5*f*

Selective prosecution, **189**–190

Self-incrimination clause, 3, 158

Sensory enhancement devices, 52–53

Sentence, **230**

bargaining, 207

Sentencing

defined, **18**

determination of sentence, 230–231

key cases, 232–235*t*

rights during, 231

Separate offense, 229

Serving

arrest warrants, 72–75

search warrants, 75–76, 77

Severance, **191**

Shepard's Citations, 14

Showup, **156**, 159–160, 162*f*

Shumate, Brett, 79

"Silver platter" doctrine, **25**

Simpson, O. J., 225

Six-month imprisonment rule, **224**

Sixth Amendment

confessions and admissions and, 139–142

in criminal procedure, **3**–4, 4*t*

defense and, 196–197

discovery and, 178–179

Size of jury, 224

"Sneak and peek" warrant, 79

Sobriety checkpoint, 125–126

Social costs and exclusionary rule, 27*f*

Sovereign entity, 10–11

Speedy trial, **221**–222

Standby counsel, 198

W